AUTISM:
EFFECTIVE BIOMEDICAL TREATMENTS

Have We Done Everything We Can for This Child?

Individuality in an Autism Epidemic

By Jon Pangborn, Ph.D. and Sidney MacDonald Baker, M.D.

September 2005 Edition

© 2005

A Publication of the Autism Research Institute's "Defeat Autism Now!" (DAN!) Project

Autism Research Institute
4182 Adams Avenue
San Diego, CA 92116

www.AutismResearchInstitute.com

PROLOGUE
Bernard Rimland, Ph.D.

This year, 2005, is the 10th anniversary of the Autism Research Institute's Defeat Autism Now! (DAN!) Project.

When we started the DAN! project in January, 1995, we knew of one child, Garrett G., who had recovered from autism through biomedical intervention. Now, a mere 10 years later, there are thousands of children who have recovered from autism as a result of the biomedical interventions pioneered by the innovative scientists and physicians in the DAN! movement.

We – Sid Baker, M.D., Jon Pangborn, Ph.D., and I – started the DAN! project for several reasons. The main reason was that we strongly disagreed with mainstream medicine's insistence (which continues today) that autism is an incurable, lifelong disability whose symptoms might be somewhat ameliorated with psychiatric drugs. Sid, Jon and I knew that the medical establishment was – and is – wrong, and set out to remedy the situation. The DAN! Project has succeeded far beyond our expectations and is moving ahead very quickly. For more about that first DAN! think-tank in 1995, see my "History of DAN!" a few pages hence.

In the meantime, back to Garrett G.: His mother, Cindy, had phoned me for advice in 1993. "I've been to 39 doctors and have spent $39,000 seeking help for my autistic child, with no results," she said. "Don't give up!" I urged. Six months later, when she phoned again, she proudly announced, I've now seen the 40th doctor, and we are really on the road to recovery!" The 40th doctor was the brilliant immunologist, Sudhir Gupta, M.D., Ph.D., whose treatment of Garrett with IVIG made a huge difference in his well-being and initiated Garrett's becoming a very normal teenager, studying to become a filmmaker. Garrett will be introduced to the audience at the Recovered Children event at our October 2005 DAN! Conference in Long Beach. Dr. Gupta hopes to be present to meet and greet Cindy and his formerly autistic patient, Garrett. There will be a number of other formerly autistic children at the Long Beach conference as well. It promises to be quite an event!

Yes, we've made enormous progress in the past 10 years, and we continue to move ahead rapidly. This volume was updated for our Boston DAN! Conference in April 2005, and has been extensively updated again for our October 2005 Conference in Long Beach. The process of detoxifying autistic children from mercury and other heavy metals, in particular, is evolving so rapidly that printed information is almost immediately outdated. For the latest on detoxification, see www.AutismMercuryDetox.com.

DISCLAIMER

Autism: Effective Biomedical Treatments is not intended as medical advice. Its intention is solely informational and educational. Please consult a medical or health professional should the need for one be indicated. The information in this book lends itself to self-help. For obvious reasons, the authors and publisher cannot take the medical or legal responsibility of having the contents herein considered as a prescription for anyone. Either you or the physician who examines and treats you (or your child) must take the responsibility for the uses made of this book

About the authors:

Jon Pangborn, Ph.D., Ch.E., received his bachelor's (1963) and doctorate (1967) degrees in chemical engineering from Syracuse University. He then served for five years as a nuclear research officer in the United States Air Force. From 1972 until 1981, he did research on alternative fuels and catalytic processes for the natural gas industry at the Institute of Gas Technology, Chicago. He became interested in human metabolism and autism in the 1970s when psychological and special educational efforts to help his autistic son yielded few positive results. He credits William Philpott, M,D,, for making the first real improvements in his son's condition through studies of diet, allergy, and metabolism. In 1981, Dr. Pangborn left the energy industry to work full-time on metabolism problems associated with childhood development. He understudied two professors of biochemistry, and with them and Dr. Philpott as advisors, set up Bionostics, an organization that provides information about nutrition and biochemistry to doctors, laboratories, and nutrition companies.

Dr. Pangborn was instrumental in introducing the active, coenzyme form of vitamin B6, pyridoxal 5-phosphate, to the U.S. nutrition industry, and he was the first to formulate alpha-ketoglutarate as a nutritional supplement, an aid for those with tissue ammonia excess. Since 1990, he has advocated and formulated enzyme supplements for autistics and others with gastrointestinal disorders. From 1990 to 1995, he was president of Doctor's Data Laboratory; from 1996 through 2003 he served as a senior consultant to Great Smokies Diagnostic Laboratory.

Dr. Pangborn is a recipient of the Herbert Rinkel Memorial Award of the American Academy of Environmental Medicine for excellence in teaching. He is author or coauthor of nine issued U.S. patents, is a Fellow of the American Institute of Chemists, and is a cofounder of Defeat Autism Now! along with Bernard Rimland, Ph.D., and Sidney MacDonald Baker, M,D. Dr. Pangborn presented his initial biochemical findings on autism to the NSAC Annual Conference in July 1984 (San Antonio, TX) – decreased cystine in blood, methionine metabolism disorder, and impaired glutathione function. In the early 1990s, he developed a laboratory test assessing liver toxicity and oversaw development of an accurate mercury analysis procedure at Doctor's Data Laboratory. From 1981 to the present, he has authored a periodically-updated flowchart of amino acid metabolism in humans, the latest edition being that of 2004, published by Kirkman Imaging.

Sidney MacDonald Baker, M.D., is a graduate of Phillips Exeter Academy, Yale University, and Yale Medical School, where he completed his residency training as Chief Resident Pediatrics in 1969 after taking time out for a mini-residency in Obstetrics and two years in Chad, Africa as a Peace Corps Volunteer. After leaving a full-time faculty appointment as Assistant Professor of Medical Computer Sciences at Yale in 1971 he became a family practitioner in a prepaid health plan in New Haven. Seven years later he took a position as Director of the Gesell Institute of Human Development where he continued a medical practice that had evolved toward an interest in biomedical aspects of chronic illness in adults and children. Dr. Baker returned to full-time practice in 1978 and currently practices in New York and Connecticut. His friendship with Dr. Bernard Rimland began in the 1970s and became the basis for the founding, along with Dr. Pangborn, of the Defeat Autism Now! Project in 1994. He is the co-author of *Child Behavior*, Harper & Row, 1982, and *Your Ten to Fourteen Year Old*, Delacorte, NY, 1988. His other books are *Folic Acid*, Keats/McGraw Hill, Chicago, 1995, *The Circadian Prescription*, Putnam, NY, 2000, and *Detoxification and Healing*, McGraw Hill, Chicago, 2003. He is associate editor of *Integrative Medicine*. Dr. Baker was the recipient of the Jonathan Forman Award, presented by the American Academy of Environmental Medicine, and the Linus Pauling Award (1999), presented by the Institute for Functional Medicine.

About DAN!

In 1994, at a lunch meeting with Dr. Rimland, Dr. Baker described his feelings of inadequacy and isolation in trying to cope with the biochemical, immunologic, and gastroenterological problems of patients with autism. Could we, he wondered, gather a small group of knowledgeable scientists, researchers, and parents to organize the pieces of the puzzle? Dr. Rimland immediately accepted this challenge, and Dr. Pangborn, a leading expert in applying broad biochemical knowledge to individual clinical decisions, joined them in founding an organization which Dr. Rimland named "Defeat Autism Now!" (DAN!). The mission of DAN! is to provide parents and professionals with a timely consensus as to the safest and most effective treatment options for children with developmental problems in the autism spectrum.

By *timely*, we mean NOW. Parents urgently need effective treatments for their autistic children, and they need these treatments immediately. Urgency exacts a toll of uncertainty about new treatments, but parents and practitioners are understandably unwilling to wait for the slow pace of medical hypothesis, funding, research, publication, and replication to provide the proven basis for public policy.

By *consensus* we mean the best accord of a group of experienced and thoughtful experts given the job of using current evidence to drive decisions for individual children. Consensus is appealing because it assembles knowledge and experience from different fields, but it does not always prevail over the insight of a single genius. Moreover, we recall that within the memory of our generation, and until the 1964 publication of Dr. Rimland's book *Infantile Autism*, the prevailing – and wrong to the point of evil - consensus among experts was that autism was the psychological result of cold mothering. The current consensus is based on the integration of persuasive evidence. The pieces of the puzzle that we have assembled from evidence relating to digestive problems, dietary intervention, nutritional supplementation, and toxic and infectious agents did not initially fit neatly together, but now these pieces are coming together nicely in ways that this book will present to you.

Our first meeting, funded by parents and other supporters of the Autism Research Institute, included about 30 researchers, clinicians and parents. Parents were then, and are now, key participants in the discovery, probing, and dissemination of treatments and systematic plans of action such as those outlined here. The DAN! ethos began with Dr. Rimland's sharing with parents and practitioners the results of surveys asking parents what works, and it is the collaboration among parents, clinicians and researchers that continues to enrich our understanding of the science behind our empirical observations. By reading this book and attending one of our two annual meetings or the many mini-DAN! workshops for clinicians, you should feel welcomed into a large family. We do not have all the answers, but we have compelling evidence to help parents and clinicians answer two key questions: "What are the best options from which to choose the next step for my child?" and "Have we done every thing we can for this child?"

> Before going to medical school I apprenticed for three months in Katmandu, Nepal with Dr. Edgar Miller at Shanta Bhawan Hospital and in little weekly clinics around the valley. After each patient, Dr. Miller would turn to me and ask, "Sidney, have we done everything we can for this patient?" I carried that question with me to medical school and still find Dr. Miller's spirit at my elbow. His question initiates a logical chain of questions that keep a focus on the individual, no matter what diagnostic label that person carries.

Acknowledgments:

We are indebted to all the patients, clinicians and researchers who have been part of the DAN! movement, and particularly to those who have attended the DAN! Think Tanks over the past decade. It is their consensus this book attempts to present, while the burden of responsibility for the accuracy and integrity of the work remains with us, the authors. Among the think tank attendees to whom we would like to express our special appreciation are Susan Owens, M.S. and Teresa Binstock, researcher. Their combined volume and quality of communication has been enormous. It was to Teresa that one of us (SMB) turned for help with the gathering and placement of citations from the scientific literature, of which Teresa has an encyclopedic command. Richard Deth, Ph.D., Jim Neubrander, M.D., Judy Converse, and Susan Owens have contributed to the text, as has Judy Gorman, who also helped edit comments we gathered from parents. Elizabeth Mumper, M.D., has given us valuable suggestions for improving the manuscript. Jaqueline McCandless, M.D., who has been a major force in training physicians in the DAN! approach, prodded Jon into expanding the nutritional supplement section into a more complete document, and also suggested improvements to his prose.

Our wives, Louise Reiner Baker and Chris Pangborn, have given emotional, intellectual, and editorial support to this project, and Chris has done a consummate job of taming and formatting Jon's diagrams.

We wish to pay affectionate tribute to Bernard Rimland, Ph.D., whose spirit of collaborative endeavor has facilitated the effective role of parents in piecing together this puzzle.

Finally, we wish to acknowledge the friendship that has joined the two authors as it passes through its third decade of collaboration, mutual affection and respect – and to celebrate the easy give and take that we continue to enjoy.

About this book:

This book is a complete revision of our previous editions of *Biomedical Assessment Options for Children with Autism and Related Problems*. It is divided into five sections. The first describes Dr. Baker's rationale for individualized treatment, presenting the seven sources of information that will help drive decisions for your child, whether you are clinician or a parent. In the second section, Dr. Baker helps you face the demands of making a plan, in which the central issue is, "What should we do next?"

Dr. Pangborn addresses the detailed information and documentation that will support your plans in the three following sections: 1) A knowledge of the chemistry relevant to the treatments we describe; 2) The use of laboratory test results; and 3) A guide to the use of nutritional supplements.

We have tried to combine the oil of accessibility with the water of technical detail and documentation. We leave it to you, the reader, to shake well according to your digestive capacity. You will find the oil on top in the form of Dr. Baker's expositions of how to think and then how to plan, with a focus on how to make the best therapeutic choices for a given child. Dr. Pangborn's parts of the book provide a detailed technical description of each of the points covered by Dr. Baker. It is Dr. Baker's role to provide you with some open ground in which to gather navigational tools and orientation, before you hit the denser woods of Dr. Pangborn's authoritative and thoroughly documented exposition. This book is not a quick read! We want you to use it according to your needs, as a map of the territory, a tour guide, and an implement for hunting and investigating.

On the cover:

The boy on the left: At 18 months of age, M. stopped talking, lost eye contact, and developed behaviors that led to the diagnosis of autism at a university child behavior clinic. His parents were assured that he would never recover and that no treatments were available other than special education programs. When I met him at age four-and-a-half, he was nonverbal and out of contact. He responded to treatment – mostly antifungal medications – over the next three years. Now he is a charming boy who wins chess championships and is an artistic prodigy. He has no trace of any symptom that could link him to the autistic spectrum from which he emerged.

On the right: B. had colic for the first four to five months and cried all day. Ear infections began around that time and he sometimes had two courses of antibiotics in a month. His first seizure occurred six days after his second DPT, given with Hib and polio injections, and he had two more seizures in the following two weeks and received phenobarbital during the ensuing year. Ear infections continued until PE tubes were inserted at 11½ months. He went on to have several sinus infections and a total of 15 ear infections in his life. As an infant he babbled but never had any words. At 10 to 13 months he could relate to others and would smile for pictures. Around 15 months his eye contact was fleeting and he was not following any commands, and his parents became concerned. He did not respond to a casein-free diet.

When I met him at age two, he had no expressive language and exhibited poor eye contact; spinning; pulling on his eye lashes; a lack of response to his name; loose, watery, explosive bowel movements daily; marked carbohydrate craving; nasal congestion; and low energy. I started him on a yeast-free diet and S. boulardii. Within two weeks his facial skin changed from being red and rough to being nearly normal. His receptive language went from being limited to two words to being almost a non-issue. He started producing expressive language in abundance and had a huge vocabulary. His eye contact became good, he interacted with others, and he was "not the same child he was five weeks ago." From that point he went on to become the bright, sociable, completely normal six-year-old he is today.

These are just two among hundreds of children who have recovered from autism. The fact of the *full* recovery of so many children tells us that it is possible. The circumstances of these children's recoveries tell us that they were due to the kinds of biomedical interventions described in this book. The message of these recoveries is, to be sure, one of hope, which cannot be completely fulfilled for all children with the knowledge available to us as of this writing. The meaning of these recoveries is that words such as "incurable," "untreatable," and "permanent" should drop from our dialog about autism. The challenge of these recoveries is to perfect our understanding of the factors that make it look easy for some children but difficult for others.

—*Sidney M. Baker, M.D.*

The History of the Defeat Autism Now! (DAN!) Project: How It Got Started, and Why It Got Started

Bernard Rimland, Ph.D.

For too many years, autism research has largely been confined to descriptive efforts (What are the symptoms? What brain areas and functions are affected?) or to trying various drugs, developed for other purposes, which might bring about reduction of symptoms. Even with such limited goals, progress has been far from encouraging.

Drugs, in particular, quite apart from their harmful side effects, have absorbed far too much time and attention. Autism has never been caused by a deficiency of Ritalin or Risperdal. I heard the following words from two psychiatrists, both mothers of autistic sons, two years apart. One physician-mother was from the East Coast, the other from California: "It is one thing to be looking for a drug in the *Physicians Desk Reference* for another mother's child. When it is your own child, the words take on a very different meaning." I'm sure that is true!

Since its establishment in 1967, the Autism Research Institute has had, as a major priority, the tracking of promising treatments for autism. Intensive study of the scientific literature, and analysis of case reports from literally thousands of parents of autistic children, convinced us that there is much that can be done now to help many autistic children. Progress in the acceptance of useful medical interventions is painfully slow – it is not uncommon for a safe and effective treatment to be available for decades before it is widely implemented. A recent example is the use of small amounts of folic acid, a very safe B vitamin, as a means of preventing severe birth defects. It is estimated that over 25,000 cases of mental retardation could have been prevented in the U.S. if widespread use of folic acid supplements had been recommended when the discovery was first announced.

To accelerate the development and dissemination of information that will be helpful to many families of autistic children, the Autism Research Institute (ARI) convened the first Defeat Autism Now! (DAN!) conference in Dallas in January, 1995. The attendees were approximately 30 physicians and scientists, from the U.S. and Europe, with special expertise in autism research and treatment. Psychiatry, neurology, immunology, allergy, biochemistry, genetics and gastroenterology were among the fields represented.

The conference was a great success: there was a cordial meeting of the minds and a very rapid consensus among the participants, most of whom had never met each other previously, as to the most useful approaches to treatment.

The participants agreed that one of the major priorities of the DAN! Project should be the publication of a document representing the best ideas and practices of those in attendance, so that they could share their expertise with physicians everywhere who were interested in bringing about real improvement in the diagnosis and treatment of autism, as quickly as possible. The document, Medical Assessment Options for Children With Autism and Related Problems (or DAN! Clinical Manual), first published in February 1996, was updated in January 1997, April 1999, September 2001, September 2002, and September 2004. It represents a consensus statement of the state-of-the-art alternative medical approach to the treatment of autism.

Follow up DAN! Conferences were held annually for five years, going to bi-annual in 2001, to further advance the treatment of autism. The conferences have produced a base of physicians who wish to employ rational, scientifically sound approaches to the diagnosis and treatment of autism, and who regard psychoactive drugs as their last choice, not their first.

The Clinical Options Manual represents the best thinking of some of the very best minds in the field of autism. The arduous work of putting together the ideas expressed at the Dallas DAN! conference, and later in innumerable letters, faxes, e-mail messages and telephone conversations among the participants, was undertaken by two exceptionally talented individuals:

- Sidney M. Baker, M.D., a graduate of and former faculty member of the Yale Medical School and former director of the Gesell Institute of Human Development, has extensive training and experience in pediatrics, allergy, immunology, neurology, biochemistry and computer science.

- Jon Pangborn, Ph.D., a fellow of the American Institute of Chemists and Certified Clinical Nutritionist, is the father of an autistic son. Now a private consultant, Dr. Pangborn was formerly president of Doctors Data, a major medical laboratory, and very probably has studied more biochemical workups of autistic patients than anyone else on earth.

Drs. Baker and Pangborn have worked together on the biochemistry of autism since the early 1980s. Although the writing of the manual is done by the Baker and Pangborn team, new ideas and careful refinement of concepts already in the manual take place at DAN! "think-tank" conferences of leading physician and researchers, which range in duration from a day to a weekend. Nine DAN! think-tanks have been convened by the Autism Research Institute thus far.

As we envision it, there are two major "consumers" of this manual:

1. Physicians who wish to apply state-of-the-art medical knowledge and technology to the process of diagnosing and treating their autistic patients.

2. Parents of autistic children who, having received a copy of the manual, will take it to the child's physician to see if that physician may be willing to undertake the intensive work-up suggested. If that physician is not interested, the parents may wish to seek another physician.

It is now very evident that there has been an enormous increase in the prevalence of autism during the past decade. In their sections of the manual, Drs. Pangborn and Baker will discuss the most plausible reasons for this unanticipated increase. One of the consequences of this huge upsurge in autism has been a great number of autistic children born into families in which one or both parents are physicians. A good many of these physician-parents, after having explored conventional medicine's approaches toward dealing with autistic children, and finding them ineffective, have joined the ranks of DAN! doctors. At the Autism Society of America's annual conference in San Diego in July, 2001, and again at ASA's conference in Indianapolis in July, 2002, the Autism Research Institute has sponsored panel presentations titled "Physicians who have successfully treated their own autistic children." Videotapes of each of these 2-1/2 hour long physician-parent panels are available from the Autism Research Institute. Jaquelyn McCandless, M.D., a board certified psychiatrist and neurologist, was about to retire when her 13th grandchild, Chelsey, was diagnosed autistic. Dr. McCandless accepted the challenge. After gent research, she adopted the DAN! approach. Her story is told in her excellent, very helpful book, *Children With Starving Brains*, also available from ARI.

Having given you a somewhat formal presentation on how the Defeat Autism Now! movement got started, let me go back a bit further in history and provide a more personal account of the experiences which led to the establishment of the DAN! Project:

It all started with the birth of my own autistic son, in March of 1956. Mark was a screaming, implacable infant who resisted being cuddled and struggled against being picked up. He also struggled against being put down. Our pediatrician, Dr. Black, who had been in practice for 35 years, had never seen nor heard of a child like Mark. Neither Dr. Black nor I, who at that time was three years beyond my Ph.D. in psychology, had ever seen or heard the word "autism." It was not until Mark was two years old that my wife, Gloria, remembered reading, in one of her old college textbooks, about children like Mark, who looked through people rather than at them, and who accurately repeated radio commercials and nursery rhymes, but did not engage in communicative speech. I went out to the garage, found the dusty box of old college texts, and there, five years after I had earned a Ph.D. as a research psychologist, I saw the word "autism" for the first time.

Autism was <u>extremely</u> rare in those days, probably occurring perhaps once or twice in every 10,000 live births. Slowly but surely, the prevalence was rising. In my summary of research on the prevalence of autism, published in an article I wrote for the *Autism Research Review International* in 1989, I reported that a number of studies showed autism to occur on average in 4.5 children per 10,000 live births. More recently, in 2003, the American Academy of Pediatrics and the Centers for Disease Control and Prevention reported that autism now occurs in 60 children out of 10,000 live births – an increase of 1500% in a decade!

Starting with the several references cited in my wife's old text, I began to read everything I could find on the subject of autism. I was appalled to find that it was uniformly believed, and presented as an established fact in every textbook, that autism was an emotional (psychological) disorder, and the only treatment recommendations were psychoanalysis or other forms of psychotherapy for both the mother and the child. The mother was required to acknowledge her guilt, and disclose why she hated the child and wished it had never been born. The child, in so-called "play therapy," was provided with a paper or clay image of a woman (his mother) and was encouraged to tear it to bits, thus expressing his hostility toward his mother, whom the psychotherapists were positive had caused his autism. There were a few drugs that were also used with autistic children, but then, as now, the idea was not to treat the autism but to slow the children down enough to make life tolerable for those who must deal with them.

I decided to read everything I could possibly find on the subject of autism, not only to learn what might be done to help Mark, but also to try to understand on what basis the psychiatrists had decided that mothers were to blame for their children's autism. After four years I had in fact read everything I could possibly find on the subject of autism, including translations of the foreign language articles I could not read myself. I learned that, despite the supreme confidence (arrogance) with which the authorities proclaimed the mothers were to blame, I could find no shred of evidence for such a belief. The book I wrote, *Infantile Autism: The Syndrome and its Implications for a Neural Theory of Behavior*, won the Century Award in 1964, and resulted, as I had intended, in destroying the belief in the "psychogenic hypothesis" that autism was an emotional disorder caused by bad mothering. Instead, I successfully argued, the biological causes of autism must be sought.

The resulting publicity – I had overnight become the world authority on autism – resulted in my receiving many letters and phone calls from other parents, as well as from a number of research scientists interested in exploring the ideas presented in *Infantile Autism*.

One of the first letters I received was from a mother in Canada who was experimenting with high doses of certain vitamins in the treatment of her autistic child. It seemed to me like rather a crazy idea, but she was reporting good results. The Canadian mother sent me a letter that she had received from her own mother, the child's grandmother, who was a nurse in a psychiatric hospital in Saskatoon. The grandmother's letter observed that two young psychiatrists, Drs. Abram Hoffer and Humphry Osmond (who later became my friends and colleagues) were experimenting with large doses of vitamin B3 on their adult schizophrenic patients. The grandmother wrote that she and the other psychiatric nurses and staff members could see quite remarkable improvement in the patients that Hoffer and Osmond were treating with "megavitamin" B3. The improvement was clearly better than that seen in the patients being treated by the other psychiatrists, who used only drugs. Nevertheless, to the surprise and disappointment of the nursing staff, the traditional psychiatrists refused to see what was so clearly evident to everyone else, that Hoffer and Osmond's megavitamin treatments were in fact effective. Since I was so keenly aware that the psychiatric establishment had shown a total lack of integrity by blaming the mother for causing autism on the basis of no data, it did not surprise me that the psychiatric establishment could also be deluding itself with regard to the efficacy of treatments. (Hoffer and Osmond had published a number of controlled double and triple blind studies supporting their initial findings. It made no difference to the psychiatric establishment, which was – and still is – hooked on drugs. ("Don't bother me with the facts – my mind is made up.")

In 1965, having been favorably impressed by the excellent results achieved by Ivar Lovaas at UCLA in teaching autistic children with behavior modification techniques (now called ABA), I founded the Autism Society of America (ASA) to provide a nationwide forum for informing parents about new and important developments. Two years later, in 1967, I founded the Autism Research Institute as a center for collecting, analyzing and disseminating research on the cause and treatment of autism.

Over a period of several years I began to hear from other mothers, in California, New York, Georgia and elsewhere that they were trying high doses of vitamins on their autistic children, and that certain vitamins seemed to be helping. There was sufficient consistency in these reports that I decided to conduct a large-scale study of the vitamins, and in the late 1960s undertook and completed such a study, based on several hundred autistic children. The results were quite positive, especially for vitamin B6. At the time of this writing I am aware of 22 studies of vitamin B6 as used in autistic children, conducted by researchers in seven countries, and all studies but one (of only nine children) have provided positive results. Adding magnesium to the B6 has repeatedly been found to be essential for best results. Thirteen of the studies have been double-blind, placebo-controlled studies. Nevertheless, a great many articles and textbooks still continue to say that vitamin therapy for autism has not been proven, or that it is unsafe. Both contentions are definitely untrue. (To answer several frequently asked questions, our studies, as well as the studies of Dr. Gilbert LeLord and his group in France, have shown that almost 50% of autistic children and adults will improve when given B6 and magnesium, and that on average, the optimal dosage is 8mg of B6 and 4mg of magnesium per pound of body weight per day.) The B6 and magnesium combination has been found to be extremely safe, and, as I noted, is effective on almost half of all the children and adults on whom it has been tried.

the years went on, I began finding more and more that the parents, especially the mothers, of autistic children were extremely effective at identifying treatments that were helpful to their autistic children. They were also very observant in detecting factors that caused their children to become worse. In 1967 we began systematically to collect such data from parents of autistic children and to include on our questionnaires items about the effects of vaccines on the children. (Many parents had reported their children to get markedly worse after the DPT shot.) Having learned that infants poisoned with mercury-containing teething lotions and diaper powders showed many of the symptoms of autism, I began collecting, in my 1967 questionnaire, information on the mother's exposure to dental amalgams while pregnant with the autistic child. I did not know then that vaccines contained significant amounts of the mercury-containing preservative thimerosal. We also began collecting information about the effects of milk and wheat on children's behavior, since many parents were telling us that their children did much better on a milk-free and/or wheat-free diet.

It was very evident that there were a number of treatments, largely discovered by the parents of autistic children, that were much more effective than the drugs being used by the psychiatric establishment, and certainly much safer.

In 1994, after a series of discussions with my esteemed colleagues Sidney Baker, M.D., and Jon Pangborn, Ph.D., we decided to call together a think-tank of exceptionally competent and open-minded physicians and scientists who were interested in the ideas that we shared, and could help us make sense of them. The approach favored by the invitees was to identify treatments -- safe treatments -- for which there is credible evidence of efficacy. Once these efficacious treatments are identified, an attempt is made to find why they work, so their efficacy can be improved.

And *that* is how the DAN! Project got started.

****

Afterword: Oh yes! You are wondering about my son Mark, who we were told to institutionalize and forget, at age 5, who was in diapers at 7 and did not ask or answer a question until age 8. Mark, now 49, lives at home with his parents, attends a day program for mentally disabled adults, takes the city bus to school, makes daily visits to the art galleries and coffee shops in the neighborhood, and has turned out to be a remarkably talented artist, discovered at age 22. Mark has been interviewed about his art on NBC, CBS, CNN and PBS. His works have been featured in a number of one-artist shows and are in the permanent collections at several galleries. He did the illustrations for his sister Helen Landalf's children's book, *The Secret Night World of Cats*. We are proud of him. Not such a bad outcome, after all!

TABLE OF CONTENTS

SECTION 1: INDIVIDUALITY
By Sidney Baker, M.D.

Your Job: Private Policy 16
Polarized Opinions 19
Attitude 21
Who Decides for My Child? 22
Parent Ratings of Treatments 24
Two Paths: Through Time and Chemistry 25
    A Time Path 25
    A Biochemical Path 27
Your Child's Story 31
The Chronological Questionnaire 31
The Big Questionnaire 34
Yeast Problems 37
Skin Problems 38
Being "Uptight" 39
Targeting Symptoms 40
    Sleep 40
    Constipation 44
Gastrointestinal Health 49
    Cleaning Up the Diet 52
    Food Additives 53
    Sugar and Artificial Sweeteners 55
    Flora 58
Laboratory Testing: General Perspective 59
Your Child's Response to Each Treatment You Try 61
Intuition 62
References 63

SECTION 2: MAKING A PLAN
By Sidney Baker, M.D.

Chart: Scheme for Considering Options for Diagnostic Trials in Children with ASD 69
Methyl-B_{12} 70
Digestive Enzymes and First-Tier Supplements 72
Antifungals 74
    Saccharomyces boulardii 79
    Nystatin or Amphoteracin B 80
    Other antifungals 81
    Additional antifungal options 83
Antibacterials 83
Parasites 84
Yeast-Free Diet 85
How to do a Five-Day Elimination and Challenge for Food, to Detect Sensitivity 92
Specific Carbohydrate Diet 93
Gluten- and Casein-Free Diets 102
Food Allergen Elimination 112
Detoxification 119
    TTFD 123
Immune Testing 125

...nsitization 128
...unization Response 129
...vention 132
Other Therapeutic Options 133
Conclusion and Final Words...137
References..138

SECTION 3: MOLECULAR ASPECTS OF AUTISM
By Jon Pangborn, Ph.D.

Preface..149
Autism in Perspective 149
    Severe Metabolic Disorders that May Feature Autism (Type 1 Autism) 152
    Acquired Metabolic Disorders with Genetic Predispositions (Type II Autism) 154
Autism at the Molecular Level 157
Why Biochemistry?..158
Methionine Metabolism...160
Creatine Formation and Energy Delivery 167
Supplementing Creatine 171
Synchronous Neuronal Processes (Richard Deth and Jon Pangborn) 171
Measles, Inflammation and Intestinal Disorder...177
Chart: Likely Chain of Events that Leads to Autism 183
Toxicities and Infectious Stressors–Revisited 185
Autism, Sex and Cognitive Abilities..187

SECTION 4: LABORATORY TESTS
By Jon Pangborn, Ph.D.

Blood Chemistry and CBC Analysis 189
Stool Analysis 190
Intestinal Permeability...191
Ammonia...191
Food Allergy Tests..192
Urinary Peptide Measurements 194
Amino Acid Analysis 195
Organic Acid Analysis...198
Fatty Acid Analysis 201
Element Analyses and Metallothionein Assessments..202
Immune Testing 206
Genomic Testing...207
Summary: Analytes of Most Significance in Autism 209

SECTION 5: NUTRITIONAL SUPPLEMENTS FOR AUTISM
By Jon Pangborn, Ph.D.

Introduction 211
Chart: Suggested Staging of Nutritional Supplements During Autism Treatment Interventions...................212
Why Are Nutritional Supplements Helpful?..213
Digestive Enzymes...216
    About Digestive Enzymes...218

Using Digestive Enzymes in Autism	220
Adverse Responses to Digestive Enzymes?	221

Vitamin B_6 and Pyridoxal Phosphate ... 223
- About Vitamin B_6 ... 223
- Using Vitamin B_6 in Autism ... 226
- Adverse Responses to B_6? ... 227

Magnesium (Mg) ... 228
- About Magnesium ... 228
- Using Magnesium in Autism ... 229
- Adverse Response to Magnesium? ... 230

Vitamin B6 With Magnesium ... 230

Taurine ... 232
- About Taurine ... 233
- Using Taurine in Autism ... 234
- Adverse Response to Taurine? ... 235

Vitamin C ... 236
- About Vitamin C ... 236
- Using Vitamin C in Autism ... 238
- Adverse Responses to Vitamin C? ... 238

Zinc (Zn) ... 239
- About Zinc ... 239
- Using Zinc in Autism ... 242
- Adverse Responses to Zinc? ... 243
- Special Strategies for Boosting Zinc ... 243
- A Possible Strategy for Reducing High Copper–Use of Molybdenum ... 244

Calcium (Ca) ... 246
- About Calcium ... 246
- Using Calcium in Autism ... 247

Vitamin A and Cod Liver Oil (Vitamins A and D) ... 249
- About Vitamins A and D ... 249
- Using Vitamin A or Cod Liver Oil in Autism ... 251
- Adverse Responses to Vitamin A or Cod Liver Oil? ... 252

Fatty Acids ... 253
- About Fatty Acids ... 253
- Using Fatty Acids in Autism ... 255
- Adverse Reactions to Fatty Acid Supplements? ... 255

Melatonin ... 256
- About Melatonin ... 256
- Using Melatonin in Autism ... 257
- Adverse Response to Melatonin? ... 258

Multivitamin/Mineral Combination Products ... 259

Probiotics ... 260
- About Probiotics ... 261
- Using Probiotics in Autism ... 262
  - Saccharomyces boulardii ... 262
  - Lactobacillus rhamnosis ... 263
  - Lactobacillus acidophilus ... 263
  - Bifidobacter bifidum ... 263
  - Streptococcus thermophilus ... 264
- Adverse Responses to Probiotics? ... 264

Vitamin B_{12} ... 266
- About Vitamin B_{12} ... 266
- Using Vitamin B_{12} in Autism ... 268
- Adverse Responses to Methylcobalamin or B_{12}? ... 270

Dimethylglycine (DMG) ... 271
- About DMG ... 271

...ing DMG in Autism	272
...dverse Response to DMG?	273
...ethylglycine	274
About TMG	274
Using TMG in Autism	275
Adverse Responses to TMG?	276
DMG or TMG with Folate and Vitamin B_{12}: Making Choices	277
Indications that Plain DMG Might be Beneficial	277
Indications that Plain TMG Might be Beneficial	277
Indications that DMG with Folate and Vitamin B_{12} Might be Beneficial	278
Indications that TMG with Folate and Vitamin B_{12} Might be Beneficial	278
DMG-TMG Choice Matrix	279
Creatine	279
About Creatine	280
Using Creatine in Autism	282
Adverse Response to Creatine?	283
Amino Acids	285
Using Amino Acids in Autism	287
Adverse Responses to Amino Acid Supplements?	289
Nutritional Supplements to be Cautious With	290
Methionine and S-Adenosylmethionine (SAM)	290
Using Methionine or SAM in Autism	292
Folate	293
About Folate	294
Using Folate in Autism	295
N-Acetylcysteine	297
About NAC	297
Using NAC in Autism	298
Lipoic Acid	299
About Lipoic Acid	300
Using Lipoic Acid in Autism	301
Glutathione	301
About Glutathione	302
Using Glutathione in Autism	303
Carnosine	305
About Carnosine	305
Using Carnosine in Autism	306
Other Nutritional Products that might be Beneficial	308
Activated Charcoal	308
Alpha-Ketoglutaric Acid or Alpha-Ketoglutarate	308
Bacopa	308
Biotin (Susan Owens)	309
L-Carnitine	312
Colostrum	312
CoQ_{10}	313
Inositol	313
Magnesium Malate	315
Selenium (Se)	316
Silymarin (Milk Thistle)	317
Vitamin E	317
Index	319

Front Cover: ARI – Autism Research on the Internet
Back Cover: Parent Ratings of Behavioral Effects of Biomedical Interventions

INDIVIDUALITY

Sidney Baker, M.D.

Individuality is the key. Even in the midst of an epidemic in which we assume that the victims all "have the same thing," respect for each person's differences is the key to finding that person's best diagnostic and therapeutic options. Only by careful listening can the clinician or researcher discover those options and begin to weave the threads of different patients' stories into a fabric that reveals a pattern.

In 1995, 32 clinicians, researchers and parents gathered to form a consensus concerning the most scientifically credible biomedical diagnostic and treatment choices available to parents of children on the autistic spectrum. The tapestry we formed is illustrated in this diagram from the first edition (1995) of this book.

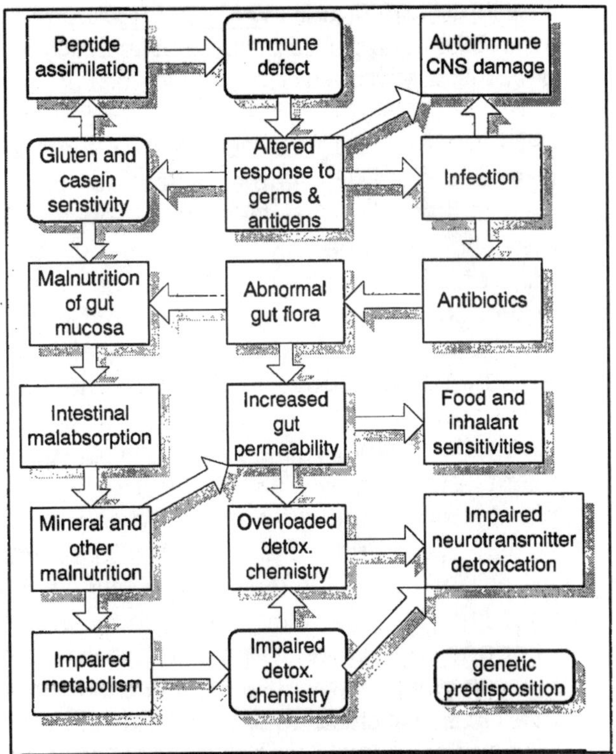

Complexity usually and ideally yields simplicity, as we refine ideas about the causes of things. The dozens of clinicians and researchers and hundreds of parents whose observations have helped shape our current notions of the toxicology, immunology and biochemistry of each child agree that the picture remains complex. Even though some children have become cured as a result of simple interventions, none of us whose opinions form the basis for this book believes that the answers to this puzzle are, or will soon be, simple. The preceding statement applies to each child as it does to the epidemic in general. Keep in mind a plain analogy: **"If you are sitting on two tacks and remove just one, you do not experience a 50% improvement." Chronic illness is, or becomes, multifactorial and requires a systems approach.**

Your dismay at the complexity of the old model in Figure 1 may take different forms depending on whether you are a parent, a clinician, a teacher or an academic. As you explore the updated version of this model in the pages that follow – one that is geared to clinical options – you will be reassured as you envision the practical application of the

Figure 1. 1995 DAN! Model of Factors in Children with Autism.

systems approach. In this approach, each component is simple and subject to straightforward strategies to determine its relevance in the overall picture for any given person. Helping you formulate such strategies is a major intent of this book.

Why are we so sure that interactions among certain biochemical, immune and toxic factors in genetically susceptible individuals are the key to understanding options for each child on the autism spectrum and to figuring out the epidemic? Pick up the newspaper and you will see that "They" don't know why there is an epidemic. "They" are darned sure it is not any of the things

SECTION ONE: RATIONALE FOR INDIVIDUALIZED AUTISM TREATMENT

...e talking about, because "there are no credible studies published in peer-reviewed medical ...als proving that any of these theories are valid." How can "They" be so wrong? Because ...y are not given to the intensive investigation of the individual child. "They" are given to going ... the library to find out what is going on. However, medical literature is generally 10 to 20 years late, because that is how long it takes for credible studies to get proposed, accepted, funded, carried out, published, repeated, and eventually incorporated into public policy. This book is not about public policy. It is about private policy concerning options for one child at a time. It is about the necessary haste we each privately feel when confronted with the demands for early intervention in children's problems.

YOUR JOB: PRIVATE POLICY

As you read forward, keep in mind the huge difference between public and private policy, because this distinction will make your job much easier: *to decide what to do next for the child in your care*. The threshold for making a good decision for a single child is tiny compared to the burden of proof for establishing public policy. Public policy is, moreover, disease-oriented, whereas private health policy is oriented almost solely toward protecting and healing the individual.

Let me give you an example: You are in charge of immunizing all of the children in the country against rubella (German measles), to protect pregnant women from exposure that would kill or deform their unborn babies. You know that after one immunization with rubella vaccine, most of the children will be fully immunized, but some will not. After two shots, the percentage of children who are fully immunized against rubella will rise further, and after three shots it will approach, but never reach, 100%. At this point, it will be high enough to prevent spread of rubella in the population, and thus achieve the goal of protecting unborn babies. Public policy would thus say that all children must have three shots.

Now let's say that you are in charge of Alexander. Just one little Alex. Private policy for Alex might be quite a different matter. He's a boy. He will never be pregnant, so he could wait until he plans a family, and get immunized only to protect his own offspring. Well, that would be pretty selfish. We assume that Alex's parents have a social obligation to protect the babies of expectant mothers in their community against the dreaded complication of intrauterine rubella infection. So, how many rubella shots should Alex get? Chances are that he is fully immunized after one shot. When it comes to the obligatory booster, what are the options? Just get the shot, figuring that re-immunization with a live virus poses no risk to him if he already has antibodies to that virus? Or check to see if he has antibodies and skip the second (or third) shot? No long-term studies have ever been published in peer-reviewed medical journals proving the safety of ANY vaccine, much less rubella, in an already-immune person. So the Alex policy might well be to take a small blood sample and send it for analysis to see if the second or third shots are really necessary for him. This would not work as a public policy, at least not in the current climate of opinion, because low cost and high compliance are very real issues as regards vaccine policy. Evaluating Alex's titer levels would work as private policy, however, because the cost in blood and money may very well be worth the investment for parents who think, as many immunologists do, that the "over-immunization" of children could be dangerous to some of them.

OK, let's take the public vs. private issue to another area and test it out. The test is, how does it work in *your* job? – that is, the job of deciding what to do next for *your* child, be you a parent or clinician. Let's say that "They" say that "we have seen no credible published studies proving the effectiveness of a gluten-free diet in the treatment of autism." (However, see Knivsberg et al.[1])

(As far as we, the authors of this book, are concerned, the published evidence is credible and persuasive; but let's accept "their" premise for the sake of argument.) You, on the other hand, have heard first- or second-hand reports that sound very persuasive, to the effect that one or more children have benefited dramatically from a gluten-free diet. You don't have to know or decide the Truth. You don't need perfect knowledge of the "treatment for autism." You only have to decide what do to next for your child. You don't have to do any blood tests. You don't have to do any urine tests. You only have to decide whether it is reasonable for you to try the diet. You don't have to do it for a year. You don't have to do it for three months. You don't have to do it for three weeks. You only have to do it for a week. At the end of the week, you have only to decide, "Shall we try it for another week?" Sure, it may sometimes take three months for a gluten-free diet to show its benefits and, rarely, it may take a year. And if you were in charge of 100,000 autistic kids, you might have to make a public policy that takes such things into account. But you are only in charge of Alex, or Andrew, or Aidan or Zoe.

So all you need is some input from a lot of other parents about what has worked for their kids, along with some explanation from clinicians and researchers as to why those things are reasonable from a scientific perspective. That is what this book is all about.

The spirit behind this book – a collaboration among parents, clinicians and researchers – really all began with the publication in 1964 of Dr. Bernard Rimland's book, *Infantile Autism*.[2] In a scholarly style, Dr. Rimland documented the evidence showing that the prevailing consensus about autism – which was that it resulted from cold mothering – was without any credible supportive evidence, and that autism instead stems from biomedical causes that call for biomedical treatments. A ramification is that the people who know the child best, his or her parents, could become part of the solution, if doctors could become educated to the new view.

Of the hundreds of classes in the curriculum that ended with my medical degree from Yale in 1964, I remember only one in specific detail, which left me uneasy. A movie was shown in a class at the Yale Child Study Center. The movie portrayed a sympathetic but quite formal child specialist discussing the options for the child of two anxious parents who sat before his imposing mahogany desk. The issue was their child's developmental problem. The message was: "Don't look for answers." Had the child been not retarded but autistic, the message would have been: "It's your fault, mother." What a crazy world! How strange it was to embark on my career as a physician with these two contradictory prejudices to bring to bear on the children I would encounter.

> WHAT I'D SAY to another parent starting the process is that they should not expect any one treatment to be a magic bullet or a cure, as this will ultimately lead to disappointment and frustration. Autism spectrum disorders tend to be highly individual and what might work for one person doesn't necessarily work for another. While we have seen that some treatments have had a remarkable effect on our son, the improvements are in specific areas of functioning only and did not effect a complete cure or reversal of all ASD symptoms.
>
> One day, perhaps, a complete cure will be found, but until that day all a parent can do is to try to use the protocols to improve different aspects of everyday living and functioning.
>
> –Richard, parent

SECTION ONE: RATIONALE FOR INDIVIDUALIZED AUTISM TREATMENT

ngborn and his wife did start to look for answers in the 1960s: "Our son wasn't quite right ...irth, and by age 3 he had no interest in his environment, or in playing with others, and ...n't interact with us. He was diagnosed as having classic infantile autism. He cried at night, ...very little, and had long bouts of diarrhea or constipation. He gradually developed severe ...ums with combative/destructive behaviors. We still bear scars from his bite marks. By the ...e he was 10 years old, he had flunked out of eleven programs for behavior modification and special education. We were advised that he was hopeless.

"Then, through a relative, we heard about a doctor, a 'clinical ecologist,' who took such cases and had remarkable progress with some. So we drove the 850 miles to his office and set up housekeeping in a motel. Although we had been told that clinical ecologists were nut cases, treated as pariahs by orthodox medical practitioners, this doctor performed really appropriate laboratory tests such as amino acid and element analyses, and enzymology studies for metabolic errors. Then he did a thorough job of food allergy testing by elimination and deliberate single-food testing. From this, we got a 'clue' that milk might be a problem. It wasn't all that evident – four, five, or even 10 days without dairy didn't seem to be all that remarkable – but it was an indication. A subsequent casein IgG test showed that our son was off-the-chart high. If 1+ to 4+ is what is usually reported, he rated 10+. Complete abstinence from dietary casein reduced his incidence of aggressive, destructive behaviors to less than 5% of the previous frequency. His amino acid test showed only trace cystine in blood and lots of methionine sulfoxide. My wife, daughter and I went on his diet and then we all did the amino acid test. Yep – he had very deficient cystine; we didn't. Addressing that biochemically has made a difference, even though he was a teenager before we got most of his labs right. Now he gets on a special bus in the morning, goes to a workshop to work like the rest of us, and earns a paycheck. He still doesn't talk much, but he's got quality of life that 'experts' denied was possible 20 years ago."

WE DREAMED ABOUT what color hair and eyes he'd have, what sports he'd play, and what he'd do when he grew up. No one dreamed of autism.

Autism affects every minute of our lives – how we sleep, what we eat, and how we spend our money. Birthdays, holidays and vacations are bittersweet – there are NO days off. We've grown thicker skins yet are more compassionate, become advocates but more earth-friendly, and become every physician's nightmare while a better health care consumer. Our family motto became, "Find a Way" – and we will.

– *a parent*

How odd it is that while Dr. Rimland's message became generally accepted throughout North America during the ensuing four decades (although it has not yet reached much of Europe, where autism is still viewed as a psychiatric problem), the concept of biomedical investigation and treatment of autism continues to be given short shrift by academics. We regularly hear from parents who have been given the "don't look for answers" lie by experts in child neurology, psychiatry and development. Parents and professionals who look for answers for individual children are pooh-poohed and marginalized.

This book focuses on treatment, and only through that window do we consider the possible causes of the epidemic. The current epidemic of autism has arisen during a time when the last vestiges of "it's your fault" are disappearing, but in a medical environment darkened by the deep shadows of the dogma that developmental problems, now including autism, result from bad luck. Most experts tell parents that their children's problem should be lived with, or treated behaviorally or educationally, without "looking for answers." A corollary to this prevailing opinion is that looking for answers is unreasonable, and abetting the search for answers is to be condemned. The parents of autistic children looking for answers have not, in that sense, made much progress in the eyes of medical professionals. In another sense, however, they have made a great deal of progress, thanks to a movement that began with Dr. Rimland's book and grew into a worldwide communication network with Dr. Rimland at its center. That network, and the parents, researchers and clinicians it has reached, are embodied in the work of the Defeat Autism Now! (DAN!) Project and its parent organization, the Autism Research Institute (of which Dr. Rimland is the founder and director). The chain of information and recommendations in this book are linked to original observations, reports, insights of parents, and published studies. Some of the involved professionals are also parents of autistic children. From reports of responsiveness to various therapies, to major insights into causative factors of the epidemic, the careful observations of parents who started out with minimal scientific background have been crucial to most of what we now know.

> WHAT I HAVE SAID to other parents starting the process (or when trying to convince them to start) is simply that the DAN! protocol and biomedical intervention work – we have our child back!!!! Our son D. is now four and a half, and after two years of this biomedical approach, D. is a happy little boy in mainstream school.
>
> At the time of diagnosis, we couldn't understand why this happened to us and how unlucky we were. Well, we now feel like the luckiest family – we were fortunate to have found Dr. Baker and after two years of treatment, our little boy is happy and almost indistinguishable from his peers. We appreciate every moment with both of our boys (including their sibling rivalry) and never take things for granted. Never give up hope – not while there are DAN! doctors fighting for our children!
>
> - Stacey, a parent

POLARIZED OPINIONS

The implications emerging from a growing body of carefully compiled anecdotal data[3] are increasingly distant from what "They" believe to be true, creating an ever-widening gap across which the two sides view each other with suspicion. The suspicion is amplified by the fact the nearly every issue involved in clinical options for our children is subject to highly polarized opinion. The issues around which opinion is polarized are:

<u>Is there an epidemic of autism?</u> Until recently, when the statistics from reliable studies became undeniably strong, positions were taken by leading experts and representatives of government, professional and scientific organizations. These positions were based on an "it couldn't be, so it can't be" thinking founded on the notion that autism is necessarily caused by genetic factors,[4] which, of course, are steady, whereas epidemics surge.

SECTION ONE: RATIONALE FOR INDIVIDUALIZED AUTISM TREATMENT

> A DOCTOR you are being entrusted with
> ...ift, a life, which has every right, desire,
> ...d ability to excel and thrive as a whole,
> ...ted light in this world. May you open your
> ...ind, practice, and heart to the job you have
> been given. May you see that people are not
> bodies meant to be suppressed but forces
> meant to thrive. May you treat parents
> expressing what they see and feel as friends
> and colleagues, not as enemies.
>
> As a parent I found our way through listening
> to other parents, the listening ear of a
> concerned doctor, watching my son's
> reactions and researching information
> constantly. My prayer goes out that other
> doctors will LISTEN to our stories, HEAR our
> words, and ACT to help all our children be
> heard as Eric has been.
>
> – Brenda, a parent

Treating the individual vs. treating the disease. The current mainstream medical paradigm is disease-oriented: find the right label for the patient's problem, and prescribe the medicine for that condition. Adherents of that school of thought naturally think that books like this one are prescriptive for a particular condition, as if we are advocating public policy. In reality, our intention is not to prescribe any set of lab tests for autism, but to offer a consensus about options you may consider while tailoring your thinking to an individual child. As illustrated by the example regarding whether or not to institute a gluten-free diet for a given child, the focus on a given child involves a different way of thinking than a focus on a disease. Focusing on a disease means paying attention to certain signs, symptoms and lab tests that give individuals membership in a certain group – a diagnostic category. Focusing on an individual means paying attention to all the ways that he or she differs from the group – ways that may drive decisions more powerfully than similarities of behavior, socialization and communication that place a given child within a diagnostic category.

Nutritional pharmacology vs. prescription-pad medicine. In medical school I was taught to believe that prescription medicines are, by their very nature, "strong," and nutrients are "weak." Thus, real doctors prescribe "real medicines" and recommendations for nutrients are wimpy. Forty years later this attitude among most doctors has strengthened, despite a growing body of scientific support for the notion that nutrients modify genetic risk, disease and behavior.[5,6]

Behavioral toxicology/allergy. Just about any part of the body can be susceptible to an adverse reaction to an allergen or a toxin. No one denies that your skin, lungs, digestive system, kidneys, heart valves or blood vessels can become inflamed or injured by allergic or toxic reactions. However, there is a prevailing belief in our medical culture that toxic or allergic reactions spare the brain in ways that make learning, behavior, and social interaction exempt from adverse effects due to small amounts of a food, pollen, mold, chemicals, dust or dander. This belief is especially odd in view of the widespread medical advocacy of pharmaceuticals to "treat" problems in learning, behavior and social interaction.

Mercury toxicity. Mercury has a long history of medicinal use, enduring through the 1960s when I was in my training and mercury-based diuretics were in common usage. Until recently, despite scientific evidence to the contrary, mercury was considered to be a relatively safe substance. As children, people in my generation played with beads of quicksilver (metallic mercury). Nowadays, a spill of such beads in our grandchildren's school room would invite an evacuation of the school and decontamination by moon-suited technicians. Still, polarization of opinion as to the dangers of mercury is maintained by a strong lobby of the American Dental Association and vaccine manufacturers who have, against the preponderance of evidence, clung to the advocacy of mercury's safety. Dentists who've insisted that mercury amalgams pose significant risks to patients, and physicians who've raised questions concerning the dangers of thimerosal in pediatric vaccines, have been marginalized by their colleagues who pooh-pooh the hazard. Similarly, representatives of the food industry have fought to minimize the risk of consuming fish with high levels of mercury.

Immunization: threshold for safety. As illustrated in our rubella example, there are inherent polarities between private and public policy regarding immunization. Beyond that dichotomy is a range of opinions. Some individuals regard all immunization as unnecessary or dangerous. Other individuals believe that the public benefits of immunization exempt vaccines from safety checks routinely enacted for other pharmaceuticals. These individuals advocate multiple simultaneous immunizations and other strategies based on medical opportunity (e.g., the immunization of newborn babies with hepatitis B vaccine) for the sake of compliance. A third group – to which we belong – feels that the potential benefits of vaccines are enormous. We also believe that specifically because many vaccines are intended for universal obligatory administration, they should meet safety standards that are higher than those for other pharmaceuticals – not lower, as has been the case during the past half century, to the detriment of public health and public trust.

Systemic effects of gut flora. "Gut flora" is a respectable medical term for the different species of bacteria and a few fungi that inhabit our digestive tract. In fact, there are 500 or so different kinds of germs inhabiting your mouth, esophagus, stomach, and small and large intestine, from which they emerge – daily, one hopes – as the major constituent of bowel movements. A dazzling variety inhabit your mouth, and an even more dazzling quantity of germs inhabit the lower digestive tract. The gut flora can be viewed as very much a body organ, with their own complex metabolism and their own capacity for health and disorder, just like the tissues of your skin, liver, lungs, muscles, brain, etc. Peer-reviewed scientific reports attest to the complex interaction between this flora and your immune system, hormone balance and nutritional status. It is a fact that gut flora are altered within hours of taking antibiotics. For reasons that are poorly understood, people have different capacities for regeneration of normal flora after antibiotics. Dr. Orion Truss published reports in the late 1970s of individuals who recovered from systemic illness thanks to treatment of what appeared to be an intolerance to the presence in their gut flora of certain fungi that were the legacy of antibiotic treatment.[7,8,9] I was one of the first to become infected by Dr. Truss's ideas, which spread like a virus among lay people and numerous physicians. Medical authorities quickly became resistant to the notion that abnormalities of gut flora produce systemic effects, and denounced this idea as heresy because it had not been "proven." So it remains to this day in the minds of many physicians, although a flurry of new studies prompt hope[10,11,12,13,14].

ATTITUDE

As you can see, this book has attitude. We are impatient with a medical profes[sion] obsessed with treating diseases with drugs rather than treating individuals wit[h]. The first part of common sense (and the topic of the next section) is the last i[n] polarized issues: Who decides for my child? The second part of common se[nse, to] discuss shortly) has to do with two simple questions that form the basis for [we] will consider while answering the fundamental question that haunts every p[arent and] clinician: Am I doing everything I can for this child?

SECTION ONE: RATIONALE FOR INDIVIDUALIZED AUTISM TREATM[ENT]

...DECIDES FOR MY CHILD?

...people – normal people – defer to professionals when it comes to important issues such ...oney, health, or education. We let other people do it for us, or to us. Our job is to pick the ...consultants; after that, we abide by our decision and have faith in, and obedience to, the opinion of our advisors. Some parents, however, maintain and exercise unusual discretion in regard to decisions governing their children. Our medical culture is wary of such parents. Sensitivity to the dangers of decisions driven by "unreasonable" expectations combines with professional tendencies to raise questions about parental discretion over matters that "are best left to the doctor." When parents reflect independent attitudes by looking for answers, and seek treatments contrary to the mainstream – such as changes in diet – the reaction of many well-trained and conscientious professionals may be anything from mild disapproval to condescension to hostility to allegations of child abuse.

This is dangerous territory for parents as well as for clinicians. I have a vivid memory from my medical student days of the ire I felt when hearing from friends about kooky treatments that my professors had taught me to believe were unproven and therefore "dangerous." Experience opened my mind, but I still recognize my former feelings in various professionals who show hostility to my kind of medicine. For licensed practitioners who enter into a collaborative relationship with parents in considering the options we present in this book, the danger is that some will be tested in the crucible of their colleagues' disaffection. Such testing has sometimes resulted in the loss of licensure by good doctors.

It *is* common sense that parents should be active, well-informed participants in the medical care of their children. Parents don't need to go to medical school to get started. They only need to learn to ask two common-sense questions. The two simple questions that we need to ask while trying to answer the fundamental question "Am I doing everything I can for my kid?" are:

Is there something my child should get for which he or she has an unmet need?

Is there something my child needs to avoid or be rid of because it is toxic or allergenic?

WHAT I'D LIKE TO SAY to doctors: please treat the individual. And, if you don't know the answer to a question, be honest about it. Being human is okay, and parents must realize and accept this too.
A professional's role is to provide advice, assistance and teaching, but parents should never become so dependent upon others that they lose sight of their child's best interests. I am frequently unsure of what should come next in my daughter's treatment plan, but I would rather feel empowered to make informed decisions than enslaved by someone else's agenda which may or may not be right for my child.

— *a parent*

JOIN A support group. Find good doctors/health care providers. Educate yourself about ASD by reading books, attending conferences, using the Internet and talking to other moms. I have learned the most from talking to other moms who have had similar experiences. These moms are a wealth of information regarding good health care providers (MDs as well as non-MD healers) and community resources.

— *Yvonne, a parent*

That's it. That is the whole strategy upon which this book is based. Maybe there is something you need to get or maybe there is something you need to avoid. Simple. All of the considerations embodied in the diagram that just intimidated you, and all of the considerations embodied in its more refined version to follow, are covered by these two questions. The focus of this book is biomedical intervention because it has helped thousands of autistic children and, as a result, it has become our expertise. We believe, moreover, that biomedical intervention should be primary because it provides the physiologic milieu needed to maximize effectiveness of other therapies and educational remedies. Keep in mind a second plain analogy: "If you are sitting on a tack, it takes a lot of behavioral therapy to help you sit still." Don't get us wrong – the DAN! consensus is strongly supportive of behavioral therapies as well as other interventions. The two questions about getting something helpful and/or avoiding something injurious frame strategies that apply to all sorts of therapeutic choices, depending on how we define "something" in the questions. For the sake of this book's purpose, "something" refers to either nutrients on the "get" side or toxins and allergens on the "avoid" side.

You may ask: If we know so much about the autism epidemic from the collective experience of thousands of parents and practitioners, then why can't we just give you the recipe? Because your kid is an individual. One of the most important lessons I have learned in 40 years of being a physician is that individuality REALLY counts. The other important lesson I have learned is that illness is a signal to change. I grant that genetic factors are important in all illness, but ancestors are easy to blame but hard to change. What can be changed is the expression of our genetic plusses and minuses. When that change comes involuntarily from environmental exposures, such as mercury toxicity, and the change is a net negative, then we may need to make complex changes to undo the damage. It appears to us that the children caught in the autism epidemic are faced with just such a proposition of simple changes whose complexity comes from knowing the priorities and sequences that suit each individual.

There are seven sources of information that may drive decisions about priorities and sequences for any individual child:

- The outcome of treatments for children like yours.
- The time path in the emergence of problems in children like yours.
- Biochemical paths of children like yours.
- Your child's history and physical exam.
- Your child's laboratory tests.
- Your child's response to each treatment you try.
- Your intuition and that of your doctor.

Of course, there is no child exactly like yours. Nor are there easy ways to find other children who are very much like yours and ask their parents what has worked for them. (We had such a system live on the Internet but it is currently in hibernation, awaiting the day when a more congenial financial and medical climate allows it to live again.) You are left with just the broad label of Autism Spectrum Disorder, which embraces an enormous variety of children. But it is at least a start, thanks to the surveys that the Autism Research Institute (ARI) has been conducting since 1967.

SECTION ONE: RATIONALE FOR INDIVIDUALIZED AUTISM TREATMENT

PARENT RATINGS OF TREATMENTS

The most recent survey conducted by ARI and published in March 2005 shows the following leaders in the competition for the treatments that have worked the best and have had the least negative effects. The number in the Better/Worse column is the numerator in the ratio of the percent of children who were reported as improving to those who were reported as getting worse on a particular treatment. For example, out of 475 reports on the drug Adderall, 34% reported improvement and 41% reported worsening. That gives a ratio of 34 to 41. Thirty-four divided by 41 = 0.8, which says that for every eight children who improved, ten got worse. Twenty-five percent exhibited no effect. Naturally, we are looking for numbers for the better/worse ratio that are at least above 1, and the higher the better. Let's take another example: gluten- and casein-free diet. Of 1,446 respondents, 3% got worse and 65% got better, yielding a ratio of 65/3 = 20. In other words, just going by the odds suggested in these data from over 23,000 parents, you might say that an average child is 20 times more likely to benefit from a gluten- and casein-free diet than to get worse. Of course, there is no such thing as an average child – average is only a concept – but you get the point of using these data to help you get an idea of the collective experience of parents with kids like yours.

# Better ÷ # Worse	Treatment (# of reports)
0.8	Adderall (475)
1.2	Prozac (1123)
1.3	Depakene – behavior (957)
3.0	Risperdal (616)
3.9	Vitamin B6 alone (620)
4.8	Depakene – seizures (627)
9.8	Nystatin (986)
11.0	Diflucan (330)
11.7	Vitamin B6 with magnesium (5780)
12.0	Folic acid (1437)
15.0	Calcium (1378)
18.0	Vitamin C (1706)
19.0	Yeast-free diet (756)
20.0	Gluten/casein-free diet (1446)
20.0	Zinc (1244)
20.0	Digestive enzymes (737)
23.0	Fatty acids (626)
23.0	Vitamin A (618)
30.0	Removing chocolate (1721)
32.0	Removing milk products (5575)
35.0	Detoxification (324)

The picture that emerges from these data is interesting. Risperdal is the only pharmaceutical with a ratio greater than 3 except for medications for seizures and two antifungal drugs. All of the high-scoring items are aimed at providing for an unmet need, or avoiding something or ridding it from the body – the latter including the two antifungal drugs. These data don't prove anything, and they don't tell you what to do, but they certainly should arouse your interest and provide some focus. "Focus!" you reply. "Why, this is just a mishmash of weird diets and vitamin supplements. If you knew what you were doing, there wouldn't be so many different treatments." Ever see a train wreck? Boyd Haley, Ph.D., Professor and Chairman of the Department of Chemistry at the University of Kentucky, describes our children as having a "biochemical train wreck." No one would claim that if you knew what you were doing, you could fix the wreck with one tool.

TWO PATHS – THROUGH TIME AND CHEMISTRY

Dr. Haley's analogy is particularly apt because a train wreck is a disaster along a particular path. Thanks in part to his detailed studies of mercury toxicity, we have a good idea of how the mishmash of measures to meet unmet needs and rid the body of mischievous substances fits together. Let me give you a glimpse of the particular path that joins the activities of the biomedical treatments reported from Dr. Rimland's tabulation of Parent Ratings, a complete copy of which can be found at the end of Section Five of this book. We can look at the path in two perspectives, one over time in a particular child, and the other by means of what biochemists call pathways, because – like assembly lines in a factory – they flow in purposeful ways that can be diagrammed with arrows pointing in the directions of flow.

> IT'S IMPORTANT to understand that working to recover a child from autism is a trial-and-error process. Many of the treatments we've tried have brought about no change, some have made my son feel sick, but some have brought about significant improvement.
>
> My son is now functioning at a level I never dreamed possible, but fairly often it's two steps forward, one step back. For most children, improvement or recovery requires a long-term, do-or-die commitment.
>
> – Jane, a parent

A time path:

Alex is born with one or more genetic predispositions that will lead to increased susceptibility to one or more ensuing environmental exposures. One genetic predisposition is being male, for which the risk of autism is four times higher than if he were female. Another is being inclined toward high intelligence, which would be expressed if he were to be spared exposure and will be expressed if his autism is cured.

> DO NOT GET THE IDEA that we think that mercury is the exclusive toxin implicated in children with autism and related (attentional) problems. It is simply the one that we currently know the most about, and it provides a model for thinking about the potential role of other toxins.

Mercury exposure from maternal dental amalgam, maternal vaccine such as RhoGam, maternal fish consumption, pediatric vaccines in early infancy, or other environmental sources (air, water, food) results in damage to the very chemistry that is responsible for detoxification of mercury and other heavy metals. It is very likely that other toxins such as pesticides can substitute for mercury in this scenario.

Antibiotics given in the first months of life increase the toxicity of mercury, and the combined effect of mercury toxicity and altered intestinal flora causes damage to Alex's digestive system, including a branch of his immune system that deals with the digestive system. This branch, the gut associated lymphoid tissue (GALT), constitutes the biggest and busiest part of the immune system. As a result, he may be more susceptible to both typical and atypical infections – the latter tending to be more hidden.

SECTION ONE: RATIONALE FOR INDIVIDUALIZED AUTISM TREATMENT

Injury to the gut is associated with symptoms such as diarrhea, constipation, and difficulty with digestion. Difficulties with digestion permit the incomplete breakdown of certain proteins, especially gluten from wheat, barley and rye, and casein from milk and milk products. Products of this incomplete digestion enter the bloodstream by way of Alex's damaged gut, which is abnormally permeable to these products (peptides).

When he is administered a vaccine combining three live viruses (mumps, measles and German measles – MMR), Alex's immune system is unable to rid his body of the live measles vaccine virus, which, instead of being transiently present in saliva, persists in his body where it can be found months or years later in his GALT as well as in his spinal fluid.[15,16,17] Susceptibility to infection leaves him vulnerable to other viruses, which may also play a role in the infectious aspect of his problems. From the beginning, he has and/or acquires special nutritional needs based on the simple or combined effects of the preceding traumas.

> AT 12 MONTHS, after constant ear infections, antibiotics, and vaccinations, our son began to slip into the world of autism, seeming deaf, with loss of muscle tone and balance, intense perseverations, and losses of language and eye contact. By 18 months of age, he was up nightly crying for hours with stomach pains, was losing weight, and was not growing properly. We knew something was terribly wrong.
>
> At 24 months he was diagnosed and we were told he may never speak. As I sat in the neurologist's office, the room became dark and I nearly fainted.
>
> – a parent

At some point in this progression, Alex begins to display symptoms related to toxicity and dysfunction of his central nervous system, and slowly or abruptly passes into a state of developmental disorganization which leads doctors to give him a label on the autism spectrum. Some children have a brush with this pathway of regression, and others become trapped in its full expression.

Here is an outline of this time-line:
1. Genetic predisposition
2. Exposure to mercury (or other toxins)
3. Antibiotics in the first months of life
4. Damage to digestive tract and its flora
5. Damage to GALT
6. Increased gut permeability
7. Absorption of food-derived peptides and antigens enter the blood
8. Anomalous live virus exposure (three-in-one vaccine) with persistence of the measles vaccine virus in GALT and central nervous system (CNS).
9. Gastrointestinal, and immunological, and CNS signs, symptoms, and laboratory evidence of inflammation and disorder.

The above time-line typically evolves during the first two years of life, usually reaching a crisis around 15 to 18 months. The interaction of the factors described under numbers 1-8 is more accurately represented in the preceding diagram than by a straight path, but we can imagine the flow of events along the path over time, occurring as a result of the mechanisms we have described.

The picture we are drawing constitutes a theory. By theory, we do not mean mere speculation, but an analysis of the relationships among a large set of facts. We will discuss the factual basis for our time-line analysis as we move forward. A key part of that factual basis is embodied in the second of the two paths I referred to above – the biochemical path.

A biochemical path:

We discuss this path here as a way to help you see how our current knowledge of one important aspect of biochemistry helps drive decisions. It will come up again later in this book. Bear in mind that the biochemical path we want you to grasp is the most important biochemical path in human chemistry, and it is relevant to problems we will all encounter before we die, so what you learn about it here will serve you in good stead in understanding options with respect to a wide variety of health problems you or your family may encounter. For now, however, simply take this lesson in biochemistry as part of our discussion of the seven sources of information that may drive decisions. You will have another shot at this chemistry in the section on molecular aspects of autism.

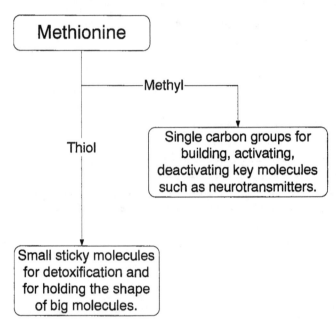

A small molecule named methionine is central to this path. Disruptions of this pathway have ramifications not only for autism and attention problems but also for cardiovascular disease, cancer, Alzheimer's disease, and just about everything else that we want to avoid.[18,19,20,21,22,23,24]

Biochemistry is one huge network of interconnected paths, some of which can kill you if just one step is missing or injured. So how can we say that one path is more important than the others?

Because the few simple steps are crucial to so many important functions, you only need to learn a few new words to find your way on this path. It starts with methionine, an amino acid which is a component in a long folded chain (you can picture this as a chain of different kinds of paperclips). If you pick up a container of protein powder at the health food store and want to know whether it is made of old shoes or something nutritious, check its content of methionine. If it is over three percent, it's OK. Methionine is the queen of the dozen essential amino acids. (Essential means two things: [1] you cannot make it in your body, but must take it in, pre-formed in your diet; and [2] it is essential in the sense of being really important.) Methionine is the most important because she brings in – and serves as a constant supply of – two precious components for your chemistry.

One is methyl groups, which consist of one simple carbon atom with some trimmings that permit it to be passed around in order to be added to other molecules that need to be synthesized, silenced or activated. Methyl groups are not just building blocks, but are tools for regulating the expression of other molecules including neurotransmitters, proteins, DNA (the source of your genetic memory) and RNA (the messenger which translates that memory into action as proteins). Methyl groups' role as building blocks is not as trivial as their simplicity implies. About

70% of the output of methyl groups from methionine ends up being used to make creatine, a key molecule in energy transfer in the body.

The second precious component is sulfur (thio- from Greek for sulfur). Sulfur's presence in garlic confers both the stickiness and the stinkiness you sense when handling it in the kitchen. The chemistry of sulfur (thiol chemistry) has to do with the delicate handling of problems of stinkiness and stickiness in the body. When our sulfur-containing molecules are optimal, we can rid ourselves properly of unwanted toxins, and we can hold our proteins in their proper shapes while still maintaining the flexibility required by an active molecule.

So here is how the pathway works. At the top, coming from your diet is methionine. It goes through transformations that end with the two destinations previously indicated.

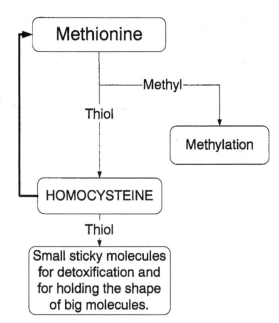

This chemistry is damaged in most children on the autism spectrum. Perhaps you have heard that biomedical intervention is "alternative medicine." Maybe you think that the biochemistry we are describing in this book is "alternative biochemistry." No such thing. There is only one biochemistry. The only difference these days in regard to the application of biochemical knowledge is the difference we pointed to earlier. In our case, we are talking about treating individuals, not diseases, by patching and repairing their broken chemistry. The chemistry you see illustrated here is the most commonly broken part in the biological train wreck called autism. In many autistic children, both branches of the methionine path are broken in ways that you may want to understand in order to grasp the use of certain supplements such as methyl B12 in accomplishing the repair.[25]

Methionine comes to you in your food. You cannot make it out of other molecules. That's why it is "essential." Food comes, say, three times daily, but in our bodies this chemistry is working all the time. Actually, this chemistry works harder at night when you are asleep and the repair and cleaning crews of your body are busy with regeneration, growth in children, and detoxification. How does your body assure a consistent supply of methionine when its source, food, is intermittent? It does so by putting into the path a means of scavenging unused methionine along the way and recycling it back to the beginning, thus providing for the optimum state of a regular supply. Here is how it works.

Along the pathway illustrated, the assembly line turns out several intermediate molecules, which we can skip over for the moment to focus on one in particular. You will want to learn its name because it will keep turning up in many places where it will catch your attention as regards heart disease, cancer, Alzheimer's, etc.[26,27,28,29,30,31] It is called homocysteine, so named because it is similar to (homo) cysteine, an amino acid farther along in this assembly line. Homocysteine is the branch point in the path where methionine can be recycled by getting its methyl group back (see diagram above).

The arrow that rises from homocysteine back to methionine is the path where a methyl group is passed to homocysteine to convert it back into methionine. The donor of the methyl group in this step is a form of vitamin B12 called methyl B12, which works with a big protein molecule (an enzyme called methionine synthase, MS) to stick the methyl group back onto homocysteine to become methionine. This step is damaged in autistic children. As a consequence, methionine supplies run short. As a further consequence of that, there is a shortage of sticky sulfury molecules at the end of the thiol path. The most important of those sticky sulfury molecules is reduced glutathione, abbreviated GSH, which is not only one of the body's chief detoxifying molecules but also the main provider of a favorable milieu for this whole system to work smoothly. What do I mean by a favorable milieu? Technically it is called redox potential, redox being a word made from two opposite forces in chemistry: reduction and oxidation.

Imagine that you are a molecule of any size. Buzzing around you are electrons which you get, give or share with other molecules. That is basically what chemistry is all about: the joining or separating of molecules according to how their electrons are shared, gained or lost. Gaining an electron is called reduction. (I know it sounds backward, but just take a deep breath and we will get through this to the easy part in another paragraph or so.) Losing an electron is called oxidation, because that's what oxygen does – it likes to steal electrons. When you strike a match, oxygen sucks zillions of electrons from the match which, in its burnt form, is "oxidized." (Oxygen is the most abundant oxidizer in our internal and external environment. Many other molecules, such as lead and mercury, have the same tendency to steal electrons, often with very negative effects.)

Back to you, the molecule. Let's say a big, burly molecule such as lead or mercury comes up to you to rip off one of your electrons. If you are lucky, vitamin C will step up and say, "Don't take her electron, take mine!" and the thief will go away content, you will be safe, and vitamin C will be imbalanced, discontent. Vitamin C turns around to vitamin E and says, "OK, hand over an electron." Vitamin E then goes after beta carotene and so on until GSH becomes the final donor who then must wait for lunch to get his electron back, meanwhile consoling himself by sharing the loss with another GSH to become GSSG[32,33] (glutathione disulfide, often improperly called oxidized glutathione). A milieu (redox potential) favorable to the chemistry under discussion – and most, but not all of the chemistry of living things – is achieved when there is no shortage of extra electrons. The members of the bucket brigade that supply lost electrons, particularly GSH, are handicapped when the redox potential is spoiled by a lack of electrons to pass around. A shortage results in a poor redox potential and a goodly supply constitutes a favorable milieu with a low level of oxidative stress.

Let us summarize. The chemistry of methylation and thiols is injured in autistic children. One site of injury is to methionine synthase (MS) which has the job of recycling homocysteine back to methionine.[34,35] As a result of that injury, thiol chemistry is impaired and GSH supplies fall short. GSH is the keeper of a healthy redox potential, so its shortage degrades the functioning of the chemistry that produces GSH. Moreover, with GSH in short supply, the mechanism by which methyl-B12 gets its methyl group becomes impaired. We need not get into the details at this point, but yet another factor (having to do in part with gluten and casein) tends to block the formation of homocysteine on its way from methionine.

With the time path and the methionine biochemical path in mind, you can begin to see how diverse treatments that appear on Dr. Rimland's surveys begin to come together. Further along we will clarify what is meant by "detoxification" – but you already have a glimpse of the fact that the methionine path is a major workhorse of detoxification. Treatments aimed at improving detoxification recently surpassed all the others in the ARI survey rating. Treatment with methyl B12 has a direct bearing on thiols, as you can now understand. (Methyl B12 treatment has not been around long enough to get a rating, but if it had been rated on Dr. Rimland's surveys it would come out a winner, as it produces a dramatic response in a very high percentage of kids.)

At this point we have explored two "outside" sources of information on which to base decisions about priorities. One is what we know about thousands of parents' ratings of the efficacy of various treatments for their kids, and the other comes from an analysis of the time-line and the chemistries of children on the autism spectrum. So far, all of the top survey-rated interventions make sense when seen from the perspective of these two paths.

Methionine path and the time path make sense out of the survey winners: RATING	TREATMENT
9.8	Nystatin (antifungal)
11.0	Diflucan (antifungal)
11.7	Vitamin B_6 with magnesium (figures in methionine pathway, and many others)
12.0	Folic acid (figures in the methionine pathway)
15.0	Calcium (corrects shortage caused by poor absorption)
18.0	Vitamin C (first member of the antioxidant bucket brigade)
19.0	Yeast-free diet (reduces exposure to mold in fungus-sensitized person)
20.0	Gluten/casein-free diet (eliminates mischievous peptides)
20.0	Zinc (corrects shortage caused by poor absorption)
20.0	Digestive enzymes (help improve digestion)
23.0	Fatty acids (correct shortage caused by poor absorption)
23.0	Vitamin A (corrects shortage caused by poor absorption)
30.0	Removing chocolate (needs further research to explain this high ranking)
32.0	Removing milk products (eliminates mischievous peptides, and milk allergens)
35.0	Detoxification (assists and/or helps repair ways of ridding heavy metals and other toxins)

Next is to look "inside" at your own child, whether you are his or her parent or a clinician.

YOUR CHILD'S STORY

Many doctors do not keep good records, which require an investment of time and energy that is incompatible with a system in which it is easy to get information (scribbles) in and hard to get it out later. Bringing a detailed questionnaire, a chronological history form and a narrative description, as well as records from previous professional contacts and laboratory tests is, then, a favor to the doctor. It is also a favor to yourself, as it helps you organize your thinking. I developed an interest in medical forms and questionnaires as an intern 40 years ago, and am still at it.

THE ONE THING THAT I FEEL IS MOST IMPORTANT when using biomedical interventions is daily record keeping. You need to have a system to keep track of what interventions you are doing and the frequency/dose. You also need to keep track of your child's response to treatment, because I guarantee that you will not be able to remember what happened last month, let alone last year.

My tracking system originally was just a spiral notebook with a line or two written each day. As we started using more and more supplements and therapies, it evolved into a chart that I fill in daily which tracks supplements and medications along with diet, sleep, speech, school, behavior and physical symptoms. I assign scores (on a scale of 1 to 7, with 4 being average) for each category for each week, and I also do a weekly overall total. I graph all of these weekly scores so I can get an overall sense of the past six months. The advantage of going to all this trouble is that I can look back and say "Well, treatment A was wonderful for speech, but we also had a lot of night-waking while on it – so what adjustment might I need to make?" So much of what we are doing is trying to restore balance to our children's metabolisms.

– Katie, a parent

THE CHRONOLOGICAL QUESTIONNNAIRE

My lowest-tech form is the chronological history. A sample follows, of the first and last pages from a form completed by the mom of a patient I first saw last year. As you can see, this format permits a very efficient presentation of an enormous amount of information describing a boy with complex problems. No other format could give me such easy access to a sense of this boy's development and its complications. As you can imagine, his mom is a contender for the gold medal in forms, but even more modest efforts – describing the timing of a dozen or so key events – are very valuable. Notice how this mother's entries summarize a complex story in just a few words.

Name Erik K. Please record: date and place of birth, introduction of changes in feeding, infections, antibiotics, moves, operations, traumas, diagnostic tests, treatments, and any other major life events including the onset or remission of any symptoms.

	Jan	Feb	Mar	Apr	May	Jun	Jul	Aug	Sep	Oct	Nov	Dec
Pregnancy 1993			Amalgam replaced 3/2. Conceived 3/30.				7/21 Rhogam (didn't need) Amniocentesis	8/5 Amnio results "normal" based on my blood			11/25 Severe Carpal Tunnel – both hands	12/26 Influenza - mild
Birth 1994 1/15/94 5:13 p.m. 7 lb. 13 oz. Palo Alto, CA.	1/11: Toxemia? 1/13: Low Amniotic fluid 1/14: Induced Labor 1/15: born 5:13 Apgars 8 & 9 1/16: Circumcision 1/17: 05:00 ICU –Seizures EEG-Abnormal CT-Normal Organic Acids- Normal Amnio Acid –incr B-Amnioisobutyric CBC Mild Thrombocyopenia Incr eosl 1/19: EEG abnrml 1/23: Released on Phenobarbital 1/27: MRI – Normal 1/30: Generalized Seizures began Antibiotics	2/3: EEG - Abnormal 2/5: Dilantin & 50 mg B6 Seizure Control 2/18: Organic Acids nl. Amino Acids – Abn but "no pattern" 2/23: Audiologist- Mild hearing loss – considered Nl	3/9 Immunize 3/17 Allergic Reaction; WBC 700; Stop using Dilantin	4/1: Sick G. Seizure 4/5: Started Formula (Enfamil) EEG - normal 4/7: "Spasm" Seizures began – not controlled until 6/11 4/8: Tegretol 4/9: 100 mg B6 4/16: All Formula Started Rolling	5/11: EEG – normal 5/19: 100 mg P5P Sitting By himself Babbling Social	6/6: Immunize 6/11: 250 mg P5P Seizure Free! First 2 teeth Fingers no longer stiff when sleeping Combat crawl Very Social	7/21 Immunize	8/11 Developmental Assessment O.K. Started full-time Daycare Very social I was worried sick, Erik was happy as a clam	Crawling	Started weaning off Tegretol Pulling to a stand Cruising	11/28 Immunize Ear Infection Antibiotics	Off Tegretol

32

	Jan	Feb	Mar	Apr	May	Jun	Jul	Aug	Sep	Oct	Nov	Dec
Age 8 2002 1st/2nd grade	1/19 Cod Liver Oil w/lemon oil	2/13 URI/Asthma Oxygen CLO w/orange essence Taurine	Multi-Vitamin Calcium	IQ test completed Possible Non-Verbal LD 4/26 IEP Vitamin E	Vitamin C		Zinc		2nd grade – No aide Began Resource Help Phosphatidyl Choline	10/2 IEP	CoQ10	B-Complex
Age 9 2003 2nd/3rd grade	Idebenone Glycine TMG	DMG	2nd tests Dr. Smith: MTHFR Color in skin 1 week after starting Folinic Acid Folocal		Methyl-Cobolamin	CoQ10	Summer school Math – satisfactory Stop Wheat Alpha-Ketoglutaric Acid Acetylcar-nitine	Calcium Multi-Mineral Stop Iron	3rd grade – No aide Resource Kaiser Genetics Taurine P5P (up 100 mg)	Kaiser Gastroenterology Phosphatidyl-Serine	Kaiser GI tests Allithiamine	Panthethine B2-5-Phosphate
Age 10 2004 3rd/4th Grade	Glycine	Acidopholous	URI – no asthma Skin on back less dry	4/14 John Wade, MD GS CSDA: Blastocystis Yeast Bacteria Thyroid Panel	5/20 Dr. Wade GPL OAT: Yeast 5/20 Bifido (2500)	6/16 Dr. Wade Vitamin: deficiencies Elevated Mercury Stop all Grain Reduce Fruit	Paramicro-cidin Cellulose Alpha-Ketoglutaric (900 mg)	Alpha-Ketoglutaric (1200 mg) Bifido (7500)				

THE BIG QUESTIONNAIRE

Another document for describing your child as an individual duplicates some of the chronological history form information, but provides for detailed information about every aspect of your child's strengths, problems, previous diagnostic tests, past and present therapies, family, social, and environmental factors. It is twenty pages long and has been through many revisions, but it has not become shorter or streamlined. It serves as a two-way instrument of communication. After filling out my questionnaire, my patients know much more about me and my way of thinking than they could learn from reading a long essay from me on the subject. The questionnaire lets them know that I am interested in details that may have nothing to do with "making a DSM-IV diagnosis" but are clues to finding the answers to the "get and avoid" questions. The questionnaire is available for any parent or physician to use in the form of a Microsoft Word document or a PDF file downloadable from the ARI website.[36] It is printed as an appendix to this book, and you are welcome to make a copy.

⇩	Symbol (0= Absent, 3= mild, 6= Moderate, 9=severe, 12= incapacitating.)	10/04	2/05
1	Hyperactive	9	6
2	Limited expressive language (regressed at 16 months) Now >200 words.	6	5
3	Poor Articulation	6	6
4	Combine words into sentences	9	9
5	Running in circles and back and forth	9	9
6	Constipation/Diarrhea	6	3
7	Intermittent Laughter	6-9	3
8	Voice modulation	9	9
9	Looking at things from corner of eyes	6	6
10	Expand variety of foods	6	6
11	Lining up toys, other items	9	9
12	Moving hands across face, eyes and in the air	6	6
13	Cradle cap	7	3
14	Brittle nails	7	7
15	Red anal ring	6	3
S	Loves music and singing		
S	Social		
S	Cuddly/Affectionate		
Lab	IgG: Almond, Coconut, Corn, Egg, Canola, Rice, Safflower, Sesame, Tomato and Brewer's Yeast (2+)		

The symptom table, of which a sample of the first four columns are shown here, delineates the major defining problems – such as poor expressive language – along with other "minor symptoms" such as cradle cap or red anal ring. As this table can be used as a flow sheet, it provides a place for scoring symptoms over time so that the "big picture" can emerge. Here, for example, we see that after the first two months of treatment, language has only increased a little, but the silly laughter, bowel problems, and red anal ring have improved a lot. Notice also that there is a conspicuous place given to the child's strengths, a very important point of discussion (especially in front of the child) at all stages of our relationship with him. A child's strengths – even an incontinently strong will – are ultimately what he or she will build on. Strengths may be overlooked in a clinical setting that focuses on everything that is wrong. It is better to assume and expect the best from your child because, in the long run, the better picture is sure to emerge. This is true both for children who become completely cured and for those who are severely damaged and don't achieve full recovery.

Michael is an example of the former. He exhibited completely normal development until 18 months of age. He had never been given an antibiotic but suffered from yeast diaper rashes, so severe that they resembled burns, from the age of six months on. These were associated with a metallic odor. He stopped talking and had complete change of personality at 18 months. In retrospect, he had what could only be described as a miraculous response to a low-carbohydrate, gluten- and casein-free diet and Nystatin, later followed by the antifungal drug Lamisil at age five. Four days after starting Lamisil he became calm, had better eye contact, and began to speak. After that he became, as it were, a Lamisil poster child. Every time we tried to stop it, he completely fell apart. Here is his father's description of one such event: "We took Michael off Lamisil three days before he was going back to school from vacation. On Monday all of the therapists wrote that he wasn't settling down and attributed his behavior to the week vacation…His reports got worse as each day went by. Finally, on Thursday, the nurse called home to ask what 'new medication' Michael was on, because he had regressed at least six months in the past few days and was out of control. When I arrived home from work that night he had just (15 minutes before) broken a glass (regular and not a 'favorite') which he had never done before. After he broke the glass he started crying, saying, 'Mommy fix it, mommy fix it.' Laura told him that it was OK and not to cry, so he ran upstairs to his room, sobbing and out of control. When I got to his room he was running into the walls and bouncing to the ground. I took him downstairs and gave him a Lamisil. He seemed better the next day at school but not the normal daily improvements as before. After four days he had a Herxheimer (die-off) reaction at 3 a.m. with metallic-smelling diarrhea. By the following Wednesday, he was back to normal per his therapists. He has never run into walls or exhibited similar self-abusive behavior prior to or since this event. He has also never sobbed so hysterically as he did that evening. It was one of the most frightening events I have ever seen. We never told anyone what we were or were not giving Michael, so the school was blind."

Here is Michael's flow sheet from my record:

⇓	Symptom (0= Absent, 3= mild, 6= Moderate, 9=severe, 12= incapacitating.) S=Strength	12/97	12/98	2/99	3/29/99	5/18/99	7/13/99	9/8/99
1	Poor language (delay)	8	4	2	2	2	0	0
2	Fatigues in language exchange	8	4	0	0	0	0	0
3	Auditory sensitivity	8	1	1	1	1	0	0
4	Fine motor problems	8	0	0	0	0	0	0
5	Peer relations problem	8	6	5	4	3	1	0
6	Eye contact problem	8	3	2	2	2	0	0
S	Computer							
S	Reading		100 word	more				

Even though Michael had strengths – played effectively with the computer at age 3½, for example – and was doing very well on diet and antifungal medications, we were so wrapped up in his problems that his parents and I were late to realize that he was destined to be extraordinarily talented: an artistic prodigy, a chess champion, and a thoroughly charming and articulate and popular boy, now age 12. (He is the boy on the left on the cover.) We might not have done anything differently, but such experiences serve as a reminder to look for and expect a lot from our children.

Another example is George, now an adult, whom I met when he was 10. Here is an excerpt of my notes from his first visit:

SECTION ONE: RATIONALE FOR INDIVIDUALIZED AUTISM TREATMENT

His mom reports a normal pregnancy and vaginal delivery. He was breastfed for a few weeks and then placed on a dairy-based formula. Solids were introduced around three months of age.

Around six months of age, George developed recurrent ear infections. Subsequent to this, he was placed on a four-month maintenance course of Amoxicillin. This chronic condition continued throughout his infancy and early childhood.

Developmentally, George was slow to meet his milestones. He did not walk until 20 months of age. By age two, however, he was walking and speaking in short sentences.

In 1985 (when he was around age 2½), George's parents noticed that he was becoming hyperactive, had reduced eye contact, and no longer responded to his name. Within a few weeks of these observations, George began making flapping and rocking movements. The consensus was that he had been developmentally OK but turned a definite corner at a certain point after 22 months of age. (The pediatrician suggested his behavior was indicative of the "terrible twos.")

His parents began to seek additional information and explanations for George's behavior. His CAT scan and audiological studies were normal. He was given the diagnosis of PDD with autistic tendencies.

From the time I met George he was caught up in a dreamy but agitated and anxious state and was constantly busy with tongue stimming, finger flicking, pacing, and generally intense but ineffective effort. It was never clear that he was able to initiate, comprehend or respond except for a very restricted communication of needs. Over the years, and despite every conceivable diagnostic and therapeutic measure, little changed except that George settled down and seemed more in touch with the world and less intensely hyper.

We often learn our best lessons from extreme examples. Michael and George represent different realizations of our hopes, but their stories each convey a lesson about how well hidden our children's strengths may lie while we are searching for answers to their troubles.

Back to the questionnaire. The data on the questionnaire that often drives decisions is from questions about antibiotics, symptoms, and the environment. A history of antibiotics in the newborn period, when babies are getting their first gut flora from those who handle them – mostly their mothers – is a risk factor for yeast problems later on. Nearly every child I have seen with a problem in the past 25 years has benefited in some way from attention paid to a yeast problem, if he or she had early exposure to antibiotics. The same goes for a history of repeated antibiotic use in the first years of life. We know that such a pattern is common and not all children who get antibiotics suffer any harm. However, when seeing a chronically ill child, the role of antibiotics cannot be dismissed without careful consideration, which I will discuss at greater length later.[37] Other yeasty clues are a history of fungal nail infections; a red ring immediately around the anus; thrush; yeasty diaper rashes (which are characterized by red areas centrally with small satellite lesions peripherally); redness and swelling of the skin

> ANTIFUNGALS were nothing short of miraculous for him. After withstanding the die-off reaction, B. began labeling within days of starting Sporonox. We have tried all antifungals and each time, B. got better and better. We also saw improvements in eye contact and socialization.
>
> – *a parent*

between the fingernails and the first knuckle; inflammation of the margin on the eye lids (blepharitis); a yeasty odor to stools or breath; silliness or silly inappropriate (drunken) laughter; craving for sugar and starchy foods; multiple allergies and/or chemical sensitivities; constipation; abdominal bloating; reflux; poor coordination; and poor attention.

YEAST PROBLEMS

Poor attention is the common denominator among tipsy patrons at a bar, who otherwise may display striking individuality in response to their consumption of yeasty beverages. There are sleepy, sad, happy, hyper, aggressive, hostile, insensitive, friendly and apologetic drunks, all of whom have consumed the same number of drinks. If tested, all would show poor gross and fine motor skills, as well as attention deficit. This analogy sparks instant recognition in parents of children who display various aspects of a state of intoxication, not with alcohol but with other congeners of the brewing process that is taking place in their gut flora.

One of the many things we do not know about this particular aspect of "gut dysbiosis" (an altered balance, quantity, location, or sensitivity to the resident germs) is where the yeasts are hiding. Swabs of the throat and cultures of the stool or specimens recovered from endoscopy fail to find yeasts with frequencies that differ between autistic and normal children in most of the studies conducted so far. This has spawned various theories about other ways in which antifungal drugs could produce their often striking effects.

> WHEN WE STARTED antifungal medications, initially the boys got worse – we had lots of irritability, smelly poops and some vomiting – all typical die-off reactions but kind of scary when you go through it for the first time. It was amazing how well activated charcoal worked to eliminate these reactions. I can remember giving one of the boys charcoal when he was whining, tantrumming and biting – 20 minutes later, he let out an enormous belch and was his usual happy self again. This was my earliest experience with just how much behavior stems from gastrointestinal issues and pain.
>
> The negatives from the antifungals faded in a few weeks and what we saw was a nice improvement in attention and academics. It was obvious from their ABA data that their work had gone up a notch. One teacher said that it was the difference between needing tangible reinforcement for every learn unit versus being able to do 10-20 learn units before breaking the rhythm. So while antifungals have not "cured" my boys, they clearly make it easier for them to focus and learn.
>
> – Katie, a parent

The jury is still out. My own observation of the similar effects of different antifungal medications seems to eliminate all possibilities except that these remedies work because they are antifungal. One of the most telling features of antifungal treatment is the die-off reaction (referred to by Michael's dad as a Herxheimer reaction), caused by a transient toxic reaction resulting from the sudden killing of certain germs. I have seen hundreds of such reactions (which can produce very scary regressive symptoms in a child) and witnessed the almost certain quenching of the bad reaction within an hour after administration of a dose of activated charcoal to absorb the toxins. The similarity of response to different medications that share only the capacity to kill fungi, and the consistent capacity of charcoal – which is inert except for its toxin-absorbing action – persuades me that the yeast problem is real and common in our children, and that the laboratory measurements to support our understanding of the phenomenon will be forthcoming. Keep in mind that most of the small intestine remains pretty much unknown territory – ten to twenty feet of a tunnel with lots of very complicated surfaces where germs are normally very scarce, but could, if present, cause the kind of mischief that clinical experience has repeatedly brought to my attention.

SKIN PROBLEMS

The skin questions on the questionnaire are another source of data that may drive decisions. Here is a list of comments pertaining to a portion of the skin, hair and nails section.

Acne	Acne is usually responsive to high-dose vitamin A, zinc and omega-3 oils. Given such a dramatic response, one may assume that the corrective nutrients met a more general need.
Athlete's foot	A fungal clue.
Bumps on back of upper arms	Unmet omega-3 oil needs. Could also be vitamin A deficiency and sometimes a form of eczema (allergy).
Dark under-eye circles	Allergic shiners, food or any allergen.
Ears get red	Allergy – food or other.
Easy bruising	Allergy – food or other or autoimmune clue, often yeast.
Eczema	Allergy, fatty acid deficiency.
Lackluster skin	A very sensitive indicator of need for omega-3 oils.
Oily skin	Omega-3 oils (also what TV used to call combination skin).
Pale skin	A basic indicator of poor health, maybe anemia.
Patchy dullness	See lackluster.
Psoriasis	A good 50% respond to antifungals; also, like cradle cap, an omega-3 need indicator.
Red face	Food allergy, yeast.
Sensitive to bug bites	Just curious – one obvious manifestation of the pervasive sensitivity of our kids.
Sensitive to poison ivy / oak	Ditto.
Shingles	Shingles, caused by the chickenpox virus and more common in kids who have received the varicella vaccine.
Strong body odor	Adrenal stress, abnormal flora.
Thick calluses	See lackluster.
Skin, itching: anus, arms, ear canals, eyes, feet, hands, legs, nipples, nose, penis, roof of mouth, scalp, skin in general, throat	Allergy to something.
Skin: stretch marks	Unmet zinc needs.
Skin, dryness of: eyes, feet/hands (any cracking, any peeling?), hair (unmanageable?), mouth/throat, scalp (any dandruff?), skin in general	Unmet omega-3 oil needs.
Nails: brittle, frayed	Unmet omega-3 oil needs.
Nails: ridges	Horizontal: growth arrest. Vertical: don't know.
Nails: white spots	Unmet zinc or other mineral.
Cracking corner of lips	Yeast problem, B-vitamin deficiency.
Flushing	Allergy – like red ears.
Tongue – geographic (map-like area of flatter texture)	Food allergy.

BEING "UPTIGHT"

Another important part of the questionnaire has to do with symptoms of being "uptight." The vernacular is eloquent in its embrace of both the nervous and muscular inference regarding tension. Here is a list of symptoms that are common in individuals with unmet needs for magnesium.[38] This is so common in adults that it is useful to give you the whole picture, from which you can extract the few items that are related to muscle twitches, tics, cramps, anxiety, insomnia and hyperactivity in kids. You may wish to copy this to serve as a checklist. In this table you will detect a unifying sense of the links among symptoms that seem different but are actually quite often the joint manifestation of the same underlying problem. An unmet need for magnesium is the most frequent such underlying problem.

Skeletal muscle:	
	Muscle cramps, including backache, neck pain, tension headache, temporomandibular joint dysfunction
	Muscle twitches
	Muscle tension
	Muscle soreness
	Chest tightness or a peculiar "I can't seem to take a deep breath" or "I have to think about my breathing" that is often interpreted as hysterical. In children, this symptom is often seen as sighing.
Other muscles:	
	Constipation
	Anal spasms –such as awaken people at night
	Urinary spasm
	Difficulty swallowing or "lump in throat," "globus hystericus"
	Difficulty with adjusting to oncoming bright headlights because of spasm of the muscles that fine-tune pupillary diameter.
	Cold hands and feet – due to vasospasm
	Loud noise sensitivity – due to abnormal tension on the stapedius muscle
	Endometriosis – due to "constipation" or reverse peristalsis of uterus/Fallopian tubes
	Menstrual cramps
	Asthma / wheezing from constriction of bronchial muscles
	Toe walking
Central nervous system:	
	Insomnia
	Anxiety
	Hyperactivity and restlessness, constant movement
	Panic attacks
	Agoraphobia
Peripheral nervous system:	
	Numbness
	Tingling
	Other abnormal sensations including "zips," "zaps," vibratory and other peculiar sensations
Cardiovascular system:	
	Mitral valve prolapse
	Palpitations
	Arrhythmias
	Vasospastic angina
	Hypertension
Other:	
	Salt craving
	Carbohydrate craving
	Carbohydrate intolerance

SECTION ONE: RATIONALE FOR INDIVIDUALIZED AUTISM TREATMENT

TARGETING SYMPTOMS

One of the questions that emerges at some point as we focus with parents on particular symptoms described in the questionnaire is "what supplement (medication, remedy) would be best for stimming, focus, sleep, appetite, anxiety, etc.?" Because medications usually target particular symptoms, it is understandable that one would carry that kind of thinking over to the treatment of children with autism. It doesn't really work that way. The idea is to keep our eye on the ball, which is the balance – or imbalance – in the web of interacting factors we have reviewed previously. There are, however, some notable exceptions. Sleep problems and the inability to poop well are two issues that lend themselves to interventions that are worth a try. These interventions may work, and when they do, they may offer insight into, and help resolve, biochemical imbalances, thus producing benefits beyond the reduction of the target symptoms.

SLEEP

Here are some suggestions about sleep:

As described below, there are "pills" you can try for sleep, without getting into "sleeping pills," which are inappropriate for extended use. However, remedies other than pills may work better, so I am describing all the sleep-related interventions here to avoid the impression that all you can do for sleep problems is to "give something."

Difficulty falling asleep, night waking and early waking can be a nightmare for parents and other family members hoping to get some rest at night. Sleep deprivation is a problem for your child as well, but it often appears that "he doesn't need much sleep" because an expected compensatory catch-up sleep or need for a nap never seems to come. Only for emergencies should sedatives be turned to. Even Benadryl (diphenhydramine), an antihistamine with sedative properties, should be used sparingly and, if never before used, should be given a trial run before use for a long car ride or air travel because a paradoxical response of hyperactivity can really ruin your day.

Here is a hierarchy of suggestions involving relatively safe substances that have the virtue of either working within one to two nights, or not working at all. Thus, you won't end up using a substance for very long unless you find it really improves the symptom.

1. Protein in the morning and carbohydrate in the evening.

This remedy has a universal application and is relevant to many aspects of human health. The scientific basis for it is explored in my book *The Circadian Prescription*.[39] The gist is that there is a marked difference between the biochemical sequences of daytime and what goes on in our chemistry at night. It is as different as night is from day. Food that supplies the different phases should be of the right sort, which turns out to be opposite to the habit of many folks: cereal and fruit, or, worse, sweet roll and coffee in the morning, and meat for dinner. I became interested in the subject when I read the studies of Charles Ehret, Ph.D., author of *Overcoming Jet Lag*[40] and noted researcher in the field of circadian (day-night cycle) physiology.[41,42] I really became hooked when I saw dramatic changes in attention and vitality as well as a host of other functions in people of all ages who took my suggestion of experimenting with the "jet lag diet" delineated by Dr. Ehret. Getting protein into the breakfast of a finicky autistic child could be impossible without the amenity of Rice Protein (Nutribiotic, Lakeport, CA 95453, 707-263-0411). This is a bland powder that is essentially 100% protein. As such, it will jack up the protein content of anything to which it is added. Thus, 30 grams (one scoop) of this powder added to any food (say fruit) that contains 30 grams of carbohydrate would give you an end product that is 50% protein, which qualifies as "high protein." Naturally, if your child has a good appetite for chicken, turkey, beef, pork, lamb, fish, beans or eggs, then you will not need recourse to rice protein. Load him or her up with these high-protein foods at breakfast and lunch, and save most of the carbohydrates for any time after 4 p.m.

My book on circadian rhythms has recipes for various high-protein shakes. If your child would take to such an offering, you may want to try such a shake or experiment by making your own based on rice protein and banana. Soy protein is OK occasionally, but I do not think it is a good steady diet for children. Whey protein is good, too, but you may not be able to guarantee freedom from casein. Egg protein is the best, if the child is not allergic to egg.

2. Dark at night, light during the day.

Under normal circumstances, exposure to full-spectrum light such as that provided by the sun or by a 2500-LUX Full Spectrum bulb (about $10 from a lighting supply or hardware store) is the most powerful stimulus for keeping our internal day-night clock set to the local time. Being out in the sun, so that your skin and eyes are exposed – I am not talking about sunbathing – in the middle part of the day will provide an influence on your body's clock that favors a good melatonin release and good sleep at night. If you use artificial light, you should be three feet or less from the light, with exposure to eyes and skin. By the same token, having complete darkness at night is essential to prevent the suppression of melatonin release that occurs even as a result of what would seem to be insignificant light exposure, such as a nightlight or flipping on the lights for a quick trip to the toilet. Whether or not anyone in your family has a sleep disturbance, it is very important to avoid nighttime light exposure.

3. Magnesium.

Magnesium supplements have a calming effect, and unmet needs for magnesium tend to make people wired in various ways listed earlier in the "uptight" table, which mentions insomnia and anxiety. A supplement of magnesium at bedtime is helpful. One of the most pleasant ways of providing magnesium to children at bedtime is with a warm Epsom salts bath (½ cup of Epsom salts [magnesium sulfate], ¼ cup of baking soda [sodium bicarbonate] and a few drops of soothing lavender oil in a tub of warm water). This also augments sulfation (one of the end products of the methionine pathway), which is askew in many autistic children.[43] (More about magnesium in the Nutritional Supplements section of this book.)

4. Tryptophan.

This amino acid (which can be purchased without a prescription as 5 hydroxytryptophan or 5HTP) is the natural precursor for the synthesis of serotonin, the neurotransmitter that typifies the chemistry of sleep. Years ago it was removed from the market after an imported batch of contaminated tryptophan caused serious illness in a number of people. It became established conclusively that the toxicity of the tryptophan-containing pills was due entirely to the contamination, and that tryptophan itself posed no threat. Eventually tryptophan was returned to the market, but only by prescription, which provides a barrier (in my mind completely unnecessary) to using straight tryptophan. 5HTP comes in doses of 50 mg (which is comparable to roughly 500 mg of tryptophan) and can be given at bedtime with a carbohydrate snack to promote better utilization of the 5HTP. The good thing about tryptophan is that it is safe and you will find out about its effectiveness in your child within a few doses. If it doesn't work, then that is the end of the story. If it does work, then it is probably the most reasonable among all the options that follow because it is tried and true, although no long-term detailed toxicity studies of tryptophan have been done in children. Rarely I have seen a paradoxical reaction (hyperactivity). Considering that tryptophan is a molecule native to the body's chemistry, it is quickly dealt with if unneeded. If I had not started prescribing tryptophan before learning about IAG elevations in autistic children, I would have been more timid in its use. As it happened, I found tryptophan to be dramatically helpful with insomnia and hyperactivity in some children, sometimes in very high doses. Considering that tryptophan is the precursor of IAG – and IAG (or its close relatives) is a potentially mischievous molecule – one might expect mischief from high-dose tryptophan. The question needs further study, but so far I have not seen IAG elevation in children on tryptophan. However, it can occur if gut dysbiosis issues are not dealt with sufficiently before tryptophan supplementation. Another question that arises with tryptophan use concerns the elevation of kynurenic acid seen on urinary organic acid measurements. Kynurenic acid, a byproduct of tryptophan metabolism, is an indicator of unmet vitamin B_6 needs when the kynurenic acid level is elevated. Such elevations tend to occur with heavy tryptophan supplementation and therefore call for extra supplementation with B_6 in the form of pyridoxal 5 phosphate – say 50 mg given in the morning if it has a stimulating effect when given in the evening, but, if not, given along with the 5 HTP.[44,45,46,47,48,49] (More about tryptophan and other amino acids in the Nutritional Supplements section of this book.)

5. Melatonin.

This hormone is normally released from the brain during a couple of hours when it reaches a peak concentration in the blood. Compared to other times of day, the sharpness of the nighttime rise and fall of melatonin looks like a church steeple if it is graphed. Its nighttime release provides the body with a kind of time stamp, allowing all the organs to feel the beat of the 24-hour rhythm of the body. It is also a powerful antioxidant. In addition, its presence flips certain switches having to do with cellular nutrition in ways that discourage cancer. Occasionally, small doses relieve insomnia in children where other measures have failed. Its use is more of an unknown in children than, say, tryptophan. I have heard anecdotal reports of melatonin having globally beneficial effects in autistic children. If the sleep benefits are significant and cannot be duplicated by other remedies listed above, then the benefit/risk must be weighed without any precise idea of the long-term risk in a given child. The adult dose of melatonin that may be effective for sleep is 0.3 to 3 mg, with a preference for the lowest effective dose. Children's doses may be scaled accordingly. As with tryptophan, a diagnostic trial of a few days of melatonin carries very little risk. Melatonin also boosts glutathione – a key product of the methionine pathway[50,51] – which is beneficial for many autistic children.

6. Herbs.

Chamomile, Milk thistle (silymarin), Kava Kava and Valerian all have reported benefits. Chamomile tea taken at bedtime has been in use for centuries. It does not taste bad and it is soothing. Milk thistle, which is used as a liver protective in cases of drug toxicity and mushroom poisoning, may exert its sleep-producing effects via its role as a promoter of basic steps in metabolism (raising levels of reduced glutathione, for example). When it works dramatically to correct insomnia in a child, I explain it by saying that the liver works on the night shift. If the liver is unhappy at night, it is more likely to be the cause of insomnia than is the brain. Providing "support" for the liver can thus correct sleep problems. Kava is in wide use. It is a calming herb that is safe enough to use for a diagnostic trial and, if dramatically effective, can be continued at moderate doses. According to reports following attribution to Kava Kava of liver damage, there is no credible evidence establishing such a connection.[52] Valerian is good, too, but it tastes so awful that it is pretty useless in kids.

7. Exercise.

I hesitate to put exercise on this list because many of the kids I know are sufficiently anxious and hyperactive that they are already expending a lot of daily energy. However, it would be amiss to neglect mention of a factor that will promote sleep in just about anyone. Whether it takes the form of lots of swimming – the preferred exercise for most autistic kids I know – or a treadmill, bike, running or dancing, exercise to the point of some degree of exhaustion is bound to be helpful to a child whose motor seems not to quit at night.

ATTITUDE AGAIN

I mentioned before that our book has attitude when it comes to the tension that exists between so-called "traditional" disease-oriented prescription-pad medicine and the emerging model of patient-oriented integrative medicine. Here is a more specific attitude regarding the decision about whether to give a particular remedy. The best time to discuss whether to use a (safe) supplement, drug, diet or other treatment is about three weeks after trying it. That is, we can sit here all day and consider whether this or that option would be worth doing, but the unpredictability of the situation – given autistic children's physiological individuality – devalues our considerations until we see if the treatment's effect is good, ill or indifferent. The first judgment based on symptoms is usually enough, but sometimes a change in a lab test will be needed as an extra measure of certainty or safety. *In other words, every treatment is really a diagnostic trial.*

Because chronic illness is chronic, we tend to have a mind-set, fostered by traditional medicine, that "you'll have to take this medicine forever." There is something in the dark side of the relationship among doctors, patients, and pharmaceutical companies that fosters that attitude. In contrast, a more practical attitude is that effective clinical strategy calls for a willingness to utter that forbidden word, "oops."

In medical school I learned a lot of new words. When you think about it, medical training involves learning to see and name invisibly small things, such as molecules, or invisibly large patterns, such as diseases. The problem occurs when we begin to think of these words for diseases as actually physical entities, and to consider them as the cause of symptoms rather than viewing them as concepts we form about groups of people who share certain signs, symptoms, and laboratory values. In the course of learning the language of medicine, we learn four words that should never be said out loud: "oops" and "I don't know." Successful collaboration between doctor and parents, in navigating the complex landscape of chronic illness in children, comes from an ongoing, leisurely, intelligent conversation in which the words "oops" and "I don't know" are allowed.

The pace of the conversation may be leisurely for the sake of thoughtful strategy and *mutual* education. The whole reason for our conversations is, however, a sense of haste. If it were not for haste, we wouldn't be writing this book. We'd just say that the government, academia and the drug companies will soon take an interest in something other than genetic etiologies and descriptive studies of autistic children, and within the next couple of decades the fog will lift from our landscape so you may know just what to do for each child's problems. Actually, most people are willing to do just that, based on the "don't look for answers" attitude. Reading this book puts you in the minority.

Haste is a factor that modulates each decision driven by the information we are presenting in this book. The sleep remedies provide examples of interventions that are all pretty quick to show results. If you are uneasy about the long-term effects of any of the listed items, you can be reassured by the fact that they are on the list to consider trying for just a few nights. Then – once you know the "benefit" side of the benefit-to-risk ratio – you can leave the remedy in place pending further, more considered but less hurried balancing of your child's chemistry or immune function. Meanwhile, your child is sleeping and you can get on with the rest of the program, which may ultimately obviate the need for the sleep remedy. In other words, the priority given to some of the options we present in this book is affected by how quickly they may yield results. Remedies with a longer lag time in showing effectiveness may wait until some of the quick things are out of the way.

For example, considering the high probability of response to a tiny injection of methyl B_{12} or to a gluten-free diet, you may figure that doing the methyl B_{12} gets first choice because it is easy to do and any positive results will usually appear within days to weeks. A gluten-free diet, on the other hand, is a big hassle and positive effects usually appear weeks to months down the road. If it should turn out that methyl B_{12} did not work but a gluten-free diet did, then repeating the trial of methyl B_{12} later on might make sense because the gluten-free diet would have changed the baseline sufficiently to renew the possibility of methyl B_{12}'s effectiveness. The point is that the sequence of most diagnostic and therapeutic steps is not cast in stone. Exceptions to some of the rules – such as cleaning the gut before doing detoxification – may cause delay from transient negative symptoms, but are only very rarely the cause of a real setback.

One of the biggest questions that comes up with regard to haste is whether one should try to do "all the tests" at the beginning of a child's evaluation and treatment. Practical considerations weigh in here. If a family travels a long distance for a consultation and may not have access to lab testing at home, say outside the United States, then trying to get a lot of baseline lab data may make sense. On the other hand, we now know – as opposed to a decade ago, when we only suspected – what most children will reveal with initial lab testing: that is, a biochemical train wreck. In many instances it is more economical of resources to use initial response to treatment as the principal diagnostic test. If initial treatments are beneficial, then lab tests will give a more refined picture of problems still requiring attention. If initial treatments are not beneficial, then the resources devoted to laboratory testing may be more justifiable.

CONSTIPATION

Constipation is an obstacle to further options. That is, if a child cannot poop, all bets are off until a means can be found to clear the way for other treatments to be put into play. This is where quick-and-dirty approaches really shine. Let's look at the constipation list before returning to this point, followed by another one that comes to mind in this connection: What should you do if doctors or teachers are accusing you of being a bad parent if you don't want to drug your child?

A daily bowel movement is normal. Not having a BM at least once a day is NOT normal. In the early part of the 20th century, the notion of a toxic bowel arose from the discovery that poops are basically wall-to-wall bacteria, leading to a medical and lay enthusiasm for enemas. Enemas had been around for a long time and have been in, certain medical contexts, thought to be a kind of panacea. That is – if there is something wrong with you and you can't poop, then first get an enema.

Let me digress with a brief story that really caught my attention. I had been asked to consult for the autistic son of a very high-profile and beloved couple who had put the coordination of the boy's care in the hands of a chiropractic physician. Their local hospital became the scene of a drama that unfolded as the boy's severe asthma attack failed to respond to the usual emergency measures and admission to the hospital was imminent. I was thousands of miles distant and helpless to offer any better options. My chiropractic colleague – also remote from the action - told the boy's parents to sign him out against medical advice, take him home, and give him an enema. Bingo! The asthma attack cleared within minutes and everyone went back to sleep, except me. I lay awake for quite a while marveling at my colleague's guts, his good call, and my job's capacity to teach me new things every day.

The discovery that fecal flora harbored pathogens (germs that cause disease) put the idea of rinsing out the bowel almost on a par with hand-washing. The pendulum swung too far. By the 1920s and 1930s, babies, children, grownups, dogs, cats and God knows what else were getting enemas for the sake of hygiene. Given the long-lasting effects of unwanted, invasive life experiences, the legacy of all of this penetration was one that children born in those days were lucky, as I was, to escape. Then the pendulum swung the other way, with the realization that things had gotten out of hand. By the time of my medical education in the 1960s, the word was that it really didn't matter if you had a BM daily, every other day, or once a week. "Irregularity" was regular for some people, everyone is different, so don't sweat, or interfere, with your "natural" pattern.

Nonsense! Moving your bowels is an essential part of the rhythmic functioning of your body, and, like eating and sleeping, should occur regularly and daily. Of course, identifying the cause of constipation makes sense. The list that follows has two purposes. One is to provide relief while the detective work is going on, so that the negative effects of constipation do not interfere with benefits from whatever treatment is put in place. The other is to help a child re-establish a repaired bowel pattern, which may be broken when the normal gastro-colic reflex (after you eat you feel like pooping) has been suppressed for whatever reasons. The reasons for constipation run the whole gamut from voluntary withholding – as, for example, in a kid who doesn't have time before school and doesn't want to do it in school – to formation in the bowel of stools that are simply too big and hard to pass, to laxity or spasms in the colon that cannot then propel its contents in the appropriate direction. Here is a list of short-term treatments you can invoke while trying to get to the diagnostic bottom of severe constipation.

1. Prunes or prune juice.

Yes, I know that dried fruit is not only heavy in carbs but also somewhat yeasty, in the sense that the normal surface flora of all fruits (yeasts) become concentrated in the drying process and therefore may be allergenic for people with yeast/mold sensitivities. But after 40 years of practice, and a sampling of the whole inventory of constipation remedies, stewed prunes come out at the top of my list.

2. Fiber.

Fiber belongs high on the list because most autistic children, especially constipated ones, have rarely tasted a fibrous vegetable. Fiber comes at two ends of a spectrum: soluble and insoluble. The latter possesses the properties of encouraging good flora, providing bulk, and offering nutrients to one's flora, which, in turn, transform fiber into substances (short chain fatty acids) that nourish the lining of the large intestine. Unadulterated food-grade cellulose is what I have prescribed over the years, but it has not always been easy to obtain. You can now order it by contacting Vital Nutrients, 860-638-3675. The dose is between a teaspoonful and a tablespoonful a day. It is very bland and can be mixed with any mushy food.

3. Magnesium.

Milk of Magnesia and magnesium citrate (comes in little bottles like soda) are saline cathartics. They are not absorbed in large quantities, and pass into the large intestine where they draw water from the tissues to produce a watery peristalsis and evacuation. Most autistic children have unmet magnesium needs. In these cases, a dose of magnesium citrate, or other kinds of magnesium as mentioned above, will relieve constipation, not as a cathartic but as a remedy for the muscle spasm that characterizes magnesium deficit – in this case affecting the bowel muscles.[53,54,55,56,57,58] If magnesium produces the desired effect only when you increase the dose, consider whether taurine supplementation may be required.

4. Senna.

This is an herbal ingredient found in Sennacot, as well as in laxative teas such as Smooth Move Tea, found in the health food store. Long-term heavy use of senna may not be good for you, but it is quite effective in getting things going in the spirit described above.

5. Olive oil.

This is the first choice among various oils. Try a tablespoon of extra-virgin olive oil daily as step number one.

6. Mineral oil.

This can be blended cold with some juices, and in that form is not too unpalatable. A dose from 1 teaspoon (5 mL) to 1 ounce (30 mL) will coat the stools and make them slippery, lubricating their exit. For a child requiring bowel retraining after losing the gastro-colic reflex, it may be just the thing to help re-sensitize him or her to the call of nature. The protocol is to escalate the dose until oil and stool simply drip from the anus, and then back off. This has to be done without risk of a public accident. No child is so unaware that he or she should be put at risk of such a memorable and humiliating defeat.

7. Castor oil.

When push comes to shove and all else fails, and constipation becomes an obstacle to other diagnostic and treatment efforts, then castor oil will do the trick. It will produce strong peristaltic waves in the bowel, so if there is a toilet-stopping stool plugging up the southern exit, the effectiveness of this approach needs to be weighed against the risk of producing intolerable cramps and splitting of the anal skin (anal fissure) when the plug is passed. The dose for adults and children 12 years and older is 1 to 4 tablespoons (15 to 60 ml) in a single daily dose. For children between the ages of two and 11, use 1/3 to 1 tablespoon (5 to 15 ml) in a single daily dose. If your child is less than two years old, consult a doctor. It is best to take it on an empty stomach, but it may be taken with juice to improve the taste. Caution: Not to be used for a period longer than one week except under medical supervision.

8. Dulcolax.

Dulcolax has some of the same properties as castor oil. It comes in suppository form, which may provide some of the lubrication needed to prevent the problem just mentioned. After a look at the inactive ingredients in the oral forms, I think you'd vote for the suppository or try a Fleet Pediatric Enema if glycerine suppositories (see #9) don't work.

(Inactive ingredients in the tablets: Acacia, acetylated monoglyceride, carnauba wax, cellulose acetate phthalate, corn starch, dibutyl phthalate, docusate sodium, gelatin, glycerin, iron oxides, kaolin, lactose, magnesium stearate, methylparaben, pharmaceutical glaze, polyethylene glycol, povidone, propylparaben, Red No. 30 lake, sodium benzoate, sorbitan monooleate, sucrose, talc, titanium dioxide, white wax, Yellow No. 10 lake.)
(Inactive ingredients in the oral solution: Citric acid, lemon oil, polyethylene glycol, sodium bicarbonate, sodium saccharin, sucrose, water purified.)
(Inactive ingredients in the suppository: Hydrogenated vegetable oil.)

9. Glycerin suppositories.

Some children accept suppositories in the spirit they are presented: a welcome relief. Some children simply don't like having something stuck up their bottoms. It is hard to tell which kind of kid you have without risking a bad reaction on the part of a child of the second type. A bad reaction can take the form of a vow never to poop again. Same thing with the response to an anal fissure or a painfully huge, hard stool. Most autistic kids have extraordinarily strong wills. You really don't want your child to exercise such a will on a battlefield where he or she is an easy winner. The two primary battlefields of that sort are whether or not to swallow a particular food or medicine, and obedience to the call to poop – even when that call originates within his or her own body.

10. Antifungal medication.

It is a tough call whether to put this at the top or the bottom of the list. Many autistic children will recover from their constipation after antifungal medication is instituted. On the other hand, you invite trouble if you give an antifungal, with its attendant possibility of a die-off reaction, without having cleared up constipation. So, the drill is to use whatever means necessary to get your child to have a BM at least once daily, and then institute antifungal treatment with the reasonable hope that success in that department will bring about resolution of constipation without further resort to any of the above remedies except magnesium (for which an ongoing need is likely for other reasons).

11. MiraLax (polyethylene glycol 3350, NF powder for solution).

Polyethylene glycol (PEG) in various forms is used in agricultural chemicals, disinfectants, hairspray (non-aerosol), herbicides, dry automatic dishwashing detergents, laundry starch preparations, lubricating oils, other hair preparations (including heat-setting wave solutions),

SECTION ONE: RATIONALE FOR INDIVIDUALIZED AUTISM TREATMENT

pharmaceutical preparations acting on the skin, pet flea and tick products (including collars), and pharmaceuticals for veterinary use. Used as a treatment for constipation, it is an osmotic agent that causes water to be retained with the stool. In normal subjects, without constipation, essentially all of an oral dose can be recovered in the stools. However, attempts at recovery of MiraLax in constipated patients are incomplete and variable. In the laboratory, MiraLax was not fermented into hydrogen or methane by the colonic microflora in human feces. So where did the MiraLax go when it was not recovered from the stools after an oral dose? *Not knowing the answer to that question is even more disquieting than the fact that safety and effectiveness in pediatric patients have not been established.* It is, however, favored by many pediatric gastroenterologists and it really works! It should not be used for more than two weeks. There are some children whose constipation is so refractory that MiraLax's effectiveness becomes a decisive point – but I would say only after *all* other measures have failed.

Susan Owens, M.S., is a parent and expert in the chemistry of sulfation as well as myriad other subjects important to the growth of our understanding of the chemistry of autism. Her contribution to DAN! meetings and the email correspondence that is shared among those of us affiliated with the DAN! organization is enormous and always helps her colleagues penetrate to the core of an issue. Here is an email from her on the subject of polyethylene glycol:

"I ran across [an article] in my more careful look at L-form bacteria. It talks about how exposure of bacteria with resistance to various antibiotics will confer to other bacteria in L-form when they are exposed to polyethylene glycol, which is what Miralax is.

"This study reminded me again of how leery I have stayed regarding giving polyethylene glycol to children with dysbiosis and possibly with leaky guts who may also have a history of being treated with various antibiotics. I took a hard look at this about four years ago when I first heard of this product being used in children with autism and heard of a few disasters associated with using it. My original concern stemmed from studying in graduate school what PEG does in merging the DNA of different cells (even from different species!) by blending their membranes creating something altogether new and changing things like the stage of differentiation of a cell type.

"Back then I did a pretty thorough look at the literature on PEG. There are many thousands of articles, but it was only necessary to go 'so deep' looking to see if my concerns about implications were substantiated by other literature. I found that there was plenty to worry about. I also looked at the approval process of the drug to see if any of these known properties and potential effects on the flora had been addressed or investigated in the approval process. The answer was no, not at all. In fact, in part of their trial, they reported a p value of one. [p values are a statistical measure of probability and are significant below a value of 0.05 – editor's note.] I had never seen anyone report a p value of one. This did not make me feel better about this product or about its approval process. I certainly am convinced it works to help constipation, but I wonder at the cost. Not only is [there] the worry of what might happen in the child you gave it to, but will some of the resistances and changes it makes to bacteria be conferred to others who won't have taken Miralax?"

LOOKING BACK

We have now reached an elevation on our path where we can take a look back over the terrain we have covered, and get a glimpse of our destination. We are approaching the end of a discussion about the sources of data that will drive our decisions about priorities among all of the options for treatment. We have decided that these decisions will involve some trial and error, in which the consequences of error should be as little as possible beyond having to utter the forbidden word, "oops." One source is the collective observations of parents reflected in the results of Autism Research Institute surveys (see Nutritional Supplements section). Another is the consensus among DAN! physicians of the time-line of main causative factors, giving us a good indication of their sequence and interactions. A third is our understanding of the biochemical pathways in and around methionine (thiol) chemistry, where measurements of abnormalities in our kids point strongly to causative factors and therapeutic opportunities. All three of these sources provide general information about many children, but the fourth source, your child's history and physical exam, provide information that is specific to him or her. We need to talk about the fifth source (laboratory data), the sixth source (your child's response to each treatment), and the seventh (intuition). Before heading up the trail, let's see if the view from our present altitude gives us enough perspective to start making some safe choices for which you do not need a doctor or a laboratory. That way you can get started and begin to gather information from the sixth source, which is what you learn from one treatment about how others may work.

You know by now that we do not think that there is a one-size-fits-all approach to our kids, even though we believe that the epidemic of autism and related disorders has causes that are common to subgroups of its victims. Individuality does not, however, spare any child from a few imperative priorities that are at the top of the list. Then there are a few that are so quick, easy, and low-risk that as soon as you are connected with a licensed physician, you can expect to get started with them.

GASTROINTESTINAL HEALTH

The imperative first priority is to clean up the gut. In a room full of well-informed DAN! practitioners presented with this statement, no one disagrees. If you do not clean up the gut, the rest of the healing effort will be more complicated and less effective. Be wary of any report you read about this or that treatment that has not worked in children with autism, if the researchers have failed to address gut issues first. So – back in the room full of DAN! doctors – who wants to tell us exactly what we mean by a clean gut? How do we know when we are done, so we are eligible for the next step? Suddenly everyone has to leave for the lavatory. That is, everyone agrees that cleaning up the gut is very important – there are pretty clear definitions of what steps are involved – but there are not such clear indications of when the objective is reached. If you are uncomfortable with that truth, then you should consider getting a refund for this book which teaches and demands tolerance for uncertainty. It comes down to this. *Deciding what to do next is pretty easy. It is what I do every day, so I am good at it, but you will also get the hang of it pretty quickly because it is not all that scary. You cannot go too far wrong by using the guidelines we are presenting here. On the other hand, deciding when you've done enough of any particular treatment that you can say it definitely didn't work, or that it worked to its max, is hard and tricky.* The hard part is that the stakes are so high, especially if you quit on something that "should" work and worked for other kids you know, and you wonder if you didn't somehow do it long enough or hard enough.

SECTION ONE: RATIONALE FOR INDIVIDUALIZED AUTISM TREATMENT

Cleaning up the gut and knowing when it is clean is just one among many strategies that will raise the same, haunting difficulty, so get used to it. It is part of the deal. And it turns out that with some experience, knowledge, professional support, and your gut feelings, you will do OK.

Anyone who has changed 2,500 diapers may be somewhat mystified by the notion of a clean gut. If, however, you recall the diaper changes that preceded the end of exclusive breast feeding, you may begin to get the idea. Breastfed babies' stools are neither sticky nor stinky. During my two years in Chad, Africa, as a Peace Corps volunteer, part of my job as a physician was to have my team teach mothers about the value of introducing solid food to their infants well ahead of the time when their toddlers were weaned. Weaning in West Africa was often abrupt, and infants became depressed and vulnerable while trying to get the hang of feeding from the family plate. Earlier introduction of solid food was part of a World Health Organization initiative to reduce mortality in this susceptible age group. The nine- to twenty-month-olds, who were the target of our intervention, spent much of their time on their mothers' backs secured with a broad wrap of cloth which could easily be loosened when mom got the signal that a BM was imminent. Swung to the ground, placed between the seated moms' feet, the kids would poop, get cleaned, and be returned to their perch without a hitch. No diapers, no mess. Along comes Dr. Baker and his crew explaining the merits of starting solid foods closer to age one than two years. The result: sudden, surprising, stinky poops and, for us, a trip back to the drawing boards of health education. Weaned infants' stools are "dirty" because of two interrelated things in the gut: food and flora. Easily digested breast milk produces a milieu in the gut that promotes a flora of less toxic, less smelly germs. Foods that aren't easily digested do the opposite, and when digestion is impaired, a result is more offensive odors. Nearly all the unattractive and attractive odors that emanate from your body are produced by germs. When the odors become really bad, you can be sure that the germs are really bad. When the germs are really bad in the gut, you can be pretty sure that something the germs are eating is promoting an unhealthy flora. When we say "clean up the gut," the agenda includes food, digestion and flora.

> TRY THE DIETS. It's not "too hard." GFCF made a dramatic difference for my boys, and paying attention to what we all eat has helped everyone in our family. You will learn more about nutrition than you ever imagined you needed to know, and that wisdom will pay off. You can use what you learn to help your other children and yourself, your parents, your brother's kids, your neighbor's kids, etc.
>
> – a parent

Here is your next opportunity to head back down the trail to the parking lot and stop at McDonald's on your way back to the lodge. If changing your child's diet is too much for you, then you are reading the wrong book. (Well, maybe not entirely. If you read ahead a little, you will find an exception that deals with the sequential priority of dietary changes.) Do I, who spent part of my career in another culture trying to get people to eat differently, think that changing diet is trivial? No. It is easier to change people's religion. People are really stuck on their food. I know I am. When I lived in Japan, breakfast was really tough. I wanted ham-u egg-u, not seaweed and mushroom soup. Tell your Italian grandmother that she cannot give pasta or a cookie to your child, and see what she says. *Illness is a signal to change, and changing food is the toughest test of just about everyone's capacity to change.* I wish I had been an optometrist instead of an optimist. "More sharp? Less sharp? Want to see better? Wear these lenses. Don't want to see better? Don't wear 'em." As it is, I have fallen into a medical practice where I get to see more rolling eyeballs than a stripper. You should have been a fly on the wall when I started telling people about the Specific Carbohydrate Diet. Parents who had developed an unreasonable confidence in my opinion were pulling on their earlobes and staring out the window waiting for me to stop telling them about yet another impossible diet. It would take forty minutes just to get people to say – after my best trapeze act – that they would read the book and think about it. Then I got parents who had already tried it to talk to the ones who were trying to run back from the end of the diving board. Time required: ten minutes.

> MY DAUGHTER, Cara, is a lovely 18-year-old woman who has lived through the ups and downs of an immune system and digestive system plagued by food sensitivities, skin rashes, bouts of diarrhea and/or constipation, yeast infections and sleep problems, among other things. She was diagnosed as being on the autistic spectrum when she was three – one of those children who had normal development until her life was seemingly upended and she started losing language.
>
> When she was about ten, and started having anxiety and panic attacks, we realized we had to do more than look to education and speech therapy to guide us as to how to help her. We had already tried some "outside the box" stuff like music therapy, sensory integration, behavioral vision therapy and auditory training, but we needed more. We had already tried appropriate meds and they turned down the anxiety, but didn't turn it off.
>
> We turned to Dr. Baker when we got truly desperate, and started looking into some biomedical approaches which later became part of the DAN! protocol. Over the years, we have made tremendous progress, but, like many parents of ASD kids, are always looking for more. We started the Specific Carbohydrate Diet last February after being on a gluten/casein-free diet (with some twists from a low-phenol Feingold program) for about seven years. (GFCF had helped greatly, but sometimes the same old problems reoccurred. We figured we had nothing to lose by making some additional changes.) Things immediately started to click. Cara's high school really noticed a difference and made mention of it in her IEP year summary, linking the diet to increased language, socialization, focus and academic success. She made High Honors for the first time ever. Family and friends have mentioned her smiling more and seeming more relaxed. She's actually talking about her future. It's made a huge difference and is well worth the extra effort. Cara's able to enjoy some foods she hasn't had for years, now that she is on the SCD. She is smiling more, and talking about cute boys, make-up, and rock n' roll, and trying harder to be social. That more than makes up for the extra cooking!
>
> – Barbara, parent

Do I understand that changing a child's diet is difficult? Yes. Do I understand that it may be hard to change the diet of a kid who will only eat McDonald's french fries, corn chips, and Diet Pepsi, and has a will bigger than Arnold Schwarzenegger's thighs? Yes. Changing the child's diet is hard, but parents like you can do it – but only if you have support from other parents who have done it before you. We can give you guidelines, but for the details you need to turn to books, websites, nutrition consultants and conversations with other parents.

SECTION ONE: RATIONALE FOR INDIVIDUALIZED AUTISM TREATMENT

Cleaning up the diet

A healthy and healing diet provides food that is varied, fresh, free of additives and chemicals – therefore organic – and free of added sugar (table sugar, or sucrose). In children who accept such a diet easily, thanks to their disposition and the cooperation of all family members, you are likely to see a rapid improvement in mood and behavior that rewards the change. In children who are addicted to the foods you are trying to eliminate, the first steps can be challenging and should be gradual. The more benefits you see from dietary changes, the more you will know that you are on the right track. That track leads to further dietary steps that may cause dramatic changes for substantial numbers of children. Here are the data from ARI's Parent Ratings,[59] sorted down by the % Better column.

DIET	Better:Worse	# of Cases
Milk-free	32:1	5574
No chocolate	30:1	1721
Wheat-free	29:1	3159
Feingold	25:1	758
No added sugar	24:1	3695
Rotation	21:1	792
Gluten/casein-free	20:1	1446
Egg-free	19:1	1096
Yeast-free	19:1	756

ARI has not yet collected data on the Specific Carbohydrate Diet, but my experience suggests that it would top the % Better list.

The experience of many of us who have taken care of kids on the autism spectrum (and those with attention deficit disorders and many other chronic illnesses) is that these kinds of diets make an enormous difference. When I see some so-called expert on TV or in the newspaper saying that dietary intervention has not been proven to have any benefits, I feel as if I am hearing a travelogue from someone who has never been there. We realize that the ARI data are rough and anecdotal, but we believe emphatically that they provide persuasive evidence in favor of trying dietary change long enough to observe effects, which then become the decisive facts.

Dietary change necessitates a family's strong commitment. That commitment in itself is bound to have an impact on any child who is the object of the intention to make such a change. Intention is, after all, the first step toward healing. Nature has such a strong impulse toward healing that intention by itself can sometimes be the trigger that promotes healing. We recognize that dietary change is such a major commitment that it has effects apart from its biological impact. To ignore or dispute the biochemical, immunological and clinical support for the notion that certain dietary changes have profound and specific biological effects is, however, just plain stupid – especially if the skeptic intends to deny the value of a diagnostic trial as a matter of private health policy.

> NO MATTER THE NAME of the diet, finding what your child can and can't eat is such a phenomenally important piece of this puzzle that the dramatic effect of removing even one specific food can forge an opening in a door whose weight was too immense to open. For Eric, we would never have found the core and center of his being, that ached to be allowed to express itself, if we hadn't discovered his unfortunate sensitivities to starches as well as his sensitivities to the chemical make-up of various foods.
>
> – Brenda, parent

Most of the children who have done well in my care have started with dietary changes, such as the basic ones to be discussed presently, plus strict avoidance of gluten and casein, yeasts and molds. More recently the Specific Carbohydrate Diet has emerged as a therapy that appears to have the highest rate of success, as measured by the percent of children benefiting and the degree of benefit in many. I do not, however, insist that all patients who come to me, never having tried any intervention, begin with major dietary changes – even though I believe that would be ideal. Instead, I strike a compromise in which major dietary changes (focusing on casein, gluten and certain carbohydrates) are placed into consideration while other therapeutic steps are enacted. Those other steps constitute cleaning up the gut with its two components, food and flora.

Food additives

You want your child to get better, but you are looking for something specific – and effective, inexpensive, safe, and undemanding – to let go. The whole idea is that changes you make to help your child get better should be tailored to your family's individual needs, and you should rightly resist the idea of one-size-fits-all methodology, especially if its remedies mess with your family's very personal choice of foods which, as I said, is sacred.

The very idea of "cleaning up" makes it sound as if we think foods are dirty, so let's start with that. Actually, food is pretty clean – although no food is completely free of various natural contaminants such as insect parts, fragments of animal waste, and just plain dirt and mold that cannot be avoided on the trail from the farm to your dinner table. Best not to think about it! When we and others who have seen people get much better from dietary changes talk about "cleaning up," we are actually talking about a few simple steps based on science, common sense, and clinical experience showing that certain substances in foods bother a significant number of people. It makes sense to answer questions about the effects of such substances before getting involved in other diagnostic and treatment options. Imagine how you would feel after months of trying a variety of tests and treatments, only to find out that the solution was in avoiding artificial dyes in your child's food.

Let's start with dyes. You probably don't use them in your kitchen. (Who boasts that mama's spaghetti sauce is tops because of the special red dye that she uses?) Rather, dyes are added to many commercial foods and medications. But what is a dye, anyway? It is a brightly-colored, sticky molecule. Its color comes from the fact that it absorbs a certain wavelength of light, and its stickiness comes from the way its atoms bind with atoms on other molecules. It is a long story, but the gist of it is that sticky, light-absorbing molecules are "biologically active," which means that they don't just float through living things but tend to get involved. Even naturally-occurring colored foods may cause mischief for some people, but here I am talking about avoiding artificially colored foods. Much of the research on food dyes has focused on children who have problems paying attention and those who are hyperactive. No one questions that some people suffer hives, digestive problems or wheezing as a result of exposure to artificial colors – as well as an infinite variety of foods, chemicals, molds, pollens, dander and dust – but the idea that behavior might be affected has met with a lot of opposition from folks who say, basically, "it couldn't be true, so it can't be true."

Here is a list of food additives that are safe for most children who are otherwise sensitive to food additives:

Acetic acid	Lactic acid
Agar-agar	Lecithin
Alginates	Mannitol
Annatto	Niacin
Ascorbic acid (vitamin C)	Pectin
Beta-carotene	Potassium bitartrate
Betanin (red color from beets)	Potassium citrate
Calcium carbonate	Potassium citrate
Calcium citrate	Potassium propionate*
Calcium propionate	Cellulose
Calcium silicate	Propionic acid*
Caramel	Riboflavin
Carbon dioxide	Sodium citrate
Carob-bean flour	Sodium proprionate*
Carotene	Sodium tartrate
Carrageenan	Sorbic acid & sorbates
Chlorophyll	Sorbitol
Citric acid	Stearic acid
Cream of tartar	Tamarind-seed flour
Curcuma	Tartaric acid
Galatine	Titanium dioxide
Guar gum	Tocopherols (vitamin E)
Iron oxide	Turmeric
Lactate (not to be confused with lactose, or milk sugar)	Xanthan gum
* may have theoretical problems because proprionate is metabolized through MMA	

A number of organizations, including the United States Food and Drug Administration, The International Food Information Council, the National Institutes of Mental Health, Children and Adults with Attention Deficit/Hyperactivity Disorder, the National Center for Learning Disabilities, the Nutrition Foundation, the American Academy of Pediatrics, the American Medical Association, The American Academy of Child and Adolescent Psychiatry, the Sugar Association, and the American Academy of Family Physicians Foundation, have published statements saying, basically, that it isn't true that some children have behavioral or cognitive reactions to food additives. With such an abundance of official pronouncements, is it any surprise that health professionals have not bothered to do their own homework? Yes, it surprises me. All one needs to do is to listen to and believe one's patients (or their parents) when they say that avoiding food colorings has made a big difference and that inadvertent exposures sometimes cause convincing, drastic symptoms. The whole issue is reviewed and discussed in an essay, "Diet, ADHD & Behavior," by Michael F. Jacobson, Ph.D. and David Shard, M.S., published by the Center for Science in the Public Interest (http://www.cspinet.org/diet.html). Another good source of documentation and practical advice on diets avoiding food additives is the Feingold Association, http://www.feingold.org. There you can get more detailed information about additives, but the basic idea is to avoid chemicals that are not part of the foods themselves.

Sugar and artificial sweeteners

The debate over the effects of sugar and artificial sweeteners has been just as polarized as the one over the behavioral toxicology of food colorings and other additives. You will have to do your own experiment to see the extent to which sugar bothers your child. Laboratory tests (urine organic acids) in most autistic children reveal a vulnerable carbohydrate chemistry. You don't have to do such a test to compare your child's mood, sleep, behavior, cognitive function and general appearance when abstaining from or pigging out on sugar. Try five days on, three weeks tapering off slowly, then five days "pigging out" (the promised "reward" for the experiment). See what happens. The reason why you need to taper off is that kids (and grownups) who have been eating a lot of sugar have set their body chemistry to expect it, with high insulin levels and the like. Pulling the rug out suddenly may set all sorts of biochemical dominos tumbling and produce crankiness, fatigue, headaches and other symptoms that can be misinterpreted as "see, he is much happier if he has Grandma's cookies, cakes, ice cream, and candy." After you have done the experiment, you should go light on sugars no matter what the results, because one of the next steps in your journey has to do with the germs in your child's gut. Many of those germs like sugar.

We will amplify the sugar issue later, when we return to a discussion of the Specific Carbohydrate Diet.

Other measures: Watch out for any food to which your child is addicted. A highly preferred food is not *always* a troublemaker, but for any adult or child with any chronic complaint, the following question frequently fingers the culprit: "Is there any food(s) that you consider to be your favorite, or that you would miss if you did not eat it every day?" Craving tends to apply in two situations: carbohydrates and allergens. Cleaning up the gut (and diet) involves avoiding or minimizing each type of substance, with cravings providing clues that one, the other, or both could be negatively affecting your child. As far as carbohydrates go, the cleaning-up-the-gut phase of treatment that we are now discussing requires minimizing craved carbohydrates such as juices, starches or sugars. As far as

> WE HAVE LEARNED to trust our instincts, have faith in our daughter, and look for and try to treat the root of the problem (not the symptoms). Kelly was vomiting and had diarrhea on a regular basis. After six months of consulting a pediatric gastroenterologist and many tests, including an endoscopy and colonoscopy, we still had few answers....There was no definite "proof" of food allergies, which we suspected to be triggering her explosive episodes. (We discovered there was a pattern: when she ate dairy, she vomited.)
>
> It was not until we consulted with DAN! practitioners that we discovered delayed reaction food allergies, of which Kelly tested positive for over 20. The gluten/casein-free diet, in addition to removal of all reactive foods, was a milestone for her. She started to sleep at night, the stomach pains and diarrhea dwindled, and her behavior improved dramatically.
>
> – *Suzie, parent*

SECTION ONE: RATIONALE FOR INDIVIDUALIZED AUTISM TREATMENT

allergens that may be suspected because of craving, the best test is avoidance and challenge. Five days off a food is usually long enough to detect improvement in any symptoms due to intolerance to that food. Three days back on the food is usually long enough to see the return of symptoms that have cleared during abstinence. No other test compares to the repeating of this routine until the association of a food with symptoms is clear. Blood, skin and other testing can be helpful indicators, but you do not want to permanently eliminate good foods such as egg from your diet just on the basis of a lab test, without confirming by avoidance and challenge that it makes a difference worth the effort of avoiding it.

Finally, before summarizing the food part of gut cleaning, we should mention that an adequate intake of water is something many of us tend to overlook. Many of our kids are very thirsty and tend to consume lots of water. If they do not, reminders and incentives to drink water are important, especially considering water's importance in detoxification, which will emerge as a central theme in treatment.

Before moving to a discussion of the flora as an object of gut cleaning, let us summarize the food issue by saying that dietary interventions of more or less strictness may emerge sooner or later depending on your capacity to make changes. For the purpose of taking the first steps, however, the minimum requirement is to work toward a diet of fresh, preferably organic, unadulterated (no additives) food that is low in sugars and starches. However, we must raise a concern that attaches to any dietary intervention.

I am indebted to Judy Converse, MPH, RD (Nutrition Care for Children, 160 MacArthur Boulevard, Suite 6, Bourne, MA 02532, judy@conversedesign.com, phone (508)743-0609; fax (508)759-5983) for describing to me a number of under-nourished children whose diets were grossly deficient as a result of heroic parental efforts to avoid "bad" foods. No practitioner or parent should try to restrict a child's diet without a basic understanding of the trade-offs. If a child's caloric intake has come substantially from wheat and dairy products, then these cannot be removed without trading in other foods of equivalent or superior quality and caloric density. Your child's measurements should be recorded and repeated monthly. A growth chart appropriate to your child's age and gender should be plotted regularly to assure that he or she is growing as expected. Your pediatrician will have one. Copy it and maintain your own copy at home.

The idea is to prevent poor outcomes caused by chronically marginal diets. Many pediatricians and parents think that a gluten-free, casein-free diet is a poor diet, so Judy works to refute this by helping parents give their children enough high-value food every day, while staying within the limits of indicated restrictions.

Here are the guidelines Judy has provided for energy, protein, and fat intakes for kids:

- Children need roughly 1,000 calories per day plus 100 calories for each year of age. Example: A four-year-old child in good nutrition status needs about 1,400 calories per day.
- Preschool-age kids who need to "catch up" in growth and gain weight require 150-250 kcal/kg (70-125 kcal/pound) of body weight per day. Extra calories should be mostly fat and carbohydrate, as these spare the protein to fuel growth. The extra fat can be a combination of olive, flax, and fish oils.

- One- to three-year-olds in good nutrition status typically need 100 kcal/kg (45 kcal/pound) of body weight per day.
- Four- to six-year-olds in good nutrition status typically need 90 kcal/kg (40 kcal/pound) of body weight per day.
- Protein requirements, minimally, are 1.2 grams/kg (.55 grams/pound) of body weight per day for one- to three-year-olds, or at least 16 grams/day; 1.1 grams/kg (.50 grams/pound) of body weight per day for four- to six-year-olds, or at least 24 grams per day. More is fine, but this is a bare minimum.
- During catch-up growth, protein requirements go up to 3.2 grams/kg (1.5 grams per pound) of body weight per day for preschool kids, or as much as 40-50 grams per day.
- Fat is usually unrestricted in kids who are not overweight. Many parents think they should not allow fats, but clinical signs of fatty acid deficiency are common in children on diets. (See the section on physical examination.)

Here are criteria for nutritional failure (which brings increased risk of infection, growth regression, or developmental and functional compromise):

- Normal nutrition status = a child who is at 90-110% of ideal weight for height
- Early malnutrition = 85-89% of ideal weight for height
- Mild malnutrition = 80-84% of ideal weight for height
- Moderate malnutrition = 75-79% of ideal weight for height
- Severe malnutrition = less than 75% of ideal weight for height

These are red flags for nutritional failure:

- A child less than age five years who is at less than 85% ideal weight for height.
- A child less than age five years who has lost weight for two months or more.
- A child less than age five years who has not gained weight for two to three months.
- A child age five to 18 who weighs less than 85% of ideal weight for height, who has lost weight for two months or longer, or who has not gained weight for six months.

Ideal weight for height is found this way:
1. Plot the child's actual height on the growth chart.
2. Plot a weight for the child on the growth chart, using the percentile found for height. Example: If a child plots at the 25th percentile for height/age, then plot the 25th percentile for weight/age. This gives the ideal weight in pounds for the child. Use this weight for the calculation below.
3. Actual weight/ideal weight x 100 = percentage of ideal weight for height.

The diet piece of this intervention must be tuned to accommodate each child's issues – which can include oral tactile defensiveness, cost of special foods, siblings on or off the diet who might help the ASD child "snitch" gluten or casein, oral mechanical capability, food sensitivities or allergies, and support or lack thereof from pediatricians, neurologists, family, and ABA or OT therapists. Common pitfalls are:

- Waiting until early intervention services end (age 3) before trying dietary interventions.
- Giving low calories, low protein, or low fats.

SECTION ONE: RATIONALE FOR INDIVIDUALIZED AUTISM TREATMENT

- Not repeating antifungal treatment periodically.
- Not changing household cooking or food prep habits to meet the child's needs.
- Stopping recommended supplements when an immediate benefit isn't seen (some may work more slowly than others).
- Introducing several changes at once in diet, supplements, meds, or therapies.
- Removing gluten and casein without putting back something of equal or greater nutritional value.
- Allowing gluten, casein, or identified food antigens as soon as improvement is obvious (assuming the child is "cured" and can now tolerate these foods).

Flora

Human beings who live exclusively by hunting and gathering consume over 100 different food sources. This is true even when they live in an environment such as the Kalahari desert or the Aleutian Islands, where a visitor from Stop and Shop would declare, "There's nothing to eat here." As it happens, the real variety in Stop and Shop, for all of its apparent plethora, is rather small. There are a few meats and fish, vegetables and fruits around the edges, and a lot of sugar, fat and salt in the middle. At the end of the day, we shoppers have a very monotonous diet compared with those hunters and gatherers. The lack of complexity in our diet at least makes changes simpler than if we, or our kids, were eating a confusing variety. Small comfort, but it is a big difference when we contrast the relative simplicity of our foods with the complexity of the germs that share our meals along the one or two dozen feet between top and bottom of our alimentary canal. This is where the definition of "clean gut" gets really tricky. We know that the flora of many kids on the autism spectrum are abnormal,[60,61] but there is no way at present to assess the quantitative distribution throughout the mouth, throat, esophagus, stomach, and small and large intestines, or to understand individual sensitivities to the germs or their toxins. For the sake of "cleaning up the gut" as a prerequisite to other treatments, including nutritional supplementation and detoxification, we have to settle for rough guidelines – and you will find a variety of opinions about these guidelines, if you survey DAN! physicians.

Negative reactions to nutritional supplements (vitamins, minerals, fatty acids, amino acids and accessory nutritional factors) and to sulfur-containing supplements and medications used for detoxification are frequent enough in our kids to call for caution. Many of these reactions are mediated by gut flora.[62,63] That is, the supplement of sulfury, detoxifying medicine may fall upon some digestive flora that have a robust appetite for that particular molecule as food. Well-fed germs are better equipped to do their thing, which is to multiply (divide, actually), thrive, and produce more of whatever they produce that is capable of causing a toxic reaction. Such reactions in people of all ages are usually interpreted as indicating that "vitamins just don't agree with me," which is only rarely the case in the strict sense of the word. The words should be "when I take vitamins, they feed my flora, which produce toxins or allergens that don't agree with me." Thus, negative reactions of this kind should be taken as a clue to the existence of dysbiosis, and treated accordingly. One way to confirm the situation in an adult is to substitute injectable for oral administration of the offending substance and observe that no negative response is elicited when the digestive tract is bypassed.

Most children on the autism spectrum are not hypersensitive to supplements, and the hypersensitivity of some has a biochemical basis that is unrelated to dysbiosis, but prudence still suggests that we generally withhold new supplements until we take steps to address the possibility of dysbiosis. Because we currently can obtain better laboratory documentation for bacterial dysbiosis than for fungal dysbiosis, there has been a recent trend toward giving antibiotics to "treat" the bacteria before going after fungi. I disagree with that priority, which depends either on guidance from a stool culture or on using very-broad-spectrum antibiotics in an effort to eliminate or reduce the numbers of undesirable bacterial flora. The problem is that we really do not know enough about the situation among 500 different germs to do more than simply kill a lot of bacteria — which we believe was one of the things that got many kids into trouble in the first place (especially when the antibiotics were given close to the time of a thimerosal-containing immunization). Stool cultures sample only a tiny fraction of the germs that may cause mischief, so with the exception of Clostridium Dificile, cultures offer very little precision as to the bacterial state of affairs in the gut. Antifungal medications are much more likely to produce a dramatic and sustained clinical response, so I favor a short course of one or two before considering that the flora have been addressed enough to say that the gut has been cleaned up. My first choice is Saccharomyces boulardii.[64,65] The next choice depends on what happens with S. boulardii. If it produces dramatic benefits that are still short of a miracle (which does happen), then a more aggressive follow-up treatment is justified by the strong evidence for a yeast problem demonstrated by those benefits. This is a good example of the sixth item on my list of factors that drive decisions: your child's response. Do not try Saccharomyces boulardii without having read further in the section on antifungals.

Saccharomyces boulardii has the advantage of acting as a probiotic. That is, it encourages the growth of normal flora. Other probiotics work by simply providing large numbers of good bacteria that make up part of the flora of the digestive tract. They are occasionally, but not often in my experience, dramatically beneficial. Infrequently, they cause unwelcome symptoms. Supplementing with one of the many probiotics is considered by many DAN! physicians to be part of cleaning up the gut.[66,67,68,69,70,71]

LABORATORY TESTING – GENERAL PERSPECTIVE

Let's turn from the detour we have taken from the path of getting things started, and consider how laboratory testing may help drive decisions about your options. Dr. Pangborn's discussion covers each test in detail. There are some laboratory tests that drive decisions, others that provide something to think about, and others that are interesting for research but are relatively useless in the confident prediction of treatment-decision outcomes for a given child. Serum ferritin, for example, is a measure of your iron stores. If its level is low, you are deficient in iron and if it is, say, above 50 mg/mL, then your iron stores are sufficient to the extent that one would not be able to blame any symptoms on iron deficiency. Between a serum concentration of ferritin of about 20 and 50 mg/mL there is a gray zone in which it becomes ever less likely with increasing numbers that iron deficiency is a problem of immediate clinical significance. If iron is deficient, a search for the cause of iron losses (such as bleeding or iron malabsorption from digestive difficulties) is called for, as is iron supplementation.

The same would be true as regards the finding of certain intestinal parasites. If you find 'em, you've got 'em; and in most cases, treatment is indicated. But what if you don't find them? Now the situation is different than in the case of ferritin. With ferritin, you will have a value that is high, medium or low. In the case of a parasite or a fungus, failure to find it in a lab test does not prove its absence. I have in my files numerous examples of individuals whose parasite test was negative (no parasite found) on one test, and positive on the next. I have many examples of negative yeast cultures in specimens in which the lab reported seeing yeasts under the microscope. I have many examples in which yeast cultures were strongly positive (large amounts of two or more different yeasts) when urine tests for fungal metabolites (chemicals made by fungi in the bowel that turn up in the urine as an indicator of bowel colonization with yeasts) were negative. I have other examples of individuals in whom the urinary metabolites were sky-high and yet stool cultures were negative.

So far I have described two types of lab results:

a. A measurement that is reliable and drives decisions directly from its value. Let's call it a decision driver.

b. A test in which a positive result is reliable but a negative result is not. Let's call it "weak negative."

A third kind of test (c) is one with complex results in which the values of the measurements require interpretation based on an understanding of the biochemical pathways under scrutiny. This is the case with tests that measure items in pathways, such as the thiols mentioned previously as well as amino acids, organic acids and fatty acids. Here we are looking, among other things, for roadblocks caused by a failure of the helpers that speed the transformation of one molecule into another. Nearly all such helpers (enzymes) depend on the assistance of vitamins and minerals (such as vitamin B_6 and magnesium, for example) to do their work. A physiological roadblock is implicated if we see lab data reflecting a pile-up of substances at one point in a pathway and a shortage just beyond that point. Various possibilities exist. It could be that the helpers and their co-factors at that point are not working, or are in short supply. Let's call that a complex test.

A fourth kind of test is an iffy test (d). Measurements of mineral nutrients are iffy. Take calcium, for example. It is the most abundant mineral in your body, but neither a serum test, nor a red blood cell measurement, nor a urine test, nor any other simple test will tell you if you have the right amount of calcium in your body. Calcium is present in different compartments of your body tissues in such widely different concentrations that measuring *here* won't tell you much about *there*. For example, the water that is outside the cells of your body – which is about one-third of your body's water – has about 1,000 times more calcium than the water contained inside cells, where calcium above a tiny concentration is downright poisonous. Individual needs for calcium may vary as much as 200-fold, so not having a simple test to tell you if you are meeting your quota is a serious handicap in health assessment. Twenty-four-hour urine calcium (that is, the measurement of calcium in a urine specimen that contains every drop of urine you pass during exactly 24 hours) is a pretty good test, but still far from perfect and not exactly simple. Mary Coleman, M.D., one of the pioneers in the biomedical assessment and treatment of autism, would not see a patient without a 24-hour urine calcium test first having been obtained. She tells a story of a patient's self-injurious behavior becoming disfiguring while his parents resisted getting a 24-hour urine specimen, which ultimately showed an unmet calcium need that was the basis for his behavior.

Many of the tests doctors do are iffy, and yet there is a tendency among us and our patients to place upon lab tests a high value because they are objective. "Subjective" is the word we use to describe a patient's report of the results from trial-and-error approaches. In general, "objective" is considered to have superior value as compared with the patient's or parents' observation-based opinion about the effect of a diagnostic trial of a particular therapy. But the longer I have been a doctor, the fewer iffy lab tests I tend to do, and the more I depend on diagnostic trials as guides.

There are two reasons for my growing parsimony with lab tests. One is that my intuition has grown, along with my patients' tolerance for my observation that the patient is often the best lab except for decision driver tests. The second is that the past decade has given us a clear picture of what we can expect from certain kinds of tests. This has helped us to define the landscape of the biochemistry and immunology of autism, so that such tests are needed more to discover how a particular child is different from our expectations than to simply confirm that he fits the usual picture. For example, earlier editions of this book stressed the desirability of extensive immunological investigation. Such tests aim at measuring various aspects of children's immune competence, which depends on a complex orchestration of cells and the substances produced by the cells, such as antibodies and signaling molecules (cytokines). Immunological evaluation done in hundreds of children over the past decade has given us a picture of an immunologic train derailment, in the sense that autistic children showed a very wide variety of defects as well as a tendency toward producing antibodies against their own tissues (autoantibodies). The many tests done on many children seem to me to have produced a good overall picture, but without many results that would drive specific decisions. Even measurement of serum IgG – the blood substance most representative of a healthy supply of antibodies against germs – turned out not to be an especially good predictor of response to intravenous treatment with immune globulins (though such measurement is a criterion that insurance companies consider necessary to approve payment for such treatment).

> NO ONE WILL EVER care about your child's outcome more than you. Get educated to be your child's advocate, and to make informed decisions about his or her treatment. Keep your own record of ALL of your child's symptoms, bowel movements, behaviors, illnesses, and reactions to everything from food to every vaccination. If your doctor ignores symptoms of concern, find a new, more informed doctor!
>
> – Linda, a parent

YOUR CHILD'S RESPONSE TO EACH TREATMENT YOU TRY

The many laboratory tests that may be helpful in finding our way to each child's best options are attractive to physicians, because such tests are an obvious part of our craft. Our craft depends for its special knowledge on a claim that we can perceive things that are invisible to the ordinary person. Epidemiology shows us invisibly large patterns. Lab tests reveal invisibly small aspects of our inner workings. Symptoms also provide messages about our inner workings. Symptoms are very helpful in acute illness, in which, for example, a painful sore, swollen pharynx and fever can readily narrow down the diagnostic options. In chronic illness, symptoms are very helpful in naming, but seldom in explaining, the exact mechanism of problems that involve a "snowball" effect in which many symptoms are secondary to the initial disordered mechanism. Chronic illness does, however, present an opportunity for symptoms to indicate progress made as the result of intervention. The key to using symptoms as a guide to monitoring progress is to focus not only on the defining of major complaints, but on the whole pattern. The defining complaints in autism are difficulties with communication, behavior and socialization. The whole pattern is made up of many other symptoms, which, however minor, may be good indicators of progress. Keep track of such symptoms with a flow sheet such as that shown earlier, or use a more elaborate version developed by a parent, Brenda Kerr (available on the ARI website).[72] Parents and physicians who keep such flow sheets are in a much better position to judge the cause-and-effect relationships between treatments and symptoms, particularly when faced by the inevitable confusion arising from doing several things at once.

INTUITION

Biomedical technicalities may so intimidate you that you distrust your own gut feelings as a source of information that will help you take on an active collaborative role with your doctors. But both logical and intuitive choices are based on data, it's just that the pathway to the decision is more evident in the former than the latter.

> WHAT I'D SAY to another parent starting this process: If any one person tells you that they have all the answers to your child's problems, run away as fast as you can.
>
> – Marisa, a parent

You may be accustomed, in your relationships with doctors, to finding that your perspective on a particular option is not entirely welcomed, even if it is backed with a handful of references that you have researched. Our profession is only slowly adjusting to the easy availability of good information that now allows for informed lay participation in decisions. Within the DAN! family, however, things are different for a few reasons.

First, as mentioned earlier, parents' ideas about what was going on with their children have frequently proven to be right, steering researchers toward investigating major factors that have now been established as causes of the autism epidemic. Second, the spirit in which the DAN! movement was founded began with Dr. Rimland's idea to gather data from parents about what works, and to provide a clearinghouse in which those data could be exchanged. In other words, the flow of information within the DAN! movement has always been bi-directional, as opposed to the usual one-way cascade of truth that only descends from the heights of academic and pharmaceutical research. Third, rapid developments in our knowledge about autism lead to a rejection of dogma and an openness to ongoing revision of what we think we know. One of our favorite quotes is from Vaclav Havel, former president of the Czech Republic: "Follow those who seek the truth but flee from those who have found it."

Intuition also plays a major role in assigning credit among various treatments that may be going on in unison. A fundamental principle of mainstream medicine is called the principle of parsimony. It is a corollary of Occam's razor, which states, "Efforts to explain a thing should not be multiplied beyond necessity" – or, stated otherwise, "All things being equal, the simplest explanation is the best." In a medical setting, the principle of parsimony tends to boil down to a strategy in which only one treatment is administered at a time, so as not to muddy the water of the therapeutic response. While generally sound, this principle can lead to strange behavior among physicians – who may, for instance, withhold gestures of support and compassion for fear of augmenting the dreaded placebo response. More to the point, however, is the reality of the train-wreck analogy, and the many issues that may properly be addressed simultaneously to support a child's whole system when it has gone out of balance. Parents often ask, when two or three therapeutic initiatives are proposed to be launched in quick succession, "If he gets much better, won't we be confused as to what was the cause?" The answer is, "If he gets much better, we can deal with it and sort it out later." Sorting it out may require subtracting one aspect of treatment, such as a food-avoidance diet that appeared – along with other steps – to have relieved some symptoms. However, intuition is a powerful tool for finding one's way out of the situation. Parents usually have a valid feeling for what is working, and they usually are proven right in the end.

> REMEMBER THAT your child has various needs. So do not exclude other therapies that your child may need. Or, put another way, don't put all your eggs in one basket. Your child has speech needs, sensory needs, social needs and others. Try to accept your child while helping him to reach his potential. This is a lot easier said than done, but is necessary for you to maintain your own life and have your own needs met. Both you and your child are a work in progress.
>
> *– Marisa, a parent*

---

1. Knivsberg AM, Reichelt KL, Nodland M. Reports on dietary intervention in autistic disorders. *Nutr Neurosci.* 2001;4(1):25-37.

2. Rimland B. *Infantile autism: the syndrome and its implications for a neural theory of behavior.* New York: Appleton-Century-Crofts, 1964.

3. Parent Ratings of Behavioral Effects of Biomedical Interventions. Autism Research Institute http://www.autismwebsite.com/ari/form34q.html.

4. Yeargin-Allsopp M et al. Prevalence of autism in a US metropolitan area. *JAMA.* 2003 Jan 1;289(1):49-55.

5. Chin RL et al. Celiac neuropathy. *Neurology.* 2003 May 27;60(10):1581-5.

6. Walsh WJ et al. Reduced violent behavior following biochemical therapy. *Physiol Behav.* 2004 Oct 15;82(5):835-9.

7. Orion Truss. Tissue Injury Induced by Candida Albicans. *Journal of Orthomolecular Psychiatry* vol. 7, no 1, 1978, pp 17-37.

8. Orion Truss. Restoration of Immune Competence to Candida Albicans. *Journal of Orthomolecular Psychiatry* vol. 9, no 4, 1980, pp 287-301.

9. Orion Truss. *The Missing Diagnosis.* Publisher: Birmingham Privately Printed 1983.

10. Vanderhoof JA, Young RJ. Current and potential uses of probiotics. *Ann Allergy Asthma Immunol.* 2004 Nov;93(5 Suppl 3):S33-7.

11. Gill HS, Guarner F. Probiotics and human health: a clinical perspective. *Postgrad Med J.* 2004 Sep;80(947):516-26.

12. Miraglia del Giudice M, De Luca MG. The role of probiotics in the clinical management of food allergy and atopic dermatitis. *J Clin Gastroenterol.* 2004 Jul;38(6 Suppl):S84-5.

13. Isolauri E. Dietary modification of atopic disease: Use of probiotics in the prevention of atopic dermatitis.*Curr Allergy Asthma Rep.* 2004 Jul;4(4):270-5.

14. Tanaka K, Ishikawa H. Role of intestinal bacterial flora in oral tolerance induction. *Histol Histopathol.* 2004 Jul;19(3):907-14.

15. Uhlmann V et al. Potential viral pathogenic mechanism for new variant inflammatory bowel disease. *Mol Pathol.* 2002 Apr;55(2):84-90.

16. Jeff Bradstreet, M.D. presentation to Institute of Medicine. www.iom.edu/includes/DBFile.asp?id=18578

17. Jeff Bradstreet, M.D. presentation to Institute of Medicine. www.iom.edu/includes/DBFile.asp?id=7498

SECTION ONE: RATIONALE FOR INDIVIDUALIZED AUTISM TREATMENT

18. Stadtman ER et al. Oxidation of methionine residues of proteins: biological consequences. *Antioxid Redox Signal.* 2003 Oct;5(5):577-82.

19. Miller AL. The methionine-homocysteine cycle and its effects on cognitive diseases. *Altern Med Rev.* 2003 Feb;8(1):7-19.

20. Lieber CS. S-adenosyl-L-methionine: its role in the treatment of liver disorders. *Am J Clin Nutr.* 2002 Nov;76(5):1183S-7S.

21. Fetrow CW, Avila JR. Efficacy of the dietary supplement S-adenosyl-L-methionine. *Ann Pharmacother.* 2001 Nov;35(11):1414-25.

22. Stadtman ER, Moskovitz J, Levine RL. Oxidation of methionine residues of proteins: biological consequences. *Antioxid Redox Signal.* 2003 Oct;5(5):577-82.

23. Miller AL. The methionine-homocysteine cycle and its effects on cognitive diseases. *Altern Med Rev.* 2003 Feb;8(1):7-19.

24. Mischoulon D, Fava M. Role of S-adenosyl-L-methionine in the treatment of depression: a review of the evidence. *Am J Clin Nutr.* 2002 Nov;76(5):1158S-61S.

25. James SJ, Cutler P, Melnyk S, Jernigan S, Janak L, Gaylor DW, Neubrander JA. Metabolic biomarkers of increased oxidative stress and impaired methylation capacity in children with autism. *Am J Clin Nutr.* 2004 Dec;80(6):1611-7.

26. Hoffer LJ. Homocysteine remethylation and trans-sulfuration. *Metabolism.* 2004 Nov;53(11):1480-3.

27. Garcia A, Zanibbi K. Homocysteine and cognitive function in elderly people. *CMAJ.* 2004 Oct 12;171(8):897-904.

28. Stipanuk MH. Sulfur amino acid metabolism: pathways for production and removal of homocysteine and cysteine. *Annu Rev Nutr.* 2004;24:539-77.

29. Kalra DK. Homocysteine and cardiovascular disease. *Curr Atheroscler Rep.* 2004 Mar;6(2):101-6.

30. Moat SJ et al. Folate, homocysteine, endothelial function and cardiovascular disease. *J Nutr Biochem.* 2004 Feb;15(2):64-79.

31. Perna AF et al. Homocysteine and oxidative stress. *Amino Acids.* 2003 Dec;25(3-4):409-17.

32. Dringen R, Hirrlinger J. Glutathione pathways in the brain. *Biol Chem.* 2003 Apr;384(4):505-16.

33. Dickinson DA, Forman HJ. Glutathione in defense and signaling: lessons from a small thiol. *Ann N Y Acad Sci.* 2002 Nov;973:488-504.

34. See cite 25.

35. Waly M et al. Activation of methionine synthase by insulin-like growth factor-1 and dopamine: a target for neurodevelopmental toxins and thimerosal. *Mol Psychiatry.* 2004 Apr;9(4):358-70.

36. Sidney M. Baker, M.D. Questionnaire for Children with Autism and Related Developmental and/or Attention Problems. http://216.117.159.91/ari/questionnaire.pdf.

37. Fallon J. Could one of the most widely prescribed antibiotics amoxicillin/clavulanate "augmentin[TM]" be a risk factor for autism? *Med Hypotheses.* 2005;64(2):312-5.

38. Magnesium Metabolism. http://www.merck.com/mrkshared/mmanual/section2/chapter12/12f.jsp (see also cites 53-58).

39. *The Circadian Prescription.* Sidney M. Baker, M.D., Karen Baar, Putnam 2000.

40. *Overcoming Jet Lag.* Charles F. Ehret, Lynne Waller Scanlon. Berkley 1985.

41. Ehret CF et al. Circadian dyschronism and chronotypic ecophilia as factors in aging and longevity. *Adv Exp Med Biol.* 1978;108:185-213.
42. Cahill AL, Ehret CF. Circadian variations in the activity of tyrosine hydroxylase, tyrosine aminotransferase, and tryptophan hydroxylase: relationship to catecholamine metabolism. *J Neurochem.* 1981 Nov;37(5):1109-15.
43. Alberti A et al. Sulphation deficit in "low-functioning" autistic children: a pilot study. *Biol Psychiatry.* 1999 Aug 1;46(3):420-4.
44. Rimland B, Callaway E, Dreyfus P. The effect of high doses of vitamin B6 on autistic children: a double-blind crossover study. *Am J Psychiatry.* 1978 Apr;135(4):472-5.
45. Moreno-Fuenmayor H et al. Plasma excitatory amino acids in autism. *Invest Clin.* 1996 37(2):113-28.
46. Hoshino Y et al. Blood serotonin and free tryptophan concentration in autistic children. *Neuropsychobiology.* 1984;11(1):22-7.
47. Kidd PM. Autism, an extreme challenge to integrative medicine. Part 2: medical management. *Altern Med Rev.* 2002 Dec;7(6):472-99.
48. Hoshino Y et al. Plasma free tryptophan concentration in autistic children. *Brain Dev.* 1986;8(4):424-7.
49. Chugani DC. Serotonin in autism and pediatric epilepsies. *Ment Retard Dev Disabil Res Rev.* 2004;10(2):112-6.
50. Martin M et al. Melatonin but not vitamins C and E maintains glutathione homeostasis in t-butyl hydroperoxide-induced mitochondrial oxidative stress. *FASEB J.* 2000 Sep;14(12):1677-9.
51. Chen ST et al. Melatonin attenuates MPP+-induced neurodegeneration and glutathione impairment in the nigrostriatal dopaminergic pathway. *J Pineal Res.* 2002 May;32(4):262-9.
52. Gruenwald J. Mueller C Skrabal, J Kava Report 2003 - [Clinical] Investigation into EU Member States and Kava Products. Phytopharm Consulting Part IIA - 4.3 March 2003.
53. Konrad M, Schlingmann KP, Gudermann T. Insights into the molecular nature of magnesium homeostasis. *Am J Physiol Renal Physiol.* 2004 Apr;286(4):F599-605.
54. Rimland B. Controversies in the treatment of autistic children: vitamin and drug therapy. *J Child Neurol.* 1988;3 Suppl:S68-72.
55. Durlach J. Clinical aspects of chronic magnesium deficit. in Cantin M, Selig M (eds): *Magnesium in health and disease*, pp. 883-909, Spectrum Press, NY 1985.
56. Holl, M, Baker, SM. Magnesium status as determined by retention of an intramuscular magnesium load: repletion and monitoring of symptoms, *J of the Am Dietetic Assn*, Suppl 90:37, 1990.
57. Seelig, M. *Magnesium deficiency in the pathogenesis of disease*, p. 367ff, Plenum, NY, 1980.
58. Baker, S.M. Magnesium Deficiency in Primary Care and Preventive Medicine: Symptom profiles in relation to magnesium loading studies. *Magnesium and Trace Elements*, 1991-1992;10:251-262.
59. Rimland, B. Edelson, SM. Parent Ratings of Behavioral Effects of Biomedical Interventions. Publication 34, August 2004. Autism Research Institute, San Diego.
60. Finegold SM et al. Gastrointestinal microflora studies in late-onset autism. *Clin Infect Dis.* 2002 Sep 1;35(Suppl 1):S6-S16.
61. Song Y, Liu C, Finegold SM. Real-time PCR quantitation of clostridia in feces of autistic children. *Appl Environ Microbiol.* 2004 Nov;70(11):6459-65.

SECTION ONE: RATIONALE FOR INDIVIDUALIZED AUTISM TREATMENT

62. Kim DH et al. Sulfation of phenolic antibiotics by sulfotransferase obtained from a human intestinal bacterium. *Chem Pharm Bull* (Tokyo). 1992 Apr;40(4):1056-7.

63. Cummings JH, Macfarlane GT. Role of intestinal bacteria in nutrient metabolism. *JPEN J Parenter Enteral Nutr*. 1997 Nov-Dec;21(6):357-65.

64. Periti P, Tonelli F. Preclinical and clinical pharmacology of biotherapeutic agents: Saccharomyces boulardii. *J Chemother*. 2001 Oct;13(5):473-93.

65. Czerucka D, Rampal P. Experimental effects of Saccharomyces boulardii on diarrheal pathogens. *Microbes Infect*. 2002 Jun;4(7):733-9.

66. Gregg CR. Enteric bacterial flora and bacterial overgrowth syndrome. *Semin Gastrointest Dis*. 2002 Oct;13(4):200-9.

67. Hart AL et al. The role of the gut flora in health and disease, and its modification as therapy. *Aliment Pharmacol Ther*. 2002 Aug;16(8):1383-93.

68. Gismondo MR et al. Review of probiotics available to modify gastrointestinal flora. *Int J Antimicrob Agents*. 1999 Aug;12(4):287-92.

69. Liebert CA et al. The impact of mercury released from dental "silver" fillings on antibiotic resistances in the primate oral and intestinal bacterial flora. *Met Ions Biol Syst*. 1997;34:441-60

70. van Furth R, Guiot HF. Modulation of the host flora. *Eur J Clin Microbiol Infect Dis*. 1989 Jan;8(1):1-7.

71. Midtvedt T. Effects of antimicrobial agents upon the functional part of the intestinal flora. *Scand J Infect Dis Suppl*. 1986;49:85-8.

72. Available as a download from http://www.autismwebsite.com/ari/

MAKING A PLAN

By Sidney M. Baker

(This section is a brief overview of clinical strategy – the details of which are described in the sections on laboratory testing and nutritional supplementation. Some repetition of the material is unavoidable and may be helpful considering its density.)

Alleviating constipation, cleaning up the diet, and initial efforts to normalize gut flora are priorities that precede all other therapeutic options. Once these gut issues have been addressed, each child's subsequent path through the landscape of possible biomedical options may be tailored to his or her individual needs. Dr. Pangborn will show you a particular sequence that would satisfy the needs of most children. Here, I would like to give you a sense of the choices you might reasonably face among several paths, depending on a few common variables that could influence the preferred order among treatment options. Writing about these options in a sequence would give the impression that this sequence is the preferred order. To avoid giving that impression, I would like you to work from a diagram that presents four different paths, illustrating that the priority among the paths may depend on circumstances.

The top sequence in the diagram follows the plan in Section Five, Using Nutritional Supplements, in which Dr. Pangborn has provided a comprehensive technical review for the practitioner and for parents who have an advanced understanding of nutrition. We, the authors, and our colleagues in the DAN! group wish to be clear that **we do not have a protocol for treating autism**. We have a way of thinking about addressing individuality in the context of an epidemic that has environmental causes. Our patients have responded to a variety of approaches that depend on the makeup of each child.

Here I present a flexible view of how nutritional supplements may be integrated into an overall scheme of diagnostic trials of diet and detoxifying remedies. These treatments fall on the two sides of our paradigm: 1) filling unmet needs, and 2) avoiding things that are toxic or allergenic. You should read Dr. Pangborn's introduction in Section Five, Nutritional Supplements for Autism – especially the four general rules – before reading on. The starting point in the center of the following diagram is cleaning up the gut, but the next choice may depend on your child's history

> IN THE PREVIOUS SECTION I PROVIDED some options for treating such vexing and specific symptoms as sleep disturbances and constipation. Please resist any inclination to view the treatment options described below as being aimed at any particular symptom, such as stimming, obsessions, poor focus, or speech problems, or any particular body part such as the gut or the brain. Each treatment, when effective, treats all symptoms, although not always to the same degree. When a particular therapy addresses a particular need to get or be rid of a crucial item in an individual's biochemical and immune balance, the result is healing the whole organism. There are drugs to put you to sleep, wake you up, make you poop, or alleviate pain. There are no drugs to heal you. Nature does the healing if you improve the milieu and break vicious cycles, in which – to give just one example – mercury poisons the chemistry (of thiols) that is chiefly responsible for the detoxification of mercury.

and physical exam, laboratory tests, response to each treatment you try, and your intuition and that of your doctor.

Here's how to read the following diagram and match it to the text that explains each of the options shown in the diagram. The triangle is simply a visual aid to finding the text that goes with that option. If, for example, you wish to find the discussion of Methyl B_{12}, then look for the paragraph in the text that is tagged with the **B** inside a triangle. If, on the other hand, you are looking for the text covering supplements, look for the Ω inside a triangle.

The reality of everyday practice is that the sequence of options may change depending on the response to a treatment. The response to a treatment is, obviously, unknown until you try that treatment. I have marked the diagram with stars that say "if negative, rather than positive effects result from this treatment, then go for the treatment indicated by the symbol inside the star." The T inside the star attached to the Antifungal Trial star says, "if you have a negative response to trials of antifungals, consider going to the Specific Carbohydrate Diet as the next step." You will find the Specific Carbohydrate Diet in the text tagged with the T in its triangle. The Ψ in the star attached to the supplement option says, "if you have negative responses to taking supplements, consider going to the antifungal trials as the next step."

I have made this diagram to provide you with an overview of some of the main options. The diagram should serve to illustrate the point that we do not have a one-size-fits-all approach to children on the autism spectrum. Autistic children are sensitive and often have odd responses to the most benign of treatments. If you feel that you are locked into a particular sequence, you could easily be stymied by a negative response. Negative responses are temporary and always provide information that serves to guide future choices.

This shape is the marker for this option and key to the text that describes that intervention.

 This shape means if you see a <u>negative</u> reaction from trying this then go to the option indicated by the enclosed symbol.

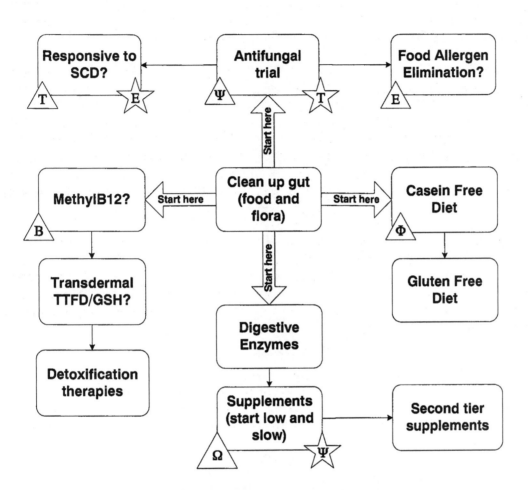

A scheme for considering options for diagnostic trials in children with autism spectrum disorders.

SECTION TWO: MAKING A PLAN

Ⓑ METHYL-B$_{12}$. Here is an intervention that beckons if you want to find out quickly if your child is dramatically responsive, as some are, to one or more injections of methyl B$_{12}$. This naturally bright-red vitamin is described thoroughly in the UNS section. Most parents quickly overcome their squeamishness about administering a tiny amount of methyl B$_{12}$ to their child with a tiny insulin syringe. Otherwise, they may easily find a relative or neighbor with the small amount of medical know-how necessary to do it for them. Some children become hyperactive after the first shot – often a useful kind of wakefulness – but methyl B$_{12}$ is otherwise exceedingly safe. In a hospital setting, injections for children are not given in the buttock because of the possibility of fecal contamination. In a home situation, with people well aware of the need for hygiene, giving the shot into the fat just below the skin at the upper outer limit of the buttocks – allowing you to deliver the injection into fat, as opposed to muscle – is simple, safe and effective.[1] If you prepare the site with a dab of EMLA® cream (available by prescription) about an hour preceding the injection, the injection is painless. Even without the EMLA® cream, the injection is trivial and usually goes unnoticed by a distracted child so long as the syringe is kept out of sight! Note that the concentrated forms of Methyl B$_{12}$ supplied by different compounding pharmacies may vary as to painlessness.

The reason for the shot has to do with the complexities of B$_{12}$'s absorption from the digestive tract – which may eventually be the preferred route, but not at first when the reliability of that route is in question.[2,3] There is some indication that transdermal methyl B$_{12}$ may work, but a diagnostic trial favors the use of a reliable route of administration: injection into subcutaneous tissue. Vitamin B$_{12}$ is a big molecule compared with other vitamins. It is made only by germs, which supply the rest of the food chain via animals who pass it along to their predators (or consumers, if you don't want to think of your family as predators). Plants don't make B$_{12}$, so strict vegans don't get any from their diet. The germs in the gut make B$_{12}$ but the kind they make isn't usually a useful kind. However, when it appears in your child's blood it may give the false impression that he or she has enough, because the lab test for blood B$_{12}$ levels (except that done by Vitamin Diagnostics Lab, Cliffwood Beach, NJ, 732-583-7773) measures false B$_{12}$ as the real thing. A better test for B$_{12}$ is a urine or blood measurement for methylmalonic acid (MMA).[4,5,6] This substance accumulates when B$_{12}$ is not at work in one of your body's assembly (actually dis-assembly) lines. When MMA is abnormally high, it is a reliable marker that B$_{12}$ is not working in that pathway from valine to succinate. Studies by James Neubrander, M.D., show that MMA levels are not predictive of a clinical response to Methyl B$_{12}$. So, regardless of the blood test results, we feel injections of methyl B$_{12}$ are worth a trial. A high blood level of B$_{12}$ is NOT a contraindication to a trial of MeB$_{12}$. The B$_{12}$ problem in autistic children has to do with getting B$_{12}$ methylated, so excesses of the wrong kind of B$_{12}$ may accumulate.

There is no completely reliable test for vitamin B$_{12}$ adequacy. In fact, blood, levels of vitamin B$_{12}$ are frequently found to be high in autistic children, giving a false impression that vitamin B$_{12}$ therapy is unneeded. There are two mechanisms to explain the false elevations. One, just referred to, is abnormal B$_{12}$ variants produced by dysbiotic gut flora; the other has to do with failure of conversion of B$_{12}$ to its useful form, resulting in a rise of the unused form in the blood.[7,8,9] Studies of the thiol pathways give the best indication. Such studies will become available from a commercial laboratory in 2006.

For the purpose of the options under discussion, everything depends on the child's response to getting a methyl-B$_{12}$ shot. The shot is needed because, at first, it is a test to see if you get a response which is immediate: same day or within two days for many children. A trial of several months of injections is needed in order to close the door on this approach as a failure when no response is seen. If the response to injectable methyl B$_{12}$ is obvious and predictable, then other routes, such as high-dose oral or transdermal administration, may offer a substitute for injection. At the moment, however, the only route of administration that we can recommend for a diagnostic trial is subcutaneous.

After a pattern of response to the shot has been worked out, you can see if high oral doses will accomplish the same thing. B_{12} and methyl-B_{12}, when swallowed as a supplement or in food, are greeted in the stomach by a transporter molecule that takes the B_{12} molecule by the hand and leads it through a few yards of small intestine and, just before reaching the appendix and the gateway to the large intestine, shows it a special "hole" through which it can and should pass into the bloodstream.[10] The B_{12} problem in children in the autism spectrum has little to do with dietary deficiency or poor absorption. It has much to do with biochemical blockages that can only be remedied by very large doses of methyl B_{12}. The very large dose acts like the high pressure needed to unblock a pipe—except that in the biochemical setting the extra pressure remains needed until healing occurs. Oral administration of even a large dose of methyl B12 does not reliably provide the kind of "pressure" needed to improve biochemistry and permit healing.

To summarize the methyl-B_{12} option: Lab tests to drive the decision are iffy. The timing of positive response – that is, how long it usually takes to see a good result manifested in behavior, attention, and/or language – is short. The timing of a negative response – that is, how long it may take before you see that no benefit results – is medium, say six weeks. The known side effect is hyperactivity, usually transient. The risk is low. The mechanism of methyl-B_{12}'s action is now well understood, thanks to the combined work of Jim Neubrander, M.D., Marvin Boris, M.D., Allan Goldblatt, P.A., Jill James, Ph.D., Richard Deth, Ph.D., and Paul Cutler, M.D.[11,12] That mechanism is likely to be at the core of the toxicology of many children affected by the current epidemic of neurodevelopmental disorders. Thus, there is a strong argument for rushing to repair one of the most broken parts of a child's chemistry – a broken part that (based on recent research) corrects itself promptly with methyl B_{12} administration. We must keep in mind that **this chemistry occurs within a web of interacting pathways, so benefits can be obtained from more than one therapeutic approach to the system.** Dr. Jim Neubrander has made a big contribution to our understanding of the clinical use of Methyl B_{12} in children on the autism spectrum, reporting his vast and growing experience at the DAN! meetings since May of 2003. Please see Dr. Neubrander's website for more detailed information, his Parent Designed Report Form, and references (http://www.drneubrander.com/).

Here are Dr. Neubrander's comments regarding the use of methyl-B_{12}:

- *Dose for approximately 85% of children: 64.5 mcg/kg/every three days.*
- *Methyl-B_{12} concentration: 25 mg/ml for lesser surface area effect, resulting in slower and more uniform rate of release.*
- *Injection should be given "high up/shallow" in the subcutaneous tissue, far away from the SQ:IM junction or the muscle itself.*
- *Adipose tissue of the buttocks is less vascular, causing slower rate of release; remember that adipose does have its own kinetic properties.*
- *During the first five weeks of methyl-B_{12} use, the clinician should allow absolutely no additions and absolutely no deletions to a child's current program. I am not saying when a clinician should do this – I do it immediately, but clinicians vary in their beliefs about when to start this and that is OK. I am saying that at whatever point methyl-B_{12} is added,*

no changes are allowed to be made. This will allow the clinician to avoid all variables, to determine whether or not a child is a methyl-B_{12} responder, and to detect any methyl-B_{12} side effects (not to be confused with similar side effects that can frequently occur with other agents, e.g. folinic acid).

- *The clinical responsiveness should be evaluated by the most sensitive and the most specific tool available to grade methyl-B_{12} responsiveness, that being the Parent Designed Report Form. There can be no exceptions to this, at least for the first five-week clinical trial. After that it should still be required for the next two reviewing cycles, because the "letter" portion of the exercise allows parents to detect subtleties they otherwise would have missed.*

- *Parents should understand and continually be reminded that it is not the intensity of the responses they see in their child that will be the most important prognostic indicator as to whether or not the child will be a mild, moderate, or significant responder over the next 1.5- to 2-year period of time, but rather the number of responses they see.*

- *If the child is a responder, the parents need to understand that the process is a slow, steady one that needs to be continued long-term, and that they should not decide that a child no longer needs methyl-B_{12} therapy based on a lack of obvious change after the first five to 15 weeks. Currently I am recommending no less than 18 to 24 months of treatment.*

- *Parents are being advised that my research indicates that many (if not most) children will experience some form of regression, and/or lack of progress they would otherwise have made, if they stop the shots.*

- *Folinic acid should be added after the first five-week clinical trial of methyl-B_{12}. It should be added alone, and the dose built up incrementally to see if it is tolerated. My research indicates that approximately 20% of children become hyper and/or cannot sleep when folinic acid is added.*

- *TMG should not be part of the protocol initially, and should only added if methyl-B_{12} fails after escalating doses or if it produces "intolerable" side effects.*

OVERVIEW OF METHYL B_{12}							
Option	Lab test	Timing (+)	Timing (−)	Side effect	Risk	Benefit	Mechanism
Methyl B12	Iffy	Hours to days	Weeks	Hyper	Low	High	Known

DIGESTIVE ENZYMES AND FIRST-TIER SUPPLEMENTS. These are another option as a first step, for the reasons outlined in the Nutritional Supplements section. Most children tolerate most supplements. If a child does not, flora should be suspected as the mediators of a negative reaction. A negative reaction to supplements that are started in low doses and increased gradually should alert us to the need to give priority to dysbiosis as a target of diagnostic trials.

Laboratory testing to determine the need for each supplement considered in the Nutritional Supplements section would be prohibitively expensive and may be iffy (see the table below). The timing of response to most supplements is quick – days to weeks – although not as quick as the response to drugs, which generally work within hours to days and set false expectations for people looking for something that "really works." The efficacy of pharmaceuticals that are aimed at human chemistry (as opposed to drugs aimed a parasites, fungi, bacteria and viruses) is illusory, because even when they seem to "really work," they hardly ever repair broken chemistry.

The side effects of supplements are generally so transient and tolerable that the strategy of simply trying the supplement to see what happens is an acceptable plan for all of the options. The risk of supplements is low and the benefits, when they are evident, are high. The mechanism of most supplements is quite well understood, but some have so many tasks in biochemistry that precision in describing their effects is impossible. For example, vitamin B_6 has about 300 different jobs in your biochemistry.

\multicolumn{7}{c}{OVERVIEW OF SUPPLEMENTS}
Option	Lab test	Timing (+)	Timing (-)	Side effect	Risk	B/W ratio**
Digestive enz.	Iffy	Days	Weeks	Constipation or Diarrhea	low	20:1
B6/Magnesium	Complex	Days	Weeks	Hyper	low	10:1
Taurine	Complex	Days	Weeks		low	NR
Vitamin C	Iffy	Days	Weeks			18:1
Zinc	Decision Driver	Days	Weeks	Nausea, which may be counteracted by taking it with carbonated water		20:1
Calcium	Iffy	Weeks	Months			15:1
Vitamin A	Decision Driver*	Weeks	Months	See note··		23:1
Cod liver oil	Complex	Weeks	Months	Fishy belches		16:1
Fatty acids	Decision Driver	Days	Months	Fishy belches		23:1
Melatonin	No	Hours to days	Days			7.3:1
Multivitamin	No	Hours to days	Weeks			NR

---

* Individuals whose blood vitamin A levels are within the lab's reference range may respond dramatically to vitamin A supplementation. The blood test is a fair indicator of excess intake, but cannot be used to exclude the possibility of an unmet need.

·· The threshold for vitamin A toxicity is quite variable. Some individuals may develop toxicity at relatively low doses, say 10,000 IU per day. Most people tolerate doses well above 50,000 IU daily for months with no adverse effects. Monitoring blood levels is helpful in preventing mischief, but symptoms are quite reliable as warning signs. Nausea, vomiting, headache and a dry, dirty-looking rash on the neck or shoulders indicate a need to suspend vitamin A supplementation.

** Better/Worse ratios are from ARI Publication 34/March 2005.

SECTION TWO: MAKING A PLAN

> K. STARTED THE B_6 SUPPLEMENTS in mid-July. Within a month we saw a child who comfortably approached strangers, interacted with peers appropriately, began napping again, asked "why" about everything, and even reasoned through problems verbally. These are tremendous improvements and ironically, he is becoming a bit of a class joker. At circle time last week, as his teacher was discussing baseball as one of her "favorite things," K. (with great empathy) stated, "Oh those poor Yankees." Even more wonderful was that he told me this story and at the end gleefully added that all his friends "thought I was so funny!"
>
> —a mom

ANTIFUNGALS. Good candidates for high-yield responses to antifungal medications include boys with cherubic appearances at age two or so, a history of antibiotic intake (especially as a newborn), silly or "drunken" behavior, a history of thrush, a yeasty odor, abdominal bloating, carbohydrate craving, and intelligence clearly detectable through the tangle of their sensory distortions and chaotic behavior. Until detoxification medications came along in the past few years, antifungal medications occupied the top of the ratings that Steve Edelson, Ph.D., and Dr. Rimland have tabulated.[13] The two that were chosen for tabulation have been nystatin, to which many yeasts are now resistant, and Diflucan, which is just one of the few effective systemic antifungal medications. Even so, the ratings indicate:

RATINGS OF ANTIFUNGALS
from ARI Publication 34/March 2005

Medication	% Worse	% No effect	% Better	Better:Worse	# of Cases
Nystatin	5	46	49	10:1	986
Diflucan	5	41	55	11:1	330
Yeast free	3	44	54	19:1	756

No other topic covered in this book is slipperier than this one, and no other area of treatment demands more of a parent when it comes to understanding not only the dos and the don'ts, but also the whys and the wherefores. The best popular books on the subject were written by the late William Crook, M.D., and are widely available. *The Yeast Connection: A Medical Breakthrough* (Vintage) is the one to start with. Dr. Crook popularized a notion first presented by Dr. Orian Truss of Birmingham, Alabama in the form of scientific presentations in 1977 and later in his book, *The Missing Diagnosis*, published in 1982. When I first heard Dr. Truss lecture in 1977, what he said rang true. I looked among my family practice patients for individuals with profiles that matched Dr. Truss's description of candidates who might respond to treatments aimed at reducing exposure to yeasts and molds. I found them easily and became convinced that the best way for a practitioner to validate Dr. Truss's point is to simply give it a try with a few patients as I had done. It is safe and quickly enlightening on the issue of the relatively high frequency of sick people whose varied symptoms have a common origin in the mischief caused by sensitivity to molds and yeasts to which they are exposed in food, air and in their own digestive flora. Dr. Truss and I had co-sponsored an international conference on the subject that gathered practitioners and academic scientists to explore the question and its clinical and research applications. The collegial spirit of that meeting contrasted sharply with that of our next conference in 1985, when speakers with affiliations to a mainstream immunology/allergy society were urged to boycott our meeting for which AMA continuing medical education credits were given by a competing society. Mainstream editorials then damned Dr. Truss's notions as heresy, and the rest is history. Go to most normal doctors and mention that you think that you might have a yeast problem, and you will likely taste the strong draught of medical condescension and disaffection with any association to heresy. The reasons for this now long history of resistance to a fairly simple, common-sense, and easily observed connection between yeasts and all sorts of illness really escape me. By the late 80's, when most of those who had editorialized against the idea had relaxed their opposition, I figured that the yeast connection's popular acceptance would soon open a crack in the wall of mainstream medicine or that the pharmaceutical industry's market instincts would promote curiosity and validating research. That has not happened, but most ordinary people you meet have heard of yeast problems in ways that make them open to the idea.

In the late 80's I continued my pediatric and general practice, which tended increasingly toward a focus on individuals with complex chronic illness, and after my seven years as Director of the Gesell Institute in New Haven, more and more on children with developmental problems including autism. I thought that I was seeing a disproportionate number of such children who were dramatically responsive to antifungal therapy because their parents had heard that I was Dr. Yeast. I did NOT as the moniker implies believe that all problems stemmed from yeast issues, but I did then and still do believe that consideration of such issues belongs high on the list of any person with complex chronic illness, whether that illness is well-named (Crohn's, ulcerative colitis, asthma, multiple sclerosis, etc.) or simply bears a descriptive tag such as reflux, depression, attention deficit, or fatigue. When I saw Dr. Rimland's reports of parents' ratings of dozens of kinds of treatments and found nystatin, a medicine for killing yeasts, at the top of the drug category, I realized that the responsiveness of kids in the autism spectrum to this sort of treatment was more widespread than my own selective practice. The importance of tending to yeast problems remains a tenet of the consensus that was formed in the first DAN! meeting in 1995. All of us feel that yeast issues, which I will define more precisely in a moment, should be high among diagnostic and therapeutic considerations for children on the autism spectrum. There is disagreement among us as to the criteria for giving up on the idea. This spectrum of opinion is the natural consequence of the basic principle that it is easy to consider or to decide doing something that is relatively safe to see if it will work (a diagnostic trial) but it is hard to know when a particular effort has been carried out with sufficient intensity or duration to justify abandoning it as a failure.

The definition of "yeast issues" is one or more symptoms that are relieved by minimizing exposure to molds and yeasts. Unlike any other allergen or toxin or germ, yeasts belong to three different domains of your environment: food, air, and the flora of your digestive tract. If you are allergic to cats, you breathe cat dander, but you don't eat cats and cats don't dwell within you. If you are allergic to wheat, you don't breathe it and do not cultivate it in your intestine. If you develop a strep infection, no one proposes that you eat strep soup or breathe strep-laced air while your immune system is trying to pursue its struggle with the strep. If you are sensitive to yeast, then your immune system may be faced by an unwelcome presence of yeasty or moldy things in the air you breathe, the food you eat, and among the 500 or so species of germs that inhabit your digestive tract. The issue is, therefore, complex. The remedy may seem simple, but it is often complex in that it demands attention to diet, environment, flora, and food and medicines that may feed the yeast in your flora.

Just about everything we know about the yeast problem is based on anecdotal evidence. During the thirty years that this evidence has accumulated and been shared among interested practitioners, the following peaks and valleys have appeared in the broad territory mapped by patients who have had dramatic responses to antifungal treatments.

SECTION TWO: MAKING A PLAN

The valleys – or gaps in our knowledge – are:

1. We do not know where the yeasts are hiding in the body. When you have a thrush infection, the white patches of fungus are evident on the tongue or inner cheeks. When you have a vaginal yeast infection, the yeasts are usually abundant on a microscope slide prepared from a swab. Not always, however. Occasionally one sees a person with the itch, the odor, the irritation, and the antibiotic story that goes with a vaginal yeast infection. But the yeast is not evident in the microscopic preparation. Or it *is* evident, but it does not grow out on culture. Or the other way around. In our kids with yeast issues – as defined by a convincing, sometimes quite miraculous, response to antifungal medication and avoidance of yeasts and molds and sugar – we often cannot find the yeasts in stool. Often we – or the laboratory – can find them under the microscope in the stools, but they do not grow on culture. Or, as in the example of vaginal yeast infections, they do not appear under the microscope but they do grow on culture. What that says is that neither culture (the defining test in microbiology) nor the microscopy is decisive. What that says to me is that *neither test can be used to drive a decision not to give an empirical trial of antifungal medication and diet*. Sooner or later the yeasts will be found – probably in the unexplored reaches of the small intestine, which is too far from the top or bottom of the digestive tract for sampling with current technology and is supposed to be sort of a microbiological desert. In an area of the body where very few germs are normally present, it may not take many to cause mischief.

2. We do not know the mechanisms by which the yeasts cause their mischief. The clinical picture of many autistic children is one of drunkenness. That is, it resembles the kind of behavior you may observe in a tavern. Check it out. The patrons have, let's say, each consumed a more-or-less identical dose of tequila, beer, or whatever. Here is one who is very happy, here is one who is quite sad, here is one who is aggressive, here is one who is silly, here is one with inappropriate laughter, here is one who is spaced out. Here is another who is scoring well in darts and another who has visual disturbances or problems with coordination. That's the problem with toxicology – there is no average person, only concepts about groups of people that may be expressed as averages of data consisting of opposite trends. The concept we form from knowing lots of kids in the spectrum who have responded to antifungal therapy is that they are intoxicated. The common feature among them is that they *all* have, like the patrons of the tavern, problems with attention. Attending is the hardest thing we all do. Think of the effort reading this book demands of you – and just wait until you get to Jon's part. Whenever something goes wrong that puts you off balance, attention is the first thing to go and its absence is pretty much universal among different individuals who are stressed in ways that may permit lots of individuality in other dimensions of their behavior.

Beyond the observation that the yeast connection in our kids looks like a form of intoxication (need I point out that everything consumed in the tavern is a product of yeast fermentation?) we do not have a clear picture as to what the yeasts that inhabit some part of our kids' intestines make in the way of substance(s) like alcohol – but not alcohol per se – that cause the drunken symptoms that we see in yeasty kids. It has been nearly a decade since William Shaw, Ph.D., first reported finding, in the urine of children on the autism spectrum, abnormally large amounts of substances known to be not of human origin but made by various bacteria and, especially, fungi of the digestive tract. The territory that Dr. Shaw opened up with his observations and his ongoing measurement of these substances at Great Plains Laboratory remains controversial. From my perspective as a clinician, I must say that comparison of laboratory values measuring fungal metabolites as well as organic acids that *are* part of my patients' own chemistry (as opposed to coming from their gut flora) show changes that correlate with treatment and improvement in symptoms. We are far, however, from nailing the exact mechanism by which the intoxication is leveraged, and it seems quite likely that none of the molecules we can now measure is the intoxicant, but it will turn out to be one present in very small amounts such as those needed to produce psychedelic changes in perception from certain mushrooms.

3. We do not know ahead of time, when we are dealing with an individual child, when we have done everything we can to confront the challenge of establishing that there is a yeast problem or that the treatments we have prescribed have had the best result we can obtain. The burden of this uncertainty lies with us practitioners. We must guide parents out on the limb where the view improves and the risk increases as we move farther from the security of the trunk. In my experience with thousands of patients over more than 25 years, the risk is tiny and the benefits of going the distance are great. What do I mean by going the distance? I call it the antifungal parade in which antifungal medications are offered in sequential short trials of about 20 days, monitoring blood tests to serve as an early indication of toxicity from the pharmaceuticals that have some toxicity. As each antifungal medication passes our reviewing stand, we ask it to tell us by the child's symptoms whether a medium, then a large dose makes a significant impact. We are looking for dramatic changes, although subtle changes may provide some insight. At the end of a series of treatments as illustrated in the following table, we elect a beauty queen – the antifungal that had the best result – or we conclude that we have pretty much exhausted our options in this area. We than have the option, depending on the circumstances, of returning to that medication to see how much more leverage we can get. I know that some practitioners say that two weeks of nystatin always does the trick or that if a lab test doesn't indicate yeast, then the game is over. But listen. Here is a typical story of an adult whose experience illustrates the dilemma.

Alina Carroll had been symptom-free for seven years after allergy injections had brought her fierce eczema under control. She had to have a measles immunization when she enrolled in an adult education program at a local college, so she had received a measles, mumps and rubella immunization in June, followed by a second measles shot in July. Six weeks later her eczema flared, leaving her covered with crusting, oozing lesions and so itchy that she could not sleep and could barely think. Because eczema is so often an expression of yeast allergy,[14,15] I wanted to be sure to cover that possibility. She went on a yeast-free diet, which had previously been helpful for her condition. Meanwhile she took a course of nystatin, followed by Diflucan, followed by Nizoral, and followed by Lamisil. Three weeks of each adds up to 12 weeks – a very long time if you are going out of your mind with itching and having to go to work every day with your skin a mess. She and I had been considering other issues including her need for increased doses of omega 3-fatty acids, the potential benefits of primrose oil (a source of the omega-6 fatty acid gamma linolenic acid), and the possibility that the immunizations may have triggered a food sensitivity. The seat of my pants still said that she could have a yeast problem. But I felt guilty proposing that she try yet another antifungal medication in the dying hopes that it would be the answer. Alina and I weighed the options while I pointed out that the package insert for Sporanox mentioned rashes as a possible side effect, though I had never seen one (nor have I in the ensuing decade). She elected to go for it. Within 48 hours she had a dramatic response, and a few days later she was free of itching and sleeping well. The decision to try yet one more antifungal was a close call, and Alina's rapid healing provided another among many similar lessons about not giving up on a reasonable suspicion.

I have had similar experiences with autistic children in whom the first two or three antifungals failed to induce a good response. This is where the decision about when to quit on a particular line of treatment gets tricky. In my experience, the safest bet is to try all the antifungals before

SECTION TWO: MAKING A PLAN

quitting, and to do so with dispatch and caution. Dispatch means a two-week trial at a regular dose, followed by a 10-day trial at double the regular dose, for a total of 24 days. With antifungals, strength is more important than length and a short course of a high dose can do wonders when a long course leaves you not knowing whether any good has come of it. Caution means regular monitoring of liver profiles and blood counts, with added kidney tests (BUN and creatinine and urinalysis) for Lamisil.

In other words, if yeast problems are part of our kids' problems as they often are, and if no lab test can drive a decision to withhold consideration of a trial of antifungal medication, and if we have no way of knowing for sure which among the various antifungals may be the best for treating this particular child's fungus problem, and if the antifungal parade is a reasonable benefit/risk deal, then I don't see a remedy for our combination of ignorance and commitment to the child's needs that does not insist on a diagnostic trial.

Mind you, this is for all clinicians a proposition fraught with the peril of our colleagues' disaffection. A decade ago one of our colleagues was taken to task and pursued relentlessly by his state's authority pertaining to practice standards. Despite his support by the state's medical board and numerous well-credentialed experts he was broken, impoverished and de-licensed for prescribing a brief trial of nystatin for a kid with poor attention. He was recently vindicated and the members of the state's authority fired with a scorching tongue-lashing from the judge. You can bet that this event, repeated in various forms in many states over the past twenty years, enlivens the fears of practitioners who want to do the best for their patients, but who also want to hang on to their livelihood. Such fears engender a sense of relief that comes with any decision to get off of yeast street and into a safer part of town. We are all aware that ethics is a subject of increasing medical scrutiny and visibility. It tends to capture our attention in the occasional life-and-death issues where the roles of men and women and God form the drama. The sum total of little everyday ethical decisions of the medical world must have ten times the collective weight of the big issues that corner the public debate. The most pernicious of the little everyday ethics slips are those driven by claims of authority by persons with no expertise (that is, personal experience) who, however well-meaning, offer or exercise caution leading to an unjustified abandonment of a potentially helpful strategy. How many pediatricians or pharmacists (both wild about prescribing Ritalin or Risperdal) scare the pants off of parents who are considering a brief trial of an antifungal that is being advertised every night on TV as the safe answer to toenail shame on the beach? How can Lamisil be relatively safe (which it is, see below) for millions of people and somehow be terribly dangerous for our kids to try for a couple of weeks? It isn't.

I am sure that you realize that I have no axe to grind. I only want to sharpen your attention to the pressures that you will encounter on the paths this book may help you travel. Recall that at the beginning I said that there were several polarized issues that influence the climate in the landscape where your path will take you. Polarization is a mild term for the tension now created by the defenders of mercury in the form of thimerosal in children's vaccines versus those of us who believe that thimerosal in pediatric vaccines has engendered the worst public health disaster in world history. Practitioners and parents who navigate the landscape of options for kids with autism will have to deal with relatives, neighbors, pediatricians, school principals, and experts on TV and in the newspaper who tell them they are wrong to look at mercury or yeast as part of the answer to their children's problems. Most people, based on that advice, will have given up looking well before they picked up this book. You must be exceptional. If so my advice is to brace yourself, try to keep your sense of humor, and hang in there.

> **FUNGUS:** *any of a major group (Fungi) of saprophytic and parasitic spore-producing organisms usually classified as plants that lack chlorophyll and include molds, rusts, mildews, smuts, mushrooms, and yeasts* (Merriam Webster Online). Actually, fungi are not classified as plants but have a separate kingdom as do animals and plants. They are like plants in that they don't have "legs" but they are like animals in that they "eat" their food rather than making it out of sunlight and air. In the grocery store you find mushrooms with the vegetables, but in scientific terms they are much more like us in that their internal chemical doings–such as the way they disassemble energy-containing molecules (sugars, proteins, fats) to get the energy for their own use–are based on pathways that are similar to or identical to those of animals including humans. The basic understanding of how sugar delivers energy (in all animals) was worked out in the brewing industry, where yeasts yielded the secrets of the citric acid (or Krebs) cycle that becomes familiar territory to all medical students and DAN! doctors who must revisit, with the help of Jon Pangborn and others, some of the things that faded from memory after we passed our exams.
>
> As you can see from the above definition, yeasts are only one of several groupings within the kingdom of fungi. Like the animal and plant kingdom, they all share certain features, which we associate with odors of moldiness, mustiness or mildew. Our noses detect a common (musty) quality among many different fungi. Similarly, our immune systems may react negatively to any kind of moldy environment even if our actual allergy tests are positive only to certain selective mold species. In other words, mold-sensitive people tend to cross-react among many yeasty, moldy, mildewy odors. Mold-sensitive people also tend to cross-react to melon and to petrochemicals, which, if you think about it, are simply very old vegetable oils that have spent millions of years buried where they fell as constituents of plants. Imagine the stench of that prehistoric compost heap the next time you get a strong whiff of diesel exhaust. The connection is remote, but it is intimate for some mold/chemical-sensitive people.

If you choose to seek treatment for intestinal yeast as a trial of therapy – that is, take the treatment and see if it convincingly helps symptoms – these are your options.

> REMEMBER THAT your child is the best laboratory. As I have pointed out before, some lab tests drive decisions, some are merely helpful for research, and some are sort of "in between." At the end of the day, however, a diagnostic trial of treatment is often the most reliable way of knowing whether a treatment is right for a given person. Diagnostic tests have dramatic utility in cases of acute illness such as strep throat or stroke, but in chronic illness, the best time to decide on the effectiveness of a relatively safe treatment is after trying it (see Section One).

<u>Saccharomyces boulardii.</u>[16,17] Twenty-five years ago, a colleague of mine, Leo Galland, M.D., told me that he had heard of this "yeast against yeast." I was incredulous that individuals with a yeast problem could benefit from taking something that seemed to me to be almost certain to provoke an allergic reaction as brewer's yeast and yeasty foods often do. Dr. Galland trusted the reports of French doctors who routinely used S. boulardii, and we started using it. It has the advantage of being readily available without a prescription. Taking S. boulardii is like swallowing a pharmaceutical company, because it takes up temporary residence in your bowel where it manufactures substances that promote healthy flora. It was discovered early in the 20th century when a French official (Boulard) was traveling in the villages of what was then French Indochina, now Vietnam. An epidemic of cholera (diarrhea from hell, caused by a bacterium) was raging, and

SECTION TWO: MAKING A PLAN

he was seeing what could be done. Visiting a particular village, he was told, "We don't have cholera here." "What do you mean, you don't have cholera? Everyone up and down the river has cholera," was the gist of his response. He ascertained that their preventative and remedy lay in a brew prepared from the surface of the litchi fruit. Saccharomyces cerevisiae (baker's and brewer's yeast) is the natural flora on the surface of most fruits, and the one Boulard came across was a strain of S. cerevisiae that favored the litchi. It has properties (described in Section Five) which include both antifungal and probiotic effects. Once swallowed, it arrives in your intestine where it sets up shop. If you stop taking it, it wakes up one day and realizes that it is not in its native habitat. At that point, or soon thereafter, it clears out of your gut. If it has done its two jobs well, it will have promoted the re-establishment of good flora while reducing the numbers of bad yeasts to a manageable level.

If you are using a stool culture to monitor success, you should wait for about a month. The lab cannot distinguish between S. boulardii and S. cerevisiae (baker's and brewer's yeast). If after your child takes S. boulardii, the lab reports isolating S. cerevisiae, it is very likely the lingering S. boulardii. If you have had a stool culture that is positive for one or another kind of yeast, you and your practitioner may be curious to see if it is gone after any treatment. So go ahead and repeat the culture, but do not take the results too seriously. As mentioned before, stool cultures are not decisive. Recall my mention of the die-off reaction that can be associated with any antifungal. Never have I seen more brutal die-off as with S. boulardii. If you see a flare of symptoms that may be indications of a mild regression or can include biting, screaming, kicking, red face, red ears, bloating, pooping behind the couch, and every manifestation of misery, then administer the contents of an activated charcoal capsule, found over-the-counter at the pharmacy or health food store (where it is sold for treating gas). In the emergency room it is used as a stopgap measure when a child comes in having swallowed grandpa's Digitalis or other poison. Activated charcoal is capable of absorbing more than its own weight of some substances (e.g. mercuric choride),[18] and its capacity to neutralize fierce die-off symptoms within about half an hour is one of the most remarkable medical phenomena that I regularly witness. The contents of a 360-mg capsule can be mixed with a small amount of whatever it takes (honey, Welch's frozen grape concentrate thawed and taken straight) to get a child to swallow it when it is delivered into the mouth with a syringe. It is a little gritty but tasteless. It should not be taken with food or medication or supplements, because it absorbs everything in its reach.

> **ACTIVATED CHARCOAL – A PANACEA**
>
> Parents who have witnessed the dramatic effects of charcoal in quenching a die-off reaction taught me years ago that it is helpful in many situations which, however mysterious, have no apparent relationship to a die-off reaction. We all have seen kids plunge into the depths of a really bad day of volatile moods, dominant among which are irritability and depression, but could include all manifestations of tavern behavior referred to previously. In these situations, charcoal is a kind of panacea. The harm in using it every day is that it interferes with the absorption of food, supplements or medicine. If it is taken on a stomach that has been empty for an hour or will stay empty for an hour (20 minutes in a pinch) one need not worry about negative effects from up to 30 doses per week.

Nystatin or Amphotericin B. Nystatin has been used in the United States for more than 50 years, after the germ that makes it was identified in a New Jersey barnyard and isolated in a New York State (NYS) laboratory. In terms of potential toxicity, when taken orally, nystatin and its close cousin Amphotericin B are in the same category as S. boulardii in that they are not absorbed into the bloodstream and only treat the digestive tract. In the past 20 years of culturing stools for fungi we have seen more and more yeasts that are resistant to nystatin, so I think Amphotericin B, which has not been widely used in the United States, is the better choice. It can be ordered from compounding pharmacies. It should be taken in its pure powder form and allowed to spend some time in your child's mouth before being swallowed, because the mouth is a favored place for yeast colonization. Moreover, it requires frequent dosage (four times per day) because it is not absorbed into the blood. Most medications, once swallowed, pass into the blood where their levels reach a peak after an hour or so and then begin to dwindle as they are detoxified in the liver and/or excreted in the urine. The effect is like a tide, rising for a period of time, and then subsiding. Taking nystatin or Amphotericin B, however, is like throwing apples into a river. They bob on downstream where at any one point you can see them go by, but then they are gone. If your child has yeasts in any part of the digestive tract from the mouth on down, these medications will be effective only while they pass through this region. After that, yeasts that were not killed can reproduce and re-establish their colonization until the next dose arrives. Nystatin and Amphotericin B should be taken at least a half an hour before or after eating, so that the medicine does not have to fight its way through food to find the yeasts! Nystatin and Amphotericin B are without any significant toxicity because each stays within the bowel. In 25 years of prescribing nystatin to thousands of individuals, I have never seen a toxic reaction.

I have, however, seen die-off reactions, occasionally of frightening intensity. Following the dietary recommendations listed above, and *avoiding constipation*, will minimize the chance of die-off. The good news is that negative reactions to antifungals with the very symptoms you are trying to treat (as opposed to novel symptoms, such as dry lips seen with Diflucan and Nizoral) are good evidence that those symptoms are connected to a yeast problem and will ultimately respond to antifungal treatment.

Other antifungals. Individuals with immune systems that are faulty because of genetic problems, infections such as human immunodeficiency virus (HIV), medications such as steroids and anticancer drugs, and/or underlying medical conditions such as diabetes are especially susceptible to yeast infections. Prior to the 1980s, when the drug Nizoral (ketoconazole) came on the market, the drugs to combat severe yeast infections were quite toxic and doctors of my generation came to view antifungal medications other than nystatin with apprehension. I find that there is a lingering fear of antifungals among my colleagues. "Liver damage" is the phrase that comes straight from the fine print of the package inserts for Nizoral, Diflucan (Fluconazole), Sporanox (Itraconazole), Lamisil (Terbinafine), and others that are coming on the market. In thousands of patients for whom I have prescribed Diflucan and Sporanox, I have seen not a single adverse reaction. I monitor "liver profile" tests, and stop the medication if I see a rise above normal. In the 1980s I had two patients on Nizoral whose liver function tests became rapidly abnormal as they developed jaundice. They recovered completely after stopping the medication. Recently a (non-autistic) patient had a reaction within two days of starting Lamisil, which temporarily affected her kidney and liver function. According to the manufacturer, hers was a reaction that occurs with a frequency of 1 in 40,000 patients. Silymarin (milk thistle) has a protective effect on the liver, so supplements of this herb, which is an effective antidote to mushroom poisoning, may guard against the hepatic toxicity of the systemic antifungal medications.

As ominous as "damage" sounds when coupled with any organ in the body, we need to keep in mind that the organ most susceptible to damage and most difficult to repair is our intestinal flora. A short course or even a single dose of antibiotics can alter your intestinal germ population[19,20,21] in ways that are enduring and difficult to repair. Antifungal medications may be necessary in that repair because they are the most effective way of combating the unwanted

SECTION TWO: MAKING A PLAN

overgrowth of fungi.[22] The very small risk associated with antifungal drugs is well balanced by the enormous benefits achieved by many individuals.

Is a trial of S. boulardii and/or Amphotericin B an adequate trial of antifungal medications? Yes, perhaps for the sake of having cleaned the gut as a precondition for initiating other therapies in our diagram. The fundamental question remains: "Are some or all of the child's symptoms caused by a yeast problem?" No lab test will give a decisive answer. A trial of antifungal medication will do so, provided the fungus in question is sensitive to the medication. So what if S. boulardii fails to work? Maybe there was no yeast problem, or maybe the S. boulardii just was not the right remedy for the particular strain(s) of yeasts involved.

Lab data can give us some help here when yeasts are identified in a stool culture. Sensitivity testing is performed (in Petri dishes or test tubes) to see which antifungal medications and natural remedies suppress the identified yeast most effectively. These tests are a very good but still imperfect guide. I have started patients on Diflucan pending the outcome of a culture, only to discover that their yeast was strongly resistant to Diflucan. On some of these occasions, when I called the patients to make a change in the treatment, I found that their symptoms had cleared so quickly and so well as to leave little doubt that the Diflucan had done the job.

The final answer to one of the primary questions I have posed is that you can never be sure that you have done everything possible to diagnose a yeast problem except by judging the response to treatment. The best you can do is to work your way through the antifungal medications as swiftly as possible, monitoring the appropriate laboratory tests to minimize risk. This can be a very tedious process, even if you adhere to a schedule of about three weeks on each antifungal. Each failure to achieve the expected results dims your hopes and makes you feel as if you are wasting your time with an expensive and potentially risky gamble. I believe that failure to see this diagnostic process through may result in missing a seemingly miraculous healing in some children.

OVERVIEW OF ANTIFUNGALS							
Antifungal treatment	*Lab test*	*Timing +*	*Timing -*	*Side effect*	*Risk*	*Benefit*	*Mechanism*
Saccharomyces boulardii	iffy	2 wks	3 wks	Die off	No	High	Unknown
Amphotericin B	iffy	2 wks	3 wks	Die off	No	High	Unknown
Systemic antifungals	iffy	2 wks	3 wks	Die off	Liver function *	High	Unknown

*As stated in the text, monitoring of so-called liver function tests is important during the use of systemic antifungals. These tests come as a panel from laboratories and are usually ordered as such. They measure in the serum the levels of total protein, albumin, globulin, total bilirubin, indirect bilirubin, alkaline phosphatase, AST, and ALT. The ones of interest while monitoring systemic antifungals are the last two, AST (aspartate aminotransferase – it was formerly called SGOT) and ALT (alanine aminotransferase – it was formerly called SGPT) which may rise slightly in response to these antifungal medications and signal caution against continuing. Bilirubin is the yellow stuff that is apparent when people are jaundiced. As mentioned in the text, I have seen a rise in bilirubin from antifungal medicines only twice in 25 years. If your child should receive antifungal medications and there is a departure from normal in the other tests, do not be concerned. If the alkaline phosphatase is reported as very elevated, it is because the lab is using adult norms for the reference range. Alkaline phosphatase, an enzyme important in bone growth, is normally very elevated in children compared with adult norms.

> WHEN THE DOOR was opened we had no choice but to walk through, because the changes in our son were undeniable. After three years we have become well-versed in dietary and biomedical treatments and our son is a true success story and testament to those treatments. [He has gone] from a two-year-old boy who repetitively opened and closed doors, was believed to have complete apraxia, and expressed no ideas of his own, to the five-year-old boy who just finished making a card for Grammy where he wrote "Happy Birth Grammy Love Eric" all by himself, and is now begging his sister to come downstairs and play with his pirate ship.
>
> – Brenda, a parent

Other antifungal options. There are a wide variety of antifungal preparations available without a prescription. These include capryllic acid, oregano concentrate, citrus seed extract, undecylenic acid, pau d'arco, and enzymes that dissolve the cell walls of yeasts (Candex). They all may be considered, although some kids either can't swallow capsules or cannot stand the taste. You may consult Dr. McCandless's book, *Children With Starving Brains*, for a more extensive discussion of non-pharmaceutical antifungals.

Antibacterials. When the normal gut flora are disturbed, the most common and accessible problem is the overgrowth of yeasts. But what about the good bacteria that are wiped out by antibiotics and replaced by the overgrowth of bad bacteria? The names of various undesirable bacteria may turn up on your stool culture report along with, if requested by the practitioner, a report of resistance and sensitivity to various antibacterial medications. If one of these germs turned up instead in a urine culture as the cause of a bladder infection – as they often do – then giving the appropriate antibiotic would be the standard thing to do. Not so with bowel germs, especially considering that antibiotics probably unbalanced healthy intestinal flora to begin with. Some individuals persist with the same bad bacteria over repeated stool cultures. The stool cultures of other patients keep shifting to show various undesirable bacteria. In either case, what you are seeing on a stool culture report of bacteria is the tiniest tip of an iceberg. Recall that in healthy individuals there are up to 500 different kinds (species) of bacteria inhabiting the gut. The vast majority of these germs are anaerobic, meaning that they thrive in the absence of oxygen. None of these can be isolated by regular culture methods, yet anaerobic bacteria are among the leading suspects as the cause of many toxic or immunologic reactions.

Efforts to rearrange your child's gut flora by killing bad germs with the hope of restoring balance by taking in good germs (probiotics) may require reducing the numbers of bad anaerobes. In some instances, this does work. Those instances are as follows. First, if your child's urine organic acids reveal high levels of dihydroxyphenylproprionate (DHPPA), taking an anti-anaerobe antibiotic works promptly to bring the level down to normal. Second, studies of autistic children with high levels of DHPPA treated with Vancomycin show clinical improvement in behavior and cognition during and shortly after the treatment.[23,24] Third, some individuals with complex chronic illness accompanied by a history of antibiotics, and lab data (abnormal pH, short chain fatty acid distribution, and culture) suggesting abnormal bowel flora may benefit from a course of a combination of two antibiotics that wipe out a major segment of bowel flora. These are Gentamycin and Vancomycin. Doctors usually use Gentamycin intravenously in a hospital setting for treating dire infections. Taken orally, like nystatin, it does not enter the bloodstream. It kills many kinds of bowel germs at an adult dose of 160 mg five times daily for three days. When combined with Vancomycin 250 mg five times daily, it will produce essentially odorless loose bowel movements by the third day. At that point, the consumption of large doses of

SECTION TWO: MAKING A PLAN

probiotics and an antifungal medication offers some hope of restoring a healthy flora while relieving symptoms that had been produced by a toxic bowel.

For a full understanding of the scientific research underlying my clinician's take on the subject, read *The Second Brain*, by Michael Gershon, M.D.[25] It is a brilliant explication of the following statement: If you are seeking the cause of harm to the brain or other tissues of the body, you need not necessarily find a harmful substance in the brain or other tissues. It is sufficient that a substance harms the gut, which by its nerve-connection to the rest of the body can evoke harm elsewhere.

Parasites

Human beings have been hosts to parasites of various descriptions, especially worms, forever, and only recently has parasitic infestation become more the exception than the rule in cultures with modern standards of sanitation. It is likely that lower rates of parasitic infestation are a trade-off against a higher incidence of various kinds of chronic inflammatory diseases. However, with the exception of a treatment for colitis that employs the deliberate introduction of intestinal worms, no one is recommending that we go back to having a lot of parasites.

If a stool examination turns up a parasite, getting it out of there is a high priority. The term parasite refers to one being living at another's expense, so it may be applied to creatures of all sizes and species, even human, if broadly interpreted. When it comes down to stools, it refers collectively to two completely different sizes and types of creatures: worms and certain single-celled organisms, but not yeasts or other fungi and not bacteria. Because the line between fungi and certain single-celled organisms is pretty thin, the term parasite is arbitrary and a little vague. A big worm (such as a roundworm) in the toilet, or even a fingernail-clipping-sized pin worm on a child's stool, produces a squeamish response in those of us living in modern cultures in which such infestations are not everyday occurrences as they were not long ago pretty much everywhere. There is at least no disagreement among doctors that worms, if found, should be eradicated. There is, however, growing agreement among some doctors that the eradication of worms from most of the population has been associated with a higher incidence of allergies and autoimmune diseases. It is as if anti-worm immune defenses left idle have caused mischief mediated by a tendency to attack innocent targets that enter our bodies via our diet or our environment, or even to attack our own flesh.

A bigger disagreement exists among doctors from two camps with regard to "minor" intestinal amoebae. These have the long double names of biological classification: Genus and species. Blastocystis hominis is the most common. Others are Dientamoeba fragilis, Entamoeba hartmanni, Endolimax nana, Entamoeba coli, and Balantidium coli. Well-trained doctors often take the view expressed in textbooks of parasitology that these germs do not generally cause severe problems, especially when compared with their virulent cousins Entamoeba histolytica and Giardia lamblia. In a tropical medicine setting such as Africa, where I practiced from 1966 to 1968, these minor parasites were indeed overlooked and left untreated because they were common and could not compete for attention with the worms and other, virulent, single-celled organisms. I returned to the U.S. from Africa with that attitude, until the current medical literature, the advice of colleagues such as Warren Levin, M.D., and experience with my own patients taught me the value of eradicating these parasites. That value often had little to do with bowel symptoms but touched on a variety of problems that can be evoked by an immune system that is unhappy about a foreign presence in the body and fights with only partial success to get rid of it. Fatigue, malaise, rashes, night sweats, headaches, and a long list of vague problems disappear with the finding and treatment of parasites.

For a number of years I had success in using natural remedies such as those derived from citrus seed and wormwood (Artemisia annua). In the late 1980s I encountered more and more treatment failures. Treatment success is defined by the results of three parasitology exams of stool specimens coming out free of parasites after treatment. Natural remedies remain an option, but I now turn to one of the following protocols (citing adult doses) as a first line of defense:

a. Bactrim or Septra (sulfamethoxazole and trimethoprim) plus Humatin (paromycin) for 14 days, using one Bactrim or Septra DS twice daily and Humatin 250 mg four times daily.

b. Yodoxin (diiodohydroxyquin) 650 mg three times daily for two weeks.

c. Flagyl (metronidazole) is usually required to treat the two more aggressive parasites: Entamoeba histolytica and Giardia lamblia. Tinidazole (from compounding pharmacies in the U.S. but widely available elsewhere in the world) may be preferable to metronidazole because of shorter duration of treatment and fewer side effects in many individuals.

When giving treatment (a) above, I make sure to provide treatment with an antifungal in order to avoid the fungal overgrowth that often accompanies antimicrobial drugs. (Paromycin works by killing normal flora as a way of starving out the parasites.)

Yeast-free diet

Somewhere early in the game, it is good to do a 5- to 14-day elimination of yeast, followed by a challenge "pig-out" of yeast to see what happens. If you find that your child is not hypersensitive to gluten but is responsive to antifungal medications (which in my experience describes a significant subset of children), then it will be important to experiment with a yeast-free diet enough to know whether it really makes a difference. The good news is that going off and on yeast usually brings prompt results when compared, say, with going off and on casein or gluten. Here is my version of a yeast-free diet.

The purpose of a yeast-free diet is two-fold. One is diagnostic and the other is for treatment. The diagnostic use of a yeast-free diet helps people discover whether or not they are sensitive to yeasts. When used in this way, the diet should be followed quite strictly and, as described later, may often be ended by a heavy consumption of yeast products to see if a reaction occurs. The second purpose of a yeast-free diet is to reduce or eliminate sources of yeasty or moldy foods in one's diet and to minimize allergic reactions to these things.

A ROCK, NOT A PEBBLE, FOR THE WELL

The reason that I find it helpful to initiate these trials with the more predictably effective medicines and strict diet is that a less stringent effort may fail to reveal the connection between treatment and relief of symptoms. In other words, an excess of subtlety may spoil the experiment. If you want to drop a rock down a deep well to hear a splash indicating that there is water, then you do better not to use a small pebble. A fair-sized rock will deliver a more decisive report. Similarly with nearly all of the interventions under discussion in his book, the strictest diet and most effective medication or supplements at eventually robust doses are needed to be able to find out if you are in the right ballpark. Once the ballpark is found, you can back off and find the least inconvenient dietary change and the lowest doses of the least risky medication or supplements that maintain the desired effect.

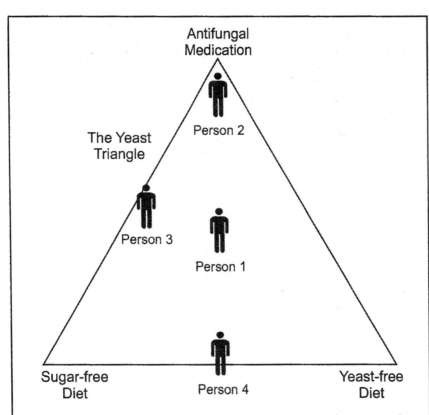

Person 1 benefits about equally from sugar-free diet, yeast-free diet and antifungal medication, and needs all three to get better. Person 2 is tolerant of sugar and yeast but needs antifungal medication. Person 3 is sugar-sensitive and needs antifungal medication but tolerates yeast. Person 4 does well on yeast- and sugar-free diet and does not need antifungal medication.

Failure to show allergy to food yeast on an elimination and challenge of yeast does not always mean that other parts of the management of the yeast problem are unnecessary. Most people do best by avoiding sugar, avoiding yeast and molds and taking an antifungal medication in order to discover the existence or the extent of a yeast problem. Failing to cover one of these three bases may prevent detection of the problem or its extent – for instance, if an individual is exquisitely sensitive to yeast in foods but only moderately responsive to avoiding sugar and killing yeast in the intestine. Keep in mind that the steps under discussion – a trial of antifungal medication and avoiding sugars and yeast - are just that: trials. Initially, they have a diagnostic purpose: finding out whether a yeast problem is part of the overall problem and, if so, what is its extent and which components (dietary yeast allergy, intestinal yeast colonization and sensitization, sugar intolerance) are more or less dominant. If it becomes clear that there is a yeast problem, then finding the right intensity, duration and combination of diet and medicine constitutes a further trial.

Remember that yeasts and molds are the normal surface inhabitants of most living things. Fruits and vegetables, when picked fresh, have a surface population of their own yeasts and molds. These are not necessarily the same ones that become abundant when food becomes moldy. Grains also have a surface population of normal molds, which appear in the flour after milling. Storage of grains and flours leaves them susceptible to the overgrowth of molds, which are inhibited by various chemicals now used in grains, flours and baked goods. Nuts and beans in the shell are not moldy when fresh, but the storage and transportation of nuts and beans from their original place of cultivation to the marketplace leaves them susceptible to the overgrowth of various molds.

The normal appearance of molds on the surface of plants and the little bit of moldiness that appears during storage and transportation of crops mean that it is really impossible to eat a strictly yeast/mold-free diet, unless one consumes only eggs, the flesh of animals, and the interior of peeled fruits and vegetables. Even milk can have fairly large amounts of yeast in it. There are some cases in which the need to investigate extreme sensitivity to molds and yeasts found in food would require consuming – temporarily – a diet consisting of completely yeast-free and mold-free foods. We call this strict yeast/mold avoidance, and its use for a period of a few days or weeks would only be for diagnostic purposes. If symptoms cleared during the consumption of such a strict yeast/mold-free diet, and then reappeared on ingestion of foods containing yeast or mold, the implication would be clear.

Usually a simplified yeast/mold-free diet is sufficient to make this point. Many foods consumed nowadays are heavily yeasty or moldy, and avoidance of these is often enough to establish the relationship between sensitivity to yeast/mold and various symptoms. A simplified yeast- and mold-free diet focuses on avoiding the most yeasty substances normally found in a healthy diet. Foods with high levels of yeast and mold include the following:

1. Leavened foods: Breads, bagels, pastries, pretzels, crackers, pizza dough and rolls are usually made with yeast as leavening. Biscuits, muffins and soda bread, as well as waffles, pancakes and some cookies made with baking soda or baking powder, are allowed. "Essene" bread is also OK. It is made with sprouted grain and no yeasts or baking powder/soda are used. Leaving aside the question of the mold – which originally grew on the grain itself or developed during storage and transportation of grain products – the baked goods in which yeast has been used are considered yeasty, and the ones made with baking soda or baking powder are considered to be permitted on a yeast-free diet.

Some flours are enriched with vitamins (see vitamin section) but for the simplified yeast-free diet, this can be overlooked. What about sourdough bread? Sourdough bread is just as yeasty as any other leavened grain product. The yeast used for making sourdough bread is a wild yeast that is usually superior to ordinary baker's yeast because it turns out lactic acid instead of alcohol. For the yeast-sensitive person, however, sourdough bread offers no advantage, and even when sourdough bread is labeled "yeast free," it should not be considered so from the standpoint of people avoiding yeasts and molds.

Wheat and rye are the only grains having enough gluten (the sticky protein) to allow for the development of the little bubbles that account for the sponginess of bread. Breads and crackers made from rice, oats, millet, corn and barley are usually successful only if some wheat flour is added. Products made with these grains are usually not leavened with yeast and can be consumed by the person trying to avoid yeast. CHECK LABELS!

2. Fermented and aged products: Fermentation was discovered before baking, when people found that the yeast naturally occurring on the skins of fruits would turn the fruit juice to wine if left in a covered container. For practical purposes, all alcohol must be considered yeasty by the person trying to avoid yeast and molds. This means that medicines, beers, wines, hard liquors and alcoholic extracts such as vanilla extract must be avoided. Many yeast-sensitive people who experiment with yeasty foods, after the diagnostic trial of stricter yeast avoidance is over, discover that they can consume high (100) proof alcoholic beverages with fewer problems than if they consume beers or wines. Distillation leaves some of the yeastier parts of the brew behind so that the end product is more refined and may be less troublesome to the yeast-sensitive person. Remember that malt is a product of the brewing industry and products containing malt should be considered yeasty.

SECTION TWO: MAKING A PLAN

Cheese is a product fermented from a variety of molds and bacteria. Some of these are quite distantly related to the family of molds referred to as yeasts, and some yeast-sensitive people can eat even quite strong cheeses without difficulty. During the yeast avoidance that is designed to detect yeast sensitivity in people, all cheeses should be avoided. This even includes cheeses that are not aged. A cheese without mold or fermented products can be made easily at home. Milk products known as "processed" are usually prepared with a substance called rennet. If real rennet is used in processing of cheeses, it is OK, but many artificial types of rennet are derived from mold products and, therefore, are not safe for the person trying to avoid yeast. Other milk products such as cottage cheese and sour cream may be made by adding vinegars or lactic acid to milk and are, therefore, "yeasty." Yogurt is fermented milk, but the germ used to make yogurt is a Lactobacillus or Acidophilus species. These bacteria are healthy, normal inhabitants of the human intestinal tract and vagina and are not related at all to yeasts or molds which are pathogenic. Yogurt without fruit can be consumed by people who are yeast-sensitive even though the milk itself, as mentioned above, may have some yeast in it. You may peel fruit and add it to plain yogurt.

3. Juices: The juices of all fruits and berries contain yeasts that came from the fruits' skin. Ciders, apple juices, commercial frozen or reconstituted orange juices and the juices of berries, etc., have an impressive content of yeasts and can be extremely troublesome for yeast-sensitive people. During the trial avoidance of yeasts, then, juices must be avoided. Freshly squeezed juices made at home from peeled fruits, in ways that keep the surface of the fruit out of contact with the juice, are permissible. Freshly squeezed juices stored for a day or two in the refrigerator at a cold temperature do not usually present much of a problem in terms of their potential yeast content. Prolonged storage of fruit juices, even when they are made at home, would raise the same question that applies to all leftovers, which tend, even in the refrigerator, to become moldy after a while. Canned pineapple juice seems to be one of the least yeasty juices and it may be tried after a person has more or less stabilized on a yeast-free diet. Apple juice made from peeled apples and orange and grapefruit juices are the main juices that can be made easily at home. It's worth noting that even the interior of fruits with unbroken skin can be found to contain live yeast, reminding us that nothing is completely yeast-free, but from a practical standpoint this probably doesn't make much difference even to the quite yeast-sensitive person. For a hot drink, lemon or orange can be squeezed into hot water.

Regular tea is made from leaves that are fermented before they are dried, so tea may be a problem and thus is not permitted on a yeast-free diet. Herbal teas are made of leaves that may carry some normal surface molds, but such teas may not be bothersome except to very sensitive individuals. Coffee is not fermented, but many yeast-sensitive people cannot tolerate coffee, whether or not it is decaffeinated.

Remember that once you have already decided that your child is sensitive to yeast, you will need to be your own judge as to the degree to which he or she can tolerate various foods that may contain some yeasts or molds. Everyone is different, and individual tolerances for coffee, tea, cheeses, juices, alcohol, etc., have to be determined on a trial-and-error basis by each person individually. If you are just beginning to do some detective work to figure out if your child is sensitive to yeast-containing foods, strict adherence to the suggestions outlined here is necessary. It would be a shame to go to the trouble of changing your child's diet for five days, and then be confused as to the results because your child consumed a little coffee or tea or other substances that may have affected the results of this little but important dietary experiment.

4. Dried fruits, condiments and sauces: Remember that most sauces and condiments are made with some vinegar or other products of fermentation as well as sugars. This applies to salad dressings, barbecue sauce, tomato sauce, soy sauce, miso, tamari sauce, mincemeat, horseradish, sauerkraut, pickles and olives. Dried fruits themselves are, of course, very "yeasty" because the drying process generally reduces the whole fruit to a small thing while the surface yeast has had a chance to proliferate during drying. You may make a salad dressing with oil, lemon juice (in place of vinegar) and some spices.

5. Mushrooms: Mushrooms are nothing but a big mold (fungus). They are, in fact, the product of molds that live in a lacy network underground and periodically push up a mushroom as part of their reproductive processes. The mushroom itself is relatively unrelated to yeasts, and some yeast-sensitive people can eat mushrooms. During a trial avoidance of molds and yeasts, mushrooms would be on the list of things to avoid. The same applies to truffles.

6. Vitamins: A number of B-vitamins are derived from fermentation. Remember the distinction between a yeast-free diet that is used to figure out how sensitive a person may be to yeast and molds in food, and the one that may be used long-term by people who already know that they are sensitive. In the first instance, the diet is used to do detective work, and it's very important that the diet be followed strictly so that we don't have to wonder – after the elimination trial is completed – whether the reason nothing showed up was that it wasn't done carefully enough. You may take yeast-free vitamins. The trouble is that we found some vitamins that are labeled yeast-free are relatively bothersome to yeast-sensitive people. There really isn't any way to study the yeast content of vitamins except by observing the reaction in people who tried them.

Germs that inhabit the gut may thrive when "fed" certain vitamins or minerals. Well-fed germs may then produce toxins that make a person sick. In my experience, most reactions to vitamins and other supplements occur because of their effects on gut flora and not because the supplements bother the person by interacting directly with his or her chemistry. The second most likely cause of distress from taking supplements is from intolerance to the excipients used in the pills. Magnesium stearate is the most common such mischievous excipient. It is a soapy substance used as an anti-caking agent to help powder flow through tubing in the pill-making process. Intolerance to this and other flow-agents is not uncommon.

7. Sugar and Carbohydrates: Some yeast-sensitive people have a lot of trouble with carbohydrates of any kind, and for most children the consumption of refined sugar is bothersome, especially when parents are trying to sort out a difficult health problem. Any parent going to the trouble of removing yeast is well advised to eliminate refined carbohydrates, such as sugars, white rice, white flour and alcohols. Whether or not a yeast-sensitive person needs to go on a low-carbohydrate diet is a matter of controversy. It really comes down to the individual, and I do not generally advise reducing carbohydrate intake unless other measures have failed to cause improvement. To be on the safe side, restriction of carbohydrates is advised when first putting your child on a yeast-free diet and an antifungal medication, and then the extent to which this is necessary can be determined by liberalizing carbohydrate intake as time goes on – while watching for adverse reactions, if any. For those whose carbohydrate intake is restricted unnecessarily, an automatic consequence is that the consumption of a relatively high-fat, high-protein diet may have its own disadvantages in the long run. I would suggest that parents implementing a yeast-free diet restrict sweet foods and save a strict limitation of carbohydrate for choices made in consultation with their children's physicians on an individual basis. Whether fruits are troublesome to people with yeast sensitivity (apart from the question of yeast on the

SECTION TWO: MAKING A PLAN

surface of the fruit) is also a matter of question at the moment. I do not recommend putting a child on a very reduced fruit intake unless you discover by trial and error that this really makes a difference. For some children, it really does. It is likely that the refinement of carbohydrates makes more difference to the person than to the yeast. That is, refined carbohydrates, lacking the nutrients removed during the refining process, probably have a negative effect more by weakening the person than by feeding the yeasts specifically.

Yeast allergy is very common, but it is certainly not the cause of everybody's problems. It does have to be considered, however, among the possibilities for a wide variety of people with many different kinds of medical and emotional problems. Doing a five-day avoidance of yeast is one of the simplest and most reliable ways to find out if such a factor may play a role in a person's health.

After strict adherence to the five-day yeast avoidance, you may choose to "challenge" your child with a relatively heavy load of yeast to see if it provokes symptoms. The challenge should be avoided if the response to being off yeast is so clear-cut that no question remains as to the relationship between yeast in the diet and symptoms. If the response to the diet is confusing or minimal or undetectable, a challenge of yeast-containing foods such as bread, cheese, vinegar and juices may provoke sufficient symptoms that a question still remains as to the extent of yeast sensitivity.

One problem with autistic children is finding a suitable food to serve as a yeast challenge. Most young autistic children do not eat lots of pickles or vinegar. Beer and wine are not on their menu. Bread, crackers, pretzels, pizza and other products leavened with yeast are the major issue, and they will have been removed in accordance with the gluten-free diet, which usually eclipses the problem of avoiding yeast. Ketchup may serve more as a sugar than a vinegar challenge, and pizza is out of the question because it is a wheat, milk and yeast challenge all combined.

The five-day yeast avoidance and challenge are usually done when nothing else is being changed, and symptoms are observed from a few minutes to two to three days following restarting yeast in the diet. The period of delay and the amount of yeast used for challenge varies considerably from person to person. On average, if your child has had a moderately impressive response to avoiding yeast, you can check it out by challenging with a piece of cheese, some orange juice, some bread and maybe some vinegar. Usually within four to eight hours definite symptoms reappear, but as noted above, this time lag may vary considerably. And casein and gluten in the cheese and bread add uncertainty.

Remember that the yeast in one's food is only part of the issue involved in this whole business. Often, finding out that a person is sensitive in some way to yeast in the diet leads us to looking at the relationship between an individual and the yeast species that live in his or her bowel and on other parts of the body. This part of the interaction between people and yeasts is treated by taking a medicine that kills yeast and by trying probiotics, so as to promote the growth of the good germs in the intestine. For instance, this can be done by taking a preparation of lactobacillus powder that is very concentrated, because plain yogurt made with this germ is not concentrated enough to introduce these germs into the bowel. The yeasts of our food, that is, baker's or brewer's yeast and other yeasts that live on plants, do not generally live inside us when we eat them as food. They are killed in the process of baking or brewing or, if consumed alive, they simply die during the process of digestion. There are instances in which human beings are colonized with baker's or brewer's yeast (S. cerevisiae); but in general, the reason for avoiding food yeast is not because of any strong tendency it has to set up housekeeping within us, but only because there is a cross-sensitivity between yeasts of all kinds. People who have trouble with yeast living in their bowel are frequently sensitive to yeast (dead or alive, cooked or uncooked) in their food.

The yeast-free diet appropriate for people who have a yeast problem varies considerably from person to person. Most people discover what their children's limits of tolerance are on their own. Some yeast-sensitive people can tolerate a fairly generous amount of yeasty foods without trouble. In other cases, parents must be extremely careful to avoid most sources of yeast and mold in their children's diet. This is best discovered by testing your child. Allergy tests are not always accurate enough to measure the degree of sensitivity one may have to various kinds of yeasts and molds in the diet. It may take months or years to come to a good understanding as to exactly what amount of yeasty foods can be consumed by a child, and what the price of consuming them may be in terms of symptoms that follow immediately or within a day or so.

The yeasts and molds that have been discussed in connection to diet and body surfaces have other relatives that live widely in the environment. About 50 common mold spores are found in the air at various times in various locations, and these cannot be avoided easily. Measures for controlling environmental molds in and around your house or workplace can sometimes help a great deal. Careful cleaning and dehumidification are the main methods to be used, but air ionization and ozonation are also very helpful.

The following yeast-free diet outline addresses only the yeast question, not gluten, casein or other issues.

Dairy products

Permitted: butter, margarine, mozzarella cheese, feta, milk (cow or goat), yogurt (plain).
Not permitted: yogurt with fruit, aged cheeses, processed cheeses (which are often made with an artificial rennet derived from fungi).

Cereals/grains

Permitted: soda bread, cakes, waffles, pancakes, popovers, cookies, biscuits, barley, corn, oatmeal, grits, rice, pasta (check label), amaranth, buckwheat, quinoa.
Not permitted: bread, sourdough bread (except that made with lactobacillus culture), rolls, breakfast cereals, crackers (check label).

Meat, poultry

All permitted (preferably organic to avoid antibiotics)

Vegetables

Permitted: all fresh vegetables, tofu (fresh), legumes (beans).
Not permitted: mushrooms, olives, capers, tempeh.

Fruits

Permitted: pineapple, avocado, banana, any fruit you can peel, any fresh squeezed juice.
Not permitted: berries, melons (they are not yeasty but tend to cross-react for people with mold allergy), prunes, dates, figs, raisins, cherries, commercial juices (concentrate, premium, in cans, in bottles).

SECTION TWO: MAKING A PLAN

Nuts

Permitted: almonds, almond butter, cashew, cashew butter, walnut, brazil, macadamia, filbert, pistachio, pecan, chestnut, water chestnut.
Not permitted: peanut, peanut butter.

Oils

All oils are permitted.

Beverages

Permitted: herb teas, mineral water, soda water, artificial sweeteners (but they are not good for you).
Not permitted: hard liquor, anything made with malt, beer, wine, cider, coffee.

Miscellaneous

Permitted: English mustard (made without vinegar), salad dressing made with oil and lemon juice.
Not permitted: catsup, mayonnaise, French mustard (made with vinegar), salad dressing made with vinegar, sweets, Chinese food (admittedly a broad and tempting category, but in general Chinese food is poorly tolerated by yeast-sensitive individuals).

How to do a five-day elimination and challenge for food, to detect sensitivity.

A number of allergy tests are available to guide us in deciding whether or not a child is sensitive to a particular food or other substance. When it comes to foods, however, the most reliable test is one of avoidance for a period of time, followed by a challenge if there is some doubt as to the results achieved during the avoidance. The food to avoid may be something that is very easy to eliminate because it is found relatively isolated in the diet. Seafood, certain citrus fruits, and potatoes or other members of the so-called nightshade family are examples of foods that usually are not mixed with other products in processed or packaged foods. On the other hand, egg products, corn products, yeasts, sugars, malt, and wheat and milk products are often presented not in their pure form, but mixed in a variety of other recipes and food processing methods that make avoidance somewhat tricky.

Once you are equipped with a list of foods containing the substance your child is to avoid, then you must prearrange a five-day period when you have relatively good control over your child's diet. A time when you are traveling or having to eat at friends' houses is not the best time to schedule this sort of experiment. Plan ahead of time by doing some shopping and store up foods that will satisfy your child's needs and make the avoidance process as enjoyable as possible. Try not to replace the food avoided with a very large amount of some other food, but if you do so, keep careful track of it on a food diary. Learn to read labels and watch carefully for ingredients that are shown on the food avoidance diet lists, so that you are able to recognize that whey comes from milk; that hydrolyzed vegetable protein is really not that different from MSG; and that vegetable gums often come from the bean family.

Once you are ready to start the five-day avoidance for a specific food(s), keep careful track in a food diary of everything your child eats. After five complete days of eliminating a food or foods, if you are totally convinced that the experiment has shown absolutely no effect, simply return to giving your child a normal diet. If, on doing so, you observe symptoms that indicate that going back to the avoided food is affecting your child in some way, then the process may need repeating in order to prove the point one way or the other. If during the five-day period you are completely convinced that the avoided food has been responsible for troublesome symptoms and you do not wish to challenge by giving your child a lot of the food in question, that is OK. If, on the other hand, you have observed some favorable change but are not sure whether it's because of coincidence or a placebo effect, try going back to giving your child the food in question in a fairly big way by having him or her "pig out" on it on the sixth day. If you have been avoiding wheat, for instance, try giving your child a big bowl of wheat cereal or a lot of bread. If you have been avoiding milk products, simply have your child drink a couple of glasses of milk. *If you have observed a major change for the better in your child's health by eliminating a particular food, do not challenge it with a big "pig out" because it may make your child very sick.* The five-day rule works most of the time. I have seen patients and heard of others who missed an important food (wheat, milk, citrus) until they extended the period of abstinence for 14 days. The period of time required for testing the reintroduction of a food is usually 24 hours. However, reactions to re-introduced foods may start as long as 72 hours after beginning challenges with a food.

If you eliminated two or three foods during the time of avoidance, return them to your child's diet at two- to three-day intervals, giving each food time to show its effects. If you observe an adverse effect from one of the foods challenged, then you will have to get back off it and wait for the effects to disappear before trying the next food.

> **TO SAY THAT** my wife and I are different people than we were three years ago when our son was first diagnosed is a vast understatement. At times we are undoubtedly more stressed and certainly financially poorer, but more importantly, I believe we are better people. We are more open-minded, thoughtful, and unpretentious. Every day we delight in the beauty and happiness of our children. Every day we gain strength from our son, whose courage and love is our inspiration.
>
> What is Autism to us…
>
> Autism is a WORD, a word that got us enrolled in educational services we needed but closed the door to the reality and depth of my son's issues. Since putting "THE WORD" aside we have been unwavering in our journey to cure our son's MEDICAL problems…not Autism. Frankly, I still can't cure Autism…but we are curing OUR SON.
>
> – *Michael, a parent*

⚠ **SPECIFIC CARBOHYDRATE DIET.** The sequence of placing antifungals ahead of trying the Specific Carbohydrate Diet is not because fungal considerations are a prerequisite to SCD, but because giving antifungals is a bigger rock to throw down the well. It's not necessarily a better rock, just one that will more often give a decisive splash sooner. That is, SCD may entail an extended period of ups and downs as it takes hold, and it requires more of a learning curve. Moreover, I have years of experience with antifungals and only caught on to the Specific Carbohydrate Diet within the past two years, so antifungals preceded SCD in my own history. So far not many of my patients who have done very well on antifungal medication have been liberated from antifungal medication thanks to, say, a year on SCD. Thus, I am wary of counting on SCD to clean up the gut in individuals who have a yeast problem as defined by having had a dramatic response to antifungal medication. On the other hand, **SCD is one of the best treatments I have found so far for many children on the autism spectrum**. It should be noted, in considering this statement, that *nearly all of my patients who have done SCD were prepared by having already undergone treatment with antifungals, detoxification therapies, gluten- and casein-free diets and supplements, so my experience with children who went straight to SCD without other interventions is limited.*

I went on SCD over a year ago. I did so only to get an idea of what it was like, and without any health expectations of my own. I lost 10 pounds easily and had more energy. I will never return to my pre-SCD diet. Family members of my patients have experienced similar and often spectacular responses to SCD, and my adult patients have benefited in numerous and diverse ways. Now that I have reflected on the fact that our human ancestors did not eat starchy foods before the development of agriculture about 10,000 years ago, I figure that a style of eating based on the principles of SCD makes a lot of sense considering that adaptation to the consumption of large amounts of sugars and starches would not easily take place over the 400 or so generations our species has produced in the last 10 millennia. The human body as it existed in the eons of pre-agricultural food-gathering culture is still what we have today, making the Paleolithic diet a very attractive notion for both preventive and therapeutic nutrition.[26]

Judy Gorman has been a central figure in a group consisting mostly of my patients' parents, dubbed "Dr. Moms" by Judy. Judy's harvesting of information from these Dr. Moms has provided insights into the use of SCD in autistic children. She has consented to share her insights in these pages.

THE SPECIFIC CARBOHYDRATE DIET, by Judy Gorman

My son, Alex, will be 11 years old in March of 2005. He is a shining example of the subclass of kids we DAN! groupies call "The Non-Responders." That is, nothing ever made Alex get better.

His history is probably very similar to those of many of your children. His life started with five days of intravenous antibiotics for what was finally determined to be a "virus of unknown origin." He was a fragile infant, a poor feeder and sleeper, and a champion at projectile spitting up. All this was followed by a monstrous physical and mental regression in his second year of life, starting directly after his MMR vaccine. Year after year, we battled diarrhea, with periodic severe constipation, abdominal distention, bloating, gas and vomiting. Alex would often go for days without touching food. By the time he was seven, his immunologist (who administered the gamma globulin infusions that kept Alex alive for many years, but who was trained at the NIH and had no sympathy for anything DAN! related) deemed him "anorexic" and told us to get ANY calories into him that we could. The type of food was irrelevant, he led us to believe, because without more calories, Alex would die.

So, we'd sit Alex down on the couch and hand him bags of potato chips. Delicious, crunchy, salty, CALORIC....and hey, even gluten/casein-free! We were desperate to get his weight up.

On page 21 of *Breaking the Vicious Cycle* (referred to later as BTVC), Elaine Gottschall quotes Dr. Samuel Gee, in an 1888 report, "On the Celiac Affliction:" **"What the patient takes beyond his ability to digest does harm."** That sentence just haunts me. Here I was, trying to make my sicker-than-sick little boy healthy – trying to get him to gain weight – by FEEDING HIM COMPLEX CARBOHRATES. Why? Because, as all of you know, THAT is what the kids want to eat: crackers, bread, pretzels, chips, candy, etc. And for heaven's sake, Alex was starving himself to death. If that was how I could get calories into him….

By the time he was eight, Alex was destroying himself and our house. In between screams, ripping his clothes off, running to the toilet 15, 16, 17 times a day to poop, he was smashing our TVs, computers, pictures, and furniture into pieces, biting and scratching himself, smashing his arms into the corners of tables to produce maximum pain….

In November of 2002, Alex finally underwent a colonoscopy and was found to have everything Dr. Andrew Wakefield had so eloquently first described in 1998: colitis, lymphoid nodular hyperplasia, cryptitis, etc. We immediately began to treat him with drugs, drugs and more drugs: 10 straight months of Prednisone, Gastrocrom, Nexium, Colazal, Azulfidine, and even immune suppressors like 6MP (which is actually a chemotherapy agent traditionally used to treat certain types of leukemia).

In late September of 2003, I got a phone call from our gastroenterologist. "Take Alex off Prednisone," he said. "He's been on too much and it's getting dangerous." (Prednisone is a synthetic version of cortisone, a steroid, which reduces inflammation in the body. If taken too long in large enough doses, amongst many other dangerous side effects, it can cause something called steroid psychosis – an insanity that can only be alleviated by stopping the drug. Now, if you can imagine a profoundly autistic kid going insane…well, it's not a pretty picture.) Without Prednisone, Alex's agony would be unbearable. One of the worst moments in my life turned out to be possibly the best thing that ever happened to Alex and me. I sat at my desk, trying not to think about putting Alex in our car and driving off a bridge, when I remembered something a mother had told me five years before at a DAN! Conference. As I stood looking at books on diet at a vendor table, this mother started to talk to me. She told me that her son was doing fantastically on a diet called the Specific Carbohydrate Diet, and got me to buy Elaine Gottschall's book, *Breaking the Vicious Cycle*.

I remembered opening it up, starting to read, and thinking, "This is INSANE! No grains! No potatoes?! No sugar?! What the hell will Alex eat?! He's already starving himself…." So, I put it on my bookshelf, thinking that I'd come back to it when I'd given everything else I was doing a try.

Then, of course, with everything else to do and to read, with this and that new treatment promising hope that for us never materialized, I forgot I even owned it.

Those five wasted years account for a lot of my current mania on the topic. If only I had done SCD then.

If only….

I came to SCD at the lowest point of our lives. I was driven to it at a time of absolute despair and desperation. However, the remarkable thing about SCD is that I have now witnessed its power to help people ranging from Alex's abhorrent state of health, and low level of functioning (i.e. most severe autistic symptoms) to children with no discernable bowel issues who, because of

SECTION TWO: MAKING A PLAN

other DAN! treatments and educational interventions, are barely on the autistic spectrum any longer.

I have told everyone who will listen that if there's to be any meaning to Alex's illness, it must come from me using my experience to help save at least one child from this agony. And to save one parent from having to say, "If only...."

There is NO excuse for not doing SCD. It is not that hard. Really. I have friends whose children are severely allergic to nuts, to eggs – yet they have these kids on SCD and their kids are getting better. There is no excuse for not doing what Sid Baker now says is "one of the best treatments for kids with autism" that he has ever seen.

So, what exactly IS the Specific Carbohydrate Diet?

To quote from Elaine Gottschall's book:

"In various conditions, a poorly-functioning intestine can be easily overwhelmed by the ingestion of carbohydrates which require numerous digestive processes. The result is an environment that supports overgrowth of intestinal yeast and bacteria....The purpose of the Specific Carbohydrate Diet is to deprive the microbial world of the intestine of the food it needs to overpopulate. By using a diet which contains predominantly 'predigested' carbohydrates, the individual with an intestinal problem can be maximally nourished without over-stimulation of the intestinal microbial population."

Bacterial microbes, by secreting toxins irritating to the lining of the digestive system, cause the tissue to try to protect itself by secreting mucus – the normal physiological reaction to irritation. Once covered by a thick layer of mucus, the intestines are unable to break down complex carbohydrates – leaving the undigested carbs in the intestines, feeding the bad bacteria. Which leads to more bacteria...which leads to more toxins. This is the vicious cycle. By starving the bacteria, keeping all complex carbs out of the digestive system, we cause the bacteria to die off.

The SCD stops the vicious cycle of malabsorption and microbe overgrowth by removing the microbes' food: sugars (specifically disaccharides). Single molecule sugars, like those found in fruit and vegetables (and honey) do not require digestive processes, but are immediately absorbed by the intestine. Therefore, they are not left in an intestine too damaged to digest them, to feed the bad flora. Inflammation decreases and the immune system can return to normal. Once the immune system functions better, it can keep the intestinal microbes in proper balance. Unlike the casein- and gluten-free diet, which only removes from the diet the sources of proteins (casein and gluten) which, undigested, can leak through the damaged intestines and cause havoc in the body, **SCD ACTUALLY HEALS THE LEAKY GUT, THEREBY NOT ALLOWING FOOD PARTICLES TO PASS INTO THE BODY AND EVENTUALLY ALLOWING ALL FOODS TO BE PROPERLY DIGESTED.**

On that day in late September, 2002, when I had pulled Elaine Gottschall's book off my shelf, dusted it off, and read the first three chapters, I realized that I needed to give this diet a try. Nothing was working. Nothing had ever worked. And so, by dinner that night, Alex was on the Specific Carbohydrate Diet.

At first, Alex got way worse. By the sixth week on SCD, I was ready to give up. I posted a desperate plea on PecanBread.com's bulletin board, describing SCD's failure to help my horribly ill son. And within an hour I got a phone call from Elaine Gottschall herself. "Don't give up," she told me. "You must promise to stick it out until at least three months." Because of that phone call, for which I will be forever grateful, I didn't give up.

And by the end of the three months, I began writing to Dr. Baker, to our immunologist, to our gastroenterologist pretty much daily (I'm sure making them rue the day I first walked into their offices) practically screaming via email, "This diet is making ALEX get better." ALEX. The little boy who NEVER got better. After three months, Alex's 15 or more bowel movements a day had become three or four. He had the first formed BM I had seen in years. He hadn't vomited once the entire three months he'd been on SCD...this from vomiting at least five times a week.

At the time of writing this, Alex has been on SCD for 16 ½ months. He has been off Prednisone and all his other gut meds (except for Flagyl, which we still use on and off) for a year now. He has gained 14 pounds since that horrible September day. He has vomited only once since being on SCD, but that was because he had a 24-hour stomach bug. The worst we ever get is four or five BMs daily, but most of the time, we're at only two or so a day, and they are mostly formed. Gone are the days of the screaming, ripping his clothes off, hitting his body against the furniture, smashing the house to pieces.

As Dr. Baker mentions above, there are ups and downs with SCD. As the body rids itself of its toxic load, it can cause a short-term worsening of bowel functioning, behavioral regressions, and so forth. This is the case with all detoxification treatments, whether they're antifungal in nature, pulling out heavy metals, whatever – toxins are toxins. And getting rid of them is not easy. When I first put Alex on SCD I did so at the same time that a very good friend was putting her daughter on it. Daily, we'd compare notes, provide each other with support...and then another of my friends joined us with her son.

By then, Dr. Baker had begun to put other patients on the diet. He'd send them to me for a chat – and we all started to talk and email daily. Then, they'd talk to their friends, who'd start their kids on the diet. Or I'd get an email or a phone call from a parent who was seeing our gastroenterologist or our immunologist....and soon, our gang was up to 30 or so parents who would take some time each day to let the rest know what was going on, compare notes, make observations.

I kept notes on our kids' progress. We saw distinct patterns in the regressions, and by keeping records, we were able to tell the new families what to expect and when. It seems that after the first year, regressions stop or at least become so mild as to be indistinguishable from the normal ups and downs of our kids. I am including these notes here, plus some more information on SCD...for those of you who don't want to say "If only" years from now.

1. <u>Regressions</u>

It appears that the worse the child's digestive problems and autistic symptoms are to start, the worse the periods of regressions are.

However, we have also all noted that after every period of regression, many of the children seem to improve in a global sense (autistic behaviors and digestive health).

SECTION TWO: MAKING A PLAN

Initial reactions upon starting SCD:

Most of our children have undergone a distinct period of die-off at the start of the diet. Symptoms may include a regression in behavior, including aggressiveness, increased hyperactivity and self-stimulatory behaviors; poor sleep; increased obsessive behaviors; tantrums; spaciness; social withdrawal; unresponsiveness; fever; and vomiting. Many of us saw a worsening of already-existing digestive troubles: that is, children with diarrhea prior to the diet got worse diarrhea after starting the diet; children with constipation got even more constipated when starting the diet. Several parents reported dark, sandy, unformed stools and also a lot of gas. Other symptoms included severe pallor of the skin, black circles around the eyes, and hiccups. One mother, however, writes: "Jack did not regress at the beginning of the diet! In fact, he was noticeably more calm and focused."

Many parents, but not all, saw an enormous increase in appetite very shortly after starting the diet. The children became ravenous, eating quantities of food way above normal.

This initial period of die-off seems to average somewhere between one and three weeks.

Several parents have reported that their children finally became toilet-trained after a very short time on the diet.

Two- to three-month regression:

Elaine actually mentions this regression on page 5 of her book. Apparently, this particular regression is common amongst people with traditional inflammatory bowel disease as well.

Most of our children underwent a regression at this time. This regression was both physical and behavioral and lasted up to 14 days for some of the children. We observed worsening diarrhea and/or constipation; gas; bloating; poor appetite; poor sleep; decreased language; decreased eye contact; increased mouthing of objects; decreased socialization; increased self-stimulatory behaviors and hyperactivity; unexplained crying; poor focus (being "out of it"); redness around the anus; increased sensory sensitivities; increased scripting and other perseverative behaviors; tantrums; black circles around the eyes; extreme skin pallor; bumpy skin; and cold-like symptoms.

It was only after this regression that many of us started seeing noticeable improvements in our children as a result of the diet. Yes, some parents saw good things almost from the start, but the majority didn't until 60 to 90 days into the diet. These improvements consist of dramatically improved bowel functioning (normal, formed, consistent bowel movements), improved attention spans, reduced self-stimulatory behaviors and hyperactivity, reduced self-abusive and aggressive behaviors, and improved sleep, appetite, mood and sociability. The parents of children who are more verbal saw increases in spontaneous language.

Five-month regression:

Again, most of us who have reached the five-month mark have seen a severe regression at almost exactly the five-month anniversary. This regression has lasted anywhere from seven to 21 days, and was mainly behavioral in nature: increased self-stimulatory behaviors and hyperactivity; increased obsessive behaviors, perseverative play and scripting; increased mood swings including manic laughing and crying; tooth-grinding; increased self-abusive behaviors and aggression; increased defiant behavior; markedly decreased attention span; decreased social interest and social language; destructive behaviors; an enormous increase in self-directed behavior; tantrums; itchy, white bumps on the legs. There was little worsening of bowel function and only mild decreases of appetite.

Seven-month regression:

This regression was marked by a severe worsening in bowel functioning and occurred in two phases (i.e. it appeared to be finished after about five to seven days, but then recurred about two days later for another five to seven days).

All the children had unformed BMs to downright diarrhea. All had enormous amounts of gas, very malodorous flatulence and constant burping. Several parents reported one day of fever. The most severely affected child also had a dramatic decrease in appetite. All had very poor sleep for several nights. Behaviorally, symptoms included a noticeable increase in self-stimulatory behaviors; dramatic increases in hyperactivity; serious decreases of attention span; enormous increases in obsessive behaviors and scripting; and decreases in social behavior.

> THE MOST IMPORTANT THING I have learned on this journey is to always trust your gut instinct first and foremost.
>
> – Jane, a parent

Nine-month regression:

For most of us, this was a severe and prolonged regression, lasting from seven to 21 days. One mother reports, "This was the worst regression of all. We saw behaviors we hadn't seen since we started GFCF, including hand-flapping, eye stims, weird yelping sounds, manic scripting, bad poops – the works. It peaked at a family dinner...she spent the almost two hours running towards the lit BBQ and repeating a line from one of her books. But when this passed we saw a jump in pretend play, and expressive language and she started to laugh appropriately."

Other symptoms include severe temper tantrums; fevers; increased stimming; gas; diarrhea; bad sleep; poor appetite; and hiccups.

2: SCD Yogurt

There have been many concerns expressed about giving autistic children the homemade yogurt that is so much a part of SCD. I can only report to you from my own experience. To date, not one of my group's parents has had to stop giving the yogurt because of an adverse effect. On the contrary, almost everyone who has tried it has seen positive changes – including parents of children who were severely casein-intolerant prior to SCD.

We all started at doses around ¼ - ½ teaspoon per day or every other day. As Alex had never shown any improvement off casein, I started the yogurt at three months on the diet, when the worst of his GI symptoms had begun to resolve. Within 24 hours of his first dose, I saw that first formed bowel movement I'd seen in years. Most of the kids who were casein-sensitive were started on yogurt at six months on the diet, if not later. Some of the children showed "die-off" symptoms such as increased scripting in language, red cheeks, increased hyperactivity and so forth. However, many parents have reported enormous increases in appropriate social behaviors with the use of the yogurt. Several parents have reported increased imaginative play and several have seen great improvement in bowel functioning.

SECTION TWO: MAKING A PLAN

3: Miscellaneous

Many parents have noted that treatments that seemed to have no effect, or a bad effect, in the past are now working well with their children. For example, methyl-B_{12} shots seem to have a much greater cognitive and language effect when the children are on SCD. We have often wondered if, in the case of supplements and meds given orally, it's because things are actually being absorbed by a healing intestine, whereas – prior to SCD – little, if any, of the supplement was actually getting into the bloodstream.

At least two parents have seen their children hit both the five- and seven-month regressions early – by as much as four weeks. However, the vast majority of us hit these almost exactly on the anniversary of those time frames.

Some favorite meals from the Dr. Moms:

As you all know, most of our kids (even the normally developing ones) are not exactly the world's champion eaters. My normally developing seven-year-old is just as unlikely to eat mussels marinara as is Alex. Actually, he's probably a lot LESS likely to eat it than Alex (after all those years of ABA feeding sessions, etc.). However, I now have friends with children as young as two and three, and as old as 22, doing SCD, and all are finding more than enough to eat for their kids. Keep in mind that the customary dietary emphasis in Europe and the U.S. on carbohydrates early in the day and protein later in the day is upside-down. Body chemistry requires protein in the morning and works better when carbohydrates are part of the evening meal (see Baker, SM, The *Circadian Prescription*, Putnam, 2000). Assuring a healthy supply of protein at breakfast time is the key point. Some suggestions:

Breakfasts (all made with nut flours as opposed to grain flours): pecan muffins, squash muffins, pancakes, waffles, fruit.

Lunches (which can be packed for school): chicken nuggets, turkey rolls, cookies, fruit, carrot sticks, muffins.

Dinners: meatballs, chicken nuggets, pizza, steak.

Besides the wonderful recipes in BTVC, there are at least two great cookbooks that I know of which feature easy and delicious SCD recipes. Both are available from Lucy at www.lucyskitchenshop.com. These are Lucy's *Specific Carbohydrate Diet Cookbook* and *Adventures in the Family Kitchen* by Raman Prasad.

PARTIAL FOOD LIST FOR SPECIFIC CARBOHYDRATE DIET:[27]

Proteins:

Allowed: All fresh or frozen beef, lamb, pork, poultry, fish and shellfish, eggs, natural cheeses (see appendix of BTVC for full list), homemade yogurt (recipe in BTVC), and dry curd cottage cheese.

Not Allowed: Processed meats such as hot dogs, bologna, turkey loaf, spiced ham, and breaded fish. Canned meats and processed cheeses.

Vegetables:

Allowed: Fresh or frozen (with no added sugar or starch), artichoke (not Jerusalem type), asparagus, beets, dried white navy beans, properly prepared lentils, split peas, broccoli,

Brussels sprouts, cabbage, cauliflower, carrots, celery, cucumbers, dill pickles, eggplant, kale, garlic, lettuce of all kinds, lima beans, mushrooms, mustard, olives, onions, parsley, peas, pumpkin, spinach, winter and summer squash, string beans, tomatoes, turnips, watercress.

Not Allowed: Canned vegetables. Grains such as: arrowroot, barley, buckwheat, bulgur, corn, millet, oats, rice, rye, triticale, or wheat or any flours, germs, pastas, starches, or cereal products made from these. Potatoes (white or sweet), yams, or parsnips. Beans (sprouts, soybeans, mung, fava, and garbanzo). Amaranth flour, Jerusalem artichoke flour or powder, quinoa flour or other grain substitutes such as cottonseed, tapioca, sago, seaweed.

Fruits:

Allowed: Fresh, raw, cooked, frozen, or dried apples, avocados, apricots, ripe bananas, berries of all kinds, cherries, fresh or unsweetened shredded coconut, grapefruit, grapes, kiwi, kumquats, lemons, limes, mangoes, melons, nectarines, oranges, papayas, peaches, pears, pineapples, prunes, dark raisins, rhubarb and tangerines.

Not Allowed: Canned fruits. Dried fruit that has been sweetened, molasses, ketchup (unless homemade), agar-agar, jams, jellies.

Nuts:

Allowed: Almonds, pecans, Brazil nuts, filberts, hazelnuts, walnuts, unroasted cashews and chestnuts. Peanut butter and other nut butters without any additives. Nut flours.

Not Allowed: Roasted nuts or peanuts in salted mixtures, beer nuts, glazed nuts.

Beverages:

Allowed: Tomato and vegetable juices. Fruit juices with no added sugar. Weak tea or coffee, herbal teas (peppermint and spearmint only). Milkshakes made with homemade yogurt and fruits and sweetened to taste with honey. Freshly squeezed vegetable or fruit juices made from the list of allowed foods.

Not Allowed: Cow milk, goat milk, soy milk, rice milk, canned coconut milk, instant coffee or tea, Postum, coffee substitutes, soft drinks.

For more information, go online to:

www.breakingthevicioiuscycle.info	Elaine Gottschall's website
www.pecanbread.com	SCD info plus an on-line bulletin board at
http://health.groups.yahoo.com/group/pecanbread/	
www.scdiet.org	SCD Web Library
www.scdrecipe.com	SCD recipes
www.lucyskitchenshop.com	SCD products, nut flours, cookbooks, etc.

SECTION TWO: MAKING A PLAN

⚠ **GLUTEN- AND CASEIN-FREE DIETS.** As you can see from the most recent ARI tabulation, of more than one thousand respondents, 65 percent reported improvement on a diet that excluded casein (a protein found in all milk products except a few whey products) and gluten (a protein found in wheat, barley, rye, and, maybe, oats).

RATINGS OF GLUTEN- AND CASEIN-FREE DIETS from ARI Publication 34/March 2005					
Diet	% Worse	% No effect	% Better	Better:Worse	# of Cases
Gluten/Casein-free	3	32	65	21:1	1446

Gluten and Casein

The flow of options so far has taken us beyond the gluten and casein question because we were propelled by the consideration of cleaning up the gut. Many experienced clinicians would take on the gluten and casein question before that of fungal overgrowth. If there were high levels of yeast metabolites in a urine organic acid test, or one or more yeasts in the stool culture, or, more so, a strong history of antibiotics and a symptom profile of "drunken" behavior, then those factors would push me toward giving the yeast a higher priority. Either way, avoidance of gluten and casein should be high on the list of diagnostic tests for children with autism spectrum problems.

So far you may have been able to stay below the radar of doctors, teachers, grandmothers, in-laws and other bystanders and participants in your efforts to sort things out with your child. However, the very idea of taking bread, pasta and milk products away from a child who already has problems is just too much for many people to endure without suspecting you of being distraught, overboard, or actually abusive. Information and encouragement from other parents and citations from the scientific literature may help, but you must be prepared to endure some pretty rough talk from various sides. Whatever you do, start slowly, not just for the sake of careful preparation but also for the sake of your child, whose withdrawal from gluten and casein may transiently provoke symptoms that will just add to his (and your) problem. While the following discussion may orient you to the problem, I urge you to consult other sources before embarking on a gluten- and casein-free diet for your child.

I was skeptical at first as my son was not a "sickly child." He ate well, was in the 90th percent for height, was physically very active, had a keen sense of balance, and enjoyed all kinds of physical activities. However, many of the local "experts" we took him to, including his pediatrician, wanted to put him on Ritalin (at the age of three) to help calm him down. Even though we didn't fully understand why he was so hyperactive and disconnected from others, as parents, we couldn't bring ourselves to put him on an amphetamine. Shortly after reading Dr. Baker's information on biomedical intervention we had him tested and the results were astounding. Dr. Baker discovered things about our son that no other doctor even looked for. As a result, our son is now 18, fully mainstreamed, driving, has six varsity letters in sports and is graduating from high school this year.

Trust your instincts, align yourself with people who want to work with you, and don't waste your time trying to convince people of what they refuse to believe or accept. You don't have the time to waste on them. You know your child best—always remember that.

– a parent

Andrew was a seven-year-old autistic child who took pebbles from my driveway and made scratches on a mirror in my office. His speech was limited to chanting the last few words that were said to him, or scripts from his videos. He made no eye contact. He was in constant motion, dashing, pacing, gesturing, grimacing, mouthing, sniffing and intermittently coming out with silly laughter. He had moments in which he showed his detailed memory of long-past events and a verbatim recall of conversations, movies or advertisements. His apparently good brain seemed poisoned with something like a psychedelic drug.

I have a vivid memory of sitting and talking with Andrew in my waiting room at a later point, trying to detect traces of the autism I had first encountered. Had I not known him before, I would not have known that Andrew could have previously been in such trouble. The difference in him was a response to a gluten-free diet.

When such changes occur in children, you can perhaps understand why witnesses to the change become zealous evangelists. More than half of the autistic children I have known who have tried a gluten-free diet have improved enough to make it worth continuing to avoid wheat, rye and barley and all products containing even traces of the protein (gluten) found in these grains but not in rice, corn, or millet. Oats are still a matter of controversy, some studies having shown no negative effect in gluten-sensitive individuals, even as some individuals report adverse reactions to them.[28,29]

The majority of psychologists, physicians, teachers, neighbors, and parents reject the idea that anything as completely innocent as bread or spaghetti could make you lose your mind. It does not seem reasonable. Nor does depriving a child of food seem appropriate when the child already has problems that limit his or her full enjoyment of life. Most people who consult me know that I will probably suggest changes in diet or supplements or other aspects of their life as part of the detective work to get to the bottom of chronic problems. Gluten avoidance is still often a hard sell. If parents, grandparents, babysitters, teachers, and therapists (who use food as a reward for performance) are not on board, making the needed changes can be impossible. Efforts to get everyone on board can bring charges of unfit parenting, and even child abuse, especially when divorce puts parents in opposition and the sympathies of the court can be recruited when an expert testifies that "there is not a shred of credible evidence" that diet can cure autism. The key word here is "credible" and it simply means that the speaker does not believe whatever evidence he or she has examined, which is never all the evidence.

In a way, there is no such thing as "all the evidence." The abundant existing evidence divides into two layers that are so separate that participants in a conversation cannot hear each other from one layer to the next. In my experience, the ultimate result of such conversations is frustration, anger, shouting, then silence. Here is how it goes:

One party to the conversation, Joe, thinks of the question in terms of the disease autism, which has been defined as a problem developing in early childhood with problems in communication, behavior and socialization. The cause is unknown and authoritative references point to no known treatment. End of story. Gluten sensitivity has nothing to do with autism's definition in the way, for instance, that the presence of strep germs has to do with the diagnosis of a strep throat. In this mindset, gluten avoidance has nothing to do with the treatment of autism, in contrast with using penicillin for the treatment of a strep throat. Joe usually points out that no double-blind, randomized, placebo-controlled studies have given statistical credibility to gluten-free diets in autism. Thus, parents or practitioners who pursue such diets are without the protection offered by scientific consensus.

The other party to the conversation, Linda, thinks of the question in terms of an individual child who carries a label based upon large numbers of children who share certain problems of communication, behavior and socialization. For Linda, the child, and not the abstract disease concept, is the focus. The focal issue is whether that particular child may or may not respond to a gluten-free diet, considering that there are credible reports of others having done so. Such reports, credible as they may be, are anecdotal and lack the standing of group statistics.

Joe is talking about treating a disease, and Linda is taking about treating individuals. Joe is talking about public health policy; Linda about private, individual health policy. Joe is talking about a scientific model for establishing proof that is necessary and suited to drug trials and can be paid for with the kinds of profits made from an effective new drug. Linda is talking about a scientific model in accordance with Edison's statement that in matters of science, "the observation of a single man may trump the collective opinion of all the experts." In my experience, most scientifically trained practitioners start out as Joes and end up more like Lindas.

When it comes to gluten, a single experience with a patient or family member is usually enough to push us over the line. I started out as a Joe and it was years after knowing of the convincing studies of Dohan and Dohan from the 1950s and 1960s that my prescription of gluten-free diets for individuals with schizophrenia and autism changed from being last-resort to near the top of the list.[30,31] Like many who have not traveled this road, I was waiting for more proof of the sort Joe requires.[32,33,34,35] Along the way, it was seeing children like Alex respond that made a believer out of me. What do I believe? I believe that you may be missing the boat if your child has any chronic symptom, and you have not tried eliminating gluten from his or her diet for somewhere between three weeks and three months to see what difference it may make.

Look at the following list. Is it any wonder that that a medical mind, like Joe's, conditioned to think that each disease has a separate cause, and each cause produces a separate disease, has difficulty believing that sensitivity to the protein in wheat (and rye, barley, and maybe oats) could produce such a diverse and growing list of conditions?

- Headache
- Fatigue
- Malaise
- Depression
- Any sort of chronic digestive problem including difficulty gaining weight, abdominal pain, diarrhea, constipation, irritable bowel, undigested food in stools
- Sjogren's syndrome (dry eyes)
- Epilepsy associated with any of the following:
    Brain calcification
    History of migraine headaches
    Hyperactivity
    Digestive problems
- Osteoporosis
- Infertility, complications of pregnancy such as miscarriage, low birth-weight infants
- Intestinal lymphoma

- Esophageal cancer
- Diabetes
- Thyroid problems
- Schizophrenia
- Gait disturbances
- Autism
- Dermatitis herpetiformis (a chronic skin condition with tiny blisters that resemble those of herpes virus infections)

There is substantial evidence of a causative association between gluten intolerance and these problems, and the list will grow as case reports of dramatic cures produced by a gluten-free diet attract the attention of researchers who can make a statistical case for a general association between gluten sensitivity and a group of individuals with similar problems.

Your child is not a group. Your child is an individual. Whether or not your child's symptoms put him or her into a diagnostic group and provide you with a label for these symptoms, you still need to make personal decisions about your child's health, looking for safe, inexpensive and relatively easy steps that may get your child out of trouble. You do not need to wait for a group for your child to belong to; all you need to do is test your child for gluten sensitivity.

There are blood tests and urine tests that are pretty reliable predictors that your child will feel better as a result of eliminating gluten from the diet. However, no blood or urine test is completely decisive. Response to a change in diet is decisive for your child. Medical research demands standard definitions for judging the effectiveness of a particular treatment. It would not do for one researcher to claim success based on treatment of people who defined their gluten sensitivity in terms of feeling better on a diet while another used a strict definition based on changes in the lining of the gut determined by biopsy. But you and Linda and I do not have to worry about disease definitions necessary for comparability of research studies. We only have to worry about safety, cost, and efficacy. Then, if a treatment like a gluten-free diet works, we can wonder about how it works and whether there might be some way around a permanent and strict avoidance of gluten.

How does a gluten-free diet work?

Of the seven food grains – rice, barley, corn, millet, wheat, oats, and rye – only wheat, rye and barley contain gluten. Some gluten-sensitive individuals react to oat. Each of the seven grains is a hybrid of wild grasses that were domesticated with the beginning of agriculture twelve to fifteen thousand years ago. The grass seeds contain starch energy stored for the day when the seed finds soil in which to germinate a new plant. The starch is enclosed in a coat of fiber and protein, which makes up less than ten percent of the resulting flour when seeds are crushed and ground in a mill.

The ancestral wild grasses of modern wheat had a few arrow-shaped kernels. These kernels fell to the ground where our ancestors could gather them, in the times before women noticed and then organized the conditions for their germination. Over a period of a few thousand years, the early farmers favored the wild grasses that produced nice fat seeds and learned how to select and then hybridize for size, taste, resistance to drought, and consistency. Consistency became a big issue after the development of fermentation gave rise to barm, the yeasty sediment formed during the production of wine and beer. Yeast-rich barm, kneaded into moist wheat flour, formed little bubbles in the dough to create raised bread. The stickier the dough, the better the bubbles;

hence a premium on flour with the appropriate stickiness. Gluten is gluey and provides the stickiness of the paste we used to use (and sometimes eat) in kindergarten. The same gluiness gives wheat the stickiness needed to make pasta as well as to form the bubbles in leavened bread. By Roman times one kind of wheat (siligo) was used for bread making, and spelt, with a lower gluten content, was used for soups. Both had kernels that stayed on the stem until harvest. By that time, the farming peoples of the Middle East had invaded and substantially replaced the original people of Northern Europe, who (like the people of the Americas, Africa and the Far East) were not adapted to the consumption of wheat because they were hunter gatherers or practiced agriculture based on corn (maize), millet (sorghum) or rice as well as tubers.

Nowadays, many descendants of the original population of Europe remain relatively poorly adapted to gluten. That means that a population of largely European origins has an incidence of gluten intolerance of about 1 in 100 people. Other populations of African, Asian, or American descent also have a high incidence of gluten intolerance.

Researchers know about the incidence of gluten intolerance largely through studies of the intestinal lining of family members of individuals with gluten-induced malabsorption (celiac disease). Many of these individuals are not (yet) sick, although their intestinal velvet has changes which, were they visible on the skin, would be clearly unhealthy. The picture of gluten intolerance has changed over the past century from scrawny, pot-bellied infants and children dying of wasting and diarrhea to a completely different spectrum of illnesses as listed above.[36,37] It is a mystery that food intolerance could devastate whole regions of the intestine. Even more mysterious is the mechanism by which gluten's mischief reaches the brain, skin and other organs remote from the gut. Keep in mind, by the way, that nothing is really very remote from anything else in the body, least of all the brain and the gut, whose chemistry are very similar. Most of the serotonin – a neurotransmitter associated with mood and sleep – is made in the gut, where it has other functions.[38] Encouragingly, gluten encephalopathies and gluten ataxias and their dietary treatment are increasingly described in mainstream medical literature.[39]

One solution to the mystery of how gluten affects the brain begins with digestion, in this case of protein. A protein is an assembly of amino acids. Imagine about twenty different shapes and colors of paper clips. Put on some good music, sit down on the floor and start assembling the paper clips into a chain. If each paper clip were an amino acid, then the first two you join together would be called a di-peptide (di=two). Add one more and it would be a tri-peptide. After that they are just called peptides until you have about 100 or so. Then it becomes a small protein. Most proteins have hundreds or thousands of amino acids, and they are folded into shapes that are kept permanent by sticky bridges, usually made with sulfur.

When you get a perm at the hair salon they put stuff on your hair (which is made of protein) to break the sulfur bridges, then set your hair before putting on some other stuff to reform the sulfur bridges. The strength of hair (try breaking a plait of just 20 strands of hair with your bare hands) is enormous, so imagine the problem of your digestive tract when you are obliged to disassemble the thousands of amino acids right down to individual paper clips, which then pass into your bloodstream to be reassembled into your very own proteins. A combination of a bath in acid (stomach) followed by a bath in alkali (small intestine), combined with the frantic work of large proteins embracing your food proteins and unhooking the paper clips at a dizzying pace, does the job. The job is more efficient because one group of enzymes breaks the paper clip chain into chunks (peptides) and the other enzyme nibbles amino acids from the ends of the chunks. The chunk-makers are proteases and the chunk-nibblers are peptidases. Gluten intolerance has to do with a failure of a particular peptidase called DPP4 (also called CD26, when the same enzyme is sticking out of a lymphocyte and apparently doing a different job within the body).[40,41,42,43] The undigested peptide that has survived because of the failure or insufficiency of DPP4 appears to cause mischief in at least two ways.

First: the undigested fragment of protein, a peptide with eight amino acids still joined together, looks familiar to the immune system. It is an instance of molecular mimicry. In this case the wheat or milk protein did not "mean to" produce a fragment that might mislead the immune system of the person consuming, and poorly digesting, the protein.[44,45] Other instances of mimicry in nature and medicine are quite "intentional," as in the case of molecules produced by fungi that mimic and block our energy-producing chemistry. In the case of gluten-derived peptides, the mimicry is purely coincidental and is based on digestive weakness among the descendents of peoples who have not been eating wheat long enough to adapt or whose digestive difficulty goes along with some other trait that has a survival benefit. Either way, many people have a gluten-related problem with digestion, and some of them have or will have symptoms caused by the triggering of an immune response against the suspicious-looking peptide.[46,47,48,49,50] What does the peptide look (or taste, or feel, or sound) like to the cells of the immune system that are constantly on border patrol? Studies have found that there is gluten mimicry with human tissue.[51,52,53,54] Because the gluten-derived peptide has similarity with at least some human tissue (eg, enterocytes), a complex defensive response occurs on the part of the immune system – reacting both to gluten and to parts of human tissue. The next step in the chain of events is damage to tissues by the antibodies aimed at the peptide. This triangle of molecular mimicry, immune response, and autoimmune damage is suspected to be a common theme in various illnesses. In summary, the first way that undigested peptides from gluten cause trouble is by stimulating an autoimmune response that damages different tissues in different people.

Second, the undigested peptide enters the bloodstream, as some peptides tend to do in the normal course of things, even though the vast majority of protein-derived amino acids enter the bloodstream only after being digested down to individual amino acids. An excess amount of undigested peptides enters the bloodstream in individuals whose intestinal lining is leaky – in the sense that unwanted molecules leak from the intestine into the bloodstream.[55,56,57,58] (See a discussion of leaky gut later in this chapter.) Peptides released from gluten when there is a failure of DPP4 possess another kind of mimicry apart from their resemblance to peptides from viruses. Gluten-derived peptides look like opium and thus have earned the name "opioid-like peptides."[59,60,61,62]

When the DPP4 enzyme fails to do its job in the digestion of substances released during the digestion of gluten (gliadinomorphin, gliadorphin and gluteomorphin) and casein (beta-casomorphins), the peptides released mimic opium and the family of drugs derived from opium: heroin, morphine, codeine, and other semisynthetic derivatives that are unequaled in alleviating pain. The way this family of molecules relieves pain is based on their molecular

> FIND A DOCTOR who listens and asks questions. If you are not comfortable with your pediatrician or specialist, find another one with an open mind who is willing and able to think outside the box. Run from anyone who wants only to enlighten and isn't open to being enlightened by you. You quickly become an expert in your field and the relationship works both ways. This will hold true at school, too.
>
> – a parent

similarity to endorphins, substances we release within our bodies when we are under the stress of exertion or injury. "Opioids" is the name of the whole family of substances that act like opium-derived drugs and endorphins.[63,64] The current understanding of this second mechanism for mischief caused by gluten is based on the finding of opioid peptides in the urine of individuals with autism and schizophrenia.[65,66] Another body of evidence comes from the experience of those like Alex, whose improvement following gluten avoidance is dramatic and not explained by any other treatment. Of the two hundred families of autistic children in my practice, more than half have stuck with a gluten-free diet after (reluctantly) trying it. A third body of evidence comes from observing the dramatic withdrawal symptoms that occur in some individuals when they come off gluten. The symptoms of malaise and irritability strongly resemble a mild version of the kinds of symptoms seen in heroin withdrawal.

DPP4 is an enzyme with three names depending on where it is working. In the gut it is DPP4 and is responsible for breaking a bond between amino acids in peptides formed during protein digestion. In the immune system it is CD26 where it is found sticking out of certain lymphocytes as part of their message-receiving apparatus. In nucleotide chemistry it is adenosine deaminase binding protein where it assists metabolism of adenosine. Insufficient adenosine deaminase activity causes elevations of adenosine (see the thiol diagram later in this section), which in turn raises levels of S-adenosyl homocysteine (SAH), which inhibits methylation. Dr. Pangborn reviews this subject in more detail, but **the key point is this link between gluten sensitivity, enzyme deficiency, and problems in methylation.**

If you decide that any of your child's symptoms may be related to sensitivity to gluten, the first rule is to embark on a gluten-free diet gradually. Unless you do all your own cooking from scratch, it is not easy to avoid gluten. Unless you are the sole source of your child's food, you will have to recruit the understanding and active cooperation of anyone who might give him or her food: other kids' parents, school personnel, brothers and sisters, and relatives. Depriving a child with problems of food that he or she likes seems at best odd, and at worst abusive, to lots of well-meaning people including some who may carry a lot of weight in your family, such as grandparents. Here are the steps.

1. Equip yourself with a guide that provides the details necessary to carry out the diet, including sources of gluten-free food, recipes, hints, and other resources. The best of such guides include *Special Diets for Special Kids*, by Lisa Lewis, and *The Cheerful Chemist's No Casein, No Gluten, Sugar Optional Cookbook*, by Sally Ramsey.

2. Let everyone know that you plan to start a gluten-free diet as of a certain date. Make it clear that the diet is for medical diagnostic purposes and will last initially for three weeks, with the proviso that it could extend to three months before you make a decision about the long term.

3. Have them read this chapter or another reference giving the background.

4. If they are not willing to provide only gluten-free food, have them agree to provide no food at all, allowing you to produce foods for your child for birthday parties, school events and lunches, and visits outside your home.

If you wish to try a gluten-free diet for your child and can exist for three weeks while making all of your child's food, then the rules are simple enough so that you could simply be sure to exclude anything made with flour from wheat, rye, barley or oats, or any other product that came originally from those sources. Most individuals with gluten-related symptoms will begin to experience relief a few days after excluding all gluten. It may take up to three weeks before you can say that avoiding gluten has *not* produced the desired effect. At that point you might want to put the gluten question on the back burner and return to a three-month exclusion of gluten as a more final test after considering other explanations for your child's symptoms. At that later date you may wish to have some lab tests that could strengthen or weaken the case against gluten.

There is no lab test that will determine decisively whether your child will respond to a gluten-free diet. There are lab tests which, if abnormal, will predict a good response to a gluten-free diet. The same tests, if normal, diminish your hopes for a good response to dietary change. Many doctors define the problem in terms of the lab test, not in terms of your child's response to a change in diet. The lab tests are, for the most part, meant to indicate celiac disease which does not necessarily have a one-to-one correlation with all of the other problems associated with gluten sensitivity.

> YOU, AS PARENTS, must learn that your child is treatable, recoverable, but only if you take steps in that direction. Serious medical conditions such as this do not get wished away. Get informed and make changes now. Do not wait for everyone else to agree with you. This experience has helped me realize in a much deeper way then ever before what I do and do not have control over. Eating well, exercising, and a healthy lifestyle did not ensure my child health for long. But researching, trying, thinking, learning and loving have made huge differences and I know they will continue to do so. I can choose to educate myself, make changes, assess, and go to the next step or I can choose ignorance. I choose knowledge. For me. For my son.
>
> – a parent

The following are options in terms of lab tests listed in order of increasing specificity:

1. Urine test for intestinal permeability, which, if it shows very low mannitol absorption, is a pointer toward malabsorption, perhaps from gluten problems.

2. Blood tests:

    a. Antibodies to wheat, rye, oats, barley. IgG antibodies as determined by an IgG ELISA may turn up in a screening test for food allergies in which your child's blood is tested for reactivity to many foods. The more and the stronger the reaction to these foods, the more likely that other, more specific tests for gluten sensitivity will turn out to be positive.

    b. Antibodies to tissue transglutaminase, endomysium, and reticulin, and gliadin (a subfraction of gluten). Elevated levels of IgA antibodies to one or more of these substances correlate strongly with celiac disease. If any of these tests is positive, it gives strong indication that you should try a gluten-free diet to see if it clears your symptoms.

SECTION TWO: MAKING A PLAN

c. Small bowel biopsy. Currently done by upper gastrointestinal endoscopy, in which a flexible tube is passed down your child's esophagus, past the stomach and into the small intestine, where small snips (biopsies) can be collected for microscopic examination. If this test shows that your child has a smoothing of the normally velvety nap of the lining of the small intestine, then you should change your child's diet and see if it corrects the abnormality. The majority of people with this abnormality are free of symptoms.

Suppose one or more of these tests is abnormal, and you change your child's diet for as long as three months but see no changes in the way your child feels or functions. Should you keep your child on a gluten-free diet indefinitely, hoping to prevent future mischief? It is a tough question that could be answered either way depending on the circumstances, but in general I would lean toward taking these lab tests seriously if they are abnormal. The problems I listed at the beginning of this chapter suggest that the stakes are quite high. On the other hand, a gluten-free diet is inconvenient.

None of the experts I have talked with believes that taking an enzyme that will do the job of DPP4 will eliminate the need for a gluten-free diet. Most, however, feel that such an enzyme – to be taken at the beginning of a gluten-containing meal – will eventually be developed. It may not permit gluten-sensitive individuals to eat bread and pasta, but it should relieve them of vigilant concern over the hidden gluten content of prepared food.

Casein sensitivity

Everything I have described regarding gluten applies to casein, one of the main proteins in milk. Just as there are people in the population who have not adapted to the consumption of certain cereal grains since the beginning of farming, so there are others who are unable to digest milk.[67,68,69,70] I have chosen to leave casein sensitivity out of the discussion until now to avoid confusion. The confusion comes with the different ways milk products can be toxic.

The first way is that a lack of a DPP4 peptidase enzyme causes incomplete digestion of the casein molecule, leaving a mischievous peptide.[71]. This problem is fully equivalent to the gluten problem, including the point that we have urine tests that identify increased levels of the peptide, caseomorphin. The peptides pass, as I have described, into the blood, where they do harm because they evoke an immune response and/or they mimic endorphins to cause changes in perception, mood, and behavior. Like everything in the blood, the peptides eventually pass through the kidneys, so some of them appear in the urine. Researchers have been able to measure these peptides for a number of years.[72,73] The tests have not yet been perfected to the point where they can reliably predict who will benefit from a change in diet. Antibodies to casein are a positive indicator, but not as much so as the antibody tests used to identify casein sensitivity as an allergic (as opposed to digestive) mechanism of casein intolerance. Small bowel biopsy is not relevant to the diagnosis of casein sensitivity because casein does not injure the bowel in that particular way.

Casein sensitivity requires a shorter interval – three weeks – in order to judge the effectiveness of an elimination diet in causing improvement in symptoms. For that reason, casein avoidance precedes gluten avoidance in our diagram and is recommended even for children with normal urinary caseomorphin peptides. I have parents who picked up Karen Seroussi's book[74] or saw a TV program or a web site or attended a DAN! meeting[75] and had their child on a strict gluten- and casein-free diet the next day. I have others who put it off for months while exploring other options. A casein-free diet is an easier sell because of the shorter interval needed to find out it if is working – often just a few days – and it is an easier food to substitute, especially for carbohydrate-craving kids hooked on bread, crackers, etc.

The second way in which milk products can be a problem does not have a clear-cut boundary with casein sensitivity as I have just described it. Milk allergy[76,77,78] comes to about the same thing: it can produce in someone, somewhere, just about any symptom you can think of. Allergy, in the usual sense of the word, has a medical implication of an immune system reaction that differs from the peptide issue I have just described. With allergy, the protein in milk (usually casein, the sticky protein familiar to you as Elmer's Glue®) causes either an immediate allergic reaction in the form of hives, eczema, swelling, itching, or digestive complaints, or a delayed reaction that can take any form. The delayed reaction is much more difficult to track to its origin because the symptoms may occur at varying intervals and intensities after eating various kinds of milk products.[79,80,81]

The third way that milk products bother people is lactose intolerance.[82,83,84,85] Lactose is the sugar common to milk from any mammal. Just as there are people from populations without a long history of consuming gluten, there are many without a long history of consuming non-human milks. Among such peoples are individuals who cannot digest lactose, a disaccharide molecule made up of two simple sugars: glucose and galactose. They lack the enzyme to separate these sugars so that each can be absorbed into the bloodstream. As a consequence, the undigested lactose travels down the digestive tract where the normal germ population consumes it. The result is bowel urgency, cramps, diarrhea, and gas within an hour after eating lactose-containing food. A test (hydrogen breath test) can distinguish lactose intolerance from other milk-related problems. If your child has symptoms outside the digestive tract from milk products, then milk allergy or casein sensitivity is the problem. If the symptoms are purely digestive, then you can distinguish between milk allergy and lactose intolerance only by doing the hydrogen breath test. The value of knowing the difference is that there are commercially available lactose-free milk products. Also, you can add lactase to milk products to make up for your child's lack of this enzyme. Lactose intolerance may or may not be associated with intolerance to (inability to digest) other disaccharides.

Karen Seroussi sent me this email summarizing her current dietary leanings and gave her permission to reproduce it here:

> "I am writing from the road, in the middle of a series of lectures I've been giving on dietary interventions. I am meeting a lot of parents in various stages of the diet(s), and getting a tremendous amount of feedback. My overall impressions are:
>
> 1. In some minority of cases, I don't think food-derived peptides are the issue at all. Generally I suspect bacteria, but of course there could be something else.
> 2. Some of these kids are sitting on too many tacks to be sure whether the diet is helping.
> 3. There are certainly lots of other kids like my son for whom the GF/CF diet is the magic bullet, provided the parents are also investigating the effects of soy, corn, allergens, yeast, and sugar, as we did, and are using effective teaching tools. In my talks, I repeatedly emphasize that GF/CF is not a

license to put a child on an all-carb diet. I recommend a trial on the SCD as a way of getting parents into the no-sugar, no-carbs mindset, with a re-evaluation each month as to whether some foods can or should be added back in, or whether the SCD is the ticket for that child and should be adhered to.

4. Some percentage of the kids are doing wonderfully well on the SCD, but many have not been able to do it due to nut and egg allergies, constipation, or weight loss. Many are doing it without medical supervision and probably need antifungals in conjunction with the diet. Many have experienced serious yeast and bacteria overgrowth on the SCD while using honey and fruit. I encourage these parents to get experienced support before giving up on the SCD, but am concerned that fanatical attitudes may be keeping some on a diet that might need modification in order to be appropriate for individual kids.

"My overall take on this right now is that the kids (and lots of the moms) probably need to be sugar- and starch-free for at least a month, with the mandatory heavy use of probiotic foods. (I am currently wildly enthusiastic about the cultured vegetables, provided you can get the stinky stuff into the kids, because they help with constipation as well as packing quite a probiotic punch.)

Some kids, it appears, cannot deviate from the monosaccharide protocol without regression. Meanwhile, several parents of those who made gains on the SCD are telling me that some low-starch GF grains added into the diet have been helpful for constipation, and have not impeded developmental progress. Since, on a practical level, it's easier to add foods back in than to keep taking them out, I think it makes sense to start strict."

FOOD ALLERGEN ELIMINATION. The priority here is somewhat flexible. If a child is very allergic or has had a food allergy test indicating a large number (say >12) of reactive foods, then the possibility exists that one or more of these foods is causing problems that will complicate the ongoing detective work. Suppose, for example, that your child's behavior is being driven to a certain extent by an allergy to egg, which makes him irritable and sleepless as well as causing skin and bowel problems. It would be a good idea to get the egg issue resolved before tackling the gluten, casein and yeast issues that lie ahead. My diagram shows a link between investigating food sensitivities and the SCD. There are two reasons for the placement of that link. One is that food sensitivity may be the result of other imbalances which, if repaired, may obviate the need for an allergy elimination diet. Allergy elimination may, then, fall lower in the hierarchy of choices because options that precede it, including SCD, may take care of the problem. A second reason is that SCD may appear to provoke allergic reactions because of the replacement of a child's usual foods with new ones, such as almond. One of my patients, who ultimately did very well on SCD, had a dramatic negative change in behavior when starting SCD until his mother took almond products – which figure heavily in SCD – out. Apart from its potential for being allergenic, almond is high in phenolic compounds, which can be troublesome especially in children with detoxification problems.

A good reason for considering food allergy at this point in the sequence is that you may be able to dismiss the question just on the basis of a good history plus good intuition. A history that completely lacks clues such as infantile colic, rashes, sleep problems, bowel symptoms, known food reactions, or allergies to dust, mold, cats, dogs, pollens, or chemicals, in a child who is not constitutionally sensitive, might lead to skipping a search for hidden food allergies at this point. Here are some thoughts on the food allergy-autism connection that may help put this question into perspective.

Many and perhaps most children with autism are overly sensitive. Of the thousands of children I have known in 40 years as a doctor, the few hundred with problems in the spectrum related to autism stand out as the most distinctively sensitive of them all. Touching, tasting, hearing, smelling and seeing are characterized not only by difficulties in processing and organization but also by a heightened, often painful, sensitivity.

What does it mean to be hypersensitive? We all know what it feels like to have sunburned skin or a reaction to the sound of chalk on the blackboard, and we can empathize with children who experience a more global sensitivity, but we physicians and scientists still do not understand what happens at the cellular or molecular level to change a person's reactivity from normal to sensitive. Even the words we use – "hypersensitive," "allergic," "intolerant," "hyper-reactive" – do not have precise definitions. Many physicians, however, would quibble if we were to say that "autistic children are allergic" as opposed to "allergic children are sensitive."

> OPEN YOUR EYES AND EARS. Look, listen, read whatever you can get your hands and eyes on. Find other parents who are working hard to help their children. They are a great resource and you will get more valuable information and strength from networking with other parents than anywhere else.
>
> – *a parent*

I was such a physician when, 30 years ago, a child psychiatrist sent me Martin Zelson for evaluation of his seasonal behavioral deterioration. Martin was on the verge of being thrown out of his school program, where he was in a group of school-aged children with severe developmental and behavioral problems, mostly on the autistic spectrum. Martin was aggressive, hyperactive and destructive. I was skeptical about hypersensitivities and only beginning to become proficient in allergy evaluation. Evaluation and treatment of Martin's inhalant and food sensitivities resulted in major improvement, enabling him to benefit more from his school program and to participate in family activities that previously would have been impossible. Symptoms of his allergic responses were cognitive and behavioral, accompanied by the absence of the kinds of symptoms we usually consider to be allergic (stuffiness, eczema, wheezing, itching).

As it turns out, I have learned in the past three decades that Martin was not an exception. Most children with problems similar to his – including children with all sorts of attention problems – have hypersensitivity to foods and inhalants. Those physicians who have taken a close look not just at these children's histories and allergy test results, but at their biochemical and immune systems, now recognize that such children tend to be in a state of inappropriate immune activation.

Let us be clear. I am not saying, "Autism is caused by allergy." I am saying that autism-spectrum children (as well as children with significant attention problems) are hypersensitive not just in the area of their primary senses, but also in their immune systems' reactions to the environment, often including reactions against certain foods. This association is a lot easier for me to

SECTION TWO: MAKING A PLAN

understand if I look at the central nervous system (CNS) and immune system from a functional, as opposed to an anatomical, point of view.

Anatomically, the CNS and immune systems are quite distinct and different. One is made up of stationary long-branching permanent cells with a compact headquarters between one's ears. The other is made up of a disseminated population of short-lived mobile cells with no specific organ to call home, although spleen and lymph nodes serve as their hostels. Pick up any textbook of anatomy, physiology, or pathology. The CNS and immune system chapters are widely separated, as are the experts who wrote the chapters. The way I see it, however, our CNS and immunity are a functional unit.

Look at it this way: the cells of both systems arise from the same origin in the neural crest of the embryo.[86] Both systems contain the only cells of our bodies that exist as permanent, undividing cells from infancy to old age. (Such long-lived cells are a subset of the otherwise ephemeral cells, lymphocytes, of the immune system.) Both systems have the job of perceiving the environment. The CNS takes in the big world of our senses, our everyday cognitive experience. The immune system takes in the microscopic or molecular world that has to do with "sensing" the constant presence of friendly or unfriendly germs, food molecules, friendly cells or unfriendly cells such as cancer.

The chemistry of the immune system perceiving its tiny environment is not very different from our nose smelling the bread baking in the oven. However, we have a direct experience of the bread, while our immune system makes us aware of its activities only when something seems to be quite wrong. The message that something is wrong may be quite delayed or obscure. The memory of your fifth birthday party when your friend Jeffrey spilled purple juice all over your new sneakers is in your CNS. That same week, when the doctor gave you your shot against tetanus, diphtheria, and whooping cough, the enduring memory of those germs was evoked in your immune system where it remains today.[87] The birthday and the immunization are stored differently in your body, but functionally they come under the same heading: perception and memory.

> WE BEGAN intensive educational services which were helpful, but something was still missing until one day, while my parents were browsing through a book store, they came across *Unraveling the Mystery of Autism* by Karyn Seroussi. I stayed up all night reading it and within a day, Brandon was gluten- and casein-free. After a year of trying to teach him where his head was, within two days of going gluten- and casein-free, he now knew six body parts. We were onto something.
>
> – *a parent*

Perception and memory are the basis for "recognition." Recognition is a term we use interchangeably to describe the day-to-day activities of both our CNS and our immune systems. Finally, both of these systems share the capacity for this mysterious process called sensitization, which is, in a way, an inconvenient or painful alteration of the memory and recognition process. Viewed from this perspective, *it is not surprising that children who have problems with taking in and processing the world express that problem on both the cognitive and immune levels. For many autistic children, immune and CNS problems are really just different aspects of the same underlying disorder.*

We try to help our children organize and integrate their cognitive world by imposing a simplified order. Such order may take the form of repetitive behavioral and linguistic exercises, or efforts to modify responses (desensitize) to sensory input. On the immune level, we try to impose a simplified order by avoidance of, or desensitization to, offending foods and inhalants. This applies whether the mechanism of the reaction to foods, for example, is "allergic" within the academic definition of the word or "intolerant" within a notion that covers a variety of mechanisms, including the mischief caused by certain peptides derived from gluten and casein.

So you have a picky kid. Your job is to help your child learn better picking. If your child chooses to limit his or her activities to monotonous behavior, you try to broaden the opportunity for cognitive experience by picking and presenting other, more useful, kinds of stimuli. If your child is sensitive to tastes, touch, smells, sights or sounds, you take steps to help him or her integrate and become less painfully sensitive to these stimuli. If your kid's immune system is picky, your job is to find the stimuli that are bothersome, and present ones that are not mischievous. In the sensory realm we are familiar with the concept of desensitization. The same is true in immunology, where allergic desensitization may begin with exposure to very small doses. Desensitization may work for food intolerances, but first you have to find out if your child is sensitive to this or that food.

When you have lots of other things to think about, should you change the diet of a child who has decided to live on French fries, smushed bagels, chocolate milk, pretzels, Twinkies and Diet Coke, rejecting all alternatives with an iron will? Yup! And when you get over the hump, you are likely to be rewarded with changes in sleep, behavior, attention and "sensitivity" that make the struggle worth it. There are several ways of checking for food allergy. Trial-and-error changes in diet are tedious, but inexpensive.

How do you find out whether a food is causing a problem? A diagnostic trial of five days of avoidance followed by three days of challenge is the most decisive. In children who have a very simple diet, avoidance and challenge is often the most appropriate tool. Otherwise there are tests that will help narrow the possibilities – to be confirmed by avoidance and challenge. There are, however, no tests on which one should base a decision to permanently take any food from a child's diet if its tendency to cause symptoms is not confirmed by avoidance and challenge. Blood tests are more reliable than skin tests because the latter focus mostly on allergies mediated by IgE – antibodies associated with immediate reactions such as inflammation of the skin, respiratory tract and digestive tract. IgG-associated allergy is more likely to be manifested as delayed symptoms and may affect any organ including the brain. Notice that I say IgG-*associated*. In immunology the role of IgG is disputed when discussion focuses on the causative mechanism of allergic inflammation. Here, however, we are not talking about IgG as the *cause* but simply as a test that serves as a marker in the blood that may single out certain foods as suspects because IgG levels are particularly high. The final test is what happens if one does or does not eat the suspected foods.

Here are ten pointers on how to deal with the results of a blood food allergy test (IgG ELISA). They apply to people with all sorts of problems.

1. Illness is a signal for change.

When I hear a person declare, "I could not possibly give up eating bread," or "How could anyone go without eating things with milk in them? Milk is in so many things," I think that I may be hearing from one of the many people whose capacity to change is not up to the challenge that

SECTION TWO: MAKING A PLAN

their illness is placing before them. But remember, so far we are talking about a short-term diagnostic change, not a permanent change, unless your body tells you that such a change is helpful.

2. Don't panic.

The test results are very helpful in sorting out symptoms of just about any kind – from seizures to rashes, from diarrhea to depression – but the foods you see marked as "positive" (+) or "reactive" are not to be forever stricken from your child's menu. This is a diagnostic test, not a treatment recipe, and the only thing you need to do with the results is to try them out for a minimum of five days, and preferably about two weeks, to see if the diagnosis "food sensitivity is causing some of my child's symptoms" is accurate. If so, then you can proceed from there. Only rarely would a person want to consider a prolonged avoidance of all reactive foods without noticing some definite improvement in symptoms.

3. Look at the total number.

Allergic people average about a dozen reactive foods. People with "no allergies" (that is, those who are not aware of having a tendency to have reactions to foods, pollens, dust, mold, chemicals and animal dander) usually have a half dozen or fewer reactive foods. People with lots of allergies tend to have as many as two dozen reactive foods (or even more). If the total number of reactive foods is a dozen or more, it is more likely that the list will reveal the cause of your symptom(s) than if you have only a few reactive foods. You can still have a serious food allergy problem if you have a small list of reactive foods, but in general, the more foods you react to on the test, the more likely it is that one or some of them account for symptoms. Remember that lots of IgG food sensitivities are compatible with increased intestinal permeability and reinforce the need to be good to the gut, using gut rehabilitation measures as well as food elimination trials. Food sensitivity may be either the cause or the effect of increased gut permeability.

4. "I've never eaten oysters or alfalfa, but my test says I'm allergic to them."

One of the first things people notice when reviewing their test results is any indication of a reaction to a food that they "never eat." They are right to be puzzled, because one thing we know about the immune system is that it is very specific and it has a very good memory. In principle, you should not be positive to foods you have never eaten. But the whole point about the immune system and illness is that mistaken identity is the source not only of puzzles but also of trouble. Your immune system may mistake a certain food for something that you have been exposed to (germs, pollens, molds, or even molecules that are part of your own molecular makeup) and develop an inappropriate reaction. That does not mean that it is easy to interpret a positive test to oyster, say, when you swear that oysters have never touched your lips, but it is not so simple as to say the test is wrong. The test is not perfect, but your immune system probably makes mistakes more often than the test does!

5. The food allergy test isn't perfect.

This test is very good at providing a list of foods which, if avoided, are likely to lead to the alleviation of symptoms. The value of the test does not, however, depend on an unvarying correspondence between any particular food and any particular symptom. Such a relationship is for you to work out by trial and error after an initial abstinence from all the foods on the list satisfies you that you are in the right ballpark. There will nearly always be foods on the list that produce no discernible change in your health when you eat them. There may also be foods that you know bother you but which are non-reactive on the test, even though you have eaten some from time to time before the test. There are many ways that foods can bother a person. Not all such ways have to do with immune mechanisms or with mechanisms for which there is any test. IgG antibodies are a good guide – I think the best there is – but they are not meant to be taken as absolutely decisive as to all the foods that could bother you.

6. IgG antibodies are a marker, not necessarily the cause of delayed allergies.[88,89,90,91]

Your immune system perceives the world of molecules just as you perceive the world around you by the overlapping use of your several senses. If you go downtown for dinner and a movie, it would be strange for you to describe some good or bad memory of the event in terms of only one of these several senses that gave you what you heard, saw, etc. You would normally invoke two or more of your senses to recall a description of the event. Similarly, the immune system has many ways of receiving, recording, and relating its experience of foods, germs, chemicals and other events that make up its experience of the world. The particular blood protein Immune Globulin type G or IgG that forms the basis the IgG ELISA is only one of several aspects of your immune system's record of its ongoing perceptions. It appears to be particularly important in delayed food hypersensitivities, just as IgE is important in reactions such as hives and swelling that occur immediately after eating a food. I do not believe, however, that IgG is the exclusive mechanism for delayed food reactivity. From experiments that I have conducted, I've concluded that IgG is a very reliable marker for allergy, and that reliability is what counts when it comes to doing detective work on the cause of difficult and mysterious symptoms.

7. "I just ate a lot of peanuts before the test..."

Whether you do this test immediately after eating a lot of peanuts or some time later does not make much difference in the results. You would have to abstain from a food for months for your IgG antibodies to go away, and even then I know of some instances in which the antibodies persist. We really do not know how long it takes for antibodies to disappear when a particular person abstains from a particular food. We do know that the test is highly reproducible in a good laboratory Many labs have failed at techniques to insure such reliability and have abandoned the test as "not reproducible." The good labs have devised modifications to the well-known basic technique of the test so that these labs can split a sample and get the same results in each half, just as they can show that your test will vary very little over a period of weeks whether you ate a lot of a particular food or not. There is a popular misconception among doctors that the IgG ELISA "just shows you what you have been eating." If that were true, individuals with the same diet would have the same results, which is far from the case. A good lab will encourage you to split samples so that the lab is blind to the fact that two samples of the same blood specimen are being tested. A physician may contact the laboratory to be provided with the protocol for splitting samples.

8. What about the plusses?

The difference between a 1+ and a 4+ reaction to a food is not as much as you might think from looking at the difference between a finger and a hand. The numbers indicate the differences in the intensity of the reaction of your blood in the lab but do not necessarily correlate with the intensity or significance of your clinical reactions. Initially a 1+ reaction needs to be considered just as seriously as a possible indicator of a symptom-causing food as does a 4+ reaction. Of course, the degree of reactivity generally correlates with the potential of a food to be the cause of symptoms, but I think it is wrong to ignore 1+ reactions when you are getting started with the detective work.

9. What about groups?

Some of the foods in the panels are tested as groups, so that positive reactions show up in all the members of the group. However, when several cereal grains (wheat, rye, oat, barley, rice, corn) or beans (legumes) come up as positive, it strengthens the impression that some or all members of that "family" are a problem. As an initial measure, however, I usually do not recommend that patients avoid members of a group if their test to that item is negative while another member of the group is reactive. For example, if a person reacts to lemon but not grapefruit or orange, then I would ask the person to avoid lemon but not the other citrus fruits.

10. So what is the bottom line?

You won't know the final value of the food allergy IgG test until you do a trial avoidance of all of the foods indicated as reactive (plus any others that you already know bother your child for some other reason). If, after two weeks of strict avoidance of the reactive foods, nothing to do with your child's health has changed, then it becomes unlikely that sensitivity to foods on that list plays a significant role in your child's symptoms. At that point you can simply re-introduce the reactive foods. If at that point, however, you notice the appearance or occurrence of symptoms whose disappearance somehow had escaped your notice, then you will have to go back to square one and repeat the two-week avoidance to see what happens. This is the "avoidance/challenge/re-challenge" phenomenon that still remains the gold standard of food sensitivity testing. If there is no change in response to either avoiding or reintroducing foods, then you can conclude that sensitivity to the tested foods is probably not an issue for your child. I say "probably" because:

a. There are some foods (particularly wheat and other gluten-containing foods, and milk products) which may test positive on IgG testing but which, in your child, are producing effects that are not really allergic but are mediated by mechanisms that take weeks or months for alleviation after avoiding the food(s); and,

b. It is still possible that a period of longer than two weeks will be needed to show an effect. Usually five days is enough. If there are other strong reasons to suspect a given reactive food (such as a history of heavy exposure during periods of stress, or a previous history of intolerance during, say, infancy or early childhood) then there may be justification for prolonging the trial of avoiding the food(s) for longer than two weeks.

> KNOW THAT THERE MAY BE some very rough patches with diet, behavior, die-off issues, etc. to soldier through. Also, in addition to building a strong relationship with a doctor in whom you trust, it is critical to have a support system of other parents who are on the same healing path and to call upon them for whatever! Another piece of advice is to STAY POSITIVE. Absolutely no one knows what tomorrow will bring. I have learned to pay attention to my gut feelings (no pun intended!!) about my child, especially regarding what is good or bad for him – nobody knows my baby like I do.
>
> – *a parent*

If there is a change in symptoms when your child avoids the reactive foods, then you will still not be sure which are the key foods. You still may not be sure how far the symptom relief may go if some symptoms have been relieved and others remain. For example, your child may have headaches and joint pain and achieve relief of only the headaches during the two weeks. You should take that as a green light to proceed with avoiding the foods, with the hope that the joint pain relief will follow in due time. After a couple of weeks of symptom relief, you may decide to simply continue avoiding all the foods without knowing which one or ones are guilty or innocent. Some children get such wonderful results that their parents are content to continue avoiding all the reactive foods. Others would like to whittle their list down to discover the key food(s). To do that you must reintroduce foods one at a time, allowing about 72 hours after beginning to give your child the suspected food once or twice daily. If your child does not develop any symptoms in the 72 hours, it is unlikely that the re-introduced food is the cause of problems and you can keep it in your child's diet. If your child does develop symptoms, remove the food, wait for symptoms to clear, and then go on to try other foods. Eventually you will develop a list of offending foods. Most children will have to simply avoid those foods or receive help in becoming desensitized. Some children will be able to eat these foods on a rotation basis, consuming the food only once every five days. The safest thing is to take the food out of your child's diet for at least six months. The possibility of successfully re-introducing the food at that point is variable from person to person and from food to food.

DETOXIFICATION

Variability is the key word in just about every test and intervention in the biomedical approach to autism. Another way to think of this is inter-individual differences. That single feature of the autism landscape dominates our efforts to find each child's safest, most efficient and most winning path. Could it be that efforts to alter the sensitivity of our kids as regards their vulnerability to negative influences on their immune system would obviate the need to fill unmet needs or avoid toxic or allergenic substances? In Minimata, Japan, where thousands were killed, disfigured or sickened by exposure to mercury contamination, many more thousands appeared to be unaffected. In your own neighborhood, most children who have been exposed to thimerosal, feast on gluten and casein and yeast in pizza, have been on antibiotics more often than not in their first years of life, and have had combined measles, mumps and rubella immunization, still appear unscathed. Reasons for increased susceptibility merit attention. Genetics are implicated, but many genetic tendencies are modifiable. Otherwise the vast sums currently being spent on genetic research would be a wasted effort to close the barn door after the horse has escaped.

The thrust of the biomedical approach is to diminish each child's sensitivity by addressing the imbalances that account for that sensitivity. If I am standing on one foot, I may be tipped over by a nudge from your thumb. I may conclude that I am very sensitive to thumb nudges unless I consider the alternative of planting both feet on the ground. Similarly, discovering and repairing unmet needs for zinc, antioxidants and other participants in thiol chemistry, or removing allergens and toxins, may be the key to re-establishment of a healthy balance in which mercury, gluten, yeast, etc. would be tolerable. But isn't there an easier way?

Sometimes it really is easy. I know children whose cognitive or behavioral problems were eliminated by antifungal treatment alone, a gluten/casein-free diet alone, or supplements alone. It makes me ask two questions. What is the difference between the responders and non-responders? Isn't there a simpler way?

SECTION TWO: MAKING A PLAN

Answers to the first question will come from tabulation of details that are costly to organize. Until the Internet bubble burst and funding stopped, we had created a website that allowed people to ask, "Is there someone else with a child just like mine, and if so, what was their path to success?" The same database that we built to provide such answers would have answered the responder-versus-non-responder question, but our project is on ice awaiting resuscitation.

The second question comes vividly to mind when subtle therapies are associated with dramatic changes in our children. By subtle, I mean having to do with mechanisms that are not revealed within the current scientific disciplines of mainstream medicine. Craniosacral therapy, acupuncture and other Chinese medicine techniques, homeopathy, NAET,[92] Bioset,[93] energy healing of various schools, and Polarity Therapy[94] are associated with very persuasive results. Practitioners who listen carefully to patients who have been treated with these methods cannot help being moved toward the empirical and away from the purely rational end of the spectrum of scientific attitudes. Rationalists are those who see what they believe. Empiricists are those who believe what they see. I started out my professional career at the former end of the spectrum and will end my career with an open mind toward a more eclectic and empirical practice in the healing arts. One cannot listen to 40 years of stories from patients, and become aware of the benefits of treatments outside the biomedical model, without coming to understand that there is more to medicine than the prescription pad, and there is more to healing than the biomedical model. The biomedical model is, however, these authors' domain. We offer our understanding of it not as the be-all-and-end-all, but as what appears to be the best bet for healing kids who have been swept up in one of the worst man-made public health disasters in history – the epidemic of autism and autism-spectrum disorders.

If mercury is one of the key links in a chain that disables thiol chemistry and injures methylation, with widespread consequences to a child's biochemical and immunologic integrity,[95,96,97,98,99,100] why then would not detoxification of mercury be among options for treatment? It may be. Ten years ago, when we first met to discuss the most reasonable options that parents should consider by way of biomedical intervention, we were not consciously aware of the epidemic– and none of us had a clue that during the coming decade we would become convinced by numerous scientific studies that this epidemic of autism might be largely an epidemic of a particular form of mercury poisoning.[101] The increasing body of research is very persuasive, and the responses of our children to heavy metal detoxification treatments are consistent with the research implicating mercury.

I was already aware of mercury toxicity as an issue to consider in evaluating patients of all ages and with all sorts of chronic problems. When one autistic patient's mom raised the question to me, I was skeptical. She had done her homework and I had not. She was right, I was wrong. She and a few others broke the story with a publication that constitutes one of those events after which nothing is the same.[102] In 2001, a group of us gathered for a think tank that produced a report offering a consensus reached with the help of experts in mercury toxicology. The report made recommendations that were updated in 2004 and were published in the spring of 2005. In the interval between 2001 and 2005, two chelation studies called attention to its importance for many autistic children.

In 2001, three physicians – Amy Holmes, Stephanie Cave, and Jane El-Dahr – presented a chelation summary at the International Meeting for Autism Research conference.[103,104] In 2002, publication of the detoxification research of Dr. Derrick Lonsdale pointed the way to the use of a form of vitamin B_1 (thiamine tetrahydrofurfuryl disulfide or TTFD) in a form (transdermal) that is effective when applied to the skin.[105] Soon thereafter, a parent's observation showed us that the combination of transdermal (TD) TTFD and TD reduced glutathione (GSH) resulted in dramatic clinical improvement in many children and was an effective means of removing heavy metals. This discovery opened our eyes to the possibility of using TD TTFD and GSH as an alternative to oral sulfur-containing medications, which cause intestinal and other side effects presumably mediated by feeding unwanted species of gut flora. The transdermal route for administering various detoxifying treatments appears to be more and more promising. I refer you to the detoxification consensus report edited by Jim Adams, Ph.D.[106]

That report will be the best place for you to seek specific guidance regarding detoxification of heavy metals. We would like to return to a lesson in thiol chemistry and a discussion of detoxification in general to provide you with helpful background information. Detoxification is a word that has historically carried, and still carries, very different meanings to different kinds of health practitioners. I have explored the topic in a book,[107] but for now, here are a few key points that may help you assess the option of detoxification for which the recent ARI survey shows the following ratings.

RATINGS FOR DETOXIFICATION from ARI Publication 34/March 2005					
Treatment	% Worse	% No effect	% Better	Better:Worse	# of Cases
Detoxification (chelation)	2	22	76	35:1	324

Granted, the numbers of cases are small and the treatment is new and, therefore, finds itself on the crest of a wave of fresh enthusiasm. However, the numbers should catch our attention in light of the solid evidence at hand that mercury is a potent poison of thiol chemistry. There is a synonym for the term thiol, which, you recall, has to do with relatively small molecules – the size of amino acids – that contain a sulfur atom. The term *mercaptan*[108] was applied to this family of molecules in the 1820s by a German chemist who composed the name from mer(cury) and cap(ture). In other words, these are *molecules that capture mercury*, which in the 1820s would have still been considered an innocent asset for a molecule because mercury was considered to be more medicinal than toxic. Nowadays we send in sulfur-containing molecules (chelators) to rescue molecules of our own biochemistry that have captured mercury to their own profound disadvantage. Indeed, when we speak of the detoxification of mercury and other heavy metals, we are generally speaking of the use of chelating medications and not the many other aspects of detoxification which are worth a brief discussion.

Brushing, clipping, combing, cutting, shampooing, picking, scratching, shaving, washing, scrubbing, blowing, breathing, coughing, sneezing, clearing, burping , defecating, flatulating, discharging, dripping, draining, menstruating, spitting, sweating, urinating, vomiting, wiping, methylating, acetylating, glucuronidating, sulfating, glutathionylating, glycinating….Ridding one's self of unwanted stuff is a lot of work.[109] Efforts at purification are age-old and involve extensions of normal grooming and excretory functions in the realms of fasting, purging, colonics, special baths, and tonics, as well as abstinence. A modern view of detoxification springs from an understanding of its biochemistry, but still the ring of the word "detoxification" is strange and old-fashioned and a little suspect in the ears of many physicians. Fact is, the energy costs for ridding ourselves of used, unwanted, and toxic molecules are substantial. In children, growth is a major budget item when it comes to putting together (synthesizing) new molecules. In adults, most of the energy spent making new molecules every day is spent on behalf of synthesizing molecules that carry metabolic waste and unwelcome toxins from the body. In other words, the process of internal "housekeeping" is one of our body's most costly

SECTION TWO: MAKING A PLAN

activities. My point is important: making sure that detoxification chemistry is working smoothly is an appropriate concern for anyone who wishes to conserve health or prevent or cure illness. The concern we have for detoxification in children with autism goes beyond a generic interest in cleansing. Instead, our concern is prompted by evidence that – in many autistic children – detoxification chemistry has been poisoned by one of the very toxins that it is designed to deal with. Here is a slightly more complex version of the thiol diagram you saw earlier:

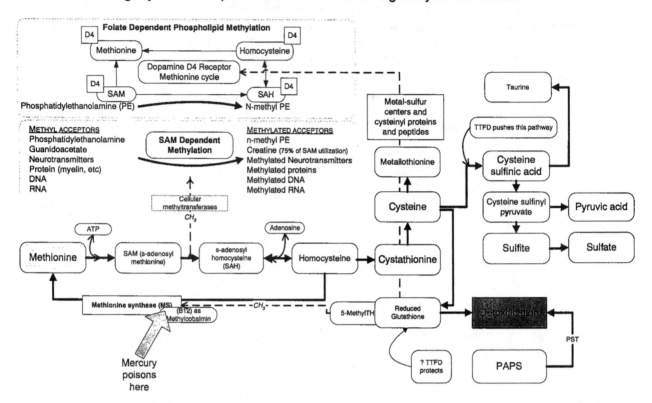

As presented here, this diagram is only part of a still larger diagram[110] that we have made to show the interrelationships among the chemical pathways of thiols, methylation, folate, and nucleotides. If you like diagrams, as I do, then you should know that Dr. Pangborn has produced a much more extensive one that covers all of the chemistry relevant to biomedical treatment in general. His big diagram can be obtained from Kirkman Laboratories, 1-800-245-8282 (outside Oregon) or 1-503-694-1600 (within Oregon).

The diagram I have shown you here is for your reference and, more particularly, to highlight the arrow indicating a target of mercury toxicity that may turn out to be the crux of the autism epidemic. This arrow carries a strong message: Either mercury is the principal cause of the autism epidemic or mercury physiology provides a model that allows us to understand and begin to search for other toxins that have combined to poison a whole generation of children.

The central role of mercury in our emerging picture of the toxicology of attentional problems in children[111] tends, at the moment, to make "detoxification" imply whatever measures we take to rid the body of mercury. On a practical level, it is an accurate snapshot of the situation at this moment. We may wish to be very cautious of falling into the most common pitfall of clinical medicine: being blinded by the obvious. The mercury-autism story is so captivating that we may fail to keep a broad perspective on the big detoxification picture. That big picture is best presented by reminding ourselves that detoxification embraces all of the ways by which a person is exposed to, recognizes, processes, and eliminates noxious substances.

Our autistic children have global disabilities in recognizing, processing, and expressing or eliminating the signals and substances they encounter. Those global disabilities at sensory, digestive, immune and metabolic levels may be healed whenever balance is restored in the broken web of biochemistry underlying the functional disabilities. Restoring balance is often progressive. When the web begins to feel the effect of balance, the web of biochemistry may reach a tipping point when healing proceeds even though all the elements of the system have not yet been repaired. It may not matter then whether one begins by repairing thiol chemistry by giving injections of methyl B12, or by chelating mercury to remove its burden on thiol chemistry. Supported by the evidence of parental reports of the efficacy of detoxification therapies, I believe that chelation and its prerequisite steps will turn out to be the best bet for the most autism-spectrum children. As this document goes to press, it appears that transdermal application of chelating agents will avoid the problems presented by their oral administration and will provide good clinical results at a low risk. The best results for each child will be achieved, however, only if the broader definition of detoxification is kept in mind – with an understanding that for a given person all of the noxious substances that affect nutrition, immunity, and detoxification are potential targets for therapy.

TTFD

Tetrahydrofurfurlydisulfide is the name of a form of vitamin B_1 (thiamine) that Derrick Lonsdale, M.D., of Westlake, Ohio had already brought to the attention of the medical world some years before he became involved in the DAN! movement, where he is now one of the principal sources of clinical acumen and scholarly wisdom. He had already established the potential therapeutic role of TTFD in connection with metabolic problems connected to vitamin B_1's role in the chemistry of carbohydrates.[112,113,114] TTFD cannot be given orally, but, because it is fat-soluble, it readily enters the bloodstream after application to the skin. (This is true of all oily substances – something to think about next time you spill kerosene, gasoline, motor oil or sun-tan oil on your skin. Your skin is waterproof but not oil-proof.) Initially, some of us seized upon Dr. Lonsdale's reports of TTFD's effectiveness in autistic children. When it is applied to the skin it usually results in the emission from the skin surface of a skunky-garlicky odor that is characteristic of the mercaptan family of chemicals. The implication of the appearance of the odor is that some toxins are being delivered to the skin.

My own learning curve took a leap when a patient's mom reported that she had obtained and started an application of reduced glutathione (GSH) cream three days after starting the TTFD cream. In the three days prior to the application of the GSH no odor had appeared. Within minutes of applying the GSH, however, my patient's room –and then the house – filled with an odor so pungent that windows needed to be opened throughout the home. I took two lessons from this experience. First, the GSH penetrated the skin and appeared to be active in my patient's body. Second, a partnership between TTFD and GSH gave rise to the latent activation of the TTFD effect.

Since then, this experience has been repeated many times in various forms, most of which are simply an enhancement of the TTFD odor with the addition of GSH. It soon became apparent that the combination of TTFD and GSH was one of the most immediately effective treatments I had seen in my patients. The down side of the treatment is the odor. No one wants to go to school with a child who smells like a skunk on garlic. That complication, as well as the occasional rash that results from the application, are dealt with in the following outline:

TTFD protocol

Begin by applying TTFD cream, 0.5 mL.(½ mL). Start putting it on a patch of skin at bedtime, choosing locations (such as the lower legs and feet) that are easily washed the next morning – to remove the skunky/garlicky odor that may form there. Re-apply it in the morning if there will be no social problems arising from having a kid smell like a skunk. Otherwise, wait until later in the day when out of the public nose and then apply the second daily dose, repeating it at bedtime. It is OK if the afternoon and evening doses are separated by only a couple of hours.

After three days, start applying ½ mL of Topical Reduced Glutathione twice daily to another part of the skin. Reduced glutathione (often abbreviated GSH) is the body's main detoxifying "usher" that combines with various toxic molecules that need to be taken from the body. Note whether the odor increases consequent to the reduced glutathione. In some instances the odor will be barely perceptible until the addition of the reduced glutathione. The enhancement of the odor on the skin after application of GSH provides persuasive evidence that the GSH gets on board through the skin and forms a detoxifying partnership with TTFD.

> TD-DMPS on December 19th and this morning. After the second application of only eight drops, G. woke up with a strong metal smell, and she was sweating. Also, the air in her room was metallic. Incredible!
> – a mom who is also an M.D.

Keep up all the applications for at least one month and observe any improvement in symptoms. If a rash develops at the site of the application, you may have to discontinue. However, the addition of the following two supplements usually permits restarting the creams with no resulting rash:

Molybdenum 300 mcg daily
Biotin 300 mcg daily

It may be preferable to start the Molybdenum and Biotin when starting the TTFD. This idea is based on the experience of a child who went off TTFD and GSH for a bad rash, waited for the rash to go away, started the Molybdenum and Biotin, and got a report from school of marked cognitive and behavioral improvement before she had restarted the TTFD and GSH – which, this time, were not associated with any rash.

If hyperactivity occurs, try activated charcoal, one capsule four to five times per day, to quench it. If the hyperactivity persists, stop the treatment.

We do not know the exact nature (beyond a membership in the family of sulfur-bearing molecules called mercaptans) of the compounds that appear on the skin and it is speculative to consider that mercury is brought out by that route. The smell on the fingers of a person applying TTFD and GSH represents the same phenomenon. Both TTFD and GSH have important roles in the body's synthetic chemistry (construction), so the benefits associated with their intended use in detoxification (sanitation) may be attributable to the multiple jobs TTFD, lipoic acid and GSH have in energy metabolism and the making of new molecules.

(A related note: The effectiveness of transdermal TTFD and GSH set the stage for the case made by Dr. Rashid Buttar for the use of transdermal (TD) dimercapto propane sulfonate (DMPS). Dr. Buttar is an expert in detoxification of heavy metals and reported dramatic success in the treatment of 19 out of 27 autistic children using TD DMPS.)

IMMUNE TESTING

Your body's defenses against invasion by unwelcome substances include your senses of touch, taste, hearing, vision, and smell. You are normally more or less aware of things that are too hot to touch, taste too bad to swallow, hurt your ears or cause you to avert your eyes, or make you flee from noxious odors.

The immune system has the same sort of defensive task but it generally works without attracting the conscious notice of your central nervous system. It employs many of the same mechanisms of molecular recognition as your senses of taste and smell but it does so without sending regular signals to your conscious brain, which would be simply overloaded if you were kept informed of the myriad of molecules in your air, food, water, intestinal flora, and your own flesh that are constantly being "tasted and smelled" by your immune system.[115,116,117] Your immune system has headquarters in your thymus gland beneath your breast bone and in your spleen beneath your left lower ribs, but is, for the most part, a disseminated system without the same sort of localization that we associate with an organ such as your liver or brain. It does, however, have a definite anatomy that consists of small nodules (lymph nodes) connected by tiny ducts that form a lacework throughout your body. The lacework includes some major tributaries that gather and recirculate a whitish fluid loaded with cells (lymphocytes) that are the main cellular constituents of the immune system. The final destination of the tributaries is the lymph duct that empties directly into a major blood vessel just beneath your left collar bone.[118,119,120] Your upper digestive tract takes advantage of this ultimate tributary to convey fat from your food directly to your blood – a different path than taken by dietary carbohydrate and protein, which are processed through your liver before gaining access to your systemic blood circulation.[121]

Except for the part-time job of moving fats, the role of the immune system's circulation is to send about molecules and cells that do the immune system's two jobs: recognizing what belongs and what doesn't belong, and doing something about things that do not belong in your body. Recognition depends in turn on two functions that are identical to what is supposed to happen in your central nervous system: perceiving the world around (and in) you, and remembering those perceptions. Perception and memory in your immune system take place below the conscious level. When your immune system is doing something about things that do not belong, the commotion may attract your attention in the form of generalized fatigue, fever, or chills, or localized itching, pain, redness, swelling, or heat. The latter symptoms are the cardinal indications of inflammation, which has microscopic features that differ between acute and chronic states.[122,123,124] Acute and chronic states of inflammation show up in the blood where the cellular components of the immune system travel during their recirculation to the tissues and then back again through the lymph ducts and lymph nodes that are continually kept up to date about the defensive needs of the body. Thus, a white blood count (WBC) enumerates the lymphocytes as a group along with other white blood cells (leukocytes) and can give a rough indication of the sorts of enemies (bacterial, viral, parasitic, or allergic) the body may be fighting at a given moment. A WBC may be quite helpful in sorting bacterial from viral causes of acute illness and may (thanks to an elevation in the number of a usually small minority of cells called eosinophils) alert us to certain parasites (mostly worms) and allergens. For the most part, however, a WBC is not much

SECTION TWO: MAKING A PLAN

help in driving decisions we make for children with autism unless they have other signs and symptoms suggestive of a chronic active infection that can diminish bone-marrow function.[125,126]

What immune system tests are helpful in driving decisions? The top of the list goes to measurement of immune globulins, the collective name of a group of sticky shapely protein molecules that are made by lymphocytes and circulate throughout the body and are delivered regularly to the moist internal surfaces of the body, particularly the digestive tract where more than half of the immune system's attention is focused.[127,128] Serum immune globulins are frequently abnormal in children with autism – but not nearly frequently or characteristically enough to make their measurement decisive in the diagnosis of autism. The measurement of the four (G,A,M,E) major immune globulins (Ig's) may be decisive in the following ways.

1. Low serum IgG may be accepted by a medical insurer as a criterion for reimbursement of treatment with intravenous immune globulins (IVIG). Some carriers demand evidence of documented bacterial infection to meet their criteria.

2. Deficient (not just a little low, but very low) IgA should be considered an exclusionary criterion for administering IVIG, which may cause complications in an IgA-deficient person.

3. High levels of IgE are a good indicator that allergy plays an important role in some aspect of a patient's problems. A low level of serum IgE is not disqualifying in regard to the allergy consideration, but a high level – relatively common in autistic children – should boost interest in finding a specific food, inhalant, dust, dander or mold that may be causing mischief.

4. As measured in quantitative immunoglobulin measurement *total* levels of IgM, the first antibody made when the immune system encounters a new substance, are not usually a helpful indicator in our children. Sometimes a different test measuring levels of IgM against a particular germ can be helpful in determining the timing of exposure to that germ.

The effectiveness of intravenous immune globulin (IVIG) was first reported by Sudhir Gupta, M.D., Ph.D., who is Professor of Medicine, University of California in Irvine. Dr. Gupta attended the first DAN! meeting and has since then been a major contributor to DAN! meetings and think tanks. He is one of the world's leading immunologists and has trained many of the rest of the world's leading immunologists. Here is a report by the mother of one of my patients, describing what happened after her son's first infusion. The benefits of subsequent infusions continue to accrue. Peter's response is not typical, but it shows why there is still a lot of enthusiasm for trying IVIG:

"Following the infusion Peter developed a fever of 104 the first night, resolved with Motrin. The ensuing nine days he was somnolent and cranky. He developed two to three watery, explosive stools daily and a remitting evening fever. Suddenly on the tenth day Peter emerged as a 'new boy.' He previously had no language and now is using appropriate language (i.e. 'Momma, I wanna, donwanna. No. shoe, Santa') and increasingly articulate babbling, on a daily basis. His eye contact improved dramatically. Previously he paid no attention to his cousin and now he initiates contact and play. He is now initiating hugs with his mom, where before he would only hug in response to his mom's approach. He is now having perfect poops for the first time in a long history of irritable bowel symptoms. His receptive language has taken a leap. He can be left ungated in rooms and will come when called and will walk with his mom without being held, whereas before he was wild."

The stickiness and shapeliness of immune globulins are related to the specific function of these molecules, which individually adhere to their targets. When immune globulins are made in response to the body's need to keep an inventory of all the molecules it encounters, each molecule of IgG, IgA, IgM and IgE (and another minor one, IgD) is crafted to form a shape that is complementary to the shape of its target. The pairing of the Ig with its target is very specific, but not so specific as to preclude cases of mistaken identity – the basis for aspects of allergy and autoimmunity. The specificity of immune pairing of globulin (antibody) with its target (antigen) forms the basis for tests for allergy and autoimmunity in autistic children, who have a high incidence of both problems. Such tests may help show – in groups of people, such as those with autism, asthma, diabetes, colitis, arthritis, or any other disease – the tendency in that group to have abnormally low or, usually, high levels of antibodies to particular environmental entities (food, mold, etc.) or tissue. If the antibodies are against molecules that make up part of your own tissue, they are called autoantibodies, which are normally present in small amounts as part of the body's inventory. Autoantibodies, when increased beyond a certain level, are either a marker or a cause of autoimmune disease.[129]

Tests for antibodies are valuable in research aimed at establishing the causes, mechanisms or complications of the groups of people just mentioned. In some cases, but not in autism, the presence of a particular antibody, or antibodies, is so closely associated with a particular disease as to be one (but usually not the sole) criterion for making the diagnosis. One example is significant changes in antibody levels to the bacteria, viruses, or parasites that cause infectious disease or their complications. For instance, a rise in antibodies against a particular strep germ (beta-hemolytic group A) goes with a strep infection and with its various autoimmune complications (rheumatic heart disease, glomerulonephritis, chorea, and PANDAS [pediatric autoimmune neuropsychiatric disorders associated with streptococcal infections]).[130,131,132] Another example involves Endomysial (IgA) and Reticulin Antibodies (IgA) which are highly predictive of celiac disease, the definition of which also includes a loss of the normal double velvet nap of the upper small intestine associated with gluten intolerance. Neither antibody is diagnostic of celiac disease or other problems related to gluten sensitivity in any given individual, and celiac disease is now known to be a spectrum with phenotypic variation.[133,134,135,136,137] Along with antibodies (IgG and IgA) to gluten (or gliadin), their presence in the serum of a large percentage of people whose health improves after gluten avoidance gives significance to research implicating gluten in many conditions.[138,139,140,141,142]

Many parents – to whom the idea of a gluten-free diet raises a mixture of doubt, fear, and anger that an already complicated situation could get more so – hope that a blood test would get them solidly on or off the hook. "If the test is normal, then we don't have to do the diet, but if the test is abnormal, then we can consider the diet with more confidence." Right? Not quite. Clearly, the correlation of such tests (and urine tests for gluten- and/or casein-derived peptides) with various manifestations of gluten sensitivity and with prediction of an eventual responsiveness to diet gives some value to such tests. The value is, however, very limited considering the stakes involved in a decision to dispense with a gluten-free diet. No test substitutes for a dietary trial to see if avoidance of a food will result in a therapeutic response that justifies the effort of avoiding that food. The preceding statement applies to all serum IgG and IgE antibody testing, the value of which is to provide a list of greater or lesser possibilities and to give some indication of the immune system's overall posture as regards antibody production. If, for example, a person's serum is reactive against many (say, more than a dozen) foods, then those data provide evidence that his or her immune system is overly sensitive. A strong implication of an overly reactive immune system can be made if more than two dozen foods provoke a reaction in the

(ELISA) test. Whether it is worth the money spent on such tests depends on your pocketbook and the stage of the investigative process. I believe that all immune testing other than quantitative serum immunoglobulins (G,A,M,E) at early stages is iffy. Sensitivity may often be the result of biochemical imbalance and may improve as the causes of that imbalance are addressed.

The "posture" I mentioned above is referred to as a TH1/TH2 imbalance, in which the TH2 side of the immune system (making antibodies against foods and bacteria) is too active and the TH1 activities of lymphocytes against viruses, fungi and cancer cells are weak. There is no single test for this balance, and the TH1/TH2 imbalances seen very commonly in autistic children are not unique to them.[143,144,145,146,147,148] Nevertheless, it would be helpful – though very expensive – to watch improvement in the indicator tests over the course of treatment. At the end of the day the child is the best lab, and no test trumps the significance of seeing clinical improvement or the lack thereof in response to therapy. Testing the TH1 side of the balance requires examination of a patient's immune cells – as opposed to the serum – which can be enumerated according to their role as killers, helpers and suppressors. These are the same cells that are monitored in patients with acquired immune deficiency syndrome (AIDS) and the trend in autistic children is toward immunodeficiency but to a very much milder degree. A full profile of cellular immunity may include, in addition to lymphocyte subsets, the effect of lymphocyte stimulation by a) Phytohemagglutinin, b) Conconavalin A, c) Pokeweed, d) Candida albicans, e) Tetanus toxoid, and f) Tuberculin. These tests are rarely of help in the management of children with autism.

DESENSITIZATION

The immune problems in autistic children suggest – and are evidenced by – a failure to respond appropriately to a variety of stimuli. These problems are generically no different from problems of perception and response to stimuli that our kids have on a global level. As such, the immunological problems are just part of a systematic problem in perception, memory, processing, and response. Desensitization refers to graduated exposure to stimuli resulting in tolerance. This process has immune counterparts to the sensory training that is so valuable in helping children overcome their tactile, auditory, visual and other sensitivities. Desensitization within the immune realm is conceptually no different, and may involve techniques that overlap with sensory training.

Allergy desensitization as done by medical doctors depends on a paradox that has been incorporated into practice over the past 100 years, at first against a tide of skepticism that put allergists at the fringes of the medical establishment. As a group, allergists have acquired professional respectability through research validating their methods, which have tended to stay within the narrow path to the high ground of proven science rather than covering the broad ground of empirical observation and practice. Thus, allergists tend to reject the idea that behavior has allergic causes except in clear association with allergic inflammation of the skin, respiratory tract and digestive tract, and only recently has delayed food allergy itself achieved a degree of recognition. Marvin Boris is a DAN! allergist/immunologist* who, over the past 30 years, has published a very valuable body of research showing the value of

---

* Board certification in Allergy and Immunology and Pediatrics does not completely define the practice of Dr. Boris and his Physician Assistant Allan Goldblatt. They continue to make discoveries in the whole range of immunological and biochemical areas within the DAN! model, making substantial contributions to its advancement.

allergy testing and treatment in individuals with attentional problems and, more recently, autism. When allergy evaluation by skin testing or blood testing is carried out by a skilled practitioner and is used as a basis for desensitization treatment, then such testing frequently leads to dramatic symptomatic improvement in children with classic allergic symptoms of stuffiness and itching as well as in children whose allergic manifestations are mostly behavioral or cognitive.

Immunization response

I referred previously to antibody testing as one way of indicating the presence of an infectious disease. What about immunizations, which are a way of evoking such a response without causing the natural disease? My experience indicates that many children with autism have abnormal responses to immunization. These abnormalities include failure of the immunization to "take" (that is, to produce the expected antibody response, ie, a missing titer to measles virus[149,150,151,152,153,154,155]), alterations of immunity due to the MMR vaccination,[156,157,158,159,160,161,162] elevated measles antibody levels after immunization with MMR,[163,164,165] and a worsening of autism following a second (booster) MMR.[166] Parents who see the connection between immunization and their child's problem are naturally guarded about following the recommended and often obligatory immunization schedule imposed by public health regulations referred to earlier. DAN! physicians as a group are strong advocates of immunization as a matter of public health, but we feel that safety issues have been ignored in the pre- and post-marketing surveillance of vaccines, which are curiously exempt from safety checks required of all other drugs and medical devices. One of the safety issues that has not been adequately assessed is that of multiple simultaneous immunizations. Another is the potential toxicity of mercury, aluminum and other components of vaccines. And, for reasons related to glutathione and intra-cellular energy status, the vaccinating of sick or recently sick children merits concern and research.

As a matter of private health policy we feel that it is appropriate for children to have as few immunizations as necessary for their individual protection and, for the sake of that goal, to have antibody testing done as mentioned earlier in the example I gave about rubella testing. Thus, in a child who is a candidate for a booster shot, an exemption from that shot would be justified if the child has serum levels of antibodies evoked by the previous shot(s) for that antigen. A single blood draw can provide such evidence in a child who has already been immunized. If a child shows a failure to immunize after a normal course of shots against, say, DPT, then that information provides some evidence toward the diagnosis of an immune defect.[167] Although more research is needed, a clinician might be wise to consider the possibility that an autistic child with a missing titer may have an immune impairment whereby his or her response to a live-virus vaccine would be insufficient to suppress the virus properly.

Testing for antibodies to the antigens present in past immunizations is not part of the repertoire of most pediatricians. Many local or hospital laboratories are not accustomed to processing orders for such testing, so misunderstandings often give rise to a need for repeat blood draws. If you plan to do such testing, you may find it easier to use a large laboratory such as Quest, so provided here are the Quest codes for a panel of testing for most of the immunizations.

Request for Laboratory Services for: Please do antibody titers to:	
Antigen	Quest lab code
Poliovirus AB (Types 1, 2, 3) (neutralizing antibodies)	8540A
Diphtheria AB, Titer Endpt	10682X
Tetanus Antitoxoid AB	50922P
Pertussis AB (IGG, A, M)	7638X
H. Influenza type B (IGG)	112565P
Hepatitis B SA QL	109009W
Measles AB (IGG)	52449W
Mumps AB (IGG)	64766R
Rubella AB)IGG)	53348W
Varicella (IGG), EIA	54031E
Diagnostic code: Immune mechanism disorder 279.9	

Antibody titers are the way immunologists determine whether an immunization has "taken," so it is surprising that the policy of public health authorities in many states is to refuse to accept antibody titers as an exemption from further immunization. I believe that the inconsistencies and confusion that appear to infect vaccine policy are a reflection of years of indifference to the scientific details on the part of scientists participating in vaccine development, manufacture and distribution. Vaccine policy is strangely remote from the physicians who implement it. When I learned about vaccines in my training, I was relieved to know that "they" had figured out exactly what I, as a practicing pediatrician, should do. I was not much more than a vending machine dispensing an immunization package that was, of course, neither of my design nor of my making. I did not realize then, as most physicians do not know now, that no vaccine has ever been submitted to a safety study lasting more than three or four weeks. Studies of the combination of vaccines to be given in one visit – I hear of children being given nine different vaccines at one time – are non-existent.

Immunization is one of the best inventions of modern medicine, yet the vending-machine phenomenon represents one of the worst trends in modern medicine: industrialization that distances the people who decide from those who implement. When the mercury exposure of babies as a result of routine immunizations was tallied and found to be enormously excessive, members of the responsible agency said, in effect, "Gee, we didn't think about that."ABor would have I, had I still been giving immunizations in the 1990s. Implementation of vaccine policy depends on the public trust, which has been betrayed with respect to the issue of thimerosal in vaccines as well as with respect to the combined measles, mumps and rubella vaccine, the safety studies for which revealed a danger that was ignored.[168,169,170,171] Dr. Pangborn discusses the way these two very different issues – toxicity of mercury and the role of the measles virus – come together in the autism epidemic. Here I would like to refer you to Stephanie Cave's book, *What Your Doctor May Not Tell You About Children's Vaccinations* (Warner Books, NY 2001), and present an outline of how the information derived from immunization titers can be put into effect.

The results of a panel of immunization titers in a child who has had some or all of his or her shots will show whether the serum levels of antibodies indicate protective levels of immunity against each of the infectious diseases tested. If protective levels of antibodies exist against the germ or virus that causes one of these diseases, it makes no sense to re-immunize that child against that germ or virus. If your doctor insists that the levels require "boosting," then you should remember that boosting really refers to the percentage in a group of children who get a "take" from a shot. Naturally, each individual in a group who is changed from not-immune to immune was "boosted," but boosting already-protected children is a different matter. There is no scientific support for such a practice, which is only assumed to be safe, without supportive evidence. The authoritative Red Book (2003 Report of the Committee on Infectious Diseases, published by the American Academy of Pediatrics) states, without supportive evidence, that pediatric vaccines may be repeated in children who are already immune. The same committee says that all pediatric vaccines can be combined in one visit, and places no limit on the number. There are no long-term studies supportive of that recommendation.

What to do about immunizations:

1. Understand that immunization is valuable and should be undertaken in each child.

2. Recognize special circumstances – especially travel – that may alter priorities for immunization against infections that are prevalent in less developed parts of the world.

3. Recognize the reality that in many communities, pediatricians and family practitioners may refuse to take patients whose parents refuse immunization. This is a highly charged issue and may give rise to accusations of child abuse by physicians whose individual zeal on behalf of your child is reinforced by a collective professional revulsion against heresy. I referred earlier to the polarization of opinions in the medical field. We physicians spend a lot of our time out on a limb and in jeopardy. Self-confidence is required and tested by heavy decisions. Sometimes, when we are sure that we are on the side of the angels, this self-confidence can become heavy-handedness. In other words, take someone who routinely and confidently faces such serious questions as, "Doctor, are you really, really sure that my child's high fever, lethargy and vomiting are just a virus and not the first sign of meningitis?" and give him or her the gift of absolute confidence in a right decision: *you must immunize your child according to the schedule of the American Academy of Pediatrics*. Never mind the subtleties of polarized thinking about who makes the best decision for your child. Your doctor is persuaded that he or she must advocate for your child, and also probably suspects that you are a nut case and have been poisoned by the Internet. So tread lightly.

4. Decide on priorities based on the realities of your child's environment and its potential for exposure. That will depend on where you live and how much exposure your child has to people, especially children. Basic knowledge of pediatric infectious disease will help. Right now there is not any pool of wild polio virus in the US. Hemophilus influenza type B (the bacterial infection – nothing to do with influenza, the viral infection for which people get "flu shots"), on the other hand, is always around. H. flu type B (for which the Hib immunization is given) is the cause of a severe croup from which healthy kids can die on their way to the emergency room, as well as the cause of a form of meningitis that can produce permanent damage even when treated relatively promptly. Tetanus spores are in the soil everywhere, so you don't have to step on a nail in the barnyard to be exposed, and you will always be at risk of lockjaw from deep dirty wounds if you live unimmunized on Planet Earth. Tetanus shots, without diphtheria and pertussis, are only available in vaccines that still contain thimerosal, so you are currently blocked from the tetanus-only option. Whooping cough is still around and may be found in old people as well as the

very young, in whom it is a pretty scary disease. Diphtheria – sore throat from hell – is less prevalent, but a disease against which your child should be protected. I suggest to my patients that they get Hib immunization started first, slowly adding immunizations according to situation and by the schedules described in Dr. Cave's book. I recommend doing titers before repeating any immunizations.

Prevention

Immunization has always been synonymous with protection. It is a sad irony that we should now limit immunization to protect children from autism or its progression,[172] as well as other problems that have yet to be associated with immunization damage. The very notion that negligent implementation of public health policy has resulted in the decimation of a whole generation of children is so unthinkable that many scientists and policy makers are still unable to stop running from the notion long enough to consider "what if?" What if the flawed epidemiologic studies provide no real reassurance that mercury from vaccines and other mercury sources, along with other toxins, have played a causative role in the current epidemic of autism? If they heed the very persuasive biological evidence that has been published for the past couple of years, how would scientists and policy makers plan to stop the epidemic? It seems to me they would need to start by considering what would be the best plan for a single future child. That plan should embrace the biomedical issues that have come to our attention as a result of listening to parents and practitioners and researchers trying to take good care of children on the autism spectrum. At the moment, the following suggestions are driven by a combination of speculation and caution. They could be adopted as private health policy for one child, even if cost and compliance present obstacles to implementing these precautions as public health policy.

1. Evaluate the environment in which the baby's future mother will carry the baby. Mercury would be at the top of the list of things to consider, but all chemicals and heavy metals should be avoided.

2. Prospective mothers should have their silver-mercury dental amalgam replaced at least six months prior to pregnancy or, if amalgam is present at the beginning of pregnancy, it should not be disturbed during pregnancy and lactation.

3. Maternal diet should be nutritionally optimum and should avoid fish and other mercury sources.

4. As thiol testing becomes commercially available, the baby's blood should be tested for these compounds as well as for zinc and copper.

5. The baby should be protected from exposure to clothing with flame retardants that contain antimony compounds.

6. Immunization:

    a. Confirm that all vaccines are thimerosal-free.

    b. Use combined vaccines only when unavoidable, as in the case of DPaT.

    c. Schedule immunizations at intervals of at least eight weeks.

d. Check blood titers before re-immunizing, and do not revaccinate a child who has protective immunity.

   e. Immunize against measles, mumps, and rubella separately.

   f. Do not immunize a child who has been ill or had antibiotics within the previous four weeks.

   g. On the day before, day of, and day after immunization, give vitamin C, zinc and cod liver oil in age-appropriate doses, which might be 100 mg, 5 mg and ½ tsp in a baby and 1000 mg, 30 mg and two tsp in a five-year-old.

OTHER THERAPEUTIC OPTIONS

Immune therapies:

Oral immune globulins.

I mentioned intravenous immunoglobulins above. The same kind of material – the globulin fraction (antibodies) from pooled human serum – can be administered orally with a quite different intention than for its intravenous use or its administration as an intramuscular shot, where it may have direct anti-infective or preventive effects due to the role of borrowed antibodies from individuals who have immunity to measles, hepatitis, etc. Intravenous immune globulins are also used because they have been shown to have positive effects in various immune-mediated diseases. In the case of oral administration of globulins the target is the gut flora, which it appears to normalize. The recent publication of a formal study by Cindy Schneider, M.D., of oral immune globulins in autistic children provided validation for an approach that many of us have been using for the past few years. The product (Oralgam) used in Dr. Schneider's study is not yet commercially available. We have been using gamma globulin for intramuscular use (Bay Gam), withdrawing it from its vial with a syringe and administering it orally with good results. To maximize the survival of the immunoglobulins through the stomach, we give the child a dose of Pepcid 10mg AC chewable (OTC) about 2 hours before the dose and have him or her avoid eating afterward, so it ends up being easier to give it (mixed in a little juice or water) either before bed or mid-morning. Studies have shown that a large amount does make it intact through the GI tract, but that blocking stomach acid with the Pepcid did improve this. Based on dosage recommendations coming from Dr. Schneider's research, a dose of Oralgam given at 420 mg/day for 8 weeks would be worth a try in children in whom restoration of normal gut flora has resisted other therapies. The positive effects seen in children in Dr. Schneider's study were statistically significant for both gastrointestinal and behavioral symptoms. A new study looking at the comparative effectiveness of other doses is underway.

Transfer factor and colostrum.

Colostrum is a secretion that precedes lactation. It is a sort of immunological gift from mother to child. It carries information regarding, among other things, the management of the gut flora that the baby is receiving from contact with its mother and other handlers. One might think that a "user's manual" designed for non-humans – such as calves - would not have much use for humans. There is a, however, a strong commonality among the flora of different animals. Bovine colostrum, or an extract from cow colostrum that concentrates a fraction called transfer factor, has positive effects in normalizing gut flora and other immunologically important functions in people of all ages.

High-dose vitamin A.

In a previous edition of this book I outlined the experience with high-dose vitamin A in treatment of acute measles infections in both undernourished and well-nourished children admitted to the hospital with potentially fatal complications of measles. The idea came after the findings of measles vaccine virus in the cerebrospinal fluid of autistic children. (ref: Bradstreet JJ, El Dahr J, O'Leary JJ, Sheils O, Anthony A, Wakefield AJ, Detection of Measles Virus Genomic RNA in Cerebrospinal Fluid in Children with Regressive Autism by TaqMan RT-PCR: A Report of Three Cases. *J. Am Physicians and Surgeons.* (2004)9:2, p. 38-44). The persistence of measles vaccine virus in children with autism had already been established by the work of Andrew Wakefield and his associates. Demonstration of virus in the central nervous system added new incentive to find a treatment that might suppress measles virus. The other measures we have discussed are aimed at improving the overall immune status of each child in many different ways that could possibly combat the abnormal persistence of a virus that does not linger in most children immunized with MMR but appears to have done so in most autistic children who have been studied. Could there be something more specifically anti-measles? There are no drugs against measles such as there are against, say, herpes or the influenza virus. However, well-conducted studies around the world have shown that 400,000 units of vitamin A administered orally on two consecutive days significant benefited children with acute measles. I suggested that perhaps a longer-term treatment with moderately high doses of vitamin A, such as I had learned to use in the treatment of teens and adults with acne, might be helpful in children suspected of having persistent measles infection. The benefits of this proposal did not outweigh the risk of causing vitamin A toxicity. Dr. Jaquelyn McCandless suggested sticking to the two-day treatment. This idea was in line with observations reported by Mary Megson, M.D., who had seen good results in children treated with vitamin A at ongoing low doses in the form of cod liver oil. The upshot of the story at the moment is that it appears prudent to administer two days worth (and ONLY two days worth) of vitamin A oil or vitamin A palmitate or micelized vitamin A in a dose of 200,000 to 400,000 IU per day. See if it makes a difference. Even though the dose seems gigantic, no adverse effects of this approach have been reported. A maintenance dose of vitamin A, as in ½ to 1 tsp of cod liver oil per day, would assure an adequate supply for general good health. It is doubtful that the vitamin A protocol that has emerged from the story just described has specific anti-measles activity, but the anecdotal support for its benefits in the behavior and health of autistic children justifies consideration of this protocol.

PPARs Agonists[1]

PPARs (peroxisomal proliferator activated receptors) are a class of regulatory protein molecules that operate inside of cells where one of their roles has to do with the modulation of inflammation. Recall that I previously characterized inflammation as a combination of redness, swelling, heat and pain such as you experience with a boil or a sore throat. It is, needless to say, a familiar and nearly universal factor in illnesses, including autism. Many illnesses and symptoms whose names end in "-itis" such as arthritis, dermatitis, pharyngitis, colitis, cystitis, conjunctivitis, and meningitis are familiar to us in the context of tissues that are afflicted with

---

[1] Agonist: a chemical substance capable of combining with a receptor on a cell and initiating a reaction or activity (Merriam Webster Online). In other words it is a chemical compound that "acts like" the one for which it is, then, an agonist, or the opposite of an antagonist.

some or all of the cardinal indications of inflammation. Other illnesses, such as cardiovascular disease, are just recently being recognized as being inflammatory in origin so that a wider view is developing concerning the role of the underlying chemistry of problems that are either florid or more subtle expressions of inflammation. Those of us who take care of children with autism have recognized for some time that inflammation is a feature of their immunological and clinical landscape, but only recently has research documented the chemical markers of inflammation in the brain of autistic children. A paper from Johns Hopkins, "Neuroglial Activation and Neuroinflammation in the Brain of Patients with Autism,"[173] published in early 2005, caught the attention of Allan Goldblatt, a very resourceful DAN! member who works with Marvin Boris. Allan had seen a paper[174] indicating that a PPARs agonist mediation could affect colitis. Other recent publications[175,176] further stimulated his thinking about the possible use of PPARs agonist medication for addressing the question of brain inflammation in autistic patients. He tried the medication, Actos (Pioglitazone HCl), for one of his autistic patients whose bowel inflammation had been unresponsive to other treatments. This patient and many subsequent patients of Allan Goldblatt and Marvin Boris have improved in all aspects of their gut and central nervous system problems, opening a new possibility for treatment. My own experience reflects theirs, with the majority of patients reporting improvement in symptoms with relatively few side effects, most of which are related to the tendency of the medication, which is ordinarily prescribed for type 2 diabetics, to lower blood sugar. It results in hunger, which may be manifested as crankiness and can be treated with food. Preliminary experience with this off-label use of a PPARs agonist suggests that it will find its way toward the top of the list of the treatment options for our children.

Every new treatment experiences an initial wave of enthusiasm which later attenuates to a lower sustained opinion as to its general effectiveness. Some such treatments, while they may remain dramatically effective for a small subset of children – and are therefore worth keeping in mind – do not hold up as mainstays among the most generally effective options. PPARs medications look like winners at the moment. Stay tuned.

Secretin

Secretin is a hormone used during upper gastrointestinal endoscopy. Intravenous infusion causes an immediate stimulation of pancreatic secretion into the small intestine, where it can be collected and analyzed.[177,178] Secretin's off-label use for the treatment of autism[179] received wide media attention, engendering a polarized reception on the part of parents of autistic children on the one hand, and a skeptical clinical and research community on the other. In the fall of 1998, Dr. Rimland and I attended a meeting at the National Institutes of Child Health and Development where experts from the National Institutes of Health, the Food and Drug Administration, and medical schools offered thoughts on how secretin might work and its potential safety in federally-sponsored studies to validate the initial claims of its efficacy. The experts were frank in expressing their lack of ideas as to whether it might work in autism by influencing the chemistry of the digestive tract, the immune system, or brain chemistry directly.

So far a few studies have been done showing that secretin doesn't work. However, the clinical effectiveness of secretin has become more credible with a meta-analysis of the earlier negative studies as reported by Walter Herlihy at the Autism Society of America Annual Meeting in July 2001. Also, a multicenter study, reported at the same meeting, gave further evidence of secretin's effectiveness in autistic children. A more decisive study failed to support claims of secretin's effectiveness in autism.[180] However, many studies have found a positive effect that some researchers call a placebo effect, even as secretin's role in brain function is increasingly documented[181,182,183,184,185,186,187,188,189,190,191]. Most physicians who have, like myself, used secretin in hundreds of children remain convinced that secretin is effective for some autistic children but are sobered by the mixed results of carefully designed studies. The only way to find out if secretin works for your child is to try it. The method with which I am familiar is intravenous infusion of a vial of Secrelux, manufactured by Goldham in Germany and available by prescription from Victoria Apoteke in Zurich, Switzerland (http://www.pharmaworld.com) or from compounding pharmacies in the United States. Other DAN! physicians and parents have tried daily doses of secretin by transdermal application in oil or DMSO. All such uses of secretin remain unapproved by the FDA. Repligen Corporation (http://www.repligen.com) holds the patent on the use of secretin (branded SecreFlo™ and used for pancreatic function tests) in autism and is currently pursuing research into its use for obsessive compulsive disorder. Although a recent study of secretin's use in severe schizophrenia failed to show a better effect than placebo, two other studies have demonstrated secretin's effectiveness in some schizophrenic individuals.[192,193,194]

Other options

Stay tuned for other options that are, as this book goes to press, experiencing a wave of interest among some DAN! practitioners and parents. Low-dose naltrexone (LDN) is one. I met its discoverer, Bernard Bihari, M.D., at the wedding reception of a mutual friend years ago and started using LDN as an immune stimulant. After learning of Dr. Bihari's studies showing positive changes in lymphocyte counts in patients with AIDS I found LDN effective in patients who had months of debility following mononucleosis infection and in other chronic viral infections. A viral shadow over the autism epidemic is cast by studies showing persistent measles vaccine virus in the lymph nodes of the digestive tract and spinal fluid of autistic children. LDN joins the other potentially anti-infective or "immune boosting" (I don't like that expression because the immune system is more complex than an elevator) interventions that I have mentioned. It has received a lot of attention recently as a result of Dr. Jaquelyn McCandless's reports on its efficacy (see McCandless J. Low-Dose Naltrexone for Immunomodulation: Clinical 8-Week Study, www.starvingbrains.com: Articles). My own experience with it over the past several years has not been as positive as I first expected. LDN is a safe treatment for a short-term trial – so keep in mind that every child is different and LDN does not have to work in most children to benefit some.

Conclusion

There is no conclusion. The search for effective biomedical treatments for children with autism and related problems is a work in progress. When you go to a doctor with just about any kind of problem you can expect to get answers that have been in place for a few years and are likely to stay in place for months or years to come. You can expect answers that have come from "above" – that is, from higher authorities as represented by the research establishment including the academic, governmental, and pharmaceutical scientists. We in the DAN! movement are now joined by some such resources and we have benefited from a growing body of research – such as the research on PPARS drugs – from outside and "above" our group. But much of what we have learned in the past decade about the biology, pathology and treatment of individuals on the autism spectrum has come up from "below." That is, it has arisen from the grassroots of a collaboration between parents and the clinicians and scientists who listen to them. This process continues, and will make parts of my section of this book obsolete within a year.

My insistence that the target of therapy is not "autism" but is the individual child will, however, remain fresh. So will the way of thinking about problem-solving that focuses on the two questions I posed earlier:

Is there something my child should get for which he or she has an unmet need?
Is there something my child needs to avoid or be rid of because it is toxic or allergenic?

I use those two questions to find my way back to the trail whenever I become baffled by the many tests and treatments that offer themselves as potentially helpful to a particular child. Then I go back to the details of the child's story and the seven sources of information that help guide us to a place where the view is clearer. Such a strategy will remain useful no matter how many new breakthroughs alter the current list of options.

This book is not a protocol. It was a big mistake back in 1995 to call the first pamphlet offering guidelines for laboratory testing a "protocol" with the implication of strict rules. Please do not think of or refer to this work as a protocol. Call it Pangborn, call it Baker, call it the "DAN Guide" or call it by its proper title, but don't call it the DAN! protocol! Thanks.

Final Words

As I usher you toward Dr. Pangborn's part of this book, I leave you with a few general points filtered from the previous pages.

- I remind myself and my patients at each point on our journey through the complex biochemistry and immunology of each child's situation that steps can be taken without full knowledge. Even if we know a hundred ways we may be able to help your child, we still just have to decide at each step what to do next.

- None of us who have been wrestling with the biomedical options for children caught in the epidemic of autism and related problems is smart enough to predict success from the next step chosen for each child.

- No lab test is good enough to predict success for any child when the step indicated by the lab test is taken.
- Your child is the ultimate expert and the best laboratory.

- Your intuition may be an efficient path from the facts to the solution.

- At the end of the day, the time to know if a given (safe) option is a good one is after you have tried it for a couple of weeks... sometimes longer.

- Knowing the facts, understanding some of the basics that Jon and I present to you in this book, will help you hone your judgment and elevate the collaboration from which thoughtful choices emerge in the relationship between clinicians and parents.

- Illness is a signal to change. Some changes, such as dietary changes, are so daunting that most parents and practitioners shun the very idea. Other changes, such as giving a pill, are relatively easy, but raise wavering doubts with increasing number of pills. Change itself is, however, the obstacle that keeps most people from pursuing biomedical choices.

SECTION TWO: MAKING A PLAN

The dominant forces in my profession have a firm notion that if people are sick, we should not burden them with choices or demands for change. Compliance is understood as a matter of "taking your medicine" which should not have to compete with other demands for alterations in diets, habits, or beliefs. Parents seeking and getting the best results tend to be the ones who are willing to try big changes.

- My profession has a deeply embedded belief that developmental problems are bad luck. The profession believes that individual parents should not look for answers. Practitioners who abet such a search tend to be viewed with disaffection.

- If the grownups believe that there is nothing that can be done – and not infrequently I have heard those word spoken by adults who don't realize that kids are listening – our children heed the negative force of that feeling.

- Our intention in this book is neither to give you answers nor even to present a complete menu of all your options, which will have changed within a few weeks of publication of this edition. Our intention is to present you with a way of thinking about problem-solving and to arm you with facts to fortify your intentions.

- Healing is a natural process toward which nature has a strong impulse. The first and sometimes the most powerful force toward promotion of healing is intention. Even children who seem to be completely inattentive have the ability to intuit your intentions as well as to comprehend your spoken and unspoken intentions.

- Find other parents who share your approach and they will help you maintain the best tools for your journey: hope and a sense of humor.

---

1. See http://www.drneubrander.com/page2.html

2. Nakano E et al. Hyperhomocystinemia in children with inflammatory bowel disease. *J Pediatr Gastroenterol Nutr.* 2003 Nov;37(5):586-90.

3. Doganci T, Bozkurt S. Celiac disease with various presentations. *Pediatr Int.* 2004 Dec;46(6):693-6.

4. Norman EJ. Urinary methylmalonic acid test may have greater value than the total homocysteine assay for screening elderly individuals for cobalamin deficiency. *Clin Chem.* 2004 Aug;50(8):1482-3.

5. Wolters M et al. Effect of multivitamin supplementation on the homocysteine and methylmalonic acid blood concentrations in women over the age of 60 years. *Eur J Nutr.* 2004 May 19;:1-10.

6. Solomon LR. Cobalamin-responsive disorders in the ambulatory care setting: unreliability of cobalamin, methylmalonic acid, and homocysteine testing. *Blood.* 2005 Feb 1;105(3):978-85.

7. Tabaqchali S. Abnormal intestinal flora: metabolic and clinical consequences. *Gastroenterol Jpn.* 1984 Aug;19(4):351-62.

8. Hill MJ. Intestinal flora and endogenous vitamin synthesis. *Eur J Cancer Prev.* 1997 Mar;6 Suppl 1:S43-5.

9. Lindenbaum J et al. Diagnosis of cobalamin deficiency: II. Relative sensitivities of serum cobalamin, methylmalonic acid, and total homocysteine concentrations. *Am J Hematol.* 1990 Jun;34(2):99-107.

10. Russell-Jones GJ, Alpers DH. Vitamin B12 transporters. *Pharm Biotechnol.* 1999;12:493-520.

11. James SJ, Cutler P, Melnyk S, Jernigan S, Janak L, Gaylor DW, Neubrander JA. Metabolic biomarkers of increased oxidative stress and impaired methylation capacity in children with autism. *Am J Clin Nutr.* 2004 Dec;80(6):1611-7.

12. Waly M et al. Activation of methionine synthase by insulin-like growth factor-1 and dopamine: a target for neurodevelopmental toxins and thimerosal. *Mol Psychiatry.* 2004 Apr;9(4):358-70.

13. Parent Ratings of the Behavioral Effects of Biomedical Interventions. Autism Research Institute http://www.autismwebsite.com/ari/form34q.html

14. McGeady SJ, Buckley RH. Depression of cell-mediated immunity in atopic eczema. *J Allergy Clin Immunol.* 1975 Nov;56(5):393-406.

15. Feuerman E, Alteras I. The prevalence of mycotic infections and the immunologic response in patients with housewives' eczema. *Mykosen.* 1976 Feb;19(2):51-4.

16. Periti P, Tonelli F. Preclinical and clinical pharmacology of biotherapeutic agents: Saccharomyces boulardii. *J Chemother.* 2001 Oct;13(5):473-93.

17. Czerucka D, Rampal P. Experimental effects of Saccharomyces boulardii on diarrheal pathogens. *Microbes Infect.* 2002 Jun;4(7):733-9.

18. Goodman, LS, Gillman, A. *The Pharmacological Basis of Therapeutics*, 4th Ed. Macmillan, 1965 p. 991.

19. Ambrose NS et al. The influence of single dose intravenous antibiotics on faecal flora and emergence of Clostridium difficile. *J Antimicrob Chemother.* 1985 Mar;15(3):319-26.

20. Shirakawa H et al. Antibiotic-induced vitamin K deficiency and the role of the presence of intestinal flora. *Int J Vitam Nutr Res.* 1990;60(3):245-51.

21. Bonnemaison E et al. Comparison of fecal flora following administration of two antibiotic protocols for suspected maternofetal infection. *Biol Neonate.* 2003;84(4):304-10.

22. Samonis G et al. Prospective study of the impact of broad-spectrum antibiotics on the yeast flora of the human gut. *Eur J Clin Microbiol Infect Dis.* 1994.

23. Sandler RH, Finegold SM, Bolte ER et al. Short-term benefit from oral vancomycin treatment of regressive-onset autism. *J Child Neurol.* 2000 Jul;15(7):429-35.

24. Sandler RH et al. Relief of psychiatric symptoms in a patient with Crohn's disease after metronidazole therapy. *Clin Infect Dis.* 2000 Jan;30(1):213-4.

25. *The Second Brain*. Michael Gershon, M.D., HarperCollins Publishers, 1998.

26. Cordain, L. *The Paleo Diet: Lose Weight and Get Healthy by Eating the Food You Were Designed to Eat*, John Wiley and Sons, Inc. Hoboken, NJ, 2002.

27. This dietary outline was compiled from material and users and contributors of www.peacanbread.com and published in *New Developments* Vol 9 No 1 of, Developmental Delay Resources, 4401 East West Highway, Suite 207, Bethesda, MD 20814, devdelay@mindspring,com, www.devdelay.org

28. Peraaho M et al. Effect of an oats-containing gluten-free diet on symptoms and quality of life in coeliac disease. A randomized study. *Scand J Gastroenterol.* 2004 Jan;39(1):27-31.

29. Hogberg L et al. Oats to children with newly diagnosed coeliac disease: a randomised double blind study. *Gut.* 2004 May;53(5):649-54.

SECTION TWO: MAKING A PLAN

30. Knivsberg AM, Reichelt KL, Nodland M. Reports on dietary intervention in autistic disorders. *Nutr Neurosci.* 2001;4(1):25-37.

31. Parent Ratings of the Behavioral Effects of Biomedical Interventions. Autism Research Institute http://www.autismwebsite.com/ari/form34q.html

32. Chin RL et al. Celiac neuropathy. *Neurology.* 2003 May 27;60(10):1581-5.

33. Chin RL, Latov N. Peripheral Neuropathy and Celiac Disease. *Curr Treat Options Neurol.* 2005 7(1):43-48.

34. Abele M et al. Prevalence of antigliadin antibodies in ataxia patients. *Neurology.* 2003 May 27;60(10):1674-5.

35. Pengiran Tengah CD et al. Multiple sclerosis and occult gluten sensitivity. *Neurology.* 2004 Jun 22;62(12):2326-7.

36. Murray JA. The widening spectrum of celiac disease. *Am J Clin Nutr.* 1999 Mar;69(3):354-65.

37. Cronin CC, Shanahan F. Exploring the iceberg–the spectrum of celiac disease. *Am J Gastroenterol.* 2003 Mar;98(3):518-20.

38. *The Second Brain.* Michael Gershon, M.D., HarperCollins Publishers, 1998.

39. See cites 31-5.

40. Fleischer B et al. Molecular associations required for signalling via dipeptidyl peptidase IV (CD26). *Adv Exp Med Biol.* 1997;421:117-25.

41. Mentlein R. Dipeptidyl-peptidase IV (CD26)–role in the inactivation of regulatory peptides. *Regul Pept.* 1999 Nov 30;85(1):9-24.

42. Fan H et al. Dipeptidyl peptidase IV/CD26 in T cell activation, cytokine secretion and immunoglobulin production. *Adv Exp Med Biol.* 2003;524:165-74.

43. Aytac U, Dang NH. CD26/dipeptidyl peptidase IV: a regulator of immune function and a potential molecular target for therapy. *Curr Drug Targets Immune Endocr Metabol Disord.* 2004 Mar;4(1):11-8.

44. Ibid.

45. Vojdani A et al. Heat shock protein and gliadin peptide promote development of peptidase antibodies in children with autism and patients with autoimmune disease. *Clin Diagn Lab Immunol.* 2004 May;11(3):515-24.

46. Dewar D et al. The pathogenesis of coeliac disease. *Int J Biochem Cell Biol.* 2004 Jan;36(1):17-24.

47. Reif S, Lerner A. Tissue transglutaminase–the key player in celiac disease: a review. *Autoimmun Rev.* 2004 Jan;3(1):40-5.

48. Duggan JM. Coeliac disease: the great imitator. *Med J Aust.* 2004 May 17;180(10):524-6.

49. Accomando S, Cataldo F. The global village of celiac disease. *Dig Liver Dis.* 2004 Jul;36(7):492-8. "In the last years our knowledge on epidemiology of celiac disease has increased: there is a wide spectrum of its clinical presentation (classical, atypical, silent and latent forms of celiac disease), and of its pathological mucosal intestinal features, which range from early and mild pictures to severe villous atrophy (Marsh stages)."

50. Hill ID et al. Guideline for the diagnosis and treatment of celiac disease in children: recommendations of the North American Society for Pediatric Gastroenterology, Hepatology and Nutrition. *J Pediatr Gastroenterol Nutr.* 2005 Jan;40(1):1-19.

51. Tuckova L et al. Molecular mimicry as a possible cause of autoimmune reactions in celiac disease? Antibodies to gliadin cross-react with epitopes on enterocytes. *Clin Immunol Immunopathol.* 1995 Feb;74(2):170-6.

52. Barbeau WE et al. Is celiac disease due to molecular mimicry between gliadin peptide-HLA class II molecule-T cell interactions and those of some unidentified superantigen? *Mol Immunol.* 1997 May;34(7):535-41.

53. Natter S et al. IgA cross-reactivity between a nuclear autoantigen and wheat proteins suggests molecular mimicry as a possible pathomechanism in celiac disease. *Eur J Immunol.* 2001 31(3):918-28.

54. Shahbazkhani B et al. Coeliac disease presenting with symptoms of irritable bowel syndrome. *Aliment Pharmacol Ther.* 2003 Jul 15;18(2):231-5.

55. Israngkun PP et al. Potential biochemical markers for infantile autism. *Neurochem Pathol.* 1986 Aug;5(1):51-70.

56. Knivsberg AM et al. A randomised, controlled study of dietary intervention in autistic syndromes. *Nutr Neurosci.* 2002 Sep;5(4):251-61.

57. Reichelt KL, Knivsberg AM. Can the pathophysiology of autism be explained by the nature of the discovered urine peptides? *Nutr Neurosci.* 2003 Feb;6(1):19-28.

58. White JF. Intestinal pathophysiology in autism. *Exp Biol Med* (Maywood). 2003 Jun;228(6):639-49.

59. Fukudome S et al. Release of opioid peptides, gluten exorphins by the action of pancreatic elastase. *FEBS Lett.* 1997 Aug 4;412(3):475-9.

60. Negri L et al. Glycodermorphins: opioid peptides with potent and prolonged analgesic activity and enhanced blood-brain barrier penetration. *Br J Pharmacol.* 1998 Aug;124(7):1516-22.

61. Meisel H, FitzGerald RJ. Opioid peptides encrypted in intact milk protein sequences. *Br J Nutr.* 2000 Nov;84 Suppl 1:S27-31.

62. Okada Y et al. Endomorphins and related opioid peptides. *Vitam Horm.* 2002;65:257-79.

63. Fields H. State-dependent opioid control of pain. *Nat Rev Neurosci.* 2004 Jul;5(7):565-75.

64. Sim MG et al. Acute pain and opioid seeking behaviour. *Aust Fam Physician.* 2004 33(12):1009-12.

65. Hole K et al. A peptide-containing fraction in the urine of schizophrenic patients which stimulates opiate receptors and inhibits dopamine uptake. *Neuroscience.* 1979;4(12):1883-93.

66. Knivsber AM et al. Reports on dietary intervention in autistic disorders. *Nutr Neurosci.* 2001;4(1):25-37.

67. Iyngkaran N, Robinson MJ, Sumithran E, Lam SK, Puthucheary SD, Yadav M. Cows' milk protein-sensitive enteropathy. An important factor in prolonging diarrhoea of acute infective enteritis in early infancy. *Arch Dis Child.* 1978 Feb;53(2):150-3.

68. Iyngkaran N et al. Intestinal brush border peptidases in cow's milk protein-sensitive enteropathy. *Acta Paediatr Scand.* 1991 May;80(5):549-50.

69. Iyngkaran N et al. Causative effect of cow's milk protein and soy protein on progressive small bowel mucosal damage. *J Gastroenterol Hepatol.* 1989 Mar-Apr;4(2):127-36.

70. Jakobsson I, Lindberg T. Cow's milk as a cause of infantile colic in breast-fed infants. *Lancet.* 1978 Aug 26;2(8087):437-9.

SECTION TWO: MAKING A PLAN

71. Heymann E, Mentlein R. Complementary action of dipeptidyl peptidase IV and aminopeptidase M in the digestion of beta-casein. *J Dairy Res.* 1986 May;53(2):229-36.

72. Reichelt KL et al. Biologically active peptide-containing fractions in schizophrenia and childhood autism. *Adv Biochem Psychopharmacol.* 1981;28:627-43.

73. Reichelt KL, Knivsberg AM. Can the pathophysiology of autism be explained by the nature of the discovered urine peptides? *Nutr Neurosci.* 2003 Feb;6(1):19-28.

74. Seroussi, K. *Unraveling the Mystery of Autism and Pervasive Developmental Disorder: A Mother's Story of Research & Recovery*, Simon and Schuster, New York, 2002.

75. For information about attending a DAN! meeting go to http://www.danconference.com

76. Bahna SL. Cow's milk allergy versus cow milk intolerance. *Ann Allergy Asthma Immunol.* 2002 Dec;89(6 Suppl 1):56-60.

77. Magazzu G, Scoglio R. Gastrointestinal manifestations of cow's milk allergy. *Ann Allergy Asthma Immunol.* 2002 Dec;89(6 Suppl 1):65-8.

78. Wal JM. Bovine milk allergenicity. *Ann Allergy Asthma Immunol.* 2004 Nov;93(5 Suppl 3):S2-11.

79. Hill DJ et al. The spectrum of cow's milk allergy in childhood. Clinical, gastroenterological and immunological studies. *Acta Paediatr Scand.* 1979 Nov;68(6):847-52.

80. Hill DJ et al. Cow milk allergy within the spectrum of atopic disorders. *Clin Exp Allergy.* 1994 Dec;24(12):1137-43.

81. Hill DJ, Hosking CS. The cow milk allergy complex: overlapping disease profiles in infancy. *Eur J Clin Nutr.* 1995 Sep;49 Suppl 1:S1-12.

82. Sinden AA, Sutphen JL. Dietary treatment of lactose intolerance in infants and children. *J Am Diet Assoc.* 1991 Dec;91(12):1567-71.

83. Villako K, Maaroos H. Clinical picture of hypolactasia and lactose intolerance. *Scand J Gastroenterol Suppl.* 1994;202:36-54.

84. Mishkin S. Dairy sensitivity, lactose malabsorption, and elimination diets in inflammatory bowel disease. *Am J Clin Nutr.* 1997 Feb;65(2):564-7.

85. Vesa TH et al. Lactose intolerance. *J Am Coll Nutr.* 2000 Apr;19(2 Suppl):165S-175S.

86. Bockman DE, Kirby ML. Neural crest interactions in the development of the immune system. *J Immunol.* 1985 Aug;135(2 Suppl):766s-768s.

87. Kurtz J. Memory in the innate and adaptive immune systems. *Microbes Infect.* 2004 Dec;6(15):1410-7.

88. Halpern GM, Scott JR. Non-IgE antibody mediated mechanisms in food allergy. *Ann Allergy.* 1987 Jan;58(1):14-27.

89. Savilahti E. Food-induced malabsorption syndromes. *J Pediatr Gastroenterol Nutr.* 2000;30 Suppl:S61-6.

90. Zar S et al. Food hypersensitivity and irritable bowel syndrome. *Aliment Pharmacol Ther.* 2001 Apr;15(4):439-49.

91. Hamilton RG, Franklin Adkinson N Jr. In vitro assays for the diagnosis of IgE-mediated disorders. *J Allergy Clin Immunol.* 2004 Aug;114(2):213-25; quiz 226.

92. Nambudripad's Allergy Elimination Treatment. See www.naet.com.

93. See www.bioset-institute.com.

94. See www.polaritytherapy.org.

95. Waly M et al. Activation of methionine synthase by insulin-like growth factor-1 and dopamine: a target for neurodevelopmental toxins and thimerosal. *Mol Psychiatry.* 2004 Apr;9(4):358-70.

96. Muller M et al. Inhibition of the human erythrocytic glutathione-S-transferase T1 (GST T1) by thimerosal. *Int J Hyg Environ Health.* 2001 Jul;203(5-6):479-81.

97. Westphal GA et al. Thimerosal induces micronuclei in the cytochalasin B block micronucleus test with human lymphocytes. *Arch Toxicol.* 2003 Jan;77(1):50-5.

98. Hoshi T, Heinemann S. Regulation of cell function by methionine oxidation and reduction. *J Physiol.* 2001 Feb 15;531(Pt 1):1-11.

99. Levine RL et al. Oxidation of methionine in proteins: roles in antioxidant defense and cellular regulation. *IUBMB Life.* 2000 Oct-Nov;50(4-5):301-7.

100. Miller AL. The methionine-homocysteine cycle and its effects on cognitive diseases. *Altern Med Rev.* 2003 Feb;8(1):7-19.

101. Bernard S, Enayati A, Redwood L, Roger H, Binstock T. Autism: a novel form of mercury poisoning. *Med Hypotheses.* 2001 Apr;56(4):462-71.

102. Ibid.

103. Holmes A et al. OPEN TRIAL OF CHELATION WITH MES0-2,3-DIMERCAPTO SUCCINIC ACID (DMSA) AND LIPOIC ACID (LA) IN CHILDREN WITH AUTISM. As submitted to IMFAR, June 2, 2001.

"Over 400 patients with autism are currently undergoing treatment for removal of heavy metals. Patients are treated with DMSA alone at doses of 10 mg/kg/dose 3 times a day for 3 days in a row (shorter duration than lead protocol to decrease side effects) with 11 days 'off' to allow metals to re-equilibrate. After at least 2 rounds of DMSA alone, the thiol antioxidant lipoic acid (hypothesized to aid in removal of heavy metals across the BBB) is added to each dose of DMSA at 2-3mg/kg/dose. In general, noticeable improvements in language, self-help skills, interaction, and core autistic features are not seen until the patient has been on DMSA with LA for 2-3 months.

"Of patients who have been on DMSA/LA for at least 4 months, these results have been noted on general global assessment by parents, teachers, and MDs: age 1-5yrs(n=40): marked improvement 35%, moderate 39%, slight 15%, none 11%; age 6-12yrs (n=25): marked 4%, moderate 28%, slight 52%, none 16%; age 13-17 (n=16): moderate 6%, slight 68%, none 26%; age 18+ (n=4): slight 25%, none 75%. For example, a boy 5yr 5mo scored in the average range on a one word expressive vocabulary test 10/00 and at age equivalent 8yr 2mo in 3/01 with no change in education or medication other than starting DMSA/LA.

"The majority of children excrete mercury, lead, and other metals, suggesting that there may be a generalized problem with metal metabolism. Side effects include transient increases in hyperactivity, self-stimulatory behavior, and loose stools. Younger children in particular respond well to this therapy with significant improvement in function."

104. DMSA Chelation efficacy PPT presentation by Jane El-Dahr, M.D. http://216.117.159.91/powerpoint/dan2002/El-Dahr.htm

105. Lonsdale D, Shamberger RJ, Audhya T. Treatment of autism spectrum children with thiamine tetrahydrofurfuryl disulfide: a pilot study. *Neuro Endocrinol Lett.* 2002

SECTION TWO: MAKING A PLAN

106. 2005 ARI Mercury Detoxification Position Paper by Jim Adams, Ph.D. (See the most current version of this evolving document at www.AutismMercuryDetox.com).

107. Baker, SM. *Detoxification and Healing.* McGraw Hill, Chicago, 2002.

108. Goldwater, LJ. "The birth of Mercaptan." *Arch. Environmental Health* 11 (4) 597, 1965.

109. Baker, SM. Detoxification: A Costly Synthetic System. *Integrative Medicine*, 3:5 October-November 2004 p. 10.

110. Baker, SM, Pangborn, J, Deth, R, Owens, S, Londsale, D. and Haley, B. The Chemistry of Autism, presented at the Autism Research Institute's Defeat Autism Now! Conference, Philadelphia, PA, May 15-18, 2003. Copies can be obtained from http://www.autism.com/ari.

111. Waly M et al. Activation of methionine synthase by insulin-like growth factor-1 and dopamine: a target for neurodevelopmental toxins and thimerosal. *Mol Psychiatry.* 2004 Apr;9(4):358-70

112. Lonsdale D. Hypothesis and case reports: possible thiamin deficiency. *J Am Coll Nutr.* 1990 Feb;9(1):13-7.

113. Lonsdale D, Shamberger RJ, Audhya T. Treatment of autism spectrum children with thiamine tetrahydrofurfuryl disulfide: a pilot study. *Neuro Endocrinol Lett.* 2002 Aug;23(4):303-8.

114. Lonsdale D. Thiamine tetrahydrofurfuryl disulfide: a little known therapeutic agent. *Med Sci Monit.* 2004 10(9):RA199-203.

115. Den Otter W. Immune surveillance and natural resistance: an evaluation. *Cancer Immunol Immunother.* 1986;21(2):85-92.

116. Kupper TS, Fuhlbrigge RC. Immune surveillance in the skin: mechanisms and clinical consequences. *Nat Rev Immunol.* 2004 Mar;4(3):211-22.

117. Minchinton RM et al. The body as fortress: innate immune surveillance. *Vox Sang.* 2004 Jul;87 Suppl1:30-4.

118. *How the Immune System Works*, 2nd Edition. L. M. Sompayrac. Blackwell Publishing, 2003.

119. *Cellular and Molecular Immunology.* Abul K. Abbas, Andrew H. Lichtman, Jordan S. Pober. Elsevier Science 2003.

120. *Immunobiology: The Immune System in Health and Disease* with CD-ROM. Charles Janeway, Paul Travers, Mark Walport, Mark Shlomchik. Taylor & Francis, Inc. 2004.

121. *Textbook of Gastroenterology*, 4th edition.. Tadataka Yamada MD et al. Lippincott Williams & Wilkins 2003.

122. Hilger RA et al. Interactions of cytokines and lipid mediators in acute and chronic inflammation. *Int Arch Allergy Immunol.* 1995 May-Jun;107(1-3):383-4.

123. Feghali CA, Wright TM. Cytokines in acute and chronic inflammation. *Front Biosci.* 1997 Jan 01;2:d12-26.

124. Cuzzocrea S, Reiter RJ. Pharmacological actions of melatonin in acute and chronic inflammation. *Curr Top Med Chem.* 2002 Feb;2(2):153-65.

125. Binstock T. Intra-monocyte pathogens delineate autism subgroups. *Med Hypotheses.* 2001 Apr;56(4):523-31.

126. Caruso JM et al. Persistent preceding focal neurologic deficits in children with chronic Epstein-Barr virus encephalitis. *J Child Neurol.* 2000 Dec;15(12):791-6.

127. Finlayson JS. Immune globulins. *Semin Thromb Hemost.* 1979;6(1):44-74.

128. Brown WR. Relationships between immunoglobulins and the intestinal epithelium. *Gastroenterology.* 1978 Jul;75(1):129-38.

129. See cites 10-11.

130. Chmelik E et al. Varied presentation of PANDAS: a case series. *Clin Pediatr* (Phila). 2004 May;43(4):379-82.

131. Snider LA, Swedo SE. PANDAS: current status and directions for research. *Mol Psychiatry.* 2004 Oct;9(10):900-7.

132. March JS. Pediatric Autoimmune Neuropsychiatric Disorders Associated With Streptococcal Infection (PANDAS): implications for clinical practice. *Arch Pediatr Adolesc Med.* 2004 Sep;158(9):927-9.

133. Frick TJ, Olsen WA. Celiac disease and the spectrum of gluten sensitivity. *Gastroenterologist.* 1994 Dec;2(4):285-92.

134. Catassi C, Fabiani E. The spectrum of coeliac disease in children. *Baillieres Clin Gastroenterol.* 1997 Sep;11(3):485-507.

135. Murray JA. The widening spectrum of celiac disease. *Am J Clin Nutr.* 1999 Mar;69(3):354-65.

136. Jevon GP et al. Spectrum of gastritis in celiac disease in childhood. *Pediatr Dev Pathol.* 1999 May-Jun;2(3):221-6.

137. da Rosa Utiyama SR et al. Spectrum of autoantibodies in celiac patients and relatives. *Dig Dis Sci.* 2001 46(12):2624-30.

138. Pellecchia MT et al. Cerebellar ataxia associated with subclinical celiac disease responding to gluten-free diet. *Neurology.* 1999 Oct 22;53(7):1606-8.

139. Hadjivassiliou M et al. Headache and CNS white matter abnormalities associated with gluten sensitivity. *Neurology.* 2001 Feb 13;56(3):385-8.

140. Poon E, Nixon R. Cutaneous spectrum of coeliac disease. *Australas J Dermatol.* 2001 May;42(2):136-8.

141. Pengiran Tengah CD et al. Multiple sclerosis and occult gluten sensitivity. *Neurology.* 2004 Jun 22;62(12):2326-7.

142. Chin RL, Latov N. Peripheral Neuropathy and Celiac Disease. *Curr Treat Options Neurol.* 2005 Jan;7(1):43-48.

143. Warren RP et al. Deficiency of suppressor-inducer (CD4+CD45RA+) T cells in autism. *Immunol Invest.* 1990 Jun;19(3):245-51.

144. Ibid.

145. Scifo R et al. Opioid-immune interactions in autism: behavioral and immunological assessment during a double-blind treatment with naltrexone. *Ann Ist Super Sanita.* 1996;32(3):351-9.

146. Gupta S et al. Th1- and Th2-like cytokines in CD4+ and CD8+ T cells in autism. *J Neuroimmunol.* 1998 85(1):106-9.

147. Romagnani S. Immunologic influences on allergy and the TH1/TH2 balance. *J Allergy Clin Immunol.* 2004 113(3):395-400.

SECTION TWO: MAKING A PLAN

148. Moss RB et al. Th1/Th2 cells in inflammatory disease states: therapeutic implications. *Expert Opin Biol Ther.* 2004 Dec;4(12):1887-96.

149. Poland GA et al. The association between HLA class I alleles and measles vaccine-induced antibody response: evidence of a significant association. *Vaccine.* 1998 Nov;16(19):1869-71.

150. Poland GA. Immunogenetic mechanisms of antibody response to measles vaccine: the role of the HLA genes. *Vaccine.* 1999 Mar 26;17(13-14):1719-25.

151. St Sauver JL et al. Associations between human leukocyte antigen homozygosity and antibody levels to measles vaccine. *J Infect Dis.* 2002 Jun 1;185(11):1545-9. Epub 2002 May 09.

152. Jacobson RM, Poland GA, Vierkant RA, Pankratz VS, Schaid DJ, Jacobsen SJ, Sauver JS, Moore SB. The association of class I HLA alleles and antibody levels after a single dose of measles vaccine. *Hum Immunol.* 2003 Jan;64(1):103-9.

153. Van Loveren H, Van Amsterdam JG, Vandebriel RJ, Kimman TG, Rumke HC, Steerenberg PS, Vos JG. Vaccine-induced antibody responses as parameters of the influence of endogenous and environmental factors. *Environ Health Perspect.* 2001 Aug;109(8):757-64.

154. Newport MJ et al. Genetic regulation of immune responses to vaccines in early life. *Genes Immun.* 2004 Mar;5(2):122-9.

155. Ovsyannikova IG et al. Variation in vaccine response in normal populations. *Pharmacogenomics.* 2004 Jun;5(4):417-27.

156. Auwaerter PG et al. Changes within T cell receptor V beta subsets in infants following measles vaccination. *Clin Immunol Immunopathol.* 1996 May;79(2):163-70.

157. Hussey GD et al. The effect of Edmonston-Zagreb and Schwarz measles vaccines on immune response in infants. *J Infect Dis.* 1996 Jun;173(6):1320-6.

158. Pabst HF et al. Differential modulation of the immune response by breast- or formula-feeding of infants. *Acta Paediatr.* 1997 Dec;86(12):1291-7.

159. Pabst HF et al. Kinetics of immunologic responses after primary MMR vaccination. *Vaccine.* 1997 Jan;15(1):10-4.

160. Valsamakis A et al. Altered virulence of vaccine strains of measles virus after prolonged replication in human tissue. *J Virol.* 1999 Oct; 73(10): 8791-7.

161. Valsamakis A, Kaneshima H, Griffin DE. Strains of measles vaccine differ in their ability to replicate in an damage human thymus. *J Infect Dis.* 2001 Feb 1; 183(3): 498-502.

162. Rager-Zisman B et al. The effect of measles-mumps-rubella (MMR) immunization on the immune responses of previously immunized primary school children. *Vaccine.* 2003 Jun 2;21(19-20):2580-8.

163. Singh VK et al. Serological association of measles virus and human herpesvirus-6 with brain autoantibodies in autism. *Clin Immunol Immunopathol.* 1998 Oct;89(1):105-8.

164. Singh VK et al. Abnormal measles-mumps-rubella antibodies and CNS autoimmunity in children with autism. *J Biomed Sci.* 2002 Jul-Aug;9(4):359-64.

165. Singh VK, Jensen RL. Elevated levels of measles antibodies in children with autism. *Pediatr Neurol.* 2003 28(4):292-4.

166. Using pre- and post-MMR growth charts, Andrew J. Wakefield, M.D., has found that some autistic children not only regressed into autism following their initial MMR but also experienced a stunting of growth velocity in the months after the MMR. Dr. Wakefield presented this information to the Institute

of Medicine and was encouraged to determine if a similar MMR-induced impairment of growth velocity occurred following such children's MMR booster. Further evaluation of the affected children's growth charts indicated that a second growth inhibition occurred following the MMR booster. Dr. Wakefield has also presented a summary of this material at a DAN! conference.

167. See sites 40-46.

168. Yazbak FE. Measles, mumps, and rubella (MMR) vaccine and autism. MMR cannot be exonerated without explaining increased incidence of autism. *BMJ.* 2001 Jul 21;323(7305):163-4.

169. Geier MR, Geier DA. Neurodevelopmental disorders after thimerosal-containing vaccines: a brief communication. *Exp Biol Med* (Maywood). 2003 Jun;228(6):660-4.

170. Geier DA, Geier MR. An assessment of the impact of thimerosal on childhood neurodevelopmental disorders. *Pediatr Rehabil.* 2003 Apr-Jun;6(2):97-102.

171. Blaxill M, Safeminds, 2004. CDC thimerosal findings in 1999 – subsequent data dilution – synopsis........http://www.safeminds.org/Generation%20Zero%20Syn.pdf – full analysis.......http://www.safeminds.org/Generation%20Zero%20Pres.pdf

172. See cite 57.

173. Vargas DL, Nascimbene C, Krishnan C, Zimmerman AW, Pardo CA. Neuroglial activation and neuroinflammation in the brain of patients with autism. *Ann Neurol* 2005 Jan;57(1):67-81.

174. Chinyu G, Su, Xiaoming Wen, Shannon T. Bailey, Wen Jiang, Shamina M. Rangwala, Sue A. Keilbaugh, Anne Flanigan, Sreekant Murthy, Mitchell A. Lazar and Gary D. Wu, A novel therapy for colitis utilizing PPAR- ligands to inhibit the epithelial inflammatory response,*J Clin Invest*, August 1999, Volume 104, Number 4, 383-389).

175. SN Murthy, DF Obregon, NN Chattergoon, NA Fonseca, D Mondal, JB Dunne, JG Diez, JR Jeter, PJ Kadowitz, KC Agrawal, DB McNamara, and VA Fonseca, Rosiglitazone reduces serum homocysteine levels, smooth muscle proliferation, and intimal hyperplasia in Sprague-Dawley rats fed a high methionine diet. *Metabolism* 1 May 2005; 54(5):645.

176. Storer PD, Xu J, Chavis J, Drew PD. Peroxisome proliferator-activated receptor-gamma agonists inhibit the activation of microglia and astrocytes: implications for multiple sclerosis. *J Neuroimmunol.* 2005 Apr; 161(1-2):113-22.

177. Hacki WH. Secretin. *Clin Gastroenterol.* 1980 Sep;9(3):609-32.

178. Chey WY, Chang TM. Secretin, 100 years later. *J Gastroenterol.* 2003;38(11):1025-35.

179. Horvath K et al. Improved social and language skills after secretin administration in patients with autistic spectrum disorders. *J Assoc Acad Minor Phys.* 1998;9(1):9-15.

180. Sturmey P. Secretin is an ineffective treatment for pervasive developmental disabilities: a review of 15 double-blind randomized controlled trials. *Res Dev Disabil.* 2005 Jan-Feb;26(1):87-97.

181. Horvath K et al. Gastrointestinal abnormalities in children with autistic disorder. *J Pediatr.* 1999 135(5):559-63.

182. Sandler AD et al. Lack of benefit of a single dose of synthetic human secretin in the treatment of autism and pervasive developmental disorder. *N Engl J Med.* 1999 Dec 9;341(24):1801-6.

183. Sandler AD, Bodfish JW. Placebo effects in autism: lessons from secretin. *J Dev Behav Pediatr.* 2000 Oct;21(5):347-50.

SECTION TWO: MAKING A PLAN

184. Dunn-Geier J et al. Effect of secretin on children with autism: a randomized controlled trial. *Dev Med Child Neurol.* 2000 Dec;42(12):796-802.

185. Roberts W et al. Repeated doses of porcine secretin in the treatment of autism: a randomized, placebo-controlled trial. *Pediatrics.* 2001 May;107(5):E71.

186. Coniglio SJ et al. A randomized, double-blind, placebo-controlled trial of single-dose intravenous secretin as treatment for children with autism. *J Pediatr.* 2001 May;138(5):649-55.

187. Horvath K, Perman JA. Autistic disorder and gastrointestinal disease. *Curr Opin Pediatr.* 2002 14(5):583-7.

188. Goulet M et al. A secretin i.v. infusion activates gene expression in the central amygdala of rats. *Neuroscience.* 2003;118(4):881-8.

189. Myers K et al. Inhibition of fear potentiated startle in rats following peripheral administration of secretin. *Psychopharmacology* (Berl). 2004 Feb;172(1):94-9.

190. Kuntz A et al. Effects of secretin on extracellular amino acid concentrations in rat hippocampus. *J Neural Transm.* 2004 Jul;111(7):931-9.

191. Koves K et al. Secretin and autism: a basic morphological study about the distribution of secretin in the nervous system. *Regul Pept.* 2004 Dec 15;123(1-3):209-16.

192. http://www.repligen.com/

193. Sheitman BB et al. Secretin for refractory schizophrenia. *Schizophr Res.* 2004 Feb 1;66(2-3):177-81.

194. Alamy SS et al. Secretin in a patient with treatment-resistant schizophrenia and prominent autistic features. *Schizophr Res.* 2004 Feb 1;66(2-3):183-6.

Author's Preface – J. Pangborn

If you take road trips, you soon realize that all cities and towns have unique street layouts. You also discover, to your dismay, that some of these are particularly prone to traffic jams. The underlying reasons can include a lack of alternative routes, too few lanes on a highway, an excessive number of intersections, or poor traffic light timing. Typically, such road systems work okay until they're stressed – when Joe's eighteen-wheeler breaks down, there's a major accident (or maybe just a flat tire), a water main breaks, or a power failure extinguishes the traffic lights.

When such events occur, the resulting traffic jams and gridlock last until someone intervenes. A tow truck removes the obstruction, the power comes back on, or police move in to direct traffic and clear intersections. Drivers are still left with a suboptimal road configuration, but it's working again. And if steps are taken to detour through-traffic onto the beltway, re-time the traffic lights, and keep a traffic cop handy, future problems are much less likely.

In many ways, an individual's genomic makeup is comparable to a street layout. We can't change this genomic makeup, any more than a driver can change a city's street layout – all we can do is make the best of it. Just as with street layouts, each genomic makeup is unique. This means that some individuals are genetically more predisposed than others to metabolic "traffic jams" and even "gridlock." The stressors that can cause these system breakdowns include opiate peptides on neuronal cell receptors, adding mercury to a cell that's trying to metabolize methionine, or having measles virus develop into a persistent infection for those with weakened immunity, allowing the virus to hijack cellular perception and response functions or stop synchronous neuronal communication.

Some children can shake off these insults, just as some lucky drivers can bypass obstructions or suffer only momentary slowdowns. Other children, however, develop lasting problems, in the form of metabolic traffic jams, until effective intervention occurs. Stressed, non-optimal metabolism can result in problems with molecular traffic – too many molecules trying to change their structures at restricted enzyme sites – and in reduced energy flow for message transmission in cells, and loss of neuronal coordination. On both a cellular and a whole-self level, knowledge of external conditions can be lacking because of a molecular traffic jam.

We call this autism, and in many cases we can improve the condition by applying individualized biomedical interventions that work to open up blocked metabolic pathways and guard against system breakdowns in the future. That's what this book is all about. J.P.

AUTISM IN PERSPECTIVE

By Jon Pangborn

Prior to about 1980, the incidence of autism was about 3 to 5 individuals per 10,000 births, with variations depending upon diagnostic criteria and geographical location.[1,2] At least two-thirds of those autistics had discernible problems soon after birth.[3] Fewer than one-third showed notable regression of social skills, speech and behavior beginning between ages one and two years. During the period 1980-1985, the incidence of autism doubled. By 1985, the occurrence of regressive autism about equaled that of the from-birth conditions,[3] suggesting that an acquired form was overtaking the mainly genetic or inborn-error types. According to ARI statistics, both general types had increased, but by 1997, late-onset or regressive autism had become at least 80% of the total.[3] By that time, the total incidence had increased by a factor of about ten, to 30 to 35 per 10,000 births, with some locales reporting twice that number.[4,5] Recent statistics released by the U.S. Centers for Disease Control and Prevention show an even higher incidence in European and Asian nations of what is now considered to be autism, or at least one major trait of ASD: six per thousand births.[6] This incidence is exceeded in at least one U.S. locale (Brick Township, New Jersey).[6] This is approximately a 20-fold increase in autism incidence in 25 years (0.0003 to 0.006). Despite some expansion of diagnostic inclusion, we still have experienced near-exponential increases in this disease. Such increases are not characteristic of inborn errors of metabolism, and strongly suggest that an acquired condition (probably with genetic predispositions) now predominates.

Acquired autism is suspected of being triggered by toxic or infectious insults piled on top of metabolic processes that aren't quite right but that could cope without such stressors. This is not unheard of in physiology and medicine. An example is inherited weakness in urea cycle enzymes, such as the ornithine-processing one (OCT), which might reduce the body's ammonia-handling capacity to perhaps 10% of normal. Typically, there's lots of reserve capacity. Individuals with this limitation may get along fine until they are exposed to ammonia, or until they contract a severe bacterial infection or gut dysbiosis. Then, the ammonia load can easily exceed the capacity of that individual's urea cycle. Severe headache (migraine), slowed speech and hearing problems (ammonia intoxication), coma and even death can then result. Or, maybe the person just experiences a lowering of IQ from brain damage. This is where I began my investigation of autism in the early 1980s. My autistic son had elevated blood ammonia, and nobody could tell me why.

According to this concept, the more we challenge with toxic and immunologic stressors, the more failures we will have in individual development. Underlying this concept model is biochemical individuality which is established by genetic differences, immune status, physiological condition, and nutritional status.

Based on ideas expressed publicly at DAN! research symposia and annual meetings, some of these stressors could be:

- Use of organic mercury (thimerosal) as a preservative in vaccinations, which have increased in number and frequency.[7,8,9,10]

- Increased vaccinations – both in total number and intensity – via multivalent shots, especially measles when given as the MMR combination.[11,12,13]

- Multiple vaccinations given in infancy (such as hepatitis B) before some have sufficiently mature metabolism and immune capabilities.[14]

- Increased environmental pollution[15] – pesticides, herbicides and fungicides, PCBs, perchlorate, military chemicals, etc.

- Use of antimony as a flame-retardant in textiles (mattresses, pads, sheets, clothing, rugs and carpets) to which infants and young children are exposed,[16] and use of brominated diphenyl chemicals as flame retardants.

- Decreased quality of nutrition during pregnancy and infancy, less breast-feeding.

- Substance abuse by moms before/during pregnancy.[17]

As portrayed by Paul Shattock, Director of the Autism Research Unit, University of Sunderland, U.K., the ability of the human population to withstand toxic and immunologic stressors follows a bell-shaped curve, most likely approximating a Gaussian (normal) distribution.[18]

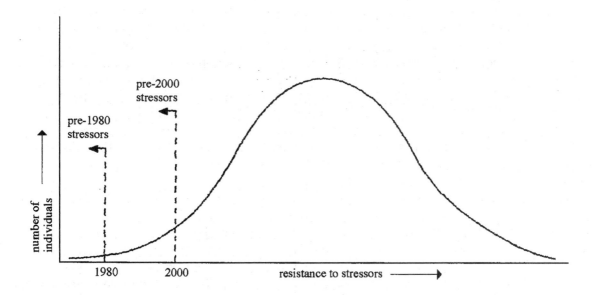

In such a distribution, the number of affected individuals is proportional to the area under the curve and to the left of the dotted data line. With the removal of thimerosal from vaccination sera during 2002-2004, we will have to wait until 2005-7 to see if the increasing incidence of autism has been arrested.

For those who are concerned about the genetic or biochemical variants that make up the autistic spectrum, two general classifications can be postulated:

Type I. This type is a severe metabolic disorder, almost certainly an inborn error of metabolism with genetic associations. These disorders feature autistic traits along with other abnormal traits that may be even more damaging than autism. There are at least two dozen of these conditions that have been reasonably well described in the literature. The ones I have looked into are listed later.

Type II. This is the newer type of autism that is primarily responsible for the near-exponential increase in its occurrence. This type involves genetic predispositions but is triggered by toxic and immunologic stressors. Like Type I, it has always been present to some degree, but now it has become prevalent because of the increased number and severity of acquired stressors. This is the kind of autism that DAN! researchers and clinicians are most concerned with.

Obviously, these two classifications could become arbitrary when metabolic disorders of genetic origin are nearly equal in severity to the effects of acquired insults. But individuals with identifiable metabolic disorders that are genetic and run in families do not make up the majority of autism cases; they are now a small minority. Our opinion is that the vast majority, something like 9 out of 10, or even 19 out of 20, would not have manifested autism had it not been for exposure to one or more of the seven bulleted stressors outlined previously.

Many severe metabolic disorders that are primarily genetic (Type I) and that may feature autism have been well described.[19,20,21] While these diseases typically feature autism in a subset of cases, a few of them almost always manifest some autistic traits. Adenylosuccinate lyase deficiency is an example.

SECTION THREE: MOLECULAR ASPECTS OF AUTISM

I have listed these diseases below for two reasons. The first is to illustrate the distinctions in my Type I and Type II classification, and to emphasize what DAN! is not trying to solve. The second reason, and the most important one, is that you need to be sure that your child/patient does not have one of these conditions. If he/she does, the DAN! approach may be of significant help, but you should also seek help from acknowledged experts in these diseases. The references for each mentioned disease can be a starting point for experienced help and therapy. Furthermore, the hereditary component of these diseases is so strong that family genetics may warrant investigation, and counseling about future pregnancy could be appropriate. Mostly, but not always, these cases are identified in early infancy. But some, like Rett syndrome, don't become obvious until after the first year of life, and then they feature regression of skills and functions as time progresses.

Severe Metabolic Disorders that May Feature Autism (Type I Autism)[19,20,21]

Readers who have not had a course in genetics or physiology may wish to skim over this outline. However, the conditions in D, Energy Transfer Deficiency, are very pertinent to the type of acquired autism with which we are mainly contending.

A. **Multiple Gene Defect/Deletion Disorders**: Genetic disasters in which whole sections of chromosomes are defective or lacking. While autism may be featured as a problem in some, even more severe mental and developmental problems are typical. There may be mental retardation, unusual stature and facial features, and other abnormal physical features.

- Maternal or paternal monosomy at 1p36: mental retardation, growth delay, seizures, hypotonia, developmental abnormalities, deafness, early puberty, cardiomyopathy. Incidence = one in 10,000 births.

- Cri-du-chat syndrome, with deletions at 5p, especially 5p15.2, causing mental retardation, developmental disorders, cataracts, and cardiovascular problems. Incidence = one in 50,000.

- Prader-Willi: 70% display paternal deletions, 28% display uniparental disomy and 2% display mutations in the region 15q11.2 to 15q13. Features variable degrees of mental retardation, obesity with constant hunger, hypotonia, neonatal feeding difficulties, stubborn behaviors with temper tantrums, and hypopigmentation. Incidence = one in 15,000.

- Angelman syndrome: about 95% display maternal deletions and about 5% display paternal disomy in the region 15q11.2 to 15q13. Features hyperactivity, underweight bodies, and ataxic gait; often characterized as "happy puppet syndrome." Mental retardation can be severe, with failure to develop speech. Incidence = one in 15,000.

- Rubenstein-Taybi syndrome with deletions at 16p13.3 (note: this is also the general locus for tuberous sclerosis type 2 and polycystic kidney disease). Features mental retardation, microcephaly and characteristic facial abnormalities. Incidence = one in 125,000.

- Smith-Magenis syndrome with deletions at 17p11.2. Features mental retardation, hyperactivity, self-destructive behaviors, delayed speech, deep hoarse voice, frequent auditory and ocular problems. Incidence = one in 25,000.

B. **Nucleoside/Nucleotide and DNA Synthesis disorders**: Enzymatic irregularities primarily causing imbalanced formation of nucleosides and nucleotides that are required for cell perception and response functions, as well as for synthesis of nucleic acids. These also are inborn metabolic errors.[22]

- PRPP Synthetase Superactivity (purine and pyrimidine syntheses are disordered).
- Adenylosuccinate Lyase Deficiency (succinylpurines excess, impaired AMP synthesis).
- Rett syndrome (various mutations in the gene that encodes a MeCpG binding protein cause DNA transcription problems).
- Histidinemia (deficient FIGlu, 5-formiminoTHF, 10-formylTHF, may feature impaired purine synthesis).

C. **Nucleoside/Nucleotide Exchange and Depletion Conditions:** Enzymatic disorders primarily causing nucleoside/nucleotide imbalances because transformation from one kind to another is inhibited. Some of these conditions may also affect RNA or DNA. Often, there is depletion or excessive wasting of purine or pyrimidine moieties or of uric acid. Immune dysregulation and cell communication problems are likely. Additionally, diseases that feature lowered ATP and/or GTP may have energy limitations such that coordinated, synchronous neuronal activities (e.g. expressive speech) are impaired. [23,24] And these too are inborn metabolic errors.

- Lesch-Nyhan disease (uridine —/→ cytidine, ATP↓, GTP↓, urate↑).[25]
- Fragile X syndrome (uridine —/→ thymidine and deficiency of a protein, FMRP, that can result in decreased neuronal plasticity and cognitive ability).[26,27]
- Tuberous Sclerosis (tuberin causes activation of GTPase, GTP ↓). Some cases of tuberous sclerosis involve contiguous gene deletions, meaning that this disease may also fit into category A.[28]
- Neurofibromatosis Type 1 (von Recklinghausen disease; neurofibromin causes activation of GTPase, GTP ↓).[29]
- Phenylketonuria (futile use of GTP to form biopterin).[30]
- Pyrimidine 5'-nucleotidase superactivity (UMP, CMP depletion).[31]
- Dihydropyrimidine dehydrogenase deficiency (dihydrouracil and dihydrothymine not formed from uracil and thymine).[32]

D. **Energy Transfer Deficiency:** Inhibitions to energy transfer for ADP → ATP, GDP → GTP. Such inhibitions slow energy conversion needed for cognitive and communicative processes. In the brain, chemical energy is transported as phosphate to ADP by phosphocreatine, providing for upgrading of ADP to ATP. ATP then phosphorylates all other nucleotides to raise their chemical energy status, including GDP to form GTP. G protein activity and much of cell signaling are dependent upon reenergizing GDP to GTP. Besides the below-listed inborn errors affecting creatine, its synthesis also depends upon the methylation capability of SAM as described below.

- Creatine Synthesis Deficiencies (inborn metabolic errors)

    (1) AGAT deficiency – guanidinoacetate and creatine deficiencies[33]
    (2) GAMT deficiency – guanidinoacetate excess, creatine deficiency[34]

- Creatine Transporter Deficiency (CRTR gene defect, an inborn error)[35]

Acquired Metabolic Disorders with Genetic Predispositions (Type II Autism)

Close examination by medical doctors and analytical testing by clinical laboratories of thousands of our autistic children from the 1980s through 2004 confirm that most do not have any of the conditions in the Type I category described above. However, many of our autistic children do have a condition that includes D(2), creatine deficiency, caused not by GAMT deficiency, but by acquired inhibition of that enzyme or by deficiency of the creatine precursor, guanidinoacetate. More about this later in the chapter on creatine formation.

The first response to autism's increased prevalence by the experienced experts in metabolism and genetics was to look for the culprit or culprits among the genes in the set of human chromosomes. A gene or genes not previously identified might be at fault, they reasoned. This isn't unreasonable considering the track record for Type I diseases. But despite spending millions of dollars and millions in other currencies as well, "the autism gene" has not been found. A single faulty gene that by itself accounts for all the increased incidence of autism is an impossibility, in my opinion. Probably, the best research effort for identifying chromosomal linkages was performed by the International Molecular Genetic Study of Autism Consortium (IMGSAC).[36]

A much more promising approach is "epigenetics," the study of how acquired influences (diet, infection, toxicity) affect the activity and expression of genes. Epigenetics is best illustrated by an example, and the example I favor is a hypothesis put forth by researchers at Baylor College of Medicine. The Chairman of the Department of Molecular and Human Genetics at Baylor is Arthur Beaudet, M.D., and he addressed the Autism Society of America (ASA) scientific conference in Indianapolis, October 2004. A publication on the Baylor researchers' epigenetics hypothesis has been authored by Jiang, Sahoo, et al.[37]

The Baylor scientists looked for genes that were associated with purely genetic diseases but were near chromosomal areas of unusual methylation in autistics. Methylation can be affected by environmental and dietary influences, and methylation of genes controls expression and limits or alters protein formation. The Baylor scientists chose a gene, UBE3A, located in the chromosomal trouble zone for Angelman's syndrome, 15q11 to q13. This gene encodes for a protein that has enzymatic activity, ubiquitin ligase. Dr. Beaudet is suspicious (as are DAN! researchers) about abnormal methylation occurring in autism, and at the Indianapolis ASA meeting, he spoke about increased dietary folate and folate-enhancing influences on methylation. With the low incidence of Angelman syndromes, the Baylor scientists admit that the role of UBE3A "may be quantitatively modest,"[37] but such epigenetic processes could play a major role in causation overall.

Here's what DAN! clinicians and researchers have found. Many autistics have oxidant stress due to metabolic limitations on glutathione synthesis and metabolism, persistent infection (measles) and intestinal inflammation, often with dysbiosis. Excessive oxidized glutathione and cytokine levels are present, and this condition perpetuates deficient methylation of homocysteine by methionine synthase. (Homocysteine supply itself is reduced by upstream metabolic problems.) Methionine synthase can become deficient in homocysteine methylation capability by contamination with toxics (ethyl mercury, thimerosal, possibly antimony). When oxidant stress occurs, ubiquitin chemistry is upregulated.[38]

What's ubiquitin?

Ubiquitin is a small protein found in cells, and it targets other proteins for degradation by attaching to them and changing their chemistry to make them susceptible to degradation. In the language of chemistry, ubiquitin "derivatizes" proteins that the cell no longer wants. Ubiquitin ligase is an enzyme that promotes attachment of ubiquitin to target proteins.

What's the connection?

Increased ubiquitin activity results from induced gene expression which changes with oxidant stress (excessive oxidation of glutathione).[39] It looks as though ubiquitin steps in and enforces decreased methylation capability in methionine synthase until oxidant stress is relieved. Unfortunately, in autism (Type II), the biochemistry that should relieve the oxidant stress is dysfunctional. In this situation, the "limited role" for ubiquitin ligase would be significantly expanded in autistic spectrum disorder. This is an example of an acquired condition (oxidant stress) upregulating the activity of an enzyme-degrading protein that is also abnormal in a purely genetic disease (Angelman) that features autism. You will need to read the chapters on methionine metabolism, creatine and synchronous neuronal processes to get a better sense of what's wrong with methylation.

The DAN! approach to the growing epidemic of autism has been to set aside purely genetic causes, which account for so few of the present autistic population. To find out what's wrong, some clinicians and scientists turned to biochemistry and immunology years ago, and their evidence has been piling up. This evidence is now undeniably pertinent to describing and treating autism.

References: Autism in Perspective

1. Coleman M and Gillberg C *The Biology of the Autistic Syndromes* Praeger Pub (1985) 53-56.
2. "Changes in the Population of Persons with Autism and Pervasive Developmental Disorders... Dept. Develop. Services, California Health and Human Services Agency (March 1 1999), Sacramento CA.
3. *Autism Research Review* vol.14, no.1 (2000) ARI 3,6.
4. "Autistic Spectrum Disorders" Dept. Develop. Services, California Health and Human Services Agency (April 2003) Sacramento CA 9.
5. Blaxill M "The Rising Incidence of Autism" from *The Global Crisis in Autism Science*, June 2001. See also DAN! May 2001 Boston Conference Proceedings.
6. CDC Website, http://www.cdc.gov: Autism Incidence, 2004 [http://www.cdc.gov/ncbddd/dd/aic/about/default.html].
7. McGinnis WR "Toxic metals in autism: focus on mercury" DAN! 2000, San Diego (Sept. 2000).
8. Holmes A. Mercury Presentation to DAN! Think Tank Symposium, Phoenix AZ, July 2000).
9. El-Dahr J "Immunologic issues in autism" DAN! Practicum 2001 Atlanta (2001).
10. Bernard S et al. "Autism: a novel form of mercury poisoning" Sally Bernard, ARC Research, 14 Commerce Dr, Crawford NJ 079-1.
11. Cave SF and El-Dahr J "What parents and professionals need to know about immunizations" Presentation at DAN! 5 Cherry Hill NJ (1999).
12. Wakefield A "The gut-brain axis in autism" DAN! 5 Cherry Hill NJ (1999).
13. Wakefield A "Virus vaccines and the gut in autism: an update" DAN! 2000, San Diego (Sept. 2000).
14. Cave S *What Your Doctor May Not Tell You About Children's Vaccinations* Warner 2001.

SECTION THREE: MOLECULAR ASPECTS OF AUTISM

15. Edelson SB "Autism: An Environmental Maladaptation" Presentation at DAN! 2 Chicago (1996).

16. Pangborn J and Smith B "Autism, antimony and methylation issues" DAN! Think Tank Symposium, Phoenix AZ (July 2000).

17. Davis E, Fennoy I, et al. "Autism and developmental abnormalities in children with perinatal cocaine exposure (11.4%). *J Natl Med Assoc* (1992) Apr; $\underline{84}$ no.4 315-319.

18. Shattock P Presentation to Oakland County Chapter Autism Society of America, Pontiac MI (May 2001).

19. Gillberg C and Coleman M *The Biology of the Autistic Syndromes* 2nd Ed. MacKeith Press (1992).

20. Sapienza C and Hall JG "Genome imprinting in human disease" Chapt.15 in Scriver C et al. Eds. *The Metabolic and Molecular Bases of Inherited Disease* 8th Ed. McGraw-Hill (2001) 417-431.

21. Shaffer LG et al. "Molecular cytogenetics of contiguous gene syndromes: mechanisms and consequences of gene dosage imbalance" Chapter 65 in Scriver CR et al. Eds 8th Ed., ibid 1291-1324.

22. Pangborn JB and Baker SM *Biomedical assessment options for children with autism and related problems* DAN! Consensus Report, ARI (Oct 2002) 21-44.

23. Von Figura K, et al. "Guanidinoacetate methyltransferase deficiency" Chapt.84 in Scriver CR et al. Eds. 8th Ed. op.cit. 1901-1902.

24. Carlson NR "Neural communication and the decision-making process", Chapt. 4, 50-62, and "Biochemistry and pharmacology of synaptic transmission," Chapt.5, 63-83, in *Physiology of Behavior* Allyn and Bacon Inc. (1977).

25. Fairbanks LD et al. "Severe pyrimidine nucleotide depletion in fibroblasts from Lesch-Nyhan patients" *Biochem J* $\underline{366}$ part 1 (2002) 265-272.

26. Nussbaum RL and Ledbetter DH "The Fragile X Syndrome" Chapt. 8 in Scriver CR et al. Eds *The Metabolic Basis of Inherited Disease* 6th Ed. McGraw-Hill (1989) 332.

27. Warren ST and Sherman SL "The fragile X syndrome" Chapt. 64 in Scriver CR et al. Eds 8th Ed. op.cit. 1257-1289.

28. Sampson JR "Tuberous sclerosis" Chapter 233 in Scriver CR et al. Eds, 8th Ed, op.cit. 5865-66, 5869.

29. Gutmann DH and Collins FS "Neurofibromatosis 1" Chapt. 39 in Scriver CR et al. Eds 8th Ed. Op. cit. 884, 887-888.

30. Pangborn JB and Baker SM DAN! Consensus Report op.cit. 23-25.

31. Page T et al. "Developmental disorder associated with increased cellular nucleotidase activity" *Proc. Nat. Acad. Sci.* $\underline{94}$ (1997) 11601-11606.

32. Webster DR et al. "Hereditary orotic aciduria and other disorders of pyrimidine metabolism" Chapt. 113 in Scriver CR et al. Eds 8th Ed. op.cit. 2664,65 and 2688-92.

33. Item CB, Stöckler-Ispiroglu et al. "Arginine: glycine amidinotransferase deficiency: the third inborn error of creatine metabolism in humans" *Am.J.Human Genetics* $\underline{69}$ (2001) 1127-1133.

34. Von Figura K, Hanefield F et al. "Guanidinoacetate methyltransferase deficiency," Chapt. 84 in Scriver CR et al. Eds. 8th Ed. op.cit. 1897-1908.

35. Salomons GS, van Dooren SJM et al. "X-linked creatine-transporter gene (SLC6A8) defect: a new creatine deficiency syndrome" *Am.J.Human Genetics* $\underline{68}$ (2001) 1497-1500.

36. IMGSAC "A genomewide screen for autism: strong evidence for linkage to chromosomes 2q, 7q, and 16p" *Am.J.Human Genet.* $\underline{69}$ (2001) 570-581.

37. Jiang YH, Sahoo T, et al. "A mixed epigenetic/genetic model for oligogenic inheritance of autism with a limited role for UBE3A" *Am.J.Med.Genetics* 131 A(1) (2004) 1-10.

38. Shang F, Gong X et al. "Activity of ubiquitin-dependent pathway in response to oxidative stress" *J.Biol. Chemistry* 272 no.37 (1997) 23086-23093.

39. Obin M, Shang F et al. "Redox regulation of ubiquitin-conjugating enzymes: mechanistic insights using the thiol-specific oxidant diamide" *FASEB Journal* 12 no.7 (1998) 561-569.

AUTISM AT THE MOLECULAR LEVEL

First, an introductory story: "Broken Water Glasses – Causation and Contributing Factors" – I.M. Klutz, Ph.D.

Years ago, I was standing before an audience, and as I introduced myself, I had the misfortune of knocking a water glass off the top of the podium and onto the floor. Of course, it broke spectacularly and splashed water about as well. I no longer needed an attention-getter or a joke. I was it. Afterward, I decided to investigate glass-breaking with the goal of preventing its reoccurrence.

A design engineer told me that glass-breaking was very definitely related to the manufacture of the glass. I asked why. He said that he and a team of design engineers had visited and inspected many glass manufacturing plants. They had characterized the shape of the shards and had determined all the common faults and flaws in glass vessels. "Well, what did you conclude?" I asked. "The design study revealed many potential faults," he replied, "but long-stemmed glasses always break when they fall to the floor. Thin-walled glasses usually break, as do tall ones. But short, thick ones break less often. And tempered or annealed glass is stronger than other glass. So, glass-breaking is related to design and manufacture, and fragile designs are inherently susceptible to breakage," he concluded.

Not really satisfied, I turned to a mechanical engineer. He became very concerned with the shape of the podium, and he built some models to test his theories. He was convinced that the podium was mostly at fault. "It's related to podium dimensions," he said. "Those with angled tops and narrow ledges often result in the glass falling and breaking. And the most important factor is podium height. Despite what design engineers might say, even fragile glasses don't break when knocked off a short podium. And wide, level podium tops drastically reduce the incidence of glass-breaking."

Still perplexed, I posed the question to some chemists. They said that glass-breaking could be reduced by using Pyrex. Plate-glass formulations and crystal were not good for strength. "It's all in the ingredients that are fed to the glass furnace," they claimed.

By now, I had heard plenty about glass-breaking, and I wasn't the only goof who had experienced it. Was there a way to protect oneself from being involved? OSHA was my next stop. They argued endlessly among themselves, but eventually, they constructed a giant matrix of interacting factors to explain glass-breaking. To test their thesis, they performed double-blind, cross-over studies of left-handed, right-handed, tall, short, farsighted and nearsighted speakers at podiums. They carefully recorded the propensities for knocking water glasses off, and finally concluded that the glass itself was not at fault. The real cause is the individual who stands at the podium and bumps the glass. If one doesn't use a podium, or even better, stays home and doesn't give speeches, then those water glasses don't break.

SECTION THREE: MOLECULAR ASPECTS OF AUTISM

As I was considering where to turn next, the building contractors appeared, rather uninvited. I hadn't asked them for advice, but by now my quest was well-known, and they were positive that they had the answer and were going out with a press release, too. Statistical analysis of 1,000 films from slow-motion cameras proved that, even though glasses were knocked off podiums, nothing really bad happened until the glasses hit the floor. One thousand films of water glasses knocked off podiums and onto pillows served as controls. No control glasses broke. The contractors were certain that it was floor material that caused the breakage. "Only a few breakages will occur on rugs," they reported, "but wood floors and linoleum floors cause frequent breakage. And despite what engineers, chemists or OSHA say, all glasses break when they hit a stone or tile floor! It's the Floor Design Administration's fault for allowing floors to be made of stone or ceramic tile."

While all of these explanations were plausible, I decided to consult someone who had an overall command of the science that seemed to be involved – a professor of physics. "Gravity, of course!" he roared. "It's what's shared in common by all glass-falling and glass-breaking events, regardless of the type of glass, shape of podium, clumsiness of the speaker, or floor materials." "But, I can't repeal gravity," I complained. "No," the professor replied, "but now you understand the general nature of the problem."

By this point, I was more determined than ever. Just to rule out any mental distortions that I might have, I decided to consult a psychiatrist. Big mistake! He explained that he and his learned colleagues had reasoned many times with falling glasses, but without effect. They still fell. Then they had reasoned with the broken pieces. But they wouldn't come back together. Then they psychoanalyzed the speakers at podiums, because it was all their fault anyway. Speakers were advised to sweep up the pieces and put them in the trash. Next, the speakers were advised to seek counseling on how to go on with their lives. In the end, the psychiatrists had solved the glass-breaking problem by renaming it "Humpty-Dumpty syndrome." My name for the event, glass-breaking, was naïve, and I had no business investigating something I was not qualified to understand.

– The End –

For those of you who are most concerned with public health issues, causations and contributing conditions are of great importance. Knowing these may lead to prevention of disease. For those of you who are parents of an autistic child, cause would be nice to know, but remedies or cures, if possible, are of paramount importance. Some of what follows in this section of this report deals with causations. More, however, deals with the biochemical and neurological conditions that we find in autism. Understanding this leads to better mastery of how biomedical options could benefit the individual.

Why Biochemistry?

For each of us, the nature of autism depends upon our frame of reference. My frame of reference is biochemistry. But often, biochemistry doesn't show cause. Instead, it shows status – what's right and wrong, what's working and not working. If you're trying to alleviate a metabolic disorder, which autism is, then this information is of prime importance. But biochemistry only hints at how things became disordered. Nevertheless, for autism, biochemistry has three important attributes:

1. Biochemical quantities can be analyzed and measured in tissue specimens, and certain ones are often abnormal in autistics. Examples are cysteine, adenosine,

adenosylhomocysteine, glutathione, tumor necrosis factor alpha, creatine and exorphin peptides. Such analyses can provide diagnosis at the molecular level.

2. These molecular quantities can be directly related to cellular perception and response. Some, when abnormal, have been correlated with autistic traits. One example is deficient brain creatine and deficient expressive speech. Another is impaired methionine synthase and disordered methylation affecting synchronous coordination of neuronal processes.

3. Some of these quantities and their precursors or associated metabolites are available as nutritional supplements or as injectables. Pyridoxine, trimethylglycine, glutathione, creatine, methylcobalamin and DPP4 digestive enzymes are examples. Trials of these as supplements can be biomedical options for remediation of autistic traits. Numerous parent and clinician reports attest to recovery by many autistics when these and other quantities are used properly.

The organized choice of appropriate biomedical options is the DAN! methodology for intervention, and it is explained in detail in other sections of this report. The purpose of this section is to illustrate some of the biochemistry that DAN!-associated researchers and clinicians have found to be at fault in autism.

What's Going Wrong at the Molecular Level in Autism?

To understand where DAN! is at in terms of both biochemical mechanisms and related therapy, you would do well to learn about three molecular processes:

1. **Methionine metabolism and its connections to methylation, oxidant stress, sulfur and folate chemistry and nucleotides, especially adenosine.**

2. **Creatine formation and energy delivery to cells, which allows them to process messages from outside in a coordinated fashion.**

3. **Methylation and operation of the dopamine D4 receptor to mediate attention to incoming messages and synchronous neuronal processing of these messages.**

Additionally, you need to learn how each of these processes can be influenced or disturbed by acquired stressors in combination with genetic predispositions for weakness. Later in this section we discuss measles virus, an extreme stressor in autism, and one that has links to the biochemistry. We believe that autism can feature both neuronal energy deficit and loss of synchronization among neuronal networks. These problems can be worsened and perpetuated by the inflammatory effects of infection.

The brain has virtually no energy storage system, and it operates on a "just in time" supply system. Each neuronal cell that participates in perception of an external stimulus, such as a verbal request, must have energy on hand to process that signal. If some of the cells have to wait for energy to arrive, then coordination by groups of neurons and synchronous processing by neuronal networks just can't occur. Neither can the appropriate response. Also, the molecules in a cell's receptors have to be in the activated form, and by activated, I mean methylated or phosphorylated. You can think about this in terms of analogies. To start a car, you need gas delivered by the fuel injectors, and you need the spark plugs to fire in the right sequence. To listen to a radio station, you need to turn the radio on, and set the tuner to that station.

SECTION THREE: MOLECULAR ASPECTS OF AUTISM

In autism, two general stressor conditions add together to cause roadblocks to methylation, sulfation, and energy delivery for cells: toxicity and inflammation. Variable genetic predispositions and nutritional status set the stage for toxicity and inflammation to occur in the individual.

Methionine Metabolism

Let's start with the part of amino acid metabolism that's most disordered in autism, methionine metabolism. I'll discuss that in parts, "region" by "region" as shown below.

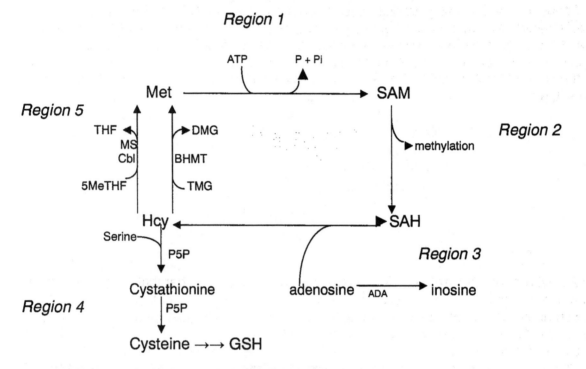

SAM = S-adenosylmethionine   MET = methionine
MS = methionine synthase   SAH = S-adenosylhomocysteine
Cbl = cobalamin   Hcy = homocysteine
P5P = pyridoxal 5-phosphate

The nutritionally essential amino acid methionine (Met) comes from dietary protein. Some of it goes into protein assembly to build or repair body tissues, and some of it goes through the open, cyclic process as shown above. It's an open cycle because only part of the methionine is regenerated; the rest is siphoned off and transformed into cysteine. Cysteine is the active part of many enzyme proteins, hormone peptides, and the antioxidant and detoxifying quantity, glutathione. Methionine that becomes cysteine must be replenished by dietary protein sources. Normally, up to 33% of methionine is recycled in human females, up to 45% in males.[1] For an individual, the split between recycle to Met or siphon-off to cysteine depends upon relative needs for methylation and antioxidant duty. We'll discuss more about this later.

Methionine carries both sulfur and a methyl group. In the body, methyl groups can be considered the currency of personality, and they can be moved from one molecule to another. When a molecule is methylated (adds a methyl group), its character is changed. Sulfur is the currency of attraction and stickiness. Sulfur-containing quantities can make structural bonds, grab and hold toxics, and release hydrogen (protons) to neutralize oxidants.

In Region 1 of this biochemical cycle, the first transformation occurs when adenosine triphosphate (ATP) combines with methionine to make S-adenosylmethionine (SAM, sometimes denoted SAMe). ATP is a high-energy molecule with lots of phosphate. Phosphate is the body's energy currency. Dropping off the phosphate (P, Pi) gives an energy push to drive the reaction Met → SAM. There already is a report that casts suspicion on energy-carrying molecules including ATP in autism, especially in the brain.[2] Also, we may have an additional problem with making SAM if magnesium is severely deficient. The enzyme that operates the Met → SAM reaction step requires magnesium.

In Region 2, SAM gives its methyl group away, which changes SAM into S-adenosylhomocysteine (SAH). About 70% of this methyl transfer goes to guanidinoacetate (GA) to change it into creatine.[3] Guanidinoacetate comes from two amino acids that get joined together, glycine and arginine. About 30% of SAM is used to methylate other things: DNA to control gene activity, serotonin to make melatonin, norepinephrine to make normetanephrine, phosphatidylethanolamine (methylated three times) to make choline, lysine to make a precursor of carnitine, histamine to inactivate it, etc.

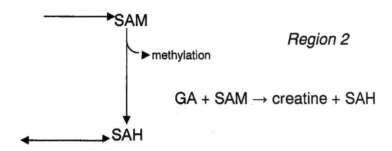

Region 2 is where we often get into big-time trouble in autism. Remember that in Type 1 autism, there are genetic versions of: (1) deficient formation of GA, (2) deficient methylation of GA to produce creatine, and (3) deficient transport of creatine. If GA is deficient, then 70% of what SAM is looking for is nowhere to be found. Imbalanced methylation or "overmethylation" of other quantities could then be occurring. If GA is present but can't be methylated, then energy delivery to cells via creatine (as phosphocreatine) will be deficient. Besides the genetic disasters that can cause such problems, we have found that creatine deficiency can also result from acquired stressor conditions combined with a number of predispositions. By themselves, such predispositions (variations in metabolism) are relatively innocuous.

The goings-on in Region 3 control the rate at which methylation occurs in Region 2. To see how this happens, we need to visit the biochemistry depicted in Region 3 of our diagram.

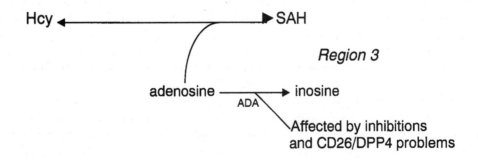

In Region 3, there is a reversible chemical change that is driven by two processes, disposal of adenosine and removal of homocysteine (Hcy). If these three substances were left alone in an enclosed area of human tissue, most of the adenosine and homocysteine would remain combined as adenosylhomocysteine (SAH). But when things are working properly, homocysteine (Hcy) is removed by methylation. Humans have two ways of methylating Hcy: transfer of a methyl group from trimethylglycine, TMG (also known as betaine), or transfer of the methyl group from methylcobalamin (methyl B_{12}), promoted by the enzyme methionine synthase (MS). In addition, Hcy can be processed out of the cycle and into cysteine (Region 4).

First, let's consider how adenosine can be disposed of. One important way is to remove its amino group; this is "deamination." Deamination is promoted by the enzyme adenosine deaminase, ADA. ADA is a zinc-containing protein; the zinc atom is located at the active enzymatic site.[4] Probably alpha-ketoglutarate cleans up the ammonia (see Nutritional Supplements section).

$$\text{adenosine + water} \xrightarrow{\text{ADA}} \text{inosine + ammonia}$$

This deamination process has a history of problems in autism. In 1982, Stubbs et al. published measurements of purine metabolism-associated enzymes in red blood cells from autistics.[5] He found that ADA was weak, and he suggested that this could have adverse influences on methylation. In the late 1970s, Daddona and Kelley reported that adenosine deaminase has two parts, the enzyme itself (ADA) and a binding protein.[6] Later came discoveries that the binding protein for ADA on lymphocytes was CD26, alias DPP4.[7,8] In the 1980s, Reichelt and others found opiate peptides of dietary origins in the urine of autistics; these peptides are called exorphins and can come from casein and gluten or gliadin.[9,10,11,12] At the mucosal surface of the small intestine, DPP4 acts as a digestive enzyme. It is supposed to digest these dietary exorphins.[13] Their presence in urine is conclusive evidence that this digestive process is deficient, and presumptive evidence that DPP4 is inhibited. In 1982, Püschel et al. published DPP4 inhibition studies using human, placental material.[14] They found that mercury, lead and organophosphates (pesticides) wreck the activity of DPP4. And in 2002, Schade et al. published a study of children with active milk allergy.[15] They determined that CD26 (DPP4) on lymphocytes is intrinsically decreased to as little as 25% of control levels, controls being lymphocytes from children without milk allergy. Many autistics have allergies to cows' milk.

So, we have four pieces of evidence in favor of adenosine deaminase not working well for autistics: Stubbs' cell measurements, the Reichelt et al. finding of high urinary exorphins, the findings by Püschel et al. of toxic inhibition of DPP4, and the milk allergy condition investigated by Schade et al. Then to top it all off, Persico found that the weaker of two adenosine deaminase phenotypes was at least twice as prevalent in autistics as in controls.[16] In humans, there are two versions of ADA, ADA1 and ADA2. ADA2 has only 80% of the activity of ADA1. In the general population, about 8% have ADA2. But in the autistic population, about 18% have ADA2.

That's a lot of circumstantial evidence for adenosine accumulating. How about real biochemical evidence? Recent blood plasma measurements of autistics vs controls by James et al. show that one in five (20%) of autistic children have significantly elevated adenosine and S-adenosylhomocysteine.[17,18] So, one undeniable metabolic problem in a significant subset of autistics is elevated adenosine, and that works against normal processing of adenosylhomocysteine into homocysteine. This also works against methylation by SAM. High SAH causes SAM to slow down its rate of methylation and, consequently, the rate of creatine formation. In fact, SAH is a competitive inhibitor of all methyltransferase reactions that produce it.[19]

The situation in Region 3 might still be rescued if we were able to pull the small amount of Hcy that can be formed away from the zone where SAH is. That would encourage more SAH to change to Hcy even though adenosine accumulates. How could that be done? We need to examine Region 4 to see how.

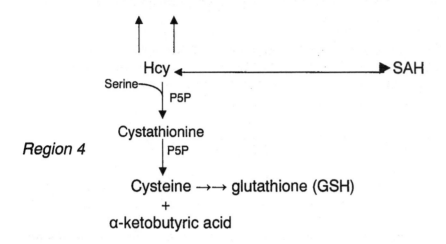

Region 4

In Region 4, some of the homocysteine leaves the cycle to be transformed into cystathionine by combining it with serine. The cystathionine is then split in two, one product being cysteine. Vitamin B_6 as coenzyme pyridoxal 5-phosphate is needed for both steps.[20]

$$Hcy + Serine \xrightarrow{B_6} cystathionine \xrightarrow{B_6} cysteine + \alpha\text{-ketobutyrate}$$

Giving supplemental vitamin B_6 should promote the kinetics or rate at which this happens. If so, then some improvement in the autistic condition should follow. Indeed it does; see the vitamin B_6 and B_6 + magnesium chapters in the Nutritional Supplements section of this report.

Evidence that the homocysteine → cysteine pathway is significantly deficient in many autistics has been found from the 1980s through to the present. My research finding presented in 1984 was that about 60% of untreated autistics had low blood plasma cystine.[21] At that time, the measurement procedure included actual plasma cystine plus a good portion of what was plasma cysteine that was oxidized to additional cystine during specimen preparation. So, those 1984 results approximated cystine + cysteine = "cyst(e)ine." Since then, Owens, James et al. and Bradstreet et al. have measured plasma cystine, cysteine or cyst(e)ine versus lab norms and versus controls (James).[22,23,24] In most cases, it was low.

Cystathionine excess would constitute a blockage as would serine deficiency or insufficient pyridoxal 5-phosphate. Serine deficiency is not seen in autism. Cystathionemia is a rare but documented error in human metabolism. One actual problem in autism is vastly reduced phosphorylation of pyridoxine or pyridoxal by ATP, using the enzyme pyridoxal kinase. Dr. Tapan Audhya and his research team reported that, statistically, autistics required ten times as much vitamin B_6 (as pyridoxine) as control individuals.[25] The increased amount is required to match the kinetics of pyridoxal kinase found in control specimens.

How tissues normally apportion Hcy between cysteine synthesis and methylation to re-make methionine depends upon needs that are imposed on enzymes, primarily methionine synthase (MS in Region 5). If oxidant stress is present, it's likely that inflammatory messengers, cytokines, are notifying the cells that contain methionine synthase. In that case, methionine synthase processes less Hcy, and more Hcy is shunted toward cysteine.[26,27,28] But in autism, Hcy often is deficient, especially so when adenosine is high. To make matters worse, cytokines, such as TNFα, may escalate to nagging mode when there's an inflammatory bowel condition that won't go away. In summary, the biochemistry in Region 3 is often stymied unless there's help from extra vitamin B_6 as pyridoxal phosphate.

The chemistry in Region 5 provides two mechanisms for pulling Hcy out of the reaction zone, thus encouraging more SAH to become Hcy. The first is methylation of Hcy by betaine (TMG), which produces DMG. DMG then provides one-carbon pieces to folate, eventually helping the supply of methyltetrahydrofolate and methylcobalamin (Cbl).

Region 5

```
              Met
               ↑           ↑
         THF ◄─┤           ├─► DMG
              MS
             Cbl|          |BHMT
     5MeTHF ────┤           └─ TMG
               |           |
              Hcy
```

The second process, and the main one as far as material flow is concerned, is methylation of Hcy by MeCbl, using the enzyme methionine synthase, MS.

The enzyme that promotes methylation of homocysteine by TMG is betaine-homocysteine methyltransferase (BHMT). This enzyme is extremely zinc-dependent. Each molecule of the enzyme needs three atoms of zinc to work, and the zinc atoms are each attached to cysteine parts of the protein.[29] BHMT is like a junior metallothionein that contains lots of cysteine and has lots of zinc binding capability. Of course, it would bind the usual sulfur-affinity metals as well – mercury, antimony, and arsenic. The chances of BHMT being 100% OK in autistics who have subnormal cysteine and deficient zinc are not good. Also, genetic variants of BHMT are being found in autistics.[30] More analytical data is needed before we can be quantitative about BHMT's problems. We do know that TMG supplements help over 45% of autistics; see the chapter on TMG in the Nutritional Supplements section of this report.

How about methylcobalamin (MeCbl) and methionine synthase (MS) in Region 5? MeCbl is bound to part of the MS complex, and it can methylate homocysteine. When it does, it normally has its methyl replaced by methyl from 5-methyltetrahydrofolate. If this works, then homocysteine can be removed and more adenosylhomocysteine might be coaxed into coming apart. But autistics have acquired problems that stall this pathway as well. The research team led by Professor Richard Deth at Northeastern University has found that the methylcobalamin part of methionine synthase is severely inhibited by mercury, very severely inhibited by thimerosal (ethyl mercury), and extremely severely inhibited by antimony.[31,32] Thimerosal, of course, has been in vaccine sera, and textiles treated with certain flame retardants are a worrisome source of antimony. More details about MS inhibition are included in the Methionine and S-Adenosylmethionine chapter of the Nutritional Supplements section of this report. But basically, there are two problems. Besides toxic inhibition of methionine synthase, we also gathered evidence that inflammation may cause MS to lose its cobalamin-rescue capability. If MS-associated cobalamin gets oxidized, it might be rescued by MS-reductase (part of the methionine synthase complex) and then methylated by the SAM-binding part of MS (see vitamin B12 discussion in Nutritional Supplements section). But this rescue activity and the SAM-binding part of MS appear to be disabled during oxidant stress and persistent inflammation. This may be an extreme consequence of the unsatisfied need for more cysteine and glutathione that I mentioned before for Region 4.

Now, why is the mercury there? We know that it has been included in many vaccines as ethylmercury (thimerosal). But most children should be able to tolerate tiny doses and detoxify it. Mercury is expelled from cells by glutathione,[33,34] and that appears to be a fundamental part of the problem – deficient glutathione. Before mercury arrives on the scene, glutathione can be deficient because of low coenzyme activity of pyridoxal 5-phosphate, and stressors and genetics that cause suboptimal processing of methionine into cysteine. Limited magnesium also can be contributory to glutathione deficit. If ethyl mercury (thimerosal) comes along, it has a particularly adverse effect on glutathione.[23] The result is mercury sequestered inside cells where it binds to and inhibits or inactivates certain enzymes such as methionine synthase, monoamine oxidase, and pyruvate dehydrogenase. While we acknowledge that other enzymes may also be impaired, our main concern here is the severe inactivation of methionine synthase.

For some children, toxicity, oxidant stress and inflammation combine to cause chronic inhibition of what methionine metabolism is supposed to accomplish. A successful remedy is direct administration of methylcobalamin as pioneered by Dr. James Neubrander. This remedy shortcuts folate, glutathione and B_{12} supply problems that might exist, and feeds methyl groups to Hcy directly via the MS enzyme system.

Region 5 problems would be worsened by some genetic predispositions. They include:

- Genetic variants or single nucleotide polymorphisms in methionine synthase or methionine synthase reductase. The latter is supposed to reduce oxidized cobalamin.

- Weakness in getting enough 5,10-methylene tetrahydrofolate to transfer methyl groups to cobalamin, as can occur with variant forms of methylene tetrahydrofolate reductase (MTHFR).

- Other metabolic problems related to folate chemistry, including histidinemia, deficient folate reductase, and disordered utilization of folates for purine synthesis.

- Genetic variants in BHMT.[30]

- Mutant activity of ubiquitin ligase gene, UBE3A (15q11-15q13, Angelman syndrome locus); ubiquitin activity changes due to changes in genetic expression during oxidant stress and inflammation and may be mechanistically involved in methionine synthase inactivation.

- Weak enzymes involved in detoxication, which might allow toxics besides mercury to affect MS.

In effect, this cyclic process for using and remaking methionine can be likened to a metabolic traffic jam for autistics. The streets (pathways) are gridlocked, but there are five escape routes:

1. Bolstering processes that reduce adenosine by supplementing DPP4, expelling mercury, and avoiding milk and casein,

2. Consuming homocysteine by pulling it to cysteine with megadose pyridoxine, perhaps with some pyridoxal phosphate as well,

3. Consuming homocysteine by pulling it to methionine with supplemental TMG.

4. Consuming homocysteine by pulling it to methionine with supplemental MeCbl.

5. Helping folate chemistry and MeCbl supply by supplementing DMG or folinic acid.

Assisting all five of the above are antioxidant, anti-inflammatory, and anti-infective measures that lower cytokine levels and allow more homocysteine to be processed by MS into methionine. This leads to improved methylation, energy transport to G proteins, and cell membrane phospholipid function.

What does not work is adding traffic to the traffic jam. Generally, adding methionine or SAM is not advisable. The parent responses on ARI Publication 34 regarding SAM supplements (see Nutritional Supplements section) show that these supplements help fewer than one in five autistic individuals. The objective is to make this chemistry cycle go faster, not to add to the cycle's burden.

What are the consequences for sulfur chemistry if the methionine methylation cycle is impeded?

- Cysteine, a metabolite produced by an offshoot of the cycle, will be limited, possibly deficient. Dietary sources assist the supply and may prevent clinical deficiency of cysteine. Measurements via amino acid analysis have found and confirmed low cysteine in autistics for more than 20 years. [21,22,18,24]

- Because cysteine is a component of many hormone peptides and enzyme proteins, some of these may be limited: oxytocin, somatostatin, thioneins (metallothionein), monoamine oxidase, betaine-homocysteine methyltransferase, etc.

- Because cysteine is the limiting amino acid for glutathione formation, glutathione may be deficient and tissue and metabolic oxidant stress may be present.

- Since glutathione is the detoxifying agent that escorts mercury and other toxics out of cells, low glutathione predisposes for the sequestering of mercury and other toxics inside cells.

- With glutathionylcobalamin being a necessary intermediate in the supply of makeup cobalamin (from cell lysosomes where it's stored as hydroxocobalamin), usable cobalamin could be limited, adding to the metabolic traffic jam.

- Cysteine also is the major source of sulfate for sulfation processes in body tissues. If sulfation is limited, a host of important metabolites may be inactive and many chemicals from foods and external sources may not be properly metabolized or detoxified.

Substances That Can or Should Be Sulfated

ENDOGENOUS METABOLITES	NATURAL FOOD CONSTITUENTS	SYNTHETIC CHEMICALS, DRUGS
Steroid hormones	Quercetin	Phenol or carbolic acid ("Lysol," some antiseptics)
Catecholamines, such as dopamine or adrenaline	Rutin	Nitrophenols
Bile acids	Vanillic acid (vanilla)	Aniline
Glycoproteins	Caffeic acid	Naphthol
Serotonin	Hesperidin	Alcohols
Tyrosine-containing peptides (e.g., cholecystokinin, thyroxine)	Salicylic acid (salicylates)	Paracetamol (acetaminophen)
Cerebrosides – molecules of lipid-sugar structure present in brain and stomach	Catechins	

Creatine Formation and Energy Delivery

OK, you've had the course on methionine metabolism problems in autism. That was, by far, the most complicated part. Now, let's apply it. What happens when methylation is impaired? What are the possible consequences to behavior? For some, there will be reduced melatonin formation with disordered sleep patterns. An autistic child who sleeps for only an hour or so, or who cries episodically at night, often has a melatonin deficit. Subnormal levels of L-carnitine and reduced beta-oxidation of fats could be another consequence. Look for mildly/moderately elevated adipic or suberic acids in urine on organic acid analyses. Elevation of these metabolites is consistent with carnitine deficit. We may also find choline insufficiency, cholinergic dysfunctions, and, unfortunately, deficient endogenous formation of betaine (which comes from choline). Intestinal peristalsis (and bowel regularity) is a cholinergic function, and constipation can be a result of weakness here. The choline problem can be part of the metabolic traffic jam. While the BHMT enzyme may have its own problems, the betaine (TMG) supply itself can be low because it originally came from either the diet or SAM's methylation of phosphatidylethanolamine to make choline. If SAM can't make enough choline, then choline may not make enough betaine (TMG). Then, homocysteine doesn't get adequately methylated by TMG, DMG can be low, and folate metabolism gets stuck. Finally, one of our biggest concerns is inadequate methylation of GA to make creatine, and this has dire consequences for cell perception and response functions.

Creatine is an amino acid that is involved in energy transfer, not only in muscle tissue but in the brain as well, where it acts as a phosphate shuttle. Phosphate transport by creatine allows energy transfer reactions to occur when the phosphate supply is separated spatially from the reactants. An example is upgrading ADP to ATP so that ATP + GDP → ADP + GTP can occur. One objective of this is to keep the G proteins in cell membranes loaded with energy so that cellular message transduction can occur. At the surface of cells, there are receptor proteins that extend through the double layer of fatty acids making up the wall of the cell. These are connected to a regulatory system for transmitting a signal, which happens when an external messenger molecule sticks to the receptor site. This regulator or "G protein" is attached to an enzyme system that initiates chemical changes inside the cell. Ionic stimulation by the G protein activates the enzymatic protein adenylyl cyclase, which changes ATP into cyclic AMP, cAMP. cAMP then acts as an internal messenger (a "second messenger"); it travels to protein kinase and activates it. Activated protein kinase phosphorylates proteins, making them biologically reactive. There are many different signaling transduction systems in cells, and different second messengers as well. cGMP is one, and phosphatidylinositol is another (see Inositol chapter of the Nutritional Supplements section).

SECTION THREE: MOLECULAR ASPECTS OF AUTISM

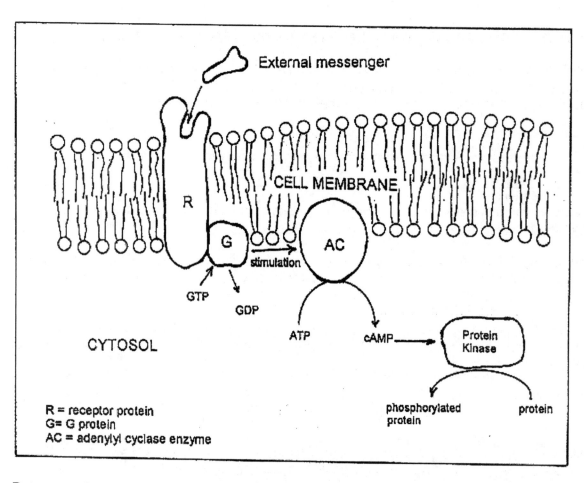

R = receptor protein
G = G protein
AC = adenylyl cyclase enzyme

But energy is required for this signal transduction, and the G protein gets it from:

$$GTP \rightarrow GDP + Pi + energy$$

However, the G protein system can't then transmit the next message until its GDP is replaced with new GTP. ATP can replenish GDP with a third phosphate. But ATP has limits to its travel permit, and it's not allowed to go where its reactivity will cause trouble. That's why phosphocreatine is needed. But first, we need to have creatine itself. G protein problems in autism were first proposed by Dr. Mary Megson.[35] We now realize that autism features inadequate energy supply to G proteins as well as inadequate methylation of lipid molecules associated with receptor and G-protein complexes.

Creatine is synthesized using parts from three amino acids: **arginine** (which usually is the limiting or least abundant one), **glycine**, and **S-adenosylmethionine**, SAM. In the kidneys, pancreas and liver, glycine combines with arginine to form ornithine and guanidinoacetate. The enzyme that promotes this first step of creatine synthesis is arginine-glycine amidinotransferase (AGAT). Lesser but significant AGAT activity exists in other tissues including heart, brain and lung. Normally, the AGAT step is the rate-limiting step of creatine synthesis.

$$\begin{array}{c} \text{Arginine} \\ + \\ \text{Glycine} \end{array} \xrightarrow{\text{AGAT}} \begin{array}{c} \text{Ornithine} \\ + \\ \text{Guanidinoacetate} \end{array}$$

(Guanidinoacetate is also called guanidoacetate or glycocyamine in various texts.)

Some of this guanidinoacetate is transported by blood to the liver and pancreas, where the second step in creatine synthesis mostly occurs. This step is methylation by SAM using the enzyme S-adenosylmethionine-guanidinoacetate methyltransferase, GAMT.

$$\text{Guanidinoacetate} \xrightarrow[\text{GAMT}]{\text{SAM} \quad \text{SAH}} \text{Creatine}$$

Besides the liver and pancreas, some GAMT activity is present in brain (neurons), ovaries and epididymal (posterior of testis) epithelial tissue.

Creatinine phosphate delivers phosphate, and in muscle, a nonenzymatic energy transfer step produces mechanical energy (muscle contraction) from chemical energy. In the process of doing this, a relatively small amount of creatine becomes creatinine.

Formation of creatinine from creatine is spontaneous (no enzyme) and irreversible. Under normal physiologic conditions, about 1% of creatine and about 2-3% of phosphocreatine are lost to creatinine per day.[36]

$$\text{Creatine phosphate} \xrightarrow{\text{Muscle}} \text{inorganic phosphate (Pi)} + \text{creatinine} + H_2O$$

Creatinine is a final waste product of energy and amino acid metabolism. It is excreted in urine, and we need to continually make new creatine to replace this loss.

As indicated above, most of our creatine survives each day. It is recycled while it participates in a shuttling or transport process that assists in supplying phosphate and chemical energy to actin or myosin in muscles.[36]

$$\text{Creatine} + \text{ATP} \xrightarrow{\text{Creatine kinase, CK}} \text{creatine phosphate} + \text{ADP}$$

$$\text{Creatine phosphate} + \text{ADP} \xrightarrow{\text{CK}} \text{creatine} + \text{ATP}$$

$$\text{ATP} \xrightarrow[\text{ATPase}]{\text{In myosin}} \text{ADP} + \text{Pi} + \text{muscle contraction}$$

$$2\ \text{ADP} \xrightarrow{\text{adenylate kinase}} \text{ATP} + \text{AMP}$$

Very significant amounts of creatine and creatine phosphate ("phosphocreatine") are normally found in brain tissue where there is no myosin or actin activity and no muscle.[3] The brain's energy consumption is mainly due to cellular communication processes, including signal transmission between neurons (synaptic processes), signal transduction across the neuronal membranes, and the attendant processes of chemical change within brain cells. When we are awake, about 80% of the energy used by the brain supports events associated with neuronal firing and recirculating of neurotransmitters.[37]

For those readers who skipped the metabolic disorders chapter, there are documented metabolic disorders associated with inadequate creatine: AGAT deficiency, GAMT deficiency, and deficient creatine transport attributed to a fault or faults in the creatine transporter gene (CTCR). All three defects can result in delayed and/or deficient expressive speech. The methylation-deficiency type (GAMT) can feature excessive blood and urine levels of guanidinoacetate, muscle dystonia in early infancy, possible regression of muscular control in later infancy, mental retardation, autistic behaviors, and self-injury.[38] Epileptic seizures are common with this problem.

There are some additional abnormal conditions reported to be possibly coincident with GAMT deficiency in some patients.[39] These may or may not occur with AGAT deficiency or CRTR defect, and biochemical explanations for them would be speculative. These conditions include:
- Mild hyperuricemia
- Mild hyperammonemia
- High lactate in cerebrospinal fluid of those with seizures
- Head circumference in CRTR defect: 4 normal, 1 macrocephalic, 2 microcephalic
- Notably abnormal electroencephalogram (lots of strange, high-amplitude spikes)
- Cranial MRI shows abnormal signals in basal ganglia, especially globus pallidus

For completeness, here is a table of analyte and genetic specifications for all three metabolic disorders with creatine.

DEFECT IN →	AGAT	GAMT	CRTR
E.C. no.	2.1.4.1	2.1.1.2	N/A
Creatinine	Low	Low	Low
Creatine	Low	Low	High in urine
Guanidinoacetate	Low	High	Normal
Faulty gene	AGAT	GAMT	SLC6A8
Chromosome locus	15q15.3	19p13.3	Xq28

What DAN! research has uncovered is that GAMT deficiency can be mimicked by an acquired defect or impairment in methylation. However, with methylation by both SAM and methionine synthase inhibited, and with transsulfuration impaired, autism includes many more problems than does just GAMT deficiency. Also of note is a finding by Alan Goldblatt and Marvin Boris, M.D., that a significant number of low-creatine autistics are low in guanidinoacetate (GA) as well.

Autism is linked to numerous abnormal lab results –

High plasma adenosine
High plasma adenosylhomocysteine
Low plasma and urine homocysteine
Low plasma cysteine
Low plasma methionine

high oxidized glutathione
high TNFα
high urine exorphin peptides
low plasma creatine, sometimes low GA
low urine creatinine

Also, the molecular problems we've found in autism correlate with biomedical interventions, such as supplements and food avoidances.

Supplementing Creatine

Obviously, supplements of creatine and creatine + GA could be of benefit to some autistics. In many cases, several grams of creatine per day are reported by parents and physicians to have a big, positive effect on speech, awareness and energy level. However, I must raise a caution flag about creatine supplements. What's needed is brain phosphocreatine. Getting from an oral creatine supplement to brain phosphocreatine requires proper operation of creatine transporters and phosphorylation promoted by creatine kinase. Unfortunately, creatine kinase is also inhibited by mercury.[40] So, oral supplements of creatine do not always work as hoped, even when creatine is measured to be low in blood. Only actual supplement trials will tell the tale. Success with creatine has not been statistically tabulated yet, and different clinicians have reported various percentages of improved patients with its use, from 10% to as high as 40%.

Synchronous Neuronal Processes – authors: Richard Deth and Jon Pangborn

Now, we address several aspects of biochemistry that relate to autistic brains:

- Besides energy delivery, why is methylation so important to cellular and whole-self awareness and response?
- Why are some autistics slow in learning or relearning appropriate responses to sensory inputs?
- What's going on with their neurons?

In the methionine metabolism chapter, we learned that normally, homocysteine is either remethylated to make methionine over again, or it is processed out of the cycle, into cysteine. Remethylation is done primarily by methylcobalamin (MeCbl) using the enzyme methionine synthase (MS), and secondarily, but importantly, by trimethylglycine (TMG) using the enzyme betaine-homocysteine methyltransferase (BHMT).

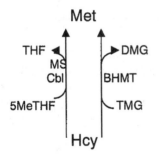

But there's more to the story, and there's more than just an energy deficit problem. Remember the radio analogy? **To produce intelligible sounds, a radio must have its power supply working and it must be tuned to the right station. We've studied the power supply (creatine, ATP). Now we have to understand the tuner's problems.**

Primates, including humans, have a neuronal cell receptor denoted dopamine D4, and it is involved in getting the cell's attention when perception and learning are supposed to occur.[41] Dopamine receptors usually are coupled to G proteins,[42] and they need energy and the right methylation environment to work properly. Besides methylation of homocysteine, the MS enzyme system is also responsible for methylating cell membrane phospholipids adjacent to and associated with the D4 receptor.[43] In the brain, methionine synthase is the only homocysteine-methylating mechanism; BHMT is not present in brain tissues and TMG cannot serve as a backup methylator. The D4 receptor gets activated by dopamine, and the first step involves adding adenosine to methionine that is in part of the D4 receptor protein.

$$ATP + Met \cdot D4 \rightarrow S\text{-adenosylmethionine} \cdot D4 + \text{phosphates}$$

This is an energy-delivery step, and somewhere along the way the ATP got its third P from phosphocreatine. Once the D4's methionine is activated to the SAM form, it can donate its methyl group (Me) to nearby phospholipids (PL) in the cell wall.

$$S\text{-adenosylmet} \cdot D4 + PL \rightarrow MetPL + S\text{-adenosylhomocysteine} \cdot D4$$

After PL methylation, we now have the D4 receptor protein with SAH where methionine was originally, and it needs to be converted back again. The enzyme SAH hydrolase starts that process by releasing adenosine.

$$SAH \cdot D4 + H2O \underset{\text{hydrolase}}{\longleftrightarrow} Hcy \cdot D4 + \text{adenosine}$$

Note that adenosine excess works against this reversible process just as it does in the regular methionine methylation cycle. And for autistics, there are multiple reasons for concern, and we have 20% with frankly high adenosine in blood.[17] The rate of methylation by SAM·D4 is controlled by the SAH·D4/SAM·D4 ratio. When SAH or adenosine accumulates, methylation decreases. Methylation of the PLs occurs on the "heads" of the phospholipids on the inner surface of the cell membrane (inner surface of the cell wall). This methylation makes the membrane more fluid or flexible, and the increased fluidity can make it easier or more difficult for membrane proteins near the D4 receptor to change shape, thereby affecting their activity.

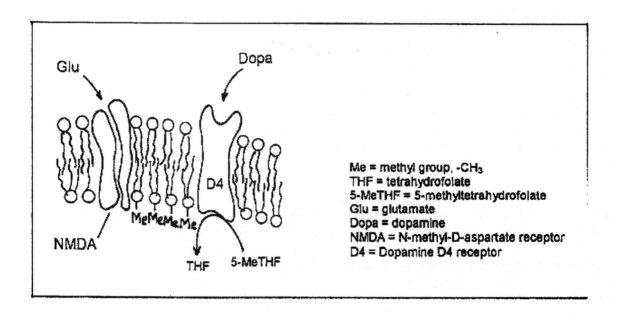

Some investigators have proposed that abnormal amounts of glutamate, acting as a neurotransmitter in the brain, are responsible for the autistic trait of not attending to sensory inputs. While we agree that this may be so, our findings are consistent with another, related situation. We think that subnormal methylation of membrane phospholipids by dopamine D4 is responsible for excessive response to glutamate by NMDA (N-methyl-D-aspartate) receptors. This, coupled with unreliable energy supplies, allows neuronal firing that is out of sequence and not coordinated with that of other neurons that participate in processing the same information.

NMDA receptor responds to glutamate, a stimulatory neurotransmitter, by opening a channel in the cell membrane that allows ions to flow through. When dopamine contacts the D4 receptor and when the adjacent PLs are methylated, opening of the NMDA receptor in response to glutamate is reduced. This decreases or stops ion flow through the channel and modulates the neuron's response to glutamate. This modulation is necessary for neuronal attention and perception, and for synchronized operation of neuronal networks. But before dealing with that, we need to complete the chemistry of the methylation cycle.

Hcy·D4 needs to become Met·D4, the form we started with. The MS enzyme controls this, and the methyl group is provided only by methylcobalamin which gets it from 5-methyltetra-hydrofolate which came from 5,10-methylenetetrahydrofolate via methylenetetrahydrofolate reductase (MTHFR). Ultimate sources of methyls are serine, glycine and one-carbon pieces that may come from catabolism of choline via TMG, DMG, and sarcosine. Formate serves as methyl precursor via these latter sources.

$$Hcy·D4 + MeCbl \rightarrow Met·D4 + Cbl$$

Methionine synthase has some important rate-controlling factors and outside influences. Insulin-like growth factor-1 (IGF-1) can stimulate (upregulate) MS activity.[27] Dopamine also does this, and it stimulates methylation of PLs by Met·D4 as well. Ethanol (alcohol in alcoholic beverages) inhibits the stimulatory signal that IGF-1 can give to MS. So, ethanol can reduce the rate at which PL methylation occurs, which reduces the effectiveness of this attention-getting mechanism for cells. Mercury at micromolar concentrations and thimerosal at nanomolar concentrations stop MS in its tracks – no measurable activity after a 60-minute exposure to 10 µM concentrations of $HgCl_2$ or 10 nM concentrations of thimerosal.[27] Lead ($PbNO_3$) at 10 µM reduces MS activity to less than 10% of normal. Aluminum also inhibits. The worst inhibitor of MS is antimony, which stops MS at nanomolar concentrations[28] (µM = amounts in millionths, nM = amounts in billionths). Clearly these toxics can interfere with MS at very low concentrations. When they interfere with MS, they also interfere with the role that dopamine-stimulated PL methylation plays in attention and cognition. As mentioned in the previous chapter, inflammatory messengers, cytokines, can also reduce methylation of homocysteine by MS. Whether or not, or to what extent this occurs in the D4 protein in neurons is a good question that merits investigation.

How does the dopamine-stimulated increase of membrane fluidity contribute to attention and learning? At this time we don't know the precise details, but the picture that is emerging indicates that it works by helping different groups of nerves to fire at the same time, in synchrony. In order to understand the importance of synchronized nerve firing, we'll first have to appreciate some basics about the wiring pattern of the brain.

The firing of nerves represents information processing. For example, in the case of vision, light enters the eye and activates millions of individual sensory neurons in the retina. Some of these neurons sense colors, while others sense edges and still others may detect texture. However, these pixels of information are not particularly useful unless we can combine them to create an image of the whole object we are viewing. Further down along the vision pathway, networks of these individual neurons (called pyramidal cells because their cell bodies look like a pyramid under the microscope) gradually combine the pixels to create the mental image of the object. Thus, the eye (the retina) breaks down the sensory experience into tiny elements, and the job of the brain is to reassemble them into a useful whole image. Synchronization of nerve firing is a critical mechanism by which resynthesis of the visual image is accomplished.

Now, imagine that another sensation is involved along with vision. Maybe you're looking at something that smells, like a sliced onion. Information from the two very different sensory systems (vision and smell) can be joined together to create a more complete, more meaningful image. However, this requires the olfactory region of the brain, located in the front, to interact with the visual region, located in the back. Integration of information from various sensory sources occurs in the cerebral cortex, especially in the frontal cortex, which is very highly developed in humans. In addition to sensory information from the outside world, the frontal cortex receives information about the internal environment such as the position of the body (e.g. legs, arms and fingers), sensations of pain, and emotional information (e.g., fear, anger). Because the information from all of these widely divergent sources has been converted into a common language, the firing rate of neurons, it can be joined together to form a highly complex perception. To create a perception, we simply have to combine the information that belongs together, and this is accomplished by bringing the firing of neurons participating in the perception into synchronization. When nerves fire together, their information content merges into a single image or perception.

During childhood development, the brain gradually creates "hard-wired" networks to facilitate synchronization. Creation of these networks represents learning. Networks are created by the development of so-called "interneurons" which link groups of the primary information-carrying pyramidal neurons to each other. Infants assemble pyramidal neurons and interneurons into networks by guiding information through them repeatedly. Repetition of experiences, learning, creates internal patterns of neuronal connections that result in efficient processing of information. Thus, the brain is a "self-organizing network." Attended sensory or emotional information (as opposed to unattended information) is the most powerful influence for creating networks. Once an interneuronal network has been formed, it can effectively interact with other networks, but again, only if they are all firing in synchrony.

Measurements of brain activity during awareness and attention show that there is an increase in synchronized firing at a particular frequency range, called the gamma frequency. This corresponds to about 40 firings per second, also known as 40 Hertz (Hz).[44] Those particular regions (i.e. networks) of the brain involved in an episode of attention fire synchronously at 40 Hz, while other regions do not. Dopamine is the most important neurotransmitter involved in causing attention, and D4 dopamine receptors appear to play a significant role in promoting synchronization and therefore in promoting attention. It is interesting that motion pictures, which create continuous visual experience, operate at about 40 frames per second, or 40 Hz. Also notable is that when we dream, increased gamma frequency synchronization can be detected, just as if we were paying attention to something. However, the object of this attention while dreaming appears to be information coming from memory circuits, rather than real sensory experience.

D4 receptors are primarily located in interneurons. During childhood development, dopamine stimulation can contribute to forming the interneuron networks. Once the networks have been formed, D4 receptor stimulation can alter the firing rates of the networks, favoring a gamma frequency. This is where PL methylation comes in. It is the more fluid membrane environment, caused by methylation, which serves to bring the neuronal network to gamma frequency so that it is able to interact with other networks that are also firing at the same frequency. Without proper methylation of the membrane phospholipids by S-adenosylmet·D4, a neuron cannot fire at the proper frequency and will not be in coordination with other neurons in the network. In a sense, dopamine-stimulated PL methylation functions like a tuner knob on a radio, bringing the tuner to the desired frequency so that information can flow from radio waves in the air to the circuits in the radio, creating sound as an output or response.

If methylation is impaired, synchronization at gamma frequency will be impaired. We believe that this is part of what's going wrong in autistic brains. At the cellular level, perception (and response) to sensory input requires that neurons be ready to receive the incoming message. All of the cells, thousands of them that are needed to receive and respond to a "hello," have to have energy on hand, and they need the right chemistry in place including enough methylated PLs between the D4 and NMDA receptor proteins. Only when this occurs can they respond in coordinated fashion, simultaneously or in sequence as may be needed. Increased dopaminergic activity increases the amount of 40 Hz oscillations and increases the brain's attention to business, but only when the above-described energy transfer and chemistry are working properly. If some of the neurons needed to acknowledge a "hello" have deficient methylation at D4 receptor sites, the "hello" is likely to be perceived as a jumbled noise of no consequence and is likely to go unheeded. That typical autistic nonresponse to a "hello" can occur if phosphocreatine doesn't show up on time, if ATP is inadequate for upgrading GDP and for making SAM·D4, if SAM·D4 can't methylate, or if MS can't process Hcy·D4 and reduce SAH·D4 levels.

Our brains are certainly amazing organs, marvels of complexity with seemingly unlimited capabilities. However, the underlying neurochemical events that allow these capabilities are fragile, and autism shows us what happens when certain pathways, particularly those involved in methylation, don't function as they should. Fortunately, our limited knowledge of these biochemical pathways, and dedicated efforts by some caring physicians, have led to treatments than can enhance methylation and bring benefit to many autistic children.

References, Autism at the Molecular Level

1. Mudd SH and Levy HL "Disorders of Transsulfuration" Chapt.15 in *The Metabolic Basis of Inherited Disease* 5th ed McGraw-Hill (1983) 525.
2. Minshew NJ, Goldstein G et al. "A preliminary 31P MRS study of autism: evidence for undersynthesis and increased degradation of brain membranes" *Biol.Psychiatry* 33 (1993) 762-773.
3. Von Figura K, Hanefeld F et al. "Guanidinoacetate Methyltransferase Deficiency" Chapt.84 in Scriver et al. eds., *The Metabolic and Molecular Bases of Inherited Disease* 8th ed, McGraw-Hill (2001) 1903.
4. Hershfield MS and Mitchell BS, "Adenosine Deaminase (ADA) Deficiency" Chapt 109 in Scriver, et al. eds, 8th ed., op.cit. 2593.
5. Stubbs, G, Litt M et al. "Adenosine deaminase activity decreased in autism" *J.Am.Acad Child Psych* 21 no.1 (1982) 71-74.
6. Daddona PE and Kelley WN "Human adenosine deaminase binding protein: assay, purification and properties" *J.Biol.Chem.* 253 no.13 (1978) 4617-4623.
7. Dong RP, Kameoka J et al. "Characterization of adenosine deaminase binding to human CD26 on T cells and its biological role in immune response" *J.Immunology* 156 no.4 (1996) 1349-1355.

8. Jeanfavre DD, Waska JR et al. "Effect of deoxyformycin and Val-boroPro on the associated catalytic activities of lymphocyte CD26 and ecto-adenosine deaminase" *Biochem. Pharmacolol* 52 no11 (1996) 1757-1765.

9. Reichelt KL, Ekrem J and Scott H "Gluten, milk proteins and autism: dietary intervention effects on behavior and peptide secretion" *J.Appl.Nutrition* 42 no.1 (1990) 1-11.

10. Reichelt KL, Knivsberg AM et al. "Nature and consequences of Hyperpeptiduria and bovine casomorphins found in autistic syndromes" *Dev.Brain Dysfunct.* 7 (1994) 71-85.

11. Shattock P, Kennedy A et al. "Role of neuropeptides in autism and their relationships with classical neurotransmitters" *Brain Dysfunct.* 3 (1990) 328-345.

12. Cade R, Privette M et al. "Autism and schizophrenia: intestinal disorders" *Nutr.Neuroscience* 3 (2000) 57-72.

13. Misumi Y and Ikehara Y "Dipeptidyl-peptidase IV" Chapter 128 in Barrett, Rawlings and Woessner eds. *Handbook of Proteolytic Enzymes* Academic Press (1998) 378-382.

14. Püschel G, Mentlein R and Heymann E "Isolation and characterization of dipeptidyl peptidase IV from human placenta" *Eur.J.Biochemistry* 126 (1982) 359-365.

15. Schade RP, Van Leperen-Van Dijk AG, et al. "Cell surface expression of CD25, CD26 and CD30 by allergen-specific T cells is intrinsically different in cow's milk allergy" *Allergy Clin.Immunology* 109 no.2 (2002) 357-362.

16. Persico AM, Militerni R et al. "Adenosine deaminase alleles and autistic disorder" *Am J Med Genet* (Neuropsychiatric Genetics) 96 (2000) 784-790.

17. James SJ "Abnormal folate-dependent methionine and glutathione metabolism in children with autism: potential for increased sensitivity to thimerosal and other pro-oxidants" Proceedings April 2004 DAN! Conference, Washington DC 59-63.

18. James SJ, Cutler P et al. "Metabolic biomarkers of increased oxidative stress and impaired methylation capacity in children with autism" *Am J Clin Nutr* 2004 Dec; 80 no.6 1611-1617.

19. Hershfield MS and Mitchell BS, op.cit. 2604.

20. Mudd HS, Levy HL and Skovby F "Disorders of Transsulfuration," Chapter 23 in Scriver, Beaudet et al. *The Metabolic Basis of Inherited Disease* 6th ed, McGraw-Hill (1989) 696.

21. Pangborn JB "Detection of metabolic disorders in people with autism" Proceedings of NSAC International Autism Conference of the Americas, San Antonio TX (1984). National Society for Children and Adults with Autism, Washington DC.

22. Owens SC, "Understanding the sulfur system" May 2003 DAN! Conference Proceedings, Philadelphia PA 65-75.

23. James SJ, Slikker W et al. "Thimerosal neurotoxicity is associated with glutathione depletion: protection with glutathione precursors" (2004).

24. Bradstreet J, the International Autism Research Center, Melbourne FL, publication of amino acid analysis results in progress, includes finding low cyst(e)ine in blood plasma.

25. Audhya T "Laboratory indices of vitamin and mineral deficiency in autism" Proceedings October 2004 DAN! Conference San Diego CA 239-274.

26. Mosharov E, Cranford MR and Banerjee R "The quantitatively important relationship between homocysteine metabolism and glutathione synthesis by the transsulfuration pathway and its regulation by redox changes" *Biochemistry* 39 no.42 (2000) 13005-13011.

27. Vitvitsky V, Mosharov E et al. "Redox regulation of homocysteine-dependent glutathione synthesis" *Redox Rep* 8 no.1 (2003) 57-63.

28. Banerjee R and Zou GG "Redox regulation and reaction mechanism of human cystathionine-beta synthase: a PLP-dependent heme sensor protein" *Arch Biochem Biophysic* 433 no.1 (2005) 144-156.

29. Breska AP and Garrow TA "Recombinant human liver betaine-homocysteine S-methyltransferase: identification of three cysteine residues critical for zinc binding" *Biochemistry* 38 no.42 (1999) 13991-13998.

30. Goldblatt A, informal report to DAN! Think Tank, January 2004, New Orleans LA. Allan Goldblatt PA-C assists Marvin Boris, M.D., at his Woodbury NY practice. Genomics testing of BHMT was performed at McGill University.

31. Waly M, Olteanu H et al. "Activation of methionine synthase by insulin-like growth factor-1 and dopamine: a target for neurodevelopmental toxins and thimerosal" *Molecular Psychiatry* 4 (2004) 358-370.

32. Deth RC, informal report at DAN! Think Tank, January 2004, New Orleans LA. Richard C Deth, Ph.D. is Professor of Pharmacology at Northeastern University, Boston MA.

33. Foulkes E "Metal disposition: an analysis of underlying mechanisms" Chapt. 1 in Goyer RA, Klaasen CD and Waalkes MP eds *Metal Toxicology* Academic Press (1995) 18-21.

34. Clarksen TW as quoted by Dalton LW in C&EN, January 9, 2004, 70. Thomas W. Clarksen is Professor of Environmental Medicine at the University of Rochester, NY.

35. Megson MN "Is autism a G-alpha protein defect reversible with natural vitamin A?" *Med.Hypotheses* 54 no.6 (2000) 979-983.

36. Granner DK "Hormone Action" Chapt.44 in Murray RK, DK Granner et al., *Harper's Biochemistry* 25th ed Appleton & Lange (2000) 541-544.

37. Shulman RG, Rothman DL et al. "Energetic basis of brain activity: implications for neuroimaging" *Trends in Neurosciences* 27 no.8 (2004) 489-495.

38. Salomons GS, van Dooren SJM et al. "X-linked creatine-transporter gene (SLC6A8) defect: a new creatine deficiency syndrome" *Am.J.Human Genetics* 68 (2001) 1497-1500.

39. Salomons, van Dooren SJM et al. "X-linked creatine transporter defect: an overview" *J.Inherited Metabolic Disorders* 26 (2003) 309-318.

40. Haley BE, private communication. Boyd Haley, Ph.D., is Professor and Chairman of the Dept. of Chemistry, U. of Kentucky. Professor Haley states that mercury assimilated into the body has inhibiting effects on many enzyme systems, including creatine kinase.

41. Deth, RC *Molecular Origins of Human Attention* Kluwer (2003) 1-22.

42. Murray RK "The Biochemical Basis of Some Neuropsychiatric Disorders" Chapt. 64 in Murray, Granner et al. eds., *Harper's Biochemistry* 25th ed. Appleton & Lange (2000) 845-847.

43. Deth RC *Molecular Origins of Human Attention* op.cit. 23-36.

44. Deth RC *Molecular Origins of Human Attention* op.cit.60-62.

Measles, Inflammation and Intestinal Disorder

After reading the chapters about methionine metabolism, methylation, and neuronal functions, you might be quite satisfied that things have been explained to a reasonable degree. But unfortunately, there's more than one way to block a cell's ability to communicate. As we've seen, messing up its internal chemistry (impeding methylation) is one way, and parking dietary opiate peptides at message-reception sites is at least contributory to this blockage.

What else can cause or contribute to a cell's not attending to external signals? Evidently, a virus, under certain, perhaps unusual circumstances, can contribute significantly to this.

Viruses are very small, live organisms of a size that lies somewhere between proteins and bacteria – about fifty nanometers to two or three hundred nanometers in size, something that can be seen by an electron microscope but not by a regular light microscope. They inhabit just about everything: animals, plants, even bacteria (bacterial ones are called bacteriophages). Bacteriophages are depicted as horrible spider-like things with a syringe-like injector apparatus in the center. Some viruses are spherical with many facets, and resemble a Buckminster Fuller "bucky ball;" some are rod-shaped, like miniature bacterial rods; and some have helix shapes. Some contain viral DNA, others just RNA.

The objective of most viruses is to find a host cell that they can invade and use to prosper and reproduce. A virus starts this by using specific proteins on its outer coat to attach to receptor sites on the surface of promising cells. In this respect, it binds just as a messenger hormone or an exorphin peptide does. Usually, a specific virus can only bind to certain types of cells in a host, and the result can be a specific disease centered in the organ that features those cells. Hepatitis virus infecting liver cells is an example. The human immunodeficiency virus favors immune cells, lymphocytes, and it looks for a protein receptor denoted as CD4 as its attachment and entry point.

Once a virus is anchored to a cell's receptor site, what happens next depends on the type of cell and type of virus. Viruses with lipid (fatty acid) outer membranes can fuse with cell membranes. "Naked" viruses, those with just a protein structure and either RNA or DNA for chromosomal structure, bind and then wait until the cell internalizes a portion of its outer surface (endocytosis) or envelops some foreign substance, as immune cells can do during phagocytosis. Viruses can use several strategies, depending upon the type of virus, to trick the cell into reproducing viral RNA or DNA. Typically, the early stages of cell invasion involve some of the cell's signaling or message transmission apparatus (including the receptor's regulatory proteins, G proteins and adenylyl cyclase). Some viruses can send signals to the cell that accelerate the incorporation of its DNA or RNA into the cell.

In autism, we are particularly, but not exclusively, concerned with strains of the measles virus. The measles virus contains a single strand of RNA and belongs to a viral subgroup called paramyxoviruses.[1] Mumps is in this group, too. They are composed of about 16,000 nucleotides, and are described as having both a protein coat and a lipid envelope. They're roughly helical in shape, and range in size from 125 to 250 nanometers. The findings by Dr. Andrew Wakefield et al. about lymphoid lesions in the mucosa of the small intestine of autistics and other developmentally-disordered children,[2,3] and the fact that they harbor measles virus (vaccination strains, to be specific), have made me pay more notice to the viral aspect.

At first, I thought that viral-caused lesions in the small intestine were just another mechanism for increased gut permeability and entry of toxins and exorphin peptides. Then came information that neurotransmitters in the gastrointestinal organs are much the same as those in the brain, although their targets and functions are different.[4] Nerves communicate directly from gut to brain so that trouble in the gut becomes an alarming situation for the brain. In fact, with autism, some of the brain's perception and response functions could be quite preoccupied with intestinal disorder and inflammation. Also, other tissues such as the liver could be receiving cytokine instructions that result in oxidant stress for autistics. To compensate, cells in such tissues might reduce methylation of homocysteine (by methionine synthase) and shift more homocysteine to production of cysteine and glutathione.[5,6,7] Jyonouchi et al. have reported notable cytokine elevations in autistics, especially tumor necrosis factor-alpha, TNFα.[8,9] This cytokine is very pro-inflammatory, and acts as a localized messenger that signals for oxidant production in cells. If upregulation of antioxidant production (e.g., glutathione) does not occur coincident with TNF-α activity, cellular oxidant stress results.[10] But before we can conclude that the toxin entry and inflammation result, at least in part, from measles, it would be wise to find evidence that the measles virus could infect and interfere with cellular processes in a persistent, chronic manner.

The questions raised about measles led me to look for documented connections between static infection and this virus. I searched for scientific evidence that some strain of measles could:

a. Infect a cell and block message processing sites;

b. Disable other message transmission activities even though it was not attached to those receptor sites; and,

c. Become a static, persistent condition without progressing through its usual disease cycle. This could allow chronic inflammation to occur.

There is at least one such description of measles that fits the above requirements exactly. The one I found was investigated and published by Slavica Krantic et al. of the Laboratory for Molecular and Cellular Biology in Marseilles, France.[11] Using human mononuclear cells from peripheral blood and Jurkat T-lymphocytes (a type of human lymphoblast), they found that the measles virus attached itself to somatostatin bindings sites on cell surfaces.

Somatostatin, a pituitary and pancreatic hormone, is a normal inhibitor of adenylyl cyclase (reduces cAMP formation). In various types of cells, somatostatin signals for: reduced glucose uptake, release of free fatty acids, enhanced calcium retention, lactogenesis, inhibition of TSH release, inhibition of growth hormone release, and inhibition of glucagon release (especially in insulin insufficiency).[12] On cells in the gastrointestinal tract, somatostatin signals for decreased cellular release of gastrin (downregulation of gastric acid production for the stomach) and decreased digestive enzyme secretion (pancreas and small intestine), and it can result in decreased delivery of dietary nutrients from the gastrointestinal tract to the bloodstream.[12] In its reduced, active form, somatostatin is a signaling peptide (a hormone) composed of 14 amino acids, two of which are cysteine, and one of these is at the carboxyl end of the peptide. If it's oxidized, it's stuck to itself or to another cysteinyl molecule by a disulfide, -S-S- bond. We don't know if somatostatin is at normal levels in autism, but it may be limited in some just as glutathione is by limited/deficient cysteine.

Obviously, attachment by measles to a cell's somatostatin binding site is not a good thing for regulation of cellular activity. Worse, on these T-cells, Krantic et al. found that the measles virus greatly reduced the function of other somatostatin binding sites, and it coupled to adenylyl cyclase in a way that reinforced the inhibitory effects of somatostatin.[13] Also, it impaired the capacity of adenylyl cyclase to be stimulated by other messengers, thus fulfilling requirements (a) and (b) above.

Measles-infected cells can proliferate because the anti-proliferative control by cyclic AMP is reduced or disabled by the virus itself. But that's not what Krantic et al. found with these cells when measles was attached to the somatostatin site. The viral infection did not proceed as expected, but became static, possibly due to the virus coincidentally switching on other chemistry that is antiproliferative.[14] So, requirement (c) is also satisfied – the possibility of chronic infection with measles has been observed with cells in vitro.

SECTION THREE: MOLECULAR ASPECTS OF AUTISM

Immunologists to whom I've shown the Krantic paper respond that it's not relevant to autism because the measles virus doesn't bind to somatostatin receptors. It binds primarily to CD46 ("membrane cofactor protein") and secondarily to another receptor, CD150 (at much slower rates). However, there is some cell receptor interaction between measles and substance P, at least in glassware on the lab bench. In vitro studies show that each will displace the other from binding sites on cultured cells.[15,16] But substance P is a small peptide with proline at every other position in its structure, and it binds to and is hydrolyzed (broken down) by DPP4, alias CD26, alias adenosine deaminase binding protein.[17] Thus, there appear to be some important, unanswered questions about where measles can bind under various circumstances. I have become convinced that there is certainly enough evidence to put measles infection high on the suspect list of mechanisms that can make cells and the whole person autistic.

Measles is a highly contagious virus that causes fatigue, runny nose, cough, fever, reddened and light-sensitive eyes, and, after several days, a rash. In the normal course of infection, the rash usually starts at the hairline of the head and spreads down the body, with pink spots one-quarter of an inch in diameter. The rash turns brown and fades after 3 or 4 days, and the fever, which can peak at 104°F, also subsides after the rash has spread. The serious complication of measles, encephalitis, occurs in 0.1% of cases, and a small percentage of those can lead to neuronal damage and mental retardation. Measles is also called rubeola.

"German measles" or "rubella" ("three-day measles") is caused by a different virus. Rubella is less contagious than measles (rubeola), and features a transient rash in which the spots do not merge, but also includes a fever. Although less severe than rubeola measles, rubella in a pregnant woman can cause damage to the fetus that results in mental retardation, birth defects or other congenital problems. Autistic children with a prenatal history of rubella were noted in the 1960s and 1970s.[18] One case of autism associated with measles (rubeola) was also recorded at that time. Eight post-natal mumps cases were also documented. As indicated previously, the mumps virus is very similar structurally to the measles virus. Coincidentally, measles, mumps and rubella are the three attenuated or inactivated viral substances in the MMR vaccine.

At the semiannual DAN! Meetings for 2000, 2001, 2002 and 2003, the general audience, typically including about 75% parents and over 1,000 in number, have been asked to raise their hands if the onset of autism in their children closely followed administration of the measles-mumps-rubella ("MMR") vaccine. There is a strong perception among parents of children with "regressive" autism that the MMR vaccine is at fault; at least 60% of the audience has held their hands up at each meeting. Yet, if we were to line up 200 infants and administer the MMR shot to each, statistics indicate that about 199 would not develop autism or autistic-like symptoms. The big question is: Why did it happen to one of the 200 (or one in 165, per recent CDC statistics)?[19] This incidence is vastly higher now than was the incidence of autism associated with "wild" measles, mumps and rubella in the 1960s and 1970s. Is it because children today have their immune systems compromised by the excessive total amount of mercury (thimerosal) accumulated from other administered vaccines? Is it because the chemistry of some of the cultured and attenuated vaccine strains is different? Is it because diets are junkier, and nutritional status is actually worse? Is it that some just can't cope with so many challenges to the immune system in infancy and early childhood? We don't know. But, we do notice that we've got three viruses that each have historical association with autism, all in the same shot!

That we have a measles problem in many present-day autistics is supported by the findings of Professor Vijendra Singh at Utah State University.[20] Professor Singh has been measuring a number of immunologic parameters in autistics, including antibodies to myelin basic protein (MBP), neuron-axon filament protein, and associations to four viruses including measles virus and human herpes virus-6. Autoantibodies to myelin basic protein were found in 65% of 112 tested autistics, indicating some degree of autoimmune response to an important protein component of myelin in brains of two-thirds of those tested. None of the 20 control children showed this. Using an analytical procedure known as Enzyme-Linked Immunosorbent Assay ("ELISA"), Professor Singh tested blood sera of autistics for antibodies to measles IgG, HHV-6 IgG, Rubella IgG, and cytomegalovirus IgG. Only the measles antibody level was found to be statistically higher in autistic children versus controls. Professor Singh then correlated the MBP antibody positives with the measles IgG antibody positives and found 90% correlation between the two. That is, 90% of the measles-responding autistics also had antibodies to MBP.[20] Of particular concern is that none of the tested autistics with positive measles IgG antibodies had experienced a wild measles infection. All had received MMR vaccinations.

In 1998, Wakefield et al. first reported finding a nodular hyperplasia condition in the lymphoid tissue of the ileal portion of the small intestine of autistic children.[21] A frequent lecturer at DAN! conferences, Dr. Wakefield has presented visual documentation of these lesions which were the first real histological findings of gastrointestinal tissue disorder in "regressive developmental disorder" or autism. Case histories tabulated in the 1998 publication showed MMR vaccination to be common to the cases that were studied, but no virology was performed at that time to prove measles involvement. Subsequent to Dr. Wakefield's documentation of ileal-lymphoid nodular hyperplasia in autistic children, this finding (without vaccine implications) was repeated and confirmed by other gastroenterologists including Timothy Buie, M.D., of Massachusetts General Hospital, and Arthur Krigsman, M.D., of New York.[22,23] In 2000, Wakefield et al. presented further, more detailed evidence of enterocolitis in developmentally disordered children.[3] Also in 2000, Kawashima et al. (including Dr. Wakefield) published a study that linked the MMR-vaccination type of measles virus to the bowel lesions in some autistics.[24] They studied eight Crohn's patients, three patients with ulcerative colitis, and nine others with autism. One of the eight Crohn's patients, one of the three colitis patients, and three of the nine autistics showed positive matches to MMR-type measles. All control cases were negative. Analytical matching was by sequencing of a telltale section of the measles virus RNA.

Additionally, a group of medical researchers in the UK and Ireland (also including Dr. Wakefield) has matched a specific type of MMR-measles virus vaccination to the virus in the lymphonodular lesions of 91 autistic and developmentally disordered children with various gastrointestinal conditions. Seventy-five of 91 developmentally disordered/autistic children had evidence of the measles virus versus 5 of 70 in the control group.[25] A further article, cited previously, by Uhlmann and Martin et al. also connects measles to inflammatory bowel disease in developmentally disordered children.[3]

Association of MMR-type measles virus with the ileal-lymphoid hyperplasia of autism remains controversial at this writing. Not all gastroenterologists who confirm the lymphonodular hyperplasia of the ileum have found or even looked for measles in the lesions. Some outright indignation has been expressed on the issue, and Dr. Wakefield has borne the brunt of dogmatic criticism (opinion). Perhaps medical orthodoxy is in denial and looks upon this as an attack on disease prevention by immunization. In reality, we have a vaccine that is probably too potent for up to 0.5% of young children who may have compromised immune and metabolic capabilities for many of the reasons that are described in this report.

In 2003, Singh et al. published more results of serological studies, this time involving 52 autistic children and 45 controls (including 15 siblings of the autistics), in which they measured antibody reaction for measles virus vaccine.[26] Elevated antibodies to measles virus vaccine were found in 83% of the autistic children but in none of the controls, including the autistics' siblings. And only the measles antibody (IgG) was statistically elevated in the autistics, not that of mumps or rubella.

In 2004, Bradstreet, El Dahr et al. reported on analysis of cerebrospinal fluid in three autistics who had been vaccinated with pharmaceutical MMR vaccine and who had developed ileal lymphoid nodular hyperplasia.[27] Additionally, the presence of measles virus of vaccine-strain type had been confirmed for these three cases by genomic assessment procedures, TaqMan probes and real-time quantitative polymerase chain-reaction (RT-PCR) analysis. These clinicians found the measles fusion gene in the cerebrospinal fluid of all three autistics. Since that publication, measles virus protein has been identified in the CNS of 25 more autistics for a total of 28 so far.[28] The fusion gene is the part of the measles virus that expresses for its binding protein – the part that sticks the virus to CD46. This is evidence that the vaccination strain of the measles virus in autistics has found its way into tissue of the central nervous system.

This finding of measles virus protein in the central nervous system is not unique to autism, although identifying the strain to be of vaccine source may be very significant. Using RT-PCR, Katayama et al. found mutated parts of measles virus in post-mortem autopsied specimens: 10 of 51 brain specimens, 9 of 51 kidney specimens and 7 of 51 lung tissue specimens.[29] There was no association, while living, of any of these 51 subjects with autism.

There is, however, one very intriguing report in the literature about measles and other paramyxoviruses. In 1982, Münzel and Koschel (Univ. Würzburg, Germany) studied methylation of the phospholipid, phosphatidylethanolamine in rat glioma cells.[30] When fully methylated by SAM, phosphatidylcholine results. With their viral strains, Münzel and Koschel found that catecholamine-stimulated beta-adrenergic receptor-dependent methylation ceased in glioma tissue that had persistent viral presence. Other methylation chemistry was unchanged. Do we now have a vaccine-strain measles virus that, if it becomes persistent due to decreased immunity, can directly disrupt methylation of phospholipids near cell receptor sites? Could vaccine measles disrupt D4 methylation?

In summary, there is strong circumstantial and correlative evidence that measles is at least partly causative of autism in what is probably a large subset, possibly a majority, of children on the autistic spectrum. If we have an individual with genetic or acquired weakness in the chemistry that operates cellular message transmission, we then have an internal susceptibility to loss of attention and perception. If messenger receptor sites are blockaded externally with exorphin peptides, then message transmission is further inhibited. If measles sticks in the wrong place, it too might interfere indefinitely with the same mechanism of cellular perception. And most intriguing is the oxidant stress and inflammation connection to decreased methylation and neuronal energy supply. These aspects need to be thoroughly researched for autism by more scientists who are not afraid of what might be discovered.

Likely Chain of Events that Leads to Autism

> Due to genetics, the at-risk child has suboptimal metabolism of one or more of: one-carbon groups or folate, transmethylation, transsulfuration, adenosine or glutathione. Food allergies, especially milk allergy, add concern.

↓

> Nutritional status may be suboptimal, particularly for vitamins A, B_6, B_{12}, magnesium and zinc. Cell defenses against toxicity and infection are hampered.

↓

> Toxic exposures occur: mercury or thimerosal, other sulfur-seeking toxic elements (antimony, arsenic), organophosphate pesticides, combinations of petrochemicals and solvents. Hampered are: DPP4 (adenosine deaminase and exorphin digestion), methionine synthase, folate chemistry, glutathione metabolism.

↓

> Methionine metabolism and methylation become deficient. Phosphate delivery to neurons via creatine is subnormal, causing unreliable and inadequate energy for neurons and networks to operate and coordinate.

↓

> Compromised cell defenses allow measles and other viruses to invade cells; abnormal nucleotide-mediated immunity allows infections to become persistent, measles in particular. Inflammation and gut dysbiosis occur.

↓

> Methylation of phospholipids near dopamine D4 receptors in neurons becomes deficient. Persistent brain infection by measles may also cause lack of neuronal phospholipid methylation.

↓

> Deficient frequency modulation (synchrony) and deficient energy modulation of neuronal networks, during the first two years of life, prevent adequate interconnection of neuronal networks. Coordinated thoughts, organized responses and expressive speech regress or do not develop, depending on age.

↓

> Inflammation (gut or brain) results in cytokine and oxidant-induced epigenetic changes such as upregulation of ubiquitin ligase (chromosome 15). Methionine metabolism is routed away from methylation toward transsulfuration (cysteine, GSH), but transsulfuration is disabled and metabolic response to inflammation is chronically deficient.

↓

> Biochemical, epistatic and infectious gridlock occurs, and neuronal network coordination remains deficient = autism.

SECTION THREE: MOLECULAR ASPECTS OF AUTISM

References – Viral Infections, Inflammation and Intestinal Disorder

1. Levine A *Viruses* Sci Am Library (1992) 218.
2. Wakefield AJ, Anthony A et al. "Enterocolitis in children with developmental disorders" *Am.J.Gastroenterology* 95 no.9 (2000) 2285-2295.
3. Uhlmann V, Martin CM et al. "Potential viral pathogenic mechanism for new variant inflammatory bowel disease" *J.Clin.Pathology: Mol Pathol* 55 (2002) 84-90.
4. Wood JD "Neuropathy in the brain-in-the-gut" *Eur J Gastroenterol Hepatol* (2000) Jun 12 (6) 597-600.
5. Mosharov E, Cranford MR and Banerjee R "The quantitatively important relationship between homocysteine metabolism and glutathione synthesis by the transsulfuration pathway and its regulation by redox changes" *Biochemistry* 39 no.42 (2000) 13005-13011.
6. Vitvitsky V, Mosharov E et al. "Redox regulation of homocysteine-dependent glutathione synthesis" *Redox Rep* 8 no.1 (2003) 57-63.
7. Banerjee R and Zou GG "Redox regulation and reaction mechanism of human cystathionine-beta synthase: a PLP-dependent heme sensor protein" *Arch Biochem Biophysic* 433 no.1 (2005) 144-156.
8. Jyonouchi H, Sun S et al. "Innate and adaptive immune responses in children with regression autism: evaluation of the effects of environmental factors including vaccination" (2001). Dr. Jyanouchi is at the Dept. of Pediatrics, University of Minnesota, Minneapolis MN.
9. Jyonouchi H, Sun S et al. "Innate immunity associated with inflammatory responses and cytokine production against common dietary proteins in patient with autism spectrum disorder" *Neuropsychobiology* (2002) 46 no.2 76-84.
10. Halliwell B and Gutteridge *Free Radicals in Biology and Medicine* Oxford U Press (1999 ed.) 334-336.
11. Krantic S, Enjalbert A et al. "Measles virus modulates human T-cell somatostatin receptors and their coupling to adenylyl cyclase" *J of virology* 71 no.10 (1997) 7470-7477.
12. Granner DK "Hormones of the pancreas and gastrointestinal tract" in Murray RK et al. eds., *Harper's Biochemistry* 25th ed (2000) 624.
13. Krantic S et al. op.cit. 7473-7474.
14. Krantic S et al. ibid.7475.
15. Harrowe GM, Mitsuhashi M et al. "Measles virus-substance P receptor interactions: possible novel mechanism of viral fusion" *J.Clin.Investigations* 84 no.4 (1990) 1324-1327; see also erratum, 86 no.1 (1990) 377.
16. Harrowe GM, Sudduth-Klinger et al. "Measles virus-substance P receptor interaction: Jurkat lymphocytes transfected with substance P receptor cDNA enhance measles virus fusion and replication" *Cellular & Molecular Neurobiology* 12 no.5 (1992) 397-409.
17. Misumi Y and Ikehara Y "Dipeptidyl-peptidase IV," Chapt 128 in Barnett, Rawlings and Woessner, eds. *Handbook of Proteolytic Enzymes* Academic Press (1998) 378-382.
18. Coleman M and Gillberg C *The Biology of the Autistic Syndromes* Praeger Pub (1985) 131-139.
19. CDC Website, http://www.cdc.gov.
20. Singh V. "Neuro-immunopathogenesis in autism" *New Foundations of Biology* Elsevier Science (2001) 447-458.
21. Wakefield AJ, Murch SH et al. "Ileal-lymphoid-nodular hyperplasia, non-specific colitis, and pervasive developmental disorder in children *The Lancet* 351 (Feb 1998) 637-641.

22. Buie T "Examining GI issues in children with autism and the effectiveness of traditional GI medicines" April DAN! 2003 Conference Proceedings, Philadelphia PA, 163-169. Timothy Buie, M.D., is at Massachusetts General Children's Hospital.
23. Krigsman A "Emerging clinical patterns of enterocolitis in autistic children" October DAN! 2003 Conference Proceedings, Portland OR, 145-153. Arthur Krigsman, M.D., practices in Woodbury NY.
24. Kawashima H et al. "Detection and sequencing of measles virus from peripheral mononuclear cells from patients with inflammatory bowel disease and autism" *Digestive Disease and Sciences* 45 no.4 (2000) 723-729.
25. Torrente F et al. "Small intestinal enteropathy with epithelial IgG and Complement deposition in children with regressive autism" *Molecular Psychiatry* 7 (2002) 375-382.
26. Singh VK and Ryan LJ "Elevated levels of measles antibodies in children with autism" *Pediatric Neurology* 28 no.4 (2003) 292-294.
27. Bradstreet JJ, El Dahr J et al. "Detection of measles virus genomic RNA in cerebrospinal fluid of children with regressive autism: a report of three cases" *J.Am.Phys.Surgeons* 9 no.2 (2004) 38-45.
28. Private communication from Jeffrey Bradstreet, M.D., Director, International Autism Research Center, Melbourne, FL.
29. Katayama Y, Kohsok K et al. "Detection of measles virus in RNA from autopsied human specimens" *J.Clin.Microbiol.* 36 no.1 (1998) 299-301.
30. Münzel P and Koschel K "Alteration in phospholipid methylation and impairment of signal transmission in persistently paramyxovirus-infected C6 rat glioma cells" *Proc.Natl.Acad.Sci.USA* 79 June (1982) 3692-3696.

Toxicities and Infectious Stressors – Revisited

Now that you know more about what's going wrong biochemically in autism, let's go back over some stressors that could contribute to the onset of autism.

What toxins or environmental stressors are we concerned about? Obviously, **mercury and thimerosal** are at the top of the list. As we saw in the discussion on biochemistry, mercury inhibits a key enzyme that's needed for methylation processes to work properly – methionine synthase. It also inhibits DPP4/CD26 and some of adenosine's metabolism. Methylation, as we've shown, is necessary for energy delivery and activation of electrochemical processes that are required for cellular (neuronal) perception and response. But what else is of concern?

Antimony is an element similar in characteristics to mercury and arsenic. Antimony inhibits methionine synthase even more than mercury does, and it interferes with several other enzymes including both monoamine oxidase (which mercury inhibits, too) and phosphofructokinase (PFK).[1] When PFK is not working correctly, carbohydrate metabolism is impeded. One consequence is increased degradation of purines in PFK-deficient muscle tissue. This results in too much ammonia, inosine, hypoxanthine and uric acid.[2] Biochemically, these aspects of antimony excess are similar to "purine autism." Antimony, as oxides and pentafluoride, is used as a flame retardant in textiles and carpets. While it may be considered inert or non-reactive in these chemical forms, there is literature and testimonial evidence that action by mildew mold can release antimony in a volatile form.[3] I've been advised by one doctor that high antimony levels were found twice in urine collected from an infant's blanket; that urine had an ammonia odor. The child's urine itself had no measurable antimony.

Antimony is of special concern because of possible toxic synergism with thimerosal or ethyl mercury. Antimony binds to sulfhydryl sites, as mercury does, and some antimony, like mercury, can be detoxified if glutathione can grab it and escort it out of the cellular environment. But before this happens, the body has another defense mechanism against antimony. That defense mechanism is methylation. SAM can methylate antimony to make methyl and dimethyl forms.

If a child has nanomolar levels of antimony and then receives ethylmercury, the amount of ethylmercury required to finish off the remaining methionine synthase capacity could be far less than it would be without antimony. And vice versa – if ethylmercury has begun to inhibit methionine synthase, then less than measurable levels of antimony might finish the job. That's what is meant by toxic synergism. A published example of toxic element synergisms in rats comes from Schubert et al., for mercury, lead and cadmium. Toxic effects of one metal can be multiplied by 50 if a little bit of another toxic metal is also present.[4] Elevated antimony levels have been found in hair of autistics, but not consistently.

Besides antimony, **brominated biphenyl compounds** are also used as textile flame retardants, and these can be combined with antimony. As of 1995, brominated chemicals accounted for 32% of US flame-retardant uses; antimony was 20%, and phosphorus or chlorine-based chemicals were 34%.[5] Researchers affiliated with the M.I.N.D. Institute, UC Davis at Sacramento CA, are investigating brominated biphenyls for links to autistic spectrum disorders.

Perchlorate, part of the chemical mix that was used for solid rocket fuels, is now in the environment of more than 20 states.[6] It's in ground and drinking water, lettuce, cow's milk and other agricultural products. While this contamination started in southern Nevada and California, it's now been found from Massachusetts to Oregon to Texas. Perchlorate displaces iodine in thyroid hormone synthesis, and it can cause decreased thyroid function. In a study of hair element concentrations reported to DAN! by Professor James Adams (Arizona State University), iodine was one of the elements that is notably lower in autistics than in controls.[7] This makes perchlorate a substance of concern in autism.

Many pesticide sprays are based on organic forms of phosphorus – "**organophosphates.**" Parathion, Malathion, Diazinon and Pirimiphos are some names that you might recognize, and there are dozens more. In 1982, Püschel et al. published studies of DPP4/CD26 inhibitors, and organophosphates, along with sulfur-seeking metals (mercury, lead, copper, cadmium), were measured to be notable inhibitors. In fact, two of the tested organophosphates had a more severe effect than did mercury (as mercuric chloride) at the same concentration.[8] So, exposure to sprays and to spray residues on foods is also of concern. Organophosphates could be guilty of initial harm to cellular defenses, making the individual more susceptible to the chain of events that leads to autism.

Another class of substances that has evidently increased significantly in our environment during the last several decades is perfluoro-octanoic acid (PFOA). Such substances give materials a nonstick, waterproof coating and are marketed as Teflon, Gore-Tex, and Stainmaster. Recent news releases state that PFOA contamination is virtually worldwide. It causes immune dysregulation and immune suppression in animals and may cause liver and testicular cancer. We have no evidence that it's linked to increased incidence of autism (because that hasn't been investigated), but it's an example of yet another pollutant that has been added to our environment during the time frame of autism's dramatic increase in incidence.

Besides measles, an infectious agent of concern is streptococcus, which produces the toxin, **streptokinase**. When DPP4 is disabled in the intestinal mucosa (by lymphoid hyperplasia, measles virus, mercury, whatever), dietary exorphin peptides such as beta-casomorphins can get into the bloodstream. They can then bind to CD26, a receptor site on the surface membrane of lymphocytes.[9] When this happens, the normal, message-receiving function of CD26 is blocked. Opiate peptide presence, at least in urine, has been verified convincingly by the clinical investigations of Reichelt, Shattock, Cade and others. Streptokinase binds to CD26 on lymphocytes. When it does, an immune response occurs as has been determined by measuring the levels of resulting anti-streptokinase IgG, IgM and IgA antibodies and anti-CD26 antibodies. Only 2 to 4% of controls had such antibody elevations. But for lymphocytes from autistics, these antibodies were elevated in 18%, 48% and 24% respectively.[9] Furthermore, when autoantibodies to CD26 are generated as a result of streptokinase binding, it becomes a form of immune dysregulation. Ethylmercury (as thimerosal), casein peptides and streptokinase all bind to CD26 sites on cell membranes. In autistics, all of these can result in autoantibody production.[9] While strep infections have not increased in incidence, as has autism, such infections could be contributory when dietary exorphins and mercury are present. DAN! clinicians have discussed the apparent overlap in some patients between autism and Pediatric Autoimmune Neuropsychiatric Disorders Associated with Streptococcal infection or "PANDAS." This is another acknowledgment that the disease we're contending with has a spectrum of causes and manifestations.

References, Toxicities and Infectious Stressors – Revisited

1. Carson, BL, Ellis HV and McCann JL *Toxicology and Biological Monitoring of Metals in Humans* Lewis Pub (1986) 24.

2. Valentine WN, Tanaka KR and Paglia DE, Chapt 94 in Scriver, Beaudet et al. eds. *The Metabolic Basis of Inherited Disease* 6th ed McGraw-Hill (1989) 2349-2350.

3. See publications by Jim Sprott, Ph.D., O.B.E. *The Cot Death Cover-Up?* Penguin Books (1996) *J. of the Forensic Science Society* 3 no.4 (1994) 199-204.

4. Schubert J, Riley EJ and Tyler SA "Combined Effects in Toxicology – A Rapid Systematic Testing Procedure: Cadmium, Mercury and Lead" *J.Toxicol.Environ.Health* 4 91978) 763-776.

5. Reisch MS "Flame retardants sales heat up" *C&EN*, Feb 24, (1997) 20.

6. AP News Story, Los Angeles January 6, 2003.

7. Adams J, Holloway CE et al. "Toxic metals and essential minerals in the hair of children with autism and their mothers" Washington DC DAN! Conference Syllabus, April (2004) 119.

8. Püschel G, Mentlein R and Heymann E "Isolation and characterization of dipeptidylpeptidase IV from human placenta" *Eur.J.Biochem* 126 (1982) 359-365.

9. Vojdani A, Pangborn JB et al. "Infections, toxic chemicals and dietary peptides binding to lymphocyte receptors and tissue enzymes are major instigators of autoimmunity in autism" *Int.J. of Immunopath and Pharmacology* 16 no.3 (2003) 189-199.

Autism, Sex and Cognitive Abilities

Populations of autistics and autistic-spectrum-disordered individuals have been surveyed for sex distribution for decades. Over the years, many different investigators, working with different subject populations, have come to a similar general conclusion: More males than females are autistic, by a ratio that's something like three or four to one. There have been several theories put forth to explain why:

- Girls get two X chromosomes, boys get one X and one Y. Many autistic traits have X-linked faults and girls have two chances to get it right; boys have only one chance.

- Testosterone amplifies the neurotoxicity of mercury, aluminum and probably other toxics, while estrogen has protective effects.

- Males require more methylation, more homocysteine recycle to methionine, and more creatine than females because of specific muscle mass and other physiologic requirements. A defect in methylation capacity affects males more than females.

- Relevant to the oxidant-stress condition of autism, differences in innate immunity between human males and females may make males more prone to inflammation and TNFα elevation than females.

- Males use their brains differently than females for cognitive activities. Males use gray matter for intensive focus on single events and tasks, and that's the majority of their thinking capacity. Females use white matter for integrative comprehension of multiple events, and that's a majority of their thinking capacity. If neuronal networks lose synchronization, who suffers most with integrative tasks? Males do, because they are more limited in this to begin with. But this may leave the male and a few females with networks that provide savant or highly-specialized skills in mathematics, puzzle-solving, art, music, etc.

If you think about this in terms of my glass-breaking story, you may come to the same conclusion that I have. None of these are wrong. They're different points of view from different frames of reference. But the last one is the most comprehensive explanation that also agrees with the scientific findings that we've come to.

My autistic son can assemble a jigsaw puzzle with the pieces upside-down faster than I can with the same pieces right-side-up. He does that by correctly picking the next-fitting piece out of all the loose pieces, usually on the first try. Many autistics learn by recognizing shapes. They appear to have built specialized neuronal networks that may not integrate well with other networks in a different part of the brain, but that operate very efficiently on their own. Our task is to fix the broken chemistry so that learning programs, like ABA, can get them to integrate neuronal networks and thus gain more integrative mental capabilities.

LABORATORY TESTS

Jon Pangborn

The strategy of choosing biomedical options for an autistic child or patient involves judgments about previous intervention outcomes, symptom status, and what else is being tried or could be tried. These judgments often can be facilitated by analytical guidance provided by lab tests. Except for serious inborn errors of metabolism, analyte levels on lab tests don't diagnose autism. (Analytes are the molecules in the specimens that lab instruments measure and that are reported on the results sheet.) There is no abnormal analyte that is common to autism in general, and I doubt there ever will be. The trained professional makes a diagnosis of autism on the basis of presented traits and behaviors.

However, laboratory tests can show aspects of the physiology, biochemistry and immunology that are disordered in a particular individual's case, and individualized interventions may be suggested by the test results. Sequential testing may then show improvement or worsening in the physiology or the amounts of substances that you may be trying to influence. As with many diseases, test results are far from foolproof and some may not reflect the clinical condition as expected.

Historically, clinicians have used lab tests to characterize what's wrong in the metabolic and immunologic makeup of autistics. Neurotransmitters, catecholamines, monoamine oxidase and other enzymes, T-lymphocytes, nutritional factors, and toxic burdens have all been surveyed. Subsets of the autistic spectrum have problems in these areas and others. Your child or patient may or may not belong to one of these subsets, but the only way to find out for sure is to do some lab work.

In this section of the report, I've outlined some of the tests that are often useful in the DAN! methodology – the orderly progression of choosing and trying biomedical options for an individual. My comments on what to look for apply particularly to the autistic patient. Not included are genetic markers for the unusual "Type I" metabolic diseases that may incidentally feature autism. These are best diagnosed by metabolic specialists who might assess structural variances in DNA or genes or chromosomes. Such conditions are often identified in infancy, and we described a number of them in the 2002 DAN! Consensus Report (Rett Syndrome, Fragile X, Lesch-Nyhan, Tuberous sclerosis, etc.). Those desiring to do chromosomal analysis might contact Baylor College of Medicine, Kleberg Cytogenetics Laboratory, Houston, Texas, 800-411-4363, or visit their website at www.bcmgeneticlabs.org.

1. Blood Chemistry and CBC Analysis

The blood chemistry test, now sometimes referred to as a "metabolic analysis" (which it isn't), includes some physiologic markers that circulate in blood serum, and the test usually is done with the patient in a fasting condition. Do this analysis first and do it before going on to more complicated and advanced analyses. Look especially for low creatinine, electrolytes out of range, and liver enzymes that are too high. Mildly elevated liver enzymes can resolve for the autistic by reducing dietary intolerance (e.g., casein, gluten), eliminating ketone excess (rebalance carbohydrate intake), or supplementing a key nutrient that has comprehensive physiological duties (magnesium, zinc, B-vitamins). If low BUN is noted, then one prospect is protein insufficiency, but another is ammonia excess with urea cycle dysfunction. High BUN can also mean ammonia excess, typically from bacterial dysbiosis. Check thyroid markers; some autistics are hypothyroid. It's also a good idea to include an iron profile with ferritin, TIBC and saturation markers. Both high and low iron conditions are occasionally found in autism. The CBC may show low RBCs or hematocrit.

Labs – None are specifically suggested, but we do advise using those that are both CLIA-licensed and CAP-certified. These are required to calibrate regularly and pass unknown survey tests to retain their certification. This process provides an impartial, nonaffiliated referee of the labs' accuracy.

2. Stool Analysis

I usually suggest this test early on; it can reveal evidence of maldigestion, dysbiosis and metabolic problems in the GI tract. Low chymotrypsin is consistent with pancreatic dysfunction, and undigested meat/vegetable fibers pretty much prove maldigestion. The bacteriology and mycology results are self-explanatory, but can be false negative and hit-or-miss with various stool specimens. Some labs provide sensitivity data for natural agents and prescriptive medications that might reduce or eliminate pathogens that are found. It's a good idea to ask for this if it's available. Anaerobes such as Clostridia are no-shows in this test; they could be there but can't be detected by these procedures. High fats in the stool suggest steatorrhea and need for lipase enzyme support. Short-chain fatty acids such as acetate and butyrate reflect on the mix of bacteria in the colon, including the no-show anaerobes. Short-chain fatty acids come from bacterial action on soluble food fibers and on lactate, which is produced by other (friendly) bacteria. Butyrate is an important nutrient for mucosal cells in the gut. Low or disordered short-chain fatty acids mean inadequate dietary fiber and/or bacterial dysbiosis.

Watch out for a stool pH that is higher than the reference range. If you see that, suspect dysbiosis (whether indicated directly or not) and consider doing a venous blood ammonia assay. Venous blood ammonias have to be obtained in a very specific way and analyzed immediately. Check with your lab for proper procedures.

Laboratories that Offer Stool Analysis:

Laboratory	Digestive Markers	Metabolic Markers	Microbiol., Mycology	Parasitology	CLIA[1] Approved	CAP[2] Approved
BioCenter				x	x	
DDI	x	x	x	x	x	
GSDL	x	x	x	x	x	x
MVCL	x	x		x	x	

BioCenter Laboratory   Wichita KS   800-494-7785; 316-682-3100
Doctor's Data Laboratory   St. Charles IL 800-323-2784; 630-377-8139
Great Smokies Diag. Lab   Asheville NC 800-522-4762, 828-253-0621
Meridian Valley Clin. Lab   Kent, WA   253-859-8700

[1] Lab is approved per guidelines of the U.S. Clinical Laboratories Improvement Act.
[2] Lab is certified by and periodically inspected by the College of American Pathologists to ensure quality control.

3. Intestinal Permeability

There are several ways to measure the integrity of the intestinal mucosa. One is with two non-metabolizable sugars that are orally ingested – a large one and a small one. The small one fits through normal mucosal porosity; the larger one does not. Subsequent urine analysis will show if too much of the larger one got through, which would imply increased gut permeability. Immunologic tests (IgM, IgA and IgG antibodies) for response to organisms that should only be in the lumen of the intestine can also be done to see if they've become invasive. Increased gut permeability is documented in autism;[1] that's how we believe exorphin peptides such as β-casomorphin get in. The value of this test is more in its assessment of gut healing than in proving increased permeability for untreated autistics. If a CF diet, GF diet or SCD helps, then you can be almost 100% certain that there was excessive permeability to toxins, peptides and large sugars (undigested disaccharides, polysaccharides). Over time, dietary intervention, digestive enzymes, probiotics and other interventions can heal the gut, and this test can be used to track the healing phase.

Reference, Intestinal Permeability

1. D'Eufemia P et al. "Abnormal intestinal permeability in children with autism," *Acta Pediatrica* 85 (1996) 1075-1079.

Laboratory Measurement of Intestinal Permeability.

The laboratories suggested below can provide a kit with complete instructions for specimen collection and mailing, as well as literature references and clinical guidance.

> Doctor's Data Laboratory, St. Charles, IL, 800-323-2784, 630-377-8139
> Great Smokies Diagnostics Lab, Asheville, NC, 800-522-4762, 828-253-0621

Laboratory Measurement of Intestinal Barrier Function

A suggested laboratory is ImmunoSciences Lab, Inc. Their test is done by blood analysis to assess three types of antibodies, IgM, IgA and IgG, for four circumstances. Category 1 indicates food allergy, Category 2 indicates antibody responses to yeasts, Category 3 indicates antibody responses to aerobic bacteria, and Category 4 indicates antibodies to anaerobic bacteria. Gut barrier dysfunction is definite when some or all of the categories have elevated IgM antibody levels. The laboratory provides a kit with instructions.

> ImmunoSciences Lab, Beverly Hills, CA, 800-950-4686, 310-657-1077

4. Ammonia

Blood ammonia is best measured very promptly after sampling at a hospital lab. Venous blood 2 to 4 hours postprandial is indicative for ammonia excess which usually is of dysbiotic origin but, in rare cases, could be due to weak urea cycle enzymes. Symptoms of ammonia excess are headache (migraine), irritability, tiredness, slurred speech or slurred speech sounds for autistics, and diarrhea. Urine ammonia is problematic and not necessarily indicative of hyperammonemia, because ammonia can be purposely generated in kidneys from glutamine to alleviate acidosis. Analytical results consistent with hyperammonemia are: intestinal bacterial dysbiosis, and BUN or urea at relatively high level. (Low BUN could mean urea cycle dysfunction and hyperammonemia). Stool pH above lab reference range, deficient alpha-ketoglutaric acid in blood or urine (by organic acid analysis), and high glutamine in blood (by amino acid analysis) are additional indicators. Usually in autism, the ammonia elevation is mild or moderate, not extreme, and oral supplements of buffered alpha-ketoglutarate can be a temporary remedy. Despite the mild degree of excess that is often seen, this condition should be addressed without delay because ammonia excess can do irreversible neuronal damage and may cause permanent losses in cognitive abilities and IQ.[1]

While 99% of increased-ammonia conditions in autism are due to bacterial dysbiosis or infection, I have seen lab work on two autistics with urea cycle OCT enzyme deficiency – an uncommon hereditary defect that hasn't been medically associated with autism.

> Laboratories: Do a test at a hospital laboratory as prescribed by a medical doctor, and follow his or her directions precisely.

Reference, Ammonia

1. Batshaw ML, Roan Y et al. "Cerebral dysfunction in asymptomatic carriers of ornithine transcarbamylase deficiency" *NEJ Med* 302 no.9 (1980) 482-485 and see editorial by S. Matthysse 516-517.

5. Food Allergy Tests

Why perform food allergy tests on autistic patients? Allergy is an immune overresponse to some substance, usually a common one, and some authorities insist that the substance include a protein or large peptide. If an autistic drinks milk and acquires casomorphins peptides that bind to neuronal receptors, there's no allergy unless the immune system then responds to the receptor-peptide entity. But that's what does happen to many autistics.[1] Antibodies and immunoglobulins are created and lymphocyte response to the receptor-peptide entity occurs. Cell surfaces, entire cells and parts of tissue could be damaged, causing inflammation and generation of cytokines such as TNFα. Elevated TNFα is documented in autistics (see AUTISM AT THE MOLECULAR LEVEL). That may cause a reduction in methionine synthase capacity, which is central to the metabolic problem in many autistics. A separate but related issue is lymphocyte expression of CD26 (DPP4), which is reduced during milk allergy.[2] Food problems that autistics have are not just metabolic intolerances; they unavoidably spill over into immunologic problems. Another reason for food allergy tests is that dietary intervention shifts the diet from poorly tolerated foods to other types of foods. But what if the "new" foods are allergens for the individual? In autism, metabolic intolerance is directly linked to immune dysregulation, including allergy, and we should assess immunologic responses to foods as part of dietary intervention.

Usually, immunologic food reactivities are judged by measuring IgE and IgG antibody levels. IgE mediation is a rapid-response mechanism, and it corresponds to prompt symptoms such as wheezing or a rash following ingestion of foods. The delayed responses, the ones that are much harder to ascribe to a particular food, are mediated by IgG. Dr. Sid Baker et al. have found IgG

Enzyme-Linked Immunosorbent Assay (ELISA) to be a very useful tool for screening for safe foods.[3,4] This was concluded after two double-blind, placebo-diet-controlled studies that validated IgG ELISA by showing a significant difference in symptom reduction in subjects avoiding IgG reactive foods as compared with IgG non-reactive foods. These kinds of tests (blood food antibody assays) are not foolproof and typically include a small percentage of false positives and negatives. Nevertheless, they provide good guidance and are an excellent starting point for finding safe foods. For autistics, we suggest avoiding foods altogether that have "+3" or "+4" results. Avoid the "+2" ones for about 30 days (or longer if your physician suggests it), then rotate by food group on a 4-day schedule. Also, rotate "+1" foods on a 4-day schedule. Food rotation can be a complex matter because of how foods are grouped by plant genus. We advise consulting a nutritionist trained in food allergy remediation if the lab test doesn't provide sufficient guidance. Cautions about casein, gluten, and carbohydrates with difficult-to-digest sugars override food allergy results. The individual may need to avoid such foods regardless of measured Ig levels.

Laboratories that Offer Food Allergy Testing

Laboratory	Offers IgG ELISA	Offers IgG	Offers IgE	CLIA Approved[1]	CAP Certified[2]
Alletess	x	x	x	x	
BioCenter		x		x	
GSDL	x		x	x	x
IL	x		x	x	
IS	x			x	
MVL		x		x	
MM		x		x	
HCD		x	x	x	
York	x	x	x	x	

Alletess Medical Lab	Rocklin MA	800-225-5404, 781-871-4426
BioCenter Lab	Wichita KS	800-494-7785, 316-682-3100
Great Smokies Diag	Asheville NC	800-522-4762, 828-253-0621
ImmunoLabs	Ft Lauderdale FL	800-231-9197, 305-486-4500
ImmunoScience Lab	Beverly Hills CA	800-950-4686, 310-657-1077
Meridian Valley Lab	Kent WA	253-859-8700
MetaMetrix	Norcross GA	800-221-4640, 404-446-5483
Hitachi Chem Diag	Mountain View CA	800-233-6278, 650-964-5461
York Nutr Labs	Hollywood FL	888-751-3388, 954-920-3728

[1] Lab is approved per guidelines of the U.S. Clinical Laboratories Improvement Act.
[2] Lab is certified by and periodically inspected by the College of American Pathologists to ensure quality control.

References, Food Allergy Tests

1. Vojdani, A., et al. "Infections, toxic chemicals and dietary peptides binding to lymphocyte receptors and tissue enzymes are major instigators of autoimmunity in autism" *Int. J of Immunopath & Pharm* 16 no.3 (2003) 189-199.

2. Schade RP, et al. "Cell-surface expression of CD25, CD26, and CD30 by allergen-specific T cells is intrinsically different in cow's milk allergy" *J.Allergy Clin Immunol* (Feb 2002) 357-362.

3. Baker SM et al. "Double blind placebo-diet controlled crossover study of IgG food ELISA, a pilot study" Presented at Am Acad Environ Med Advanced Seminar, Virginia Beach VA Oct. 1994.
4. Baker SM et al. "You are NOT what you eat: double blind placebo diet controlled study of IgG ELISA, pilot II" Am. Coll for Advancement in Med Semi-Annual Meeting San Diego CA Nov 1994.

6. Urinary Peptide Measurements

There are three types of peptides of concern in autism:

1. The common dietary dipeptides anserine and carnosine;
2. The peptide form of detoxified indolylacrylic acid, which comes from malabsorbed tryptophan (its nickname is IAG); and,
3. The exorphin peptides, such as casomorphin and gluteomorphin, that bind to receptor sites on neurons, immune cells (lymphocytes) and certain intestinal mucosal cells.

Anserine and carnosine come from meat, fish and poultry. Both contain beta-alanine. Beta-alanine tends to block conservation of taurine in the kidneys, and it interferes with the formation of creatine. Both dipeptides chelate copper and can increase uptake of copper from the GI tract,[1] which can be harmful in autism. Anserine and carnosine are measured in urine (primarily) and usually in blood plasma as part of amino acid analysis; see that test description for more information.

IAG is indolylacrolylglycine. It's a peptide formed from tryptophan, when tryptophan is not properly digested. Tryptophan can be metabolized by normal and dysbiotic intestinal bacteria. It can then be absorbed into the blood and further metabolized by the liver, where IAG is formed. A chemical that appears temporarily during this process attacks cell lipid membranes. IAG can be elevated in autistics when digestion of protein and peptides is disordered. Evidently, IAG can also be elevated if organophosphate pesticides affect liver metabolism of tryptophan. Paul Shattock's research team in Sunderland, U.K., has studied IAG and found it to be frequently elevated in the autistic population.[2] If the lab test shows high IAG, serotonin formation may be disordered, intestinal dysbiosis and/or pesticide exposure are likely, and liver stress is possible – another reason for mildly elevated liver enzymes on a blood chemistry panel. High IAG from malabsorption suggests that digestive peptidase enzymes need enhancement by enzyme supplementation. It also suggests pancreatic insufficiency. Measurement of urinary IAG can be the deciding factor when determining whether to supplement tryptophan and 5-hydroxytryptophan. Gut bacteria can do mischief with either when there is malabsorption.

The exorphin peptides, such as beta-casomorphin 7, were discovered by Drs. Reichelt, Knivsberg, and others with a laboratory procedure called high-performance liquid chromatography, "HPLC."[3,4] Using this procedure, the exorphin findings were duplicated and confirmed at other research centers such as the University of Sunderland, U.K., and the University of Florida at Gainesville.[5,6] These exorphins result from incomplete digestion of casein, a major protein found in dairy products.

During the last ten years, measurement of urinary exorphin peptides has provided an analytical means of tracking gastrointestinal response to special diets and/or use of digestive enzymes in clinical research. The researched options, use of casein-free or gluten-free diets and/or enzymes, have been established as beneficial for various groups of autistics under study.[6,7,8,9] We accept these as valid biomedical options that you should try for the individual under your care. Outcomes – an individual's response to dietary intervention and use of digestive aids – have to be determined for the individual. These outcomes, not exorphin peptide tests, will drive your decision to stick with or discontinue the option.

> The laboratory that offers urinary IAG measurement is Antibody Assay Lab, Austin, TX, 800-522-2621, 512-873-3311

References, Using Peptide Measurements

1. Rodwell VW "Conversion of Amino Acids to Specialized Products" Chapt 33 in Murray, Granner et al. Eds. *Harper's Biochemistry* 23rd ed (1993) 327.
2. Shattock P "International perspective on toxins and treatment options" Spring DAN! Conference Syllabus, Philadelphia, May 2003 33,37.
3. Reichelt KL, Knivsberg A-M et al. "Probable etiology and possible treatment of childhood autism" *Brain Dysfunct* 4 (1991) 308-319.
4. Reichelt KL, Knivsberg A-M et al. "Nature and consequences of hyperpeptiduria and bovine casomorphins found in autistic syndromes" *Dev.Brain Dysfunct* 7 (1994) 71-85.
5. Shattock P, Kennedy A et al. "Role of neuropeptides in autism and their relationships with clinical neurotransmitters" *Brain Dysfunct* 3 (1990) 328-345.
6. Cade R, Privette M et al. "Autism and Schizophrenia – Intestinal Disorders" *Nutritional Neuroscience* 3 (2000) 57-72.
7. Knivsberg A-M, Reichelt KL et al. "A randomized, controlled study of dietary intervention in autistic syndromes" *Nutr.Neurosci* 5 no.4 (2002) 251-261.
8. Brudnak MA, Rimland B et al. "Enzyme-based therapy for autism-spectrum disorders – is it worth another look?" *Med.Hypoth.* 58 no 2 (2002) 422-428.
9. Reichelt KL and Knivsberg A-M "Why diet is useful in some autistic children: results so far" Presentation at DAN! Portland Conference, 2003; DAN! Fall 2003 Syllabus 91-99.

7. Amino Acid Analysis

There are ten reasons to do an amino acid analysis of an autistic's blood plasma or urine. They are:

- To assess dietary protein adequacy. Primarily, this assessment is made by comparing the measured level of nutritionally-essential amino acids (methionine, phenylalanine, threonine, tryptophan, lysine, leucine, isoleucine, valine and histidine) with reference ranges. Other, nonessential amino acids such as glutamine, glycine and asparagine can aid in this assessment.

- To determine if the methionine methylation cycle is adequate. If it is, we expect cystine or cysteine, homocystine or homocysteine, cystathionine and methionine to be within normal limits. Additional analytes that may not be available for quantitation but which bear on this aspect are adenosylmethionine and adenosylhomocysteine.

- To check 24-hour creatinine level in the case of a 24-hour urine analysis. Creatine and creatinine are subnormal for many autistics. Low creatine in blood plasma is consistent with (but does not prove) energy delivery deficit to cells. Low brain creatine and phosphocreatine can result in a deficiency of expressive speech.

- To assess maldigestion and malabsorption:

    a. Low blood levels of the essentials plus high levels of anserine and/or carnosine are consistent with incomplete digestive proteolysis (maldigestion).

    b. Especially low blood threonine is consistent with impaired transport across intestinal mucosa (contributes to malabsorption). Threonine is the slowest traveler in this respect.

    c. Especially low blood levels of methionine, phenylalanine, tyrosine and tryptophan as a group are consistent with gastric dysfunction.

    d. Especially low levels of valine, leucine and isoleucine are consistent with pancreatic dysfunction, as is high anserine and/or carnosine.

- As an initial assessment of folate and cobalamin (B_{12}) balance and function. Homocysteine, beta-aminoisobutyric acid, sarcosine and glycine should not be excessive. High serine (occasionally) and high histidine (rarely) can mean a deficiency of folate as tetrahydrofolate. Both have other, more common reasons for being elevated. Beta-AIBA is specific to B_{12} as adenosylcobalamin, high beta-AIBA means low AdoCbl (occasional in autism). High homocysteine could be due to methylcobalamin deficit, folate imbalance or deficit, a deficiency of vitamin B_6 as pyridoxal phosphate, or serine deficit. Serine deficit and high homocysteine are unusual in autism.

- To alert one to the possibility of ammonia excess per elevations of glutamine and glutamine in any combination with: asparagine, glycine, serine and alanine. If urea is low with glutamine elevation, then urea cycle enzyme disorder is possible.

- To check the functional activity of vitamin B_6 as pyridoxal 5-phosphate *provided that* dietary protein is adequate and digestion is working properly. False normals occur when amino acid levels are low and metabolism enzymes that use coenzyme P5P are not challenged. Consistent with deficient P5P coenzyme activity are:

    low or high cystathionine   high tryptophan

    high leucine, isoleucine and/or valine   high beta-alanine

    high tyrosine   high threonine

    high serine

- To check the functional activity of magnesium. Magnesium may be dysfunctional as an enzyme activator if any of the following are observed in amino acid results:

    low phosphoethanolamine with normal or high ethanolamine

    elevated citrulline

    elevated methionine (but low S-adenosylmethionine if measured)

    taurine is low in blood, low in urine, or high (wasting) in urine when not being supplemented.

- To check for the presence of excessive yeast or fungi. High alpha-aminoadipic acid with normal or low lysine is consistent with yeast or fungal dysbiosis.

- To check markers for bacterial dysbiosis, high gamma-aminobutyric acid (GABA) and/or beta-alanine. While GABA is a neurotransmitter in the CNS, measurable quantities in urine suggest dysbiosis, urinary tract infection or bacterial contamination of the specimen. High blood levels of GABA occur in sepsis. Beta-alanine has three sources:

dietary peptides (anserine, carnosine), gut bacteria, and catabolism of pyrimidine nucleotides. High beta-alanine in the kidneys, for whatever reason, can result in urinary wasting of taurine and magnesium.

Blood plasma amino acid measurements show what is being transported at a point in time. Overnight fast, before-breakfast plasma measurement is conventional practice. Such sampling reduces dietary influences and accentuates metabolism influences. For autism, however, this test highlights the deficiency in cystine or cysteine and related methionine methylation cycle analytes.

24-Hour urine amino acid measurements show what is high and what is low over a 24-hour period, provided that renal function is reasonably normal. The circadian rhythm is not a complicating factor. Overall nutritional status is influential, as are metabolism processes, and the dipeptides carnosine and anserine are highlighted, as are beta-alanine and taurine.

Generally, urine amino acid analysis is more diagnostic than plasma analysis because of the 24-hour period and because there are more distinctive patterns in urine related to problems in enzymatic activity, cofactor adequacy, and transport. But, for autistics, the urine test often doesn't show the low cystine/cysteine problem as well as blood plasma does.

Ideally, both a 24-hour urine and plasma should be measured during the same time period. Age, toilet training, behavior and patient cooperation can be factors in sampling. Proper urine amino acid analysis should include a urine creatinine measurement. If your patient has poor renal clearance or renal failure, do a blood plasma analysis.

For autistics, when urine is analyzed, I very strongly prefer results that are NOT ratioed to creatinine. Dividing a low amino acid level by a low creatinine level yields a false normal result or maybe even a contradictory high result.

Amino Acid Analysis Laboratory Information

Laboratory	24-hr urine	Spot urine	Fasting plasma	Supplement schedule[1]	CLIA Approved[2]	CAP Certified[3]
DDI	x		x	x	x	
ELN	x		x		N/A	N/A
GPL		x			x	
GSDL	x		x	x	x	x
MM	x		x	x	x	

Doctor's Data Inc   St. Charles IL   800-323-2784, 630-377-8139
European Lab of Nutrients   Utrecht, NL   31-(0)300-287-1492
Great Plains Lab   Lenexa KS   913-341-8949
Great Smokies Diag Lab   Asheville NC   800-522-4762, 828-253-0621
MetaMetrix Lab   Norcross GA   800-221-4640, 404-446-5483

[1] Lab report includes a supplement schedule for needed amino acids if appropriate.
[2] Lab is approved per guidelines of the U.S. Clinical Laboratories Improvement Act.
[3] Lab is certified by and periodically inspected by the College of American Pathologists to ensure quality control.

8. Organic Acid Analysis

Organic acids can be thought of as amino acids without nitrogen (no amino group). In other words, they are composed of carbon, hydrogen and oxygen and are a very basic form of carbohydrate. In many cases, organic acids in body tissues come from catabolism of amino acids, and when this happens, the body has to deal with the released nitrogen (or ammonium ion). Often, it does so by adding the amino group to a very important organic acid, alpha-ketoglutaric acid. In this exchange, amino acids such as leucine, isoleucine and valine become keto-organic acids while pre-existing alpha-ketoglutaric acid becomes glutamic acid.

A much larger source of organic acids is dietary carbohydrate. Carbohydrates are processed by body tissue into another very important organic acid called pyruvic acid (or pyruvate). Most pyruvate is destined to be biochemically changed into energy inside cell mitochondria. Mitochondria are islands inside cells that are insulated from the water of the cell by a membrane. Only certain metabolites are allowed to cross the mitochondrial membrane, and pyruvate is one of them. Inside mitochondria, amino acids are processed into organic acids, fats are broken down and turned into chemical energy, and pyruvate from carbohydrate joins these processes. Like the fats, pyruvate is enzymatically converted to acetyl-coenzyme A, which enters the Krebs citric acid cycle. This cyclic process allows release of hydrogen that is subsequently combined with oxygen (from respiration) to release energy. While amino acids are the molecules of structures, enzymes, peptides, immune and detoxication processes, organic acids are the molecules of energy. The citric acid cycle accounts for 90% of the transfer of energy stored in food into chemical energy (ATP) for operation of body processes. When we measure organic acids in urine, part of what we are observing is the efficiency with which we "burn" our foods to obtain energy.

Laboratories that DAN! clinicians often use have constructed special versions of organic acid profiles, and they include various analytes that are not on traditional organic acid tests. Adrenal catecholamines and bacterial/yeast-source sugars and organic acids are some of these non-traditional analytes. Currently, some of the analytes attributed to dysbiotic flora are controversial. Other sources are claimed for some of them, and test specificity in these matters is uncertain.

Most laboratories offer organic acid analysis with urine as the specimen, and virtually all of them ratio the actual measured levels to creatinine. So, beware of out-of-range-low creatinines that are used to "normalize" organic acid results. From my experience, at least one in three profiles done for autistic patients has "inflated" results due to division of mostly normal organic acid levels by subnormal creatinine.

All the laboratories listed below provide interpretive commentary along with test results, or on request. Therefore, I haven't included lengthy explanations of what abnormals and combinations of abnormals might mean. Instead, I restrict my remarks to what is often seen for autistics, and what is not explained well enough (in my opinion) by usual laboratory commentary.

- Elevated FIGlu (formiminoglutamic acid) means that folate metabolism is disordered, possibly with folate trapped in some form due to enzymatic deficiencies or B_{12} metabolism problems. For autistics, high FIGlu rarely means that folate overall is deficient. Giving folic acid rarely helps; giving folinic acid may help. Giving cobalamin or methylcobalamin has a higher probability of helping. In unusual cases, neither folinic acid nor methylcobalamin helps. FIGlu can be elevated due to deficient coenzyme function of pyridoxal phosphate, because the FIGlu-processing enzyme requires it. Particular disorders in purine synthesis can imbalance and trap folate in a way that no form of B_{12} can completely undo, and we have not yet found any way to normalize FIGlu in those unusual cases.

- Methylmalonic acid (MMA) is a metabolite that increases when B_{12} is dysfunctional as adenosylcobalamin. Some autistics do have this problem, but most need methylcobalamin. But if they do need adenosylCbl, then cells can transform methylcobalamin into it as well or better than they might with cyanocobalamin or hydroxocobalamin. Methylcobalamin, hydroxocobalamin, and adenosylcobalamin all are available as injectables, but it is inadvisable to use adenosylcobalamin because adenosine processing is often faulty in autistics.

- Pyroglutamic acid is often seen to be high or low; it is a metabolite of glutathione and of hydrolysis of dietary peptides. If "pyroglu" is high, it could be of dietary origin, especially if protein or peptide powders, shakes or "supplements" are used. "Pyruoglu" that's not of dietary origin comes from incomplete reassembly of glutathione after it has come apart while doing some metabolic task. Glutathione comes apart when it transports nutrients across membranes or does "phase II" (conjugation) of detoxication. Extremely high pyroglu may be metabolic pyroglutamic aciduria, a rare, hereditary disorder that severely depletes glutathione. Pyroglu needs ATP and the enzyme 5-oxoprolinase to become glutamate, after which it might be reused to make glutathione (GSH). Magnesium supplements may help since Mg deficiency limits GSH synthesis. High pyroglu in urine does not prove that GSH is deficient, but GSH supplements often help. Low pyroglu corresponds more closely to low GSH and usually resolves when GSH is supplemented. It may resolve for autistics when combinations of methylcobalamin, TMG, DMG and folinic acid are used.

- Alpha-ketoglutaric acid: Low usually means either that manganese is deficient (in which case isocitrate is probably high), or there is an ammonia load (isocitrate normal or low). Isocitrate is the precursor of alpha-ketoglutaric acid. Low alpha-ketoglutarate is an occasional but serious finding with autistics; please refer to the Nutritional Supplements Section. High alpha-ketoglutarate also occurs, but only occasionally. The enzyme that's usually at fault when it's high requires magnesium, thiamin, lipoic acid, vitamin B_3 as NAD, riboflavin as FAD and coenzyme A (which comes from cysteine and pantothenate). Use straight riboflavin, not FAD; use straight thiamin, not the phosphate.

- Pyruvate: A high result is usually a problem very similar to that of alpha-ketoglutaric acid. Toxicity by mercury, arsenic or antimony will damage the enzymes that both pyruvate and alpha-ketoglutarate need. These toxics poison the lipoic acid portion of the enzyme complexes. Thiamin usually provides the best help when pyruvate is high, but seems to be a bit less helpful for high alpha-ketoglutarate.

- Lactate: High lactate is occasionally seen in autism, and then we've got some problems that some clinical labs may not explain or account for very well. Lactate is pyruvate's cousin; it is not lactose – that's milk sugar. Lactate comes in two versions that are very different in source and metabolism: D-lactate and L-lactate.

  Blends of both, D,L-lactate, are in some types of cheese, candy and confection foods. Also, D,L-lactate is made by "lactic acid" bacteria. Some bacteria are especially proficient in making D-lactate (Lactobacillus leishmanii). Some bacteria have an enzyme, lactic acid racemase, which can transform D-lactate into L-lactate and vice versa.

Humans do not have lactate racemase in body tissues. Humans have lactate dehydrogenase, which handles L-lactate but not D-lactate. In the intestines (colon mostly), bacteria use their enzymes to convert both D- and L-lactate to short-chain fatty acids: acetate, propionate and butyrate. With dysbiosis, this may be inadequate, and excessive D-lactate can be absorbed into the blood.

L-lactate is an end product of glucose metabolism that occurs when there is not enough oxygen (anaerobic conditions). When muscles run low on oxygen, muscle activity produces lactate instead of pyruvate. L-lactic acidosis can also occur as a result of exposure to carbon monoxide, seizures, shock, and contamination by some toxic substances.

Now, did your lab report L-lactate, D-lactate, or D,L-lactate as being elevated? Most labs report D,L (both as one analyte), and if the report doesn't specify, then it's D and L together. Normally, the vast majority of lactate in blood or urine is the L-form. A finding of too much D is consistent with severe intestinal dysbiosis or infection. Giving thiamin, magnesium and other nutrients that help internal pyruvate metabolism is very unlikely to help D-lactic acidosis/D-lactic aciduria. Curing the infection or dysbiosis should help. Be sure to eliminate any dietary sources.

If L-lactate is high, the problem could be pyruvic acidosis. If so, correcting the high pyruvate condition usually corrects high lactate as well. When pyruvate is normal and L-lactate is high, there could be some form of lactic acidosis, for which there are many potential causes. The clinician is referred to the Metabolic Acidosis chapter in *Harrison's Principles of Internal Medicine* for general information and for procedures for differential diagnosis. Some autistics have mild L-lactic acidosis until detoxification is successful, and some develop it temporarily while detoxification is underway. Some nutrients that can aid cell respiration and tissue oxygenation may also alleviate L-lactic acidosis: coenzyme Q_{10}, the herb Ginkgo biloba, DMG, malic aid (magnesium malate), alpha-ketoglutarate, iron (if low), B12 and folate (if anemia is present), etc.

- High fumaric or malic acids: When this occurs in autistics, it's usually gut dysbiosis with production of look-alike carboxylic acids that are absorbed, and then inhibit citric acid cycle enzymes. Clearing the gut and replenishment with proper flora usually corrects high levels of fumaric and malic acids.

- High citric acid: After acetylcoenzyme-A enters the citric acid cycle, it combines with oxaloacetic acid to form citric acid. Occasionally, organic acid test results on autistics include elevated citric acid. From my experience, there are three reasons for this. The first is that either the lab's reference range is lower or "tighter" than it should be, or else the raw citric acid result was divided by a low creatinine result. The high citric result may not be confirmed when a urine sample from the individual is sent to a hospital reference lab; I've asked doctors to use the Hospital for Sick Children in Toronto for such confirmation. Valid high urine citrates suggest two conditions. The first is oxidant stress, which is common in untreated autistics. A reduced sulfhydryl (-SH) group, as with reduced glutathione, is needed for enzymatic processing of citrate in the citric acid cycle. Second, if the pancreas has limited function, it may be pushing less bicarbonate into the small intestine, and the small intestine may be too acidic for many peptidase and other enzymes to work properly. I've had occasion to observe this with several autistics when they ate cream of wheat and were being monitored by a Heidelberg pH gastrogram instrument. Chronically-elevated urine citric acid may indicate need for a bicarbonate supplement about an hour after meals. It may also indicate that there would be a benefit to use of Secretin, and of course, antioxidant therapy.

Laboratories That Offer Organic Acid Analysis

Laboratory	Urine Analytes	CLIA Approved[1]	CAP Certified[2]
GSDL	x	x	x
Great Plains	x	x	
MetaMetrix	x	x	

[1] Lab is approved per guidelines of the U.S. Clinical Laboratories Improvement Act.
[2] Lab is certified by and periodically inspected by the College of American Pathologists to ensure quality control.

Great Smokies Diag Lab	Asheville NC	800-522-4762, 828-253-0621
Great Plains Lab	Lenexa KS	913-341-8949
MetaMetrix Lab	Norcross GA	800-221-4640, 404-446-5483

9. Fatty Acid Analysis

With autism, we are concerned about the fatty acid composition of cell "walls," because certain fatty acids assist message transmission through the wall. Actually, a cell wall is a lipid membrane composed of a double layer of fatty acids positioned side-by side. Controlled passageways through the membrane allow certain elements to enter, and there are signaling ports or binding sites (proteins) to which water-soluble messengers attach to make an announcement about external conditions. Protein systems traverse the fat-soluble lipid membrane, and carry the news to the inner working of the cell to provoke an appropriate response. External binding sites are not used by lipid-soluble messengers, such as steroids or sex hormones. They can directly traverse lipid membranes and find their receptors inside the cytosol.

The fatty acid makeup of cell membranes is important for integrity and protection of the cell. Disordered fatty acid makeup of cell membranes is an invitation to invasion by toxic elements, protein toxins and viruses. When fatty acids are measured for an autistic, we recommend that cell membrane fatty acids, or phospholipids, be the test of choice, not free fatty acids in the bloodstream. Usually, labs measure membrane fatty acids using erythrocytes (red blood cells).

The two major types of membrane fatty acids are the omega-3 type and the omega-6 type. The omega-3s are:

- Alpha-linolenic $18:3\omega3$
- Eicosapentaenoic $20:5\omega3$
- Docosapentaenoic $22:5\omega3$
- Docosahexaenoic $22:6\omega3$

The omega-6s are:
- Linoleic $18:2\omega6$
- Gamma-linolenic $18:3\omega6$
- Dihomogamma-linolenic $20:3\omega6$
- Arachidonic $20:4\,\omega6$

Cell membrane fatty acids are those with 18 to as many as 24 carbons, and most of them are unsaturated to some extent. In erythrocytes, the major fatty acids are docosapentaenoic, docosahexaenoic, linoleic, dihomogamma-linolenic and arachidonic. The most common abnormality in autism is depressed levels of omega-3 fatty acids, especially docosahexaenoic acid, DHA.[1,2] Also, the relative amount of "polyunsaturated" fatty acids is important. These are the fatty acids that give fluidity and flexibility to membranes. Fully-saturated fatty acids in cell membranes are much less flexible, and they can impede message transmission and make the cell walls less durable. DHA is an important brain lipid. In cell membranes DHA contributes to fluidity, correct receptor function and interaction with lipid hormones (estrogen, progesterone, angiotensin). Per animal studies, DHA suppresses oxidant stress by reducing nitric oxide production.[3]

Laboratories That Offer Fatty Acid Analysis

Laboratory	Offers RBC FAs	CLIA Approved[1]	CAP Certified[2]
BioCenter	x	x	
GSDL	x	x	x
MetaMetrix	x	x	

[1]. Lab is approved per guidelines of the U.S. Clinical Laboratories Improvement Act.
[2]. Lab is certified by and periodically inspected by the College of American Pathologists to ensure quality control.

BioCenter	Wichita KS	800-797-7785, 316-682-3100
Great Smokies Diag Lab	Asheville NC	800-522-4762, 828-253-0621
MetaMetrix Lab	Norcross GA	800-221-4640, 404-446-5483

References – Analysis of Cellular Fatty Acid Content

1. Stoll AL "Omega-3 Fatty Acids in Autism" Presentation at DAN! 2002 Boston MA, May 2002, Conference Syllabus 26-43.

2. Stoll AL and Hardy PM "Omega-3 Fatty Acids in the Pathophysiology and Treatment of Autism" Presentation at DAN! 2001 Atlanta GA May 2001.

3. Komatsu W, Ishihara K et al. "Docosahexaenoic acid suppresses nitric oxide..." *Free Radic Biol Med* **34** no.8 (2003) 1006-1016.

10. Element Analyses and Metallothionein Assessments

Four tissues – whole blood, packed blood cells (unwashed erythrocytes), urine and hair – have commonly been used to assess element levels in autistics. Element analyses that measure total amounts have been used almost exclusively. Elemental analysis measures the entire amount of each reported element that is in a specimen, regardless of how that element is partitioned and regardless of chemical form. For elemental analysis, the tissue specimen is digested, often in heated acid, to decompose and dissolve everything. The digested specimen that goes into the element-measuring instrument is a clear liquid. The instrument is usually an induction-coupled plasma mass spectrometer (ICP-MS). The digested specimen is heated to plasma temperatures (ten thousand degrees) which strip the electrons off the nucleus of each element. Then the nuclei traverse an electromagnetic field to a detector which is tuned to count the nuclei of each type of element. Almost everything from lithium (atomic weight of 4) to uranium (atomic weight of 238) can be accounted for with this technology, although not all of these elements are reported.

This measurement procedure is considerably different from traditional clinical analysis of electrolytes or minerals done in a blood chemistry analysis. For example, the traditional blood analyzer can report inorganic phosphate in blood serum, although it is often incorrectly termed "serum phosphorus." It isn't; it's just the inorganic phosphate fraction that is in blood serum. Element analysis by ICP-MS cannot measure phosphate and can't directly measure the chemical form of any element. But it can measure the total amount of an element in a digested specimen – total phosphorus, for example. The total phosphorus in blood is all organic and inorganic fractions added together.

For autistics, we're interested in any tissue showing elevations of toxic elements, such as mercury, arsenic and antimony. We're also concerned about imbalances of some essential elements (such as high copper, low zinc), and we'd like to correct deficiencies of essentials. Deficiencies that are often seen include those of magnesium, manganese, molybdenum and sometimes calcium (per urine). Low selenium is seen, but at an incidence about that of the general population. Iron can be high or low; usually it's normal. The best way to assess iron (as previously noted) is via ferritin, TIBC and saturation parameters, not by element analysis.

Whole blood shows what's being transported at a point in time, including what's bound to the surface of cells and what's been tucked away inside cells. It's a convenient compromise between plasma or serum and cells or RBCs. If we're looking for toxic elements, we have only hours or a few days to catch them in serum or plasma unless detoxication is actively occurring. With whole blood, we have days to weeks because most toxic elements are held for weeks in red blood cells. RBCs have a lifespan of about 120 days, and are constantly dying, being catabolized, and being replaced by new (clean) ones. So, after a point-in-time exposure, the clock is ticking on whole blood and cells as an indicator of that exposure.

Looking for toxic elements in packed RBCs lengthens the time interval for meaningful results to perhaps 10 weeks or so, partly because of element concentration factors. For example, with organic mercury, the ratio of RBC-to-plasma content becomes 10 or 20 to one in a matter of hours. Ninety to 95% of blood organic mercury rapidly goes into the RBCs.[1] This form of mercury stays around for weeks with a biphasic disappearance: 7.6 hours half-time for rapid dispersal to other tissues, and 52 days half-time for the slower phase of dispersal. So, there's often a better chance of finding the smoking gun in the cells instead of the plasma, serum, or whole blood. That's one reason that cells are a preferred tissue for element analysis. Another reason is that some essential or beneficial elements have more functional meaning in cells; magnesium is an example.

Urine shows only part of what the body is getting rid of. Biliary secretion into the intestine and fecal excretion are very important too, especially for mercury that the body detoxifies on its own. But when a synthetic sulfhydryl agent such as DMSA or DMPS is used, most sulfur-bound toxic element excretion then occurs via the urine. Urine has also been used to assess calcium status in autistics because it's virtually impossible to check on body calcium stores by measuring blood levels. Please note, however, that some toxic elements won't be found in urine unless detoxication (what the body does on its own) or detoxification (what the doctor does) is occurring. In autism, we believe that glutathione deficit plus oxidant stress inhibits removal of mercury from cells and allows it and other toxic substances to be sequestered almost indefinitely in body tissues.

SECTION FOUR: LABORATORY TESTS

I advise assessing toxic element burden by measuring urine elements twice, once without use of a detoxifying agent and then again during use or immediately afterward. One benefit of measuring twice is to see if sulfur goes up in the urine soon after ingestion of an orally-administered agent, such as DMSA. If the sulfur amount doesn't go up, then a no-change for the toxic elements could be a false negative result. If sulfur does go up but toxic elements don't, then there are no available toxic elements in the blood. (But they still might be hidden inside organ tissue.) And watch out for creatinine-ratioed results when creatinine is deficient. Such results artificially inflate the amounts of elements that are really coming out. Please contact a laboratory of choice for details about how, when and how long to collect urine for elemental analysis.

Hair is an excretory tissue; it carries elements out of the body. Look at any hair element analysis, and you'll see that sulfur is by far the most abundant element that's reported, about 50,000 ppm or 5% by weight. That's due mostly to the cysteinyl residue in hair protein, which binds elements that have sulfur affinity. These elements include antimony, arsenic, mercury, cadmium and lead. Hair cysteine also binds some friendly elements that like sulfur – zinc, copper, selenium, manganese and molybdenum.

But there's a big caveat for using hair to assess toxic element burden. Hair won't work for toxic elements that are sequestered in other tissues and that don't circulate in blood. If the element doesn't get to the hair follicle, it won't be in the hair. That's what often happens with mercury in untreated autistics. The mercury excess is there, and shows in the urine following provocation, but it's not in the hair initially.[2,3] Mercury goes up in hair once detoxification and detoxication get going, and it goes down after body burden has normalized or after detox has ceased. Be wary of the levels of sulfur-seeking toxic elements in hair test results when sulfur itself is deficient. Deficient hair sulfur is a reason for false-negative findings about toxic elements. Also, be wary of hair results when titanium, nickel and iron are high. Often these high levels signal external contamination of the hair.

Hair analysis has been a useful research tool for illustrating that mercury can hide from detection in autistics. For this very reason, it is not recommended for routine diagnostic purposes, while it may be valuable for research. There are some elements, antimony for example, that deserve further investigation to elucidate their possible roles in autism. Hair analysis may become a good way to find and monitor such elements in the future.

Hair shows us a history of what was circulating weeks to months ago. One inch of hair adjacent to the scalp at the nape of the neck reflects circulating element levels for the last couple of months. Nowadays, most labs with ICP-MS technology can get ± 10% accuracy with 0.25 grams of hair. Amounts less than that may cause results to be inaccurate. Finally, hair levels often don't correspond to blood levels even for some circulating elements. That's because blood transports and hair excretes. Elements that participate in metabolic imbalances can be displaced from normal in hair tissue and may show a trend that's different from blood. If you choose to use hair element analysis, have an experienced professional do your interpretive work. Don't expect valid results for hair that has been permed, dyed, or bleached. Such hair has had its elemental composition irreversibly changed.

Element Analysis Laboratory Information

Laboratory	Blood cell analysis	Urine analysis	Hair analysis	CLIA approved[1]	CAP certified[2]
BioCenter	x	x	x	x	
DDI	x	x	x	x	
ELN		x	x	N/A	N/A
GSDL	x	x	x	x	X
GPL		x	x	X	
MetaMetrix	x	x	x	x	

[1] Lab is approved per guidelines of the U.S. Clinical Laboratories Improvement Act.
[2] Lab is certified by and periodically inspected by the College of American Pathologists to ensure quality control.

BioCenter	Wichita KS	800-797-7785, 316-682-3100
Doctor's Data	St. Charles IL	800-323-2784, 630-377-8139
ELN	Utrecht, NL	31-(0)-30-287-1492
Great Smokies Diag Lab	Asheville NC	800-522-4762, 828-253-0621
Great Plains Lab	Lenexa KS	913-341-8949
MetaMetrix Lab	Norcross GA	800-221-4640, 404-446-5483

Special mention is due to Bill Walsh, Ph.D., who has intensely studied copper/zinc ratios in autistics. He has measured the ratio of blood serum copper to blood plasma zinc and finds this ratio to be typically high (about 1.6 ± 0.5) for autistics compared with that for normal controls (about 1.15 ± 0.20). Measuring copper and zinc in serum and plasma is fine; they are not declining with time as a toxic would after a period of exposure. Blood serum/plasma for zinc and copper can be ordered from most of the large clinical laboratories such as Quest and LabCorp.

Dr. Walsh's copper/zinc findings plus my observations about low cysteine in autistics led him to suspect and investigate metallothionein's involvement in autism.[4] Medical staff at Dr. Walsh's clinic, the Pfeiffer Treatment Center, now located in Warrenville, Illinois, sent many blood specimens from autistics to an environmental lab for metallothionein analysis. (Before 2004, this analysis was not available at clinical laboratories.) Statistically significant low metallothionein was found for the autistic patient population vs. controls, and these results are being prepared for publication.

Thioneins are small proteins that contain a very high number of cysteinyl residues. Twenty molecules of cysteine are used to make the various thioneins which contain about 60 to 70 amino acids in all. Each cysteinyl residue has a sulfhydryl group (-SH) and the sulfur in this group readily trades its hydrogen for metals like zinc, copper, cadmium or mercury. Once attached, such metals are held strongly by these proteins which have then become "metallothioneins."

There are four different kinds of metallothioneins denoted MT-I, MT-II, MT-III and MT-IV. MT-IV is found in the mucosal tissue of the gastrointestinal tract, where it protects other proteins (brush-border enzymes such as DPPIV) from attack by toxic elements that would otherwise bind to the sulfhydryl sites on these other proteins. MT-IV binds and holds copper in villous cells of the intestinal mucosa, thus preventing excessive uptake of this element. This copper is ultimately excreted by villous shedding of these cells.[5] There is no known genetic link between the chromosomal locus for MT expression (16q13) and autism, but with subnormal cysteine, deficient MT is a likely prospect. MT-1 and MT-II are ubiquitous in body tissues and act as toxic metal collectors and as delivery agents for zinc. MT-III is active in the brain, where part of its job is controlling neuronal growth.

A laboratory test that provides quantitative assay of metallothionein levels in blood is:

> Great Plains Laboratory, Lenexa, KS, 913-341-8949

A laboratory that provides analysis of metallothionein function in blood cells (lymphocytes) using stimulation by a metal challenge is:

> Immunosciences Lab, Beverly Hills, CA, 800-950-4686, 310-657-1077

References, Element Analyses and Metallothionein Assessments

1. Tsalev DL and Zaprianov ZK *Atomic Absorption Spectrometry in Occupational and Environmental Health Practice* vol. 1, CRC Press (1983) 160, 161.
2. Holmes AS, Blaxil MF and Haley BE "Reduced levels of mercury in first baby haircuts of autistic children" *Int.J.Toxicology* 111 no.4 (2003) 277-285.
3. Adams JB, Holloway CE et al. "Heavy metal exposures, developmental milestones, and physical symptoms in children with autism" Fall DAN! 2003 Conference Presentation/Syllabus, Portland Oct 2003 71-89.
4. Walsh WJ, Usman A et al. "Metallothionein and Autism" Pfeiffer Treatment Center, Naperville IL Oct 2001.
5. Culotta VC and Gitlin JD "Disorders of Copper Transport" Chapt 126 in Scriver CR et al. eds. *The Metabolic and Molecular Bases of Inherited Disease* 8th ed. McGraw Hill (2001) 3107-3110.

11. Immune Testing

Food allergy tests were described previously, as were the complete blood count (CBC), element analysis (zinc), and amino acids. Analytes in these tests are involved in immune functions. Also, intestinal barrier immunology testing was mentioned, along with intestinal permeability measurements, and they are very important in autism. But further specific testing may uncover other fundamental problems, such as an undetectable titer (no response) to measles, or aggravating problems such as other viral infections, or evidence of imbalanced immune system molecules that evoke oxidant responses or inflammation. Before doing such tests, parents and physicians should discuss how test results might alter therapy for the individual.

We know from the work of Professor Singh and others that for many autistics, there's a static measles infection with related autoimmune response to myelin basic protein – a protein in the myelin sheath that surrounds neuronal cells. But we don't have enough evidence that specific antiviral therapies counter this. On the other hand, symptomatic recovery often follows the normalization of fundamental biochemistry of methylation, transsulfuration, energy flow and nucleotides. On the side of immunologic testing, there are two positive aspects: (1) gaining knowledge about what's wrong in this realm, whether or not it can be directly addressed by a specific therapy, and (2) monitoring the progress of the individual while you make your way through the field of biomedical options.

For autistics, a viral panel or panels can be ordered to assess the degree of immune system vigilance for measles, mumps, rubella, various herpes viruses, cytomegalovirus, and Epstein-Barr virus (EBV). All of these are seen from time to time in autistics as problem infections, and "blood titer" tests are available to show which may be affecting the individual. These viruses and other infectious agents (Streptococcus and Chlamydia) can produce substances that mimic neuron-specific antigens, setting up appropriate and inappropriate (autoimmune) responses.

Immune cells in autistics are often out of balance. Natural killer (NK) cells are loafing or seem to be on vacation, and the immune response normally mounted by cells against fungi and viruses (sometimes referred to as "Th 1") is not up to par. Meanwhile, humoral response ("Th 2") is over-accentuated, which often leads to allergic-like responses. Additionally, the various types of T-lymphocytes that do much of our immune duties are skewed in number. Lab tests are available to assess lymphocyte types, NK cell activity, "helper" cell function and immunoglobulin levels.

Also measurable are some messenger molecules that bring news about immune response needs to cells: interleukins IL-1,2,6, and 10, tumor necrosis factor-alpha and gamma (TNFα, TNFγ), and interferon-gamma (IFN-γ). These messengers or "cytokines" can be calling for help and getting inadequate cellular response. Our tissues then increase the amounts of these cytokines so as to amplify the message. But what often results is oxidant stress and inflammation, instead of appropriate and effective immune response. Elevated levels of TNFα are commonly found in autistics and have been associated with immune and inflammatory responses to dietary proteins.[1] Oxidant stress, which increases TNFα, is associated with increased attempts by cells to form more cysteine and glutathione from homocysteine and less methionine.[2,3,4] Therefore, oxidant stress, inflammation and TNFα act to decrease methylation in many autistics, and TNFα may be used as a marker to monitor the extent to which antioxidant efforts and immunotherapy therapy are successful.

A laboratory that offers all of these tests plus others for characterization of an individual's immune function is:

Immunosciences Lab, Beverly Hills, CA, 800-950-4686, 310-657-1077

References, Immune Testing

1. Jyanouchi H, Sun S and Itokazu N "Innate immunity associated with inflammatory responses and cytokine production..." *Neuropsychobiology* 46 no.2 (2002) 76-84.
2. Halliwell B and Gutteridge JMC *Free Radicals in Biology and Medicine* 3rd Ed, Oxford Sci.Pub. (1999) 335-336.
3. Vitvitsky V, Mosharov E et al. "Redox regulation of homocysteine-dependent glutathione synthesis" *Redox Rep* 8 no.1 (2003) 57-63.
4. Bannerjee R and Zou GG "Redox regulation and reaction mechanism of human cystathionine beta-synthase: a PLP-dependent hemesensor protein" *Arch.Biochem Biophys* 433 no.1 (2005) 144-156.

12. Genomic Testing

In the last several years, it has become practical to study isolated parts of the human genome and look for places where one nucleotide has been replaced by another in selected genes. The human genome includes a large number of slight variations, or polymorphisms. Many are being explored for linkage to disease. These genetic variations can result in a protein that has one amino acid replaced by another, and this alters the character of the protein to some degree. These variants are called single nucleotide polymorphisms or SNPs. Small samples of humans – fewer than 300 people – were surveyed, and well over a million SNPs were found in each sample.(*Chem.Engineering News* Feb 21, 2005, 13). If the variant protein is an enzyme, there can be several possible consequences:

- Insignificant change in reaction rates or kinetics (no disease or disorder results).
- Faster kinetics (not usually, but it happens).
- Slower kinetics (often happens).
- More substances are acted on, and the enzyme is less specific in its actions.
- Fewer substances are acted on, and the enzyme does only part of its expected job.
- The enzyme doesn't work at all. (We should know about this without genomic tests, because completely dead enzymes leave an obvious pile of unprocessed material. If this is related to illness, it's usually identified in infancy.)

For autism, several SNPs have been found that actually relate to the transmethylation and transsulfuration that are disordered per conventional lab tests for the related metabolites (such as cysteine, adenosine, and methionine). Those SNPs that are under scrutiny include:

- MTHFR: methylene tetrahydrofolate reductase.
- MTRR: methionine synthase reductase.
- BHMT: betaine-homocysteine methyltransferase.
- ADA: adenosine deaminase.
- COMT: catechol-O-methyltransferase.
- Groups of genes responsible for proteins and enzymes that look after detoxication chemistry in body tissues, including cytochrome P450 genes, CYPXXX, glutathione transferase or conjugation enzymes (GSTs), and glutathione peroxidase (GPx).

Genomics testing is an analytical option that you may wish to explore at any time during the course of the biomedical intervention. The genetic makeup won't change with diet or nutrition or with supplement use or detoxification, but the individual's biochemistry will be influenced by these interventions. The point is that genomics shows underlying predispositions, while biochemical and immunologic testing show what's actually happening. Genomics sets the layout of streets and alleys. The biochemicals, adenosine, folate, B_{12}, methionine, etc. are the traffic on the streets. The traffic jam that we call autism is due to gridlock on those streets. But it doesn't have to be that way. Traffic jams can be cleared and traffic can flow smoothly when the biochemical gridlock is broken – maybe by supplementing methylcobalamin or TMG or folinic acid. When we do this, we are making metabolic manipulations that alleviate or compensate, at least in part, for the individual's genetic predispositions and acquired stressors.

Genomic testing is fine for research on autism and is the only way to really pin down predispositions that contribute to autism when stressors are piled on. But, is genomic testing valuable for the individual? How will it influence treatment? Will you try methylcobalamin, vitamin B_6, DMG, etc. regardless of the outcome? That's for you to decide. Several DAN!-

trained clinicians routinely measure SNPs that reflect glutathione function. Their use of glutathione –how much for how long, and whether to administer it and NAC intravenously – depends on these test results. To me, this seems to be a very valid use of genomic analysis for individual patients.

I do wish to caution about genomic profiling or other fishing expeditions that measure/report all kinds of SNP variants. We've all got them; some of us have lots of them. The vast majority have no illness or disease associations. DAN! research first focused on abnormal metabolites related to chemistry that is essential for cell and self capabilities of perception and response. In addition, we focused on organ disease that is prevalent in autism such as intestinal problems. Then, we went looking for corresponding SNPs that could be predispositions for these autism-related problems. Some of these are prevalent in the autistic population. If you try to work from the other direction, not only do you have to wade through lots of extraneous genomics, but you can be deceived as well. Need an example? Let's take MTHFR – methylene tetrahydrofolate reductase. That's the enzyme that processes folate into the form that assists conversion of homocysteine to methionine.

Many autistics have variant SNPs for MTHFR. Typically, weak MTHFR predisposes to homocystinuria. Counter to this, autistics as a group have low homocystine; homocystinuria is rare in autism. For many autistics there are significant problems "upstream" of MTHFR. Homocysteine is low because the metabolic sequence is hung up before we even get there. Adenosine and adenosylhomocysteine are often high; they precede formation of homocysteine. Folate is hung up at getting one-carbon pieces from DMG to make folate forms that precede those that interact with MTHFR. Giving more folate because of MTHFR SNP variance in autism can make matters worse.

Balanced in favor of genomic testing is human curiosity. What is genetically unusual about my son or daughter with autism? If you as a parent want to know, you should check with your doctor and maybe look on the Internet, because laboratory capabilities for this are changing rapidly. One lab that is CLIA-licensed and CAP certified and that offers some SNP analysis is Great Smokies Diagnostics of Asheville, NC, 800-522-4762, or 828-253-0621 for those outside the 800 calling area. Another organization that has a business alliance with a laboratory that does genomic testing is Integrative Genomics; their website address is www.integrativegenomics.com.

SUMMARY – Analytes of Most Significance in Autism

I've listed the analytes that I find to be most useful in helping physicians decipher the biochemistry and immunology that has gone wrong in autism. Clinicians can discuss how best to measure these with selected laboratories. These are my favorites for reasons that are discussed elsewhere in this report. Other analytes can certainly be useful, perhaps even more than any of these for a given individual. The ones I have chosen pertain to autism's chemistry as we understand it, and they do not include analytes that are markers for what I have categorized as Type 1 autism – profound metabolic errors of genetic origin. These analytes pertain to Type 2 autism, genetic predispositions plus acquired stressors.

Blood plasma cysteine
Blood or cell GSH or GSH/GSSH ratio
Plasma methionine
Plasma SAM and SAH (hard to measure with existing lab capabilities)
Plasma adenosine

Serum creatine
TNFα (check with lab for specimen requirements)
Urine taurine and beta-alanine
Erythrocyte DHA and other cell membrane fatty acids
Venous blood ammonia
Intestinal flora (stool analysis)
Specific Food IgE and IgG levels (or food avoidance trials)
Pyruvate, lactate, and pyroglutamic acid (pyroglu) (organic acids)
Urine toxic elements, especially mercury, in pre- and post-challenge specimens
Erythrocyte elements – essential and toxic, must include magnesium

USING NUTRITIONAL SUPPLEMENTS FOR AUTISM

By Jon Pangborn

Introduction

> - **Improving nutritional status should be an initial strategy.**
> - **Food intolerances and maldigestion lead to intestinal dysbiosis and leaky gut.**
> - **Some nutritional supplements are beneficial initially while others can be detrimental if given before prerequisite treatments.**

From my experience, improving nutritional status should be an initial strategy for helping the autistic individual, and one of the first actions should be intervention on dietary matters. As described by Dr. Baker in a previous section, cleaning up the diet comes first. Then comes assessment of whether or not an exclusionary diet will be of benefit. Cleaning up means avoiding foods with synthetic colors or flavors, omitting excess sugar and highly processed carbohydrates, and avoiding food that we all would consider to be "junk." Exclusionary diets that have shown benefit for many autistics are: casein-free diet (excludes dairy foods and anything known to contain casein), gluten-free diet (excludes wheat, oats, rye, barley and spelt and anything known to contain gluten), and the "specific carbohydrate diet" (explained in Dr. Baker's section). Getting dietary matters settled is really a prerequisite to success with nutritional supplementation.

Why should we attend to foods and diet first? With some, I admit it seems to make no difference. But with many, it makes a huge difference. That's because many autistics have food allergies and gastrointestinal dysfunctions that lead to malabsorption and intestinal distress. In autism, these problems are usually specific to certain foods such as dairy products, cereal grains, or carbohydrates that contain certain disaccharide sugars. When these foods are eaten regularly, the malabsorption process constantly provides undigested food substances to the lower small intestine and large bowel. These are places where such substances don't belong. Undigested food at those locations becomes a nutrient source for dysbiotic flora – pathogenic bacteria, yeast, fungi and possibly parasites. Dysbiotic flora can cause or add to inflammation and to abnormal mucosal permeability ("leaky gut"), which may adversely influence the entire gastrointestinal process. Bowel irritability, rapid intestinal transit with inadequate digestion, abnormal pH conditions and diarrhea are some of the gastrointestinal woes that can result. Adding certain nutrients, like amino acids, to this situation is likely to make things worse. There is no guarantee that the dysbiosis won't flourish when some supplemented nutrients – in ready to use (bioavailable) form – are provided. So, we have two lessons to learn.

Lesson One: some nutritional supplements, but not others, can be part of the earlier stages of intervention, along with dietary changes if necessary. Typically, nutritional supplements that are beneficial during dietary intervention include: digestive enzymes, vitamin B_6 with magnesium, cod liver oil (vitamins A and D), vitamin C, zinc, calcium, taurine, and maybe melatonin. Blends or combination formulas of B_6, other vitamins and assisting nutrients usually are tolerated then as well. Essential fatty acids may also be beneficial, along with the antioxidant protection of vitamin E (as well as vitamin C and taurine). Other nutritional supplements can cause problems, including behavioral disasters, if used at this stage. Examples might be amino acids (except taurine),

SAMe, carnosine, and choosing wrong on DMG versus TMG. Detoxifying agents are very ill advised at early stages of intervention.

Lesson Two: After digestion is working, food intolerances have been addressed and intestinal dysbiosis has been treated, a second tier of supplement options can be explored. These include vitamin B_{12} (or methylcobalamin) and folate (or folinic acid), DMG or TMG, glutathione, amino acid supplements, carnosine, carnitine, SAMe (S-adenosylmethionine), and immune system aids (colostrum, herbals). And in between these two stages of nutritional supplementation, when the population of intestinal flora is being addressed, comes the need to supplement probiotics.

SUGGESTED STAGING OF NUTRITIONAL SUPPLEMENTS DURING AUTISM TREATMENT INTERVENTIONS

<u>First-Tier Options</u>

Digestive enzymes
Vitamin B6 and magnesium
Taurine
Vitamins C and E
Zinc
Calcium
Vitamin A, cod liver oil
Fatty acids
Melatonin
Multivitamins, multiminerals

Activated charcoal
Silymarin (milk thistle)
Probiotics
S.boulardii as needed
a-Ketoglutaric acid

<u>Second-Tier Options</u>

More vitamin C
Antioxidant formulations
N-acetylcysteine
Glutathione

DMG, TMG
MethylCbl, folinic acid
Amino acids
Creatine
L-carnitine
CoQ_{10}
Mg malate
Carnosine

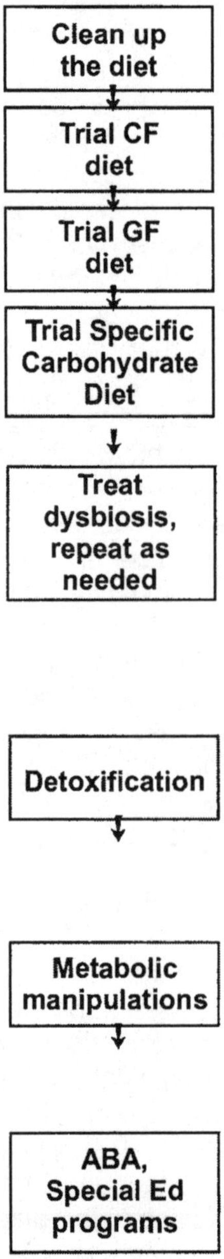

```
Clean up the diet
       ↓
Trial CF diet
       ↓
Trial GF diet
       ↓
Trial Specific Carbohydrate Diet
       ↓
Treat dysbiosis, repeat as needed
       
Detoxification
       ↓
Metabolic manipulations
       ↓
ABA, Special Ed programs
```

Notes for Suggested Staging chart:

1. Some supplements are intended for intermittent use (as needed): activated charcoal, S.boulardii, alpha-ketoglutaric acid, silymarin, N-acetylcysteine.
2. Treatment for dysbiosis may have to be repeated every so often while probiotics or "anti-yeast" nutrient use should be continuous for most individuals.
3. Inositol (for obsessive–compulsive behavior) can be tried in the first-tier group as an aid to diet adjustment and to facilitate behavioral changes.
4. Trying creatine before mercury detoxification can result in a negative response (mercury blocks formation of creatine phosphate). By blocking pyruvate dehydrogenase, mercury can also negate the potential positive effects of L-carnitine, CoQ_{10} and Mg malate.

Nutritional supplements in the first tier are those for consideration during early interventions. They are nutrients or foods that should help or even be synergistic with adjustments to the diet. First-tier supplements should not provoke or worsen intestinal dysbiosis. Also, they should not overload an autistic's limited capacity for detoxication nor should they spread an existing contamination. That means, we don't start with items like N-acetylcysteine, glutathione, or amino acid blends. We also want to hold off on nutrients that can't be used until gastrointestinal functioning is improved. Oral vitamin B_{12} could be an example. Notice I said oral. Injectable methylcobalamin, methylCbl, is a different matter entirely. If the doctor has a therapeutic strategy that includes early use of injected methylCbl, I have no problem, provided that other issues (diet, digestion, dysbiosis, etc.) are promptly addressed.

How an oral nutrient is accepted and utilized depends upon how healed the digestive process is and upon the individual's metabolic status. Amino acids can't be properly processed unless B-vitamins are adequate and functional. In addition, there's a logical order for many of the nutrients themselves. Taurine is needed for formation of bile salts. Bile salts facilitate uptake of lipids including vitamins A and D. Vitamin D helps assimilation of calcium. If you remove dairy products from an autistic's diet, you remove perhaps 75% of his/her dietary calcium, and calcium then needs to be supplemented. So, very early on we're going to try the taurine option. Our first-tier nutritional supplement options will begin with digestive enzymes and will then be expanded to: vitamin B_6, magnesium, taurine, vitamin C, zinc, calcium, vitamin A, essential fatty acids (especially DHA), and multivitamin/mineral combination products. All of these can be tried during dietary adjustment periods and before confronting dysbiosis.

Why Are Nutritional Supplements Helpful?

- **Many digestive enzymes have evidence of deficiency in autistic-spectrum disease.**
- **Some vitamins are needed at therapeutic doses to potentiate metabolic processes that are impaired for many autistics.**
- **Impaired metabolic processes include transmethylation, transsulfuration, imbalanced methionine metabolism, and deficient and disordered glutathione metabolism.**
- **Special diets can create need for nutritional supplements.**

There are several major reasons for autistic individuals benefiting from various nutritional supplements. The first is imperfect digestion of foods and/or limited diet, causing less than adequate uptake of dietary-source nutrients. Evidence of hindrances to digestion and absorption of food-source nutrients comes from studies and from clinical metabolic findings related to maldigestion, including:

- Horvath et al., *J.Pediatrics* 135 no.5, (November 1999) p.559-563: 69% with reflux esophagitis, 66% with chronic duodenitis, 58% with lower than normal digestive capacity for carbohydrates.

- Horvath and Perman, *Curr.Opin.Pediatrics* 14 (2002) p.583-587: many autistic children with chronic diarrhea, others with stool impaction, some abnormal behaviors connected to GI dysfunction.

- Bradstreet J. unpublished study of stool fat content presented at DAN! Atlanta Conference, May 2001: differential analysis of stool fats and total fats shows fat malabsorption in more than 50% of tested autistic children; this frequently indicates need for supplemental lipase.

- Kushak R and Buie T, "Disaccharidase Deficiencies in Patients with Autistic Spectrum Disorders" presented at DAN! New Orleans Think Tank, Jan.2004: lactase deficiency in 58-65% (age dependent), isomaltase/palatinase deficiency in 30% to 40%. There is a lower percentage with maltase deficiency. These are enzymes that break down complex sugars into simple sugars like glucose and fructose. These enzymes (disaccharidases) are very frequently deficient in autistics with intestinal inflammation (77% for lactase, 64% for isomaltase).

- Reichelt, Shattock, Cade, and many others have published on the presence of dietary peptides in the urine of autistics. Many of these peptides come from protein in cereal grains and dairy products. Peptiduria is direct evidence of protein maldigestion.

If there is maldigestion of carbohydrates, fats and proteins in autistics as a group, then it would be unlikely for them to have normal or adequate nutritional status without supplementation.

The second reason for supplements helping is that certain nutrients, such as vitamins B_6 and B_{12}, may be needed at higher-than-normal dietary amounts to potentiate metabolic processes. Many vitamins act as coenzymes – helpers to enzymes that promote chemical changes in body tissue. Vitamin B_6, for example, becomes pyridoxal 5'-phosphate, P5P. As a coenzyme, P5P assists many metabolic steps, including three of the steps in the essential amino acid methionine becoming taurine: homocysteine → cystathionine, cystathionine → cysteine, cysteine sulfinate → hypotaurine. Hence, an oral supplement of vitamin B_6 can help the rate at which methionine is used to make other beneficial amino acids such as cysteine and taurine. Giving vitamins for enzyme potentiation is accepted medical practice in metabolic dysfunctions where inhibited chemistry can be appropriately benefited.

Thanks to the efforts of many clinicians and scientists, we now know that many autistics have imbalanced metabolism of methionine, impaired methylation and disordered transsulfuration. They have deficient cysteine and glutathione formation, and excessive oxidized glutathione relative to the active, reduced form. These autistics may benefit from nutrients that can improve this biochemistry or partially compensate for it. Some nutritional supplements that can directly assist with these problems are B_6 with magnesium, B_{12} and sometimes folate, TMG (betaine) and reduced glutathione. The trick is knowing when to use these and other nutrients, and how much. Also very important is knowing what not to use. With autism, the simple adage "supplement what's deficient" can lead to disaster. Homocysteine is low per blood analysis in many autistics. Would you supplement homocysteine? I hope not. And supplementing methionine or its ready-to-methylate form, SAM (or SAMe), can lead to big problems even though they would normally help methylation. In the nutritional supplement descriptions that follow, I will do my best to advise and suggest about the whens, hows, and when-not-tos.

But, while we're still on the whys of nutritional supplementation, there is a third reason that sometimes becomes important. Many autistic-spectrum children and adults are on diets that exclude certain types of foods – dairy products, cereal grains and foods containing gluten, or specific carbohydrates. These exclusions may be due to allergic responses, metabolic problems, or digestive limitations. Or without knowing the biomedical reason, some autistic individuals may just function better when certain types of foods are avoided. When you as a parent or clinician remove a class of foods from an individual's diet, you should also consider the adequacy of essential nutrients in the diet. This is another reason for considering use of nutritional supplements. We strongly advise all parents and guardians of those on exclusion diets to consider caloric adequacy of proteins, fats and carbohydrates as well as adequacy of individual essential nutrients. If you have questions about this, we recommend that you consult with a licensed, DAN!-trained nutritionist or dietician.

There is an interesting bit of history to nutritional supplement use in autism. Long before we had any inkling of what chemistry might be affected in autism, Dr. Bernard Rimland and other parents observed that some supplemental nutrients produced beneficial effects in autistics. Dr. Rimland had read about vitamin B_6 correcting tryptophan metabolism so it would form more serotonin and niacin and less of a wasted byproduct (xanthurenic acid). Also, there was some early published evidence that vitamin B_6 could help with behavior and mental function. So, Dr. Rimland asked Adele Davis, a pioneer in environmental concerns and nutrition, to help formulate a comprehensive B_6 supplement for autistics. Once the formulation was worked out, he asked for help in developing it into a saleable product. Only one nutritional product manufacturer stepped forward to do the testing and production trials – Kirkman Laboratories. Eventually, Nu-Thera was born (1969) – the first combination product designed for autism. It was a vitamin B_6-based product that included all nutrients that were thought to be related to B_6 and its functions.

Some years later, Dr. Rimland decided that it would be a good idea to keep track of individual responses by autistics to various single nutrients and to medications (drugs) as well. The parents would observe and record the responses – better behavior, worse behavior, or no change. They would send the information to the Autism Research Institute on a provided form, and ARI would tally and summarize the responses once each year. This summary has become ARI Publication 34. The latest update is that of March 2005 (ARI Publ.34, March 2005); see last page of this book.

Autistic-spectrum individuals have varying degrees of autistic traits. That's because autism isn't just one disease but is the possible outcome of many disease conditions. As a result, responses to supplements vary. The "best" response to a single supplement goes to melatonin (61% better). The "worst" response goes to SAMe, S-adenosylmethionine (only 19% better, with 15% worse). You might note that this is completely consistent with impaired ability of SAMe to methylate. Melatonin is made from serotonin with methylation by SAMe. But if SAMe is inhibited from methylating (by elevated adenosylhomocysteine), then giving more of it does little good. So, even with individuality, there are common themes to the results of this tracking effort.

The descriptions that follow are a compendium of information on about 40 nutritional supplements, including use of digestive enzymes with meals. This compendium is written for the clinician and trained nutritionist. Parents with nutrition training or experience should learn from it as well. Many of these supplements have tabulated responses on ARI Publication 34 (included

SECTION FIVE: NUTRITIONAL SUPPLEMENTS FOR AUTISM

at the end of this section). From our experience and those of DAN! clinicians, these supplements can be of help if used properly. The "properly" part depends on the supplement and is explained in the information to follow. Choosing a supplement for a trial period at various doses is a biomedical option that is open to you. And the more you know about a supplement, the more likely you are to choose and use wisely.

There are, however, four general rules that apply to use of all supplements.

1. **Always start with a low dose. You may not see any change, and that's a signal that you could increase the dosage and watch for an effect.**

2. **Discontinue the supplement if there are adverse effects, except that in a few cases, such as digestive enzymes or perhaps probiotics, "worse" may precede "much better." But often, worse means worse permanently, so stop the supplement if the worse is much worse or continues unabated. Also, you should discontinue a supplement that has no apparent benefit or that worsens a laboratory test result that is related to it.**

3. **Introduce new supplements one at a time with few exceptions. B_6 and magnesium together is an exception. Combination products (Super Nu-Thera, ASD-Plex) are a blend of many nutrients, and they can be tried. If there's a problem, however, there is no way to figure out which ingredient is not tolerated without one-at-a-time testing. That means purchasing individual ingredients. Having to do this is unusual, but it happens.**

4. **Keep records religiously. What wasn't successful can be as important as what was. Write down the symptoms of worsening if it occurs, because you might want a future retrial of that supplement. Don't forget to include dosages and brands in the record.**

DIGESTIVE ENZYMES

- Enzymes are NOT a substitute for an exclusionary diet.
- Autistic-spectrum individuals often benefit from –
    - Digestive peptidases, especially DPP4
    - Lipases for digestion of dietary fats
    - Disaccharidases for digestion of complex dietary sugars
- Most digestive enzymes designed for autism should be taken at the beginning of each meal
- Digestive enzyme dosage depends on the amount of food that's eaten, not the age or weight of the individual.
- Often there is an initial period of worsened behavior and traits when enzymes are started due to reduction of exorphins and die-off of dysbiotic flora.

While the diet is being adjusted or immediately thereafter, you should give digestive enzymes a trial. And let's have an understanding at the outset – digestive enzymes are not a substitute for an exclusionary diet. The first order of business is to determine if some type of diet is beneficial as described previously, by Dr. Baker. If it is, do it. You can wait until the diet issues are completely settled and then put in the enzymes, or you can try the enzymes along with trial diets. But make only one change at a time. I usually advise doing a casein-free (CF) diet for a 30-day trial period. After two or three weeks of the CF trial, add digestive enzymes. Then wait a couple of weeks before beginning a 45-60 day gluten-free (GF) trial. After that, maybe a trial of the specific carbohydrate diet. That means the digestive enzymes are present for the GF and SCD trial periods, and just part of the CF trial period. While improvements often are prompt with the CF diet, they can be quite delayed with the GF diet. For older children and teens, the GF trial may have to be considerably longer, 3-6 months, before improvements become obvious.

Will the enzymes obscure the effects of the GF and SCD trials? Perhaps to some moderate degree they will. While enzymes usually do not immediately shut off prompt immunologic response to foods that are allergenic for an individual, they do tend to reduce delayed or possibly IgG-mediated responses. For autistics, two primary purposes of supplemented enzymes are: (1) to break apart or digest peptides that could be absorbed to disrupt cellular perception and response processes, and (2) to reduce or shut off the inappropriate food supply to the lower small intestine and large bowel – the food supply for dysbiotic flora. This latter purpose includes digestion of disaccharide sugars from carbohydrate foods. But supplemental enzymes cannot be depended upon to be 100% effective in finding and digesting all of the peptide and disaccharide molecules. Even with digestive enzyme use, you'll usually be able to see the effects of dietary gluten if there are ill effects for the individual. Sometimes, a deliberate gluten test meal at the end of a long avoidance period tells the tale. Also, you're likely to see some temporary side effects of the enzymes as well, as explained below.

There are some additional reasons or benefits to enzymes, besides the two primary ones enumerated above. One is that their use will compensate to a significant degree for mistakes in the diet. No matter how careful you are, mistakes are going to happen. Besides, food labels do not always provide full disclosure of contents. Did you know that casein may be in canned salmon and tuna? And gluten is added to all kinds of processed foods. Watch out for "textured vegetable protein;" it contains gluten.

Another reason is the dietary shift itself – if there is one. When a class of foods is excluded, another class or other classes are usually increased. Excluding dairy and grains, for example, often shifts the diet toward more meat and poultry. This makes more demands on protein-digesting enzymes and may provoke protein maldigestion in some individuals. If that happens, then one of the primary purposes of going on a diet is defeated, and an inappropriate food supply will again be created for dysbiotic flora. Regardless of enzyme use, always try to maintain a reasonable balance among total protein, total carbs and total fats.

Summary so far: Why Supplement Digestive Enzymes?

1. **To reduce/eliminate exorphins and other dietary peptides that may interfere with cellular processes.**
2. **To reduce/eliminate inappropriate food matter, especially complex sugars and carbohydrates, that allows dysbiotic gut flora to flourish.**
3. **To compensate for mistakes in the diet.**
4. **To compensate for a diet that shifts to food groups in higher amounts than the individual is used to eating.**

About Digestive Enzymes

Digestive enzymes, the natural ones in our gastrointestinal tracts and the supplemental ones that come in capsules, are proteins that have the catalytic ability to disassemble large food molecules. Digestive enzyme supplements come from plant or animal sources (classified legally as "foods") and they can help us to digest food when they are taken with a meal. The different types of digestive enzymes include: proteases for breaking proteins down into peptides and peptidases for breaking peptides down to individual, free-form amino acids or short-chain peptides. Short-chain peptides are dipeptides (two amino acids linked together) and perhaps some tripeptides (three amino acids linked together). Lipases split dietary fat molecules into smaller pieces (glycerol and fatty acids). Amylases break dietary starch down into simpler carbohydrates like disaccharides or monosaccharide sugars. Sometimes additional enzymes are present that break down the cellular structure of plants – cellulases, hemicellulase and xylanases. Disaccharidases break complex sugars down into simple sugars. As mentioned previously, we often need disaccharidase help in autism: lactase (for processing milk sugar into glucose and galactose), and maltase and isomaltase for processing some complex sugars into simple ones like glucose or fructose. When nutritional supplements are needed, digestive enzyme supplements are usually needed also, because they improve the body's ability to extract needed nutrients from food.

A natural peptidase enzyme of particular interest in autism is dipeptidylpeptidase IV (DPP4).[1] DPP4's job is to break apart peptides that have the amino acid proline at every other position in the peptide molecule. Such peptides, "exorphins," have morphine-like action on neuronal cells. Beta-casomorphin 7, from casein, is such a peptide:

Tyrosine-proline-phenylalanine-proline-glycine-proline-isoleucine

So is gliadorphin (gliadinomorphin), from gliadin from gluten:

Tyrosine-proline-glutamine-proline-glutamine-proline-phenylalanine

DPP4 cleaves peptides such as these at the second bond (a proline-amino acid bond) from the N-terminal end (the left end as written and where H_2N- is understood to be attached). Thus, DPP4 acting successively on beta-casomorphin 7 causes:

Tyr-Pro / Phe-Pro-Gly-Pro-Ile
Tyr-Pro / Phe-Pro / Gly-Pro-Ile
Tyr-Pro / Phe-Pro / Gly-Pro / Ile

In the human digestive tract, only DPP4 can do this. But, DPP4, like many enzymes, is subject to inactivation or poisoning by external substances. During the 1980s and 1990s, Reichelt, Cade and others found undigested exorphin peptides in the urine of autistics.[2,3,4,5] These findings are consistent with impaired and deficient activity of DPP4. In 1982, Püschel et al. examined DPP4 from human placenta and found that it is inactivated by mercury (mercuric chloride), organophosphates (pesticide sprays), zinc and cadmium chlorides, and lead acetate.[6]

Here, we've come upon a fifth reason for supplementing digestive enzymes – to compensate for certain toxic exposures or contaminations. Such exposures may be an underlying cause of many of the gastrointestinal-related problems found in autistics. During detoxification therapy, circulating toxics may increase the need for enzyme supplements.

The exorphin peptiduria presented by autistics is consistent with deficiency of DPP4 digestive activity. There also are autism connections, explained elsewhere in this book, between the DPP4 protein as a digestive enzyme and adenosine deaminase binding protein and cluster differentiation factor CD26, which is a binding and signaling site on lymphocytes. All these are the same protein. The plant-source analog of DPP4, when taken orally, has digestive activity in the stomach and small intestine, but its molecular form is much too large to be absorbed. Further, adenosine deaminase binding protein and CD26 are human-form cell-membrane proteins that grow out of cells and protrude through the lipid membrane. Supplemental DPP4 enzyme is a plant-source protein; its amino acid sequence is different from human DPP4. DPP4 cannot substitute for CD26 internally, and is probably, itself, digested in the small intestine.

You will find in the literature that there can be immune response to CD26 in autism.[7] This is related to the fact that certain exogenous (from outside the body) molecules or substances bind to human CD26. Some casein peptides (casomorphins) do this; they'd have to for intestinal DPP4 to digest them. But mercury in Thimerosal form also binds to DPP4/CD26 (everywhere), as does the toxin from strep germs, streptokinase. This does not mean that oral, plant-source DPP4 analog causes immune response or dysregulation. That's what's going on with the natural, human CD26 in the autistic's body. The supplemental DPP4 analog is supposed to digest exorphin peptides. If these peptides are not digested and if they get into the bloodstream, then they can bind to cellular CD26-adenosine binding protein and cause trouble.

Now, let's switch to carbohydrate digestion, which has been found faulty in autistics by Horvath and others and by Kushak and Buie.[8,9,10] Lactase, which digests the milk sugar, lactose, is the disaccharidase enzyme that is most often weak in autistics. Lactose, a disaccharide sugar, is glucose attached to galactose. Lactase in the small intestine separates lactose into glucose and galactose. Lactase is most active at a pH of 5.4 to 6.0 (slightly acidic), and the pancreas has to put adequate bicarbonate into the much more acidic food matter coming from the stomach for lactase to work. For whatever reason, though, lactase deficiency is present in at least 60% of tested autistics.[9,10] So, lactase must also be in digestive enzyme formulations for use in autism.

Three other disaccharide sugars also are known to be not digested well by autistics:
    Maltose: glucose + glucose with a 1→ 4 glycosidic bond
    Isomaltose: glucose + glucose with a 1→ 6 glycosidic bond
    Palatinose: glucose + fructose with a 1→ 6 glycosidic bond

The difference between maltose and isomaltose is how the two sugars are linked together; two different digestive enzymes, maltase and isomaltase, are needed, one for each. Palatinose uses the isomaltase enzyme for digestion. Because many autistics have maltase and isomaltase/palatinase deficiencies too, these also need to be provided as supplemental digestive enzymes.

A word of caution is very much in order about enzyme names. Most commercial digestive enzymes, and natural ones too, have multiple common names. That's because these enzymes have both primary and various secondary activities.

For example, in humans, the enzyme system that includes lactose digestion is the "beta-galactosidase complex." The lactase enzyme itself has synonyms: beta-D-galactoside galactohydrolase, or beta-1,3-galactosidase, or lactase. Its enzyme commission number is unequivocal; it is E.C.3.2.1.23. The enzyme that acts on maltose is E.C.3.2.1.20, the "glycoamylase complex." It's variously called: alpha-glucosidase, or alpha-D-glucosidase, glucohydrolase, or glucoinvertase or maltase. And the enzyme that handles isomaltose and palatinose is E.C.3.2.1.10, the "sucrase-isomaltase complex." It's also called oligo-1,6-glucosidase or dextrin 6-alpha-D-glucanohydrolase, or palatinase or limit dextrinase. Problems can arise when other enzymes (not these specific E.C. ones) have similar names. Such enzymes often have other undesirable activities, and they should not be used as substitutes for the real ones. An example would be limit dextrinase, which actually is E.C.3.2.1.41. While that enzyme digests maltose, it can also produce maltose from starch and has negligible isomaltase activity. The lesson here is to use digestive enzymes from a trusted source. Don't hesitate to ask questions of the manufacturer/provider, and expect sensible and forthright answers. The interested biochemist or enzymologist may wish to consult:

- White and White, *Source Book of Enzymes*, CRC Press; new editions are published periodically.
- Semenza G, Auricclio S and Mantei N "Small Intestinal Disaccharidases", Chapter 25 in Scriver et al. eds, *The Metabolic and Molecular Bases of Inherited Disease* 8th ed, vol. 1 McGraw-Hill (2001) p.1623-1650.

Finally, a few words about lipase, the digestive enzyme that breaks complicated dietary fats into two types of molecules that can be absorbed more easily – fatty acids and glycerol. For years, we saw elevated fats in the stools of autistics when a stool or digestive stool analysis was done. At the Atlanta DAN! Conference in May 2001, Jeff Bradstreet M.D. (Melbourne, FL) spoke about this. Over 50% of his autistic patients showed some degree of excessive stool fat per the Great Smokies Diagnostic Lab CDSA test. (Other labs now offer this too; see Laboratory Tests section.) When this problem gets bad enough (steatorrhea), fatty acid, vitamin D and calcium deficiencies can occur. The temporary, and sometimes long-term, remedy is to provide lipase orally with meals.

Using Digestive Enzymes in Autism

The general rule is to follow the manufacturer's or provider's instructions for use. Most of the enzymes offered for autism are plant-based. Some come from highly refined aspergillus strains, and the refining has removed the allergenic substances that used to be a problem with supplements from this source. Nevertheless, do a careful trial with just one capsule before a meal to check for tolerance. Use of digestive enzymes can provoke temporary symptoms which I will discuss below, but these symptoms usually appear after a day or two of use and may continue for a week to two weeks. So, tolerance or intolerance to enzymes can be problematic.

Enzyme formulations for autistics contain protein analogs of the human enzyme forms. These analogs can be quite stable and typically remain active over wide pH ranges (acid-base conditions). Most are designed to work at pH 1.5 to above 7 and begin digestion (or do all their digestive work) in the stomach. This includes the peptidases such as DPP4 analogs. So, the usual procedure is to give digestive enzymes that are formulated for autism just before or at the beginning of each meal – not afterward. Alternatively, gelatin encapsulated enzymes can be opened and the enzyme powder can be sprinkled on the food. The amount to be given depends upon the size of the meal, not the size of the person. The specifics of how much depend on enzyme potencies – follow the label or provided instructions.

A comprehensive enzyme formulation for an autistic should contain:

- **Several peptidases – to break peptides apart; many proteases also have peptidase activities. So, while peptidases may not be specifically named, they may be there. Bromelain, papain and alkaline proteases have peptidase activities.**

- **DPP4 activity.**
- **Some amount of lipase – to aid digestion of fats and uptake of lipids.**
- **At least one type of amylase – for digestion of starch to sugars.**
- **A glycoamylase – for breaking glucose away from starches or polysaccharides.**
- **And key disaccharidases – lactase, maltase, isomaltase and sucrase.**

We do have a tabulation of parent responses to use of digestive enzymes by autistic children – ARI Publication 34/March 2005. So far, there have been almost 750 such responses –

Digestive Enzymes Parent Response Tally, responses = 737

Behavior or Traits Improved 56%	No Discernible Effect 42%	Behavior or Traits Worsened 3%

Adverse Responses to Digestive Enzymes?

Based on many parent responses, it isn't uncommon to have a period of "worse before better" with digestive enzyme use in autism. Many parents have contacted me directly, describing a worsening of autistic traits, sometimes (increased) hyperactivity and irritability. Almost always, this is a temporary phase.

When digestive enzymes with DPP4 are used, the exposure to dietary opiate peptides is further decreased as more casein and gluten are digested by the enzymes. This usually brings about a period of opiate-like withdrawal, which may last 5 to 10 days or longer in some cases. During this period, the individual may become irritable or tantrum, develop hyperactivity, experience an increase in stimming, or present increased levels of inappropriate behavior or regression. Cravings for discontinued foods can occur which may potentiate these withdrawal symptoms. Not all children experience withdrawal or adverse reactions when starting the enzymes; prior elimination of casein foods from the diet can significantly lessen or eliminate withdrawal symptoms. This is the reason for starting these enzymes several weeks after starting the CF diet trial. In that case, the first week of the CF diet trial may produce some withdrawal symptoms.

Decreasing undigested food in the lower gastrointestinal tract can lower or eliminate a food supply that may have fostered the growth of dysbiotic, possibly pathogenic flora. Remember that autistics often have increased permeability of the gut wall,[11] which allows for an increased toxic burden. A temporary result of using digestive enzymes can be die-off of dysbiotic flora with consequent release of even more toxins. The die-off period usually does not last more than a week, but may continue longer with persistent, adaptable dysbiotic strains.

With more complete digestion of dietary protein comes a more normal amount of free-form essential and protein amino acids. In a few individuals, this can lead to a third effect if there is an underlying problem with transport and metabolism of amino acids. An example of such a problem is malabsorption of the essential amino acid tryptophan which can lead to an increase in indolylacryloylglycine ("IAG"). With this problem, increased tryptophan (from better digestion) leads to a toxic organic acid, indoleacrylic acid. This organic acid is detoxified by attaching glycine to it, forming IAG. So, an occasional consequence of digestive enzyme use is temporarily increased IAG (see the Laboratory Tests Section of this report). Vitamin B_6 (with magnesium), adequate iron, and proper antioxidant balance help to normalize tryptophan metabolism.

So, an initial period of adverse response to digestive enzymes can occur in some autistics. If this problem period continues beyond two weeks, please consult a "DAN doctor" or other knowledgeable health professional. Clinical laboratory tests can be informative in cases of prolonged problems – a comprehensive diagnostic stool analysis, an amino acid analysis (24-hour urine preferred for this situation but fasting plasma is OK), and a food allergy workup. (Food allergies can cause inflammation of the intestinal mucosa and worsening of the responses described above.)

Also, a capsule of activated charcoal, taken three times per day (away from meds and supplements) may reduce or stop adverse symptoms. Charcoal does this by absorbing toxins from dysbiotic flora before the toxins can cross into the bloodstream.

References – Digestive enzymes

1. Misumi Y and Ikehara Y "Dipeptidyl-peptidase IV" Chapt. 128 in Barrett AJ, Rawlings NO and Woessner JF, eds: *Handbook of Proteolytic Enzymes* Academic Press (1998) 378-382.
2. Reichelt KL, Hole K, et al. "Biologically Active Peptide-Containing Fractions in Schizophrenia and Childhood Autism" *Neurosecretion and Brain Peptides*, Martin JB, Reichlin S and Bick KL eds, Raven Press (1981) 628-643.
3. Reichelt KL, Ekrem J and Scott H "Gluten, Milk Proteins and Autism: Dietary Intervention Effects on Behavior and Peptide Secretion" *J.Appl. Nutrition* 42 no.1 (1990). 1-11.
4. Reichelt KL, Knivsberg AM et al. "Nature and Consequences of Hyperpeptiduria and Bovine Casomorphins Found in Autistic Syndromes" *Dev. Brain Dysfunct* 7 (1994) 71-85.
5. Cade R, Privette M et al. "Autism and Schizophrenia: Intestinal Disorders" *Nutritional Neuroscience* 3 (2000) 57-72.
6. Püschel G, Mentlein R and Heymann E "Isolation and Characterization of Dipeptidyl Peptidase IV from Human Placenta" *Eur. J. Biochem* 126 (1982) 359-365.
7. Vojdani A, Pangborn JB et al. "Infections, toxic chemicals and dietary peptides binding to lymphocyte receptors and tissue enzymes are major instigators of autoimmunity in autism" *Int.J.Immunopath and Pharmacol* 16 no.3 (2003) 189-199.
8. Horvath K, Papdimitriou JC et al. "Gastrointestinal abnormalities in children with autistic disorder" *J. Pediatrics* 135 no.5 (1999) 559-563.
9. Horvath K and Perman JA "Autistic disorder and gastrointestinal disease" *Curr. Opinion in Pediatrics* 14 (2002) 583-387.
10. Kushak RI and Buie T "Disaccharidase deficiencies in patients with autistic spectrum disorders" presented at the DAN! New Orleans Think Tank, January 2004.
11. D'Eufemia P, Celli M et al. "Abnormal intestinal permeability in children with autism" *Acta Paediatr* 65 (1996) 1076-1079.

VITAMIN B_6 AND PYRIDOXAL PHOSPHATE

- Vitamin B_6, pyridoxine, must be metabolized into pyridoxal 5-phosphate (P5P) to be active for coenzyme use.
- Analytical studies show that, as a group, autistics have remarkably slow phosphorylation of pyridoxine and pyridoxal.
- Vitamin B_6 needs depend upon individual metabolism requirements. For autism, needed amounts can greatly exceed those that government agencies recommend for the general population.
- 21 of 22 consecutive clinical studies have shown beneficial effects for autistics with much larger than RDA amounts of B_6.

First isolated and identified as a vital nutrient in the 1930s, vitamin B_6 or pyridoxine is actually found in various chemical forms in foods such as nuts, fish (especially salmon and herring), liver and meats, brown rice, and most vegetables. Pyridoxine is stabilized as a commercial vitamin with hydrochloride to form pyridoxine·HCl. In this form, it is sour tasting, acidic, and is best tolerated with food.

About Vitamin B_6

To be useful in the body, vitamin B_6 must be processed into its coenzyme form, pyridoxal 5-phosphate. This is a two-step process that has two possible sequences. The first step of one sequence is phosphorylation by the enzyme pyridoxal kinase. In humans, this is now considered to be a zinc-dependent enzyme that transfers some phosphate from ATP to pyridoxine to make pyridoxine phosphate.[1] Next, a coenzyme form of vitamin B_2 (FMN) promotes oxidation of pyridoxine phosphate to pyridoxal phosphate. Without adequate FMN, pyridoxal formation can be quite slow.[2,3] Under some conditions, the order of these steps can be reversed with oxidation occurring first. The coenzyme form of B_6 is often abbreviated as P5P or PLP, and the chemical name is pyridoxal 5'-phosphate. Most P5P is formed in red blood cells and liver cells. Once it is formed, it can be transported to other cells or tissues where it is needed. Transportation across cell membranes requires dephosphorylation, but once formed, pyridoxal is preserved.[1] When the P5P coenzyme form is supplemented orally, it is dephosphorylated before it enters gut mucosal cells, and the pyridoxal form is absorbed into the bloodstream. The advantage of a pyridoxal supplement is that it bypasses the pyridoxine phosphate oxidase (FMN or B_2-assist) step; it still needs to be rephosphorylated in tissues where it does its work.

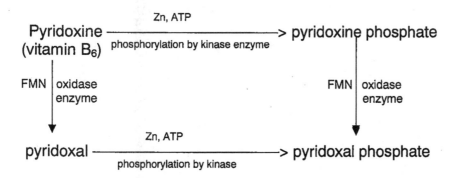

Making coenzyme P5P from vitamin B_6 (FMN assists and accelerates.)

SECTION FIVE: NUTRITIONAL SUPPLEMENTS FOR AUTISM

So, pyridoxine or pyridoxine·HCl is the vitamin, and pyridoxal phosphate, P5P, is the active coenzyme form in body tissues. When P5P does its work inside cells, one of its tasks is to move amino groups around. When it does this, P5P temporarily becomes pyridoxamine phosphate, and pyridoxamine itself can also be transported in and out of cells. Natural food forms of vitamin B_6 include all of these: pyridoxine, pyridoxal, pyridoxamine, and their phosphorylated forms.[4]

The amount of P5P that is needed depends upon the efficiencies and peculiarities of an individual's P5P-related metabolism. For essential nutrients, our government (the National Research Council) has set amounts that, for a while, were called RDAs (Reference Daily Allowances).[5] On labels, you'll find DRIs (Dietary Reference Intake). In some government publications on nutrition, DRIs are embellished with EARs (Estimated Average Requirement), AIs (adequate Intake) and ULs (tolerable Upper intake Levels).[6] Statistically, these amounts are calculated to prevent clinical problems from nutrient deficiency or excess. For vitamin B_6, the adult RDA, DRI, and the daily value have been fixed for decades at 2.0 milligrams per day. This is the amount that the experts from the NRC's Food and Nutrition Board and/or the Institute of Medicine believe to be adequate to ensure that a healthy person will not develop a disease caused by B_6 deficiency. This government-specified amount has nothing whatsoever to do with how much B_6 is needed by an individual with a metabolic disorder involving B_6-dependent enzymes. Such disorders may be hereditary or acquired as with toxic contamination. People with these kinds of problems require far more B_6 as a potentiating factor for sluggish or impaired cellular processes.

P5P is considered to be more potent for most individuals than is pyridoxine·HCl.[7] This belief stems from uncontrolled clinical studies of a small number of B_6-deficient adults, some of whom were given P5P and some pyridoxine·HCl. From laboratory tests of erythrocyte function of P5P (ery. glutamate-pyruvate transaminase kinetics), it was found that 50 mg of P5P for five days produced the same favorable effect as 500 mg of pyridoxine·HCl. However, the effects of both forms at lower doses were not studied, so the potency difference over a range of possible doses is uncertain.

Why not measure the blood level of vitamin B_6 to see if it's needed? This is usually pointless for two reasons. The first is that it's cheaper and faster to simply try the nutritional supplement and observe the results. Are attention, speech, eye contact, and other cognitive abilities improved or not? Also, the real test of nutritional adequacy rests with the biochemistry that the nutrient influences – not with the nutrient's quantitative level in blood, urine, cells, etc. It's whether or not there's enough to get the metabolism job done efficiently. Many autistics have blood pyridoxine levels within lab norms, and some have high blood plasma or serum levels, but cellular P5P may be a bit on the low side. The problem is that lots of P5P may be needed to potentiate cellular enzymes that are impaired or sluggish. From the standpoint of methionine metabolism, adequate B_6 (along with folate and B_{12}) is the amount that normalizes SAH, cysteine and the other players in this metabolic sequence. This amount also depends on levels of other nutrients or cofactors that are involved, such as cobalamin (B_{12}) and folate. Adequate vitamin B_6 is the amount that produces a satisfactory clinical response and functional improvement in the individual.

A recent research study by Dr. Tapan Audhya provides some answers to why, in part, many autistics should benefit from large doses of vitamin B_6.[8] Using groups of autistic children, Dr. Audhya measured several B_6 and P5P parameters. First, he determined that in normal (control) children, a single 500 mg dose of pyridoxine produced a maximum blood concentration 2 hours later. In autistic children, the times to maximum concentration ranged from 5 to 15 hours later. So, absorption of the vitamin appears to be slower in the autistics and with considerable variation. Also, the peak P5P concentration in the blood of autistics was only about 60% that of the controls. So, processing of the vitamin to the coenzyme form is slow and less complete in many autistics. Next, using measurements of P5P coenzyme kinetics in red blood cells (how fast the P5P works as a coenzyme), Dr. Audhya found that a huge increase in dosage was required by the cells of autistics. To get the same kinetics that 2 mg (per Kg of body weight) pyridoxine provides for a normal child, he had to use, on average, 21 mg/Kg body weight, over ten times as much, in the autistics. In other words, the coenzyme function of P5P is somehow seriously attenuated in autistics, and therefore, much more P5P is needed.

Does medical science acknowledge efficacy and safety of large (pharmacologic) doses of vitamin B_6, and if so, what for? Paraphrasing some authorities who have written medical textbook articles covering the subject of pharmacologic doses of pyridoxine:

- With a low or inadequate B_6 diet, depletion to the point of disease can occur in 11 to 27 days in various individuals. Megadoses or pharmacologic doses of B_6 are used to alleviate certain metabolic and neurologic diseases. In carpal tunnel syndrome, 50 to 200 mg/d pyridoxine for over 12 weeks is of benefit to some but not all with the condition. Vitamin B_6 is impaired or inactivated by drugs such as D-penicillamine (Cuprimine), cycloserine, Isoniazid (for tuberculosis), and L-dopa. Naturally-occurring B_6 antagonists include: agaritine and gyromitrin (mushrooms), canavanine (jack beans), and linatine (flax seed meal). Doses of B_6 up to 500 mg/d have been safe for periods as long as 6 years. Doses above 500 mg/d may produce a reversible neuropathy. Sauberlich HE, *Laboratory Tests for the Assessment of Nutritional Status* 2nd Ed, CRC Press, 1999 p 71-102.

- For methionine metabolism disorder at cystathionine, pyridoxine at 250 to 500 mg/d can be beneficial – Mudd SH, HL Levy and JP Kraus, "Disorders of Transsulfuration" Chapter 88 of Scriver C et al. eds, *The Metabolic and Molecular Bases of Inherited Disease* 8th ed, McGraw-Hill (2001) p. 2023.

- For beta-alanine excess, cellular (fibroblast) concentration of pyridoxine was increased 5 times from 0.02 millimolar to 0.10 millimolar which "abolished" the cellular toxicity of beta-alanine – Gibson KM and C Jacobs "Disorders of Beta- and Gamma-Amino Acids in Free and Peptide-Linked Forms" Scriver et al. eds., *The Metabolic and Molecular Bases of Inherited Disease*, op.cit. p. 2987.

- In seizure cases, where CSF glutamate is excessive or GABA is deficient, doses of pyridoxine should be sufficient to resolve the seizures and lower glutamate to below toxic threshold levels. For seizure disorders, pyridoxine may be therapeutic, and 10 to 1000 mg/d may be needed. This need may be lifelong. Gibson KM and Jacobs, ibid. p.2093.

- For remediation of amino acid decarboxylase deficiency (a human phenotype that presents with hypotonia, poor feeding in infancy, rolling eyes, irritability, sleep disturbances and developmental delay) up to 400 mg/d pyridoxine augments beneficial effects of L-dopa and certain medications – Blau N et al. "Disorders of Tetrahydrobiopterin and Related Biogenic Amines" Chapter 78 in Scriver et al. eds. *The Metabolic and Molecular Bases of Inherited Disease* op.cit. p.1760.

SECTION FIVE: NUTRITIONAL SUPPLEMENTS FOR AUTISM

Using Vitamin B_6 in Autism

In the 1960s, a few clinicians began to observe that use of large doses of vitamin B_6 coincided with reduction of some of the traits of autism and lessened some of the inappropriate behaviors that may also be present. Since that time, 21 of 22 consecutive studies have shown beneficial effects for autistics with pharmacologic doses of vitamin B_6, often accompanied by magnesium.[9]

In 1997, Dr. Rimland summarized the dosage findings of 18 consecutive studies of B_6 use in autism.[10] His finding is that the optimal dose is about 8 milligrams per pound of body weight per day (about 17 mg/Kg/day). Dr. Audhya found it advisable to not exceed 20 mg/Kg/day. From my experience, not all autistics who benefit from B_6 supplementation need large doses; many do well at lower or moderate dose levels.

What do we think vitamin B_6 is doing biochemically that makes it beneficial for many autistics? Similar to trimethylglycine (TMG) or methylcobalamin (MeCbl), vitamin B_6 as P5P can help accelerate sluggish metabolism of methionine (Met). Methionine metabolism is sluggish if S-adenosylhomocysteine (SAH) is high. It's also sluggish if methylcobalamin or 5-methyltetrahydrofolate is inadequate or if methionine synthase is inhibited. One way to speed up methionine metabolism is to pull homocysteine out of the recycle loop by changing it into cystathionine and then cysteine. Enhanced levels of vitamin B_6 can do this. In fact, P5P is required three times to process homocysteine via cysteine into either sulfate or taurine. And removing homocysteine serves to pull SAH apart into adenosine and more homocysteine. Getting rid of excess SAH allows methylation to proceed, including that which is needed for creatine formation, phospholipid methylation, melatonin synthesis, catecholamine balance, and methylation of cytosine in DNA to control gene expression.

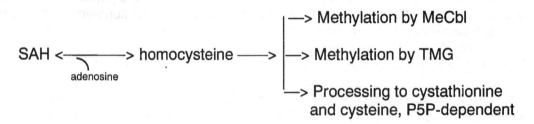

Because autism is not one disease but a set of traits featured by many disease conditions, and because of biochemical individuality, not all autistic children benefit from supplemental B_6. Those who do will gain most benefit from doses that compensate best for their individual condition. Hence, there is no hard and fast rule about how much B_6 to use. Trials of oral B_6 from about 1 or 2 mg/Lb/day up to about 8 mg/Lb/day are suggested for all. Some will do better when some P5P is added to the pyridoxine·HCl dose. Discontinue it if adverse effects are seen. Do not exceed 500 mg/d without medical supervision. A low starting dose to check tolerance could be about 1 mg/Lb of body weight per day.

Based on parent responses to the Autism Research Institute (ARI Publication 34/March 2005), the statistics are –

Vitamin B_6 (alone) Parent-Response Tally, responses = 620

Behavior or Traits Improved	No Discernible Effect	Behavior or Traits Worsened
30%	63%	8%

These statistics become much more favorable (47% improved) when magnesium is used in conjunction with pyridoxine·HCl. But before we go on to magnesium, it is important to consider why a small minority (8%) of individuals display limited tolerance to vitamin B_6 alone. This can be manifested by irritability, hyperactivity or worsening of behaviors and autistic traits. Intolerance to B_6 is certainly not a common occurrence, but when it does occur, parents and clinicians are often puzzled.

Adverse Responses to B_6?

We know of five circumstances in which individuals can display limited tolerance to vitamin B_6. These are:

1. <u>The vitamin is given without adequate food</u>, and the inherent acidity of pyridoxine·HCl causes stomach upset. Or, the individual already has marginal gastric hyperacidity with limited ability to control acid-base balance, and pyridoxine·HCl adds to the problem regardless of food. Breakfast is the preferred meal; lunch is OK. Use of B_6 and other B vitamins may cause insomnia if taken with supper or during the PM hours.

2. <u>Zinc is severely deficient</u> to the point where pyridoxal is not adequately phosphorylated to form P5P. The pyridoxal kinase enzyme that does this phosphorylation needs zinc. Without adequate zinc, an inactive pyridoxal excess may block pyridoxal phosphate activity.

3. <u>Amino acid or monoamine levels may be deficient</u> and the extra P5P then skews the relative amounts of these and may even deplete some of them further. Turning alanine into pyruvate, and depletion of tyrosine or Dopa are examples. In such cases, review of dietary adequacy, use of digestive aids that include protease and peptidase enzymes, and amino acid supplementation can all be beneficial. But don't supplement amino acids until gut dysbiosis is corrected.

4. <u>An impure grade of pyridoxine is used</u> and the tiny but potent amount of interfering vitamers actually blocks P5P function. This may be a cause of peripheral neuropathy when large quantities of vitamin B_6 are given.[11] Discontinuing the vitamin supplement allows the neuropathy to resolve, and use of pyridoxal 5-phosphate may actually accelerate the recovery process. Because of additional processing during the manufacture of P5P, this form can be more pure than pyridoxine.

5. <u>Magnesium is required when vitamin B_6 is used</u> in significant doses in those autistics who have limited sulfotransferase activity. Evidently, magnesium is nutritionally and physiologically synergistic with vitamin B_6 or P5P, and sometimes in autism this really matters. This brings us to the topic of magnesium.

References

References are listed after the VITAMIN B_6 WITH MAGNESIUM discussion.

MAGNESIUM, Mg

> - **Magnesium is important as an activator of phosphate and energy-transfer enzymes.**
> - **Magnesium is necessary for assembly of glutathione and conversion of methionine to SAM.**
> - **Simultaneous use of magnesium and vitamin B_6 is strongly advised.**

Magnesium, an element (sometimes called a "mineral"), is important because it activates certain enzymes, helps maintain ionic balance in and around cells, and can be part of structural tissues. Many enzymes need metal elements to make them work – zinc, copper, iron, manganese, molybdenum, cobalt and magnesium are elements that do this in humans.

About Magnesium

Magnesium is most important for energy delivery in cells because it activates "kinases," enzymes that transfer phosphate. It's also necessary for assembly of glutathione, which can be limited or deficient when magnesium is.[12,13,14] Some magnesium-dependent enzymes' jobs that are important to autism:

- To make SAM from methionine (enzyme: methionine adenosyltransferase). Methionine, when converted to SAM, becomes the big-time methyl donor in body tissues. It gives away a methyl to change the character of many molecules that are methyl acceptors. Examples are the methylation of (acetylated) serotonin to make melatonin and methylation of guanidinoacetate to make creatine.

- To make methylated adrenal hormones (catecholamines) like metanephrine (methylated adrenalin) from epinephrine, (enzyme: catechol-O-methyltransferase).

- To make activated sulfur forms required for sulfation, APS (enzyme: ATP sulfurylase) and PAPS (enzyme: APS kinase).

- To phosphorylate all the nucleosides making them nucleotides: guanosine to GMP, GDP, GTP; cytidine to CMP, CDP, CTP; uridine to UMP, UDP, UTP, etc. (enzymes: different kinases).

- To assemble glutathione from its three component amino acids: cysteine, glycine and glutamic acid (enzymes: gamma-glutamylcysteine synthase and glutathione synthase).

Some physiological responses to magnesium supplementation can be:[15,16]
- Less constipation and easier and more regular bowel movements
- Improved muscle relaxation and muscle rest
- Decreased "tics," muscle jerks or spasms
- Improved mood
- Improved appetite

With nutritional supplements, many elements have to be provided in a form that combines the specific nutrient or element with carrier or companion substances that form a molecule or "mineral." An example is magnesium in the form of magnesium glycinate chelate. Magnesium is a very reactive element, but in the glycinate-chelate form it is surrounded and protected by molecules of the amino acid glycine. Several magnesium glycinate chelates are commercially available, and they vary in content from about 10% to about 20% magnesium. So, at best, a 100-milligram supplement of Mg in this form actually weighs 500 milligrams, and it could weigh as much as 1000 milligrams. That's why it often takes multiple tablets or capsules for adequate nutritional supplementation.

As an oral nutritional supplement, magnesium is available as amino acid chelates, such as glycinate chelate, as oxide (buffered), and as salts of aspartate, malate, and gluconate. Magnesium is present in dolomite along with calcium, but bioavailability of this form is poor. (Bioavailability means ability to be readily taken in and used by body tissues. Dolomite does not dissolve easily, so the body's ability to extract calcium and magnesium from it is limited.) Liquid supplements may contain magnesium as the chloride or sulfate, and these are very bioavailable forms. The adult RDI or "Daily Value" for magnesium is 400 milligrams per day (mg/d). Effective nutritional amounts for children depend upon the form of the supplement and upon the individual need, but often range between 50 and 250 mg/d as magnesium.

Using Magnesium in Autism

As with vitamin B_6, many trials of magnesium have been carried out by parents and doctors for autistic individuals. From these trials, we learn that the effective Mg supplementation range is 3 milligrams to 8 milligrams per kilogram of body weight per day. (Or 1.5 mg to 4 mg per pound of body weight per day.) For a 25-Kg (55-lb) four- to six-year-old, for example, this is 80 to 220 mg/d of a magnesium supplement as elemental magnesium. An initial low-dose trial of magnesium would be 0.5 to 1.0 mg/Kg of body weight (1 to 2 mg per pound) and not more than 100 mg in any case.

For autism, magnesium is best used in conjunction with vitamin B_6. When used alone, neither is as effective as are both when used together. Magnesium or magnesium with vitamin B_6 can be beneficial for autistic individuals when introduced during initial stages of dietary intervention. Magnesium and magnesium with vitamin B_6 are best tolerated with food, often with breakfast, and this holds true for multivitamin and multimineral supplements that include these nutrients (BrainChild, ASD-Plex, Super Nu-Thera).

Magnesium (only) Parent-Response Tally, responses = 301 (ARI Publ.34/March 2005)

Behavior or Traits Improved	No Discernible Effect	Behavior or Traits Worsened
29%	65%	6%

Magnesium plays an important role in helping sulfate do its job in body tissues, and this can be especially important to autistics. In fact, sulfation rates are reduced in some forms of autism.[17,18] In a study using human cells, Dr Rosemary Waring showed that magnesium assists sulfation rates including that of phenolsulfotransferase.[19] When supplied to the cell, adequate magnesium can compensate for sulfation rates that might otherwise be slowed by pyridoxal phosphate.[19,20] Probably this is one reason behind numerous clinical observations that, for autism, magnesium, when taken with vitamin B_6, produces more beneficial effects than B_6 or Mg alone.[10]

Based on Waring's studies with human cells, for whatever amount of pyridoxine is taken, at least 10% of that amount of magnesium (as elemental magnesium, by weight) should also be taken to enhance the sulfation chemistry. At least this amount of magnesium is included in various nutritional combination products often suggested for autism such as Super Nu-Thera,

Brain Child Nutritionals and ASD-Plex. These supplements do provide adequate Mg, at least from the standpoint of synergism with vitamin B_6.

Adverse Response to Magnesium?

As shown in the table above, there were a few adverse reactions to magnesium supplements. The most commonly-reported problem seems to be looser bowel movements or diarrhea and irritability associated with diarrhea. Magnesium often does stimulate bowel movements and looser stools. If this is a problem, reduce the Mg intake. You may have to switch supplements or give B_6 and Mg separately. You should discontinue the Mg until the reason for persistent diarrhea is understood and the condition remedied. Intestinal dysbiosis, food intolerances, medications and excessive amounts of other nutritional supplements can also cause diarrhea. Dietary intervention, such as gluten avoidance, may be required before magnesium is well tolerated. Chronic diarrhea also may be a marker for Secretin need or gastrointestinal disorders such as pancreatic dysfunction.

As with other mineral supplements, a worsening in behavior or function may not be due to the mineral or element itself. It could be due to the salt form or to the other chemical part(s) of the supplement. Magnesium citrate is notorious for causing loose stools and can be used therapeutically as a cathartic. Magnesium oxide that is not buffered may contain a bit of residual magnesium hydroxide and upon dissolution, some ionized magnesium hydroxide (as well as ionized magnesium chloride) could be formed. The result could be something that's too alkaline. Some residual magnesium hydroxide may be in other magnesium forms as well, including glycinate chelates. When magnesium is taken with vitamin B6 (see below) or in a blend of nutrients, this acid-base pH problem is dampened out by the other ingredients.

When the magnesium carrier nutrients (the other part of the supplement: glycine, aspartate, malate, sulfate, gluconate, etc.) are the troublemakers, the best thing to do is discontinue that kind or brand of supplement. Wait three or four days, then start with a different kind of magnesium. Form, amount and individual tolerance are all important to magnesium supplementation.

References

References are listed after the VITAMIN B_6 WITH MAGNESIUM discussion.

VITAMIN B_6 WITH MAGNESIUM

B_6 and magnesium work synergistically in many important processes. According to more than 5000 parent responses reported to ARI, nearly one-half of autistic patients benefit from the combination of B_6 plus magnesium (ARI Publ.34/March 2005).

Vitamin B_6 with Magnesium Parent-Response Tally, responses = 5780

Behavior or Traits Improved	No Discernible Effect	Behavior or Traits Worsened
47%	49%	4%

The amounts of B_6 (pyridoxine.HCl) and magnesium that have been beneficial are tabulated below.

Weight Kg / Lb	Vitamin B_6, Suggested Amounts, mg/day	Magnesium, corresponding minimum amounts, mg/day
15 33	Up to 250	At least 66
20 44	Up to 340	At least 88
30 66	Up to 500*	At least 132
40 88	Up to 500*	At least 176
50 110	Up to 500"	At least 220

*Exceed only under medical supervision

SUMMARY

- **Use vitamin B_6 with magnesium.**
- **Start these supplements (or a blend that contains both) early in nutritional intervention – when dietary intervention is assessed.**
- **Use both with food, preferably breakfast.**
- **Test various amounts to achieve the most beneficial response.**
- **Discontinue if there is worsening, and consider the intolerance factors.**
- **Associated nutrients may be needed or may provide further benefit: increased dietary protein, digestive aids, amino acid supplements if appropriate, zinc, other B-vitamins.**

References - Vitamin B_6 and Pyridoxal Phosphate, Magnesium, and Vitamin B_6 with Magnesium

1. Merrill AH, Henderson JM et al. "Metabolism of B_6 by human liver" *J.Nutr.* 114 (1984) 1664-74.
2. Clements JE and Anderson BB "Pyridoxine (pyridoxamine) phosphate oxidase activity in the red cell" *Biochimica et Biophysica Acta* 613 (1980) 401-409.
3. Clements JE and Anderson BB "Glutathione reductase activity and pyridoxine (pyridoxamine) phosphate oxidase activity in the red cell" *Biochimica et Biophysica* Acta 632 (1980) 159-163.
4. Kutsky RJ *Handbook of Vitamins, Minerals and Hormones* 2nd Ed, Van Norstrand Reinhold Co. (1981) 234.
5. Recommended Dietary Allowances, 10th Ed, Food and Nutrition Board, NRC – National Academy of Sciences (1989).
6. "DRI: Dietary Reference Intakes" Food and Nutrition Board, Institute of Medicine, National Academy Press, 2000.
7. Personal communication from William H. Philpott, M.D., to J. Pangborn, Ph.D. in 1984. Functional B_6 activity tests (EGPT-P5P Stimulation Index Test) were performed at Monroe Medical Research Laboratory (George Miroff, Ph.D., Director), Monroe, NY.
8. Audhya T "Laboratory indices of vitamin and mineral deficiency in autism" Fall DAN! 2002 Conference Proceedings pgs 239-244, San Diego, Oct 27, 2002. Reprint available from Vitamin Diagnostics, Cliffwood Beach NJ, 732-583-7773.
9. Rimland BR "Studies of high-dosage vitamin B_6 (and often with magnesium) in autistic children and adults", 1965-2003, on the ARI Website: http://www.autism.com.

SECTION FIVE: NUTRITIONAL SUPPLEMENTS FOR AUTISM

10. Rimland B "What is the 'right' dosage for vitamin B_6, DMG and other nutrients in autism," *Autism Research Review International* 11 no.4 (1997) p.3.

11. Windebank AJ "Neurotoxicity of pyridoxine analogs is related to coenzyme structure" *Neurochem. Pathology* 3 no.3 (1985), 159-167.

12. Mills BJ, Lindeman RV and Lang CA "Magnesium deficiency inhibits biosynthesis of blood glutathione and tumor growth in the rat" *Proc Soc Exp Biol and Med* 181 (1986) 326-332.

13. Abbott JJ, Pei J et al. "Structure prediction and active site analysis of the metal binding determinants in gamma-glutamylcysteine Synthetase" *J Biol Chem* 276 (45) Nov. 2001 42099-42107.

14. Gogus A and Shapiro L "Large conformational changes in the catalytic cycle of glutathione Synthetase" *Structure* (Cambridge) 10 (12) Dec. 2002 1669-1676.

15. Shils M "Magnesium" Chapt 8 in Shils M, Olson JA and Shike M, *Modern Nutrition in Health and Disease* vol.1, 8th ed, Lea & Febiger (1994) 164-184.

16. Baker SM "Magnesium in Primary Care and Preventive Medicine: Clinical Correlation of Magnesium Loading studies" *Magnesium and Trace Elements* (S.Karger AG, Basel, Switzerland) 10 (1991-92) 251-262.

17. Waring RH et al. "Biochemical Parameters in Autistic Children" *Dev. Brain Dysfunct.* (1997) 10 40-43.

18. Waring RH and LV Klovrza "Sulphur Metabolism in Autism" *J.Nutr. & Environ. Medicine* (2000) 10 25-32.

19. Waring RH, RM Harris and VL Griffiths "The effects of pyridoxal 5-phosphate on sulfotransferase activity: action on tyrosyl protein sulfotransferase and phenol sulfotransferase" April 2003, research report to ARI, available on ARI website, http://www.autism.com.

20. Bartzatt R and JD Beckmann "Inhibition of Phenol Sulfotransferase by Pyridoxal Phosphate" *Biochem. Pharmacology* (1994) 47 (11) 2087-2095.

TAURINE

- Taurine and magnesium have synergistic actions, and taurine is a magnesium-sparing nutrient.
- Taurine is needed for formation of bile salts which assist assimilation of essential lipids, including vitamins A, D and E.
- Taurine is a powerful antioxidant that neutralizes hypochlorite, OCl^-.
- Taurine supplementation should be in place before trying TMG and sometimes before methylcobalamin.

Although it has not been tracked statistically by parent responses, many DAN! doctors have reported excellent results with taurine. In fact, one of the first heroic responses in autism happened with a patient of Dr. Baker, and he presented that case report to the National Society for Children and Adults with Autism (NSAC) in 1984.[1] This was a typical autistic boy with bowel dysfunction, major sleep disorder, and lots of allergies. He was on haloperidol prescribed by a previous physician, and vitamin B_6 with magnesium had allowed the haloperidol dose to be halved. Following the first dose of taurine, the boy slept through the night for the first time in his life. Next came improved bowel regularity and improved attention in his special classes. His parents considered taurine to be the most successful therapeutic intervention in their son's life.

About Taurine

Taurine is an almost unique "amino acid." Typical amino acids carry at least one amino group, and one of them is attached to the carbon next to the organic acid (carboxyl) group. Taurine is different. It doesn't have a carboxyl group. Its acid part is a sulfonic acid ($-SO_3H$ instead of $-COOH$). And, its amino group ($-NH_2$) is not next to the sulfur-acid part; it's at the other end of the molecule. This structural difference makes taurine very special. While it cannot become part of a protein structure, taurine is active ionically and can react or combine with substances in ways that ordinary amino acids cannot.

In leukocytes, taurine assists oxidant response (during phagocytosis) by limiting the abundance of hypochlorite ion (OCl^-) and, in turn, limiting tissue oxidation and inflammation.[2] Taurine actually combines with OCl^- to form a stable, less harmful chloramine, but one molecule of taurine is sacrificed to destroy each hypochlorite ion. A metabolic precursor of taurine, hypotaurine, also does this. As a necessary amino acid for bile salt formation, taurine combines with unneeded or excess cholesterol to form taurocholic acid, which is secreted into the intestines for removal.[3] Again, one molecule of taurine is used to remove each molecule of cholesterol. In doing this, taurine assists virtually all the biochemical modes of detoxication by helping to provide the biliary excretion pathway. Further, taurine itself binds to some foreign substances or "xenobiotics" and detoxifies them as well.[4] Additionally, taurine is reported to help in balancing glutamate and GABA (neurotransmitter) levels.[5]

Taurine is present in the heart at higher concentrations than in any other organ. It balances electrolyte levels and helps to keep the rhythm within norms.[6] When performing this function, taurine is not used up but rather acts ionically at cell membranes to control the flux of sodium, magnesium, potassium and calcium ions. In body tissues globally, taurine is magnesium sparing because when it's low, magnesium tends to leave cells and enter the blood plasma.[7,8] Any excess of plasma magnesium is quickly lost to the urine.

There are some problems with taurine supply in autism. It can be derived from dietary intake of meat, fish, and fowl, especially shellfish and seafood. However, shellfish and seafood may have to be avoided or eaten only in small amounts when mercury is an issue. Taurine can be formed endogenously from cysteine, but this formation is dependent upon oxygenase enzyme activity and upon adequate pyridoxal 5-phosphate. In fact, taurine is at the very end of the metabolic pathway that begins with the essential amino acid methionine and progresses through many of the sulfur-containing amino acids that we now know to be potential problem areas in autism: methionine, SAMe, S-adenosylhomocysteine, homocysteine, cystathionine, cysteine, cysteine sulfinic acid, hypotaurine – then comes formation of taurine. Taurine may be inadequate in autistics when cysteine is subnormal (as measured, usually, by plasma amino acid analysis).

Human mothers' milk contains taurine as 33% of all free-form amino acids.[9] That accommodates the difficulty that infants (and young children) have with the formation of taurine from methionine or cysteine. For them, taurine is a nutritionally essential amino acid.

Besides the difficulties in making taurine in body tissues, there is the possibility of losing it via urinary wasting. Structurally, taurine looks to renal tubules like another unusual amino acid – beta-alanine. When both are present, they compete for reabsorption. The result can be taurine wasting in urine.[10] So, we need to be concerned about conditions that lead to excesses of beta-alanine. These are:

SECTION FIVE: NUTRITIONAL SUPPLEMENTS FOR AUTISM

1. Maldigestion of meat, fish or fowl with excessive uptake of the dipeptides carnosine and anserine. Both contain beta-alanine.

2. Bacterial dysbiosis or infection. Some bacteria can produce high amounts of beta-alanine. Friendly bacteria use beta-alanine to synthesize the vitamin pantothenate: pantoic acid + beta-alanine = pantothenic acid. But with dysbiosis, this beneficial biochemistry can go awry.

3. Increased catabolism of pyrimidines. The nucleotides, nucleosides, and bases that are structured from pyrimidine molecules can lead to formation of beta-alanine when they are catabolized. UTP, UDP, UMP, uridine and uracil are direct sources of beta-alanine. Thymidine and thymine can be sources if they are enzymatically transformed into uridine moieties. One metabolic error disease that can manifest as autism or PDD is pyrimidine nucleotidase superactivity; it features accelerated dephosphorylation of uridine phosphate. Beta-alanine can then be elevated. Dihydropyrimidine dehydrogenase deficiency (decreased utilization of uracil and thymine) may also feature elevated beta-alanine.

Using Taurine in Autism

Assessing need for taurine based on results from amino acid analysis can be a tricky proposition. High taurine in the urine may mean wasting and deficiency of taurine in tissues or in the vicinity of cell membranes. High taurine in blood plasma can mean increased inflammatory response or breakdown of leukocytes, lymphocytes or hemolysis of erythrocytes. But if taurine's precursors are low, particularly cysteine or cystine, then it's likely that supplies of taurine are limited. Because of the analytical ambiguities, it's probably best to give taurine an empirical trial, especially if vitamin B_6 and magnesium have been of some help. Taurine helps body tissue hold on to its magnesium, and that's why I suggest trying it right after vitamin B_6 with magnesium. Because taurine is needed for formation of bile salts and bile salts facilitate uptake of dietary lipids, taurine supplementation should precede supplementation of vitamins A, D and E and essential fatty acids. It should also precede calcium supplements, which vitamin D assists. And it is wise to have taurine in place before trials of TMG, because, at first, TMG tends to decrease cysteine and taurine formation.

Usually, a supplement of 100 to 250 mg/day is adequate for 2- to 5-year-olds, and 250 to 500 mg/d suffices for 6- to 12-year-olds. Amounts higher than 2 grams/day in adults may have undesirable influences on electrolyte balances and adrenal function. Use of taurine to reduce seizures in some forms of epilepsy is documented.[11,12] In such cases, taurine is thought to counteract excitatory neurotransmitter excesses and to normalize glutamate levels.[11]

Because much of our taurine comes from cysteine metabolically, the supply of cysteine is critical to taurine adequacy. Seizures can occur with taurine insufficiency, and sometimes preexisting seizure conditions are alleviated by supplementing it.[5,13,14,15,16,17] This becomes quite important with use of some nutrient interventions that are described later – trimethylglycine, TMG with folinic acid and methylcobalamin, and possibly even injectable methylcobalamin. Those interventions cause homocysteine to be transformed directly into methionine, bypassing the route to cysteine. While they can open up the methylation roadblock and eventually result in improved cysteine and glutathione levels, there is an unavoidable initial period where cysteine and taurine may actually decrease further. So, I strongly recommend having a taurine supplement in place before trying these more advanced options.

If you are using carnosine and find that it has noticeable benefit, then taurine could be beneficial as well. The reason is that carnosine includes beta-alanine, which can cause urinary loss of taurine. Metabolically, taurine does not improve sulfate supplies or sulfation because humans cannot extract sulfate from it. Some bacteria can do this, but it's doubtful whether intestinal bacteria would provide significant sulfate from it. So, taurine should not be considered as a sulfate source.

Adverse Response to Taurine?

Adverse responses to appropriate amounts of taurine are evidently quite uncommon. During the more than 20 years that I have suggested taurine use, reports to me of problems have numbered less than a dozen (out of thousands who have tried taurine as a nutritional supplement). If the electrolyte levels are already imbalanced in a certain way and are not corrected by homeostasis, then taurine, in significant amounts, could worsen the imbalance. Intolerance can occur in hyperkalemia conditions (excessive blood potassium), Addison's disease, and insulin deficiency if gram quantities of taurine are used. This is because it mediates the flux of electrolyte minerals across cell membranes. As with all supplements, start at a low dose (100 or 250 mg/d depending on body weight or age). We are cautioned by clinical researchers not to use more than about 2000 mg/d (2 grams/day), and large doses can produce effects that are opposite to what would be expected.[11]

References - Taurine

1. Baker SM "Diagnostic and therapeutic strategies in an autistic child with a positive response to taurine", Proceedings of the 1984 NSAC and International Autism Conference of the Americas, July 1984, San Antonio TX 8-23.
2. Babior BM and Crowley CA "Chronic granulomatous disease and other disorders of oxidative killing by phagocytes" in Stanbury JB et al. *The Metabolic Basis of Inherited Disease* 5th ed McGraw-Hill 1983 1960-1965.
3. Mayes PA "Cholesterol synthesis, transport & excretion" in Murray RK *Harper's Biochemistry* 23rd ed, Appleton & Lange 1993 273-275.
4. Wright CD Tallan HH and Lin YY "Taurine: biological update" *Ann.Rev.Biochem* 55 (1986) 444-445.
5. Van Gelder NM "Rectification of abnormal glutamic acid levels by taurine" in *Taurine*, Huxtable R and Barbeau A eds, Raven Press 1976 293-302.
6. Huxtable R "Metabolism and function of taurine in the heart" in Huxtable R and Barbeau A *Taurine* Raven Press 1976 99-119.
7. Durlach J and Rayssiguier Y "Données nouvelles sur les relations entre magnésium et hydrates de carbone" *Magnesium* 2 (1983) 174-191.
8. Welty JD, McBroom MH et al. "Effect of taurine on heart and brain electrolyte imbalances" in Huxtable and Barbeau, eds, op.cit. 155-163.
9. Picone T "Taurine update: metabolism and function" *Nutrition Today* July/Aug 1987 16-20.
10. Scriver CR and Perry TL "Disorders of ω-amino acids in free and peptide-linked forms," Chapter 26 in Scriver et al. eds, *The Metabolic Basis of Inherited Disease* 6th ed. McGraw-Hill 1989 758-759.
11. VanGelder NM, Sherwin AL et al. "Brain Research" 94 (1975) 297-306.
12. Airakseinen EM, Oja SS et al. "Effects of taurine treatment on epileptic patients" *Neurochemistry and Clinical Neurology* Alan R. Liss Inc. (1980) 157-166.

SECTION FIVE: NUTRITIONAL SUPPLEMENTS FOR AUTISM

13. Barbeau A and Donaldson *J Archives of Neurol* 30 (1974) 52.
14. Bergainini L, Mutani R et al. *Eur.Neurol* 11 (1974) 261.
15. Barbeau A, Tsukada Y and Naohide I in *Taurine* ibid. 256-261.
16. Mantovani J and DeVito DC *Archives of Neurol* 36 (1979) 672-674.
17. Airakseinen EM, Oja SS et al. in *Neurochemistry and Clinical Neurology* Battisin L, Hashim G and Lajtha A eds. Alan R Liss Inc. (1980) 157-166.
18. Wright CE, Tallan HH et al. "Taurine: biological update" *Ann Rev Biochem* 55 (1986) 434.

VITAMIN C

- **Besides keeping stools loose and bowels regular, there are seven documented metabolic functions of vitamin C; each could be important to an autistic individual.**
- **Vitamin C supplementation has a very high benefit ratio (18 to 1) for autistics (number improved ÷ number worsened = about 20).**

Vitamin C's chemical name is ascorbic acid, and it can be combined with elements (minerals) to make salt forms such as calcium ascorbate, magnesium ascorbate, potassium ascorbate, etc. All can provide the functions of vitamin C. Of single nutrient supplements that ARI has tabulated responses for, vitamin C has the highest benefit ratio (got better / got worse), 16 to one! Only about 2.5% of parents report problems; almost 40% report improvement.

About Vitamin C

Many mammals can synthesize their own vitamin C from glucose. Ascorbate is not really a vitamin for them, it's a natural biochemical that they make. For them, dietary intake merely supplements their own vitamin C synthesis. Cats and dogs can make anywhere from 5 to 40 mg of vitamin C per day per kilogram of body weight. Animals that aren't very careful about their diets can make much more (and need it) – goats 32 to 190 and rats 40 to 200 mg/Kg per day.[1] The same authoritative reference that states these amounts (*New England Journal of Medicine*, April 3, 1986) also states the US Government-established recommended dietary allowance for humans in the same units of measurement, 0.9 mg/Kg per day. Humans cannot form vitamin C because we lack a required enzyme. So for us, ascorbate is a vitamin. It looks like we've been shortchanged here, doesn't it? Actually, the Food and Nutrition Board of the National Research Council has made some minor progress on this issue. In the 1970s, the adult RDA for vitamin C was 45 mg/day. In the late 1980s it became 60 mg/day, a 33% improvement. Looking at the January 2003 edition of *Facts and Comparisons*, a handbook widely used by pharmacies, the RDA or DRI still is 60 mg but the experts are beginning to hedge upward.[2] If you use nicotine (smoke or chew tobacco), you should take at least 100 mg/d. "The average protective dose is 70 to 150 mg/day" (for adults, "protection" is not explained). For scurvy, 300 to 1000 mg/day is stated. For enhanced wound healing, 200 to 500 mg/d for 7 to 10 days, and for severe burns, 1000 to 2000 mg/day are stated. Also mentioned in this edition of *Facts and Comparisons* is: "...up to 6 grams per day has been administered parenterally to healthy adults without evidence of toxicity." But there are warnings for diabetics and those with disordered chemistry that causes recurrent kidney stones. For those individuals, high-dose vitamin C might be detrimental.[2]

What exactly does vitamin C do in the human body? And why would it be beneficial in autism?

1. Vitamin C neutralizes harmful oxidants such as the hydroxyl radical, OH^-, and it can regenerate vitamin E.[3,4] Many autistics are under oxidant stress per the findings of Michelson,[5] Pangborn,[6] James,[7] McGinnis[8] and others. Reducing hydroxyl radical damage can only help.

2. When ascorbate participates in oxidant-quenching reactions, the resulting forms of ascorbate (ascorbate radicals) are relatively harmless because they are neither strongly oxidizing nor reducing. Also, used (oxidized) ascorbate is easily recycled back to active ascorbate by enzyme systems that use NADH or NADPH.[9]

3. Vitamin C is a helper or promoter for the enzyme that changes dopamine into norepinephrine (noradrenaline).[10] This is a very necessary step in adrenal catecholamine metabolism, and it precedes methylation steps that balance catecholamine levels.

4. Vitamin C is a helper or promoter for the enzyme in tyrosine metabolism that transforms hydroxyphenylpyruvate to homogentisic acid.[10] This helps balance the phenylalanine-tyrosine-catecholamine system.

5. Ascorbate is required for efficient formation of L-carnitine.[11] L-carnitine is an inside-the-cell carrier of fatty acids needed for normal utilization of fats for energy ("beta-oxidation" of fatty acids). If you've done organic acid analyses on autistics, have you found elevated adipic or suberic acids? These are fatty acids that didn't or couldn't go through normal processing, possibly because of inadequate L-carnitine.

6. There are some peptide-hormones that have been mentioned by various investigators as possibly not behaving very well in autism. Examples are oxytocin, vasopressin and cholecystokinin. You may wish to look up the literature on these hormones. Balanced chemistry of these hormones involves adding nitrogen (amination) and the monooxygenase enzyme that does this is assisted by ascorbate.[11]

7. Ascorbate helps folic acid metabolism by assisting the conversion of folic acid to folinic acid.[2] This is obviously beneficial to many autistics, considering the recent advantageous use of folinic acid by many DAN doctors.

A few words about natural, food-source vitamin C are in order, because a nutritional supplement is intended to add to food-source intake. Heating foods to above 175° C (above about 350°F) begins to degrade its vitamin C content, and above 190°C (about 375°F), vitamin C is destroyed. Oxidized copper ions (cupric, Cu^{++}) are a catalyst for oxidizing ascorbate to dehydroascorbate. So, cooking utensils with copper inside may not be so good for vitamin C's longevity.

Really good food sources of C are: broccoli, collards, horseradish, kale, parsley, turnip greens, black currant, and guava. Moderate vitamin C sources are; citrus, strawberries, papaya, beet greens, cabbage, cauliflower, chives, watercress, mustard greens and spinach. Except for strawberries and maybe citrus, how many autistics eat these foods?

When taken orally, vitamin C promotes looser stools and easier bowel movements. It works against the formation of bowel impactions. Magnesium supplements can also help with this. The amounts of vitamin C required for regular bowels vary with the individual and are usually above 20 mg/Kg body weight per day. Some individuals may require considerably more. In their gastrointestinal study of autistics, Horvath and Permian found stool impaction in 19% of autistic disordered children (n=112); none of the age-matched controls had this problem.[12]

Using Vitamin C in Autism

Vitamin C is an ingredient in some of the popular blend products for autism. "ASD-Plex" powder contains 400 mg per rounded teaspoon, and "Super Nu-Thera" contains 250 mg per 3 caplets. Vitamin C is widely available in capsules with contents ranging from 250 to 500 or 750 mg, and big tablets may contain 1000 mg. Be advised that most health food store vitamin C is corn-based in its manufacture. Some autistic individuals have food allergies including corn allergy. Use of hypoallergenic vitamin C that is (at least) 99.9% pure is advisable, because of the relatively large amounts often needed.

For autistic children weighing less than about 50 Lbs (23 Kg), 250 mg/d is the usually suggested amount, and that is the initial trial dose as well. For children at 50 to 100 Lb, 500 mg/d or more (per physician's direction) can be used. Usually, 500 to 1000 mg/d is the absolute minimum that is adequate for autistic individuals weighing over 100 Lbs. Here's how parents of autistics have scored vitamin C.

Vitamin C, Parent Responses to ARI, n= 1706 (ARI Publ. 34/March 2005)

Behavior or Traits Improved	No Discernible Effect	Behavior or Traits Worsened
41%	57%	2%

Vitamin C adequacy is tough to pin down analytically. Urine analysis is provided by several clinical laboratories, and what's important is the amount of urine ascorbate, not the oxidized dehydroascorbate. Finding some unoxidized, active ascorbate in urine is a necessary condition for vitamin C adequacy. But such a finding is not "necessary and sufficient." The "sufficient" part means that there's enough to satisfy the seven functions plus regular bowel movements.

There is a published report of high-dose vitamin C (4 to 8 grams/day) causing increased urinary excretion of uric acid (induced uricosuria) in susceptible individuals.[13] At the same time, blood plasma uric acid decreased in these individuals. Thus, vitamin C in large doses may increase renal clearance of uric acid. The effect of this on autistic individuals with purine metabolism disorders is uncertain. But if you have a Lesch-Nyhan patient or any individual with elevated uric acid, blood or urine, it would be wise to monitor levels and check for precipitates or crystals in the urine if high-dose vitamin C is used. The problem here is low solubility of calcium urate and stone formation in the kidneys and renal tract.

Adverse Responses to Vitamin C?

Of the 1706 responses, only 37 (about 2%) reported problems – usually excessively loose stools or diarrhea. The usual remedy is to find out why there's diarrhea in the first place and to discontinue vitamin C. A lesser amount may be appropriate, as may be dietary intervention that lessens food reactivities and irritable bowel conditions.

Multi-element buffered vitamin C may be the answer when amounts over 500 mg/d are to be used. Such formulations combine ascorbic acid (moderately acidic) with mineral ascorbates (moderately alkaline). This produces a supplement for which there is much better bowel tolerance. Also, multi-element buffered C replenishes elements (calcium, magnesium, potassium, etc.) that can be lost in urine when large quantities of ascorbate are used.

References - Vitamin C

1. Levine, M "New concepts in the biology and biochemistry of ascorbic acid" *N.E.J.Med* 314 no.14 (Apr.1986) 892-902 – see page 897.
2. *Drug Facts and Comparisons* Jan 2003 page 19a Wolters Kluwer Health, St.Louis MO.
3. Babior BM and Crowley CA Chapter 90 in Stanbury et al. eds. *The Metabolic Basis of Inherited Disease* 5th ed McGraw-Hill (1983) 1965.
4. Forehand JR Nauseef WM and Johnston RB, Chapter 114 in Scriver et al. eds. *The Metabolic Basis of Inherited Disease* 6th ed McGraw-Hill (1989) 2784.
5. Michelson AM, Chapter 17 in Autor AP ed., *Pathology of Oxygen* Academic Press (1982) 278-279.
6. Pangborn JB "Detection of metabolic disorders in people with autism" Proceedings, NSAC Annual Conference, San Antonio TX, International Autism Conference of the Americas (July 1984) 36-39.
7. James SJ "Abnormal folate-dependent methionine and glutathione metabolism in children with autism: potential for increased sensitivity to Thimerosal and other pro-oxidants" Spring DAN! Conference Proceedings, Washington DC (April 2004) 59-63.
8. McGinnis WR "Oxidative stress and autism" Alternative Therapies 10 no. 6 (2004).
9. Buettner GR "The pecking order of free radicals and antioxidants: lipid peroxidation, α-tocopherol, and ascorbate" *Arch. Biochem and Biophys* 300 no.2 (1993) 535-543, see esp. 539-540.
10. Levine M op.cit. p 893.
11. Levine M. ibid, p.893.
12. Horvath K and Permian *J. Curr Opinion Pediatrics* 14 (2002) 583-587.
13. Stein HB et al. "Ascorbic-acid-induced uricosuria", *Ann Inter Med* 84 (1976) 385-388.

ZINC, Zn

- **Recent clinical studies show a high copper-to- zinc ratio in blood for about 85% of autistics.**
- **Zinc assists digestion, methylation, immune response and nucleotide balance. Zinc supplements help the autistic child accept changes in diet.**
- **Zinc assimilation depends on gastrointestinal conditions, supplemental forms and assisting nutrients.**

We have provided a rather extensive discussion of zinc because it is actually reported to be subnormal in many autistics and because it can be quite difficult to normalize cellular levels by supplementation. When it is measured in relation to copper in blood serum or plasma, copper is relatively elevated. The serum zinc level often is marginal or subnormal. Before dealing with why and what to do about it, we need some knowledge about zinc itself.

About Zinc

An essential element or mineral, zinc is required by many enzymes in the body as an activator or structural component.[1] Additionally, this element participates in the mechanisms of storage and release of insulin from the pancreas,[2] and it is essential for lymphocyte functions and proper immune response.[3] Infants who are breast-fed acquire zinc as zinc citrate in mothers' milk,[4] and this is one of the preferred supplemental forms. The normal human requirement for daily intake of zinc from the diet increases from 3 mg for a 10-15 pound infant to at least 15 mg/day for an adult, and lactating mothers typically need 25 mg/day.[5]

Nutritional causes of zinc deficiency include poor quality of diet or a monotonous diet of foods that are insufficient in the element (some cereal diets, processed grains and pasta, diets that exclude meat and seafood).[6] Gastrointestinal disorders, especially of the pancreas or small intestine, may cause zinc deficiency, often with loss of nutrients via diarrhea.[6] Zinc may be displaced by copper in some tissues if copper uptake is excessive, as may be the case when cysteine and thioneins are insufficient. This can also happen with excessive uptake of small peptides from meat, fish or poultry (carnosine, anserine).[6,7,8] These small peptides grab copper ions and form a chemical complex that enables them to carry the copper into the bloodstream.

Besides supporting lymphoid tissue, zinc stabilizes thiol (sulfur) and phospholipid (phosphorylated fats) in membranes, and it helps to stabilize RNA and DNA structures. Also very important are zinc's many roles as an enzyme activator or stabilizer. Some enzymes that require zinc are:

- Carbonic anhydrase, the enzyme that makes bicarbonate out of carbon dioxide generated in cells by respiration.[9] This allows acid-base balancing in body tissues and is required for the production of stomach acid.

- Carboxypeptidase, a digestive enzyme secreted by the pancreas into the small intestine. It helps digest dietary peptides by cleaving amino acids from peptides at the organic acid or "carboxyl" end.[10]

- Leucine (*leucyl*) aminopeptidase, a digestive enzyme secreted by the pancreas into the small intestine. It helps digest dietary peptides by cleaving branched-chain essential amino acids (leucine, isoleucine, valine) from the peptides at the N-terminal or amino group end.[11]

- Alcohol dehydrogenase, an enzyme that processes ethanol, which foods may contain and intestinal yeast can produce. It begins a sequence that changes ethanol into useful "acetyl" forms.[12]

- Copper-zinc superoxide dismutase, an enzyme that assists in cellular handling of oxidant chemicals and ions.[13]

- Alkaline phosphatase, a group of enzymes that remove phosphate from biochemicals when the pH is above 7 (alkaline).[14] When there is tissue damage or repair occurring, this enzyme removes phosphate from pieces of RNA/DNA so that disassembly can proceed prior to rebuilding the tissue.

- Betaine-homocysteine methyltransferase (BHMT), the enzyme that processes trimethylglycine into dimethylglycine, and at the same time makes methionine from homocysteine.[15] This enzyme works in parallel with the folate-methyl B_{12}-methionine synthase process for the same purpose except that BHMT then makes DMG, which provides one-carbon pieces for folate metabolism and purine nucleotide assembly.

- Cytidine deaminase, the enzyme that processes cytidine into uridine (these are pyrimidine nucleosides), a step that also is required for proper immune response.

Deficiency of cytidine deaminase in mice results in a huge overgrowth in (harmful) intestinal microflora and in lymph node hyperplasia of the small intestine.[16]

- Adenosine deaminase, one enzyme that looks after unneeded or excessive adenosine (and toxic deoxyadenosine).[17] Elevated adenosine can lead to elevated S-adenosylhomocysteine, impaired methylation, and immune dysregulation.[18]

So, zinc participates in many physiological processes of concern in autism, from digestion to immune function to methylation to nucleotide balance. Theoretically, an acute zinc deficiency, if focused on betaine-homocysteine methyltransferase and adenosine deaminase, could stall methionine metabolism. If this resulted in inadequate methylation and deficient creatine formation in the brain, then deficiency of expressive speech would probably result. While we make no pretensions that zinc deficiency itself is an autism-causing condition, we do raise the issue because it seems to be an aggravating or contributing factor for many victims of this disease.

Zinc deficiency in autistics is not universal; neither is high copper. But in the last decade, a majority of autistic children were noticed to have blood or blood cell zinc levels below laboratory norms, and this has been found repeatedly by different clinicians. The findings of the first Defeat Autism Now! Conference in Dallas, Texas, in January 1995 were recorded in a 1996 Consensus Report. That report includes mention of low zinc and of evidence of zinc dysfunction relative to dietary peptide excesses.[19] These findings differ dramatically from those published by Coleman and Gillberg in 1976, in which elevated serum zinc was measured in autistics versus controls.[20] They found the autistic mean zinc concentration to be 171 mcg% (n=64), versus 112.5 mcg% for control individuals (n=69). In Coleman's studies, there was no statistically significant difference in serum copper concentrations; the mean was normal at about 120 mcg% for both autistics and controls. In contrast to this, Walsh reported in 2001 that the blood concentration ratio, serum copper ÷ plasma zinc was 1.63 for autistics (n=503) and 1.15 for age-matched controls (n=25).[21] But, Walsh also stated that this relative copper/zinc excess was seen in 85% or 428 of the 503 subjects. Seventy five, or 15%, of the 503 did not have remarkably abnormal blood copper/zinc ratios. Not stated was how many of the 503 had absolutely low zinc per the laboratory reference range.

These divergent findings do not leave us with a dilemma because we know that some important characteristics of autism and ASD have changed very significantly since the 1970s. The incidence has increased from about 3 per 10,000 to about 6 per 1,000 births (0.0003 to 0.006), or a 20-fold increase. Further, in the 1970s, about 70% showed abnormalities from birth. Now, over 80% show onset and regression between ages 1 and 2 years. We may have had a zinc utilization disorder in one or two per 10,000 in the 1970s and we may still have this. But it's swamped by 50 per 10,000 who now have copper excess relative to zinc, including many with absolutely deficient zinc.

Why is copper elevated? Walsh attributes that to metallothionein deficiency, which would be a logical consequence of cysteine deficiency and impaired processing of its essential precursor, methionine. In the mucosal tissue of the digestive tract, one of metallothionein's duties is to collect copper ions so that they are not excessively absorbed. There is, however, another concern. With inflammation, and especially with chronic infection (as may be present in the gut tissue with dysbiotic flora), copper is redistributed from the liver to the blood. A quantity known as leukocyte endogenous mediator may be involved, and it is a normal physiological response to infection.[22] This process increases blood copper levels and may even cause hypercupremia in acute infectious response. So, part of the remedy for lowering or normalizing blood copper levels may be appropriate use of antibiotics and antifungals and improvement of gastrointestinal function (and diet) so that the intestinal infection and inflammation are removed and digestion is improved.

Maldigestion and malabsorption can, by themselves, result in increased copper uptake. Maldigestion of meat, fish, or poultry can create unusually high concentrations of two dipeptides in the small intestine, anserine and carnosine. Anserine comes from chicken, turkey, duck, rabbit, tuna and salmon. Carnosine comes from beef, pork, tuna and salmon. Both can be high when digestive peptidase function is inadequate in the small intestine, or if excessive amounts of these foods are consumed (diet is imbalanced). Anserine and carnosine are powerful copper collectors. They can form a chemical complex with intestinal copper ions and transport that copper into the bloodstream[8] – especially if metallothionein isn't on the job. Additionally, once zinc becomes scarce, many zinc-requiring digestive enzymes may be weak, making anserine and carnosine levels higher and copper uptake even worse. This applies to anserine and carnosine because their digestive enzyme, carnosinase, is itself a zinc-requiring enzyme.[8] My observation is that about 20% of untreated autistics have elevated anserine and/or carnosine per 24-hour urine amino acid analysis.

The issue of why zinc is subnormal in many autistics is complex. Surely, part of it is the maldigestion and malabsorption that goes along with digestive enzyme weakness, food allergies and intolerances. Zinc supplements often are necessary but not sufficient to correct the problem. Gastrointestinal functioning has to be improved or normalized, which may require dietary interventions and regular use of digestive enzymes. There is virtually no hope of correcting zinc deficiency while there is chronic diarrhea. Furthermore, uptake of some essential elements, including zinc and copper, is controlled to some extent by thiols (sulfur-bearing molecules, including metallothionein), that patrol the mucosal tissue in the gastrointestinal tract. Glutathione (only slightly) and cysteine are reported to assist the transport and uptake of zinc, and both are sulfur-bearing quantities.[23,24]

For some, this means that the copper-zinc balance can be normalized only after diet, digestion, and transsulfuration chemistry are working properly. In some cases, this means getting rid of most toxic element excesses (mercury, arsenic, antimony) as well. The bottom line is that we should strive to get zinc up to a normal level in blood and get copper down to where it's supposed to be. Don't be discouraged if months go by and treatment progresses without zinc cooperating. Eventually, it will. If it doesn't, the answer usually isn't higher doses of zinc. It's more work on diet, gastrointestinal conditions and metabolism.

Using Zinc in Autism

Effective forms of nutritional zinc supplements include: citrate (human mothers' milk form), amino acid chelates, and zinc salts of picolinate, gluconate, aspartate, and alpha-ketoglutarate. Oral zinc sulfate is available but often causes stomach upset. Zinc can be beneficial for autistic individuals when introduced during initial stages of dietary intervention, because it may improve both appetite and taste. Zinc is in the saliva protein "gustin", which has a major role in the sensation of taste. Clinicians, nutritionists and parents all report that zinc supplements typically help autistic children accept new foods in their diets. Often, zinc is included in multivitamin and multimineral blends that are best tolerated with meals. Vitamin B_6 as pyridoxine.HCl assists zinc absorption, at least in animal studies.[25] For some, separate zinc supplements may work best, and they should be given away from meals or in the evening, several hours after supper. You may wish to try additional and separate zinc supplements if, after a month or two, the supplement blend-with-meal regimen does not improve the measured zinc status (blood or blood cell zinc level). Large amounts of supplemental zinc may slow the digestive action of dipeptidylpeptidase 4 (DPP4). Both human and supplemental DPP4 do not contain zinc, and human DPP4 is inhibited by significant amounts of zinc.[26] This is why we advise against giving large doses of zinc with meals. It can be given with snacks, juice or tolerated treats, and some do well with small amounts (~10 mg) with each meal. What is not advisable is giving 30 or 45 mg of zinc with a single meal.

The low-dose start level could be 5 mg/day for a small child, but most commercial supplements have 15 mg as the smallest unit dose or capsule content. 15 mg/day is the US FDA RDI for zinc.

The amounts of zinc that usually are effective are tabulated below. Your doctor may wish to increase these amounts. Some individuals do require more.

WEIGHT Kg / LB	ZINC, mg/day
20 44	5-15
30 66	7-20
40 88	10-30
50 110	12-35
60 132 and over	15-45

The Autism Research Institute has kept a tally of success and failure with zinc supplement use in autism per parent responses (ARI Publ.34/March 2005):

Zinc Parent-Response Tally, responses = 1244

Behavior or Traits Improved 47%	No Discernible Effect 51%	Behavior or Traits Worsened 2%

Adverse Response to Zinc?

It's hard to come up with a physiological reason for intolerance to zinc at low doses or dietary levels, or to levels that are just 2x or 3x the DRI. One reason would be severe copper deficiency, which is uncommon in the general population and rare in autism. Usually, a worsening of behavior following a zinc supplement is due to the substance that the zinc is combined with. Trying a different form (such as switching from picolinate to gluconate or citrate) could solve the problem. Adverse reactions to large doses of zinc can occur, but such doses are well beyond what we have tabulated above.

Special Strategies for Boosting Zinc

Because normalizing zinc level can be a difficult, frustrating and lengthy endeavor, we've included some strategies and ideas that may help.

- For some autistics, it's best to not give zinc with meals. Try twice a day between meals.
- Don't give zinc along with calcium, iron or folate.
- Don't give zinc along with phosphorylated nutrients such as phosphatidylcholine, phosphorylated lipids, pyridoxal phosphate, etc.

- Do give oral glutathione if it's tolerated. And a small dose of L-histidine can help too. Like cysteine, histidine can complex and transport zinc.[24] But it can do this for copper too,[25] so don't use histidine with food when the objective is to lower copper and raise zinc levels. Beneficial amounts would be 25 mg of GSH and 100 mg of L-histidine with 15 mg of zinc. Besides histidine and cysteine/cystine (which we do not recommend here), three other amino acids, lysine, glutamine and threonine, can bind zinc,[28] but information on assisting zinc assimilation with these is lacking. WARNING: About one in 250 to 500 autistics has a metabolic condition known as histidinemia/histidinuria – too much histidine already. You'll only know this by doing an amino acid analysis. Do not give histidine when histidinemia is present.

- If you do use histidine with zinc, then give these between meals, midmorning or midafternoon. Histidine in the evening may cause insomnia.

- Watch for urinary zinc loss during detoxification treatments that use chelating agents. Some (D-penicillamine and EDTA) are known to remove zinc, and others may have that effect in an autistic individual whose sulfur and elemental biochemistries are abnormal. Larger supplemental doses of zinc may be needed at appropriate times during detoxification therapy.

- A physician may opt to use zinc acetate, a zinc form with very high bioavailability. It has FDA-approved orphan drug status for copper overload conditions.[29] The trade name is "Galzin;" the sponsor is Lemmon Co and Teva Pharmaceuticals of North Wales, PA.

- Zinc often rises to satisfactory levels in blood serum or plasma before it does so in red blood cells. Much of erythrocyte zinc is bound to the cell plasma membrane. If RBC zinc stays low, perhaps the cell membrane is deficient in certain fatty acids that should be there, or there's something wrong with membrane binding/transport of zinc. An RBC fatty acid analysis might be helpful. In cases like this, the supplemented amount of zinc is usually not the problem.

A Possible Strategy for Reducing High Copper – Use of Molybdenum

One strategy for reducing copper retention in body tissues is to supplement molybdenum. Molybdenum can be of benefit if it is used in reasonable amounts. Molybdenum, Mo or "moly" as chemists call it, is an activator of an enzyme, sulfite oxidase, that helps process sulfur in our tissues. That enzyme oxidizes toxic sulfite into usable sulfate for sulfation. Copper can be retained excessively in cells if moly is deficient. A packed RBC analysis for elements usually is a good telltale for status. A reasonable supplement of moly, usually as sodium molybdate, may help coax excess amounts of copper out of cells. A reasonable amount means 25 to 250 micrograms per day as Mo. I'm not a fan of giant megadoses of moly. That's because high doses can have detrimental effects on the same sulfur chemistry that correct amounts would benefit. Besides sodium molybdate, other forms also are available – molybdenum citrate, tetrathiomolybdate, ammonium molybdate. I don't care for the citrate because the Mo seems to be at the wrong oxidation state for enzyme use, and I don't like ammonium anything for autism. Tetrathiomolybdate has been used to good benefit by Dr. Anju Usman, who practices in Naperville, Illinois, and by the Pfeiffer Treatment Center, in Warrenville, Illinois. By the way, the best food source for natural molybdenum is buckwheat, with lima beans in second place (from Dr. Carl Pfeiffer's book, *Mental and Element Nutrients*, Keats [1975] 284).

References - Zinc

1. Harper HA et al. *Review of Physiological Chemistry* 17th ed, Lange Med Pub, Los Altos CA (1979) 590-591.
2. Brennan M. "Extracellular pH plays role in insulin release" C&EN p.32 (Mar 4, 1996).
3. Myrvik QN "Immunology and Nutrition" Chapt.41 in Shils ME et al., eds. *Modern Nutrition in Health and Disease* 8th ed, vol. 1 Lea & Febiger (1994) 647.
4. Hurley LS and B Lönnerdal "Zinc binding in human milk: citrate versus picolinate" *Nutrition Reviews* vol 40 no.3 March 1982 65-71.
5. NRC Food and Nutrition Board, Committee on the Tenth Edition of the RDAs, *Recommended Dietary Allowances* 10th ed, National Academy Press, Wash DC 1989, Summary table after page 284.
6. King JC and CL Keen "Zinc", Chapter 10 in Shils et al. eds. Op.cit. 214-230.
7. Culotta VC and JD Gitlin "Disorders of Copper Transport" Chapt 26 in Scriver et al. eds *The Metabolic and Molecular Bases of Inherited Disease* 8th ed., McGraw-Hill (2001) 3107.
8. Scriver CR and TL Perry "Disorders of ω-Amino –Acids in Free and Peptide-Linked Forms, Chapter 26 in Scriver et al. eds, *The Metabolic Basis of Inherited Disease* 6th ed McGraw-Hill (1989) 765.
9. Martin DW et al. *Harper's Review of Biochemistry* 20th ed Lange Medical Publ. (1985) 44,659.
10. Lehninger AL *Biochemistry* 2nd ed, Worth Publ (1978) 560.
11. Lehninger AL ibid. 561.
12. Martin DW et al. *Harper's Review of Biochemistry* 20th ed, op.cit 131,245.
13. Paik HY et al. "Serum extracellular superoxide dismutase activity as an indicator of zinc status in humans" *Biol Trace Element Res* 69 (1999) 45-57.
14. Martin DW et al. *Harper's Review of Biochemistry* 20th ed. Op.cit. 62,659.
15. Breksa AP 3rd, Garrow TA "Recombinant liver betaine-homocysteine S-methyltransferase: identification of three cysteine residues for zinc binding" *Biochemistry* 38 no.42 (1999) 13991-13998.
16. Fagarasan S et al. "Critical roles of activation-induced cytidine deaminase in the homeostasis of gut flora" *Science* 298 (Nov. 2002) 1424-1427.
17. Wilson DK et al. "Atomic structure of adenosine deaminase complexed with a transition-state analog: understanding catalysis and immunodeficiency mutations" *Science* 252 (May 1991) 1278-1284.
18. Hershfield MS "Immunodeficiency Diseases Caused by Adenosine Deaminase Deficiency and Purine Nucleoside Phosphorylase Deficiency" in Scriver CR et al. *The Metabolic and Molecular Bases of Inherited Disease* 8th ed (2001) 2585-2625.
19. Baker SM and Pangborn JB *Clinical Assessment Options for Children with Autism and Related Disorders: A Biomedical Approach* Autism Research Institute, San Diego (January 1996) 21,23.
20. Coleman M and Gillberg C *The Biology of the Autistic Syndromes* Praeger (1985) 102,103.
21. Walsh WJ et al. "Metallothionein and Autism," Pfeiffer Treatment Center, Naperville IL (Oct 2001) 5.
22. Harper HA *Review of Physiological Chemistry* 17th ed, Lange Med Pub (19790 589.
23. Menard MP and Cousins RJ "Effect of citrate, glutathione and picolinate on zinc transport by brush border membrane vesicles from rat intestine" *J.Nutrition* 113 91983) 1653-11656.

SECTION FIVE: NUTRITIONAL SUPPLEMENTS FOR AUTISM

24. King JC and Keen CL "Zinc" Chapt.10 in Shils et al. eds *Modern Nutrition in Health and Disease* 8th ed (1994) 2115.

25. Evans GW and Johnson EC "Effect of iron, vitamin B_6 and picolinic acid in zinc absorption in the rat" *J. Nutrition* 111 (1981) 68-75.

26. Püschel G et al. "Isolation and characterization of dipeptidyl peptidase IV from human placenta" *Eur.J. Biochem* 126 (1982) 359-365.

27. Danks DM Chapter 58 in Stanbury et al. eds. *The Metabolic Basis of Inherited Disease* 5th ed. McGraw Hill (1983) 1253.

28. Prasad AS "Nutritional zinc today" *Nutrition Today* (Mar/Apr 1981) 4-11.

29. *PDR for Nutritional Supplements* Thomson 1st ed (2001) 535.

CALCIUM, Ca

- **Low calcium has been postulated for a subset of autistics per urine levels. Calcium supplementation is behaviorally beneficial for 35%.**
- **Diets that avoid dairy products significantly increase the need for calcium supplements.**
- **Choosing the best supplement form or forms requires consideration of biochemical individuality.**

The element calcium is necessary not only for bones and teeth, but also for cell signaling processes and hormonal messenger activities. Strictly speaking, minerals are forms of elements combined with other elements to make salts or oxides, but in nutrition "minerals" and "elements" are used synonymously. The minerals (elements) that humans are known to need for good health are "essential minerals:" calcium, sodium, potassium, magnesium, phosphorus, chloride, sulfur; and a number of trace minerals: iron, zinc, copper, chromium, manganese, selenium, iodine, and molybdenum. Of all these, only two have been consistently found to be subnormal by tissue or fluid analysis in subsets of the autistic population: zinc (discussed previously), and calcium. (Magnesium need usually is determined functionally; quantitative analysis of blood or urine typically shows a magnesium concentration that is within lab norms.)

About Calcium

For autistics, the findings of low calcium have been those of urine analysis. With normal dietary calcium, a finding of low urine levels implies subnormal dietary uptake or malabsorption. Over 30 years ago, calcium was found to be low in autistic children with celiac disease or with a history of colic.[1] Since then, low or marginal calcium levels per hair or urine analysis have been observed from time to time at higher frequencies than in the normal population. One might conjecture that poor digestion, including fat malabsorption, is part of the mechanism that limits uptake of dietary calcium. This abnormality does not show in blood, which can be deceptively normal even in gross calcium disorders such as osteoporosis. And hair calcium levels can be high and deceptive when calcium metabolism is disturbed.

Besides the finding of subnormal calcium that may be a secondary part of the disease process for some autistics, there also is the major issue of calcium sufficiency when a casein-free diet is followed. Excluding dairy products, especially milk, means excluding a major source of calcium. For the typical child, milk may provide 75% of the total dietary calcium intake.[2]

Using Calcium in Autism

Below, we tabulate the calcium needs of children to provide an idea of the magnitude of the alternative-calcium source problem when dairy is excluded from the diet.

Age (years) nominal	Weight (lbs.)	Calcium RDA, mg/d*[3]	Mg/d needed in substitute if milk is excluded
0.5-1	20	800	600
1-2	29	800	600
4-6	44	800	600
7-10	62	1200	900
11-14	99	1200	900

* While the FDA RDA is a nominal 1000 mg calcium per day, up to 1200 is recommended by the National Academy of Sciences – National Research Council.[3]

Part of the calcium that substitutes for milk in the diet can be in nutritional supplement form – capsules, tablets or powders that include calcium in various forms. Moms and dads are urged to attempt to quantify how much calcium may be in rice milk, soy milk or whatever foods substitute for milk. If these amounts don't add up to about three-quarters of your child's RDA for calcium, a nutritional supplement is in order.

As with many other nutritional supplements, parents have responded to ARI about beneficial or adverse response to calcium. Here's the scorecard as of March 2005 (ARI Publication 34).

Calcium Parent-Response Tally, n=1378

Behavior or Traits Improved 36%	No Discernible Effect 62%	Behavior or Traits Worsened 2%

Note that for these results, the casein-free diet and calcium adequacy issues are not expressly included. Some of the 35% may have been on such a diet, some certainly not. So, calcium benefits 35% before the problem of nutritional adequacy is even considered!

After estimating how much supplemental calcium is needed, the next problem is the form. There are many kinds of calcium supplements, and many sometimes confusing claims about them. We cannot possibly deal with them all, so here are some words of wisdom that come from experience and from experts. These have been chosen because they cover most of the commonly encountered questions from parents.

Is calcium carbonate a good form for an autistic person to use? (Carbonate includes eggshells and coral forms.) Yes, provided that it is combined with another, more soluble, form. Using two or more forms of calcium evens out the absorption period for uptake from the gastrointestinal tract. Also, the possibility of calcium carbonate not being absorbed when there isn't enough stomach acid is not a big issue in autism. It can be an issue for people with some forms of

SECTION FIVE: NUTRITIONAL SUPPLEMENTS FOR AUTISM

environmental illness or chemical sensitivity, and often is an issue for the elderly. Dr. Timothy Buie, of Massachusetts General Children's Hospital, stated at a recent DAN! Meeting: "I have examined the gastrointestinal tract of over 500 autistic children, and I've yet to find the first one with gastric hypochlorhydria[4]." The value of calcium carbonate is its calcium "density" – it's 40% calcium by weight versus about 20% for most citrates, and less than 10% for most organic salts such as gluconate. If your child needs 200 mg of supplemental calcium, that's 500 mg of calcium carbonate (one capsule), or 1000 mg of citrate (two capsules), or over 2000 mg of gluconate (more than four capsules).

Is all calcium citrate a good idea? Probably not. Citrate is not completely processed in many autistics, and urine organic acid tests frequently show that higher-than-normal amounts of citrate are excreted. This may be secondary to several physiological problems: decreased demand for bicarbonate by a malfunctioning pancreas, decreased sulfhydryl presence in the citric acid processing enzymes, oxidant stress, or interference with citric acid cycle enzymes by mimic compounds from dysbiotic gut flora. Regardless, hundreds of milligrams of extra citrate may not be a good idea for many autistics.

Is calcium lactate a good idea? Calcium lactate is a calcium salt of lactic acid (not lactose). As with citrate, urine organic acid tests for autistics have shown elevated lactate, but this occurs less often than elevated citrate does. And, for that matter, pyruvate may also be elevated. Pyruvate, lactate and citrate are all clustered near the same place metabolically, and that place seems to have problems in many autistics. So, I'd avoid lactate supplements unless I knew from analytical testing that it would be okay for the individual. Calcium lactate is nominally 18% calcium. 100 milligrams corresponds to 455 milligrams of lactate; 500 mg of Ca means 2275 mg of lactate.

Can I count the calcium that's in calcium ascorbate as part of the calcium supplement? You can count only about one-third of it. Up to two-thirds is going to come out in the urine as a companion ion to dehydroascorbate and unused ascorbate, depending upon magnesium status. With plentiful magnesium, less calcium is wasted in this way (at the expense of magnesium).

Should vitamin D be in the calcium supplement? Probably yes, or it should be in companion supplements. The same 5-year-old child who needs 800 mg/d of calcium also needs 400 IU of vitamin D per day. This is 10 micrograms of cholecalciferol.[3] See the text on Vitamin A and Cod Liver Oil. Cod liver oil contains vitamin D and some vitamin A formulations really are A and D combined. So, some supplemental vitamin D may already be in the supplement schedule.

When is the best time to take a calcium supplement? With meals and not when zinc is taken. (Zinc is best taken away from big meals.)

<u>*References – Calcium*</u>

1. Coleman M. *The Autistic Syndromes* North-Holland Publishing (1976) p.199-204, 214-216.
2. Robinson CH *Normal and Therapeutic Nutrition* 14th ed, MacMillan Pub.Co. (1972) p.109.
3. Food and Nutrition Board of US, NRC, *Recommended Dietary Allowances*, 10th ed, National Academy Press (1989) Foldout page 285.
4. Timothy Buie, M.D., specializes in pediatric gastroenterology and nutrition at Massachusetts General Hospital for Children, Boston, MA.

VITAMIN A and COD LIVER OIL (Vitamins A and D)

> - Vitamin A and beta-carotene have a history of confusing units of measurement and recommended amounts.
> - Vitamin A has a high benefit ratio with autistics, and cod liver oil is an excellent form that also includes vitamin D.
> - While vitamin A definitely enhances immunity, megadose use against entrenched measles virus has not been very successful.

Vitamin A is called the "anti-infective vitamin."[1] Pharmacologically, it is defined to be one molecular structure, "all-trans-retinol." In nature (animals, not plants), there are several vitamin A-like molecules having vitamin A activities of various degrees. Fish oils, especially cod liver oil, contain several vitamin A forms, predominantly the esterified retinyl palmitate form.[1] Esterified means that it's attached to another molecule which often increases the stability of the vitamin. Fish oils also contain some vitamin D. While plants do not contain vitamins A or D, they do contain a precursor for vitamin A, provitamin A or beta-carotene. Vitamin A is of interest in autism because it seems to improve immune function and because it may not be well absorbed from food sources. Vitamin D is of interest because uptake can also be limited and because calcium may be deficient.

About Vitamins A and D

One confusing aspect of vitamin A is its units of measurement. Another is how much should be ingested daily or periodically. In older literature on vitamins you will find vitamin A measured in International Units (IU). 1.0 IU of vitamin A is (was) 0.30 micrograms of all-trans-retinol, and 1.0 IU of vitamin A as beta-carotene is (was) 0.60 micrograms of beta-carotene.[2] For many years, the RDA (adults) was simply 5000 IU/day. All this has been superseded by new units of measurement and new recommendations. The units in current use are retinal equivalents (RE). 1.0 RE is the same as 3.33 IU of vitamin A.[3] 1.0 RE = 1.0 micrograms of all trans-retinol = 6.0 micrograms of all trans-beta-carotene.[4] Yes, there are lots of beta carotene forms too, and over 500 natural carotenoids have been identified. The all-trans form of beta-carotene is the most potent in terms of being transformed to vitamin A.

The "new" government-recommended amounts for vitamin A, stated in either RE or micrograms (they are the same now) are:[5]

AGE/CONDITION	VITAMIN A (RE)
Birth-6 months	375
6 months-1 year	375
1-3 years	400
4-6 years	500
7-10 years	700
Pregnant female	800
Lactating female	1300 (first 6 months)
Lactating female	1200 (second 6 months)
Males 11 and older	1000

Medical warnings about excessive use of vitamin A during pregnancy stem from the possibility of birth defects which have been rare in humans, but have occurred with incidences of concern in animal studies.[3] Actual vitamin A toxicity from hypervitaminosis A is rare.

Because a stable, solid (powder) form is needed for most nutritional supplements, a synthetic esterified form is often used, retinyl acetate. You need about 15% more retinyl acetate to equal a desired amount of vitamin A. About 1150 RE of retinyl acetate provides the same activity as 1000 RE of all-trans-retinol.

If you're using beta-carotene to provide vitamin A activity, you need to know three things. First, beta-carotene is stored and converted to vitamin A at your liver's convenience. Human infants and some young children don't make this conversion efficiently. In some, the conversion is extremely limited. It isn't possible to produce hypervitaminosis A by taking large doses of beta-carotene. But if large amounts are used, the skin may turn reddish-brown from lots of stored beta-carotene. Second, if you have pure, all trans-beta-carotene, then to get 1000 RE you typically need about 6000 micrograms of that type of beta-carotene. With other types, more is needed. Third, if you have a natural blend of provitamin A carotenoids, from some plant source, then to get 1000 RE you need 12,000 micrograms of the mixed carotenoids.[3] Usually, the beta-carotene in liquid gel capsules is a blend of mixed provitamin A carotenoids.

Now, what about realistic concerns for large doses of vitamin A? Excluding pregnancy, there is both anecdotal evidence and published data showing that megadoses can be consumed without harm of toxic effects. While 800 to 1000 RE is the upper level that often is recommended for nutritional purposes, therapeutic limits in non-pregnant, non-lactating humans are vastly higher:[6]
- Adults 1,000,000 IU daily for 3 days
- Adults, 500,000 IU daily for 2 months
- Adults, 50,000 IU daily for longer than 18 months

(IU units are quoted from the original source.)

Large doses of vitamin A have been used therapeutically and safely to enhance the immune system, to reduce mortality in HIV-infected children, to diminish the growth of malignant cells (cancer) and as a treatment for acne.[3]

At excessive dosage levels, vitamin A may induce symptoms and disease conditions categorized as vitamin A toxicity or "hypervitaminosis A." Such symptoms depend upon: the oral dosage level, acute or chronic dosing schedule, intestinal absorption, and patient weight, or perhaps age. Vitamin A is absorbed from the small intestine, and absorption efficiency depends upon biliary function (bile salts), lipase activity and the level of fats in the diet. Uptake of vitamin A can be very impaired if biliary or pancreatic functions are impaired. In such cases, large amounts of vitamin A or water-soluble forms may be needed for effective vitamin A nurture or therapy. Symptoms consistent with vitamin A toxicity are: headache, nausea, vomiting, dizziness or vertigo, blurred vision, and dry scaly skin rash, often at the back of the neck.[6] A clinical laboratory finding consistent with hypervitaminosis A is elevated calcium in blood serum (hypercalcemia).[6]

If cod liver oil is used, then supplemental vitamin D is also provided. Vitamin D still is measured in its international units (IU), and the standard vitamin form is cholecalciferol, also known as vitamin D_3. 1.0 IU of vitamin D is 0.025 micrograms of cholecalciferol, and 400 IU (nominal RDA amount) is 10 micrograms of cholecalciferol.[5]

In terms of the old IU units for vitamin A, cod liver oil contains about 10% as much vitamin D (IU) as it does vitamin A (IU). In other words, if a cod liver oil capsule contains 1000 IU of vitamin A, it typically contains about 100 IU of vitamin D. In RE units, for each 300 RE of vitamin A, there's about 100 IU of vitamin D. This varies from batch to batch because not all codfish are alike. With various batches or lots of cod liver oil, it's possible to find 80 or 90 IU or 120 to 130 IU of vitamin D for each 300 RE of vitamin A. This is somewhat important because vitamin D can also be in multivitamin formulations, and it can be in calcium formulations as well. While vitamin D is not toxic at two or three times the RDA, it may be at levels above that.

What is sunlight and vitamin D all about? In animal-source foods, there is a natural precursor to vitamin D, 7-dehydrocholesterol (cholesterol minus a hydrogen atom). When it's in skin tissue and exposed to ultraviolet light, this provitamin D form is changed to become vitamin D_3[7]. Then in the liver, D_3 adds a hydroxyl, and then in the kidney, it adds one more hydroxyl to become the active hormonal form. Consuming adequate cod liver oil bypasses the sunlight part of the process and provides the form that fish (who don't get much sunlight) use for their metabolism.

Using Vitamin A or Cod Liver Oil in Autism

There are two stages of vitamin A usage that health professionals have tried for vitamin A supplementation in autism. Stage one is use of nutritional amounts to ensure adequacy and to possibly help with some biochemical mechanisms of cellular perception and response. These amounts follow the previous tabulation but are presented again in all the units of measurement to alleviate confusion.

Daily Nutritional Amounts of Vitamin A as all trans-retinol

Age	RE	IU	Micrograms	Approx. tsp. cod liver oil
Infants	375	1250	375	1/4
1-3 years	400	1333	400	1/3
4-6 years	500	1667	500	1/3
7-10 years	700	2333	700	1/2
Females>10 yrs	800	2667	800	1/2
Males >10 yrs	1000	3330	1000	2/3

Capsules, tablets, and teaspoons contain fixed quantities that are not necessarily graduated in the above amounts. But, there is flexibility in the amount that can be used as a supplement. It's perfectly OK to use amounts that are up to double those listed above; no toxicity should occur while added benefits may. For decades, males/females over 10 years took 5000 IU (1500 RE), and many supplement companies still provide this as the unit dose or amount in a capsule/tablet. And it's ok to give 2500 IU (750 RE) to children. Cod liver oil is a liquid given by teaspoon or eyedropper. The same amounts of vitamin A as cod liver oil also are fine for adults (5000 IU) and children (2500 IU). Very young children or infants probably should be supplemented with half the 2500 IU dose, or 1250 IU (375 RE). That's usually about one-quarter of a teaspoon of cod liver oil (read the product labels!).

ARI has compiled parent-response statistics on use of vitamin A in autism, and adverse reactions to nutritional levels are uncommon (2%), see ARI Publication 34/March 2005.

SECTION FIVE: NUTRITIONAL SUPPLEMENTS FOR AUTISM

Vitamin A Parent-Response Tally, n=618

| Behavior or Traits Improved 41% | No Discernible Effect 58% | Behavior or Traits Worsened 2% |

There is no parent response tally for vitamin D.

In 1999, Dr. Mary Megson postulated that vitamin A can help alleviate defective G-alpha protein function in autism.[8] The G-alpha protein is part of a cell's signal transmission system located in the outer (plasma) membrane. It gives an energy push by dephosphorylating GTP to form GDP. This chemical change provides energy to some of the chemistry that moves a message from outside the cell into the cell's inner workings. It's a necessary part of cellular perception. While Dr. Megson did this research with patients who had family histories of G-alpha protein defect, DAN! studies and many others of autistic populations do not find defective G-alpha protein frequently or as a commonality in autism. However, there is very strong evidence of energy supply deficit to brain cell G-proteins in autism. (See previous chapter on Autism at the Molecular Level.) So, Dr. Megson has identified an important area of probable molecular dysfunction. Whether or not vitamin A supplements help cellular perception when brain ATP or phosphocreatine (energy delivery molecules) are insufficient is not known. There are numerous anecdotal reports of improvement with supplementation of nutritional amounts of natural vitamin A (as in cod liver oil).

Dr. Megson also reports enhancement of beneficial effects when Bethanechol (bethanechol chloride, urecholine) is used in conjunction with vitamin A. Bethanechol is a prescriptive, choline-like substance that stimulates the parasympathetic nervous system. It's acknowledged to aid urination and reduce esophageal reflux, and it may help biliary and pancreatic functions. Dr. Megson finds that with vitamin A, bethanechol improves some autistic traits such as poor eye contact and sociability. As a prescriptive medication, usage of bethanechol should follow package insert or doctor/pharmacy instructions.

The second-stage use of vitamin A is to combat entrenched viral infections, those that seem static and unaffected (or at least unconquered) by the autistic's immune system. This use of vitamin A is controversial among the DAN! medical cadre. Antiviral use involves megadose amounts of vitamin A, up to 100,000 IU/day (30,000 RE/day) for short periods (days). While DAN! doctors do not report incidence of hypervitaminosis A in older children or adults with these amounts, neither do they report any consensus of viral cures or normalization of viral titers including measles. While there are anecdotal reports of significant improvement, most do not show such responses with megadose A. Therapeutic dosing of children with megadoses of vitamin A should be done only under the direction of a physician.

Adverse Responses to Vitamin A or Cod Liver Oil?

A very small subset of humans seem to have allergic-like sensitivity to palmitic acid or palmitate, and this may actually be a "cross-reactivity" to something else. Palmitate is a fatty acid (saturated hexadecanoic acid, from palm oil), and food allergies usually involve proteins or peptides, not fatty acids. Yet respected allergists, such as Theron Randolph, M.D., have reported sensitivity to palm oil and palmitate. So, one possible remedy is to switch to another type of vitamin A, perhaps to vitamin A acetate, even though it is a synthetic form. If a child shows reactivity to coconut on a food allergy test and has trouble with vitamin A palmitate, then you have a good reason to try another type of vitamin A.

Adverse responses to hypervitaminosis A are well documented,[6] but are expected to occur only with megadose usage.

References – Vitamin A

1. *The Merck Index* 12th Ed., Merck & Co., Whitehouse Station, NJ (1997), entry 10150 pg 10150.
2. Harper HA, Rodwell VW, Mayes PA, eds. *Review of Physiological Chemistry*, 17th ed 149.
3. *Drug Facts and Comparisons*, Wolters Kluwer Health, St. Louis MO, 6 (Jan 2000 update).
4. *Recommended Dietary Allowances*, 10th Ed, Food & Nutrition Board, NRC, National Academy Press (1989) 80.
5. Ibid. 285 (foldout sheet at end of book).
6. *Drug Facts and Comparisons*, op.cit. 7.
7. Harper HA et al. op. cit. 151-152.
8. Megson MN "Is Autism a G-alpha protein defect reversible with natural vitamin A?" *Med. Hypotheses* (2000) 54 979-983s.

FATTY ACIDS

> - **Cell walls are membranes composed of fatty acids.**
> - **Unsaturated fatty acids give cell walls flexibility and are required for proper supply of nutrients and relay of messages to cells.**
> - **Many autistics are subnormal in docosahexaenoic acid (DHA), a polyunsaturated, omega-3 type of fatty acid.**

The cells in our bodies have protective membranes that enclose them – "cell walls," as they're sometimes referred to. A cell's wall is really a membrane composed of fatty acids that keeps water-soluble stuff, toxins and microorganisms outside and separated from the special water-soluble substances inside (in the cytosol). The inside of a cell typically has many compartments and centers of activity such as mitochondria, Golgi complexes and lysosomes; these also are contained by lipid membranes. The cell wall membrane has a double layer of fatty acids, as do mitochondria. Lysosomes and Golgi complexes have single-thickness fatty acid membranes.[1] These membranes are not completely continuous. They have channels for nutrients and wastes to pass in and out, and they have binding sites (proteins) where messengers can dock – to signal the cell about external happenings and requirements. Our body builds these membranes out of fatty acids that it processes from dietary sources. In autism, cell membrane composition is especially important because the kinds of fatty acids adjacent to messenger binding sites have a strong effect on message transmission and cellular understanding of external events.[2,3,4,5]

About Fatty Acids

Fatty acids come in many varieties, some from the diet and many made or altered in body tissues. These molecules are chains of carbon atoms with an organic acid group, a carboxyl group, -COOH, at one and, and a methyl group, $-CH_3$, on the other end. Chemists number these carbon atoms, starting with the carbon in the carboxyl group as number "one." The last carbon at the opposite end of the chain, the one in the methyl group, either has a number or is referred to generically as the "omega" (ω) carbon. The names of fatty acids typically refer to the total number of included carbon atoms. For example, decanoic acid (10 carbons) is:

$CH_3CH_2CH_2CH_2CH_2CH_2CH_2CH_2CH_2COOH$.

Because of its electron structure, each carbon atom has four arms or bonds that it uses to attach to other atoms. Methane, for example, is CH_4, a carbon atom holding on to four hydrogen atoms. In the fatty acid chain shown above, except for the ends, each carbon holds another carbon on each side plus two hydrogens. This structure is called "saturated." It results in straight-chain molecules that stack together easily, forming solid shapes rather than flexible membranes. At body temperature, saturated fatty acids with chains containing more than 10 carbons are solidified if they are grouped together (decanoic acid melts at 30°C, dodecanoic or lauric acid with 12 carbons melts at 44°C).

Cells can't live with solid, inflexible sheets of fat for a membrane, so they are composed mostly of flexible, "unsaturated" fatty acids. In unsaturated fatty acids, two or four or six or more of the carbons are joined in pairs by double bonds. In order to do this, some hydrogen atoms are omitted (dehydrogenation). An important cell membrane fatty acid, docosahexaenoic acid or DHA, has 22 carbons with six pairs of double-bonded carbons (six double bonds). In the shorthand of the chemist, DHA is 22:6;4,7,10,13,16,19 because it contains six double bonds located between carbons 4 and 5, 7 and 8, 10 and 11, etc. An alternative nomenclature calls this same molecule 22:6ω3 or 22:6n3 where n is used instead of ω, and the first of the six double bonds starts at the third carbon from the omega end. (Sorry, I didn't make up this nomenclature; it's traditional chemistry.)

```
22 21 20 19 18 17  16 15 14  13 12 11  10 9  8   7 6   5   4 3   2  1
CH₃CH₂CH=CHCH₂CH=CHCH₂CH=CHCH₂CH=CHCH₂CH=CHCH₂CH=CHCH₂CH₂COOH
```

DHA is a very important and abundant lipid in brain tissue.[6] In cell membranes, it contributes to fluidity, correct receptor function and interaction with lipid hormones such as estrogen, progesterone, and angiotensin. An animal cell study shows that DHA has antioxidant capability through suppression of nitric oxide synthase expression.[7] Cell membrane fatty acids are those with 18 to as many as 24 carbons, and most of them are unsaturated to some extent.

Unsaturated fatty acids have flexibility and angles or kinks in their shape. If they contain 20 carbons, they can be processed by the body into biologically active entities called eicosanoids. Eicosanoids include prostaglandins and thromboxanes which may be inflammatory, anti-inflammatory, or active in other ways in body tissues.

The two major types of membrane fatty acids are the omega-3 types (which DHA is), and the omega-6 type. Some omega-3s are:

- Alpha-linolenic   18:3ω3
- Eicosapentaenoic   20:5ω3
- Docosapentaenoic   22:5ω3
- Docosahexaenoic   22:6ω3

Some omega-6s are:

- Linoleic   18:2ω6
- Gamma-linolenic   18:3ω6
- Dihomo-γ-linolenic   20:3ω6
- Arachidonic   20:4ω6

Using Fatty Acids in Autism

While we do not have parent response tallies for improvement vs. worsening with fatty acid supplements, we do have many testimonial reports of benefits from their use by autistics. Levels of both omega-3 and omega-6 types can be depressed in autistics, as measured by erythrocyte membrane analyses. Perhaps this is consistent with elevated fats in stools of autistics who are not taking lipase enzymes. A common abnormality in autism is a depressed level of omega-3 fatty acids, especially docosahexaenoic acid, DHA.[8,9]

There are some sensible prerequisites to use of fatty acid supplements by an autistic individual. Supplements of taurine, and perhaps glycine as well, should be in place. These amino acids are needed to make bile salts, which emulsify and make conjugates and "micelles" of dietary fats and fatty acids.[10] This process is necessary for uptake of most lipid nutrients from the small intestine. Without adequate amounts of bile salts, fatty acid supplements can, like fats in food, pass right on through without being absorbed.

Next, some antioxidants should be in place, at least vitamins C and E. Taurine is also an antioxidant. Some vitamin A as beta-carotene can also be helpful. Of course, vitamin E and beta-carotene are "oils," and their uptake is enhanced by bile salts as well.

Amounts of omega-3 fatty acids that have been helpful range form 20 to 60 mg per Kg of body weight. So, a 25-Kg (55-lb) child would be expected to benefit from 500 to 1500 mg/d of omega-3 fatty acids, but the fatty acid or "essential" fatty acid content in a capsule usually is only 20 to 35% of the whole. So, it may take three or four 1000-mg soft-gel capsules to provide 1000 mg of omega-3 fatty acids. And the DHA is only a fraction of the omega-3 content, 30 to 50% in most supplement products. Thus, three 1000-mg soft-gel omega-3 fatty acid capsules usually provide about 300-500 mg of DHA.

Adverse Reactions to Fatty Acid Supplements?

Adverse reactions to fatty acid supplements are uncommon, and are usually related to spoilage. Break open a capsule and smell it. It should have a fresh, "nutty" aroma. If it smells rancid, toss out the lot. Also, always check the expiration date or "best if used before" date on fatty acid/essential oil packaging. Keep it refrigerated before and after opening.

Giving too much at one time can cause intestinal or bowel symptoms including gas for some individuals. Start with one capsule/day and work up to the desired amount. Be sure that taurine and glycine and lipase are being supplemented too.

References - Fatty Acids

1. Lehninger A *Biochemistry* 2nd Ed, Worth Publishers (1975) 28-36.
2. Deth RC *Molecular Origins of Human Attention* Kluwer (2003) 23-36, 142-145.
3. Murphy MG and Byczko Z "Effects of membrane polyunsaturated fatty acids on adenosine receptor function in intact N1E-115 neuroblastoma cells" *Biochem Cell Biol* 68 no.1 (1990) 392-395.
4. Murphy MG and Byczko Z "Further studies on the mechanism(s) of polyunsaturated fatty acids-mediated increases in intracellular cAMP formation..." *Neurochem Res* 17 no.11 (1992) 1069-1071.
5. Ottoboni F and Ottoboni A "Can attention deficit-hyperactivity disorder result from nutritional deficiency?" *J Am Phys & Surg* 8 no.2 (2003) 58-60.

6. Galli C, Marangoni F and Petroni A "Modulation of arachidonic acid metabolism in cultured rat astroglial cells by long-chain N-3 fatty acids" in Bazan, Murphy and Toffano eds. *Neurobiology of Essential Fatty Acids* Adv. Exp.Med.& Biol. Vol.318 Plenum Press (1992) 117.

7. Komatsu W, Isihara K et al. "Docosahexaenoic acid suppresses nitric oxide production and induceable nitric oxide synthase..." Free Radical Biol Med 34 no.8 (2003) 1006-1016

8. Stoll AL "Omega-3 Fatty Acids in Autism" presentation at DAN! 2002 Boston MA May 2002, Conference Syllabus 26-43.

9. Stoll AL and Hardy PM "Omega-3 Fatty Acids in the Pathophysiology and Treatment of Autism" Presentation at DAN! 2001 Atlanta GA, May 2001.

10. Martin DW, Mayes PA *Harper's Review of Biochemistry* 20th ed, Lange Med Pub (1985) 622-629.

MELATONIN

- **Formation of melatonin requires methylation of serotonin by SAM.**
- **Melatonin helps regulate circadian rhythm, sleep, intestinal motility, and antioxidant chemistry, and it upregulates phosphorylation of vitamin B_6.**
- **Melatonin has the highest benefit score for any single oral nutrient reported by parents to ARI – helping 58% of autistics.**

Melatonin is a hormone-like substance that the body makes, by methylation, from serotonin. Many parents of autistics have reported that just one or two milligrams per day have helped their autistic child with sleep and behavior. It has one of the very best parent response scores for a single nutrient supplement (58% improved with it!).

About Melatonin

Melatonin is a neurohormone that is made in the pineal gland from serotonin. A neurohormone is a natural body chemical that signals the nervous system to do something. Formation of melatonin occurs by adding an acetyl group to serotonin (from acetyl coenzyme A) and then methylation of acetylserotonin by SAMe.[1] Most melatonin is formed during the day, and it is released from the pineal gland at night. Melatonin supplies are dependent upon those of serotonin and upon the methylation process.

Serotonin, also a hormone, comes from the essential amino acid tryptophan, and tryptophan uses two cofactors to become serotonin: biopterin and pyridoxal phosphate (from vitamin B_6). Biopterin is a cofactor needed for metabolism of phenylalanine, tyrosine and tryptophan, and it is made in body cells from the nucleotide GTP. Once formed, serotonin can influence a number of body processes. In the blood, it can act as a vasoconstrictor – an agent that decreases the diameter of blood vessels. In the central nervous system, serotonin is an inhibitory or calming neurotransmitter associated with neurons in the back part of the brain that extend both to the forebrain and down to the spinal column. Serotonin, also called 5-hydroxytryptamine or "5-HT," moves in and out of the neuronal synapse to effect chemical signaling or message transfer for this kind of cell. When serotonin is insufficient in the central nervous systems of mammals, hunger, anxiety, and insomnia may result. There is little if any interchange between the serotonin in blood, most of which is formed in the abdominal tissues, and serotonin in the brain. The blood pool and the brain pool cannot compensate for each other's insufficiency or excess. In fact, blood and brain levels may be opposite to one another if the tryptophan supply is depleted by making lots of serotonin in abdominal tissues. This might happen if the body is trying to constrict capillary blood flow from the intestines because there is intestinal dysbiosis and toxicity. In the autistic spectrum, there is a significant subgroup with abnormal serotonin levels, and this can directly affect melatonin supplies.

One published study with rats shows that melatonin in abdominal tissues influences gastrointestinal functions.[2] It increases the movement (intestinal motility) of the digesting food mass in the gastrointestinal tract. One mechanism for this is thought to be modulation of the motility effects of cholecystokinin, and melatonin is said to help coordinate the process of digestion.[2] Cholecystokinin is a sulfated intestinal hormone; it is postulated by Dr. Rosemary Waring to have subnormal function in some autistics.[3]

Melatonin is considered to be a regulator of human circadian rhythm. It can induce sleep when other influences for sleep are inadequate.[4] Melatonin can cause phase shifts in the body's daily clock that sets times for sleep and wakefulness. This leads to the concept of using melatonin to counter insomnia. One possible mechanism for this is sensitization of adenylate cyclase, which melatonin does in certain cells of the pituitary gland.[5,6] Cellular perception often depends upon adenylate cyclase which is an enzyme that participates in message processing by cells. Melatonin also is reported to influence tissue and organ activity via G-protein-coupled receptors.[7]

There is also a report that melatonin upregulates the enzyme pyridoxal kinase in brain tissue.[8] This is the enzyme that forms pyridoxal phosphate or pyridoxine phosphate from pyridoxal or pyridoxine. Pyridoxal 5-phosphate is the active coenzyme form of vitamin B_6; see chapter on Vitamin B_6. Phosphorylation of pyridoxine is the step that Dr. Audhya found to be very slow in autistics.

Finally, there are literature reports of antioxidant and anti-cytokine activity of melatonin.[9,10] A cytokine is a protein or peptide that is released from inflamed tissue, and tumor-necrosis-factor alpha (TNF-α) is a cytokine that may be elevated in autism. TNF-α may cause decreased sulfation capability.[11] Melatonin helps to regulate the expression of antioxidant enzyme genes.[12] It protects against lipid peroxidation by hydrogen peroxide,[13] and it scavenges the hydroxyl radical[11] (as does vitamin C) which means that melatonin helps to protect DNA from oxidant attack. Melatonin is considered by some to be an antioxidant vitamin.[14] Of course, it's a vitamin only to those who cannot make enough of it in their own bodies, and this group appears to include a majority of autistic spectrum individuals.

Using Melatonin in Autism

These observations and the relationship of serotonin to melatonin are important for two reasons. There is a historical finding that about 20% of autistics have high levels of serotonin in blood, while a small percentage, perhaps 5%, have low blood serotonin. Currently, these percentages are uncertain because they predate the autism increase that began in the 1980s. Most important, melatonin has the highest "got better" response of all individual nutritional supplements.

Melatonin, Parent Responses to ARI n= 573 (ARI Pub. 34/March 2005)

Behavior or Traits Improved 61%	No Discernible Effect 30%	Behavior or Traits Worsened 8%

The daily amount of supplemental melatonin is small, typically one or two milligrams taken one hour before bedtime. Parents of autistic children usually report improved sleep with melatonin: less insomnia, decrease or elimination of crying at night, and less daytime irritability.

If you've done some laboratory tests to assess nutritional status, you may have gotten results that are consistent with an expected benefit from melatonin as a nutritional supplement. Laboratory test results considered to be consistent with melatonin providing some benefit are:

- Deficient methionine per plasma or urine amino acid analysis.
- Deficient tryptophan per plasma amino acid analysis.
- Deficient or elevated tryptophan per urine amino acid analysis. Elevated urine tryptophan often indicates urinary wasting. It can also indicate deficient processing of tryptophan into its various metabolites, including serotonin.
- Elevated urine indolylacryloylglycine ("IAG"). This is a small peptide that can result from tryptophan that is not properly digested and absorbed from the small intestine.
- Abnormal (deficient or excessive) serotonin in whole blood or blood platelets.
- Biopterin or tetrahydrobiopterin deficiency, elevated phenylalanine in blood or urine, or PKU.

Also consistent with need for melatonin and maybe serotonin are insomnia, irregular sleep patterns and persistent bouts of night crying.

Adverse Response to Melatonin?

Melatonin has powerful hormonal effects and is taken up from blood circulation by all body tissues including the brain.[15] But when its effects are no longer called for, the body has to dispose of it. That's done by adding a hydroxyl group (-OH) to the carbon at "position 6" of the molecule ("6-hydroxylation" in the parlance of chemistry). Hydroxylated melatonin is then sulfated or conjugated by glucuronic acid.[15]

Tsuchiya and Hayashi, in researching liver chemistry and detoxication in autism, have discovered and published that 6-hydroxylation does not work well in autistics.[16] And, of course, sulfation can be subnormal per the research of Rosemary Waring et al.[17,18] Most likely, adverse responses by autistics to melatonin are attributable to problems with maintaining balanced amounts and getting rid of unwanted amounts efficiently. The most common complaint is disturbed sleep patterns instead of better quality sleep. If your child or patient doesn't do well with melatonin, discontinue it, or try time-release formulations.

References – Melatonin

1. Rodwell VC "Conversion of Amino Acids to Specialized Products," in Murray et al., eds, *Harper's Biochemistry*, 25th ed (2000), 342-354.

2. Delagrange P et al. "Therapeutic perspectives for melatonin agonists and antagonists" *J.Neuroendocrinology* 15 no.4 (2003) 442-448.

3. Waring RH and LV Klovrza "Sulfur metabolism in autism" *J.Nutrtitional & Environ.Med* 10 (2000) 25-32.

4. Cajochen C K Krauchi and A Wirz-Justice "Role of melatonin in the regulation of human circadian rhythm" *J.Neuroendocrinology* 15 no.4 (2003) 432-437.

5. Lincoln GA, H Andersen and D Hazlerigg "Clock genes and the long-term regulation of prolactin secretion..." *J.Neuroendocrinology* 15 no.4 (2003) 390-397.

6. Barrett P, C Schuister et al. "Sensitization: a mechanism for melatonin action in the pars tuberalis" *J.Neuroendocrinology* 15 no.4 (2003) 415-421.

7. Johnston JD et al. "Gonadotrophin-releasing hormone drives melatonin receptor..." *Proceedings, Nat. Acad.Sci* (USA) 100 no.5 (2003) 2831-2835.

8. Anton-Tay "Pineal-brain relationships" in Wolstenholme and Knigt, eds, *The Pineal Gland*, Churchill Livingston, London (1971) 213-237.

9. Bonilla A et al. "Melatonin increases interleukin-1beta and decreases tumor necrosis factor alpha..." *Neurochemistry Research* 28 no.5 (2003) 681-686.

10. Saski M et al. "Melatonin reduces TNF-☐ induced expression of MAdCAM-1 via inhibition of NF-Kappa B" Brit Med.Coll *Gastroenterology* 2 no.1 (2002).9.

11. Waring R "Disordered transsulfuration in autism" Proceedings of DAN! Fall 2002 Conference, San Diego, Oct 26, 2002.

12. Mayo JC et al. "Melatonin regulation of antioxidant enzyme gene expression" *Cell Mol.Life Sci* 59 no.10 (2002) 1706-1713.

13. Mayo JC et al. "Protection against oxidative protein damage..." *Biochim. Biophys. Acta* 1620 no. 1-3 (2003) 139-150.

14. Tan DX et al. "Melatonin: a hormone, a tissue factor, a paracoid and an antioxidant vitamin" *J.Pineal Research* 34 no.1 (2003) 75-78.

15. Rodwell VW *Harper's Biochemistry* 25th ed op.cit. 354.

16. Tsuchiya H and T Hayashi "A possible link between beta-carboline metabolism and infantile autism" *Medical Hypotheses* 55 no.3 (2000) 215-217.

17. O'Reilly BA and RH Waring "Enzyme and sulphur oxidation deficiencies in autistic children with known food/chemical intolerances" RH Waring Ph.D., Dept of Biochemistry, Birmingham University, Edgbaston, Birmingham UK.

18. Waring RH and JM Ngong "Sulphate metabolism in allergy-induced autism – relevance to the disease aetiology" RH Waring Ph.D., Dept of Biochemistry, Birmingham University, Edgbaston, Birmingham UK.

MULTIVITAMIN/MINERAL COMBINATION PRODUCTS

Previously, I described a number of single nutrients that can be very beneficial to many autistics per the experience of clinicians and parents. All of these can usually be used to good advantage in early stages of intervention. Also, there is a long-standing product for autism that enhances vitamin B_6 coenzyme function that is a combination supplement – "NuThera" or "Super NuThera." This product is a combination of nutrients that assist vitamin B_6 biochemically, and B_6 itself is present in relatively high amounts. These supplements, the single nutrients and Super

NuThera, are focused supplements – focused on a nutrient that has a track record for helping to alleviate autistic traits and/or inappropriate behaviors.

There are also general nutritional supplements, those that include all or most all of the vitamins, essential elements (minerals) and perhaps other supporting nutrients. While focused supplements usually contain relatively large amounts of the key nutrient of interest, general nutritional supplements contain many nutrients in smaller amounts. Sometimes general nutritional supplements contain amounts that are close to RDA or DRI (daily reference intake) levels, and sometimes they have higher but intermediate amounts. Often, there is additional benefit to using a general supplement – a multiple vitamin and mineral or "one-a-day" type supplement – in addition to the focused nutrients described previously. There are a number of these now available and suggested for autistics. Which works best depends strictly on the individual. Only trials can determine which one or ones do the best job as a general supporting supplement. As a rule, autistics do better with complete nutritional support, with the exception that some nutrients may already be high or imbalanced – copper and folate for example. If one nutritional objective is to normalize a high copper/zinc status, then it would be better to not have much or any copper in the supporting general supplement.

ARI does not have parent response statistics for general nutritional supplements of any brand. Your choice in this matter should be made solely on how much it helps the person in your care. Usually, these kinds of supplements are best tolerated with meals and the meal usually chosen is breakfast.

PROBIOTICS

> - **In the war against dysbiotic gut flora, probiotics can provide both mop-up and occupation functions that promote healthy conditions.**
> - **One species, Saccharomyces boulardii, is a hired gun that exterminates other yeast; afterward, it leaves.**
> - **Lactobacillus rhamnosis is particularly beneficial, but efficacious formulations require refrigeration.**
> - **Watch out for casein in probiotics formulations.**
> - **Probiotics won't implant and flourish, and only large daily doses will show beneficial effects, if prerequisites haven't been attended to: food intolerances, maldigestion, constipation, pancreatic dysfunction (intestinal acidity), deficient biliary function.**

One reason for dietary intervention in autism is to reduce the amount of undigested food that otherwise finds its way to the lower small intestine and the large bowel. Undigested food in these locations promotes dysbiosis – the growth of abnormal and sometimes pathogenic flora. Intestinal dysbiosis leads to mucosal inflammation, increased gut permeability, and entry of toxins and peptides to the bloodstream. Following the biomedical options that Dr. Baker presented in the previous section of this report, prescriptive medicinals will most likely be required to kill off the dysbiotic flora. Little of this initial cleanup work can be done by supplementing friendly flora, with the exception of Saccharomyces boulardii, which is a yeast killer. Good-guy flora and dysbiotic, bad-guy flora are both killed by most antibiotics. The purpose of friendly flora supplements (probiotics) is to repopulate the gut with the good guys. If beneficial flora implant and flourish, then they can help keep the pathogens at bay.

About Probiotics

There are many types of probiotics organisms, species, subspecies and "strains" that you will encounter if you dig into the kinds of probiotics supplements that are sold by nutritional supply houses. It is way beyond the scope of this report to describe the characteristics of all the probiotics organisms that are sold. Instead, I will mention a select few and discuss some of the general characteristics that you should be looking for in a really beneficial type or brand. The important message is that probiotics usually are needed continuously, like digestive enzymes, and they are always a good option after treating dysbiosis with antibiotics or powerful herbals.

First, you must realize that probiotic organisms are sold in a dormant state with some included, supporting nutrients. The hope is that they will grow and multiply in the autistic's intestinal tract. But implanting, growth and multiplying depend upon gut conditions. If pancreatic or biliary functions are poor and the pH conditions of the lower small intestine or large bowel are abnormal, there may be no growth or multiplication. If the diet is wrong, if there are too many active food allergies, if the pancreas doesn't put enough bicarbonate into the chyme, if bile synthesis is disordered, etc., then no brand of probiotics may flourish. When such intestinal problems are present the individual may show benefit from 25 to 50 billion or so live, colony-forming-units (CFU) taken daily, while 5 billion or so is of little benefit. And virtually no live probiotics colonies can be cultured from the stool specimens of such individuals. This happens all too frequently with autistics, and hype about changing brands is just that – hype. The prerequisite care and interventions for normalizing intestinal processes, described by Dr. Baker, are essential to growing a friendly, beneficial flora in the gut.

Next, probiotics flora have a "shelf life" – they're dying off daily in the jar whether refrigerated or not (refrigeration helps considerably but doesn't stop this). Beware of brands that "don't require refrigeration." My experiences with these have been most disappointing for autistics. Such non-refrigerated types often exclude some of the most beneficial flora, such as Lactobacillus rhamnosis. And many have low counts of live CFUs when tested independently. So, keep the jar refrigerated and purchase a good brand (one that needs refrigeration) to start with.

Finally, probiotics in autism are for establishment and maintenance of healthy gut flora and for gut healing after some prerequisite interventions are accomplished. These interventions are: diet changes if necessary, use of digestive enzymes, use of some basic nutrients that improve bowel regularity (magnesium, vitamin C), treatment for intestinal dysbiosis, and perhaps more extensive interventions by a qualified gastroenterologist. Often, in autism, probiotics alone cannot alleviate the initial dysbiosis because they cannot implant and multiply in the diseased intestine, which is why they are so often "deficient" initially per stool analysis. The only exception to this problem is S. boulardii which kills other yeast without implanting or colonizing in gut mucosal tissue.

If gut conditions allow implantation and growth, can probiotics help alleviate remaining food reactivities and gut inflammation? Yes. Frequently-referenced studies by Finnish clinicians showed that a type of Lactobacillus given regularly to infants with food allergy alleviated the allergic symptoms and intestinal inflammation.[1,2]

Does it matter if a probiotics strain has been grown on dairy products or casein? Yes, if the objective is to eliminate dairy products, casein and casomorphins peptides from the diet, and to stop allergic responses to milk. Lactose intolerance alone is unlikely to be an issue because that intolerance is typically a matter of quantity, and only a tiny amount of lactose comes from probiotics grown on dairy products. However, tiny amounts of protein (casein) can provoke allergic responses, and produce enough casomorphins peptides to cause neurotransmitter problems in some autistics. Probiotic organisms consume and process food in order to grow and multiply. If a given probiotic strain can be cultured on milk, or if it ferments milk, then products containing it may or may not be dairy-free. This is because branded product versions of that strain may be manufactured by growing it on other materials (not dairy). If a strain or product cannot be cultured in milk and cannot ferment it, then it's probably dairy-free in its manufacture. Lactobacillus acidophilus may or may not be dairy-free. Lactobacillus rhamnosis doesn't have to be grown in dairy product broth, yet it will ferment lactose.

What's so good about probiotics; what do they actually do? According to the experts, they can do the following:

- **They predigest food molecules (sugars and proteins) that may be difficult for us to deal with.**[3] Lactose, for example, is converted to glucose and galactose by lactobacilli.

- **They synthesize some vitamins for us; pantothenate and biotin are important examples.**[4] If lactobacilli act on milk, cheese, or yogurt (which some autistics must avoid) they can make riboflavin, niacin, pyridoxine, folate and B_{12}.[5]

- **Antinutritional substances in some foods can be reduced in quantity by certain probiotics strains.**[6] Trypsin-inhibitor in soy, phytate in grains and some oligosaccharides that cause intestinal discomfort are examples.

- **Some lactobacilli and bifidobacteria can make antibiotic-like substances that don't hurt them but do inhibit the growth of various dysbiotic flora and food-borne pathogens.**[7,8]

- **There is considerable evidence that probiotic flora reduce intestinal toxicity by reducing bacterial beta-glucuronidase. Too much beta-glucuronidase can release toxic substances from their detoxified form. Connections between probiotics and inhibition of carcinogenesis have been made.**[9,10,11]

Using Probiotics in Autism

There are five probiotics organisms that I believe are particularly beneficial to maintaining intestinal health in autism. Other, unmentioned species may also be beneficial, but these five are usually required.

Saccharomyces boulardii is a yeast that kills other yeast such as Candida.[12,13] S. boulardii is a subspecie type of Saccharomyces cerevisiae, which has been described as a yeast killer system.[14,15,16] Gastrointestinal examinations by several experienced gastroenterologists conclude that the occurrence of yeast overgrowth in untreated autistics does not exceed that of healthy control children.[13,17] But this is a moot point if the digestive disaccharidase enzyme trehalase is weak – as has been demonstrated for other digestive disaccharidases in autistics (lactase, maltase, sucrase/isomaltase/palatinase). Trehalose, a sugar, comes from yeast and fungi, and it needs to be digested.[18] While trehalase has not been clinically assayed by intestinal biopsy for autistics, this has been proposed to clinical researchers (by me). If this enzyme is weak, as are other disaccharidases,[19,20] then a normal amount of intestinal yeast will produce abnormally high levels of undigested trehalose. One solution is to reduce the intestinal yeast level to below what is considered normal (below 1000 CFU per gram of feces as measured by stool analysis). This can be done by occasional or periodic use of S. boulardii as an oral probiotic. We do not recommend continual daily use of billion-plus amounts. Effective, as-needed amounts depend on the individual and whether potential yeast-fostering nutrients or supplements are also being used and how much. Yeast-fostering substances include alpha-lipoic acid, DMSA, cysteine, cystine and N-acetylcysteine, and sometimes glutathione. Sometimes S. boulardii at 2 billion CFU per day is needed, sometimes 2 billion, 3x per day, is needed. Please refer to Dr. Baker's comments for more information on use. S. boulardii comes from a form of baker's yeast; the bottle needs to be refrigerated; and it does not colonize well in the human intestine. It does its hatchet job on other yeast and then leaves. S. boulardii is killed by antifungals like Diflucan or Sporonox, so don't use it along with medicinal antifungals.

Lactobacillus rhamnosis is very similar to the famous "Lactobacillus GG" that is sold under the "Culturelle™" brand name. Pure L. rhamnosis need not contain any casein or dairy products. L. rhamnosis was the "DDS#1" strain of Dr. Khem Shahani and the University of Nebraska Department of Dairy Science.[21] For many years, it was considered to be a dairy-free subtype of Lactobacillus acidophilus, and for awhile after that it was named "L. caseii." Given near-normal intestinal conditions, L. rhamnosis implants and colonizes with a vengeance in the mucosa of the lower part of the small intestine. (Some claim that it colonizes in almost the entire small intestine.) This would be an individual happenstance that depends on local conditions throughout the small intestine. L. rhamnosis does produce antibiotic-like substances that inhibit growth of some pathogenic flora, so it helps maintain a population of beneficial gut flora. It grows on sugars such as rhamnose (which L. caseii does not), galactose, fructose, lactose, maltose and glucose.[22] Rhamnosis is very acid-resistant and survives normal stomach acidity on its own. In fact, enteric-coating a rhamnosis supplement makes its usefulness dependent on normal pancreatic function – something that can be very questionable in many autistics. L. rhamnosis should be one of the first probiotics used after antibiotic therapy. Daily amounts of 10 to 20 billion CFU can be beneficial initially and may be needed as long as intestinal conditions cannot be adequately normalized. Once normalized, lesser amounts should be adequate. Keep this one refrigerated.

Lactobacillus acidophilus is the "old reliable" in the world of probiotics. But if avoidance of dairy/casein is an objective, ask the vendor or manufacturer for a statement that the product is dairy-free. L. acidophilus produces acidophilin,[23] a broad-spectrum antimicrobial that works against pathogens that might be in food. Like rhamnosis, acidophilus has been observed to decrease or stop diarrhea due to dysbiotic flora. L. acidophilus can implant in the mucous membranes of the mouth, throat and small intestine. In women, it can grow in and protect the vaginal tract. Some strains require refrigeration; some do not. Regardless, refrigerating it will preserve its potency longer. Most strains are quite acid stable, and like rhamnosis, survive normal stomach conditions.

Bifidobacter bifidum (also called Bifidobacter lactis) is thought to produce a natural antibiotic similar to acidophilin, but B. bifidum colonizes in the large bowel below where acidophilus grows. So. L. acidophilus and B. bifidum complement each other with respect to location and antimicrobial functions. Bifidobacterium anaerobes have been found to predominate in the colon of healthy infants who are breast-fed and much less so for infants who are not.[24] Bifidobacteria help to balance the acid-base balance in the bowel. While bacterial action and putrefaction can produce ammonia, which is basic (high pH), B. bifidum reduces putrefaction and produces short-chain organic acids (acetic, lactic) which lower the pH.[25,26] Obviously, there needs to be a balance between these and other processes so that bowel pH remains within healthy limits. B. bifidum (or lactis) can be grown in a dairy-product broth, or it can be dairy-free and grown in a broth of sugars such as dextrose. Refrigeration may or may not be required for this one; refer to the product label. But again, refrigerating can help shelf life whether specified or not.

Streptococcus thermophilus is the fifth usually-needed probiotics organism. This good-guy bacterium does not implant and colonize in the human GI tract, but it helps the others do so, and it helps digestion, particularly of milk and dairy products.[27,28] Not all autistics need to avoid dairy for reasons of allergy or casomorphin peptide problems. But about 60% of autistics have some "degree" of lactose intolerance and the "degree" is a quantity issue. Some might tolerate one glass of milk per day but not three or four. S. thermophilus makes lactase, the enzyme that digests lactose. S. thermophilus (and another bacterium, Lactobacillus bulgaricus) are used to make yogurt, so thermophilus is in the food supply and has been for a long time. When thermophilus gobbles up lactose, it produces lactic acid, which usually improves the intestinal environment for Acidophilus and Bifidobacter. A clinical study published in Thailand documented prevention of diarrhea in infants by B. bifidum and S. thermophilus when used together.[28] This combination was postulated to prevent rotavirus from causing gastroenteritis and formula milk from causing diarrhea due to lactose intolerance.

Adverse Responses to Probiotics?

Despite our intention to use most probiotics for healing and maintenance of intestinal health, these organisms can displace other (dysbiotic) or pathogenic flora. Toxins from their die-off can evoke symptoms, and one course of remedial action is use of oral activated charcoal. This is especially true for Streptomyces boulardii, the "hired gun" for purposely exterminating yeast and fungi. Die-off symptoms from its use are expected. Symptoms of headache, hyperactivity, temporary diarrhea, stimming and irritability are not uncommon but should resolve in a week or so if intestinal dysbiosis is the problem.

Sometimes, the "dose" is too high and the die-off can be made more gradual and tolerable with use of fewer capsules per day or a fractional capsule. Most powdered probiotics in gelatin capsules can be spread on food, and a third or half of a capsule may be plenty to start with.

Other problems could arise from the stabilizing nutrients and additives in a particular brand of probiotics. If milk allergy is a problem, double check the dairy-free aspects of the brand you are using. Sometimes just changing the brand does the trick.

References – Probiotics

1. Majumaa H and Isolauri E "Probiotics: a novel approach in the management of food allergy" *J.Allergy Clin Immunol* 99 no.2 (1997) 179-185.
2. Salminen S, Isolauri E and Salminen E "Clinical uses of probiotics for stabilizing the gut mucosal barrier: successful strains and future challenges" *Autonie van Leeuwenhoek* (Kluwer) 70 (1996) 347-358.
3. Friend BA and Shahani KM "Nutritional and therapeutic aspects of lactobacilli" *J.Appl.Nutrition* 26 no.2 (198r)125-153.
4. Harper HA, Rodwell VW and Mayes PA *Review of Physiological Chemistry* 17th ed, Lang Med Pub (1979) 169, 171
5. Friend BA and Shahani KM, op.cit. 128.
6. Friend BA and Shahani KM ibid. 128-129.
7. Babel FJ "Antibiosis by lactic culture bacteria" *J. Dairy Science* 60 (1977) 815-821.

8. Friend BA and Shahani KM op.cit. 129.

9. Goldin BR, Swanson L et al. "Effect of diet and L. acidophilus supplements on human fecal bacterial enzymes" *J. National Cancer Inst.* 64 (1980) 255-262.

10. Marteau P, Pochart P et al. "Effect of chronic ingestion of a fermented dairy product containing Lactobacillus acidophilus and Bifidobacterium bifidum on metabolic activities of the colonic flora in humans" *Am.J.Clin Nutrition* 52 (1990) 685-688.

11. Friend BA and Shahani KM op.cit. 130-133.

12. Berg R, Bernasconi P et al. "Inhibition of Candida albicans translocation from the gastrointestinal tract of mice by oral administration of Saccharomyces boulardii" *J.Infect Dis* 168 no.5 (1993) 1314-1318.

13. Elmer GW, Surawicz CM, McFarland LV "Biotherapeutic agents. A neglected modality for the treatment and prevention of selected intestinal and vaginal infections." *JAMA* 276 (1) (1996 July 3) 29-31.

14. Mitterdorfer G, Mayer HK et al. "Clustering of Saccharomyces boulardii strains within the specie cerevisiae using molecular typing techniques" *J.Appl.Microbiol* 93 no.4 (2002) 521-530.

15. Van der Aa, Kuhle A and Jesperson L "The taxonomic position of Saccharomyces boulardii..." *Sys.Appl.Microbiol.*26 no.4 (2003) 564-571.

16. Magliani W, Conti S et al. "Yeast Killer Systems" *Clin.Microbiol.Revs* 10 (July 1997) 369-400.

17. Horvath K and Papadimitriou "Gastrointestinal abnormalities in children with autistic disorder" *J.Pediatrics* 135 no.5 (1999) 559-563 (see p. 562).

18. Rosseneu SLM, van Saene HKF, et al. "Aerobic throat and gut flora in children with autistic spectrum disorder and gastrointestinal symptoms" *Proceedings DAN! Conference*, Fall 2003, Autism Research Institute, October 3, 2003, Science Session Syllabus 63-70.

19. Semenza G, Salvatore A and Mantei N "Small-intestinal disaccharidases" Chapt.75 in Scriver et al. *The Metabolic and Molecular Bases of Inherited Disease* 8th ed, vol. 1 (2001) 16223-1650 (see 1630).

20. Horvath K and Papadimitrious op.cit. 562.

21. Horvath K and Perman JA "Autistic disorder and gastrointestinal disease" *Curr Opinion in Pediatrics* 14 (2002) 583-587.

22. Verbal statement made by Professor Khem Shahani to Claire Farr of Klaire Laboratories and to me, 1994. Subsequently stated as such in Klaire Laboratories product catalogs.

23. "Lactobacillus rhamnosis" in *Rosell's Probiotics Update*, referenced information pamphlet, 1997 edition, The Rosell Institute, Inc. 8480 St. Laurent, Montreal, Canada H2P 2M6.

24. Friend BA and Shahani KM, op.cit. 129.

25. Saavedra JM, Bauman NA et al. "Feeding of Bifidobacterium bifidum and Streptococcus thermophilus to infants in hospital for prevention of diarrhoea and shedding of rotavirus" *The Lancet* 344 Oct. 15, 1994 1046-1049.

26. Langendries JB, Detry J et al. "Effect of a fermented infant formula containing viable Bifidobacteria on the fecal flora composition and pH of healthy full-term infants" *J. Pediatric Gastroenter Nutr* 21 (1995) 177-181.

27. "Bifidobacteria" in *Rosell's Probiotics Update*, 1997, op.cit.

28. Saavedra JM, Bauman NA et al. op.cit.

29. Nopchinda S et al. "Effect of bifidobacterium Bb 12 with or without Streptococcus thermophilus supplemented formula on nutritional status" *J Med Assoc Thai* 2002 Nov; 85 Suppl.4: S1225-31.

SECTION FIVE: NUTRITIONAL SUPPLEMENTS FOR AUTISM

VITAMIN B_{12}

> - Vitamin B_{12}, cobalamin, participates in two metabolic processes in humans. One, methylation of homocysteine to make methionine, is of great concern in autism.
>
> - Oxidant stress and limited supply of 5-methyltetrahydrofolate can expose cobalamin to oxidation.
>
> - It's the making of methylcobalamin that is hurt by toxic elements and thimerosal, but this can be circumvented by administering methylcobalamin.

Vitamin B_{12} is called cobalamin because the element cobalt is located at the center of its activity. Decades ago it was known as anti-pernicious anemia factor; B_{12} deficiency may cause pernicious anemia. That disease features gastrointestinal disturbances and deficient red blood cells, which are also malformed. Lack of intrinsic factor can be causative; it participates in absorption of B_{12} and is secreted by the gastric mucosa. Since the 1920s when vitamin B_{12} was first isolated, then as "extrinsic factor," we've learned that insufficiencies can have many consequences other than anemia. These consequences depend upon what other metabolic weaknesses and predispositions or nutritional deficits are present.

About Vitamin B_{12}

Vitamin B_{12} exists in several chemical forms in body tissues. It is stored in the lysosomes of cells as hydroxocobalamin, also called hydroxycobalamin or B_{12a}. In this form, cobalt is at the +3 oxidation state. This is not an active, coenzyme form of the vitamin. Upon signaling for its need, hydroxocobalamin (OHCbl) is secreted from the lysosomes and combined temporarily with glutathione, forming glutathionylcobalamin (GSCbl). This occurs in the cytosol of cells.[1] GSCbl then can stay in the cytosol where cobalamin +2 or B_{12r} is delivered to the methionine synthase enzyme complex, or it can enter a mitochondrion where it is processed further into adenosylcobalamin. In human metabolism, we know of only two coenzyme uses of cobalamin: (1) adenosylcobalamin for processing methylmalonate into succinate, and (2) methylcobalamin for processing homocysteine into methionine.[2] With autism, we are primarily concerned with how cobalamin supports the function of methionine synthase (MS), an enzyme that methylates homocysteine.

The methionine synthase (MS) complex exists in two general forms, one with three enzyme-assisting domains and one with four domains. We're not sure about the tissue distribution of these, but we know that the liver contains at least the four-domain version.[3] To see what happens to cobalamin in the four-domain MS, let's continue with the GSCbl molecule that's in the cytosol. Suppose MS needs a "new" Cbl because its old one is ruined beyond repair. When our GSCbl molecule arrives at MS, it gets reduced to Cbl+1 by the methionine synthase reductase (MS reductase) part; glutathione departs the scene. Then the S-adenosylmethionine-(SAM)-binding domain of MS methylates Cbl+1 to make methylcobalamin, MeCbl+2. When homocysteine (Hcy) arrives at MS, the active site catalyzes the transfer of the methyl group from MeCbl+2 to Hcy forming methionine (Met). Cobalamin is left, bound to its domain on MS as Cbl+1. From then on, 5-methyltetrahydrofolate (5-MeTHF) delivers methyls to the Cbl domain of MS, and those methyls are used to make Met from Hcy.

[Diagram: Lysosome OHCbl → (GSH, H₂O) → GSCbl → Cbl⁺¹ → MeCbl (via SAM→SAH); MeCbl/Cbl cycle with Met/Hcy and MeTHF/THF. Mitochondrion branch: reductase, ATP → P, Pi → AdenosylCbl.]

This process of methyl transfer repeats and repeats until, by accident or design, Cbl+1 gets oxidized to Cbl+2. As Cbl+2, it can't accept a methyl from 5-MeTHF. The oxidation occurs after Cbl has given away its methyl and before it gets a new one from 5-MeTHF. The two evident risk factors for oxidation of Cbl are oxidant stress and limited 5-MeTHF supply. Inflammation, oxidant stress and limited GSH predispose to oxidation, and phenotypically-weak methylene tetrahydrofolate reductase (MTHFR) predisposes to limited availability of 5-MeTHF.

Oxidized Cbl can be rescued by the MS reductase part of the enzyme complex.[3] Cbl+2 can be reduced back to Cbl+1, methylated once by SAM from the SAM-binding domain, and it's ready to go again. But when this happens, the SAM becomes S-adenosylhomocysteine, SAH. And if SAH is already high, as we know it is in at least 20% of autistics,[4] this rejuvenation-methylation of Cbl can be inhibited too. Of considerable importance is the possibility that oxidation of Cbl may not be an accident. It may occur by design and may involve some of the signaling molecules in oxidant stress and inflammation, such as TNF-α (tumor necrosis factor-alpha), or GSSG or hydrogen peroxide. Purposeful shutdown of Cbl methylation stops MS from making methionine from homocysteine. Instead, homocysteine is fed to the metabolic sequence that forms cysteine and GSH. The GSH is needed to combat the oxidant stress condition.

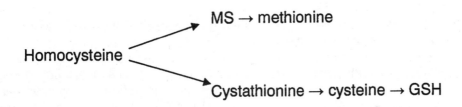

SECTION FIVE: NUTRITIONAL SUPPLEMENTS FOR AUTISM

What about the three-domain version of MS? That version lacks the SAM-binding domain, and it can't, by itself, repair oxidized Cbl. How it gets itself going is an area of ongoing research. MS must have MeCbl+2 from somewhere to do the first methylation of Hcy. Maybe that version can use 5-MeTHF initially, or it imports Cbl as MeCbl+2 – we don't know at this time.

What we do know is that several toxic substances inhibit MS by interfering with the cobalamin-processing part. Research by Professor Richard Deth's team at Northeastern University has demonstrated that exposure of the MS complex to mercury, thimerosal, lead, antimony, ethanol and other substances harms the enzyme's kinetics.[5] After such exposures, the enzyme can't do its job when cyanocobalamin or GSCbl is supplied. But it begins to work again when MeCbl is provided. This demonstrates analytically that delivery of reduced cobalamin and its methylation is the mechanism that's vulnerable to toxic inhibition.[3] We believe that's why methylcobalamin works so well in autism. Also, we now have more analytical evidence that Thimerosal is a neurotoxin that can cause depletion of glutathione, a condition consistent with methionine synthase inhibition.[6]

The FDA RDA and "Daily Value" for vitamin B_{12} is 6 micrograms for an adult.[7] The National Academy lists other B_{12} amounts: 0.7 mcg for ages 1-3, 1.0 mcg for ages 4-6, 1.4 mcg for ages 7-10, and 2 micrograms/d for humans over 11 years of age.[8,9] Usually, it is sold in a stabilized form, cyanocobalamin or CNCbl, and this form has to be changed in body tissues, probably via the glutathione mechanism, into either MeCbl or adenosylCbl. Vitamin B_{12} has very low toxicity, and oral and injectable doses of 1000 to 2000 mcg (1 to 2 mg per day) have no adverse effects.[10,11]

Animal food products are the natural dietary source of vitamin B_{12}. Except for bacteria and microorganism content, vegetables and plant foods are devoid of this vitamin.[12] Vegetarians may be low in B_{12} and vegans deficient, unless they use nutritional supplements. Proper gastrointestinal function is necessary for B_{12} absorption from the diet. In the stomach, free B_{12} is bound to intrinsic factor (IF, a glycoprotein). This protects the B_{12} itself from being digested. The B_{12}-IF couple finds receptor sites in the ileal region of the small intestine where they are separated and B_{12} is absorbed.[13] B_{12} has a peptide-like structure, and without IF, it would be partly disassembled. If this occurs, B_{12} deficiency is likely. Moreover, onset of such deficiencies can be insidious because B_{12} disappears slowly; its biological half-time in humans is about 400 days.[13]

The reduced, coenzyme forms of vitamin B_{12}, methyl and adenosylCbl, can be oxidized by nitrous oxide (anesthetic)[14] and are unstable in direct sunlight. In fact, the vitamin decomposes and chars when heated above 190°C (375°F).[15] Prolonged exposure to heat at temperatures below 190°C can also damage this vitamin, and the methyl and adenosyl forms are more fragile than cyanocobalamin.

Using Vitamin B_{12} in Autism

Vitamin B_{12}, primarily as injectable methylcobalamin, has been used to very good advantage. There are at least five reasons for this.

1. The ileal lymphoid nodular hyperplasia and inflammation discovered by Wakefield et al. disturbs the mucosal tissue in the ileum of the small intestine,[16,17] where B_{12}-intrinsic factor is supposed to bind with subsequent absorption of the B_{12} part. So, limited uptake of dietary B_{12} can be a consequence of this hyperplasia condition.

2. Glutathione in the active form, GSH, is subnormal in many autistics,[4] and metabolism of glutathione is abnormal also.[18,19] This probably limits the conversion of lysosomal B_{12} into its active, coenzyme forms.

3. In the autistic population, there is a higher-than-usual percentage of phenotypical variance for methylene tetrahydrofolate reductase (MTHFR).[20] This means that, proportionately, fewer autistics are able to efficiently convert 5,10-methylene THF to 5-methylTHF. And 5-methylTHF is what feeds the methyl to B_{12} for methionine synthase action. We also suspect and are investigating genomic problems with methionine synthase reductase. Subnormal activity of this would greatly increase need for supplemental, reduced cobalamin.

4. The alternate pathway for methylation of homocysteine is via betaine:homocysteine methyltransferase (BHMT):

$$TMG + homocysteine \xrightarrow{BHMT} DMG + methionine$$

A majority of tested autistics have variant genetic expression of BHMT per genomic analyses.[21] This increases the methylation burden of folate, B_{12} and methionine synthase.

5. Because adenosine is already high in at least 20% of tested autistics[22] and because it causes down-regulation of methylation, use of adenosylCbl is not advisable for those individuals.

When all of these concerns are combined, only methylcobalamin makes sense as a supplement. We advise waiting on use of high-dose oral methylcobalamin until diet and dysbiosis issues have been addressed because uptake is so dependent upon proper gastrointestinal function. This suggested restriction does not apply to injectable methyl Cbl. A doctor may wish to establish whether an autistic patient responds positively to methylCbl, which is an excellent indication that methylation is inhibited. Diet, digestion and dysbiosis must still be confronted whether methylCbl helps or not.

Dr. James Neubrander has pioneered injection of vitamin B_{12} as methylCbl. After exploring different dosing schedules, he has settled on 64.5 micrograms per Kg of body weight every third day.[23] This is not oral nutritional supplementation – it's a shot usually given by parents following detailed instructions from a medical doctor. See Dr. Sidney Baker's section of this report for more details. Also, Dr. Neubrander has a website: www.drneubrander.com.

Oral use of B_{12} as methylCbl can be done singly or in conjunction with a B-vitamin complex, a broad-spectrum nutritional supplement, or DMG or TMG. Gastrointestinal problems make oral methylCbl supplementation most effective after diet and dysbiosis problems have been addressed. And sometimes, a trip to the gastroenterologist is necessary to deal with more severe intestinal issues.

As expected, oral amounts that are effective can depend greatly on intestinal uptake. As of this writing, methylCbl is not widely available from nutritional supply houses. When available, it is packaged in gelatin capsules and as a powder to be mixed with food or drink. For those autistics or parents choosing oral methylCbl, I suggest using 2x to 3x the injectable therapeutic amount (daily equivalent) or about 40 to 60 mcg/Kg body weight per day. Often, it takes a lot of oral methylcobalamin to get the chemistry to work. If the autistic person is able to comply, absorption under the tongue is also effective. An appropriate oral trial dose is 20-40 mcg/Kg for five days.

Adverse Responses to Methylcobalamin or B_{12}?

The first question I always ask is: Were you giving taurine as an oral supplement? If not, go back and read the chapter on taurine.

Sometimes, DMG is needed. Methylcobalamin pulls homocysteine straight over to the methionine camp. Some homocysteine is meant to be reacted with TMG to produce DMG as well as methionine. Methyl B12 could be converting more of the homocysteine than it's entitled to. If DMG then goes low, folate metabolism will be impaired. So, DMG may be needed along with methylcobalamin. For a few, maybe TMG is needed. Sometimes, folate is needed in some form; usually, folinic acid works best. These needs are individual situations that are best decided by supplement trials.

Are you also trying to give methionine or SAM? Don't. If you want to know why, skip ahead to the chapter on methionine and S-adenosylmethionine.

Not every autistic needs methylcobalamin or any form of vitamin B_{12}. While MeCbl evidently has a very high benefit ratio (being compiled by ARI as I write this), it's certainly not 100%. So, if you didn't see the response you hoped for, there are many more biomedical options to try.

References - Vitamin B_{12}

1. Rosenblatt DS and Fenton WA Chapter 155 in Scriver et al. Eds *The Metabolic and Molecular Bases of Inherited Disease* 8th Ed McGraw-Hill (2001) 3912-3913.
2. Harper HA, Rodwell VW and Mayes PA *Review of Physiological Chemistry* 17th Ed Lange Med Pub (1979) 180.
3. Deth RC and Waly M "Effects of mercury on methionine synthase: implications for disordered methylation in autism" Spring DAN! 2004 Conference Syllabus, Washington DC, April 2004 73-86.
4. James SJ "Abnormal folate-dependent methionine and glutathione metabolism in children with autism..." Proceedings/Syllabus, Spring DAN! 2004 Conference, Washington DC (April 2004) 60.
5. Waly M, Olteanu H, Banerjee R et al. "Activation of methionine synthase by insulin-like growth factor-1 and dopamine: a target for neurodevelopmental toxins and Thimerosal" *Molec.Psych* 9 no.4 (2004) 358-370.
6. James SJ, Slikker W, Melnyk S, et al. "Thimerosal neurotoxicity is associated with glutathione depletion: protection with glutathione precursors" *Neurotoxicology* 26 (2005) 1-8.
7. *PDR for Nutritional Supplements* Thompson PDR, 1st Ed, (2001) 484.
8. NRC *Recommended Dietary Allowances* National Acad Press (1989) 285 (end foldout page).
9. *Drug Facts and Comparisons* Jan 2000 update, Facts & Comparisons. Walters Kluwer Health (2000) 4.
10. Sauberlich HE *Laboratory Tests for the Assessment of Nutritional Status* 2nd Ed CRC Press (1999) 147.
11. Rosenblatt DS and Fenton WA, op.cit 3922.
12. Sauberlich HE, op.cit. 139.
13. Harper HA et al. op.cit. 181.

14. Sauberlich HE, op.cit. 139-140.
15. Kutsky RJ *Handbook of Vitamins, Minerals and Hormones* 2nd Ed Van Nostrand Reinhold Co (1981) 244.
16. Wakefield AJ, March SH et al. "Ileal-lymphoid-nodular hyperplasia, non-specific colitis, and pervasive developmental disorder in children" *The Lancet* 351 (Feb 28, 1998) 637-641.
17. Wakefield AJ, Anthony A et al. "Enterocolitis in children with developmental disorders" *Am J Gastroenterology* 95 no.9 (2000) 2285-2294.
18. Pangborn JB "Detection of metabolic disorders in people with autism", Proceedings, Annual Meeting And Conference, NSAC, San Antonio TX (July 1984) 38-39.
19. Michelson AM, Chapter 17 in Autor AP Ed. *Pathology of Oxygen* Academic Press (1982) 278-279.
20. Boris M and Goldblatt A "The association of 5,10-methylenetetrahydrofolate reductase (MTHFR) gene polymorphisms with autistic spectrum disorders" Proceedings Fall DAN! 2004 Conference, Los Angeles (Oct 2004) 175-182.
21. Goldblatt A and Boris M. Verbal Report to DAN! Think Tank, New Orleans, Jan 2004.
22. James SJ op.cit. 60,61.
23. Neubrander JA "Biochemical context and clinical use of one specific member of the five-member vitamin B_{12} family, methyl-B_{12} (methylcobalamin)" Proceedings, Fall DAN! Conference, Los Angeles (Oct 2004) 279-280.

DIMETHYLGLYCINE (DMG)

- **DMG provides chemical parts needed for folate to do its many jobs.**
- **For autism, relatively high doses of DMG can have positive results for speech and eye contact; the data set is anecdotal but huge, n=5000.**
- **Start with low trial doses.**

Dimethylglycine is an amino acid that has helped thousands of autistic individuals when used at relatively high doses. In the body, dimethylglycine or DMG comes from betaine or TMG, and that comes from choline. But in autism, this process of DMG formation may be impeded, and that can cause folate metabolism to be imbalanced.

About DMG

DMG is the amino acid glycine with two attached methyls that can be given away. When DMG gives away the first methyl, it becomes sarcosine, and the donated methyl can add onto tetrahydrofolate (THF). Depending upon how the donation process works, the THF can become 5,10-methyleneTHF or it can become 10-formylTHF. 5,10-methyleneTHF and 10-formylTHF are special forms of folate that can provide carbon pieces needed for assembly of purines or purine nucleosides. These molecules lead to nucleotides such as phosphorylated adenosine (AMP, ADP, ATP) and phosphorylated guanosine (GMP, GDP, GTP). Nucleotides are required for cellular processing of information and cellular response (including immune response). Additionally, 5,10-methylene THF is needed for balanced pyrimidine metabolism; it allows uridine (as dUMP) to become thymidine (as dTMP). Fragile X syndrome may result if uridine is inhibited from becoming thymidine, and there are other genetic/metabolic faults that can result in fragility of the X chromosome besides 5,10-methyleneTHF deficiency.

The sarcosine that came from DMG can also give away a methyl to become glycine. That second methyl can also go to THF, forming either 5,10-methyleneTHF or 10-formylTHF. Furthermore, glycine itself can break apart and allow THF to become 5,10-methyleneTHF. Eventually, all that is left of the original DMG are bicarbonate and ammonium ions. So, disassembly of DMG provides chemical parts that are essential for folate metabolism. The special forms of folate that result are needed to construct the molecules of cellular perception and response – purines and pyrimidines. Also, methylated folate is needed by cobalamin and methionine synthase to process homocysteine into methionine, which becomes SAM. And SAM is needed to make creatine for cellular energy delivery. SAM also activates the dopamine D4 receptor system, which gets neuronal cells to pay attention to incoming signals. All of this is hindered if DMG is inadequate.

From published clinical research on DMG, we provide the following synopses or summaries:

- In a small population study (8 male autistics, 4 to 30 years of age), which was double-blinded and placebo-controlled, low-dose DMG supplementation in one-month trials did not significantly improve autistic traits as measured by several rating scales. However, the methodological weakness of "low dosage" and small sample size are acknowledged by the researchers.[1]

- In a larger trial (37 children, ages 3 to 11) including autistics and those with pervasive developmental disorder, both those on DMG and those on the placebo improved per two rating scales.[2]

- Animal studies of the gastric effects of oral DMG lead to the conclusion that it has antioxidant activity as a free radical scavenger and that it can protect gastric mucosal cells.[3]

- DMG has immunomodulating properties. In humans predosed with DMG and then exposed to streptokinase, leukocyte inhibition factor was notably decreased (PMN leukocytes are more active with DMG).[4] Note that streptokinase is one toxin that binds to CD26/DPP4 on the surface of lymphocytes in autistics.[5]

Using DMG in Autism

Many clinicians have reported elevations of folate in blood serum for some autistics. Irritability, hyperactivity and stimming are reported to increase when these same individuals supplement folate. In fact, reactivity to folic acid supplements is not uncommon in autism. Conjectured is a block or "trap" in folate metabolism, a situation where folate accumulates in some form because a needed helping nutrient, cofactor, or enzyme is inadequate. Also postulated is poor transport of folate from serum into cells with some anecdotal reports indicating low RBC folate. But when DMG is supplemented, we have a huge number of reports about reduced irritability, hyperactivity and stimming, and the beginnings of improvement in speech. In fact, improved behavior and/or speech is reported in over 40% of autistics per nearly 5000 parent responses to ARI.

To be effective, relatively large doses of DMG are needed, and these amounts vary considerably from individual to individual. Usually, DMG is provided in unit doses of 125 mg, in a capsule or tablet. Often at least three capsules or tablets are needed per day, and considerably more may be required to achieve maximum benefit. But the low-dose, trial amount should be what is listed below for a 20-Kg (44-Lb) individual. **Do not start DMG at high doses**.

The suggested continual dosage range for DMG is tabulated below, and even higher amounts may be beneficial and may be recommended by the attending physician. One parent reported, at a DAN! Conference, great success with 2000 mg/d (16 tablets over a 24-hour period) for a 15-year-old autistic.

Body Weight Kg / Lb	DMG Dose* Range, mg/d
20 44	125-375
30 66	190-560
40 88	250-750
50 110	300-900
60 132	375-1100
70+ 154+	450-1300

* This is approximately the dose range that corresponds to the Parent Tally statistics, below. More may be given if medically advised.

Dimethylglycine Parent Response Tally, Responses = 5153, ARI Publ.34/March 2005

Behavior or Traits Improved 42%	No Discernible Effect 51%	Behavior or Traits Worsened 7%

Adverse Response to DMG?

As tabulated above, seven out of 100 individuals on the autistic spectrum have "trouble" with DMG. This trouble usually is more stimming or hyperactivity. Biochemically, there are two circumstances that we know of that could cause problems. The first is that folate, as tetrahydrofolate, is insufficient or unable to accept and utilize the one-carbon chemical pieces that DMG provides. Supplementing folinic acid and vitamin B_{12} as methylcobalamin along with DMG may solve the problem. (See subsequent texts on DMG or TMG with folic acid and vitamin B_{12}.)

Some individuals do best on DMG, some on DMG plus folate and B_{12}, some on TMG, and some on TMG plus folate and B_{12}. Read on for more about this.

References - DMG

1. Boman WM and JA Richmond "A double-blind, placebo-controlled, crossover, pilot trial of low dose dimethylglycine in patients with autistic disorder" *J.Autism Dev.Disord* 29 no 3 (1999) 191-194.

2. Kern JK, VS Miller et al. "Effectiveness of N,N-dimethylglycine in autism and pervasive developmental disorder", *J.Child Neurol* 16 no.3 (2001) 169-173.

3. *Hariganesh* K and J Prathiba "Effect of dimethylglycine on gastric ulcers in rats" *J.Pharm.Pharmacol.* 52 no.12 (2000) 1519-1522.

4. Graber CD, JM Goust, et al. "Immunomodulating properties of dimethylglycine in humans" *J.Infect.Dis* 143 no.1 (1981) 101-105.

5. Vojdani A, JB Pangborn et al. "Infections, toxic chemicals and dietary peptides binding to lymphocyte receptors and tissue enzymes are major instigators of autoimmunity in autism", *Int J Immunopath Pharm* 16 no.3 (2003) 189-199.

TRIMETHYLGLYCINE (TMG)

> - **TMG methylates homocysteine to form methionine and, in doing this, it becomes DMG.**
> - **Trimethylglycine (not betaine•HCl) can have positive results on speech and eye contact.**
> - **Start with low trial doses, have taurine supplements in place.**

Trimethylglycine or TMG is also called betaine, because it was first identified in beet juice. Also, there is another form manufactured for aiding gastric hypochlorhydria, betaine hydrochloride. That is not the form of interest here, and betaine•HCl is not recommended for autism, unless small amounts are needed before meals for gastric acidification. This need is unusual in autism.

TMG is DMG with one more methyl group attached; TMG holds three methyls. And just to refresh the memory of those who have skipped directly to this section, "methyl" is the chemists' nickname for a group of atoms that consists of one carbon with three attached hydrogens, and a hook (a "bond") that allows attachment of the whole methyl group to some molecule. In the shorthand of chemistry, a methyl group is $-CH_3$. Adding a $-CH_3$ to a molecule changes its character and behavior just as adding one to homocysteine causes it to become one of the most important amino acids in all of human metabolism, methionine.

About TMG

In the body, methyls are often traded from one molecule to another, and TMG acts as a methyl bank with virtually a single purpose. It regularly gives away one of its methyls to homocysteine, a transient amino acid that comes originally from the nutritionally essential amino acid methionine. Methylation of homocysteine is a recycling process that helps to replenish the supply of methionine. Methionine itself becomes the body's biggest dealer in methyls when it changes into SAM or SAMe (S-adenosylmethionine). After SAM has given away its methyl, it becomes S-adenosylhomocysteine and then homocysteine. Once formed, homocysteine has two possible paths to follow: it can become cysteine (goes to taurine or glutathione or sulfate, etc.), or it can be remethylated to become methionine all over again. Obtaining a methyl from the TMG bank is one way that homocysteine returns to being methionine. The enzyme that promotes this is betaine-homocysteine methyltransferase, BHMT. Once TMG is minus one of its methyls, it is DMG. As explained in the prior chapter, DMG is essential for folate chemistry. Folates participate in formation of purine and some pyrimidine nucleotides. These nucleotides are essential for cellular perception and response including immune response. In addition, the methylfolate that comes from folate and DMG is needed by cobalamin and methionine synthase for the second way of making methionine from homocysteine.

```
        TMG → DMG → methyls and one-carbon parts
         ↓ methyl              ↓
        transforms         balance folate, purine,
        homocysteine       pyrimidine metabolism;
        into methionine    provide methylfolate for
                           transforming homocysteine
                           into methionine
```

Some pertinent scientific articles about TMG are briefly summarized here:

- In the cytosol of cells, betaine uses the enzyme betaine-homocysteine methyltransferase to make methionine out of homocysteine.[1] When this happens, the resulting DMG is shuttled into the mitochondria of the cell where the other methyl give-away steps and some folate biochemistry occur.

- Two studies on the use of betaine supplements to aid in reducing excess levels of homocysteine have been reviewed and summarized by Werbach.[2] In both cases, very large daily doses of betaine were used (6000 mg), and no adverse effects were reported.

Using TMG in Autism

I almost put TMG in with the group of supplements to be cautious about. That's because some of its proponents don't realize that some autistics are so low in cysteine, and so limited in taurine and glutathione, that sudden trials of high-dose TMG can have detrimental effects on antioxidant and neurological functions. TMG makes methionine, not cysteine, out of homocysteine. Cysteine supply controls formation of taurine and glutathione. So, do two things. **First, have taurine supplements in place, and second, start with low doses of TMG.** Generally, the adverse effects are temporary, lasting only for hours or days, after which glutathione levels should improve. The initial trial period is where most trouble occurs.

Generally, it is wise and safest to start trials with DMG as described previously. If DMG does not provide satisfactory benefits, try DMG with folate/B_{12} or try TMG (not betaine•HCl). **Always start with low doses.** As with DMG, parents have reported improved behavior and functioning with TMG. Based on 289 responses to ARI, we have (ARI Publ.34/March 2005):

Trimethylglycine Parent Response Tally, Responses = 434

Behavior or Traits Improved	No Discernible Effect	Behavior or Traits Worsened
42%	44%	14%

Note that the improved percentage is the same, 42% for TMG and 42% for DMG. Also, for those who tried both, there is a 72% overlap. DMG helped 72% of those whom TMG also helped. This suggests that the most significant biochemical mode of help is via the supply of one-carbon pieces for balanced folate, purine and pyrimidine metabolism. An abundant supply of methylated folate helps methionine synthase process homocysteine into methionine, and TMG has the added benefit of changing homocysteine into methionine via the BHMT enzyme as well.

As with DMG, relatively large, continual doses of TMG are usually needed for beneficial effects, and individual variations in need can be large. Amounts exceeding those in the table below may also be beneficial (see reference 2) but should be taken under medical supervision. The low-dose test amount for initial trials of TMG should be that listed for 20-Kg (44-Lb) individuals.

Body Weight Kg / Lb	TMG Dose* Range, mg/d
20 44	150-500
30 66	250-800
40 88	350-1050
50 110	450-1300
60 132	550-1600
70+ 154+	600-2000

Recent clinical research by Dr. Jill James shows that after TMG (and folinic acid) supplementation, the ratio of reduced to oxidized glutathione improves – less of the oxidized and more of the active reduced form.[3] This indicates that TMG is helping to relieve the methionine-methylation traffic jam as it increases levels of methionine, SAM and glutathione.

Adverse Responses to TMG?

Are you also using taurine? If not, start the trial over after taurine has been used for a week or so, and continue the taurine while TMG is used. Are you using betaine·HCl? Don't, it's too acidic. The name and synonyms of what you should be using are: trimethylglycine, betaine, glycine betaine, oxyneurine, and lycine. What you should not be using is betaine hydrochloride, betaine HCl, pluchine or trimethylglycine hydrochloride.

Because TMG becomes DMG and DMG needs tetrahydrofolate directly and vitamin B_{12} indirectly, TMG may not be beneficial without supplementing folate (or folinic acid) and vitamin B_{12} as well. Supplement trials will show you this, and there are some analytical or lab test clues – see next chapter.

Please refer back to the diagram in the About TMG section. TMG pushes homocysteine to methionine and not to cystathionine, cysteine, glutathione, etc. Many autistics show marginal or subnormal cysteine in blood plasma by amino acid analysis. At first, TMG supplementation enhances methionine and works against cysteine formation; this is dictated by the chemistry. Eventually, however, cysteine levels have to improve as do levels of GSH per the clinical findings.[3] It may take hours or days for the methionine-methylation traffic jam to clear. So, don't start out with big doses of TMG, because there's a "worse before better" aspect to this biochemistry for some individuals.

References - TMG

1. Sandu C, P Nick et al. "Association of betaine-homocysteine S-methyltransferase with microtubules" *Biol.Chem.* 381 no.7 (2000) p 619-622.
2. Werbach MR *Nutritional Influences on Illness* 2nd Ed, Third Line Press, Tarzana CA (1993) p.87.
3. James SJ "Increased oxidative stress and impaired methylation capacity in children with autism: metabolic biomarkers and genetic predisposition" Proceedings, Fall DAN! 2004 Conference, Los Angeles (2004) 143-150.

DMG or TMG with FOLATE and VITAMIN B_{12}: Making Choices

> - DMG and TMG work synergistically with folate and vitamin B_{12} in different ways; needs depend upon the individual.
> - Laboratory test results can provide hints for choosing DMG or TMG and whether B_{12} and folate might also be needed.
> - When undecided, choose DMG trials first.
> - Actual trial outcomes are the deciding factors.

As described in the previous texts for DMG and TMG, methylation of folate is one of the major functions of these nutrients. Folate or folic acid (which becomes tetrahydrofolate, THF, in cells) is a companion nutrient for DMG and TMG. There are, however, some individuals, a minority subset of autistics, who react adversely to supplemental folic acid. Therefore, some nutritional suppliers provide DMG and TMG with and without folate and vitamin B_{12}. And recently, folinic acid, methylcobalamin and DMG or TMG combinations have become available. Occasionally, B_{12} is needed to relieve bottlenecks in the metabolism of folate, called "folate traps." If its metabolism is working properly, B_{12} can be methylated by methylated folate, and the resulting methylcobalamin can then add the methyl to homocysteine to make methionine. Methylcobalamin activity is the major way for homocysteine to become methionine. The TMG → DMG route, while essential for DMG formation, is considered to methylate lesser amounts of homocysteine than methylcobalamin.

Indications that Plain DMG might be Beneficial

If you've done some laboratory tests to assess nutritional or physiological status, you may have gotten results that are consistent with an expected benefit from DMG. Laboratory test results considered to be consistent with DMG providing some benefit are:

- An amino acid analysis with low cysteine, cystine or cyst(e)ine. Adenosylhomocysteine and homocysteine are not elevated.
- An amino acid analysis showing high histidine.
- A vitamin analysis showing high folate (in blood serum).
- Adverse reaction and worsened behavior following folic acid supplements or methylcobalamin.

The only nutritional concern with plain DMG and TMG is low folic acid. When DMG comes apart and gives away its methyl parts, the body needs folate as an acceptor. In the absence of folate, DMG can produce formaldehyde. So, be sure that folic acid is adequate when DMG is used.

Indications that Plain TMG might be beneficial

If you've done some laboratory tests to assess nutritional status, you may have gotten results that are consistent with an expected benefit from TMG. Laboratory test results considered to be consistent with TMG providing some benefit are:

- An amino acid analysis with elevated adenosylhomocysteine or homocysteine, homocystine, or homocyst(e)ine.
- An amino acid analysis showing methionine and/or SAM deficiency.
- A vitamin analysis showing high folate (usually total folate forms in whole blood or blood serum).
- Adverse reaction and worsened behavior following folic acid supplements or methylcobalamin.

I have not included low cystine or low cysteine as indicators of TMG need. That's because TMG's methylation of homocysteine causes cysteine formation to be bypassed. However, cysteine and glutathione levels may improve after a few days of TMG use if it is able to clear the traffic gridlock in the methionine-methylation cycle.

Indications that DMG with Folate and Vitamin B_{12} Might be Beneficial

If you've done some laboratory tests, you may have gotten results that are consistent with an expected benefit from DMG plus folate and B_{12} as nutritional supplements. Laboratory test results considered to be consistent with need for these are:

- An amino acid analysis with low cysteine, cystine or cyst(e)ine and with low or low-normal methionine.
- Adenosylhomocysteine and homocysteine are not elevated.
- A vitamin analysis indicating low folate.
- Metabolic analyses showing high "FIGlu" or high "MMA."
- A hair element analysis showing deficient cobalt. (Cobalt is the element that activates vitamin B_{12}, cobalamin.)

Indications that TMG with Folate and Vitamin B_{12} Might be Beneficial

If you've done some laboratory tests to assess nutritional status, you may have gotten results that are consistent with an expected benefit from TMG plus folate and B_{12} as nutritional supplements. Laboratory test results considered to be consistent with need for these are:

- An amino acid analysis with elevated adenosylhomocysteine, homocysteine, homocystine, or homocyst(e)ine.
- An amino acid analysis showing methionine and/or SAM deficiency.
- Metabolic analysis or organic acid analysis showing high urine "FIGlu" or high urine "MMA."
- A vitamin analysis indicating low folate.
- A hair element analysis showing deficient cobalt.

DMG-TMG CHOICE MATRIX

	DMG	DMG + Folate* + B$_{12}$*	TMG	TMG + Folate* + B$_{12}$*
Poor speech development	x	x	x	x
Poor eye contact	x	x	x	x
Has hyperactivity		x		x
Cystine or cysteine is low	x	x		
Adenosylhomocysteine high			x	x
Homocystine is high			x	x
Methionine and/or SAM low			x	x
Histidine is high	x			
Folate is high	x		x	
Reacts to folate	x		x	
Folate is low		x		x
Urine "FIGlu" high**		x		x
B$_{12}$ shots worsen	x		x	
Low cobalt per hair element analysis		x		x
Urine "MMA" high		x		x
Glutathione is low		x		x

Add up all the x's that apply. Whichever product gets the most x's is your first choice. If you get fewer than three x's for each of the four possible products, then it is not likely that any of the four will be of great benefit. If you get a tie between DMG and DMG + Folate + B$_{12}$, make DMG your first choice. If you get a tie between TMG and TMG + Folate + B$_{12}$, choose TMG. If you get a tie between DMG and TMG, choose DMG. However, no formula is infallible. The right product is the one that the autistic individual does the best with. Note also that plain DMG has the least percentage of adverse responses, 7%, while TMG has twice this.

* The new generation of these supplements uses folinic acid and methylcobalamin.
** Impairments in purine synthesis or unusual folate traps may cause FIGlu to be elevated regardless of supplemental forms of folate/B$_{12}$.

CREATINE

- **Creatine, as phosphocreatine, carries energy needed for cellular communication processes.**
- **70% of SAM's methylation activity is formation of creatine from guanidinoacetate.**
- **A major subset of autistics present low creatine or symptoms consistent with this.**
- **Metabolic errors are documented for creatine deficiency and for its transport. Deficient expressive speech and other autistic traits are presented in such cases.**

Creatine is an amino acid that is involved in energy transfer, not only in muscle tissue but in the brain as well. In these tissues, creatine acts as a phosphate shuttle. At the molecular level, phosphate is the currency of energy in body tissues. Adding phosphate to a molecule requires an energy input, but subsequent release of phosphate also releases this chemical energy. Phosphate transport by creatine allows energy transfer reactions to occur when the energy supply is separated spatially from the substances or cells that need it. An example is energizing ADP to ATP so that ATP + GDP → ADP + GTP can occur. This reaction transfers the energy from ATP to GDP, re-energizing it. And GTP is what G-proteins require for message transmission at the cell membrane/cytosol interface. When we consider this chemistry, we are dealing with a problem that can be central to the trait of expressive speech deficit in autism. In fact, a major objective of the methionine recycle loop (where methyl group give-away occurs followed by remethylation of homocysteine to get the methionine back) is to provide adequate creatine. Creatine deficit can coincide with and be causative of expressive speech deficit.

About Creatine

Creatine is synthesized by using parts from three amino acids, arginine (which usually is the limiting or least abundant one), glycine, and S-adenosylmethionine (SAM). In some autistics, we suspect that methylation by SAM is restricting creatine synthesis. This can occur when adenosine and/or adenosylhomocysteine are excessive, folate as 5-methylTHF is deficient, methylcobalamin is deficient, or oxidant stress or toxicity blocks cobalamin's participation in methionine synthase activity. How does all this work? Let's start with how creatine is made.

Primarily in the kidneys, pancreas and liver, glycine combines with arginine to form ornithine and guanidinoacetate. The enzyme that promotes this first step of creatine synthesis is arginine-glycine amidinotransferase (AGAT). Lesser but significant AGAT activity exists in other tissues including heart, brain and lung. Normally, the AGAT step is the rate-limiting step of creatine synthesis.

$$\text{Arginine} + \text{Glycine} \xrightarrow{\text{AGAT}} \text{Ornithine} + \text{Guanidinoacetate}$$

(Guanidinoacetate is also called guanidoacetate or glycoamine in various texts.)

Some of this guanidinoacetate is transported by blood to the liver and pancreas, where the second step in creatine synthesis mostly occurs. This step is methylation by SAM using the enzyme S-adenosylmethionine-guanidinoacetate methyltransferase, GAMT. About 70% of SAM's duty is methylating guanidinoacetate to form creatine and SAH (S-adenosylhomocysteine).[1]

$$\text{SAM} + \text{Guanidinoacetate} \xrightarrow{\text{GAMT}} \text{SAH} + \text{Creatine}$$

Besides the liver and pancreas, some GAMT activity is present in brain (neurons), ovaries and epididymal (posterior of testis) epithelial tissue. But this reaction slows down when SAH, S-adenosylhomocysteine, accumulates. And it will accumulate at locales in cells where adenosine processing is impaired. That's because SAH has to give away its adenosine to become homocysteine, the next substance in methionine metabolism.

$$\text{SAH} + \text{H}_2\text{O} \xleftrightarrow{\text{hydrolase}} \text{Adenosine} + \text{Homocysteine}$$

This reaction is "reversible," but actually favors SAH. If adenosine accumulates, the reaction is driven back toward SAH, which impedes the GAMT step and reduces creatine formation. From previous chapters, adenosine can accumulate for several reasons, and does in 20% of autistics per analytical testing.

After creatine is formed, it can become an energy carrier by adding phosphate, which it acquires from ATP using the enzyme creatine kinase, CK. Creatine phosphate then delivers high-energy phosphate some distance away where another pool of ADP needs it. This is a relatively fast and efficient way to upgrade the distant ADP. In muscle, a nonenzymatic energy transfer step produces mechanical energy (muscle contraction) from chemical energy, and in the process, forms some creatinine from creatine. Formation of creatinine from creatine is spontaneous (no enzyme) and irreversible. Under normal physiologic conditions, about 1% of creatine and about 2-3% of phosphocreatine are lost to creatinine per day.[2]

$$\text{Creatine phosphate} \xrightarrow{\text{Muscle}} \text{inorganic phosphate (Pi)} + \text{creatinine} + H_2O$$

Creatinine is a final waste product of energy and amino acid metabolism. It is excreted in urine. And that's why a continual, daily makeup of new creatine is required.

The vast majority of creatine is not wasted as creatinine; it is recycled while it participates in the phosphate (energy) shuttling or transport process. This process assists in supplying chemical energy to actin or myosin in muscle.[3]

$$\text{Creatine} + \text{ATP} \xrightarrow{\text{Creatine kinase, CK}} \text{Creatine phosphate} + \text{ADP}$$

$$\text{Creatine phosphate} + \text{ADP} \xrightarrow{\text{CK}} \text{Creatine} + \text{ATP}$$

$$\text{ATP} \xrightarrow[\text{ATPase}]{\text{in myosin}} \text{ADP} + \text{Pi} + \text{muscle contraction}$$

$$2\,\text{ADP} \xrightarrow{\text{adenylate kinase}} \text{ATP} + \text{AMP}$$

Very significant amounts of creatine and creatine phosphate ("phosphocreatine") are normally found in brain tissue where there is no myosin or actin activity and no muscle.[1] Much of the brain's energy consumption is for cellular communication processes. This includes signal transduction between neurons (synaptic processes), signal transduction across the neuronal membranes and the attendant processes of chemical change within brain cells. Energy is transferred, changed in form and consumed by perceiving, thinking and responding.

Our brains have virtually no stored energy reserves to operate these chemical and electrochemical processes. A few minutes without oxygen or nourishment from the rest of the body causes cessation of the brain's sensory processing and response. The rapid, "just in time" energy delivery system, operated by creatine phosphate, helps to keep G proteins supplied with ready-to-go GTP. G proteins are in the lipid membrane (cell wall) attached to receptor proteins, and they regulate transmission of incoming messages. To be active in signal transduction, the guanosine nucleotide has to be in GTP configuration. The GTP part of a G protein is degraded to GDP by the GTPase part of the receptor as the signal is transmitted. The GTP → GDP degradation provides the energy to push the signal from the receptor in the cell membrane on to the next part of the signal-processing system. Once GTP has changed to GDP, that particular G protein receptor cannot transmit another signal until it's given another increment of chemical energy.[4] That increment comes from replacing the spent ADP with a new GTP, and the spent GDP has to be rejuvenated for reuse. That rejuvenation comes from ATP that got its third P from creatine phosphate.

$$ATP + GDP \xrightarrow{\text{Nucleoside diphosphate kinase}} ADP + GTP$$

For cellular communication to be efficient, there has to be an immediate and adequate supply of ATP. Communication processes will be inhibited if ADP or GDP accumulate. Transfer of energy from chemical to electrical (and to mechanical) forms also is required to generate a response once the neuronal network of the brain has decided to issue one. This requires phosphate transport as well.

Besides the two enzymatic steps of creatine formation, AGAT and GAMT, another molecular process is crucial to the supply of creatine and phosphate. That process is accomplished by the "creatine transporter" (CRTR, or CRT in some texts). Intercellular transport of creatine is needed to get it from places of assembly to places of usage. At this writing, the exact configuration of the creatine transporter system has not been described. It is suspected to consist of a polypeptide (cDNA composed of 635 amino acids) and 12 associated transmembrane proteins.[5] Two sodium ions (Na^+) are transported for each creatine molecule. Na^+-driven transporters, like the one for creatine, also transport GABA, serotonin, dopamine and other catecholamines, and taurine.[5]

Documented metabolic errors are associated with all three creatine formation and delivery processes, AGAT, GAMT, and the CRTR gene. And all three defects produce delayed development of speech, lack of expressive speech, and sometimes other autistic traits.[6,7,8,9]

Using Creatine in Autism

If it's so important to coordinated neuronal processes, cellular perception and responsiveness, and speech, why not use creatine early on? You might be able to, and I'm told by the clinicians that perhaps one of ten autistics has a fantastic, beneficial response to oral creatine. But, there can be some "bumps in the road" with creatine. In some, contrary to the chemistry explained above, there is elevated creatine, per blood serum analysis, and adverse response to creatine supplements. One possible problem is toxicity, such as mercury, which can stop creatine kinase from doing its job of loading the creatine truck with phosphate. Phosphorylation of creatine is inhibited by mercury.[10] Another problem may be acquired interference with the creatine transporter system. So, if you use creatine early on, and it doesn't work, don't discard that option permanently. It might work later when it can be transported and phosphorylated better.

Another tactic is to give guanidinoacetate (GA) with creatine. Alan Goldblatt and Marvin Boris, M.D., have reported at DAN! think tanks that lab tests have shown that GA is deficient in many autistics who also are deficient in creatine. They have used supplements of 200 mg of GA twice per day (along with supplemental creatine) with good results.

Relatively large, therapeutic amounts of oral creatine are needed to be effective. DAN! clinicians have used amounts ranging from 300 to 1000 mg/Kg body weight per day, in divided doses. Von Figura, Hanefeld et al. state that 350 to 2000 mg/Kg are therapeutic in GAMT deficiency and that 20,000 mg/d (adults?) produced no serious side effects.[11] Because large amounts are required to gain beneficial response, be sure to obtain this supplement from a reputable supplier. Small concentrations of impurities can add up when large amounts are used.

There are some analytical indications and physical traits that can be clues to creatine insufficiency:

1. **Hypotonia, low muscle mass, and "floppy baby" condition are all consistent with inadequate creatine. However, deficient brain creatine/phosphocreatine can occur when muscle development and function appear normal.**
2. **Deficient blood serum creatine.**
3. **Deficient urine creatinine (clearance is okay, but the quantities in urine and blood are subnormal). Be wary of urine creatinine concentrations below 300 mg/liter.**
4. **Abnormal (high or low) guanidinoacetate in blood serum.**
5. **Elevated ornithine or beta-alanine per amino acid analysis. Both interfere with formation of guanidinoacetate.**

Here are some "normal" levels that I have found in the literature. While your laboratory should have its own reference range, I would not expect such ranges to be wildly different from these guidelines:

- Normal human plasma or serum creatine is reported to range from 25 to 125 micromoles per liter (µM/l).[12]
- With a molecular weight of 131, normal plasma serum creatine would also be 3.28 to 16.4 milligrams per liter (mg/l).
- Normal urine creatine is -[13]
  Age 1-5 years, 4-8 mg/Kg/24 hrs
  Age 6-12 years, 2.5-5 mg/Kg/24 hrs
  Teens/adults, 2.5-3.5 mg/Kg/24 hrs, and women typically excrete more creatine than men.
- Normal plasma/serum creatinine is –[14]
  Age 1-5 years, 0.3-0.7 mg/dl (and 0.3 is worrisome)
  Age 6-12 years, 0.5-1.1 mg/dl
  Teens/adults, 0.7-1.5 mg/dl
- Normal urine creatinine is –[15]
  Age 1-5 years, 12-18 mg/Kg/24 hrs or 30-80 mg/dl
  Age 6-12 years, 15-22 mg/Kg/24 hrs or 40-120 mg/dl
  Teens/adults, 20-30 mg/Kg/24 hr or 50-160 mg/dl, and men typically excrete more creatinine than women.
- Normal guanidinoacetate is –[16]
  Plasma/serum, 0.52-1.14 µM/l
  Urine, 63-429 µM/l
  Cerebrospinal fluid, 0.023-0.087 µM/l

Adverse Response to Creatine?

Is it pure material? Did you get it at the local health food store where bodybuilders buy it and use it by the wheelbarrow-full? This type may not be pure enough for an autistic child whose detoxication capacity is limited.

Are you detoxing (mobilizing) mercury at the same time that you are using creatine? If so, phosphorylation via creatine kinase isn't going to work very well.

Measure blood creatine and find out if it's already high. And, if you can, measure it in urine too. High may also mean that the creatine transporter system is impaired or defective. While defects in CRTR (transporter gene) have been considered rare, recent clinical research brings this "rarity" into question.[17] It may be a rather common defect.

References – Creatine

1. Von Figura K, Hanefeld F et al. "Guanidinoacetate Methyltransferase Deficiency" Chapter 84 in Scriver et al., eds., *The Metabolic and Molecular Gases of Inherited Disease* 8th Ed., McGraw-Hill (2001) 1903.
2. Wyss M and Kaddurah-Daouk R "Creatine and Creatinine Metabolism" *Physiological Reviews* 80 no.3 (2000) 1113-1114.
3. Martin DW "Contractile & Structural Proteins" Chapt. 34 in Martin DW, Mayes PA et al. eds., *Harper's Review of Biochemistry* 20th ed, Lange Medical Publications (1985) 488.
4. Granner DK "Hormone Action" Chapter 44 in Murray RK, Granner DK et al. *Harper's Biochemistry* 25th ed., (2000) 541-544.
5. Von Figura K, Hanefeld F et al., op.cit. 1901.
6. Von Figura K, Hanefeld F et al., ibid 1898.
7. Salomons GS, van Dooren SJM et al. "X-linked creatine transporter (SLC6A8) defect: a new creatine deficiency syndrome" *Am.J.Human Genetics* 68 (2001) 1497-1500.
8. Salomons GS, van Dooren SJM et al. "X-linked creatine transporter defect: an overview" *J. Inherited Metabolic Disorders* 26 (2003) 309-318.
9. Item CB, Stöckler-Ipsiroglu S et al. "Arginine: Glycine Amidinotransferase Deficiency: The third inborn error of creatine metabolism in humans" *Am.J.Human Genetics* 69 (2001) 1127-1133.
10. Private communication from Professor Boyd Haley, Chairman, Chemistry Dept., U. of Kentucky.
11. Von Figura K, Hanefeld F et al., op.cit. 1904.
12. Salomons GS, van Dooren SJM et al. (2003) op.cit. 315.
13. Krupp MA, Tierney LM et al. *Physicians' Handbook* 20th d, LMP (1982) 201.
14. Composite of several references: Von Figura K, Hanefeld F. op.cit. 1899; Krupp MA, Tierney LM et al. *Physicians' Handbook* 20th ed, LMP (1982) 202; Jacobs DS, Kasten BL *Laboratory Test Handbook* 2nd ed, Lexi-Comp (1990) 171.
15. Composite of several references: Von Figura K, Hanefeld F op.cit. 1899; Krupp MA, Tierney LM et al. *Physicians' Handbook* 20th ed, LMP (1982) 201; Jacobs DS, Kasten BL et al. *Laboratory Test Handbook* 2nd ed, Lexi-Comp (1990) 169.
16. Von Figura K, Hanefeld et al. op.cit. 1899.
17. Salomons GS, van Dooren SJM op.cit. 309.

AMINO ACIDS

> - Many untreated and treated autistics present deficiencies of essential amino acids.
> - Amino acid supplements should not be used until dietary intervention, digestion and dysbiosis issues have been addressed.
> - An amino acid analysis is a guide to supplementation. Compounding pharmacies can supply a customized product based on the analysis.

When humans eat vegetable or animal proteins, our digestive processes are supposed to break these proteins into smaller pieces, single, free-form amino acids or very short-chain peptides (two or three amino acids still connected together). These smaller molecules can be absorbed through the mucosal cells of the small intestine. Absorbed short-chain peptides are further digested by peptidase enzymes in the blood, liver, kidney and other organs. The objective is to form a pool of free-form amino acids that can be reassembled in specific sequences to make human proteins, peptides and some very specialized products. Among the specialized products formed from one or more amino acids are: creatine, serotonin, melatonin, adrenal catecholamines, glutathione, melanins (biochemicals that give color to tissue), porphyrins, purines and pyrimidines (and their nucleoside and nucleotide forms).[1] Nucleotides are the molecules that participate in cellular function and information processing. Amino acids are used to construct enzymes, antibodies, immunoglobulins and hormones, and they help to operate detoxication chemistry. Detoxication is the body's cleanup process, the getting-rid-of unwanted, perhaps harmful substances. Amino acids combine with or conjugate toxic substances, they get rid of excess nitrogen as urea, and they form bile salts from cholesterol using the amino acids glycine or taurine. Bile and urine are the two major fluids that carry toxics out of the body.

Obviously, when digestion goes wrong, the supply of amino acids can run short, and the processes that depend upon them can go wrong as well. My experience is that protein maldigestion can be quite accurately assessed by amino acid analysis. Test results showing decreased essentials and elevated dietary peptides (usually, anserine and carnosine in urine) are analytic evidence of incomplete digestive proteolysis -- maldigestion. This can occur with gastric dysfunctions, such as insufficient stomach acidity, or, as is hypothesized to happen in some types of autism, insufficient pancreatic function. With malabsorption, some of the needed dietary nutrients, including amino acids, are carried to the large intestine and may be lost in the stool. Malabsorption is suggested by very low threonine, together with low essentials, while the dietary peptides may be within normal limits. Threonine is an essential amino acid and is the slowest one to cross from the lumen of the small intestine into the portal blood.[2]

The nutritionally essential amino acids are:

Leucine, Isoleucine and Valine: are "branched-chain" essential amino acids needed for collagen tissue formation. These are called "branched-chain" because the carbon chain in each one is forked or branched. Assimilation of these is quite dependent upon pancreatic and mucosal peptidases, digestive enzymes that work in the small intestine. In autism, levels of leucine, isoleucine and valine may be low if peptidase function is weak. Deficiencies of leucine, isoleucine and/or valine are not typical in autism, but they seem to occur in about one in three or four autistics per urine amino acid analysis.

SECTION FIVE: NUTRITIONAL SUPPLEMENTS FOR AUTISM

Methionine: brings sulfur and methyl groups into the body, does methylation when it becomes "SAM," and is the essential precursor of cysteine and taurine. Methionine assimilation is somewhat dependent upon adequate stomach acid and pepsinogen becoming pepsin. However, insufficient stomach acidity and inadequate pepsin are not reported to be common in autism. Yet, prior to interventions, methionine is low in about half of autistic children, per blood plasma analysis. This is ascribed to deficient recycling of homocysteine to methionine via methionine synthase.

Phenylalanine: is the precursor of tyrosine, which forms the adrenal catecholamines, and the part of thyroglobulin to which iodine attaches to make thyroid hormones. Phenylalanine is low in some autistic children. However, it is high in PKU or phenylketonuria, which may feature autism. PKU is rarely found now as an untreated condition.

Tryptophan: is the precursor of serotonin and melatonin. Tryptophan can be low in blood in some autistics if maldigestion or malabsorption occurs. In such cases, tryptophan can be changed into indolylpropionic acid by gut bacteria. This is absorbed into the bloodstream and converted to indolylacrylic acid in body tissues. Indolylacrylic acid is a toxic organic acid. It is detoxified by combining it with glycine to form indolylacryloylglycine, "IAG." Recent research on IAG suggests that it may also be formed when internal metabolism of tryptophan is disturbed.[3] If this happens, urine or plasma tryptophan can be elevated rather than depleted. Occasionally, tryptophan is used to form excessive amounts of serotonin in abdominal tissues, and the availability of tryptophan (to become serotonin) may be then limited in the CNS. Serotonin produced in abdominal tissues acts as a vasoconstrictor. It decreases capillary blood flow in the intestinal mucosa and restricts uptake of toxins (from dysbiosis) or peptides and undigested parts of food (from maldigestion). If serotonin is low in the CNS, consequences can be low melatonin and poor sleep patterns, and increased sensitivity to light and sound. Elevated blood serotonin is reported to occur in about 25% of autistics,[4] but this statistic predates the notable increase in the occurrence of autism since 1980.

Lysine: is a major component of muscle protein. It is the link point in aminotransferase enzymes ("transaminases") between the enzyme and the coenzyme, pyridoxal 5-phosphate. Lysine is commonly deficient in autistics before dietary intervention.

Threonine: is the essential precursor of serine and glycine. It is one of the few amino acids that allow glycoprotein formation – attachment of a carbohydrate or sugar to a protein. Cell membranes contain glycoproteins as do blood group substances, the compounds that make blood types different. Immunoglobulins, interferon, and cell-cell recognition substances include glycoproteins. These structures are essential for proper immune function. Blood or urine threonine is often low in medically defined malabsorption syndromes, but it is only occasionally found to be low in autism.

Histidine: is the precursor of the hormone histamine. Before about 1985, this amino acid was considered to be essential only for infants. It is now considered to be essential for adults as well.[4] Histidine is usually provided by a dietary dipeptide that is digested either in the small intestine or internally – carnosine. Anserine, a sister peptide, contains methylated histidine, and we may or may not derive histidine from that source. Histidine is very important in autism. Some of it is processed to form "FIGlu" (formiminoglutamic acid). FIGlu combines with tetrahydrofolate to make 5-formimino-tetrahydrofolate. This is eventually changed into folate forms that are needed for purine synthesis (10-formylTHF and 5,10-methenylTHF). An uncommon disease condition, histidinemia (with histidinuria) can feature autistic-like traits.[5]

Cysteine may be considered a nonessential or conditionally essential amino acid because much of the need can be supplied by methionine. By my own estimates, about 50% to 65% of cysteine normally comes from methionine. The remainder is from direct, dietary sources (cystine + cysteine + related other forms). Cysteine is the rate-limiting amino acid for formation of glutathione; it contributes significantly (depending on diet) to taurine synthesis, and it is the major source of sulfate for sulfation. Cysteine is low/deficient, per amino acid analysis, in many autistics.[6,7,8]

Using Amino Acids in Autism

From reading the above, it's understandable why you'd want to supplement amino acids as soon as you can find some and while you're doing dietary intervention. DON'T! Here's why.

- Cystine, cysteine and N-acetylcysteine or NAC are culture media for the Candida genus of yeast.[9] Also, cystine or cysteine or NAC supplementation will mobilize toxics (such as mercury) from sequestered sites inside cells. But this mobilization will not necessarily cause detoxication and may worsen the extent of the contamination. Wait until the gastrointestinal tract is healthy and functional, and wait until metabolism is improved, especially that of glutathione, and wait until oxidant stress is alleviated.

- Glutamine when malabsorbed and chewed on by dysbiotic bacterial flora produces succinic acid.[10] Most elevations of succinic acid found by organic acid analysis of the urine of autistics come from glutamine and resolve when the digestive function is normalized. Succinic acid can have toxic effects when it's not in the cellular compartments where it is supposed to be.

- As mentioned previously, tryptophan can become indolylpropionic acid, indolylacrylic acid (quite toxic) and then, IAG (a detoxified form).[11]

- Clostridia ingesting phenylalanine, tyrosine and tryptophan produce hydroxyphenylproprionic acid (HPPA) which, when hydroxylated in the liver, becomes the dihydroxyl form, DHPPA. From these same amino acids, Clostridia also produce lots of substances of varying toxicities: para-cresol, phenylacetic acid, phenyllactic acid, phenol, indole, indoleacetic acid, and indoleproprionic acid.[12]

If your attitude has now changed and you're wondering, "Why would I ever give amino acids to an autistic?", then I've succeeded in raising the caution flags. Amino acid supplements can be very beneficial in many cases of autism. But they should not be used until after the "gut issues" have been successfully addressed. Free-form amino acids are very readily taken in through the mucosal tissues of our digestive tracts and should be absorbed before they reach the lower part of the small intestine.

In 2002, I did a survey of over 60 urine amino acid analyses on autistic children, ages 3-9. These kids (47 males, 14 females) had gone through diet trials, and many were on special diets. They had been treated with antifungals and antibacterials and were on probiotics supplements. However, only a few were reported to be on digestive enzymes, which definitely help protein digestion and amino acid adequacy. Here's what I found. (Cyst(e)ine is excluded because urine isn't a good specimen for assessing its adequacy,)

Deficient taurine or taurine wasting	62%
Deficient lysine	59%
Deficient phenylalanine	54%
Deficient methionine	51%
Deficient tyrosine	38%
Deficient leucine	36%
Deficient glutamine	33%
Deficient valine	30%
Deficient asparagine	26%

The deficiencies may have resulted from the special diets, but more likely, they have persisted since before intervention. This is supported by many other amino acid analyses performed pretreatment that I've looked at over the years. Pretreatment analyses show as many or more deficiencies. Remember, changing the diet and killing bad flora are cleanup procedures. They don't necessarily repair digestive dysfunctions that may have been preexisting conditions, and they don't ensure nutritional adequacy.

Various blends of essential and protein amino acids are available OTC and from nutrition company sources. A unique blend that matches the above 'average" needs of autistics (as I determined them) is available from Kirkman Laboratories of Lake Oswego, OR.

The most accurate way to learn which amino acids are needed for an individual, and how much, is to do an amino acid analysis. I'm partial to 24-hour urine (not ratioed to creatinine) because it tells a 24-hour tale. Plasma is okay, but it is a fasting test that is a snapshot in time of what's circulating in the blood. Urine shows what's left over after a whole day's physiological activities. If there's too little left over, then more is needed. When urine is used to judge amino acid status, renal clearance should also be judged as okay by your doctor. He or she can assess this from a simple blood chemistry test. I strongly advise not ratioing 24-hour urine analyte levels to creatinine because both creatine and creatinine are often deficient in autistics. Dividing a low amino acid level by a low creatinine gives a false normal result.

The amino acid reports may come with a supplement schedule. If not, the parents/practitioner will need to consult a professional nutritionist for guidance about supplementation. The supplement schedule from a lab report can be filled by a compounding pharmacy upon receiving a doctor's prescription appended to the supplement schedule page. Some compounding pharmacies are:

Apothecary, Bethesda MD, 800-869-9160, fax 301-493-4671
ApotheCure, Dallas TX, 800-969-6601, fax 800-687-5252
College Pharmacy, Colorado Springs, CO, 800-888-9858, fax 800-556-5893
Creative Compounds, Wilsonville, OR, 877-585-6111, fax 503-570-2831
Falls Pharmacy, Snoqualmie, WA, 877-392-7948, fax 425-888-6870
Hopewell Pharmacy, Hopewell NJ, 800-792-6670, fax 800-417-3864
Key Pharmacy, Kent, WA, 800-878-1322, fax 206-878-1114
Lee Silsby Pharmacy, Cleveland OH, 800-918-8831, fax 216-321-4303
University Pharmacy, Troy MI, 248-267-5002, fax 248-267-5003
Wellness, Birmingham AL, 800-227-2627, fax 205-369-0302

Taurine is usually not accounted for correctly by supplement schedules unless they are based on blood plasma levels. In urine, high taurine (when it is not being supplemented) almost always means urinary wasting and need for taurine. (See previous chapter on taurine.)

We do not have Parent-Response statistics for amino acid use by autistics (not included on ARI Publication 34).

Adverse Responses to Amino Acid Supplements?

With adverse responses, the first concern should be: is gut dysbiosis still present? That's most often the problem. I strongly advise taking natural, herbal-type antifungals/antiyeast supplements whenever cystine, NAC or even glutathione is used orally.

The next concern is rapid transit in the gastrointestinal tract, which may be coincident with diarrhea or runny stools. If that's not dysbiosis, then it's usually intolerance or reactivity to a food or medication. The problem is that the fast transit may be allowing the amino acids to reach the large bowel (where lots of bacteria reside). If that's going on, then don't give amino acid supplements. Ditto for the opposite case, constipation. Amino acids may make things worse with constipation.

Ensure that there is B-vitamin adequacy and also adequate supplements of minerals, especially magnesium and zinc. These are needed for metabolism of amino acids.

Health professionals are cautioned that some unusual metabolic conditions have contraindications for amino acid supplementation. Some of these are as follows:

- Hyperammonemia – no amino acids until the condition is completely understood, then maybe none, or only selected ones.
- Renal failure (poor kidney clearance), do not give amino acids if this is the case.
- Histidinemia – avoid histidine.
- Cystinuria – avoid cystine, cysteine, NAC, and limit glutathione; measure blood plasma for status of lysine, arginine and ornithine.
- Lysinuric intolerance – avoid lysine.
- Methionine and SAM are often poorly tolerated in autism, regardless of blood/urine levels.
- Hartnup syndrome – avoid tryptophan.
- Hyperphenylalaninuria – avoid phenylalanine; determine if tyrosine is needed.
- Tyrosinemia – avoid tyrosine.
- Branched-chain amino acid excesses – avoid leucine, isoleucine and valine, at least until the biochemical reasons are understood.

References - Amino Acids

1. Murray RK, Granner DK et al. *Harper's Biochemistry* 23rd Ed, Lange Med. Pub (1993) 326-362.
2. Robinson C. *Normal and Therapeutic Nutrition* 145h Ed. MacMillan Pub (1972) 47-48.
3. Shattock P. Presentation to the Oakland County Chapter, Autism Society of America, Pontiac MI, May 2001.
4. Recommended Dietary Allowances 10th Ed, National Research Council, Food and Nutrition Board, National Academy Press, Washington DC (1989) 53.

SECTION FIVE: NUTRITIONAL SUPPLEMENTS FOR AUTISM

5. Bremer HJ, Duran M et al. <u>Disturbances of Amino Acid Metabolism: Clinical Chemistry and Diagnosis</u> Urban & Schwarzenberg (1981) 270-274.
6. Pangborn J. Proceedings of the International Autism Conference of the Americas, NSAC, San Antonio TX (1984) 45-47.
7. Owens SC "Understanding the Sulfur System" Spring DAN 2003 Conference Syllabus, Philadelphia PA, May 2003 65-75.
8. James SJ "Abnormal folate-dependent methionine and glutathione metabolism in children with autism: potential for increased sensitivity to Thimerosal and other pro-oxidants." Spring DAN 2004 Conference Syllabus, Washington DC, April 2004 59-72.
9. Griffin DH *Fungal Physiology* John Wiley & Sons (1981) 124.
10. Chalmers RA and Lawson AM *Organic Acids in Man*, Chapman and Hall (1982) 195.
11. Jepson JB "Hartnup Disease" Chapter 66 in Stanbury J et al. *The Metabolic Basis of Inherited Disease*, 4th ed. McGraw-Hill (1978) 1566-1568.
12. Elsden SR, Hilton MG and Waller JM "The end products of the metabolism of aromatic amino acids by Clostridia" <u>Arch Microbiol</u> 107 no.3 (1976) 283-288.

NUTRITIONAL SUPPLEMENTS TO BE CAUTIOUS WITH

There are seven supplements that may provide significant benefits for some, but that have produced worsening in many as well. I advise caution and careful observation if these are tried. These seven are:

- Methionine, the essential amino acid that brings sulfur and methyl groups into the body.
- SAM or S-adenosylmethionine, the active, methylating form of methionine.
- Folate, the vitamin that processes one-carbon groups into usable forms, like methyl.
- N-acetylcysteine, a more stable form of cysteine that can help with glutathione supply.
- Carnosine, a dipeptide that can help when seizures are part of the problem.
- Lipoic acid, a reducing and detoxifying cofactor (sometimes called a vitamin).
- Glutathione, a reducing and detoxifying factor known to be subnormal in many autistics.

METHIONINE AND S-ADENOSYLMETHIONINE (SAM)

> - **Methionine and SAM supplements hinder as many as they help.**
> - **If you wish to try methionine, use only pure L-methionine. Do NOT use D,L methionine.**
> - **There is a negative outcome for one out of five autistics from supplementing SAM and there is no discernible benefit for another three out of five.**

The active, methyl-group-donating form of methionine has adenosine attached to its sulfur atom and is nicknamed "SAM" or SAMe." To become SAM, methionine acquires its adenosine from adenosine triphosphate, ATP, leaving the phosphates behind. SAM then has to find a home for its methyl. A big home in need of methyls is guanidinoacetate; when methylated it becomes creatine. If guanidinoacetate is low, then SAM is kind of stuck, and this whole process slows down. After SAM is able to give away its methyl, it's no longer SAM, it's S-adenosylhomocysteine, or SAH. Then SAH needs to come apart into two pieces, adenosine and homocysteine. But SAH can't come apart if there is too much of either of these two hanging around. One destination for the homocysteine is the enzyme methionine synthase, which should have its cobalamin "loaded" with a methyl group. If so, the cobalamin gives its methyl to homocysteine, which changes it to methionine. Then 5-methyltetrahydrofolate reloads the cobalamin with a new methyl group, making it ready for the next round.

Adenosine also needs a place to go. One place is to adenosine deaminase, where it loses its amino group and become inosine. But to do this, adenosine deaminase needs its binding protein, and that protein is our old friend DPP4 or CD26. The other possibility is for adenosine, phosphate and energy to remake adenosine phosphate nucleotides, AMP, ADP, and ATP. If all this works okay, we have an ongoing cyclic process that continually methylates things and recycles amino acids to make methionine and SAM.

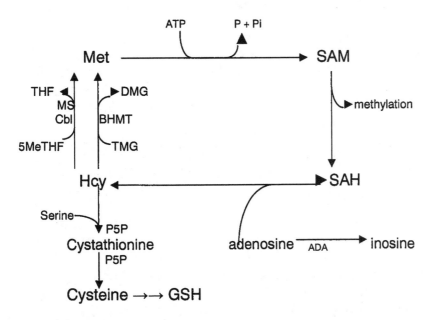

SAM = S-adenosylmethionine
MS = methionine synthase
Cbl = cobalamin
P5P = pyridoxal 5-phosphate

Under normal circumstances, supplementing methionine or SAM probably enhances the above process and increases methylation rates if tissues need that. But for many autistics this chemistry is anything but normal. With variations in type and degree of disorder in the autistic spectrum, we have:

- Not enough guanidinoacetate (unusual, but does occur).

- Creatine excess (unusual, caused by transporter defects or mercury inhibition of creatine kinase).

- Adenosine excess (multiple causes, 20% of so-far tested autistic population – Dr. Jill James).

SECTION FIVE: NUTRITIONAL SUPPLEMENTS FOR AUTISM

- Adenosylhomocysteine excess (also about 20% of ASD population).
- Homocysteine <u>deficit</u> (still quantifying, maybe 40-50% of ASD population).
- Methylcobalamin deficit (a majority of the ASD population, causes include toxic inhibitions, oxidant stress, and reduced supply of 5-MeTHF).
- Oxidant stress and inflammation which results in purposeful reduction of methylation of Hcy, probably with the objective of shunting Hcy to cysteine (relative occurrence unknown but suspected to be high).
- Subnormal kinetics of Hcy → cysteine (cysteine is low per blood plasma in about 60% of the ASD population). Phosphorylation of pyridoxal and pyridoxine is very slow in autistics – Dr. Tapan Audhya.

In summary, for autism, this cyclic process has multiple problems that cause rate restrictions and congestion. The molecules don't flow freely, they're caught in a traffic jam. With many autistics, methionine or SAM supplements can be likened to adding cars to the traffic jam. Traffic doesn't go any faster, there's just more of it.

We do not have parent-response statistics on methionine at ARI. We do have them for SAM, and they're not very good. SAM has about the highest "got worse" percentage (about 15%) of all nutritional supplements. Also, it has the lowest "got better" rating of any tallied nutritional supplement, only 19%.[4]

SAM Parent Response Tally, responses = 62

Behavior or Traits Improved	No Discernible Effect	Behavior or Traits Worsened
19%	66%	15%

Using Methionine or SAM in Autism

Some nutritional supply companies provide the synthetic form, D,L-methionine. Absolutely, positively without exception do not ever use this form of methionine as a nutritional supplement for autism. Use only all-natural L-methionine. Use of D,L-methionine will cause oxidation to methionine sulfoxide by peroxynitrite,[5] and methionine in both D- and L-configurations will be wasted in the urine because the D-form cannot be efficiently processed or racemized (changed to L-).[6,7,8] Giving D,L-methionine is like adding a drunk driver to the traffic jam.

Amounts of L-methionine that may be beneficial are 10 to 20 mg/Kg of body weight, given in divided doses, not to exceed 2000 mg/day total. Methionine is usually provided in capsules or tablets in 500 mg amounts, and 500 mg is the maximum amount per day that should be used on a trial basis. With young children, use less (for the trial period) by opening the capsule or breaking the tablet in half. (Use about 250 mg/d for children under 5 years of age.)

Both methionine and SAM are absorbed into the blood from the small intestine. Neither is known to provoke yeast or fungi overgrowth or bacterial dysbiosis, so they can be tried any time after supporting nutrition is in place: especially B_6, magnesium, B_{12}, and perhaps folate.

SAM needs to be enterically coated to protect it from disassembly by stomach acid; hence most SAM supplements are tablets. These won't work if the pancreas has deficient function or if bicarbonate secretion into the small intestine is deficient. When this part of digestion works as it should, SAM concentrations will peak in the blood 3 to 5 hours after tablet ingestion.[9] SAM is usually provided in 200-mg or 500-mg amounts (per tablet) and effective doses are 5 to15 mg/Kg body weight per day. Safety for doses above 1600 mg/d is not documented.[10] Do the initial trial with just 500 mg. (Breaking the SAM tablet in half to get a smaller dose means that it is no longer protected by the enteric coat, so don't do that.)

References – Methionine and SAM

1. Mudd SH and Levy HL "Disorders of Transsulfuration" Chapter 25 in Stanbury et al. eds *The Metabolic Basis of Inherited Disease* 5th Ed McGraw-Hill (1983) 525.
2. Granner DK "Regulation of Gene Expression" Chapter 41 in Murray RK, Granner DK, et al., eds *Harper's Biochemistry* 25th Ed, Appleton & Lange (2000) 477.
3. Waly M, Olteanu H et al. "Activation of methionine synthase by insulin-like growth factor-1 and dopamine: a target for neurodevelopmental toxins and Thimerosal" *Molec Psych* 9 no.4 (2004) 358-370.
4. ARI Publication 34 updated March 2005, Autism Research Institute, 4182 Adams Ave, San Diego CA 92116.
5. Pryor WA Jin X and Squadrito G "One- and two-electron oxidations of methionine by peroxynitrile" *Proc.Natl Acad Sci* (USA) 91 (1994) 11173-11177.
6. Crim MC and Hamish NM "Proteins and Amino Acids" Chapt.1 in Shils et al. eds *Modern Nutrition in Health and Disease* 8th Ed Lea & Febiger (994) 3,4.
7. Mudd HS and Levy HL, op.cit. 527.
8. Pangborn JB, personal observation of numerous 24-hour urine amino acid analyses of autistics intentionally or unintentionally given D,L-methionine. In autism, increased stimming, irritability and hyperactivity can occur with use of D-methionine, and methionine and methionine sulfoxide (if measured) are invariably at excessive levels (versus reference ranges) when the D-form is used.
9. *PDR for Nutritional Supplements*, Thompson PDR, 1st Ed. (2001) 441.
10. *PDR for Nutritional Supplements* ibid. 413.

FOLATE

- **Folate is a carrier of one-carbon pieces which are used to assemble or alter nucleotides, and folate brings methyls to cobalamin for use in methionine synthase.**
- **When utilization of these one-carbon pieces becomes impeded, folate can be trapped and can accumulate in one form while another is depleted.**
- **For autism, folinic acid (5-formyltetrahydrofolate) is the most versatile supplement form; ordinary folic acid is not tolerated by some.**

The name folate comes from the Latin "folium" for leaf, and folic acid does come from leafy vegetables, such as spinach and parsley, but it also comes from meats, grains and beans. Many different types of yeast and some bacteria can synthesize it, too.[1]

About Folate

Folate exists in nature with various amounts of attached glutamic acid. The vitamin is defined to be pteracylmonoglutamate or folate with just one attached glutamic acid molecule, and that's called folic acid or folacin.[2] Decades ago, the various glutamic acid attachments caused confusion about what the vitamin was. The triglutamate was "fermentation factor," the heptaglutamate was a yeast-source type. It's been called vitamin Bc, Vitamin M, and anti-anemia factor.

To be used in the body, all but one of the glutamates have to be clipped off (enzymatically), and it has to be chemically reduced by addition of hydrogen atoms. The reduced coenzyme form of vitamin B_3 can do this.[2]

$$\text{Folate} + \text{NADPH} + H^+ \rightarrow H_2\text{folate} + \text{NADP}^+$$
$$H_2\text{folate} + \text{NADPH} + H^+ \rightarrow H_4\text{folate} + \text{NADP}^+$$

H_4 folate is "tetrahydrofolate," abbreviated as THF or H_4F. Dietary folate is useless to us without this reduction by the coenzyme form of niacin; both NADH and NADPH can do this.

Once we have H_4 folate or THF, we have a molecular truck that can acquire, carry and give away chemical pieces that are composed of one carbon (always), some hydrogen, and maybe an oxygen and a nitrogen atom. THF can carry methyl, $-CH_3$, methylene, $=CH_2$, formyl, -CHO, formimino, -CH=NH, and methenyl, -CH=, groups. And THF can also serve as a platform for interchanging these one-carbon pieces. Now, what's all this chemical transport and change good for?

- As 5-methylTHF, folate provides a methyl group to cobalamin to form methylcobalamin. Via methionine synthase, methylcobalamin methylates homocysteine to (re)make methionine.

- As 5,10-methyleneTHF, folate is a cofactor for transforming the pyrimidine nucleotide deoxyuridine into deoxythymidine (as monophosphates). Deficiency of this folate form is considered to be one possible cause of Fragile X syndrome.[3]

- As 5-formiminoTHF, folate handles what the amino acid histidine has provided, and allows it to be transformed into the 5,10-methenyl form.

- As 5,10-methenylTHF, folate provides a reactive carbon group for synthesis of purine nucleosides, such as adenosine and guanosine.

- And 5,10-methenylTHF can allow the methenyl group to become 10-formylTHF, and that also is used for purine nucleoside formation.

So, folate is one of the vitamins that is absolutely necessary for operation of the methionine methylation cycle. Also, it's required for formation of the molecules that transfer energy for cellular perception and response functions. A road map of how the forms of folate are related and how they interact with vitamin B_{12} (cobalamin) is provided below. We need this to understand what's often going wrong in autism, and why various forms of folate may help or hinder the condition.

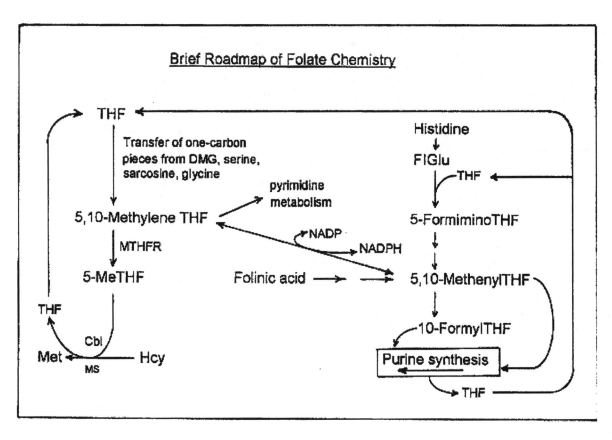

Using Folate in Autism

I know of three forms of folate that can be used nutritionally or therapeutically:

1. Folate or folacin is the health food store form and usual nutritional supplement form that's in multivitamins. That's the kind with one attached glutamate that has to be reduced by NADH or NADPH to make THF.
2. FolaPro™, which is provided by Metagenics, Inc, and is 5-methylTHF.
3. Folinic acid which is 5-formylTHF, stabilized as a calcium salt, and available in injectable form (prescription) and in oral form as capsules or tablets (OTC).

Over recent decades, the DRI, Daily Value for this vitamin has been stated inconsistently, and this has been a source of confusion for many of those concerned with nutrition. Going back to the 1970s and 1980s, the RDA, recommended dietary allowance, was 400 micrograms (400mcg) per day for an adult.[4] This was the FDA RDA for food product labeling, and it remains so today as the "Daily Value" on labels. However, in 1989 the Food and Nutrition Board of the National Research Council, NRC, restated the RDA levels to be: 200mcg/d for adult males over 10 years, 180 mcg/d for adult females, 80 mcg/d for children ages 4 to 6 years and 100 mcg/d for children ages 7 to 10 years.[5] These levels are in the pharmacists' *Drug Facts and Comparisons*[6] book as well as in the 10th edition of the NRC's RDA book. Reconsideration and realization that metabolic diseases (neural tube defects, homocystinuria) can be due to inadequacy in human phenotypes caused the Food and Nutrition Board (now under the auspices of the Institute of Medicine) to go back to 400 mcg/d as the Dietary Reference Intake, DRI. So, the Food and Nutrition Board, the IOM and the NRC now have restated the adult folate need to be 400 mcg/d.[7]

Problems with folate or B_{12} metabolism can cause or contribute to the metabolic traffic jam that often is present in autism. These problems are sometimes referred to as folate traps or methyl traps, places where one form of folate accumulates because of difficulty with an enzymatic process. Usually, "folate trap" refers to accumulation of 5,10-methylene THF due to weakness of the reductase enzyme that is supposed to change this form into 5-methylTHF. The weak enzyme is methylene-tetrahydrofolate reductase, MTHFR. The MTHFR gene has variants, and human carriers of the variants can have MTHFR activities that are low enough to contribute to homocysteinemia. Homocysteinemia is rare in autism for two reasons. First, in many there is an upstream bottleneck at adenosine and adenosylhomocysteine that throttles homocysteine formation. Second, when 5,10-methylene THF accumulates, it tends to drive the conversion of glycine to serine.

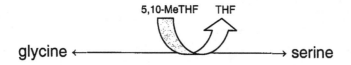

This, in turn, drives whatever homocysteine is present toward cystathionine (especially because we're usually giving significant doses of vitamin B_6):

$$\text{Homocystine + serine} \xrightarrow[\text{Cys beta synthase}]{\text{P5P}} \text{cystathionine}$$

In autism, there can be at least two more folate traps. One is expected to occur when cobalamin is oxidized and glutathione is insufficient, which can result in methionine synthase having reduced activity. One consequence is elevated 5-methylTHF because there's no home for all the methyls that are available (assuming MTHFR produces normal or near-normal 5-methylTHF amounts). Another trap occurs if purine metabolism is impaired. This could trap folate as 10-formylTHF and maybe as 5,10-methenylTHF. Referring to the folate road map, a marker for this could be elevated FIGlu in the face of adequate nutritional folate and B_{12}. Supplementing folate in that case could, very conceivably, drive FIGlu even higher, as would supplementing histidine. Indeed, Dr. Sidney Baker has had several autistic patients where supplements of all kinds of folate simply increased urine FIGlu excretions.

The most versatile supplemental form is folinic acid because it's already reduced, already has a one-carbon moiety on board, and it can be transformed into any of the other forms (except formimino, which isn't an end-use form anyway).[8] 5-MethylTHF is an end-use form, and it can be a dead-end form. Once our tissues make 5-methylTHF, there's no going back; it's on a one-way street. 5-MethylTHF has to meet up with reduced cobalamin to get rid of its methyl. That's fine if cobalamin and methionine synthase are ready to go. Unfortunately, they often aren't in autism, and that's why Dr. Neubrander and others are having such success with injected methylcobalamin. That the metabolic traffic jam is up against a real throttle point (or a dead-end street) is confirmed by the fact that the doctor (or parents) have to keep injecting methylcobalamin, daily or perhaps 3 times a week, to gain and maintain improvements.

Folic acid levels in blood are often found to be high in untreated autistic individuals. That has been interpreted to mean that folate is not needed, and some have construed excessive folate as a cause of autism. With our clinical research activities in DAN!, we have learned that the situation is not that simple. While one form of folate is excessive, perhaps causing the blood serum level of total folate to be above a lab's reference range, specific folate forms can be low.

This observation is based on clinical reports about supplementing or injecting folinic acid or methylcobalamin. This problem with specific folate forms is also consistent with the 42% of 4918 autistics who improved with DMG and with DMG plus methylcobalamin plus folinic acid (a supplemental form that has been widely used).

My experience is that DMG or TMG with folate as folinic acid, or separate folinic acid, perhaps adjunctive to injected methylcobalamin, has the best chance of working in autism. You may wish to try 5-meTHF, FolaPro™, if you have reason to believe that cobalamin, glutathione, methionine synthase and methionine synthase reductase are adequate and cooperating with each other. If they're not, neither 5-meTHF nor ordinary folate is likely to be beneficial.

References - Folate

1. Kutsky R *Handbook of Vitamins, Minerals and Hormones* 2nd ed Van Norstrand Reinhold Co (1981) 269-274.
2. Harper HA, Rodwell VW and Mayes PA *Review of Physiological Chemistry* 17th Ed (1979) 172-173.
3. Nussbaum RL and Ledbetter DH "The Fragile X Syndrome" Chapter 8 in Scriver CR et al., Eds. *The Metabolic Basis of Inherited Disease* 6th Ed. McGraw-Hill (1989) 332.
4. Harper HA, Rodwell VW and Mayes PA, op.cit. 605.
5. *Recommended Dietary Allowances*, 10th Ed., National Research Council, National Academy Press (1989) 285, (end sheet foldout).
6. *Drug Facts and Comparisons* "Recommended Dietary Allowances of Vitamins and Minerals" Facts & Comparisons (Kluwer) January 2000, 4.
7. *Dietary Reference Intakes for Thiamin, Riboflavin...* Institute of Medicine, Nat Acad Press (1998) 196 and end foldout sheet.
8. Rosenblatt DS and Fenton WA "Inherited Disorders of Folate and Cobalamin Transport and Metabolism" Scriver CR et al. Eds., *The Metabolic and Molecular Bases of Inherited Disease* 8th Ed. McGraw-Hill (2001) 3900, 3906.

N-ACETYLCYSTEINE

- **NAC use can increase glutathione levels, but it can foster yeast dysbiosis as well.**
- **NAC, by itself, is not an efficient or safe detoxifier for toxics such as mercury.**

The reduced and very reactive amino acid cysteine is not an easy nutrient to manufacture, package, tolerate or utilize correctly. It's somewhat more stable, tolerable and useful in the form called "NAC," N-acetylcysteine.

About NAC

N-acetylcysteine is the reduced form of cystine with an acetyl group ($COCH_3$) attached to the nitrogen of what otherwise would be its amino group.[1] NAC has a 30-year history of therapeutic use as an expectorant in veterinary practice, and as an antidote for acetaminophen poisoning in humans.[1] As a nutritional supplement, NAC is an antioxidant which protects against the hydroxyl radical, hydrogen peroxide, the superoxide ion, and hypochlorous acid (present in bleach and containing the hypochlorite ion which is generated in humans in leukocytes).[2] NAC can increase cellular levels of glutathione,[3] and the glutathione can then help with detoxication, leukotriene synthesis, transport of amino acids, and protection of enzymes and metabolites that carry sulfur.[4]

NAC has been made available in health food stores as a nutritional supplement, usually in capsules or tablets containing 200, 250 or 500 mg. In addition, it is often included in antioxidant blends or combination products that provide other reducing agents or antioxidants such as vitamin C, vitamin E, taurine, and/or grape seed extract.

Using NAC in Autism

N-acetylcysteine has been used with the objective of increasing glutathione amounts to more normal levels, and some have sought to use it directly as a detoxifier. While it is often beneficial, two different problems have been frequently encountered with its use. The first is promotion of yeast dysbiosis in the intestines. I acknowledge and accept the findings of Horvath, Buie, and Rosseneu that yeast overgrowth is not more common in untreated autistics than in matched controls.[5,6,7] But after a few weeks of oral cystine or NAC (or alpha-lipoic acid), this situation becomes very different. Cystine is a culture medium for the Candida genus of yeast.[8] Cystine is two cysteines linked by a sulfur-to-sulfur bond, so cystine is oxidized cysteine. Inside organisms, cystine (Cys_2) reacts with glutathione (GSH) which pulls it apart (and may use up glutathione which has to be resynthesized).[9]

$$Cys_2 + GSH \rightarrow \text{gamma-glutamylcystine} + \text{cysteinylglycine}$$

Or, inside a cell[10]:

$$Cys_2 + GSH \rightarrow GS\text{-}Cys + Cys$$

This gives the organism (including human cells) access to cysteine. So cystine, cysteine and, to some extent, GSH can feed yeast growth. Apparently, NAC also feeds it because stool analyses on autistics fed that supplement typically show Candidiasis if robust anti-yeast measures are not in place. Anti-yeast measures include daily supplements of nutrients such as caprylic acid, olive leaf extract, oregano, garlic and/or goldenseal extract. Regular use of probiotics also helps. Once or twice a week, Saccharomyces boulardii may be needed, and medicinal antifungals may be required for periodic rescue of the situation. That's problem one with NAC use.

Problem two is uncontrolled binding and movement of toxics having high affinity for sulfur and thus for cysteine. One of the highest affinities known, and the highest one listed in my textbook, is that of divalent mercury ion, Hg^{++} (mercuric).[11] When enough cysteine finds some Hg^{++}, virtually all of the Hg^{++} becomes very tightly bound to cysteine:

$$Cys + Cys + Hg{++} \rightarrow CysHgCys$$

Chemists measure how complete a reaction is by ratioing the amount of product (CysHgCys) to the amount of remaining reactant ($Cys + Cys + Hg^{++}$) after they've been in contact for a long time ("equilibrium"). In this case, it doesn't take long, usually just seconds, for all of the Hg^{++} to be bound to the nearby cysteine if there's enough of it. The equilibrium constant, the ratio of CysHgCys ÷ ($Cys + Cys + Hg^{++}$), is 10 followed by 43 zeros. Nothing's perfect, but this reaction comes as close as chemistry can.

Now, we've gotten rid of the mercury – or have we? Who says that cysteine (or NAC for that matter) will escort mercury out of the body? Nobody does – no reference, no toxicology study, no clinical evidence of this at all. If cysteine could do this (as glutathione does), then there would be no need for BAL, DMSA, DMPS, etc. In fact, NAC, cystine and cysteine do not detoxify by themselves. But they can move mercury around, perhaps spreading the contamination, and their use may make the sequestering of mercury more difficult to undo. It takes another cysteine-like molecule to grab mercury and dispose of it, by carrying it to urine or bile – which is why the body has glutathione and why your doctor uses DMSA or DMPS. He or she may wish to use NAC along with these agents. But don't use NAC or cystine by themselves for detoxing; they don't work that way. When they are used as nutritional supplements, wait until detox trials prove that mercury excess is not a problem.

References - NAC

1. "Acetylcysteine. N-Acetyl-L-Cysteine". Entry #89, *The Merck Index* 12th Ed. Merck & Co. 1996.
2. Aruoma OI et al. "The antioxidant action of N-acetylcysteine: its reaction with hydrogen peroxide, hydroxyl radical, superoxide, and hypochlorous acid" *Free Radical Biology & Medicine* vol.6 Pergamon Press 1989 593-597.
3. Meister A "Glutathione metabolism" *Methods in Enzymology* vol.251 Academic Press 1995 3-7.
4. Beutler E "Nutritional and metabolic aspects of glutathione" *Annu.Rev.Nutr.* 9 (1989) 287-302.
5. Horvath K, Papadimitriou JC et al. "Gastrointestinal abnormalities in children with autistic disorder" *J.Pediatrics* 135 no.5 (1999) 559-563.
6. Buie T, Statement at DAN! Think Tank, New Orleans, January 2004; Dr. Timothy Buie is a practicing gastroenterologist at Massachusetts General Children's Hospital with extensive experience in examining autistic patients.
7. Rosseneu SLM, van Saene HFK et al. "Anaerobic throat and gut flora in children with autistic spectrum disorder and gastrointestinal symptoms" Proceedings (Syllabus) Spring DAN 2000 Conference, Washington DC 101-105.
8. Griffin DH *Fungal Physiology* John Wiley & Sons (1981) 124.
9. Meister A and Larsson A Chapter 31 in Scriver et al. Eds. *The Metabolic Basis of Inherited Disease* 6th Ed McGraw-Hill (1989) 855-856.
10. Gahl WA Renlund M and Thoene JG, Chapter 107 in Scriver et al. Eds. ibid. 2621.
11. Chaberek S and Martell AE *Organic Sequestering Agents* John Wiley & Sons (1959) 548.

LIPOIC ACID

> - **Lipoic acid is required for operation of the citric acid cycle and catabolism of branched-chain essential amino acids; it's a powerful antioxidant, an efficient detoxifying agent for sulfur-seeking toxic elements, and it can assist mercury detoxification when DMPS or DMSA are used.**
>
> - **Unfortunately, lipoic acid often fosters severe intestinal yeast infections in autistics in spite of ongoing anti-yeast measures.**

Lipoic acid or alpha-lipoic acid is an essential cofactor for human metabolism, yet it is not a true vitamin. It does not have an RDA or RDI or Daily Value amount for nutritional intake. That's because it is considered to be made in adequate amounts endogenously, but exactly how is unknown.[1] It is necessary for energy metabolism because operation of the citric acid cycle depends on it, and it's needed for catabolism of the branched-chain amino acids, leucine, isoleucine and valine.

About Lipoic Acid

The chemical structure of this cofactor looks like what might result if we crossed DMSA with a short-chain fatty acid. It has eight carbon atoms, an organic acid group (-COOH or carboxyl) on one end, and two sulfur atoms on the other end – and it's water soluble, too. Lipoic acid comes in two versions: reduced, with the sulfur as sulfhydryls (-SH), and oxidized, with the sulfhydryl hydrogens replaced by a disulfide bond (-S-S-). A descriptive chemical name for it is 6,8-dithio-octanoic acid.

```
CH2-CH2-CH-(CH2)4-COOH           CH2-CH2-CH-(CH2)4-COOH
 |    |                           |    |
 SH   SH                          S————S
    Reduced form                     Oxidized form
```

Both forms function directly as cofactors, acting to assist thiamin diphosphate, the active form of vitamin B_1, in "dehydrogenase" enzyme complexes that are used to process pyruvate into acetyl coenzyme A and alpha-ketoglutaric acid into succinyl CoA for citric acid cycle use.[2] Besides being an enzymatic cofactor, reduced alpha-lipoic acid is a powerful antioxidant. It can scavenge and neutralize hydroxyl radicals, peroxynitrite, hypochlorite and hydrogen peroxide.[3] And, the reduced form can be a chelator or complexing agent for metals that have affinity for sulfur, such as arsenic and mercury. In fact, lipoate in the pyruvate dehydrogenase enzyme complex is a molecular target for both arsenic and mercury.[4]

When acting as a cofactor, oxidized lipoic acid displaces thiamin from its temporary binding with pyruvate (or alpha-ketoglutarate), and an instant later, it is displaced, in reduced form, by coenzyme A (CoA). The reduced lipoic acid (HS-L-SH) can then reduce (activate) the coenzyme form of riboflavin, FAD, and that, in turn, can reduce (activate) the coenzyme form of niacin, NAD. So, reduced lipoic acid has considerable chemical reducing and antioxidant capacities.

Lipoic Acid Use by Pyruvate Dehydrogenase

Pyruvic acid → (Pyruvate dehydrogenase, with Thiamin and CoA) → acetyl CoA + CO_2

S-L-S ⇌ HS-L-SH
FAD ⇌ FADH₂
NAD ⇌ NADH + H

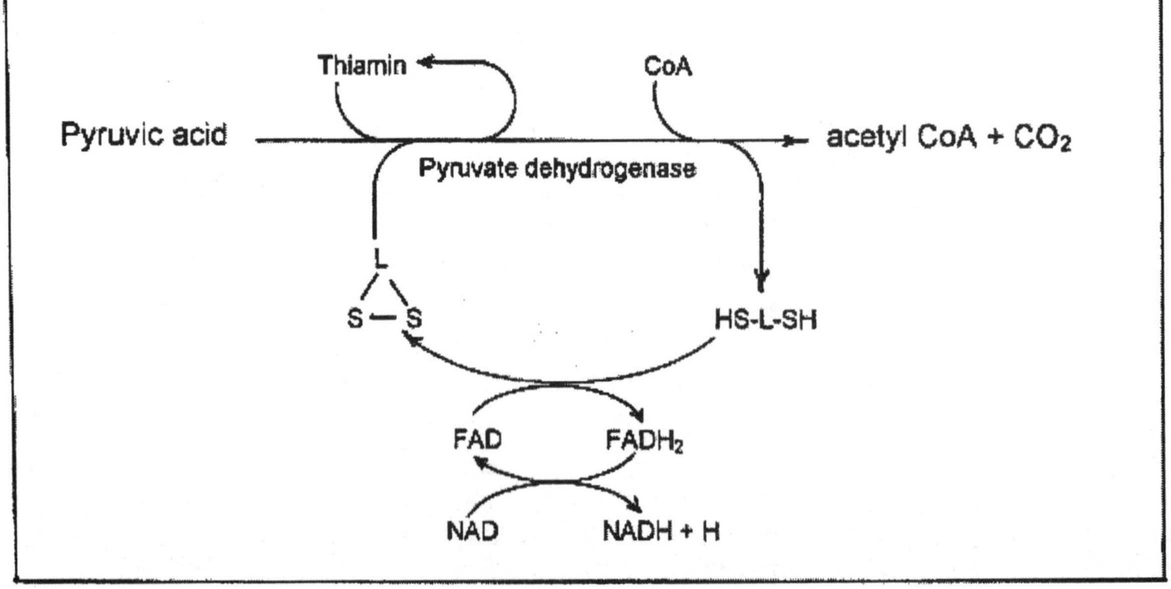

Using Lipoic Acid in Autism

Lipoic acid has been used as a nutritional supplement for autistics who present with elevated pyruvate, who are considered to have oxidant stress, and who have increased body burden of mercury – in conjunction with other chelating agents (usually DMSA). The DAN! Mercury Detoxification Consensus Group Position Paper of May 2001 included lipoic acid as an assisting nutrient to DMSA for mercury removal. Since that time, an unanticipated problem has occurred very frequently. The new DAN! position paper (2005) on detoxification includes lipoic acid as a substance to be wary of (as we do here). Like cystine, oral lipoic acid promotes growth of yeast and fungi in the intestinal tract – especially, it seems, in many autistics. It is so potent at doing this that anti-yeast measures (capryllic acid, herbals, even periodic Saccharomyces boulardii) often can't keep up. So, while it's a great antioxidant and a good co-detoxifier, the resulting intestinal yeast problems often make it more bother than it's worth. Like cystine and cysteine, the oxidized and reduced forms make no difference in this respect. Yeasts love both.

Lipoic acid or alpha-lipoic acid is provided in gelatin capsules or tablets, usually containing amounts of 50 or 100 or 300 mg. All these amounts and more have been used as daily supplements for autism without reported problems except that of intestinal yeast overgrowth. Hypoglycemia, low blood sugar, is a possible contraindication for lipoic acid because it does tend to lower blood glucose levels.

References – Lipoic Acid

1. Hendler SS and Rorvik D Eds, *PDR for Nutritional Supplements*, 1st Ed, Thompson PDR, Montvale NJ (2001) 17.
2. Murray RK, Granner DK et al. *Harper's Biochemistry* 25th Ed Appleton & Lange (2000) 184-5, 195-196
3. Hendler SS and Rorvik D, op.cit. 18.
4. Murray RK, Granner DK et al. op.cit. 197.

GLUTATHIONE

> - **Glutathione, GSH, participates in control of oxidant stress, detoxication, immune response, insulin and glucose metabolism, nutrient transport and mediation of inflammation.**
> - **In autism, the quantity of GSH is reduced and the ratio of oxidized to reduced glutathione is elevated.**
> - **Occasional adverse responses have occurred with oral and injected GSH.**
> - **Clinical research has shown significant improvement in the reduced/oxidized glutathione ratio when TMG and folinic acid are used.**

In the last two and a half decades, the natural tripeptide, glutathione, has become one of the most popular topics for clinical study with over 63,500 citations listed in "PubMed." Glutathione influences detoxication, oxidant/antioxidant balance, immune response, insulin and glucose metabolism, transport of nutrients across membranes, and mediation of inflammation via leukotrienes.[1,2] It is required for metabolism of vitamin B_{12} (see Vitamin B_{12} discussion). Frequently, glutathione has been measured to be subnormal in blood or erythrocytes of autistics and too much of it is in the inactive, oxidized form.

About Glutathione

Reduced, active glutathione, GSH, is a tripeptide composed of glutamic acid, cysteine and glycine, and the cysteinyl part (in the middle) carries a very reactive sulfhydryl group –SH. Synthesis of GSH is magnesium-dependent; magnesium deficiency hinders the formation of GSH.[3] The sulfhydryl group can trade its hydrogen for a bond or connection to atoms or molecules with affinity for sulfur. Bonds are formed with other sulfur compounds such as cysteine (pulling apart cystine to some degree), or with itself to form GSSG while releasing two hydrogens and acting as a chemical reducing agent. Reducing hydrogen peroxide is an example:

$$H_2O_2 + 2\ GSH \xrightarrow{GPx} 2H_2O + GSSG$$

The enzyme that promotes this reaction, GPx, is glutathione peroxidase. The red blood cell version of GPx needs selenium for catalytic activity. This mechanism also works to protect lipids or fatty acids from oxidation.[4] Once GSSG is formed, it has to be rescued from its oxidized state and reduced back to its active GSH form. The enzyme that promotes this is glutathione reductase, GR. Although NADPH is the preferred reducing reactant, NADH will also do this.[5]

$$GSSG + NADPH + H^+ \xrightarrow{GR} 2GSH + NADP^+$$

Studies indicate that healthy mammals (including humans) maintain at least 98% of intracellular glutathione as GSH, and at least 90% of extracellular glutathione also as GSH.[6,7,8,9] Oxidant stress tends to increase the proportion of oxidized glutathione, GSSG.[10,11,12,13] The supply of NADPH for GSSG reduction comes primarily from glucose 6-phosphate dehydrogenase in a part of human glucose metabolism known as the "hexose monophosphate shunt."

$$\text{Glucose 6-P} \xrightarrow[\text{dehydrogenase}]{NADP^+ \quad NADPH+H^+} \text{6-phosphogluconate}$$

NADPH is also provided by other processes including the citric acid cycle (malate to oxaloacetate) plus proton-translocating transhydrogenase[14] and the glycolysis of glucose or fructose to pyruvate (glyceraldehyde to bisphosphoglycerate).[15] These are all processes of carbohydrate and energy metabolism, and they are crucial to GSH supply.

Besides antioxidant work, GSH binds elements that might otherwise attach to and inactivate proteins, hormones and enzymes that contain sulfur. Metals that bind to GSH, roughly in order of decreasing affinity, are: mercury (Hg^{++}), free iron (Fe^{+++}), cadmium, nickel, copper, lead, cobalt, zinc, and selenium.[16] Mercury is reported to be escorted out of cells by GSH.[17,18]

Over the years, a controversy has festered over whether oral glutathione is beneficial. My opinion is a definite yes, for most individuals. There are exceptions, some being autistics.

Dietary GSH is absorbed into the bloodstream from the lumen of the small intestine; most absorption occurs in the jejunum.[19,20,21,22] Not all dietary/oral GSH is digested. Research has demonstrated that direct, intact intestinal absorption of dietary GSH occurs as well as absorption via partial hydrolysis followed by resynthesis in cells.[19,21,22,23,24] The ability of significant amounts of GSH to survive normal peptidase digestive activity is attributed to the unusual peptide structure of GSH which features cysteine bound to the gamma rather than to the alpha carboxy group of glutamic acid.[1,13,19] Use of oral GSH as a nutritional supplement has been explicitly mentioned by leading authorities on GSH.[13,19,20,25,26] If dietary GSH is insufficient, oxidative stress, toxicity, and cell damage may occur to mucosal cells in the small intestine.[22,23,25]

Using Glutathione in Autism

The substance that typically limits the amount of GSH that can be synthesized in cells is cysteine.[27] Cysteine and GSH are often subnormal in autism and the ratio of GSSG to GSH is too high (typical of oxidant stress).[28,29,30] So, there is an undeniable need for GSH by many autistics. However, several problems, some of them rather severe, have been reported with use of supplemental GSH.

First, over time, some have developed intestinal yeast overgrowth with oral GSH. Not as many nor as severely as happens with lipoic acid, but it has been a bothersome side effect. Of course, this does not occur with transdermal or intravenous administration, offered by some pharmacies or clinicians respectively.

Second, in a few cases, there have been some very bad prompt responses to intravenous administration of GSH, including a few seizure cases. Also, a few prompt behavioral problems, probably not yeast-related, have occurred with oral GSH. The biochemical reasons or the physiological basis for these problems remains speculative. One speculation is that there really isn't enough NADPH to recycle GSSG into GSH. After the infused GSH is used, which may occur in minutes to a few hours, there's more GSSG and even less NADPH. If that's occurring, then a more correct therapy would be a nutritional strategy for producing more NADPH; supplements of magnesium malate might do that. And a second speculation is that GSH from outside a cell doesn't quite do what GSH inside a cell does when it comes to mercury transport. GSH inside the cell pulls mercury and other toxics out. If some of the additional, external GSH breaks down to cysteine or cysteinyl pieces and there are toxics present outside of a cell, does some get pulled inside? If there is mercury or there are toxics in the intestinal mucosa, do some of them get pulled in by oral GSH? Finally, was insulin decreased to critical levels in the very few with severely bad responses to intravenous GSH? These unknowns and occasional bad experiences make GSH a nutritional supplement to be cautious about with autism.

A paper presented by Jill James at the October 2004 DAN! Conference showed the beneficial clinical effects of betaine (TMG) and folinic acid.[30] These supplements increased cysteine and GSH levels and decreased the GSSG/GSH ratio significantly in a three-month intervention trial with 20 autistic children. Total GSH was raised an average of 25% from baseline levels and the GSSG/GSH ratio was halved with daily supplements of betaine (1000 mg bid) and folinic acid (800micrograms bid). So, in autism, attacking the biochemical problem of impaired methylation achieves another desired result – better glutathione levels – without having to give glutathione itself. To me, this is yet another example of biomedical intervention that attacks the roadblocks that have throttled methylation and thiol (sulfur) chemistry in many autistics.

References – Glutathione

1. Beutler E "Nutritional and metabolic aspects of glutathione" *Ann.Rev.of Nutrition* 9 (1989) 287-302.
2. Arias IM and Jakoby WB Eds *Glutathione: Metabolism and Function* Raven Press (1976).
3. Mills BJ, Lindeman RD, Lang CA "Magnesium deficiency inhibits biosynthesis of blood glutathione and tumor growth in the rat" *Proc.Soc.Exper.Bio.Med.* 181 (1986) 326-332.
4. Mayes PA, Chapter 53 in Murray, Granner et al. eds, *Harper's Biochemistry* 23rd Ed (1993) 593.
5. Beutler E "Nutritional and metabolic aspects of glutathione" op.cit. 289.
6. Bannai S "Turnover of glutathione in human fibroblasts in culture in *Glutathione: Storage, Transport and Turnover in Mammals* eds Sakamoto Y et al. Japan Sci Soc Press, (1983) 41-51.
7. Beutler E Chapt 74 of Stanbury, Wyngaarden et al. eds. *The Metabolic Basis of Inherited Disease* 5th Ed. McGraw-Hill (1983) 1633.
8. Meister A "Glutathione metabolism" in *Methods of Enzymology* 251 (1995) 3.
9. Halliwell B and Gutteridge JMC *Free Radicals in Biology and Medicine* 3rd Ed. Oxford Univ Press (2000) 142.
10. Ormstad K and Orrenius S "Metabolism of extracellular glutathione in small intestine and kidney" in *Glutathione: Storage, Transport and Turnover in Mammals*, Sakamoto et al. eds. Japan Sci Soc Press (1983) 107-125.
11. Sies H "Reduced and oxidized glutathione efflux from liver" in *Glutathione: Storage, Transport and Turnover in Mammals* op.cit. 63-88.
12. Jenkinson SC Marcum RF et al. "Glutathione disulfide formation occurring during hypoxia and reoxygenation of rat lung" *J.Lab.Clin.Med.* 112 no.4 (1988) 471-480.
13. Bray TM and Taylor CG "Tissue glutathione, nutrition, and oxidative stress" *Canadian J Physiol.Pharmacol* 71 (1993) 746-751.
14. Mayes PA Chapt 14 in Murray RK, Granner DK et al. Eds *Harper's Biochemistry* 25th Ed. Lange Med Pub (2000) 146.
15. Mayes PA Chapt 19 in Murray RK, Granner DK et al. eds. ibid.192.
16. Chaberek S and Martell AE *Organic Sequestering Agents* John Wiley & Sons (1959) 548 (using cysteine as a model for GSH binding of metals).
17. Foulkes E "Metal disposition: an analysis of underlying mechanisms" Chapt 1 in Goyer RA, Klaasen CD and Waalkes MP eds. *Metal Toxicology* Academic Press (1995) 18-21.
18. Clarksen TW as quoted by Dalton LW in C&EN, January 9, 2004, p.70. Thomas W. Clarksen is Professor of Environmental Medicine at the University of Rochester, NY.
19. Vincenzini MT, Favilli F and Iantomasi T "Intestinal uptake and transmembrane transport systems of intact GSH; characteristics and possible biological role" *Biochimica et Biophysica* Acta 1113 (1992) 13-23.
20. Hagen TM et al. "Fate of dietary glutathione: disposition in the gastrointestinal tract" *Am.Physiological Society*, 0193-1857-90 (1990) 6530-6535.
21. Linder M DeBurlet G and Sudake P "Transport of glutathione by intestinal brush border membrane vesicles" *Biochemical and Biophysical Research Communications*, Academic Press 123 no.3 (1984) 929-936.
22. Vincenzini MT, Iantomasi T and Favilli F "Glutathione transport across intestinal brush-border membranes: effects of ions, pH, $\Delta\Psi$, and inhibitors" *Biochim et Biophys Acta* 987 (1989) 29-37.

23. Hagen TM et al. "Bioavailability of dietary glutathione: effect on plasma concentration" *Am Physiol Soc* 0193-1857-90 (1990) G524-G529.
24. Vincenzini MT, Favilli F and Iantomasi T "Glutathione-mediated transport across intestinal brush-order membranes" *Biochim Et Biophys Acta* 942 (1988) 107-114.
25. Martensson J, Jain A and Meister A "Glutathione is required for intestinal function" *Proc. Nat Acad Sci USA* 87 (1990) 1715-1719.
26. Tateishi N and Sakamoto Y "Nutritional significance of glutathione in rat liver" in *Glutathione: Storage, Transport and Turnover in Mammals* op.cit. (1983) 13-38.
27. Meister A "Glutathione Metabolism" op.cit. 6,7.
28. Pangborn JB "Detection of Metabolic Disorders in People with Autism" Proceedings of NSAC Annual Meeting and International Autism Conference of the Americas, San Antonio TX (1984) 32-51, esp. page 46.
29. Owens SC "Understanding the sulfur system" Proceedings and Syllabus, Spring DAN! Conference, Philadelphia PA, (May 2003) 65-76, esp. page 66, 70 (diagram).
30. James SJ "Increased oxidative stress and impaired methylation capacity in children with autism: metabolic biomarkers and genetic predisposition" Fall DAN! Conference, Los Angeles CAN (October 2004) 143-160

CARNOSINE

- **Carnosine is a dietary peptide that contains histidine and beta-alanine; it's present in meats and fish.**
- **There are credible clinical reports of carnosine reducing seizures and improving speech and other autistic traits.**
- **Problems with its use have occurred, and there are several worrisome aspects for carnosine use in autism.**

Carnosine is a natural dipeptide that has meat and fish as dietary sources. Over the years it has been used nutritionally and therapeutically for enhancement of muscle mass and alleviation of muscular dystrophy. Recently, it has been used clinically, with some success, in alleviating autistic traits in autistic-spectrum children.

About Carnosine

Carnosine is a dipeptide – beta-alanyl-L-histidine – and the beta-alanyl part is the unusual amino acid, beta-alanine (not alanine, as may be incorrectly stated in commercial descriptions). Regular L-alpha-alanine is a protein-forming amino acid that we derive from dietary protein. The "alanine" in carnosine is different in chemical structure, does not participate in protein formation, and can interfere with membrane transport of other amino acids, primarily taurine.[1] Carnosine is similar to a slightly larger peptide, homocarnosine, and both can be synthesized in the brain in glial cells.[2] Both are considered to have neurotransmitter functions, but homocarnosine is 100x more prevalent than carnosine in human brains. Homocarnosine, when disassembled (hydrolyzed), yields histidine and gamma-aminobutyric acid (GABA). GABA in the brain or CNS can have seizure-alleviating actions.

Using Carnosine in Autism

Noting the beneficial effects ascribed to homocarnosine, Dr. Michael Chez et al. tried therapeutic use of L-carnosine on a group of autistic children in a placebo-controlled study. They reported improvements in socialization, communication and behavior.[3] When I questioned Dr. Chez about the types of autistic individuals that he had most success with by using carnosine, he replied that the individuals with seizures showed the most significant benefits.[4]

I must also disclose that a number of parents of autistic children have contacted me about very adverse responses to carnosine. However, none of these reports (to me) involved seizure patients. One child became severely hyperactive, and the hyperactivity lasted for days after carnosine was discontinued. Two became aggressive and destructive, and several lapsed deeper into isolation and noncommunication while taking carnosine. What's going on?

Dietary carnosine comes from beef, pork, tuna, salmon, and perhaps other animal meats and fish as well. Years ago, Dr. William Philpott correlated elevated urine or blood carnosine levels and a diet of carnosine foods with onset of behavior and speech disorders for children with environmental sensitivities. These children were not disassembling enough of the dietary carnosine, and it was being absorbed directly into their blood in excessive amounts.[5] Per other studies, elevated carnosine and carnosinase deficiency may or may not be coincident with neurological disorders.[6] Carnosine levels must be balanced, and the enzyme that disassembles carnosine into histidine and beta-alanine is a zinc-dependent protein called carnosinase. Obviously, carnosinase is weak in zinc deficiency. Many autistics are reported to be low in zinc, and oral zinc supplements may or may not be effective in rectifying a functional zinc deficiency. My experience is that carnosine is elevated, per urine amino acid analysis, in about 20% of the autistic population. So, a carnosine-handling problem may already be in place for a subset of the autistic population. Oral carnosine would then be contraindicated. Probably, a 24-hour urine amino acid analysis is the most indicative test for this.

The next condition that should be ruled out or corrected before using carnosine is blood copper/zinc ratio excess. Carnosine is a copper chelator,[7,8] and copper is almost invariably in the diet, especially in meats, shellfish, legumes, mushrooms, whole-grain cereals, nuts and chocolate.[9] Copper cooking utensils and sometimes copper water pipes can add more. If the copper is there, carnosine can carry it into the portal blood from the gastrointestinal tract, especially when sulfur, cysteine and metallothionein are deficient. Thioneins, acting in the intestinal mucosa, should collect excess copper because they have higher affinity for it than do most food components. However, deficient thioneins activity and excess copper uptake has already been reported in autism by Dr. William Walsh.[10] When this copper guardianship mechanism isn't adequate, oral carnosine could worsen the copper/zinc imbalance, regardless of whether zinc is also provided.

Next come two problems with the beta-alanine that can be derived from carnosine by carnosinase. First, beta-alanine competes with taurine for conservation in kidney tubules.[1] Elevated beta-alanine causes urinary wasting of taurine and that, in turn, can cause urinary wasting of magnesium.[11] So, if supplemental carnosine is used, a urine amino acid analysis during the period of use is a wise investment. If taurine is elevated in the urine and taurine is not being supplemented, then it's being wasted, especially if beta-alanine is also elevated. In that case, there's a 99% chance that magnesium dysfunction will occur unless it is also supplemented (along with taurine). And by the way, just supplementing taurine (instead of carnosine) can alleviate seizures in many cases.

The second problem with beta-alanine is interference with formation of guanidinoacetate, the precursor of creatine.[12] If creatine is low by blood analysis, then supplementing that may be the most beneficial course. Deficiency of guanidinoacetate is a seizure-provoking disorder that also can feature speech deficiency and mental retardation.[13,14]

In summary, carnosine is most beneficial for individuals with autistic spectrum disorder if they also present with seizures. But you may wish to occasionally monitor by laboratory tests some of the metabolites and nutrients that could be affected over time. And, be wary of carnosine use if:

- Carnosine is already high by urine amino acid analysis.
- Taurine is being wasted in urine, also per amino acid analysis.
- Taurine is low in blood, per plasma amino acid analysis.
- Blood Cu/Zn is excessive or zinc is deficient.
- Creatine is deficient in blood.

Carnosine is available from nutritional supply houses in gelatin capsules usually containing 200-mg amounts. Most have reported benefits from taking three to six capsules per day (600 to 1200 mg). Supporting nutrients would be zinc, magnesium, taurine, and vitamin B_6. Vitamin B_6 helps to lower beta-alanine by transamination.

References - Carnosine

1. Scriver CR and Perry TL "Disorders of ω-amino acids in free and peptide-linked forms," Chapter 26 in Scriver, Beaudet et al. *The Metabolic Basis of Inherited Disease* 6th Ed (1989) 758-759.
2. Gibson KM and Jakobs C, Chapter 91 in Scriver, Beaudet et al. *The Metabolic and Molecular Bases of Inherited Disease* 8th Ed (2001) 2097.
3. Chez MG, Buchanan CP et al. "Double-blind, placebo-controlled study of L-carnosine supplementation in children with autistic spectrum disorders" *J.Child Neurol* 17 no.11 (2002) 833-837.
4. Verbal statement by Dr. Michael Chez at the M.I.N.D. Institute Autism Focus Meeting, UC Davis, Sacramento CA July 2004.
5. Philpott WH and Philpott K "Carnosinase Enzyme Deficiency" Inst. For Bio-Ecologic Medicine, Hollywood FL, June 1984. Possible availability from WH Philpott M.D., PO Box 50655, Midwest City OK 73140.
6. Gibson KM and Jakobs C, op.cit. 2097-2098.
7. Rodwell VW "Conversion of Amino Acids to Specialized Products" Chapt 33 in Murray, Granner et al. Eds. *Harper's Biochemistry* 23rd ed (1993) 327.
8. Scriver CW and Perry TL, op.cit. 265.
9. Robinson CH *Normal and Therapeutic Nutrition* 14th Ed, MacMillan (1972) 639.
10. Walsh WJ, Usman A et al. "Metallothionein and Autism" Pfeiffer Treatment Center, Naperville IL October 2001 4-15.
11. Durlach J and Rayssiguier "Overview of relationships between magnesium and carbohydrate metabolism" *Magnesium* 2 (1983) 174-191 (S. Karger AG, Basel, in French).

12. Wyss M and Kaddurah-Daouk R "Creatine and creatinine metabolism" *Physiological Reviews* 80 no.3 (2000) 1107-1189.

13. Item CB, Stöckler-Ipsiroglu S et al. "Arginine:glycine amidinotransferase deficiency: the third inborn error of creatine metabolism in humans" *Am J Hum Genet* 69 (2001) 1127-1133.

14. Stromberger C, Stromberger G, et al. "Clinical characteristics and diagnostic clues in inborn errors of creatine metabolism" *J. Inherited Metab Dis* 26 no.2 (2003) 299-308.

OTHER NUTRITIONAL PRODUCTS THAT MIGHT BE BENEFICIAL

Activated Charcoal:

This was mentioned in connection with treating gut dysbiosis. It's provided in gelatin capsules, and when the charcoal is released in the GI tract, it absorbs and adsorbs (surface-sticking) volatiles and toxins. Don't use it at the same time that medications or nutritional supplements are given. One to three capsules per day between meals and away from supplements/medications can lessen "die-off" symptoms. Stools will darken with its use. No adverse reactions during its use have been reported to me.

Alpha-Ketoglutaric Acid or Alpha-Ketoglutarate

This is a natural metabolite formed in the citric acid cycle inside cells, and it goes just about everywhere in body tissues. It balances amino acid metabolism, helps to make carnitine and glutamine, and most importantly, it ties up ammonia. Alpha-ketoglutarate extends the body's natural buffering system for ammonia, and it can be very beneficial for those with elevated blood ammonia which, in autism, is usually a sign of bacterial dysbiosis. High stool pH is consistent with ammonia excess in the bowel and may indicate need for a blood ammonia analysis. Also consistent with ammonia excess are high hippuric acid with low benzoic acid in a urine organic acid analysis, and high glutamine in a urine or plasma amino acid analysis. Alpha-ketoglutaric acid is a keto-structured organic acid, and supplements should have it in buffered form so that it is not too acidic when used. Effective amounts vary with ammonia levels, but are often in the range of 15 to 60 mg/Kg body weight per day, in divided doses, with meals. Usually, it is packaged in gelatin capsules containing 300 mg. The only instances of problems known to me have been for improperly buffered alpha-ketoglutarate products. Adults have consumed as much as 6000 mg/d (20 capsules) of properly formulated alpha-ketoglutarate with only restlessness and hyperactivity as side effects. This natural biochemical also is an antidote for exposure to toxic amines and cyanide.

Bacopa

An herbal product from ayurvedic medicine, Bacopa helps cognitive function and may improve speech and communication abilities. It's usually provided as an extract from the leaves of the plant (Bacopa monnieri) together with ground-up leaves – 100 mg or so of extract plus 300 or 400 mg of leaf material per capsule. Robert Elghammer, M.D., of Danville, Illinois, has reported very good results for Bacopa without detrimental side effects. The usual dosage is two or three capsules per day, taken with meals. It works best in the later stages of intervention, after diet and gut problems have been addressed.

Biotin

This section on biotin contributed by Susan Costen Owens

Some common experiences in the lives of children with autism may predispose them to biotin deficiency. Scientists have learned that some portion of the biotin we use comes from our intestinal flora, and not from the food in our diets, but unfortunately, no one has quantified the amount of biotin our flora produces. Scientists also have not yet determined which microbes are the most responsible for making the biotin we need, but they do know that the very abundant e. coli is one of the biotin producers.[1] Additionally, vitamin B6 inadequacy, which is often seen in autism, may make it difficult for the flora to produce biotin.[2] Also, because children with autism frequently have problems with dysbiosis and diarrhea, intestinal microbes may not be able to produce enough biotin from food. The reduced transit time may make it difficult for intestinal cells to absorb adequate biotin from food or flora. This problem of reduced absorption would be shared by other vitamins and minerals as well.

Antibiotics that are frequently used may kill some of the biotin-producing microbes. Among these antibiotics is the commonly used pediatric antibiotic amoxicillin, whose dose has been increased from 20 mg/kg/day to 90 mg/kg/day in the last decade or two. Also, the penicilllin that is given for PANDAS, a condition which seems more prevalent than one would expect in autism, is also a biotin depleter. Other antibiotics that may kill organisms that make biotin are sulfa drugs, macrolides, quinolones, and tetracycline derivatives. Some anti-epileptic drugs are also biotin depleters, such as hydantoin derivatives and phenytoin.[3]

The usefulness of biotin can be compromised if the enzyme that removes biotin from proteins and recycles it, called biotinidase, is not functioning well.[4] (For testing for biotinidase, see reference 5 cited at the end of this chapter.) Inborn errors in the genes that make biotinidase have been associated with autism. For instance, in one family, a child whose biotinidase deficiency was not discovered and thus not treated developed autism, but when his younger brother was found to be biotinidase deficient on neonatal screening, he was treated with biotin and did not develop autism.[6] Biotinidase deficiency is addressed by high doses of biotin: even as high as 10-40 mg/day.[4]

Importantly, biotinidase has been found to be the same protein as lipoamidase, which performs a similar function for lipoic acid.[7] For that reason, and because the two vitamins also share membrane transport with pantothenic acid, the status of lipoic acid should also be checked in anyone suspected of biotinidase deficiency. It also may be of interest that biotinidase helps to release GPI-anchored proteins[8] at the cell surface and biotin has a newly characterized role in modifying histones in the nucleus, providing gene regulation.[9]

Biotinidase activity can be seriously depleted by the commonly used anti-epileptic medication depakote or valproic acid.[10] It would be unwise to prescribe this drug for seizures without first checking biotin and biotinidase status, because biotin deficiency itself can cause seizures. Problems in the liver can compromise biotinidase activity, so elevated liver enzymes should raise suspicions.[11]

Magnesium is important to biotinidase activity.[12] That means that people with low magnesium may be more prone to see signs of biotin deficiency. Equally, high dose supplements with biotin may bring on signs of magnesium deficiency, such as the onset of tics or leg cramps that resolve with magnesium supplement.[13] Some children also develop problems sleeping with higher doses of biotin, and that may be related to biotinidase using up magnesium.[14]

There are many nutrients and some drugs that may share transport with biotin, so large disproportionate doses may interfere with biotin trafficking. Among those vitamins are lipoic acid, pantothenic acid, thiamine, and among the drugs are salicylate and other substrates of the monocarboxylate tranporter.[15,16,17] With transporter competition, blood levels might actually increase while biotin activity would be reduced.

Biotin is utilized at a much greater rate whenever there is cell proliferation,[18] which is important when considering the effects and requirements of immunological events.[19] This may explain why biotin deficiency signs may first show up when a child has been sick or vaccinated or has been through a time of rapid growth. Eosinophilia is also associated with biotin deficiency.[20] Lack of biotin will involute the thymus, a change which may be associated with risk for autoimmune reactions.[21,22]

The stepped up cell proliferation of pregnancy may explain why biotin deficiency may begin in utero. Biotin deficiency is quite common during pregnancy, but rarely tested. Even marginal deficiency in the mother may harm the fetus and lead to birth defects or fetal death.[23] For that reason, any history of fetal loss is an important part of a mother's history and her biotin status should be monitored in future pregnancies. Anecdotal reports suggest leg cramps may occur in some mothers who may have been biotin deficient in pregnancy, and some children who developed clinical signs of biotin deficiency that resolved on biotin supplements (including hair loss) were born with unusually full heads of hair!

Carboxylase enzymes need biotin to function, so the most prevalent test for biotin deficiency has been elevations of compounds that rise when carboxylases are not functioning properly. These compounds which should be reported on organic acid tests are: hydroxyisovaleric acid, hydroxypropionic acid, methylcrotonylglycine and methylcitric acid.[24] Lactic acid also tends to be elevated. Even though these tests are useful to detect some types of biotin deficiency, there are serious neurological conditions responsive to biotin that are not accompanied by abnormal results on these tests.[25] This may be due to the fact that different organs store biotin and are depleted at different rates and under different conditions. This seems to be a major issue in the basal ganglia.[17,]

If a cluster of the clinical signs of biotin deficiency are present, a trial of biotin supplement may be in order even when the set of biotin-related organic acids are normal. In some of the conditions responsive to biotin reported in the literature, the effective dose was extremely high and a trial using only the RDA would not have produced results. For that reason, please refer to the literature for guidance on high doses related to particular symptoms, and know that some children have had basal ganglia-related issues such as OCD improve on high dose biotin therapy, but for others, these issues got much worse or appeared initially on high dose biotin. Most of the negatives reported appeared after the dose went over 10 mg./day.

Clinical signs of biotin and/or biotinidase deficiency [3,4,26] include:

- developmental delay
- hypotonia
- jaundice
- seizures
- ataxia
- hearing loss
- neuropathy
- breathing problems

- secretory diarrhea
- eczematous and other skin rashes
- hair loss
- immune dysfunction
- mucocutaneous candidiasis
- metabolic acidosis
- keto-lactic acidosis

References—Biotin

1. Cronan JE Jr. Expression of the biotin biosynthetic operon of Escherichia coli is regulated by the rate of protein biotination. *J Biol Chem.* 1988 Jul 25;263(21):10332-6.

2. Ikeda M, Hosotani T, Ueda T, Kotake Y, Sakakibara B. Effect of vitamin B6 deficiency on the levels of several water-soluble vitamins in tissues of germ-free and conventional rats. *J Nutr Sci Vitaminol (Tokyo).* 1979;25(3):141-9.

3. http://www.umm.edu/altmed/ConsSupplements/Depletions/VitaminHBiotincs.html.

4. http://www.emedicine.com/ped/topic239.htm.

5. Biotinidase Deficiency is tested via a lymphocyte enzyme activty assay which is performed at Baylor Medical and the University of Maryland Genetics Lab.

6. Zaffanello M, Zamboni G, Fontana E, Zoccante L, Tato L. A case of partial biotinidase deficiency associated with autism. *Neuropsychol Dev Cogn Sect C Child Neuropsychol.* 2003 Sep;9(3):184-8.

7. Nilsson L, Ronge E. Lipoamidase and biotinidase deficiency: evidence that lipoamidase and biotinidase are the same enzyme in human serum. *Eur J Clin Chem Clin Biochem.* 1992 Mar;30(3):119-26.

8. Oizumi J, Hayakawa K. Release of anchored membrane enzymes by lipoamidase. *Mol Cell Biochem.* 1992 Sep 22;115(1):11-7.

9. Narang MA, Dumas R, Ayer LM, Gravel RA. Reduced histone biotinylation in multiple carboxylase deficiency patients: a nuclear role for holocarboxylase synthetase. Hum Mol Genet. 2004 Jan 1;13(1):15-23.

10. Schulpis KH, Karikas GA, Tjamouranis J, Regoutas S, Tsakiris S. Low serum biotinidase activity in children with valproic acid monotherapy. *Epilepsia.* 2001 Oct;42(10):1359-62.

11. Pabuccuoglu A, Aydogdu S, Bas M. Serum biotinidase activity in children with chronic liver disease and its clinical significance. *J Pediatr Gastroenterol Nutr.* 2002 Jan;34(1):59-62.

12. Branson JP, Attwood PV. Effects of Mg(2+) on the pre-steady-state kinetics of the biotin carboxylation reaction of pyruvate carboxylase. *Biochemistry.* 2000 Jun 27;39(25):7480-91.

13. Roffe C, Sills S, Crome P, Jones P. Randomised, cross-over, placebo controlled trial of magnesium citrate in the treatment of chronic persistent leg cramps. *Med Sci Monit.* 2002 May;8(5):CR326-30.

14. Durlach J, Pages N, Bac P, Bara M, Guiet-Bara A, Agrapart C. Chronopathological forms of magnesium depletion with hypofunction or with hyperfunction of the biological clock. Magnes Res. 2002 Dec;15(3-4):263-8.

15. Daberkow RL, White BR, Cederberg RA, Griffin JB, Zempleni J. Monocarboxylate transporter 1 mediates biotin uptake in human peripheral blood mononuclear cells. *J Nutr.* 2003 Sep;133(9):2703-6.

16. Pacheco-Alvarez D, Solorzano-Vargas RS, Gonzalez-Noriega A, Michalak C, Zempleni J, Leon-Del-Rio A. Biotin availability regulates expression of the sodium-dependent multivitamin transporter and the rate of biotin uptake in HepG2 cells. Mol Genet Metab. 2005 May 16; [Epub ahead of print]

17. Zeng WQ, Al-Yamani E, Acierno JS Jr, Slaugenhaupt S, Gillis T, Macdonald ME, Ozand PT, Gusella JF. Biotin-Responsive Basal Ganglia Disease Maps to 2q36.3 and Is Due to Mutations in SLC19A3. *Am J Hum Genet.* 2005 Jul;77(1):16-26.

18. Stanley JS, Mock DM, Griffin JB, Zempleni J. Biotin uptake into human peripheral blood mononuclear cells increases early in the cell cycle, increasing carboxylase activities. *J Nutr.* 2002 Jul;132(7):1854-9.

19. Wiedmann S, Eudy JD, Zempleni J. Biotin supplementation increases _expression of genes encoding interferon-gamma, interleukin-1beta, and 3-methylcrotonyl-CoA carboxylase, and

decreases expression of the gene encoding interleukin-4 in human peripheral blood mononuclear cells. *J Nutr.* 2003 Mar;133(3):716-9.

20. Tanaka M, Yanagi M, Shirota K, Une Y, Nomura Y, Masaoka T, Akahori F. Eosinophil and foam cell accumulation in lungs of Sprague-Dawley rats fed purified, biotin-deficient diets. *Vet Pathol.* 1995 Sep;32(5):498-503.

21. Moretti P, Petrelli C, Petrelli F, Gabrielli MG, Palatroni P. Relationships between biotin and thymus morphology, and thymic and plasma peptides controlling DNA transcription. *Thymus.* 1990 Mar;15(2):79-92.

22. Taub DD, Longo DL Insights into thymic aging and regeneration..*Immunol Rev.* 2005 Jun;205:72-93.

23. Sealey WM, Stratton SL, Mock DM, Hansen DK. Marginal maternal biotin deficiency in CD-1 mice reduces fetal mass of biotin-dependent carboxylases. *J Nutr.* 2005 May;135(5):973-7.

24. Mock DM, Henrich-Shell CL, Carnell N, Stumbo P, Mock NI. 3-Hydroxypropionic acid and methylcitric acid are not reliable indicators of marginal biotin deficiency in humans. *Nutr.* 2004 Feb;134(2):317-20.

25. Ozand PT, Gascon GG, Al Essa M, Joshi S, Al Jishi E, Bakheet S, Al Watban J, Al-Kawi MZ, Dabbagh O. Biotin-responsive basal ganglia disease: a novel entity. *Brain.* 1998 Jul;121 (Pt 7):1267-79.

26. http://www.mericon-industries.com/biotin3.htm.

L-Carnitine

This is a natural transporter molecule that carries fatty acids into cell mitochondria so that the fatty acids can be metabolized or broken down to acetyl-CoA pieces. Most of this acetyl CoA then goes into the citric acid cycle which provides hydrogen, bicarbonate, and energy for synthesis of ATP. L-carnitine has been used to good advantage when autism, at the molecular level, involves mitochondrial dysfunctions. Analytical and diagnostic markers for carnitine need include low levels of blood carnitine, high urine or blood levels of unusual fatty acids (adipic, suberic, octenedioic), elevated blood triglycerides, myopathy and chronic fatigue. Relatively large amounts of L-carnitine are needed therapeutically, usually 25 to 100 mg/Kg body weight per day in divided doses. Do not ever use D,L-carnitine. The D-form actually inhibits carnitine function. Usually, carnitine is sold in a stabilized but very bioavailable form, acetyl-L-carnitine, which is fine for use in autism. This supplement may be tried at any time during the course of biomedical interventions including early ones, but it works better after dietary intervention and resolution of gastrointestinal issues.

Colostrum

This is a natural liquid produced in the mammary glands of mammals including humans. Its secretion precedes that of milk for infant feeding, and it contains immune factors, essential nutrients, and growth factors. The commercial colostrum that you can purchase from nutritional supply houses comes from milk cows. So, if you need a casein-free diet for an autistic, ask for assurance or a certificate of analysis stating that the colostrum has undetectable casein content. Also, the cows should be "organic" ones – no pesticides or herbicides in what they eat and no added hormones or antibiotics. I don't think there is any special remedial benefit that colostrum provides in autism, but it can act as an immune booster to all children with immune weakness or dysregulation. It seems most helpful in combating common flu or "cold" viruses, but it doesn't solve the entrenched measles problem that many autistics have. About a teaspoon or two of liquid colostrum per day is said to be effective for immune support.

CoQ$_{10}$

Coenzyme Q$_{10}$ is a natural molecule that occurs in the mitochondria of cells. It does its work after L-carnitine has delivered fatty acids to the inner part of mitochondria, and after these have been turned into chemical fuel (acetyl CoA). While the fuel is being consumed by the citric acid cycle, protons (H+) are produced. At the same time, electrons have to be moved and then combined with protons in a biochemical manner that produces chemical energy (ATP). CoQ$_{10}$ is one form of coenzyme Q or "ubiquinone" that enables electron and chemical energy transfer to occur. Because some types of autism feature energy deficit at the cellular level, CoQ$_{10}$ supplements may be helpful. Amounts that are reported to be beneficial are 3 to 6 mg/Kg of body weight per day. CoQ$_{10}$ is easily oxidized (it's a reducing agent when exposed to oxidants), so don't leave the bottle open, keep it out of sunlight, and give it at the same time that vitamin C and/or E are given.

Inositol

Once considered to be a vitamin, inositol can be formed in body tissues from dietary sugars once they become glucose-6-phosphate. Inositol also is present in the diet, coming from fish, meat, poultry and dairy products. Cereal grains and nuts are a source of fully-phosphorylated inositol which we call phytate. Plain inositol is also known as myoinositol, and phytate is myoinositol hexaphosphate. Myoinositol is a 6-carbon ring with no double bonds, and there is one hydrogen and one hydroxyl (OH) attached to each of the six carbons.

There are several nutritional supplement forms of inositol: myoinositol (usually in B-vitamin complex formulations), myoinositol hexaphosphate (less desired because it chelates iron +2, calcium, zinc and copper), phosphatidylinositol (which may be in choline or phosphatidylcholine formulations) and inositol hexanicotinate (a non-flushing, usually high-dose niacin supplement). Some dietary myoinositol-hexaphosphate is dephosphorylated in the small intestine at the brush-border zone of the mucosa by phytase, and that is added to dietary myoinositol for absorption. When that happens, however, nearby element ions (minerals) can be made into insoluble phosphates. Insoluble phosphate metal salts, such as zinc phosphate, are not bioavailable and are lost in the feces.

An important therapeutic use of this chemistry is alleviation of obsessive-compulsive behaviors or obsessive-compulsive disorder, OCD (Fux, Levine et al Am.J. Psychiatry 153 no.9 [1996] p 1219-21). Initial studies by Fux et al. used huge doses of inositol, but later trials indicate that lesser amounts, such as 2000 mg/d (adults), are effective at alleviating OCD in some individuals. Because a significant fraction of the autistic population presents with obsessive-compulsive behaviors, some parents and doctors have tried health food store inositol. Testimonial evidence is that it can be beneficial, and I've not received any news of adverse reactions to it. The PDR for Nutritional Supplements (Thomson, 2000 p.223) states, "No significant adverse effects noted...use of daily dose of 8.8 grams of inositol hexaphosphate taken for several months."

SECTION FIVE: NUTRITIONAL SUPPLEMENTS FOR AUTISM

Dr. Miriam Jang, who practices in California, has used inositol extensively for both OCD and aggressive behaviors in autistic-spectrum children and adults. She finds that the lower doses are often effective for obsessive-compulsive behaviors, but higher doses, up to 10 grams/day, may be needed to alleviate aggressive, destructive behaviors, especially in adults. Dr. Jang also reports that inositol, given as a powder, is sweet-tasting and she's not aware of any adverse effects. She reports success with inositol for a 25-year-old who was going to be institutionalized because of the danger of physical harm to others in his family. Ten grams of inositol per day alleviated that problem, and the individual became a calmer, safer family member.

Inositol is a nutrient that deserves more study by scientists and clinicians dealing with autism. Dr. Jang's clinical successes indicate that there's something more to inositol than its vitamin-like properties. Its benefits are likely to be associated with the interactions that phosphorylated inositol has with cell message-transmission and subsequent phosphorylation of proteins. Inositol phosphate is not known to phosphorylate ADP to ATP (as creatine phosphate can) and it does not phosphorylate GDP to GTP (as ATP can). Instead, phosphorylated inositol is involved later, as a "second messenger," operating internally at the interface of the cell membrane and cytosol.

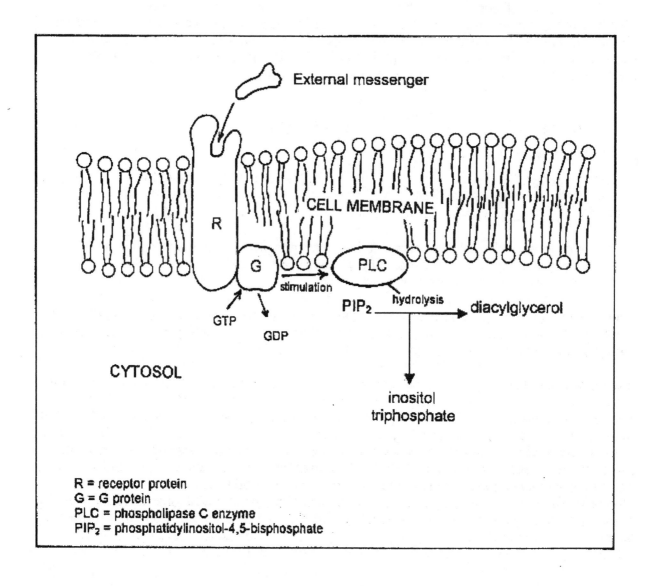

Inositol as phosphatidylinositol-4,5-bisphosphate is hydrolyzed to diacylglycerol and inositol triphosphate (ITP) by the enzyme phospholipase C following a signal from the receptor plus G-protein system. Diacylglycerol remains in the cell membrane and provides a chemical signal to another enzyme, protein C kinase. Inositol triphosphate leaves the membrane, and goes into the cytosol where it can release calcium to initiate a series of chemical responses. Recent investigations show that it can provide phosphate for protein phosphorylation. (York JD and Hunter T, *Science* 306 17 Dec 2004, 2053-2055.)

Unneeded inositol is catabolized to D-glucuronic acid, which may then be combined with phosphorylated uridine to form UDP-glucuronate. This may be used as a conjugating agent for detoxification of many hydrophobic substances and xenobiotics. D-glucuronate also is processed into phosphorylated D-xylulose, which can be used in the metabolic sequence known as the hexose monophosphate shunt. This sequence generates NADPH which is needed for regeneration of reduced glutathione, GSH, from GSSG.

Magnesium Malate

This is a salt form of malic acid, which participates in the citric acid cycle and in the "malate shuttle." In the citric acid cycle (in cell mitochondria), the malate-to-oxaloacetate step generates hydrogen to make NADH. Malate carries hydrogen and gives it away in this metabolism step.

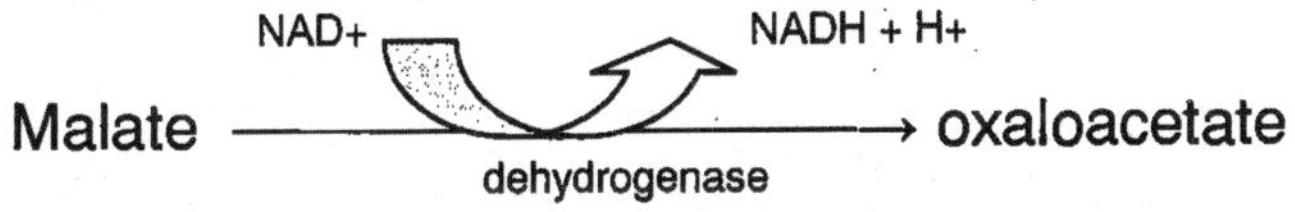

$$\text{Malate} \xrightarrow[\text{dehydrogenase}]{\text{NAD}^+ \quad \text{NADH} + \text{H}^+} \text{oxaloacetate}$$

Oxaloacetate can then be changed into alpha-ketoglutarate (change requires vitamin B_6 as P5P) and alpha-ketoglutarate can exit the mitochondrion and enter the cytosol. There, it is changed back to oxaloacetate and the reverse of the above reaction occurs:

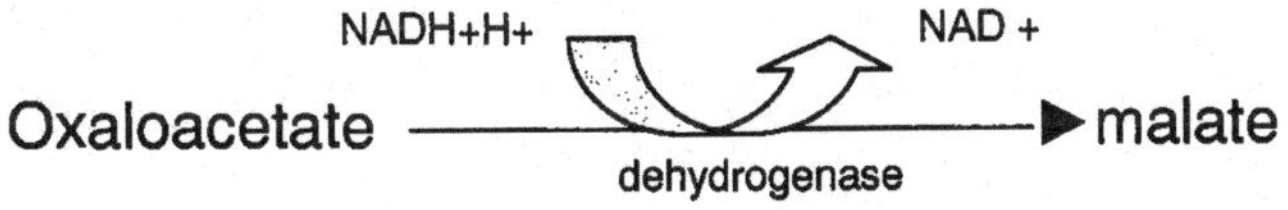

$$\text{Oxaloacetate} \xrightarrow[\text{dehydrogenase}]{\text{NADH} + \text{H}^+ \quad \text{NAD}^+} \text{malate}$$

Malate can then go back into the mitochondrion. This may seem like a useless circle of events, but it isn't. What's happening is a shuttling process that transports hydrogen (chemical reducing capacity) into mitochondria by malate.

If we provide malate as a nutritional supplement, it can get into the cell cytosol and then into the mitochondria. This preserves some cytosolic NADH and it provides hydrogen (antioxidant capacity) to mitochondria. And this should help the oxidant stress and excessive GSSG/GSH ratio condition that is present in many autistics. In effect, malic acid, in a safe form such as magnesium malate, is a reducing nutrient or antioxidant supplement for cell mitochondria. Beneficial amounts, per testimonial experiences that I'm aware of, are 5 to 10 mg/Kg body wt per day. Magnesium malate may be hard to find in health food stores; it has been used for alleviation of chronic fatigue syndrome. I'm not aware of problems with use of magnesium malate as a first-tier supplement, perhaps along with other magnesium forms and/or vitamin C.

Selenium, Se

The element selenium is acknowledged to be active in only two enzymatic processes in humans:

1. Glutathione peroxidase (GPx). GPx catalyzes glutathione's reduction of peroxides to water. In doing so, oxidized glutathione is produced.

2. Removing one iodine atom from thyroid hormone T_4 to produce T_3, which is the most active form of thyroid hormones.

In both enzymes, selenium is bound into an amino acid of cysteinyl structure, "selenocysteine," which is at the active site of the protein. We now understand that selenocysteine acts as a single amino acid when these enzyme proteins are assembled; the selenium is not added on later. Obviously, many important metabolic processes depend upon glutathione and thyroid functions, so selenium deficiency can have serious consequences.

Twenty years ago, I investigated GPx activity in autistics and found it to be subnormal; others also found this. My first response was to look for selenium deficiency. I did not find that by either hair or packed RBC analyses furnished to me on a patient-anonymous basis by doctors. Since then, various investigations by others have not produced convincing evidence that selenium is subnormal in autistics as a group. Selenium may be deficient in individuals, with an occurrence that is not noticeably different form the general population. However, we do have evidence that glutathione peroxidase activity is subnormal in some autistics. Consequently, it's possible that selenocysteine is limited in autism. Also possible is toxic element binding to selenocysteine in glutathione peroxidase; mercury and silver are documented to do so.

Selenium also binds to sulfur in sulfhydryl groups, and it binds to cysteine and glutathione which typically are subnormal in autistics. Also, selenium is detoxified by methylation (subnormal in autism) and excessive selenium results in an increased requirement for NADPH. This causes us to be careful about how much selenium an autistic might need, if any. If too much selenium is given, the main binding agents may not be adequate, and NADPH could become (more) deficient. Then, selenium can do mischief by binding to the wrong molecules. If too little selenium is present, then when biochemistry and physiology improve, we may lack adequate selenocysteine for enzyme building. A guide for selenium supplementation can be an elemental analysis, and for this element hair is an accurate, but lagging, indicator. RBC Se is also acceptable. Blood serum, plasma and urine are not reliable for Se, because they reflect recent dietary intake, not retention and utilization.

Here are some supplemental guidelines for selenium from the Food and Nutrition Board of the USNRC.* Selenium, at these or in similar amounts, can be used as a first-tier supplement along with vitamin C and possibly vitamin E. One beneficial form is selenomethionine, and we are not concerned about methionine at microgram levels.

Age (years)	Micrograms/day
1-3	20
4-6	20
7-10	30
Males 11-14	40
Males 15-18	50
Females 11-14	45
Females 15-18	50

* 10th Ed RDA, NRC, National Academy Press, 1989

Somewhat more than these amounts may be needed when Se is measured to be deficient or when maldigestion and malabsorption are present. But double these amounts is not a good idea unless under medical supervision.

Silymarin (Milk Thistle)

Silymarin is a mixture of three flavonoids derived from the seeds of the milk thistle plant (Silybum marianum). The plant is sometimes called milkweed because of its sticky, milky sap. Silymarin protects liver cells from many hepatotoxic chemicals, and there is considerable pharmacologic and clinical evidence behind its use for hepatitis and cirrhosis (Facts & Comparisons Review of Natural Products Monograph Jan 1997). It protects against liver damage form medicinals, phenothiazine drugs, and even Amanita mushroom poisoning. So, milk thistle extract or silymarin is an excellent herbal supplement to use when doing battle with intestinal dysbiosis. Toxins that escape capture by activated charcoal can target liver cells, and silymarin can counteract these destructive effects. It does this by stimulating RNA and DNA synthesis in liver cells. Also, it protects the outer cell membrane "cell wall" by blocking certain binding or entry sites that toxins might use. Milk thistle/silymarin is available in capsule or tablet forms containing seeds, extracts and sometimes combinations of these. Units of potency can be stated as milligrams of silybin (one of the three silymarin flavonoids) or mg of silymarin. Daily amounts in the range of 5 to 10 mg/Kg body wt work well but more may be needed – consult your doctor in this during dysbiosis treatments and during detoxification therapy if organic xenobiotic chemicals are an issue.

Vitamin E

Natural, food-source vitamin E is a mixture of tocopherols, the most active one being d-alpha-tocopherol (per the traditional US Pharmacopoeia assay procedure). D-alpha tocopherol has become the chemical form that is defined to be vitamin E; other tocopherols don't count as far as RDA, DRI or Daily Value product label amounts are concerned. The other tocopherols (beta, gamma, delta) and tocotrienols also have vitamin E activity and have differing antioxidant capacities. The biologic activities of the various tocopherols are still being explored. Some documented functions are:

- Prevention or reduction of oxidation of cellular and blood plasma lipids, especially polyunsaturated fatty acids.
- Reduction or elimination of erythrocyte fragility and hemolysis.
- Preservation of active sulfhydryl-bearing biochemicals such as cysteine, glutathione and many enzymes.
- Reduction of hepatic tissue necrosis in cysteine/glutathione-deficient animals.
- Protection of tissues from oxidant attack by ozone or nitrous oxide.
- Reduction of susceptibility to neuromuscular diseases, particularly in children.

While we don't have vitamin E deficiency in autistics as a group, we do have oxidant stress with limited glutathione and too much oxidized glutathione. We have inflammation and we appear to have inflammatory inhibition of methylcobalamin function for methionine synthase. So, vitamin E use as an antioxidant is a good idea for autistics. I urge use of vitamin E supplements that include mixed tocopherols. Natural, food-source antioxidants usually have multiple but similar chemical forms and they work either synergistically or in complementary fashion. You're much better off using mixed tocopherol-vitamin E plus vitamin C plus taurine plus GSH-enhancing strategies than you would be by giving huge megadoses of just d-alpha-tocopherol.

The Food and Nutrition Board of the NRC has listed very small RDA levels of vitamin E (d-α-tocopherol) for children, about 4 to 10 milligrams per day (10th Ed RDA, NRC, National Academy Press, 1989). These small amounts won't do the job in autism.

For synthetic, solid, d,l-α-tocopherol acetate, 1.0 mg = 1.0 IU.
For natural, solid d-α-tocopherol acetate, 1.0 mg = 1.36 IU
For natural, liquid d-α-tocopherol, 1.0 mg = 1.49 IU

I recommend the following dose ranges for d-α-tocopherol, and if possible, include additional tocopherols as well by using a mixed-tocopherol product. Higher amounts may be beneficial, but seek medical direction before doing that. Vitamin E can be used as a first-tier supplement, along with vitamin C, for added antioxidant protection.

Age (years)	IU/day
1-3	15-30
4-6	25-50
7-10	40-80
Males 11-14	50-100
Males 15-18	60-120
Females 11-14	45-90
Females 15-18	50-100

* 10th Ed RDA, NRC, National Academy Press, 1989

Index

A
acetyl-L-carnitine, 312
N-acetylcysteine (NAC), 287, 297-299
N-acetylcysteine supplement, 297, 299
activated charcoal, 80, 124, 222, 264, 308
Actos, 135
ADA. See adenosine deaminase
Adams, Prof. James, 186
Adderall, rating as autism treatment, 24
adenosine
    accumulation of, 162
    synchronous neuronal processes and, 172
adenosine deaminase (ADA), 162, 208, 241
adenosine excess, 291
adenosylcobalamin, 199, 266
adenosylhomocysteine excess, 292
adenylate cyclase, 257
adenylosuccinate lyase deficiency, 153
advocacy byparents, 22-23
AGAT, 168, 280, 282
AGAT deficiency, 153, 170
aged products, on yeast-free diet, 87-88
alanine aminotransferase (ALT), 82
alcohol dehydrogenase, 240
alkaline phosphatase, 82, 240
alkaline proteases, 220
all-trans-retinol, 249, 250, 251
allergy, 20
    defined, 192
    desensitization, 128-133
    five-day avoidance/challenge test, 90, 92, 115, 118
    food allergen elimination, 69, 112-119
    food allergy test, 115-119, 192-193
    skin problems, 38
allergy desensitization, 128-133
alpha-ketoglutaric acid, 199, 308
alpha-lipoic acid, 299
aluminum, methionine synthase and, 173
amino acid analysis, 18, 195-197, 278, 288
amino acid supplements, 287-289
amino acids, 285-289
ammonia, blood level, 189, 191-192, 289
amoebae, intestinal, 84
amoxicillin, 309
Amphotericin B, 80-81, 82. See also nystatin
amylases, 218, 221
anemia, 266
Angelman's syndrome, 152, 154
anserine, 194, 242, 286
antibacterials, 83
antibiotics
    biotin depletion from, 309
    in first months of life, 25, 36
antibody testing, 109, 127, 130
antifungal drugs, 69, 74-84
    for constipation, 47
    die-off reaction, 35, 37, 47, 80, 81, 99
    individual case studies, 35, 36
    rating as autism treatment, 24, 30, 74
    side effects, 81
antimony, 150, 173, 185, 203
antimony toxicity, 185-186
antioxidants, 255

APS kinase, 228
arginine, 168
arsenic, 203
Artemisia annua, 85
ASA. See Autism Society of America
ascorbic acid. See vitamin C
asparagine level, 288
aspartate aminotransferase (AST), 82
ATP sulfurylase, 228
Audhya, Dr. Tapan, 163, 224, 257
autism
    biochemical path to development of, 27-31, 183
    epidemic, 19, 149-150
    gender and, 25, 187-188
    old model, 15
    prevalence, 8, 149-150
    recovery, 5
    scenario for develoment of, 26, 183
    Type I, 151, 152-154, 161, 209
    Type II, 151, 154, 209
    See also autism treatments
Autism Now! conferences, 6, 7
Autism Research Institute, 7, 9
Autism Society of America (ASA), 9
autism treatments
    decision-making, 22-23, 43-44
    nutritional supplements. See nutritional supplements
    ratings, 24-25
    See also individual forms of treatment
autoimmune response, 181, 206
avoidance/challenge/re-challenge, 118

B
Bacopa, 308
Bactrim, 85
baked goods, on yeast-free diet, 87, 91
Baker, Dr. Sid, 192-193
baker's yeast, 80
Balantidium coli, 84
barbecue sauce, on yeast-free diet, 89
Bay Gam, 133
Beaudet, Dr. Arthur, 154
behavioral toxicology, 20
beta-alanine, 194, 234, 235
beta-alanyl-L-histidine, 305
beta carotene, 249
beta-casomorphin 7!, 218
beta-galactosidase complex, 219
betaine (TMG), 72, 164, 167, 171, 214, 274, 303. See also trimethylglycine
betaine-homocysteine methyltransferase (BHMT), 164, 165, 171, 208, 240, 269, 274
bethanechol, 252
beverages
    on Specific Carbohydrate Diet, 101
    on yeast-free diet, 92
BHMT. See betaine-homocysteine methyltransferase
Bifidobacter bifidum, 263-264
Bifidobacter lactis, 263
Bihari, Dr. Bernard, 136
bile salts, 285
bilirubin, 82

biochemistry, 27, 28, 158-159
    creatine synthesis, 280-282
    folate chemistry, 294-295
    inositol, 314
    methionine metabolism, 27-29, 108, 154, 159, 160-166, 195, 214, 226
    S-adenosylmethionine (SAMe), 291
    vitamin B12 action, 266-268
biopterin, 256
biotin, 124, 309-310
biotin deficiency, 309-310
biotinidase, 309
biotinidase deficiency, 309, 310
Blastocystis hominis, 84
blood, elemental analyses, 203
blood ammonia, 191-192
blood chemistry, laboratory testing, 189-190
Boris, Dr. Marvin, 128, 135, 170, 282
bowel lesions, 181
bowel movements, 45. *See also* constipation; gastrointestinal health
brain, 159
    neuronal function, 171-175
    as self-organizing network, 174
bread, on yeast-free diet, 87, 91
breakfast, on Specific Carbohydrate Diet, 100
Breaking the Vicious Cycle (Gottschall), 94
brewer's yeast, 80
bromelain, 220
brominated biphenyl compounds, 186
Buie, Dr. Timothy, 181
BUN, 189-190
Buttar, Dr. Rashid, 125

C
calcium, 246-248
calcium carbonate, 247-248
calcium citrate, 248
calcium lactate, 248
calcium level, 203, 246
calcium supplement, 73, 213, 247-248
    dosage chart, 247
    rating as autism treatment, 24, 30, 247
caloric intake, 56
Candex, 83
capryllic acid, 83
carbohydrate craving, 39
carbohydrates, 214
    best eaten in the evening, 40-41
    chemistry of, 55
    craving for, 39
    digestion, 219
    as source of organic acids, 198
    on yeast-free diet, 86, 89-90
carbonic anhydrase, 240
carboxypeptidase, 240
cardiovascular system, magnesium deficiency and, 39
carnitine, 312
carnitine deficit, 167
carnosinase, 306
carnosine, 194, 235, 242, 286, 305-307
carnosine supplement, 306-307
Carroll, Alina, 77
casein, antibodies to, 110
casein-free diet, 18, 55, 69, 102-105, 110-112
    rating as autism treatment, 24, 30, 52

casein sensitivity, 110-112
casomorphin, 110, 194, 218
castor oil, for constipation, 46-47
catechol-O-methyltransferase (COMT), 208, 228
catecholamines, 286
cathartics, 46
Cave, Dr. Stephanie, 120, 130
CBC analysis, 190
CD26, 108, 162, 187, 192, 219
celiac disease, 106, 109, 127
cell membranes, fatty acid makeup of, 201, 253
cellulases, 218
central nervous system (CNS), 114
    magnesium deficiency and, 39
cereals, on yeast-free diet, 91
chamomile, 42
charcoal. *See* activated charcoal
cheese, on yeast-free diet, 88
chelating agents, 299, 301
chelation, 121, 244
children
    dietary guidelines for, 56-57
    ideal weight for height, 57
Children With Starving Brains (McCandless), 8, 83
chocolate-free diet, rating as autism treatment, 24, 30, 52
choline insufficiency, 167
chromosomal analysis, 189
chronological questionnaire, 31-33
The Circadian Prescription (Baker), 39
circadian rhythm, 40, 41
citrate level, 248
citric acid cycle, 200, 299, 308, 313, 315
citric acid level, 200-201
citrus seed extract, 83, 85
Clinical Manual, 6, 7
clostridia, 287
CNS. *See* central nervous system
cobalamin, 165, 166, 266. *See also* Vitamin B12
cod liver oil supplement, 73, 250-252
coenzyme Q_{10}, 313
coenzymes, 214
coffee, on yeast-free diet, 88
colostrum, 133-134, 312
COMT. *See* catechol-O-methyltransferase
condiments, on yeast-free diet, 89, 92
constipation, 67, 167
    amino acids and, 289
    reasons for, 45
    remedies for, 44-48
Converse, Judy, 56
copper, 194, 203
copper chelation, 306
copper level, 241-242, 244
copper/zinc ratio, 205, 239, 240, 306
copper-zinc superoxide dismutase, 240
cravings, 39, 54, 221
creatine, 167, 279-284
    blood plasma level, 195
    formation and energy delivery, 159, 167-170
    phosphate transport by, 167, 280
    synthesis, 280-282
creatine deficiency, 279, 283
creatine excess, 291
creatine level, 279, 283, 291
creatine phosphate, 169, 281
creatine supplement, 171, 213, 282-284

creatine synthesis deficiencies, 153
creatine transporter (CRTR), 282
creatine transporter deficiency, 153, 170
creatine transporter gene, 170
creatinine, 169, 189, 195, 281, 288
cri-du-chat syndrome, 152
Crohn's disease, 181
Crook, Dr. William, 74
cystathionemia, 163
cystathionine, 163
cysteine, 160, 166, 234, 287
cysteine deficiency, 241, 275
cystine, 278
cytidine deaminase, 240-241

D
D4 receptors, 172, 174
dairy products, on yeast-free diet, 91
DAN!. See Defeat Autism Now!
Davis, Adele, 215
deamination process, 162
decarboxylase deficiency, 225
decision-making, 22-23, 43-44
Defeat Autism Now! (DAN!), 19
    history, 3-10
Depakene, rating as autism treatment, 24
Depakote, 309
desensitization, 128-133
Deth, Prof. Richard, 164, 268
detoxication, 285
detoxification, 29-30, 69, 119-123
    mercury, 120, 299, 301
    rating as autism treatment, 24, 30
dextrin 6-alpha-D-glucanohydrolase, 220
DHA. See docosahexaenoic acid
DHPPA. See dihydroxyphenylproprionate
die-off reaction
    activated charcoal for, 308
    antifungal drugs, 35, 37, 47, 80, 81, 99
    digestive enzyme use and, 221
    probiotics use and, 264
Dientamoeba fragilis, 84
diet
    avoiding food additives, 55
    carbohydrate best eaten in the evening, 40-41
    dietary guidelines for children, 56-57
    food additives in, 53-55
    food allergen elimination, 69, 112-119
    and gut cleaning, 56
    protein best eaten in the morning, 40, 41
    sugar and artificial sweeteners, 55-58
    See also casein-free diet; gluten-free diet; milk-free diet; Specific Carbohydrate Diet; yeast-free diet
dietary change, 50-53, 67. See also casein-free diet; diet; gluten-free diet; milk-free diet; Specific Carbohydrate Diet; yeast-free diet
difficulty falling asleep, 40
Diflucan, 74, 77, 81
    rating as autism treatment, 24, 30, 74
    side effects, 81
digestion, of proteins, 106-107
digestive enzyme supplements, 216-222
    adverse responses to, 221-222
    rating as autism treatment, 24, 30, 221
digestive enzymes, 69, 72-73

digestive tract. See gastrointestinal health
dihydropyrimidine dehydrogenase deficiency, 153, 234
dihydroxyphenylproprionate (DHPPA), 83
diiodohydroxyquin, 85
dimercapto propane sulfonate (DMPS), 125, 299
dimethylglycine (DMG), 164, 271-273, 276, 277-279
dimethylglycine supplement, 272-273
    adverse response to, 273
    dosage, 273
    with folate and vitamin B12, 277-279, 297
    parent rating of, 273
dinner, on Specific Carbohydrate Diet, 100
dipeptides, 218
diphtheria virus, antibodies to, 130
disaccharidases, 216, 218, 221, 262
6,8-dithiooctanoic acid, 300
DMG. See dimethylglycine
DMPS. See dimercapto propane sulfonate
DMSA, 299, 301
DNA synthesis disorders, 152-153
docosahexaenoic acid (DHA), 202, 254
dopamine, 174
dopamine receptors, 171
DPP4, 107, 108, 110, 162, 192, 218, 219, 221, 243
dried fruits, on yeast-free diet, 89
dry skin, 38
Dulcolax, for constipation, 47
dyes, in foods, 53-54
dysbiosis, 37, 196, 213, 234, 260-261, 289, 317

E
early waking, 40
eczema, 38, 77
Edelson, Steve, 74
egg-free diet, rating as autism treatment, 52
egg protein, 41
Ehret, Charles, 40
El-Dahr, Dr. Jane, 120, 182
element analyses, 202-205
Elghammer, Dr. Robert, 308
Endolimax nana, 84
endomysium antibodies, 109
enemas, 45
energy transfer deficiency, 153-154
Entamoeba coli, 84
Entamoeba hartmanni, 84
Entamoeba histolytica, 85
enterocolitis, 181
environmental stressors, 150, 185-187
enzymes, requiring zinc, 240-241
epigenetics, 154
Epson salts bath, 41
essential amino acids, 285-287, 299. See also amino acids
estrogen, mercury neurotoxicity and, 188
exercise, 43
exorphins, 162, 194, 217, 218
extrinsic factor, 266

F
fatty acid analysis, 201-202
fatty acid deficiency, 57
fatty acid supplement, 73, 254-255
    rating as autism treatment, 24, 30
fatty acids, 253-255
Feingold diet, rating as autism treatment, 52

fermented products, on yeast-free diet, 87-88
ferritin, 59
fiber, for constipation, 46
FIGlu. *See* formiminoglutamic acid
finger nails, 38
first-tier nutritional supplements, 69, 72-73, 212
five-day avoidance/challenge, 90, 92, 115, 118
Flagyl, 85
flame retardants, 150, 185, 186
fluconazole. *See* Diflucan
folacin, 295
FolaPro™, 295
folate, 293-297
folate metabolism, 198
folate supplement, 276, 293, 295-297
    DMG or TMG with, 277-279
    dosage, 295
folate traps, 296
folic acid levels, 296
folic acid supplement, rating as autism treatment, 24, 30
folinic acid, 72, 293, 295, 296, 303
food additives, in diet, 53-55
food allergen elimination, 69, 112-119
food allergy tests, 115-119, 192-193
food dyes, 53-54
5-formimino tetrahydrofolate, 294
formiminoglutamic acid (FIGlu), 198-199, 286
5-formyltetrahydrofolate, 293, 295
fragile X syndrome, 153, 271
fruit juices, on yeast-free diet, 88
fruits
    on Specific Carbohydrate Diet, 101
    on yeast-free diet, 91
    yeast on outer surface, 86
full-spectrum light, for sleep rhythm, 41
fumaric acid level, 200
fungal infections, 36-37. *See also* antifungal drugs; yeast infections
fungi, 79. *See also* antifungal drugs; yeast infections

G
G-alpha protein, 167, 171, 252
GA. *See* guanidinoacetate
GABA. *See* gamma-aminobutyric acid
Galland, Dr. Leo, 79
GALT. *See* gut associated lymphoid tissue
Galzin, 244
gamma-aminobutyric acid (GABA), 196, 305
GAMT, 169, 282
GAMT deficiency, 153, 170
gastro-colic reflex, 45
gastrointestinal health, 49-51
    amino acids and, 285
    amoebae, 84
    dietary change, 50-53
    digestive enzymes, 218-220
    gut cleaning, 56, 58-59
    gut dysbiosis, 37, 196, 213, 234, 289, 317
    gut flora, 21, 67, 83
    ileal-lymphoid nodular hyperplasia, 181-182, 186-187, 268
    infant digestive tract, damage to, 25-26
    intestinal barrier function, 191
    intestinal permeability, 109, 191
    malabsorption, 285
    small intestine lesions, 178-179
    Specific Carbohydrate Diet and, 95-96
    worms, 84
    zinc, 242
    See also intestine
Gee, Dr. Samuel, 94
gender, autism and, 25, 187-188
gene defect/deletion disorders, Type I autism, 152, 189
genomic testing, 207-208
Gentamycin, 83
German measles. *See* rubella
Gershon, Dr. Michael, 84
Giardia lamblia, 85
ginkgo biloba, 200
gliadin antibodies, 109
gliadinomorphin, 218
gliadorphin, 218
glucose 6-dehydrogenase, 302
glutamate, 173
glutamine, 287
glutamine level, 288
glutathione (GSH), 29, 42, 123, 165, 166, 199, 228, 242, 269, 275
glutathione deficit, 165
glutathione disulfide (GSSG), 29, 302
glutathione supplement, 301, 303
glutathionylcobalamin (GSCbl), 166, 266
gluten, 106
gluten-free diet, 55, 69, 102-110, 127
    rating as autism treatment, 24, 30, 52
gluten intolerance, 106
    symptoms, 104-105
glycerin suppositories, for constipation, 47
glycine, 168, 272, 280
glycine supplement, 255
glycoamine, 169, 280
glycoamylase, 221
Goldblatt, Allan, 128, 135, 170, 282
Golgi complexes, 253
Gorman, Alex, 94-97
Gorman, Judy, 94
Gottschall, Elaine, 94, 95, 96, 98
grains
    gluten-containing, 105
    on yeast-free diet, 91
GSCbl. *See* glutathionylcobalamin
GSH. *See* glutathione
GSSG. *See* glutathione disulfide
guanidinoacetate (GA), 161, 168, 169, 280, 282, 291
guanidoacetate, 169, 280
Gupta, Dr. Sudhir, 126
gustin, 242
gut associated lymphoid tissue (GALT), 25
gut cleaning, 56, 58-59
gut dysbiosis, 37, 196, 213, 234, 289, 317
gut flora, 21, 67, 83

H
H. influenza, antibodies to, 130
hair analysis, 204
Haley, Boyd, 25
heavy metals, detoxification, 121
hemicellulase, 218
hepatitis virus, antibodies to, 130
herbs, 42-43
Herlihy, Walter, 135
Herxheimer reaction, 37

high-protein shakes, 41
histamine, 286
histidine, 244, 286
histidinemia, 153
Hoffer, Dr. Abram, 9
Holmes, Dr. Amy, 120
homocarnosine, 305
homocysteine, 28-29, 154, 162, 163, 164, 166, 196, 209, 214, 267
    kinetics of, 292
    methylation of, 274
homocysteine deficit, 292
horseradish, on yeast-free diet, 89
HPPA. See hydroxyphenylproprionic acid
5HTP, 41-42
Humatin, 85
hydrogen breath test, 111
hydroxocobalamin, 266
hydroxycobalamin, 266
hydroxyphenylproprionic acid (HPPA), 287
hyperammonemia, 191-192, 289
hypervitaminosis A, 250

I
IAG. See indolylacrolylglycine
ICP-MS. See induction-coupled plasma mass spectrometer
IgA, 127
IgE, 127
IgE antibodies, 127, 192
IgG, 127
IgG antibodies, 127, 192
IgG level, 126
IgM, 127
ileal-lymphoid nodular hyperplasia, 181-182, 186-187, 268
immune cells, 207
immune system, 114, 125
    chemistry, 114
    colostrum and, 133-134, 312
    of infant, damage to, 26
immune testing, 125-128, 206-207
immunizations, 16, 21, 132-133, 150
    abnormal response to, 129
    effect of, 26
    guidelines for, 131-132
    MMR vaccine, 26, 180
immunologic stressors, 150-151
indolylacrolylglycine (IAG), 42, 194, 221, 286, 287
indolylacrylic acid, 286, 287
indolylpropionic acid, 287
induction-coupled plasma mass spectrometer (ICP-MS), 202, 203
Infantile Autism: The Syndrome and its Implications for a Neural Theory of Behavior (Rimland), 8, 17
infectious stressors, 186-187
inositol hexanicotinate, 313
inositol supplement, 213, 313-314
insomnia, 42
interneurons, 174
intestinal barrier function, 191
intestinal dysbiosis, 37, 196, 213, 234, 289, 317
intestinal lesions, 178-179
intestinal permeability, 109, 191
intestine
    barrier function, 191

    dysbiosis, 37, 196, 213, 234, 289, 317
    ileal-lymphoid nodular hyperplasia, 181-182, 186-187, 268
    lesions, 178-179
    permeability, 109, 191
    See also gastrointestinal health
intravenous immune globulins (IVIG), 126
intrinsic factor, 268
iron deficiency, 59
iron level, 203
isoleucine, 285
isoleucine deficiency, 285
isomaltase, 218, 221, 262
itching, 38
itraconazole. See Sporanox
IVIG. See intravenous immune globulins

J
James, Dr. Jill, 276, 303
Jang, Dr. Miriam, 314
juices, on yeast-free diet, 88

K
kava kava, 42, 43
ketoconazole. See Nizoral
kinases, 228
Kirkman Laboratories, 215, 288
Koschel, K., 182
Krantic, Slavica, 179
Krigsman, Dr. Arthur, 181
kynurenic acid, 42

L
L-alpha-alanine, 305
L-carnitine, 312
laboratory testing, 59-61, 72, 189-209
    abnormal results indicating autism, 170
    amino acid analysis, 18, 195-197, 278, 288
    antibodies, 109, 127, 130
    for autism, 209-210
    blood ammonia, 191-192
    blood chemistry, 189-190
    CBC analysis, 190
    element analyses, 202-205
    fatty acid analysis, 201-202
    food allergy tests, 115-119, 192-193
    genomic testing, 207-208
    gluten-free diet indicated, 109
    hydrogen breath test, 111
    immune testing, 125-128, 206-207
    intestinal barrier function, 191
    intestinal permeability, 109, 191
    liver profile tests, 81
    metallothionein assessment, 205-206
    organic acid analysis, 198-201
    for parasites, 59-60, 84-85
    stool cultures, 59, 60, 80, 81, 190
    urinary peptide measurements, 194-195
    venous blood ammonia assay, 190
    viral panel, 207
lactase, 218, 219, 221, 262
lactate level, 199-200, 248
lactobacilli, 262
Lactobacillus acidophilus, 263
Lactobacillus caseii, 263
Lactobacillus rhamnosis, 260, 263

lactose, 111
lactose-free diet, rating as autism treatment, 24, 30
lactose intolerance, 111
Lamisil, 78, 81
LDN. *See* low-dose naltrexone
lead, methionine synthase and, 173
leavened foods, 87
LeLord, Dr. Gilbert, 9
Lesch-Nyhan disease, 153
leucine, 285
leucine aminopeptidase, 240
leucine deficiency, 285, 288
Levin, Dr. Warren, 84
light exposure, for sleep rhythm, 41
limit dextrinase, 220
lipases, 216, 218, 220
lipoic acid, 299-300
lipoic acid supplement, 301
liver profile tests, 81
Lonsdale, Dr. Derrick, 120
Lovaas, Ivar, 9
low-dose naltrexone (LDN), 136
lunch, on Specific Carbohydrate Diet, 100
lysine, 286
lysine deficiency, 286, 288
lysosomes, 253

M
magnesium, 228-229
    biotinidase and, 309
    unmet need for, 39
magnesium chloride, 230
magnesium citrate, 46, 230
magnesium deficit, 39, 46, 161, 196, 203
magnesium glycinate chelate, 228-229
magnesium hydroxide, 230
magnesium malate, 315
magnesium oxide, 230
magnesium stearate, 89
magnesium supplement, 41, 199, 229-231
    adverse response to, 230
    for constipation, 46
    dosage chart, 231
    rating as autism treatment, 229
    responses to, 228
    vitamin B6 action and, 227
    vitamin B6 with magnesium, 24, 30, 73, 214, 229-231
malabsorption, 285
malate, 315
maldigestion, amino acids and, 285
malic acid, 315
malic acid level, 200
maltase, 218, 221, 262
manganese level, 203
McCandless, Dr. Jaquelyn, 7-8, 134, 136
measles, 178-180
    MMR immunization, 26, 180
measles virus, 178, 180
    antibodies to, 130
    in cerebrospinal fluid, 134
    protein of, 182
meat, on yeast-free diet, 91
Medical Assessment Options for Children with Autism and Related Problems See *DAN! Clinical Manual*
megavitamin treatment, 9

Megson, Dr. Mary, 134, 168, 252
melatonin, 42, 167, 215, 256-258, 286
melatonin supplement, 73, 257-258
mercaptans, 121, 124
mercury, 165, 185, 203
    detoxification, 120, 299, 301
    hair analysis for, 204
    methionine synthase and, 164, 173, 185
    testing for, 203
mercury exposure, maternal, 25
mercury toxicity, 20-21, 120
    diagram, 122
    in infancy, 25
    MMR vaccine, reaction to, 180
    sex hormones and, 188
metabolic analysis, 189
metabolic disorders
    Type I autism, 151, 152-154, 161, 170
    Type II autism, 154
metabolism, digestive enzymes, 218-220
metallothionein assessment, 205-206
metallothionein deficiency, 241
metanephrine, 228
5,10-methenyl tetrahydrofolate, 294
methionine, 27, 160, 286
methionine level, 286, 288
methionine metabolism, 27-29, 159, 160-166
    methylation cycle, 108, 154, 164-166, 195, 214, 279, 294, 303
    speeding up, 226
methionine supplement, 292
methionine synthase (MS), 29, 162, 171, 172, 173, 185, 266-288
methionine synthase reductase (MTRR), 208
methyl B12 supplement, 29, 30, 69, 70-72, 100, 268-270
methyl groups, 27-28
methyl traps, 296
methylation, 108, 154, 164-166, 195, 214
    adenosine and, 172
    creatine and, 279
    folate and, 294
    impaired, 303
    importance of, 171, 185
    remethylation, 174
methylcobalamin (MeCbl), 164, 165, 171, 173, 199, 269, 270
methylcobalamin deficit, 292
5,10-methylene tetrahydrofolate, 271, 296
methylene tetrahydrofolate reductase (MTHFR), 165, 173, 208, 209, 267, 269
methylmalonic acid (MMA), 70, 199
5-methyltetrahydrofolate (5-MeTHF), 266, 294, 296
metronidazole, 85
milk, on Specific Carbohydrate Diet, 101
milk allergy, 111, 192
milk-containing products
    lactose intolerance, 111
    milk allergy, 111
milk-free diet, rating as autism treatment, 24, 30, 52
milk of magnesia, 46
milk products, on yeast-free diet, 91
milk thistle, 42-43, 81
Miller, Dr. Edgar, 3
mincemeat, on yeast-free diet, 89
mineral oil, for constipation, 46
MiraLax, for constipation, 47-48

miso, on yeast-free diet, 89
The Missing Diagnosis (Truss), 74
mitochondria, 198, 315
MMA. *See* methylmalonic acid
MMR immunization, 26, 180
molybdenum
    for reducing high copper, 244
    with TTFD therapy, 124
molybdenum citrate, 244
molybdenum level, 203
moving the bowels, 45
    See also constipation; gastrointestinal health
MS. *See* methionine synthase
MT-I, 206
MT-II, 206
MT-III, 206
MT-IV, 205
MTHFR. *See* methylene tetrahydrofolate reductase
MTRR. *See* methionine synthase reductase
multivitamin, 73, 259-260
mumps, 178
    antibodies to, 130
    MMR immunization, 26, 180
Münzel, P., 182
muscles, magnesium deficiency and, 39
myelin basic protein, autoantibodies to, 181, 206
myoinositol, 313
myoinositol hexaphosphate, 313

N

NAC. *See* N-acetylcysteine
naltrexone, 136
nervous system, magnesium deficiency and, 39
Neubrander, Dr. James, 71, 165, 269
neurofibromatosis Type 1!, 153
neurofibromin, 153
neurohormone, 256
neuronal function, 171-175
night waking, 40
nighttime light exposure, 41
Nizoral, 81
NMDA receptor, 173
Nu-Thera, 215, 229-230, 259-260
nucleoside/nucleotide exchange and depletion
    conditions, 153
nucleoside/nucleotide synthesis disorders, 152-153
nutritional failure, criteria, 57
nutritional supplements, 20, 67-68, 211-216
    N-acetylcysteine (NAC), 287, 297-299
    adverse reactions to, 58
    alpha-ketoglutaric acid, 199, 308
    amino acids, 285-289
    ARI Publication 34!, 215
    benefits of, 213-214
    Bifidobacter bifidum, 263-264
    biotin, 124, 309-310
    calcium, 24, 30, 73, 213, 247-248
    carnosine, 194, 235, 242, 286, 305-307
    caution to be used with, 290-293
    cod liver oil, 73, 250-252
    coenzyme Q_{10}, 313
    colostrum, 133-134, 312
    creatine, 171, 213, 279-284
    digestive enzymes, 69, 72-73, 216-222
    dimethylglycine (DMG), 164, 271-273, 276,
        277-279
    DMG or TMG with folate and vitamin B12, 277-279
    fatty acids, 24, 30, 73, 254-255
    first-tier supplements, 69, 72-73, 212
    folate, 276, 277-279, 293-297
    glutathione, 301, 303
    glycine, 255
    guidelines for use, 216
    inositol, 213, 313-314
    L-carnitine, 312
    Lactobacillus acidophilus, 263
    Lactobacillus rhamnosis, 260, 263
    lipoic acid, 299-300
    magnesium malate, 315
    magnesium supplements, 41, 46, 199, 227, 228,
        229-231
    melatonin, 73, 257-258
    methionine, 290-293
    methyl B12, 29, 30, 69, 70-72, 100, 268-270
    molybdenum, 124, 244
    multivitamin, 73, 259-260
    probiotics, 59, 83, 260-264
    rating as autism treatment, 24
    recordkeeping, 216
    S-adenosylmethionine (SAMe), 290-293
    Saccharomyces boulardii, 59, 79-80, 82, 260,
        262-263
    second-tier supplements, 212
    selenium, 316-317
    silymarin, 81, 317
    staging of, 212-213
    Streptococcus thermophilus, 264
    taurine, 73, 232, 234-235, 255, 275, 306
    trimethylglycine (TMG), 171, 274-279
    vitamin A, 24, 30, 73, 134, 249-253, 255
    vitamin B1, transdermal, 120-121
    vitamin B3 megavitamin treatment, 9
    vitamin B6, 9, 42, 163, 215, 223-227
    vitamin B6 with magnesium, 24, 30, 73, 214,
        229-231
    vitamin B12, 268-270
    vitamin C, 24, 30, 73, 238-239
    vitamin D, 248, 251
    vitamin E, 317-318
    zinc, 24, 30, 73, 242-244, 248
    See also antifungal drugs
nuts
    on Specific Carbohydrate Diet, 101
    on yeast-free diet, 92
nystatin, 74, 77, 80-81, 83
    rating as autism treatment, 24, 30, 74

O

obsessive-compulsive disorder (OCD), inositol for, 313
Occam's razor, 62
oils, on yeast-free diet, 92
oligo-1,6-glucosidase, 220
olive oil, for constipation, 46
olives, on yeast-free diet, 89
omega-3 fatty acids, 254, 255
omega-6 fatty acids, 254
opioids, 108, 162
oral immune globulins, 133
Oralgam, 133
oregano concentrate, 83
organic acid analysis, 198-201
organophosphates, 186

Osmond, Dr. Humphry, 9
Owens, Susan, 48, 309
oxidant stressors, 165
oxidized glutathione. *See* glutathione disulfide

P

P5P. *See* pyridoxal 5-phosphate
palatinase, 220, 262
palmitate, 252
PANDAS. *See* Pediatric Autoimmune Neuropsychiatric Disorders Associated with Streptococcal Infection
papain, 220
paramyxoviruses, 178
parasites, 59-60, 84-85
parent advocacy, 22-23
parents
    decision-making by, 22-23, 43-44
    intuition, 62
    maternal mercury exposure, 25
    recordkeeping by, 31-36
paromycin, 85
pau d'arco, 83
Pediatric Autoimmune Neuropsychiatric Disorders Associated with Streptococcal Infection (PANDAS), 187, 309
PEG. *See* polyethylene glycol
peptidase supplements, 216
peptidases, 220
peptides, 214
    urinary peptide measurements, 194-195
perchlorate, 186
perfluoro-octanoic acid (PFOA), 186
peripheral nervous system, magnesium deficiency and, 39
peroxisomal proliferator activated receptors (PPARs), 134
pertussis virus, antibodies to, 130
pesticides, 186
PFOA. *See* perfluoro-octanoic acid
phenolsulfotransferase, 229
phenylalanine, 286, 288
phenylketonuria, 153, 286
Philpott, Dr. William, 306
phosphate transport, by creatine, 167, 280
phosphatidylinositol, 313
phosphocreatine, 169, 281
phytate, 313
pickles, on yeast-free diet, 89
Pioglitazone, 135
pluchine, 276
poliovirus, antibodies to, 130
polyethylene glycol (PEG), for constipation, 47-48
polymorphisms, 208
poultry, on yeast-free diet, 91
PPAR agonists, 134-135
PPARs. *See* peroxisomal proliferator activated receptors
Prader-Willi syndrome, 152
prednisone, 95
private policy, vs. public policy, 16-18
probiotics, 59, 83, 260-264
    adverse response to, 264
    Bifidobacter bifidum, 263-264
    Lactobacillus acidophilus, 263
    Lactobacillus rhamnosis, 260, 263
    Saccharomyces boulardii, 59, 79-80, 82, 260, 262-263

    Streptococcus thermophilus, 264
proteases, 218
protein shakes, 41
proteins
    best eaten in the morning, 40, 41
    digestion, 106-107
    requirements for children, 57
    on Specific Carbohydrate Diet, 100
Prozac, rating as autism treatment, 24
PRPP synthetase superactivity, 153
prunes/prune juice, for constipation, 45
psoriasis, 38
public policy, private policy vs., 16-18
purine autism, 185
pyridoxal 5-phosphate (P5P), 163, 196, 214, 223, 226, 257
pyridoxal kinase, 227, 257
pyridoxine. *See* Vitamin B6
pyrimidine 5'-nucleotidase superactivity, 153
pyrimidines, 153, 234, 271
pyroglutamic acid, 199
pyruvate, 199, 200
pyruvate dehydrogenase, lipoic acid use by, 300
pyruvate level, 248
pyruvic acidosis, 200

R

Randolph, Dr. Theron, 252
recognition, 114
recordkeeping
    chronological questionnaire, 31-33
    nutritional supplements, 216
    symptom table, 34-36
regressions, Specific Carbohydrate Diet (SCD), 97-99
remethylation, 171
reticulin antibodies, 109
retinyl acetate, 250
Rett syndrome, 153
rice protein, 40-41
Rimland, Dr. Bernard, 3, 8, 17, 18, 19, 29, 62, 74, 75, 215
Rimland, Mark, 8, 10
Risperdal, rating as autism treatment, 24
rotation diet, rating as autism treatment, 52
rubella, MMR immunization, 26, 180
rubella virus, antibodies to, 130
Rubenstein-Taybi syndrome, 152
rubeola. *See* measles

S

S-adenosylhomocysteine (SAH), 161-163, 226
S-adenosylmethionine (SAMe), 161, 168, 215, 228, 274, 279, 290-293
    biochemistry, 291
S-adenosylmethionine supplement, 290, 292-293
Saccharomyces boulardii, 59, 79-80, 82, 260, 262-263
Saccharomyces cerevisiae, 80, 262
salad dressings, on yeast-free diet, 89
salt craving, 39
sarcosine, 271, 272
sauces, on yeast-free diet, 89
sauerkraut, on yeast-free diet, 89
SCD. *See* Specific Carbohydrate Diet
Schneider, Dr. Cindy, 133
The Second Brain (Gershon), 84
second-tier nutritional supplements, 212

secretin, 135-136
seizures
    carnosine for, 307
    taurine supplement for, 306
    vitamin B6 supplements for, 225
selenium, 316
selenium deficiency, 316
selenium level, 203
selenium supplement, 316-317
senna, for constipation, 46
Septra, 85
serotonin, 256, 257, 286
serotonin level, 286
Seroussi, Karyn, 110, 111, 114
SGOT, 82
SGPT, 82
Shahani, Dr. Khem, 263
Shattock, Paul, 150, 194
Shaw, William, 76
short-chain fatty acids, in stool, 190
short-chain peptides, 218
silymarin, 81, 317
Singh, Prof. Vijendra, 180-182, 206
single nucleotide polymorphisms (SNPs), 208, 209
skin problems, 38
sleep difficulties, 40-43
small bowel biopsy, 109
small intestine lesions, 178-179
Smith-Magenis syndrome, 152
SNPs. See single nucleotide polymorphisms
sodium molybdate, 244
somatostatin, 179
sourdough bread, 87
soy protein, 41
soy sauce, on yeast-free diet, 89
Specific Carbohydrate Diet (SCD), 51, 53, 69, 93-101, 112
    food list, 100-101
    initial reaction to, 98
    online resources, 101
    regressions and, 97-99
    yogurt, 99
Sporanox, 81
steatorrhea, 190
steroid psychosis, 95
stool cultures, 59, 60, 80, 81, 190
streptococcus, as stressor, 186-187
Streptococcus thermophilus, 264
stressors, 150-151, 165, 185-187
succinic acid, 287
sucrase, 221, 262
sucrase-isomaltase complex, 220
sugar, on yeast-free diet, 86, 89-90
sugars, 55-58
sulfamethoxazole, 85
sulfation, 41, 48, 166-167, 214, 228
sulfur chemistry, 28, 121, 166
Super Nu-Thera, 229-230, 259-260
symptom table, 34-36
synchronous neuronal processes, 159, 171-175
systems approach, 15

T
tamari, on yeast-free diet, 89
taurine, 232-234
taurine deficiency, 288

taurine level, 288
taurine supplement, 73, 232, 234-235, 255, 275, 306
tea, on yeast-free diet, 88
Teflon, 186
terbinafine. See Lamisil
testosterone, mercury neurotoxicity and, 188
tetanus virus, antibodies to, 130
tetrahydrofolate (THF), 271, 294
tetrahydrofuryryl disulfide (TTFD), 120
tetrathiomolybdate, 244
textile flame retardants, 150, 185, 186
TH1/TH2 imbalance, 128, 207
THF. See tetrahydrofolate
thiamin, 199
thiamine tetrahydrofuryryl disulfide (TTFD), 69, 120, 123-125
thimerosal, 150, 165, 173, 185, 187, 219
thiol chemistry, 28, 121
thioneins, 205
threonine, 285, 286
threonine level, 285, 286
thrush infection, 75
thymidine, 271
thyroid hormone, synthesis of, 186
Tinidazole, 85
tissue transglutaminase antibodies, 109
TMG. See betaine; trimethylglycine
tocopherols, 317
tomato sauce, on yeast-free diet, 89
tongue, allergies and, 38
toxic stressors, 150-151
transaminases, 286
transfer factor, 133-134
transglutaminase antibodies, 109
transsulfuration, 214
trehalase, 262
trehalose, 262
trimethoprim, 85
trimethylglycine (TMG), 171, 274-279. See also betaine
trimethylglycine hydrochloride, 276
trimethylglycine supplement, 275-276
    dosage, 275-276
    with folate and vitamin B12, 277-279
    parent rating of, 275
Truss, Dr. Orion, 21, 74
tryptophan, 41-42, 194, 286, 287
    malabsorption of, 221
    metabolism of, 194
TTFD. See Tetrahydrofuryryl disulfide
tuberin, 153
tuberous sclerosis, 153
Type I autism, 151, 152-154, 161, 209
Type II autism, 151, 154, 209
tyrosine level, 288

U
UBE3A gene, 154, 165
ubiquinone. See coenzyme Q_{10}
ubiquitin, 154-155, 165
ubiquitin ligase gene, 165
undecylenic acid, 83
Unraveling the Mystery of Autism (Seroussi), 114
unsaturated fatty acids, 254
urea cycle, 150, 196
urinary peptide measurements, 194-195
urine, elemental analyses, 203-204

Usman, Dr. Anju, 244

V
vaccines. See immunizations
vaginal yeast infection, 75
valerian, 42, 43
valine, 285
valine deficiency, 285, 288
valproic acid, biotinidase depletion and, 309
Vancomycin, 83
varicella virus, antibodies to, 130
vegetables
    on Specific Carbohydrate Diet, 100-101
    on yeast-free diet, 91
    yeast on outer surface of, 86
venous blood ammonia assay, 190
viral panel, 207
viruses, 178
vision, 174
vitamin A, toxicity, 73, 250
vitamin A acetate, 252
vitamin A palmitate, 252
vitamin A supplement, 73, 249-253, 255
    adverse response to, 251, 252-253
    government recommended amounts, 249
    high-dose, 134, 250, 252
    measuring, 249-250
    rating as autism treatment, 24, 30, 252
vitamin A toxicity, 73, 250
vitamin B1 supplement, transdermal, 120-121
vitamin B3, 9
vitamin B6, 9, 73, 163, 196, 214, 223-224
vitamin B6 supplement, 42, 225-227
    adverse responses to, 227
    dosage chart, 231
    Nu-Thera, 215, 229-230, 259-260
    rating as autism treatment, 24, 226
vitamin B6 with magnesium, 214, 229-231
    dosage chart, 231
    rating as autism treatment, 24, 30, 73, 230
vitamin B12, 29, 276
    absorption, 70
    blood levels, 70
vitamin B12 deficiency, 268
vitamin B12 supplement, 268-270
    adverse responses to, 270
    DMG or TMG with folate and vitamin B12, 277-279
    dosage, 268
    methyl B12, 29, 30, 69, 70-72, 100, 268-270
vitamin C, 29, 236-238
vitamin C supplement, 73, 238-239
    adverse responses to, 238-239
    rating as autism treatment, 24, 30, 238
vitamin D, 213, 249
vitamin D supplement, 248
vitamin E, 29, 317-318
vitamin E deficiency, 317
vitamin E supplement, 318
vitamins
    as coenzymes, 214
    on yeast-free diet, 89
    See also individual vitamins
von Recklinghausen disease, 153

W
Wakefield, Dr. Andrew, 95, 178, 181
Walsh, Dr. William, 205, 306
Waring, Dr. Rosemary, 229, 258
weight, ideal weight for height, 57
What Your Doctor May Not Tell You About Children's Vaccinations (Cave), 130
wheat-free diet, rating as autism treatment, 52
whey protein, 41
worms, eradication, 84
wormwood, 85

X
xylanases, 218

Y
yeast allergy, 90
The Yeast Connection: A Medical Breakthrough (Crook), 74
yeast cultures, 60
yeast-free diet, 77, 85-93
    food list, 91-92
    rating as autism treatment, 24, 30, 52, 74
yeast-free vitamins, 89
yeast infections, 37-38, 75-79
    amino acid supplements and, 287
    lipoic acid fostering, 299, 301
    See also antifungal drugs; fungal infections
yeasts, 79
    on fruits and vegetables, 86-87
Yodoxin, 85
yogurt
    on Specific Carbohydrate Diet, 99
    on yeast-free diet, 88

Z
Zelson, Martin, 113
zinc, 239-242
    copper/zinc ratio, 205, 239, 240, 306
    vitamin B6 action and, 227
zinc acetate, 244
zinc citrate, 242
zinc deficiency, 240, 241
zinc level, 203, 239, 244
zinc sulfate, 242
zinc supplement, 73, 242-244, 248
    adverse response to, 243
    dosage chart, 243
    rating as autism treatment, 24, 30, 243

NOTES

NOTES

NOTES

NOTES

NOTES